PSYCHOLOGY APPLIED

GEORGE W. CRANE, Ph. D., M. D.

*Northwestern University Psychologist; Consultant in Business
and Industrial Psychology; Five Years Research Psychologist
under auspices of the National Research Council of
America, and the Carnegie Institution of
Washington, D. C., Author of the two
syndicated newspaper columns entitled
"TEST YOUR HORSE SENSE"
and "THE WORRY CLINIC."*

HOPKINS SYNDICATE, INCORPORATED
HOPKINS BUILDING
MELLOTT, INDIANA
1967

TO
MY FATHER AND MOTHER
APPLIED PSYCHOLOGISTS
PAR EXCELLENCE

INTRODUCTION

Pedagogy is a major field of Applied Psychology. So classroom teachers merit a long overdue salute! They are really educational "salesmen". They can protect this great Republic with its superb "free enterprise" system far better than armies or navies.

President Frederick L. Hovde of Purdue University recently addressed a Detroit convention on the vital importance of better communications in business and industry.

"Better economic education," he said, "is a MUST if a free society is to survive!"

We teachers need to widen our scope and thus show American youth why they pledge allegiance to a Republic instead of a Democracy in the salute to our flag (Pp. 661–665).

The Declaration of Independence also states that we are entitled only to the "pursuit of happiness" and not "happiness" itself. Yet many welfare agencies are confusing that concept.

Many college graduates also lack the understanding of "net" vs. "gross" income. Recently a clergyman with $6,000 salary grumbled about dental surgeons and morticians in his parish who took in $17,500 per year. But that $17,500 was "gross" and a doctor or mortician with $17,500 gross income still doesn't take home any more net income than the $6,000-per-year cleric!

Dartnell Corporation recently showed that the cost of the average personal letter sent out by any private business firm runs $2.44 (Pg. 817), yet thousands of college graduates can't believe this basic fact.

Every Liberal Arts graduate would be a far better citizen if he first had received a diploma from a topnotch Business College!

All good teachers function as versatile salesmen of ideas and idealism. In medicine and dentistry we now stress the "organismic" instead of the former "organic" viewpoint, for doctors operate on total personalities; not just upon an appendix or infected molar. Superlative teachers also follow that same "organismic" strategy.

"Pull up the shades. I don't want to go home in the dark," were the dying words that O. Henry whispered to his nurse.

Our modern Applied Psychologists are thus giving mankind scientific illumination in social relationships so that people may be able to LIVE in the light of God's wisdom. Theoretically, we should never have divorces or juvenile delinquency or strikes and lockouts or war. For psychology is the ally of morality.

Psychology, however, is the latest science to bud from the parent trunk, philosophy, so it hasn't had time to show its full value. Please remember that we didn't possess even a successful intelligence test till 1905 A.D., when the Binet-Simon Scale was developed for youngsters. And 1918 marks our first great adult test of mental "horse power", otherwise labeled I.Q. It caused the Employment Manager thereafter to go ritzy and have his title listed in gold leaf as "Personnel Director."

Although Harvard University was founded in 1636, and over 1,800 other American colleges have arisen during the succeeding centuries, almost all the scientists therein relatively ignored mankind. Instead, they looked through their telescopes at the distant heavenly bodies, and through their microscopes at insects or bacteria but it wasn't till almost the start of this 20th century that anybody suggested:

"Let's reverse things, for a change, and look at the MAN at the eyepiece of those telescopes or microscopes!"

In 1869, our famous Library of Congress thus contained thousands of volumes dealing with chemistry and metallurgy, physics and astronomy, medicine and music, but it held only one book dealing with such vital psychological matters as salesmanship. Yet salesmanship is one branch of Applied Psychology which has been basic to all business since remote antiquity. It has furnished much of the taxes to operate governments.

Indeed, salesmanship began when the serpent sold Eve on a forbidden brand of fruit, yet we hadn't made a full analysis of the sales situation till the year 1907, when A. F. Sheldon added the fifth element to our current sales formula: Attract attention; maintain interest; create desire; get action; and produce permanent satisfaction.

Apparently, our human attention had been so extroverted upon external reality that we had seldom thought to analyze man himself, although a few great exceptions stand out in history.

Thus, Aristotle may very properly be regarded as the leading Applied Psychologist in the centuries before the birth of Christ. Jesus was the greatest Applied Psychologist of all time, and Shakespeare undoubtedly takes the laurels during the Middle Ages.

With the beginning of the 20th century, however, we suddenly became aware of mankind as a primary subject for scientific study. Psychology then began to cut loose from the maternal apron strings of the philosophy departments in our leading universities, and set up its own courses in the curriculum.

Closely paralleling this innovation came the birth of many constructive social service organizations, such as the Rotary Club in 1905, the Boy Scouts in 1910, Kiwanis in 1915, Lions in 1917, Optimist in 1919 and Civitan in 1920. These male organizations function much as the various "home missionary societies" of women in our different churches. This 16-year span from 1905 through 1920 was a unique period of psychological awakening. It bore out the prediction made by Dr. J. McKeen Cattell in 1903, when he said:

"The nineteenth century witnessed an extraordinary increase in our knowledge of the material world and in our powers to make it subservient to our ends; the twentieth century will probably witness a corresponding increase in our knowledge of human nature and in our power to use it for our welfare."

The unsung heroes of Applied Psychology are actually the teachers in college classrooms, whose enthusiasm is doing a remarkable "selling" job for our vital science. They are taking small enrollments in psychology and actually doubling (sometimes trebling) them by their own skillful use of psychological principles.

In the more progressive Liberal Arts and Business Colleges they are now channeling all their psychology students through an orientation course in Applied Psychology. This method gives the pupils a panoramic view of the many practical fields where psychology helps them earn a living. It also whets their interest in enroling for advanced courses.

Thus, the University of Iowa, as well as Iowa State, have employed over 1,000 copies of *Psychology Applied* per year and Pace College has exceeded 1,200.

Dr. Thomas O. Burgess (Concordia) typifies these versatile professors who help account for this zooming interest. He pioneered hypnotherapy and created teaching clinics therein for American dentists and medics. And his college classes are overcrowded.

Prof. J. A. Donatelli (Mercyhurst) is another dynamic classroom teacher whose students have become such enthusiasts, they have actually petitioned for additional classes. I also owe him thanks for many suggestions.

Dr. Roy E. Hoke (King's College) was a pioneer researcher but likewise combines the teaching art so perfectly that he has about 500 students each year in Applied Psychology. He is a real Titan.

Sister Anne Cawley (Mt. St. Scholastica) likewise used Applied Psychology to help "spark" greater interest in the entire department. And Sister Mary of St. Michael trebled her classroom enrolments, prior to her becoming a talented college president.

Dean E. M. Cooke (Carson-Newman) used clever experiments in his classroom teaching and thus "dressed up" his lectures so students never wanted to "cut" his classes. Professors H. C. Evans, Jr. and R. F. Koonce do the same.

Dean Francis L. Richardson and his talented colleagues, Professors Armin Ripplemeyer and Earl H. Dawes, have made Belleville College famous for Applied Psychology!

Applied Psychology (called "Human Relations" or "H-R") is now regarded as vital to success in business and professional fields as well as Liberal Arts. Among the more than 1,000 college classroom adoptions of *Psychology Applied*, note the wide variety of famous educators and schools below:

W. F. Vaughan (Harvard)
Chas. Schweitzer (Rutgers)
J. H. Baker, Jr. (U. of Puerto Rico)
G. H. Peters (Panhandle A & M)
T. L. Purnell (Penn. Milit.)
Robert P. Kite (G-J Morticians)
Pres. A. R. Kennett (Va. Southern)
Pres. A. B. Mackey (Trevecca)
Glenn W. Samuelson (E. Baptist)
Dean W. B. Hammer (Estherville)
Warner Sizemore (V. Forge Milit.)
H. G. Miller (Chicago Chiropody)
Capt. R. H. Meeker (N. M. Milit.)
R. F. Keeler (Minn. Bible)
Stanley Brown (Friends Bible)
V. E. Kekter (N. D. St. Science)
Pres. C. E. Butterfield (N. W. Bible)
Pres. J. L. Lusby (Ky. Christian)
F. C. Bean (Connor's St. Agr.)
Pres. M. O. Kirkpatrick (King's Bus.)
Pres. Otto Madland (Madison Bus.)
Pres. Jack Jones (Jones Bus.)
Pres. H. E. Pope, Jr. (Okla. Acctg.)
Pres. Wayne L. Huff (Cecil's Bus.)
Pres. Harry Green (Phillips Bus.)
Pres. D. W. Miller (Curry College)
Pres. L. R. Stevens (Stevens-Henager)
Pres. Frank 'Harwood (Massey Bus.)
Pres. S. J. Drake (Drake Bus.)
Pres. C. A. Neale (Hammel-Actual)
Pres. J. F. Kane (Lakeland Inst.)
Pres. Gerald Wickham (Bliss)
Dean R. Perreault (W. C. Teachers)
Dean F. H. Gilliland (Devil's Lake)
Dean F. L. McCallum (Owosso)
Pres. J. A. Rodeira (Fla. Central)

Pres. K. S. Bennion (L. D. S.)
C. S. Simkins (Johnson Bible)
R. V. Phillips (Pa. Coll. Optometry)
R. E. Dougher (N. Y. State)
Thomas Painter (Waynesboro)
Larry Doyle (Barrington)
Beth Clark (Penn. Milit.)
Dean D. E. Matthews (Stevens-H)
Robert M. Blacker (Walsh School)
Joann Macmillan (Worth College)
V. T. Pinkerton (Midland)
Dean Ethel M. Neal (Waynesboro
C. B. Bigby (Dentsville)
Francis Crnarick (Altoona)
C. C. Hurst (Cecil's)
Felicidad Sycip (Azusa)
A. R. Stanford (Fla. Bible)
W. C. Walker (Ricks Coll.)
R. A. Tesseneer (Murray St.)
C. W. Zull (Saginaw Inst.)
Glenn W. Erickson (NW. Coll.)
M. D. O'Connor (Rockhurst)
Sister M. Eugenia (Coll. St. Rose)
M. B. Levinson (U. Palm Beach)
A. Stewart (New Trier)
F. W. Eiseman (Gulf Coast)
R. J. Bradley (Pikeville)
Jule Barnett (NW Sch. Comm.)
A. E. Kanniwischer (E. Baptist)
W. R. Montler (Altoona)
James D. Greer (Spartanburg)
Dorothy Powell (Bapt. Memorial)
L. E. Anderson (Columbia Basin)
E. C. Christenbury (Ch. God)
Walter L. Thomas (Cent. Pilgrim)
Margaret Stober (NW. Sch. Comm.)
J. H. Tobias (Altoona Sch. Comm.)
H. N. Donnan (N. Greenville)
A. K. Mehren (Racine Teachers)
Frieda Gipson (National Coll.)
Pres. Pauline Young (Young's Bus.)
David King (Lain Techn. Inst.)
L. E. Gilbreath (Hutchinson Coll.)

Bessie G. Sharpe (Gardner Sch.)
Robert J. Fiedler (Starbuck)
Jean LaBella (Burdett Coll.)
Ettabel Aasheim (Modern Bus.)
R. B. Solomon (Gulf Coast Coll.)
George Rountree (Piedmont Coll.)
R. K. Wilson (Twin Falls)
Stanley Brown (Friends Bible)
Ester Small (Burdett Coll.)
Virginia L. Graham (Meridian Coll.)
W. E. Schenck (Eric Fromm, Inc.)
Evelyn Stinchfield (Burdett)
B. C. Murdock (Wesleyan)
Father James McManamon (Quincy)
R. B. Nell (U. Baltimore)
F. S. Rankin (King, Tenn.)
T. J. Eskridge (Newberry)
Earl Fitz (Grand View Coll.)
H. W. Peterson (Ft. Dodge)
Helen French (Mason City)
R. W. Erickson (Miss. State)
W. F. Scott (Muscatine)
Frank Matthews (Penn. Milit.)
Paul A. Williams (Century)
Pres. O. J. Kersten (Warren)
T. H. Cutler (U. of Denver)
Chas. J. Snell (Houghton Coll.)
F. L. Watson (Cent. Christian)
K. E. Gillming (Baptist Bible)
Halice Wiggs (Millikin U.)
W. A. Sprague (E. Ky. State)
Albert Bartz (U. N. Dakota)
Dean Sweetland (Cecil's)
Paul F. Barkman (Taylor U.)
L. J. Brown (Sterling Morton)
Dean J. F. Loper (Muscatine)
E. R. Price (E. Miss. Coll.)
L. H. Mendenhall (William Penn)
D. W. Boles (Devil's Lake)
Pres. A. V. Calhoon (Hampton Roads)
Roxy Lefforge (Huntington)
Chas. S. Montgomery (Milligan)
Harold K. Fink (Florida)

Many state and national conventions of physicians, dentists, morticians, clergymen and teachers have graciously invited me to address them in recent years. And the usual topic they request is "How to Get Along Harmoniously With People".

Famous J. L. Hudson's Department Store in Detroit also asked me to speak to all 12,000 of its employees. These included the 4,000 at the sales counters, plus the 8,000 additional employees in the accounting, advertising, remodeling and other departments. They counted off, army style, in units of 1 to 12. Then I took the 1,000 who were #1, and lectured to them at 9:30 A.M., followed by 1,000 who were #2, and whom I addressed at 10:30. In the afternoon, I handled 1,000 more at 2:30 and the 4th group of 1,000 at 3:30.

This routine was followed out the next two days till I had covered the entire group of employees and management. And the topic I was specifically requested to elaborate was "How to Get Along Harmoniously With People" (at home and in the store).

All livewire psychology professors realize that students are keenly interested in this same topic. So *Psychology Applied* is written to help open the eyes of all first year students to the many practical fields in psychology where they may later specialize and earn an adequate salary.

Many professors thus report a doubling or even trebling in the number of beginning psychology students who decide to take a major in the field, after they have studied *Psychology Applied* and been enthused by dynamic teachers.

Every good teacher is an enthusiast for his subject so he appreciates all relevant teaching aids that help dramatize education and fascinate his pupils.

Alas, there are still some professors who have a dyspeptic attitude toward teaching and who deliver boring lectures that drive first year students AWAY from such courses. But good teachers utilize all relevant psychological aids and stage materials for motivating students TOWARD, instead of AWAY from, their subject matter.

Superb teachers recognize interesting textbooks and all other dramatic aids to pedagogy. But dull teachers apparently can't distinguish between a boring book versus a dynamic textbook, which is one reason why Morpheus appears in far too many college classrooms even at this late date!

So I wish to salute my dynamic psychology colleagues who are making Applied Psychology a vital, fascinating subject for the 18 and 19-year-olds on over 1,000 campuses. May their tribe increase! For they are the stellar salesmen of ideas that justify colleges! (See Dr. Glenn Frank's comment, P. 199-200).

Dr. L. W. Hess asked his large sections in Applied Psychology to vote as to which chapter in this textbook they liked most and found that about 90% chose Ch. XVIII, entitled "Psychology Goes to Church". That should reassure older Americans concerning the religious idealism of the youthful leaders of the present generation. On pp. 590 and 658, I shall include tributes to additional outstanding psychology teachers who combine moral zeal with effective classroom pedagogy.

Psychology should never lose its initial interest for students, since it is the most vital science of all! Although physicists and chemists may gloat over their Atomic or Hydrogen Bombs, we psychologists deal with a far more powerful force, namely, human personality.

The explosive force of Christ's personality hit this planet over 19 centuries ago, yet it is still growing more potent each day. Atomic and Hydrogen Bombs are finite. Their power is gone with a "Poof."

But Christ's "bombshell" personality has blasted billions of tons of granite and limestone from the face of this earth. However, those fragments have not been death producing like shrapnel. Instead, they have fallen back into orderly array as tens of thousands of churches, hospitals, college buildings, YMCA, YWCA and CYO Halls.

When teamed up with religion, psychology thus becomes the most important science of all, with the greatest hope for improving civilization. At our final graduation ceremony from this earth it helps us banish O. Henry's fear of "going home in the dark" but meanwhile it permits us to LIVE zestful, happy and constructive lives.

TABLE OF CONTENTS

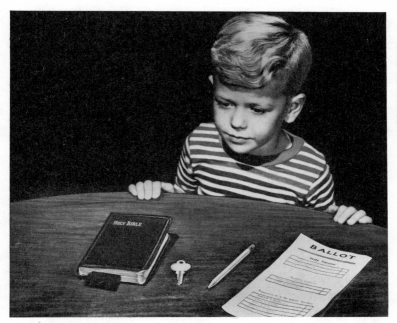

A Message For Independence Day

Will You Leave These To Your Children?

Men have died to leave you these four symbols of freedom:

A door key—your right to lock your door against illegal government force and prying. (Fourth Amendment, U.S. Constitution)

A Holy Bible—symbol of your right to worship as you wish. (First Amendment, U.S. Constitution)

A pencil—freedom to speak or write what you think, whether you agree with the government or not. (First Amendment, U.S. Constitution)

And a free ballot—your right to choose the kind of government you want—your protection against government tyranny. (Article I, U.S. Constitution)

These symbols of our independence have no meaning in countries where government controls every-thing . . . for there the individual man or woman has *no* freedoms.

Today, after 188 years of American freedom, there are people who are trying to give our government more and more control over our way of life. "Let the government start," they say, "by taking over the doctors, the railroads, and the independent light and power companies."

If they succeed, *you* will be controlled eventually, too. Then what freedoms will you be able to pass on to your children? What will Independence Day mean to them?

Tune in "Crusade in Europe."
Watch the television program which has received more awards than any other.
Monday nights at 10
WXYZ-TV • Channel 7

The DETROIT EDISON Company

(An outstanding advertisement, reprinted by courtesy of the Detroit Edison Company. This ad is adapted from one that has been run widely by the business-managed, tax-paying Electric Light and Power Companies of America.)

How Well Do You Know People?

Imagine yourself a publisher, selling books to the general public. Which one of each pair of book titles below would you select in order to sell the greater number of volumes? Place a check mark before one of each pair.

- [ ] Battles of a Seaman
- [ ] Privateersman

- [ ] Ten O'Clock
- [ ] What Art Should Mean to You

- [ ] The King Enjoys Himself
- [ ] The Lustful King Enjoys Himself

- [ ] Pen, Pencil and Poison
- [ ] The Story of a Notorious Criminal

- [ ] The Truth About Patent Medicine
- [ ] Patent Medicine and the Public Health

- [ ] The Art of Controversy
- [ ] How to Argue Logically

- [ ] The Art of Courtship
- [ ] The Art of Kissing

- [ ] An Introduction to Einstein
- [ ] Einstein's Theory of Relativity Explained

- [ ] Nietzsche: Who He Was and What He Stood For
- [ ] The Story of Nietzsche's Philosophy

- [ ] Quest for a Blonde Mistress
- [ ] Fleece of Gold

- [ ] Markheim's Murder
- [ ] Markheim

- [ ] How to Improve Your Conversation
- [ ] The Secret of Self-Improvement

- [ ] Eating for Health (Vitamins)
- [ ] Care of the Skin and Hair

- [ ] The Facts About Fascism
- [ ] The Truth About Mussolini

- [ ] The Mystery of the Iron Mask
- [ ] The Mystery of the Man in the Iron Mask

At their conventions or society meetings, I have personally administered this motivation test to over 250,000 editors, physicians, dentists, lawyers, engineers, advertisers, salesmen, merchants and parent-teachers. Others have given this test to over 1,000,000 adults. Scores of 13 to 15 are Very Superior; 10 to 12 are Superior; 7 to 9 are Average; while 1 to 6 are Below Average. The actual sales volumes are found in Chapter I.

Psychology Applied

CHAPTER I

METHODS OF MOTIVATING HUMAN BEINGS

The application of psychology consists chiefly of the manipulation of stimuli so that they will set off the desired habit patterns in the subjects under consideration. In some cases, of course, as in education, it becomes necessary to develop habitual responses which are not present originally. It is evident, therefore, that the applied psychologist must be familiar with the native habits or instincts possessed by mankind, as well as with the laws of habit formation and modification. He must also learn the varieties of stimuli which are capable of affecting the sense organs of the human being, and know the relative effectiveness of each.

His study will soon bring out the fact that human beings can be motivated and controlled by substitute or symbolic stimuli which, like the abbreviations in shorthand, represent other things, such as objects and actions. In this classification fall spoken and written words, pictures, graphs, figures, musical notes, money, and signs. The major portion of this book will consist of the development and utilization of symbolic stimuli by teacher, clergyman, salesman, employment manager, politician, writer, parent, physician, and lawyer. We shall begin with a consideration of those fundamental neural pathways which serve as the foundation for human motivation.

Bases of Motivation. There are two general bases of motivation, whose distinctions are of more academic than of practical significance inasmuch as it is almost impossible to separate their effect in the human adult.

(1) INSTINCTS. These potent bases, frequently regarded as

early conditioned reflex chains, are determining factors in the behavior of both animals and man. They make their incidence from the fetal state until puberty, and actively influence behavior until the menopause, in the case of sex, and until death in respect to the others. Their number has been variously listed by numerous authors, almost all of whom have given too many. This error is easily appreciated when we recognize that a multitude of habits take root in these basic reflex chains, and become so intimately interwoven with them as to defy later dissociation. Here is our classification of instincts:

(a) *Self-preservation.* Under this category fall a group of motive bases, such as hunger, elimination, respiration, pugnacity, fear, desire to avoid physical pain and to escape curtailment of movement.

(b) *Love.* This term is employed in its broadest sense to include parental, filial, "sweetheart", and sexual attachment, the first three of which are probably admixtures of social conditioning with the more basic erotic reflexes.

(2) HABITS. These motive bases are legion, and serve as the differentiæ for human and infrahuman behavior. Animals below man share most of the instinctive behavior with him, but man alone is capable of that complex elaboration of habits which culminates in language and our social inheritances.

Although hunger is an instinctive motive base, it is habit superimposed upon the instinct which determines whether we shall dine upon Shredded Wheat or oatmeal; upon lamb or pork or beef. It is, moreover, this superstructure of habits that constitutes the immediate concern of those who are interested in motivating and controlling their fellows.

In the age of the Neanderthal, for example, the sex urge expressed itself directly and quickly. When a desirable stimulus—a young Neanderthal maiden—appeared within the vision of a mating-bent man, he could take her by sheer superior strength, speed, or size of club. Recalcitrant in-laws with crushed skulls may have marked the path to the cavernous domicile of the newlyweds.

Nowadays such behavior is taboo. When a young man wishes to possess a girl who has peculiarly stimulated his erotic mechanism, he may, as his past habits dictate, arrange for a formal introduction, or else begin after the fashion of informal modern youth. Thereafter follows a series of "dates" interspersed with candy, flowers, telephone conversations, *billets-doux,* and reciprocal presentation to the prospective in-laws. An engagement ring ensues, followed by increased and thrilling tactual stimulation; then marriage and a "one-room kitchenette and bath" or a cabin in the hills. The entire courtship, unlike the three-minute Neanderthal romance, may continue for years, depending chiefly on the man's skill in handling symbolic stimuli, both in the presence of the girl and also in the sanctum of his employer.

In summarizing the bases of motivation, therefore, we may state that instincts and habits are the neural foundations of human activity. The former are usually more potent than the latter, although habits may change the course of instinctive behavior. Because habits become so bound up with instincts, moreover, they form the immediate concern of those who wish to motivate their fellows. The next section will elaborate this point.

Coaxing vs. Clubbing. Fishermen realize that they cannot drive either bass or suckers to take hold of their hooks by use of threats or scorpions. They must entice the fish; they must pull them on from in front, instead of trying to drive them on from behind. And, of course, they must adjust their type of bait to the food habits of the species they seek. Furthermore, they realize that the food habits of the fish vary with their chemical condition so that what is effective in one month may not be so effective the next. In short, motivation involves a knowledge of the specific habits and instincts, plus a realization of the specific stimuli that will set off or ignite those habit patterns.

The same stimulus, therefore, will always and invariably produce the same response if the subject to whom it is presented is unchanged. The difficulty in human motivation is the fact that we cannot look at a person and from external appearance discover that today he has a toothache, or indigestion, or that he is raging with himself and the world at large because he lost a twenty-dollar bill, or because his stocks have dropped three points. As a result, we may never be able to attain perfection and an invariable infallibility in dealing with human beings. But a diligent and scientific study of mankind will enable us to be eminently successful, for it does not require every vote in the nation to put a president in the White House.

The art of coaxing people is worthy of study. True, the club may at times be effective, but even animal trainers today are finding that they obtain better results by using the fishball or lump of sugar, than by wielding the lash.

There is a marked psychological difference in the output under the two methods. When forced to labor, we do just as little as possible in order to get by; we are resentful meanwhile, and fatigue more quickly in consequence. When enticed to productivity, we work with more enthusiasm and pride in our products; we like our superiors or employers, and we feel less fatigue. Regarded purely from the economic angle, therefore, coaxing is far better than clubbing.

Goddard[4] has shown us an admirable example of this, when he describes how John, an adult in chronological age but with the mental attainments of a seven-year-old child, came down to the barns one morning and said he wasn't going to plow that day. The supervisor could have compelled him to harness his horses and get his plow in action, but he didn't. Instead, he

---

"I would alter the motto, 'If at first you don't succeed, try again,' to 'If at first you don't suceed, try another method.'"   —Sir William Lever expressed sympathy and concern over the condition of John's health. He urged John to go to the house and go to bed, so that he would get better more quickly, as they didn't have any one who could plow as straight a furrow as John, and they certainly couldn't get along without him. He was too good a man not to be missed.

John stayed around the barn, however, and a little later the supervisor again met him, and urged him to go to bed, for they wanted him back as soon as possible. They didn't wish to send another man out with John's team and plow, for the other man wouldn't do as good a job. Still John remained. When for a third time the supervisor urged him in like manner, John said he wasn't going to bed. He felt better, and was going to plow.

All day long John plowed, whistling at his job, and cutting every furrow just as neatly as he possibly could. There was no resentment in his mind; he didn't sulk and pout, and do a careless job. What produced the change in John? Not any tangible stimulus like ice cream or cake, or a shiny new rifle, or a suit of clothes, or a pocketknife. It was simply a few sentences uttered within his hearing. Those sentences had no market value in dollars and cents, nor could they be carried around like a pocketknife and shown to other workers. They were just little puffs of air that struck John's eardrums. However, they were very special puffs of air to which a definite meaning attached. They were symbolic stimuli. To John they meant that he was a leader, a desirable person who was valued highly by his "boss." They inflated his ego. John, a lowest grade of moron, could be affected by these symbolic stimuli so that he would stick to his plow all day. A dog or other infra-human species cannot be motivated to ten hours of hard effort even with a thousand complimentary phrases.

The effectiveness of symbolic stimuli as bait was also presented in the famous story of Benjamin Franklin and the grindstone. They work equally well, however, with groups of persons, as advertisers and speakers can attest. In the public schools today we have stimulated the children to eat spinach and other forms of green vegetables by constructing charts with such terms as green beans, lettuce, cabbage, spinach, and others at the heads of columns. The children have the privilege of writing their names under each vegetable they ate the preceding day. And it is a distinct honor for a youngster to be able to see his name under several vegetable headings. They vie with one another to see who can have eaten the greatest number of vegetables. Social prestige is now involved.

Actually, under this system the children go home and ask their mothers to have spinach and other vegetables. In some cases I have known the youngsters even to do errands and housework in order to bribe their parents to increase the variety of vegetables on the menu, for possession of a blue or gold star next day puts them among the èlite.

One of the best examples of motivating a whole population is to be found in the popularization of the Irish potato. This beneficial tuber, when it had been introduced into England by Raleigh, encountered concerted opposition and prejudice. The laymen abused it in print, and the priests thundered at it from the pulpit. It was supposed to sterilize the soil in which it was planted, and cause all sorts of ailments.

But Thomas William Coke appreciated its potentialities as a means of staving off famine among the poorer classes, and determined to spread its cultivation. He began with his own neighbors and tenants, but they were indignant. For five years he couldn't induce them to grow potatoes, even though he resorted to mild attempts at coercion, and finally offered them land rent free. It wasn't until he himself had grown the large Ox Noble variety that he was able to get any farmers to concede that perhaps " 'twouldn't poison the pigs."

In marked contrast were the tactics employed by Parmentier of France. This young apothecary had encountered the potato during confinement as a prisoner of war. While his fellow prisoners were protesting at the outrage of having to dine on such "ungodly provender", he thoughtfully inquired about the methods of cultivating and cooking the new food.

Upon his return to France, he procured an experimental farm from the emperor, in which he planted potatoes. When it was time to dig them, at his own expense he hired a few soldiers to patrol all sides of his famous potato patch during the daytime. Meanwhile he conducted distinguished guests through the field, digging a few tubers here and there, which they peeled and devoured with evident gusto. At night, however, he withdrew his guards. A few mornings later one of the guards hastened to Parmentier with the sad news that thieves had broken into the potato patch at night, and had dug part of the crop.

Parmentier was overjoyed, much to the surprise of his informant, and exclaimed, "When the people will steal in order to procure my potatoes, their popularity is assured."

The psychological phases of coaxing, therefore, consist of placing stimuli before the subjects which will lead to pleasurable results. We have pointed out the superiority of coaxing to the more painful process of clubbing. The method is effective on animals, children, and large groups of adults. The art of coaxing individuals, of course, involves a more intelligent analysis of their bases of motivation than does the use of the whip, but it obtains far better results in most cases, and therefore is worthy of study by all those who wish to deal effectively with human beings in a business or social way. To be most successful, however, the one who wishes to employ this method must give heed to the importance of concrete stimuli, which we shall now discuss.

Specificity in Appeals.

Appeals are simply stimuli to habit systems developed in the nervous tissue, and accordingly they operate as do all habit stimuli. One rule of habit is that the more specific the stimulus, the more immediate will be the response. The restaurant's slogan, "We serve good meals", is too general to cause an active flow of saliva with the attendant whetting of the appetite. We don't find sensory cells, such as taste buds, that are sensitive to "meals". But we do have taste buds that are sensitive to sweet, salt, sour and bitter. Therefore, sugar, strawberry shortcake, ice cream, or vinegar, lemons, persimmons, and quinine do have the power to set up salivary action.

We may grade stimuli with reference to their nearness to the sensory mechanism of the human body, into several degrees. Remaining in the gustatory realm, we may call sugar and sugar foods, such as candy and pastries, stimuli of the first degree. Stimuli of the second degree are those symbolic stimuli like the spoken or written words: sugar, cake, pie, candy. Stimuli of the third degree, therefore, consist of those generic spoken and written words, such as foods, meals, menus, diets.

In motivating people we shall find it an invariable axiom of psychology that *stimuli of the first degree are more effective than stimuli of the second degree, while stimuli of the second degree are more effective than those of the third degree.* It is apparent, of course, that we cannot carry sugar, or silks, automobiles, or pianos around with us constantly, so the science of human motivation resolves itself chiefly into using second and third degree stimuli. These are what we shall designate as symbolic stimuli.

Too many salesmen, speakers, teachers and leaders in general include an undue number of third degree stimuli in their dealings with others. And third degree stimuli seldom if ever elicit response for the very obvious reason that our habits are not developed in accordance with these vague, diffuse words and ideas. We don't ignite gasoline or wood with flame in general, but with specific sparks or matches. We don't grow enthusiastic over "service", "greater efficiency", "greater safety", etc. But we do throw off our lethargy when we find two deliveries henceforth instead of one; when we realize that tomorrow under this new filing system our clerk will file seventy-three more vouchers than she could possibly file today; when we discover that tomorrow with the installation of one of these new electrical guards over each wall switch, not a workman in the factory can touch a live wire, as did Brown last week, with whose widow we just settled for $5,000.

Snow[12] gives the following excellent example of how even the mental appreciation of a saving of $190 on a piano was too vague a stimulus to produce action, until the salesman gave it more immediacy by translating dollars into social prestige and maternal duty:

A piano salesman had been working for a certain sale for two weeks. The prospect was a widow who was buying the piano for her daughter. She had intended to buy a higher-priced piano until this salesman came on the ground and showed her a saving of $190 in buying his piano.

Then she decided that she would rather have the higher-priced piano for her daughter—that the extra prestige in its name was worth $190—satisfaction and pride.

The salesman was up against it. His strong talk on the $190 saving that had started things his way was ineffective now. He sat down at the demonstrating piano and as he ran his fingers over the keys seized the opportunity to do a little hard thinking.

"My only argument is the same quality at $190 less price," he reflected. "But she doesn't care so much for $190 as for that high-sounding name on the other piano. That's vanity—and the only motive I have to play on is money."

Then an idea occurred.

If vanity was a motive in buying a piano, couldn't he . . .

Well, here is what he did:

"Of course, you know, Mrs. Houston," he said as he stopped playing and turned round on the bench, "how you enjoy a piano depends more on the one playing it than on the piano itself. By

---

"If you educate a man, you educate an individual; if you educate a woman, you educate a family."   —Dr. Charles D. McIver the way, what instructor are you going to have for your daughter?"

"Miss Martin," the lady replied.

"Hum!" returned the salesman, "I would advise you to have Professor Habicht."

"Mercy!" she exclaimed. "He charges $5 for half-hour lessons! I cannot afford it."

"Miss Martin charges $2 a lesson, I believe?"

"Yes."

"Then," said the salesman, "the $190 you plan to spend by buying this other piano, is going to cost your daughter 60 *lessons* that she *might* have with Professor Habicht.

"Sixty lessons under Habicht is too big a thing to overlook, Mrs. Houston, when your daughter's musical ability is at stake."

He got the woman to thinking about what the $190 *would buy,* and finally sold the piano.

It is apparent that money may frequently be a third degree stimulus until the subject himself, or the salesman, translates it into a second degree stimulus, after which action is more likely to follow. This translation process is clearly portrayed in an unusual type of advertisement of tooth paste, shown in Exhibit 1. This pre-war advertisement proved very successful. But contrast our present higher food prices with those shown here. Laws of psychology don't change but the dollar value does!

From the standpoint of psychology, therefore, specficity in appeals becomes imperative if old habit systems are to be re-aroused. One characteristic of habit is that the response is conditioned to a definite stimulus, and no other stimulus is effective unless it was also present in the learning situation and so became a conditioned or symbolic stimulus. We have advanced the three general types of stimuli as measured by their effectiveness upon the individual, showing that first degree stimuli are most satisfactory in their results but are often inconvenient to use. The problem confronting the applied psychologist, as a consequence, is chiefly that of selecting second degree stimuli in preference to the more vague third degree kind. This selective process is advisable regardless of which of the following motives is being employed:

With that $3 you save
ON YOUR TOOTH PASTE

BUY 20 QUARTS OF MILK

The average person, using a tube of tooth paste a month, saves $3 a year by switching from a 50¢ dentifrice to Listerine Tooth Paste. There are hundreds of useful and pleasant things you could buy for that sum. Milk, bread, and eggs, are just the beginning of a list that would cover many pages.

or

BUY 6 DOZEN EGGS

or

BUY 30 LOAVES OF BREAD

Acclaimed by millions, this tooth paste won on merit

Over four million persons have switched to Listerine Tooth Paste in nine years—and have kept right on using it. They are delighted with its better results.

Many of them were first attracted by its economy, half the usual price, 25¢ instead of 50¢.

But a mere saving of money could not possibly have held them. Especially the millions of women, whose first care is always to look their best. To them we had to offer a remarkable cleansing and polishing power. That is what you will find in Listerine Tooth Paste. It will give you new ideas about how white your teeth can be. And new pleasure in brushing them.

This unusual cleansing and polishing power is due chiefly to a *special polishing agent*. It cleans off tartar and tobacco-stains, dirt, decay, and discolorations—leaving teeth healthily white and flashing, as Nature meant them to be.

Yet, even though dirt cannot resist this polishing agent, it is too gentle ever to do your tooth enamel the slightest harm.

And after you finish brushing your teeth, you will be grateful, too, for the clean, fresh, tingling after-taste in your mouth—the effect you associate with Listerine itself.

We Save — You Benefit

We are able to give you a dentifrice of such extraordinary quality at half the common price—for two reasons. First, we have developed ultra-efficient and economical methods of manufacture and distribution. Second, quick and immense demand (over 4,000,000 users in 9 years) calls for production on a great, cost-cutting scale.

You want to improve your teeth and cut down your expenses. Try Listerine Tooth Paste today, and see how it will help you do these things. Lambert Pharmacal Co., St. Louis, Mo.

25¢

Ad No. 3460 R1*

EXHIBIT 1. An early example of the economy appeal in which the saving is translated into second degree stimuli. Courtesy of Lambert and Feasley.

The Relative Strength of Motives. Since instincts are such basic motive forces in human life, it is evident that any listing of the relative strength of motives will undoubtedly show a high ranking for such factors as we have placed under *self-preservation* and *love*. In the following table from Starch[14] are presented the general motive headings ranked in order of strength by 74 men and women, when given the instructions, "Ask yourself in connection with each one how important it is in determining your own actions from day to day. Write 10 after the very strongest motives, and a number between 0 and 10 after the others, according to their relative strength or importance."

Motives	Per Cent	Motives	Per Cent
Appetite-hunger	9.2	Respect for Deity	7.1
Love of offspring	9.1	Sympathy for others	7.0
Health	9.0	Protection of others	7.0
Sex attraction	8.9	Domesticity	7.0
Parental affection	8.9	Social Distinction	6.9
Ambition	8.6	Devotion to others	6.8
Pleasure	8.6	Hospitality	6.6
Bodily Comfort	8.4	Warmth	6.5
Possession	8.4	Imitation	6.5
Approval by others	8.0	Courtesy	6.5
Gregariousness	7.9	Play-sport	6.5
Taste	7.8	Managing others	6.4
Personal appearance	7.8	Coolness	6.2
Safety	7.8	Fear-caution	6.2
Cleanliness	7.7	Physical activity	6.0
Rest-sleep	7.7	Manipulation	6.0
Home comfort	7.5	Construction	6.0
Economy	7.5	Style	5.8
Curiosity	7.5	Humor	5.8
Efficiency	7.3	Amusement	5.8
Competition	7.3	Shyness	4.2
Cooperation	7.1	Teasing	2.6

EXHIBIT 2. Relative strength of motives as determined by introspection.

"I don't wait for moods. You accomplish nothing if you do that. Your mind must know it has got to get down to work."   —Pearl Buck

The disadvantages attaching to the method by which these data were obtained are twofold: (1) the subjects have difficulty interpreting several of the general terms into specific applications, and hence do not fully understand their full implications; (2) the subjects are not always competent judges of their own behavior. In other words, what they think they do and what they actually do are not always identical.

A better method, whenever it is feasible, is to place definite stimuli before the group, and then note to which they respond most readily and most often. An analysis of the returns from advertisements in which each of the above motives is in turn the chief appeal, would be more reliable. This sort of thing has been done by Haldeman-Julius[5] who sold the Little Blue Books solely through newspaper and magazine advertisements. These books are designated only by their titles, of which he listed 1260. The titles are subdivided under such headings as Humor, Love, Health, etc., but no title has any pictorial illustration to give it an advantage over any other title. Buyers sent their orders direct, so there was no personality factor of a salesman intermediary to influence the readers. Exhibit 3 shows some of the most popular books.

In Exhibit 3 we see the preferences of approximately one million annual purchasers of the 5-cent Little Blue Books, which were advertised in media ranging from *Harper's* and *Review of Reviews* to *Liberty* and the *Chicago Tribune*. Because of the wide variety of advertising media, and the small cost of the books, these data are rather significant. It might be added that analysis of the sex of the purchasers indicates that 70 per cent are men and 30 per cent are women. This fact probably explains why some of the female sex books outsell those for men. The males are buying them, too. Sex analysis of the buyers is difficult, however, since many women, if order-

---

"I have never known a man who died from overwork, but many who died from doubt."   —Dr. Charles Mayo

Title of Book	Copies Sold Annually
Prostitution in the Modern World	129,500
What Married Women Should Know	112,000
What Married Men Should Know	97,500
Woman's Sexual Life	97,500
Man's Sexual Life	78,500
How to Improve Your Conversation	77,000
How to Improve Your Vocabulary	76,000
Toasts for All Occasions	55,000
How to Write Letters	53,500
Book of 500 Riddles	53,500
Care of the Skin and Hair	52,000
Best Jokes of 1926	50,500
Spanish Self-Taught	47,000
French Self-Taught	46,500
Hints on Public Speaking	46,500
What Do You Know	45,500
Facts About Fortune Telling	44,000
How to Psycho-Analyze Yourself	43,000
Facts About Venereal Disease	41,500
How to Fight Nervous Troubles	39,000
Facts to Know About Music	37,000
Eating for Health (Vitamins)	36,000
The Secret of Self-Improvement	36,000
Psychology for Beginners	35,000
100 Best Books to Read	32,000

EXHIBIT 3. Relative strength of motives as indicated by orders for Little Blue Books.

ing sex books, either have them sent in their husbands' names, or else sign only their initials.

When the twenty-five book titles are inspected closely they may be resolved into the following classification: (1) Sex; (2) Social Improvement; (3) Humor; (4) Personal Appearance; (5) Education; (6) Occultism; and (7) Health. It will be seen from a comparison with Exhibit 2 that the order of merit of these appeals does not coincide with those given by Starch's subjects. Health apparently loses rank whereas Humor markedly gains.

If we combine the results obtained by Starch with those of

Haldeman-Julius we find that motives follow closely the instincts which were cited earlier in the chapter. It is generally conceded that hunger precedes sex, with self-esteem or the desire for prestige and an inflated ego running a close third. The latter is probably an admixture of habits and instincts. The writer would be inclined to include pugnacity fourth, with its modern correlates, rivalry and competition. It is to this motive base that speakers and salesmen frequently appeal in short-circuiting reason with emotional stimuli. In the ensuing section we shall discuss the relative strength and quantity of motives as they affect the choice or decision of an individual.

Motivation and Will Power. The *Will* is not regarded as a mysterious force by which we can arbitrarily decide to go right instead of left, quite apart from all of our previous experiences. Such terms as "will" and "will power" belong in the category of third degree verbal stimuli and need to be simplified before they are understandable. They are no more esoteric than the tipping of a balance when five pounds are in one scale pan and six pounds in the other. The scales or balance does not "will" to go down on the side which is heavier.

In similar fashion human choice of action is determined in three ways: (1) by placing additional weights on the side where action is desired; (2) by removing weights from the other scale pan; (3) by a combination of the two preceding methods, whereby some weights are added to the positive side while others are removed from the negative. These weights, moreover, are motives, often dignified by being called reasons. "Selling points" are the weights placed on the side where action is desired and "objections" are the weights on the opposite scale pan.

A curious commentary on human behavior is the fact that the negative weights (objections) do not have to be removed invariably by destroying them through a logical process, although this plan is more effective for permanent satisfaction.

As long as the subject forgets the objections, that is, as long as his attention is completely absorbed by the "selling points", the negative weights do not exist for him at the moment.

In the majority of decisions the salesman (hereafter we shall use salesman as a generic term to cover everybody who motivates his fellows, whether it be minister, parent, teacher, or friend) works with both sides of the scales, placing positive weights on the one pan and definitely removing the opposing weights from the other by answering the objections in a satisfactory manner. But even here, he attempts to keep the attention of the subject focussed on the positive pan, carefully avoiding any negative suggestion which might arouse hostile "weights".

But an enthusiastic salesman with a sense of dramatic values and a rapid oral delivery, coupled with plenty of specific sensory words which he chooses for their speed in igniting basic habitual and instinctive nervous patterns, can take a group of otherwise intelligent citizens and lead them on a lynching party, or a snake-dance down the boulevard; can sell them a set of books they will never use thereafter, or some submerged real estate. After all, there is artistry in the technique of such a human motivator, even though we must frown upon unethical phases of his results. As a matter of fact, this type of salesmanship defeats its own end, for the customer feels tricked and disgusted, instead of satisfied with himself and his purchase.

For sheer speed of producing action, however, the above method is excellent. The dramatic presentation keeps the subject's curiosity whetted by suspense, and the rapid-fire delivery doesn't allow him opportunity for those mental flash-backs during which objections are likely to come into the forefront of his attention. Then, too, the inner or chemical environment of the subject sometimes makes him more susceptible to certain stimuli, just as roast beef is far stronger as a stimulus to a starving man than to one who has just gorged himself to satiety. He finds it more difficult, therefore, to think contrary ideas.

In "The Haunted Lady"[3] we find an exceptionally clear-cut example of a tremendous decision made by a very upright and intelligent young woman, whose entire previous and subsequent life was exactly opposed to her brief tragic step. Lack of will power, some would describe it, but we prefer the analogy of the scale pans with a temporary shifting in weights due partly to an unusual concatenation of sexual motivation. In Exhibit 4 we have attempted to show the motive forces for and against her step during the three stages: Before, During, and After. Later she excused herself for her behavior in the 9 P. M. period by saying that she must have been mad, that she had suffered a case of temporary insanity. Viewed in the light of her physiological environment at 4 A. M. and the normal stimuli then affecting her, it was impossible for her to understand why she had transgressed.

Her behavior resulted from the cumulative effect of a number of factors. Had any one of these factors been absent, she might have acted quite differently. If her son had cried out, if the moon had not been shining, if she had not read the lustful poetry, or if she had had a toothache, the scale pans might have remained in their normal position. In like manner, the behavior of every person depends upon four types of factors: (1) the inherited mechanisms, including quality of nervous tissue, sense organs, etc.; (2) his acquired experience, involving the sum of his habit patterns; (3) the physiological state of his body—his intra-cutaneous environment; and (4) the stimuli affecting his sense organs at the moment.

In illustrating these, we may state that we don't expect a hen to swim, nor a feeble-minded child to enter college. Inheritance is a partial determinant of development. But habit also

---

"There is no worse evil than a bad woman, and nothing has ever been produced better than a good one."   —Euripides

3 P. M.

MOTIVES TO MORALITY	MOTIVES TO IMMORALITY
All positive	*All negative*

Husband present whom she really
loves.
Adored son also present.
Married state emphasized by
home surroundings.
Religious and home training entirely moral.

9 P. M.

All negative	*All positive*

Husband gone on trip, and his
memory not in focus of her
immediate attention.

Son asleep, and his memory not
in focus of attention.

Away from household stimuli;
seated in garden.

No church bells, thoughts of mother or other home training
stimuli in her mind.

Romantic stimuli all about her:
moon, roses, Spring.
Physiological state probably attuned to Spring sexual accele-
ration.
Just been reading wanton poetry
urging many loves ere age kills
passion.
Frantic fear she's growing old
and away from romance.
Man appears who once kissed her
before her marriage and set her
pulse leaping.
Thinks him a handsome god as
moonlight glints his dark hair
when he kisses her hand.
His kiss enflames her more, and
when he crushes her lips to his,
all else is oblivion.

4 A. M.

All positive	*All negative*

Husband gone, but his memory
vivid in her attention.
Son asleep, but in next room
where she is aware of him.
Back amid normal household environment and stimuli.
Conscience vividly demonstrating
her religious and moral up-
bringing.

EXHIBIT 4. Example of the shift in motive forces causing a young woman
to act in total disregard of all her previous habits. The boxed motives in the
middle panel designate not objections overcome by reason, but simply supplanted in the focus of attention by other motives.

enters into behavior. A stimulus is not capable of igniting a given response until that response is built into the nervous system. References to Biblical and Shakespearean narratives and characters leave the average audience largely un-illuminated, although Lincoln constantly illustrated his speeches with such material. As regards the physiological condition, we have already described its effect on the immediately preceding pages. Its influence is probably more important than we have heretofore thought. The hyperthyroid's excitability and excessive irritability is the opposite of the cretin's sluggishness and dull mentality, largely because of excessive functioning of the thyroid gland in one case, and its hypo-function in the other. The seasonal mating of infrahuman animals, the salt hunger of cattle, and the nervousness and excitement of the smoker who finds himself without tobacco, are instances of organic changes in the intra-cutaneous environment that render them peculiarly susceptible to certain extra-cutaneous stimuli.

The preceding examples show that what is called the Will is simply the response to the sum of motives leading the individual to one kind of behavior in contrast to those influencing him in the other direction. This choice or decision depends upon the four factors previously cited, to wit, his inherited mechanisms, his acquired experience, his chemical environment, and the specific stimuli affecting his sense organs at the moment. It is valuable to remember, moreover, that inhibiting ideas can be dispelled either by answering them or by keeping the subject's attention so focussed upon the positive form of action that he forgets them. In the next section we shall continue our discussion of the conflicts involved in decision.

Conflicts Among Motives. Most of the decisions which we are forced to make in life are not between such simple extremes as good in contrast to bad, but between the good and that which is a bit better. There are, of course, numerous exceptions and plenty of unhealthy conflicts, which we shall mention in greater detail when we discuss psychiatry. To show the choice between two pleasures we need mention only the interesting experiment by Moss[10] in which he placed hungry white male rats in a central compartment, with a female in the oestrual period in one adjacent compartment, and food in another. From previous experience in the situation the rats had learned that if they chose the female, they could not get the food, and conversely. Five male rats were used, after a starvation period of seventy-two hours. Four of them chose the food, demonstrating to the extent of this one experiment, at least, the greater potency of food over a sex stimulus. Other experiments by Moss corroborated this finding.

A caution to bear in mind in such experiments is the physiological or intra-cutaneous environment of the subjects. Young and old rats are not as susceptible to sex stimuli as are rats in their prime. And some strains of rats are more highly sexed than are others. When one states that a certain motive produced a certain action in a certain subject, one must be sure to bear in mind the nature of the subject and generalize only for that type of subject under identical conditions. This, of course, Moss has done, but the layman frequently overlooks such very necessary precautions.

When a young person is deciding upon the college or university which he wishes to attend, he encounters a conflict of motives. And his decision, like that of the young woman's in Exhibit 4, will depend upon the number and weight of the arguments for one school in contradistinction to the other's. Decision is made on the basis of the motive pull exerted in one direction as opposed by that in the other. One must bear in mind the caution that one selling point for product "A" may outweigh ten selling points for product "B"; so it isn't number alone, but rather the weight or pull or the sum of the motive forces that determines the human as well as the scales response.

"There are no gains without pains."   —Benjamin Franklin

When Mark Antony was confronted with his great crisis of deciding between Cleopatra and the love and power which she could offer him, as opposed to Octavia and his imperial position in the world, he demonstrated behavior no different essentially from that of the youngster who has to give one of his two playthings to his little brother or sister.

The difference between logical decisions and impulsive decisions is simply the fact that in the former we carefully inspect the contents of both pans of the scales under little or no emotional excitement, whereas impulsive decisions are usually made under some emotional tension, and with little or no attention to the contents of one pan of the scales. Exhibit 4 is an instance of impulsive decision. In emotional turmoil we become restricted in our thinking; hence, the usual number of associated ideas do not come to our attention, and we don't have occasion to perceive the negative or opposing arguments that would otherwise likely be present.

Conflicts among motives, therefore, simply denote that the individual is attempting to determine which course of action will lead to the greatest pleasure. These conflicts may exist between two laudable and socially approved motives, or between a good and a socially decried motive. The bad motive, however, holds intrinsic pleasurable capacity or it would forthwith lose its power to cause a conflict. Moreover, an immediate pleasure may be contrasted with a remote one which is greater. The subnormal person and the animal usually select the immediate satisfaction. This tendency, therefore, is probably true of all persons, although the intelligent individual is more capable of selecting the deferred pleasure. Impulsive decisions are usually those made with reference to an immediate pleasurable stimulus in contrast to a greater but delayed reward.

The Motive Force of Symbolic Stimuli. When the child sees a candy bar for the first time it has no gustatory significance whatever, and gives rise only to an optical effect. After he eats the candy bar, and several subsequent ones, we find that the sight of the candy bar alone becomes sufficient to cause a flow of saliva—to make his mouth water. This process by which an originally inadequate stimulus, through repeated association with the natural or adequate stimulus, becomes capable of calling forth the response originally subject only to the adequate stimulus, is called *conditioning*. Thus, words become substitute or symbolic stimuli, replacing objects and actions. As shorthand symbols were devised as an economy in time and effort over use of the more cumbersome words, so words in turn are symbols by which we can more speedily and easily deal with objects and events in our environment. We have discussed the fact that words fall into the second and third degree classification of effective stimuli. But pictures, numbers, musical notes, in fact, anything used to denote something else, belong in the group of symbolic stimuli.

By means of words, therefore, we can symbolically dangle juicy beefsteaks, delicious peach shortcake, roses, automobiles, radios, silks and satins—indeed, any object we have in mind, before our subjects. We can make them thirsty. We can discuss savoury viands before a group that wasn't hungry until we began talking, and in a few minutes have them so restless from hunger sensations that they can scarcely sit still. We can discuss sleep, relaxation, perfect repose, pleasantly flaccid muscles, and deep restful slumber until we have the listeners in an artificial sleep, or a natural one.

Words can make the tears flow; they can wrench a staid personality from its moorings, incite it to lofty endeavor and noble deeds, or lead it to a lynching party and human ignominy. Words can make men lend a helping hand directly or through the medium of their contributed dollars, or can place bayonets in their grasp with which they viciously rip open the intestines of those same persons to whom they previously lent a friendly hand. Words, as in the mouth of an Iago, can destroy the sweetest faith of pure love, or they can build the highest type of human trust and confidence out of originally casual acquaintanceship. Words can sculpture a beautiful manhood or womanhood out of a helpless bit of animate human flesh, or they may render it bestial and cruel. They may build a small company into a billion dollar industry, or drive a great corporation into bankruptcy.

However, words are not effective stimuli unless in the personalities on whom they are employed, habit systems are already developed which may be ignited by such stimuli. Like pulling the trigger of the rifle, no energy discharge results unless a cartridge (habit) is present to be acted upon. This fact is illustrated in the quotation: "Give not that which is holy unto the dogs, neither cast ye your pearls before swine, lest they trample them under their feet, and turn again and rend you." Salesmen of every type must learn that a polysyllabic vocabulary is not effective on minds trained only to monosyllabic verbal stimuli. So, too, all of us who hope to deal successfully with our fellows must be adept in the employment of symbolic stimuli, since they are the most widely used motivating forces. "I am by calling a dealer in words," said Rudyard Kipling in a speech before the Royal College of Surgeons, "and words are, of course, the most powerful drug used by mankind."

"Give me the right word and the right accent, and I will move the world," says Joseph Conrad. This is not poetic hyperbole. The world moves as its human cogs. Note the following example of such specificity. A woman went into a shoe shop to buy a new pair of slippers. The salesman obligingly did everything he could to fit her, but in vain. At last he exclaimed, "Lady, I cannot fit you. One of your feet is larger than the other." The customer was incensed. She went to the young fellow's manager, who happened to have overheard his clerk's comment. He asked to see if he couldn't solve the difficulty. She sat down and the manager examined her feet. "Madame," he exclaimed seriously, "one of your feet is *smaller* than the other. What you need is a smaller size of shoe." He sent her away happy, and with a higher priced pair of slippers. The young clerk later said to his manager, "Why, I told her the same thing you did." But he was wrong. Words possess distinctive personalities, just as human beings do. Two words, like two brothers, may be so much alike that they belong to the same family—they may be synonyms—but like the brothers they are also very different in many characteristics.

Hotchkiss[7] has effectively brought out this distinction in the following: "We can speak of a *bunch* of flowers, but a bunch of girls is a *bevy*; a bevy of elephants is a *herd*; a herd of thieves is a *gang*; a gang of angels is a *host*; a host of wolves is a *pack*; a pack of geese is a *flock*; a flock of acrobats is a *troupe*; a troupe of bees is a *swarm*; a swarm of pigs is a *drove*; a drove of horsemen is a *troop*; a troop of fish is a *school*; a school of partridges is a *covey*; a covey of police is a *squad*; a squad of editors is a *staff*; a staff of salesmen is a *crew*."

The sixteen synonyms above do not exhaust those that we have in the English language for the idea of a group, but they clearly demonstrate that one word cannot be substituted for its twin without frequently giving rise to vague feelings of unpleasantness. Note the effect of "a gang of angels". A Spanish medical student recently told me of one of his experiences here in the United States. Having learned English only in the past four years, he was not fully cognizant of all its idiomatic usages. When the American college girl whom he was escorting to the annual ball entered the room where he was waiting, he noted her beautiful dress, and sought to compliment her. "What a lovely nightgown you have on," he said. "What?"

"There is one thing stronger than all the armies of the world and that is an idea whose time has come."   —Voltaire exclaimed the surprised girl. "I say, you are wearing a beautiful nightgown," he repeated, thinking she had not heard him aright the first time. In discussing this incident later he defended himself by saying, "How should I know that evening gown and nightgown weren't the same? My teacher told me I could use 'evening' and 'night' interchangeably."

Although a person with a protein hunger which specifically craves beefsteak, will dine upon pork or lamb or beans in the absence of his favorite, he will be much more satisfied by, and hence much more easily motivated by, the perfect stimulus of the moment. Fish, too, if sufficiently hungry, will bite on a variety of bait, but the alert fisherman endeavors to employ the most effective bait. In dealing with human beings, an incorrect or mediocre type of appeal may produce results of a sort but intelligent motivation demands a conscious effort to sift the best stimuli from the neutral and negative, realizing always that what is best at one moment may not be best at a later time, even with the same subjects.

The motive force of symbolic stimuli, therefore, depends upon the specific type of appeal employed, its relevancy to the immediate condition of the subject at that moment, and the neural patterns which are already developed in him. Polysyllables, as we have already mentioned, will not motivate people with no habits conditioned to polysyllables. Symbolic stimuli are the chief instruments of persuasion, but the applied psychologist must know of what his stimuli are symbolic as regards the group which he wishes to influence. Among other things this involves feeling tone.

Motivation and Feeling Tone. We have stated that words and other symbolic stimuli may possess personalities. There are caste systems among words in much the same fashion as among people. We actively or vaguely resent moving a term up or down from its accustomed level. These personality qualities attaching to symbolic stimuli are conditioned in much the fashion that salivary flow is conditioned to a visual stimulus, such as a gum wrapper. The word "skinny" in the phrase, "She was a skinny maiden", is definitely out of place, because "maiden" has a semi-poetic connotation, whereas "skinny" is suggestive of a vacant-lot baseball diamond, and freckled-faced boys, dirty and decidedly unfeminine. "She was a slender maiden", is all right. No verbal note is struck that is discordant with the motif of the sentence. Even, "He was a skinny kid," isn't bad, despite the slang, for "skinny" has a masculine connotation, as does "kid".

In earlier languages all nouns possessed gender—masculine, feminine, or neuter. Although we do not classify them in such fashion today, many words, including adjectives and nouns, have developed a feminine or masculine quality, partly from excessive use by one sex or the other. Which of the following words, for example, suggest masculine usage and which feminine: *gorgeous, bawl, cute, weep, cry, marvelous, cunning, kid, gosh, dainty?* It is partly on the basis of the choice of words employed by an author that the listener can usually determine whether it is a man or woman who is writing. But the setting or contextual environment of words also influences their feeling tone. Despite the fact that "skinny" and "slender" are approved English words, one of them has more desirable feeling tone than the other. In advertising copy as well as in ordinary speech, one should endeavor to avoid the terms with unfavorable connotation, inasmuch as they call attention away from the idea being advanced. In Exhibit 5 are listed two sets of verbal stimuli with obviously different feeling tone. Those words under the "Negative" heading are somewhat unfavorable in general usage, although there are many occasions when they fit the general mood of the moment, or of the verbal picture being created, better than do their more polished synonyms.

POSITIVE FEELING TONE	NEGATIVE FEELING TONE
Plump	Fat
Intestines	Guts
Aroma	Smell
Nude	Naked
Inexpensive	Cheap
Girl	Female
Decayed	Rotten
Intoxicated	Drunk
Child	Brat
Saliva	Spit

EXHIBIT 5. Paired synonyms illustrating pleasant versus unpleasant feeling tone.

Polysyllables are frequently found to possess more favorable feeling tone than monosyllables, probably owing in part to their less frequent association with the unpleasant situation, as well as their usage by a more educated class. Words apparently are known by the company they keep. If used excessively by vulgar people, the most desirable term may ultimately give rise to a feeling of coarseness. Some of these reasons just outlined explain our preferences for certain male and female Christian names. Our experience with people possessing these names emotionally colors our attitudes toward them. These experiences do not necessarily involve personal contact. We may encounter the name in fiction, belonging to hero or villain, or it may suggest French, German or Jewish backgrounds, and as we have been favorably or unfavorably conditioned to these nationalities, we may react accordingly. In Exhibit 6 are listed the preferences of two adult women from quite similar home environments as regards racial background, social and economic factors. In almost every instance, they later explained, their judgments were made from personal contacts with people of these names. The agreement between the two raters is probably rather close for this type of situation. It will be noted that both sets of names cover a fairly wide range of races or nationalities.

Male Names	Mrs. C.	Miss B.	Female Names	Mrs. C.	Miss B.
Peter	2	8	Rachel	1	1
John	1	1	Anna	9	4
Algernon	6	6	Belinda	5	6
Gilbert	3	4	Bertha	10	9
Herman	7	7	Geraldine	3	5
Patrick	4	10	Janet	2	3
Richard	5	2	Maud	7	7
Maurice	9	5	Minnie	6	10
Henry	8	3	Nora	8	8
Jacob	10	9	Priscilla	4	2

Exhibit 6. Expression of preferences for male and female names by two female raters.

From the psychological viewpoint, therefore, feeling tone denotes the unpleasant or the pleasant habits which have been conditioned to a given stimulus apart from its obvious and most apparent response. These affective habits are usually of an emotional type, and are not always predictable from *a priori* thinking. It is essential that stimuli possess pleasant connotations if they are to evoke approach and appropriative behavior. It is because of the avoidance reaction engendered by unpleasant feeling tone that advertisers in general refrain from using illustrations which produce horror, fear, or nausea. In motivating people by print, as we shall describe below, it is necessary not only to employ second degree stimuli which arouse basic neural patterns, but which are free from unpleasant emotional connotation.

Motivation by Print. Through the medium of the newspaper and magazine, the billboard and the book, symbolic stimuli can repeatedly exercise their effect upon human behavior.

Although we shall devote later chapters to this subject, it is appropriate here to cite some of the interesting data that Haldeman-Julius presents regarding the sales volume of some of his Little Blue Books before and after he had changed their titles. Unless a book sold 10,000 copies annually, he had it

OLD TITLE	YEARLY SALE	NEW TITLE	YEARLY SALE
The Tallow Ball (Maupassant)	15,000	A French Prostitute's Sacrifice	54,700
Privateersman	7,500	Battles of a Seaman	10,000
Fleece of Gold	6,000	The Quest for a Blonde Mistress	50,000
The Mystery of the Iron Mask	11,000	The Mystery of the Man in the Iron Mask	30,000
The King Enjoys Himself	8,000	The Lustful King Enjoys Himself	38,000
None Beneath the King	6,000	None Beneath the King Shall Enjoy This Woman	34,000
Ten O'Clock	2,000	What Art Should Mean to You	9,000
Markheim	Few	Markheim's Murder	7,000
Pen, Pencil and Poison	5,000	The Story of a Notorious Criminal	15,800
"Patent Medicine" and the Public Health	3,000	The Truth About "Patent Medicine"	10,000
Art of Controversy	Few	How to Argue Logically	30,000
Nietzche: Who He Was and What He Stood For	10,000	The Story of Nietzsche's Philosophy	45,000
An Introduction to Einstein	15,000	Einstein's Theory of Relativity Explained	42,000
The Truth About Mussolini	14,000	The Facts About Fascism	24,000
Poems of Evolution	2,000	When You Were a Tadpole and I Was a Fish	7,000

EXHIBIT 7. The influence of new titles on the next year's annual sale of copies of Little Blue Books.

"Be not simply good—Be good for something." —Thoreau

sent to the "hospital" where he doctored its name, hoping by a change of words to render it a stronger motive to buying. In Exhibit 7 are listed some of the volumes before and after hospitalization. These data furnish probably the best example of the influence of specific words and phrases as motive forces, that we have in the literature. According to Mr. Haldeman-Julius the magical words in titling, as shown by his records, are: *Truth, Life, Love, How to, Facts You Should Know*. A close inspection of Exhibit 7 will disclose the following important findings: (1) An intimation of sex greatly accelerates the pulling power of a title; (2) Vague titles (Markheim, Ten o'Clock) do not ignite habitual tendencies; so are less effective than specific titles; (3) A man's products or inventions apparently are more interesting than the man; (4) Titles intimating dramatic or narrative contents (The Truth About; The Story of) have more motive force than purely expositional titles; (5) Polysyllables don't pull as strongly as shorter words.

Specificity is the keynote underlying the improvement of all the above title changes, as a quick glance will show. Vague stimuli do not start the thought process in any definite direction. They are as static as a highway sign that reads "Ten Miles" but fails to indicate to or from where. The title "The Art of Kissing", sold 60,500 copies against 17,500 for "The Art of Courtship". Here is just another example of specificity in contradistinction to generality as a motive force. "Kissing" is much more definite to the reader than is "Courting". It is the difference between a second degree stimulus, such as lamb chops, and the third degree stimulus, food.

The emphasis heretofore in titling has been upon shortness. The fewer words employed, the better was supposed to be the title. The publisher just mentioned opposes this view, saying that there is no yardstick measurement for a good title. The majority of the titles in the previous exhibit demonstrate that increasing their length apparently had no adverse effect upon their appeal, provided the increased length gave more specificity. Publishers, advertisers and publicists in general may profitably keep this suggestion in mind. Too frequently in the past one has had to read a novel in order to understand the significance of the caption under which the volume was sold. Figurative and far-fetched titles may have poetic significance, but they don't seem to be very strong as motivating forces.

A good movie title should be dynamic instead of static, meaning it should hint as to the plot even BEFORE we have seen the picture. A popular actor's name can help offset a static title, as in *Gone With The Wind*. Rate these:

Movie Title	Dynamic	Static
Hatari -------------------	-----	-----
Demetrius & the Gladiators -	-----	-----
Cleopatra ----------------	-----	-----
The Seven Year Itch ------	-----	-----
Broken Bow --------------	-----	-----
Return of the Fly ----------	-----	-----
House of Fright -----------	-----	-----
Call Me Bwana -----------	-----	-----
The Alamo --------------	-----	-----
Information Received ------	-----	-----
Dial M for Murder --------	-----	-----
Gone With the Wind ------	-----	-----

Failure to use the motive force of a dynamic and dramatic title is not only poor business, but it places an undue load upon the actor's name that accompanies it. It is like putting out a number of entirely new commercial products with little or no advertising copy or cuts to illustrate the uses of the new goods, and then sticking an old, reliable slogan on the container or carton as the sole sales point. A slogan, an actor's name or a storage battery cannot constantly be drained of motive force, and still remain fully charged. There must be reciprocity between name and goods. The movie title should "pull" along with the actor's name for maximum effect.

Before leaving Exhibit 7 too far behind it might be interesting to call attention to the last title in the list. The change of name increased the sale 5,000 copies annually. But when the new caption was also taken out of the "Poetry" classification and placed under the heading, "Humor", the annual sale increased to 21,000 copies. A similar change was wrought in Shelley's "Defense of Poetry", which jumped from 1,500 copies when listed under the "Miscellaneous" heading, up to 6,000 copies when classified under "Cultural Helps".

The motivation of people by print, therefore, involves primarily the use of specificity in words, which usually means second degree stimuli. These words must fall in the categories of the fundamental motive bases if they are to be most effective on the mass of mankind. They must, moreover, be free from unpleasant emotional coloring, else they will not lead to approach behavior. In being specific, moreover, they will usually be more effective when not in the superlative degree, since superlatives tend to produce negative behavior or "sales resistance". The following section will dwell upon this phase of print stimuli.

The Motive Force of Sincerity. The familiar adage that truth is stranger than fiction might be paraphrased to read that truth seems to be a stronger motivating force than superlatives and exaggeration. This result occurs because truth or sincerity gives rise to a feeling of confidence and trust, where superlatives develop a feeling of skepticism. The use of the phrases, "Fire Sale" and "Bankruptcy Sale" show an attempt to draw customers by giving an ostensibly adequate reason for the intimated low prices. Because such slogans have been overworked, and because the public has learned that the prices were not always lowered, many individuals deliberately stay away from such business houses. A large store, such as Marshall Field's, which possesses a very high reputation for honesty in dealing with its patrons, doesn't need to use such blatant devices for assuring its customers that they will get their money's worth. The latter have already been educated to expect full value. In order to demonstrate the value of sincerity, we offer the following illustration.

HART, SCHAFFNER & MARX

Chicago, Feb. 28, 19__

Editor of *Printers' Ink*: We are sending you a copy of an advertisement which brought remarkable results for one of our customers, together with a little story on the accompanying sheet, which tells about it.

We know that you often make use of articles of this kind, and believe that this one will be of interest to your readers.

Hart, Schaffner & Marx.

Here's an advertisement that sold 100 suits in one day in a very small clothing store whose previous high record for a single day's business had been nineteen garments.

In addition it was used as an object lesson in honest advertising in the School of Commerce of Northwestern University, and proved so convincing that a number of students and even an instructor or two took advantage of the sale to replenish their wardrobes.

The store is located on a residence street in Evanston, Ill., nationally known as the "classic" or "highbrow" suburb of Chicago.

The clothes which it was desired to sell were the left-overs of several seasons, in colors, styles and materials which had not proved popular with discriminating buyers.

"You couldn't give those clothes away in Evanston," said the manager of the store. "Our trade is the most fastidious in the country."

You know every merchant, no matter where located, thinks he has a particular kind of trade, or some special situation which makes his problem different from all others.

The advertising department of Hart, Schaffner & Marx, however, thought that human nature in Evanston was very much the same as anywhere else, and persuaded the manager to run the advertisement.

It appeared Thursday and Friday afternoons.

There was a crowd in front of the store when it opened on Saturday.

When it closed that evening just two of the suits remained—one so small no one could get into it, and one which seemed to have been designed for a fat man in a circus.

At least 250 men had applied for the suits during the day, and as a number of the early comers bought more than one suit, the great majority necessarily was disappointed.

One result of the advertisement was that since it appeared sales of higher-priced clothes have been much larger than before.

(Below follows the advertisement)

$20

Beginning Saturday, February 19

We'll be frank about this.

These suits have been in stock for two or three seasons.

They are not in the very latest styles.

Some are in colors and patterns that have not proven most popular.

Some seem to be just as attractive as any we have, but for reasons
we can't explain, haven't sold well. But—

Every one is all wool.

Every one is well tailored.

Every one is in perfect condition.

You see men—well dressed men, too—wearing suits just like them
every day, suits they've had for a season or two.

Why not get one or two of these suits now when you can get them
at one-third or one-fourth of the original price?

Sale opens Saturday morning, February 19.

It won't last long.[2]

(Taken from *Printers' Ink*)

The force of truth is felt frequently by the audience, which
will render marked attention to an otherwise unpolished
speaker who is so deeply and sincerely concerned with the project under discussion that the listeners are unable to do aught
but heed his words. In fact, sincerity backed by a little emotional enthusiasm is one of the best attention-holders possessed
by the public speakers. But we shall defer such topics as motivating children, juries, and audiences until later in this book.

It is sufficient in this chapter to emphasize the fact that there
must be instinctive or habitual bases of a neurological nature
on which the motive operates. We have conceived of motives
as stimuli, or clusters of stimuli, that set off motor activity of
some sort through the mediation of an inherited or acquired
functional linkage of neurones. From this viewpoint the odor
of a piece of cheese may be considered the motive for the random movements of the rat which ultimately lead to his suc-

---

"A hermit is a deserter from the army of humanity."   —Southgate cessfully threading the maze. Here the motor response follows an external food stimulus. The same type of motor response, even in the absence of the cheese odor, will also follow irritation of sensory cells in the walls of the stomach, which is, incidentally, the usual maze learning stimulus. In the latter case, the stimulus is a specific internal sensory one. Frequently it is called hunger, but this word popularly seems to cover a portion of the motor response, so we have avoided using it. It is a common event for an intra-cutaneous sensory stimulus to be confused with its gross motor response, since the latter is more evident to the other senses.

The psychological explanation of the motive force of sincerity, therefore, concerns the fewer inhibitions which are aroused thereby. Trickery gives rise to unpleasant feelings, and is consequently repellent, as we have learned by experience. From our social environment we have acquired not only language but also the knowledge that unscrupulous persons employ it to our hurt. Because of our contacts with persuaders of all sorts, moreover, we have found that superlatives and a stretching of truth usually go hand in hand with such persons. We try to be on our guard, therefore, against anything which indicates that we may be caught in a trap, which means anything that is unreal or insincere. Sincerity, on the other hand, does not give rise to this "sales resistance" with its inhibitions; so we are motivated much more easily thereby.

REFERENCES

1 ALEXANDER, F. G., *The History of Psychiatry* (Harper & Row, 1966).
2 CRANE, G. W., *How to Motivate Patients* (Cal. Dent. Mag., Mar. 1967).
3 GALLISHAW, J., *The Only Two Ways to Write a Story* (Putnam's, 1928).
4 GODDARD, H. H., *Psych. of Normal & Subnormal* (Dodd, Mead, 1919).
5 HALDEMAN-JULIUS, E., *The First Hundred Million* (Simon & Schuster, 1928).
6 HEBB, D. O., *A Textbook of Psychology* (Saunders, 1960).
7 HOTCHKISS, G. B., *Advertising Copy* (Harper, 1924).
8 HUDSON, R. L., *Sir, I Have a Problem* (Crowell, 1959).
9 MONTGOMERY, G. H., *Why People Like You* (Taplinger, 1963).
10 MOSS, F. A., *Applications of Psychology* (Houghton Mifflin, 1929).
11 PEALE, N. V., *Stay Alive All Your Life* (Prentice-Hall, 1960).
12 SNOW, A. J., *Psychology in Business Relations* (McGraw-Hill, 1930).
13 STRINGHAM, E. J. *Listening to Music Creatively* (Prentice-Hall, 1960).
14 STARCH, D., *Principles of Advertising* (Shaw, 1923).
15 WHARTON, D., *Shoplifting — Newest Crime Wave* (Family Weekly,
    March 17, 1963

CHAPTER II

THE PSYCHOLOGY OF LEARNING AND MEMORY

The basis for all learning consists of some animal tissue which is plastic enough to be affected by changes impressed upon it, and yet sufficiently retentive to keep a record of such influences. Simple animals like the amoeba, possessing no neurone cells or processes, and with no eyes, ears, or other sense organs, can nevertheless react to various stimuli in the environment. The amoeba possesses sensitivity, motility, and conductivity, despite its obvious lack of nervous tissue. Its responses to its surroundings are called *tropisms,* which Hunter[17] defines as "any unlearned form of response not under the control of a nervous system".

Lacking a nervous system, however, the amoeba can not store up the effects of its experiences in various situations, as can higher forms of animal life, and therefore profits little from experience in its watery habitat. The snail, on the contrary, has been conditioned to physical contact until it has formed a habit. If we take a snail and place food before it, we find that it makes expansive movements in the direction of the food. If, however, we now touch a definite spot on its body with the point of our pencil, the snail immediately retracts. Thereafter, if we simultaneously place the food before it and at the moment of expansive movement touch its body with our pencil point we find that eventually, instead of retracting to the pencil contact, it seems to expand and approach the food more readily. At length, we can omit the food altogether, after which stimulation with the pencil point alone will elicit the expansive or food getting behavior. The negative reaction to the pencil contact which originally was produced, has now been conditioned to a positive response. The snail has developed a

---

Courage is a habit. The coward is afraid and shows it, while the brave man, though quaking, puts up a bold front.

habit by contact with the special environmental situation which we have employed.

But the snail cannot learn a more complex type of habit, such as that of choosing between a right and left opening, one of which leads to the surface and air, while the other is closed below the surface of the water. The ant, however, can acquire more complex habits and learn to thread a maze. It is curious that the ant in learning a maze uses the sun, or the electric light—at least, some constant source of illumination—as a fixed point around which it orients itself. If, after the ant has learned the habit of successfully threading the maze, we were to turn the maze board around so that the light now is at the left where it previously was on the right side, the ant is as helpless as a tyro, and must begin all over again.

The so-called homing instinct of bees, as well as of pigeons, is now considered to be only a homing habit acquired by the individual after hatching. Bees have been taken out over arid wastes, and bodies of water, not so far but they could easily fly back again if they knew the way, and they have never returned. From much greater distances over fertile territory they have returned quickly. It seems that they must have developed a set of landmarks of some sort by starting out in ever increasing circles of flight over the fertile land. The same explanation is thought to clarify the homing of pigeons.

White rats and guinea pigs have been the popular types of animal employed in psychological laboratories for learning experiments involving the maze. Differences between rats have been noted which lead us to feel that, if we had mental tests for rats, we would probably find different levels of intelligence to parallel the human species. Some rats are morons, others normal, and once in a century we might even encounter an Aristotle.

It is interesting to observe a rat in process of learning the maze. He enters blind alleys as well as open ones. Eventually by a trial and error process he arrives at the reward box. With succeeding attempts on successive days he gradually eliminates some of his errors. The rat apparently learns the maze from the reward box backward toward the starting point. During the last quarter or third of his course he makes fewer errors and runs faster and more certainly. The human being learns the maze using both the end and the starting point as orientation centers, with the middle third of the maze being the most difficult region. After the rat has perfectly mastered the maze we may endeavor to find how adaptable or intelligent he is, by closing the main path and opening a detour through a previous blind alley.

Now when we place the rat at the starting point he races through the accustomed paths until he bumps against the partition which we have used to close the alley. If he is a moron rat, and the closure is in the section of the maze near the starting point, he goes back to the starting point and begins all over again, bumping into the partition as before. His behavior resembles that of the child reciting a piece of poetry who reaches a line where he is blocked by inability to remember the next word, and then returns to his starting point for a fresh attempt, apparently feeling that mental momentum will carry him through. An intelligent rat will choose the detour after a few more trials—indeed, some brilliant rats will learn on one attempt—but the moron rat continues to choose the old pathway and bump into the partition. It may require a score of trips to the starting point for fresh attacks before he seems to acknowledge defeat, and search for a new course.

The same perseverance in old habits, and refusal to attempt the formation of new and more adequate adjustments is true of human beings, too, and bears the name conservatism. Youth finds it easy to adopt new ideas and motor habits because it has few old ones at variance with the new. Age, however, finds it necessary to break established routine and habit in order to adopt the novel, and, disliking to expend effort and lower its prestige by acknowledging inadequate previous adjustments, it endeavors to retain the old by fiat. Observe the following reply written by the school board of Lancashire, Ohio, in 1828

A. D., to a group of citizens who had asked permission to hold a debate in the schoolhouse on the practicability of railroads:

"You are welcome to use the schoolroom to debate all proper questions in, but such things as railroads and telegraphs are impossibilities and rank infidelity. There is nothing in the word of God about them. If God had designed that his intelligent creatures should travel at the frightful speed of 15 miles an hour by steam, he would have foretold it through his holy prophets. It is a device of Satan to lead immortal souls astray."

The Laws of Learning. In the region where the end-brush of one axone makes connection with the dendrites of the succeeding neurones is found that animal tissue which is both modifiable and retentive. These regions—called the synapses—number billions, and furnish the neurological bases for intelligence. To explain how they operate we can draw a crude analogy to the action of the rat in a new maze. Let us assume that the rat represents a nervous impulse; that each straight section of the maze constitutes an entire neurone with its processes, and that the point where an alley joins any other alley is the synapse. The rat is dropped into the maze from our hand. In much the same fashion a nervous impulse is dropped into the neural maze at a neural starting point, which is a rod or cone cell in the retina, or a Meissner tactile corpuscle of the palm, etc., by some physical or chemical force.

As the rat progresses along a straight stretch of unbranching pathway, so the neural impulse passes over a single neurone. When a fork in the path occurs (synapse), the rat and the nervous impulse may take either branch. Neither knows which is the correct turn. If the wrong fork is taken, the rat enters a blind alley and the nervous impulse innervates an ineffectual muscle or gland. Since the goal has not been reached, the rat may come back to the fork and take the other branch. The nervous impulse doesn't come back, but new impulses are constantly being set up at the starting point, because of the continued action of fire, or light, or sound on the sense organ. At last success crowns the efforts of both. The rat gets his cheese, and the nervous impulse innervates the muscles that lead to removal of the fire, dazzling light, biting cold, etc.

It is apparent that if only one fork (synapse) were involved, at the outset fifty per cent of the rats would be right by chance alone. The interposition of more forks (synapses) between starting point and finish prolongs the learning process.

If, in the above analogy, the rat is placed in the maze the second day, or if the stimulus sets up a nervous impulse at a later date, it may by chance alone omit some of the blind alleys previously traversed and enter some of the blind alleys previously ignored. But *always* the impulse and the rat traverse the correct pathway before they effect success. Thus the right course is chosen every day. If we assume that we have not precluded the factor of odor in the maze, we can readily see that more rat odor will soon attach to the correct pathways than to the less frequented wrong alleys, and each succeeding day will increase this effect. The nervous impulse, too, leaves an effect in the synapse which we call lessened resistance, and this enables each succeeding impulse to follow the correct pathways more readily. Since our rat, let us assume, is now following the paths where his odor is strongest, we can readily appreciate that anything which will increase the odor will make it easier for him to follow the right pathway. On a *priori* grounds, therefore, we can make the following logical predictions concerning habit formation: (1) The more times the rat traverses the correct pathway, the more odor will attach to it; (2) The longer the rat spends in the correct alleys, the greater will be the odor he leaves there; (3) The greater the lapse of time since he last tried the maze, the less will be his odor on the paths. Remembering that the rat's scent is homologous to the reduced resistance to the nervous impulse, we may now state the laws of learning.

(1) *Law of Frequency.* Of two neural pathways, the one which has functioned most often will, other things being equal, offer less resistance to the subsequent passage of a nervous im-

pulse. This law is embodied in the statement that practice makes perfect; that repetition leads to perfection.

(2) *Law of Duration.* Of two neural pathways, the one which has functioned longer will, other things being equal, offer less resistance to the subsequent passage of a nervous impulse.

(3) *Law of Recency.* Of two neural pathways, the one which has functioned last will, other things being equal, offer less resistance to the subsequent passage of a nervous impulse.

The three laws stated above give the specific functional reasons for synaptic modification. There are numerous other primary or secondary laws of habit which may readily be resolved into these more basic ones. The Law of Vividness holds that the more vivid of two experiences will be retained longer than the less vivid. The Law of Primacy affirms that the first experience of a type is likely to be remembered longer than subsequent ones. But Adrian's All-or-None Law precludes our having large impulses and small impulses running over a given neural arc; so vividness must be explained in terms of longer duration, greater repetition, or the formation of additional habits which may be conditioned simultaneously with the given neural arc. For any given elementary habit, therefore, Frequency, Duration, and Recency explain the functional effect on the synapse.

The Role of Intention and Attention in Learning. Not only must one attend to stimuli which are to be remembered, but one must have sufficient motivation to keep attending. One may look casually at a page of printed verses, reading them one hundred times, and yet not be able to recite them from memory. If one is given an equally difficult page and instructed to memorize all the material thereon, it may be possible to have all the verses committed to memory in thirty readings. The latter example represents the intention to remember. Wherein lies the difference? The one hundred exposures to the printed words cannot be said to have been ineffectual as visual stimuli, for you may have read the page aloud each time, thus tying the motor expression to the visual stimuli. In short, when you read a page thirty times with the intention to remember it, why can you recall far more than when you read the page one hundred times without intending to remember?

By recalling the three rules for learning, we gain some aid. Although optical reaction to the printed words has been tied to the oral expression through the same neural arc in each case, the greater frequency of one stimulus has been partly offset by the slower reading for reproduction in the case of the other. If, however, the thirty slow readings do not surpass the one hundred rapid readings in the time during which the neural arc was being exercised, we still have not entirely solved the problem.

As a matter of fact, in the second illustration above conditions were different in still another respect, namely, rote memory was modified in part by logical memory. Connections between words were noted which were ignored during the one hundred readings. Moreover, the reader kept trying to formulate succeeding words without looking at them on the printed page, and then, when he failed, corrected himself from the page. These additional motor responses were instigated by his realization of the need for later reproduction of the verses.

An interesting example of the above situation can be demonstrated for the reader's satisfaction by timing some one who has been requested to write the alphabet backwards, beginning "z y x . . . c b a". Then have the same individual write the alphabet in the normal order. It requires at least three times as long to write it in the inverted order as in the normal way. Although the average American has experienced "j" just as many times beside "i" as beside "k", he finds it much easier to write "i j k" than "k j i". We tend to think forward, not backward, a fact which advertisers can utilize to great profit. "When You Need a New Collar—Buy an Arrow" is much more effective than "Buy an Arrow—When You Need a New Collar", because the real life situation finds the man without a collar. "I Need a New Collar" is his thought. If he has been exposed to the former advertising slogan, his thoughts flow right along in a-b-c-d-e order, which means that he immediately recalls "Buy an Arrow". If the second slogan had been used in advertising, however, and the man had thought, "I Need a New Collar", the phrase "Buy an Arrow" would not have come to his mind so readily.

The importance of attention in learning is great. Although one can learn without attending to the maximum of one's ability, unless material is in the focus of attention while learning occurs, one cannot by a voluntary effort recall nor utilize the habits acquired. There are different degrees of attention, which we have attempted to show graphically in Exhibit 8. In the normal waking state there is always a focal point of maximum attention, but one is also aware in lesser and lesser degree of marginal stimuli. To be under voluntary control, however, stimuli must be brought into the focal circle of attention when memorized. For example, a man goes into a grocery to buy a can of beans. "What kind do you want?" asks the clerk. The customer doesn't know; in fact, he can't remember any branded lines. "What kind have you?" he counters. "Oh, we have Heinz, Van Camp's, Campbell's, Totem, and White House", is the reply. The purchaser instantly recognizes several brands, and selects the one whose advertising has probably fallen within his field of vision most often. Circle No. 2 probably illustrates the degree of attention which he has given to such advertisements.

In Exhibit 8 it is advisable to explain the meaning of Circles No. 3 and 4. Stimuli which lie in Circle No. 3 include those sounds, lights, and pressures to which we respond as in sleep, and of which we have but slight recollection thereafter. "Hunches" and woman's intuition may belong here. In Circle No. 4 fall the stimuli and habits which are entirely outside the subject's recall, such as the pupillary reflex conditioned to a bell, as in Cason's[5] experiments.

Act the way you'd like to be and soon you'll be the way you act!

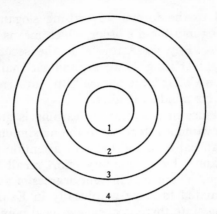

EXHIBIT 8. Showing degrees of attention. Stimuli in Circle No. 1 give rise to habits under the subject's voluntary control. Those in No. 2 are not under voluntary control, but are recognized when called up. In No. 3 the habits are vaguely conscious. In No. 4 both stimuli and habits are unknown to Subject.

Attention may be focussed now on one point, now on another. Thus, a stimulus in Circle No. 3 may usurp the focal point, in which case it then will lie in Circle No. 1. While reading a book we may suddenly become aware of a movement in the margin of our field of vision, and turn our head to see if it is a mouse. There are certain *Objective Determinants of Attention* which will force the subject to focus upon them. We shall present them in the following classification.

(1) *Change.* This usually involves movement, and is considered the most effective objective determinant. The flashing on and off of electrical advertising signs depends on this factor for part of its effectiveness. The gestures and changes in tone of the speaker, as well as the attention value of the directive motions of the orchestra leader are also effective for this reason.

(2) *Uniqueness or Novelty.* This factor probably obtains its effectiveness because of Change. The unique is different, which is the essence of change. However, the latter has a connotation of movement or spacial change, whereas novelty usu-

ally involves a qualitative change; so we shall make a separate heading for this factor.

(3) *Size.* Other things being equal, the larger of two objects will attract one's attention first. In advertising this is appreciated, and used as an argument in favor of the full page advertisement. The effectiveness of the quarter, half and whole page advertisements does not vary in the ratio: 1: 2: 4, however. As regards the total efficiency of such spaces, Strong[28] has determined that they approximate the ratios: 1.00: 1.41: 2.00. The efficiency of space increases approximately as the square root of the area, and not directly as the area. Efficiency of an advertisement, however, is not solely a function of the size. A full page advertisement, for example, eliminates the distracting effects of adjacent cuts and copy.

(4) *Intensity.* A thunderclap will usually break through the most concentrated attention. Richly saturated colors, and intense gustatory and olfactory stimuli are capable of capturing one's attention. The employment of color in advertising demonstrates in part the use of this method of forcing the reader to glance in the direction of a given advertisement.

(5) *Duration.* This factor in an intermittent form is called Repetition. Up to a certain point duration is effective as a means of compelling attention. Beyond that point adaptation sets in, and we become consciously oblivious to the stimulus. The loud tick-tock of a grandfather's clock is ignored by the dweller, at least until it stops. The cessations of sound may, from its fulfilling Rule (1) above, again command our attention.

(6) *Color.* Although part of the effectiveness of color may be explained under the heading Intensity, there is some evidence that hue alone, even when very unsaturated, is more compelling than black and white.

If you go through the proper motions, you'll soon begin to feel the corresponding emotions!

The attention of pedestrian, audience, reader, and child is *caught* by one or more of the foregoing objective determinants. But the next step is *holding* the attention, which involves an appreciation of the *Subjective Determinants of Attention,* which will be listed as follows:

(1) *Purpose or Attitude of the Moment.* The average man is not very observant of adult masculine attire until he heads for the city for the purchase of an overcoat, suit, hat, or shoes. Then he suddenly takes cognizance of his own sex, watching to see whether overcoats that others are wearing are double-breasted or belted, checkered or plain. Coats now fit in with his purpose or attitude of the moment, so they hold his interest. Having become overcoat conscious, he may even retain an active interest in men's coats for a few days following his purchase, but his interest soon begins to lapse. Herein he shows one of the sex differences distinguishing men from women. Women are usually alert to styles whether they are shopping bent or not.

(2) *Duty or Social Obligation.* This heading explains why men will study materials and labor attentively day in and day out at work which intrinsically is not interesting. The pay check at the end of the week is interesting, and the particular job in question is simply a means to an end. True, the work ultimately becomes habitual, in which case it does possess intrinsic interest, as shown in the next heading below. The difference between many a textbook and a novel is explicable on the basis of headings (2) and (4).

(3) *Earlier Education—Habits.* Individuals tend to see in life what they have been trained to see. The artist takes note of the pictures in the homes which he visits; the musician instantly observes the grand piano; the outdoor man sees the fishing tackle and guns in the host's den or study, and the grammarian notes the language employed by those around him. Trade journals are developed for those whose business and professional habits set them apart from others of mankind.

Speakers and advertisers must take these differences into consideration in order to hold the attention of their respective publics.

(4) *Instinctive Tendencies.* The reason one sex is interested in the other is obvious from this heading. Our movies are better attention holders than many political addresses and sermons, because they strike at fundamental motive bases, whereas politicians and clergymen don't always tie up their talks to fundamental urges. In a survey at New Haven some years ago, for example, six hundred copies of *True Story Magazine* were sold to the Yale students in contrast to one copy of *Century Magazine.* Moreover, material which holds the attention of people because of instinct is much less tiring in its effect than that which holds them through Duty or Social Obligation. Six or eight hours of study in one night is quite fatiguing, but college men and women will spend an equal amount of time together, often in active exercise, and not feel at all worn out, thus illustrating the psychical phase of fatigue. It is possible to employ instincts as an attention holding device by such apparently irrelevant material as coal. Here is a coal advertisement, for example, showing a cozy living room with an open fire before which two attractive youngsters are seated, while the caption and copy explain that there is no danger of these kiddies taking cold when XYZ coal is used.

In concluding this topic we may state that Intention aids the learning process by causing the subject to keep the new material in the focal circle of his attention-field, thereby insuring a conscious control of and ability to reinstate the new habits acquired. It greatly reduces the number of repetitions necessary for successful reproduction. Besides Intention, of course, the subject's Attention is an invaluable ally in learning. We have distinguished between the six objective determinants of attention and the four subjective determinants. The former serve as attractors of attention while the latter hold it after it is once caught. In controlling human behavior, however, the applied psychologist must make sure that the objective determinants attract the subject to the desired form of behavior, not away from it. In the latter case they are distracters, and therefore produce inefficiency.

The Effect of Motivation on Learning. From the paragraphs immediately preceding, it is obvious that any device that will tie up closely with fundamental motive bases of human nature will hold the attention. And learning cannot progress very rapidly and successfully unless the subjects concentrate. Verbal coaxing and verbal clubbing are demonstrated on a group of 106 fourth and sixth grade pupils reported by Hurlock.[18] They were divided into four classifications for the purpose of the experiment, as shown in Exhibit 9. Problems in addition were given the children. After the first day's test, the members of the Control Group took the daily examination in a separate room so they would be entirely unaffected by the other procedures of the experiment. "Each day, before the test papers were given out, the names of the children of the Praised Group were called out by the experimenter, and the children were asked to rise, come to the front of the room and face the class. They were then praised for the excellence of their work of the preceding day, as shown both in the improvement made and the general superiority over the other members of the group. They were encouraged to do better, to try to avoid any careless mistakes, and to add as many problems as the time permitted. Following this, the members of the Reproved Group were called out and were severely reproved for poor work, careless mistakes, lack of improvement over the preceding day's work, and general inferiority to the other members of the class. The members of the Ignored Group heard the praise and reproof given to the two other groups, but they themselves received no recognition whatever." In Exhibit 10

The most undeveloped territory on the face of this earth lies just north of a man's hatband!

AVERAGES

GROUPS	FIRST DAY	SECOND DAY	THIRD DAY	FOURTH DAY	FIFTH DAY
Control ____11.81	12.34	11.65	10.50	11.35
Praised ____11.81	16.59	18.85	18.81	20.22
Reproved __11.85	16.59	14.30	13.26	14.19
Ignored ____11.84	14.19	13.30	12.92	12.38

EXHIBIT 9. Showing total results in average scores for the various groups of school children, with 26, 27, 27 and 26 pupils of both sexes in the groups, respectively.

are plotted curves to illustrate the data in the preceding table. It will be apparent that the Praised Group did almost twice as well as the Control Group.

The effect of motivation on learning, therefore, is to increase the efficiency of the process. This result occurs because the attention of the subject is held more closely and continuously upon the task or problem at hand. Increasing the motivation means enhancing the strength of those subjective determinants of attention described in the preceding section. The value of different motives, and the significance of specificity in appeals were explained in Chapter I. A bonus in industrial plants, or praise and honors in school and social life are some of the chief methods employed in motivating persons to learning. Throughout the life of the individual, moreover, motivation will be effective in accelerating the learning process.

The Effect of Age on Learning. The ability to learn increases up till adulthood and then remains fairly constant until senescence sets in. The somewhat popular opinion that children learn more rapidly than adults is not correct. The ability to learn is both a function of innate intelligence and acquired knowledge or vocabulary. Since the neural connections do not reach their maximum efficiency until about the

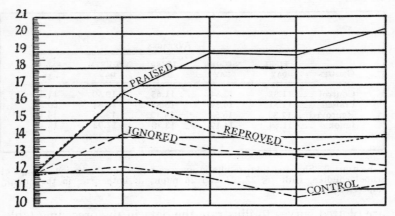

EXHIBIT 10. Graphic representation of the data in Exhibit 9.

age of sixteen years, the child is obviously handicapped in reasoning capacity when competing with adults.

The vocabulary factor is quite important in learning. Other things being equal, the man who possesses a vocabulary of 10,000 words is superior in learning capacity to the man who has only 7,500 words. Words are not only individual habits of vocal enunciation, but they also represent fineness of mental distinctions that have already been made concerning elements in the environment, and which can be used for future thinking. They are like various kinds of mental chisels with which one carves out knowledge concerning his milieu. The more such chisels he possesses, the more and finer discriminations he can make when confronted with a new situation.

To the savage a modern automobile is just a large moving object—more elephantine than anything else he can think of. To the modern man it consists of wheels, spokes, hub caps, radiator, speedometer, headlights, tires, steering wheel, and a hundred or more other things. Moreover, the modern man sees many of these things, while the savage misses them, especially if the exposure to the machine is brief.

Poffenberger[26] gives the average vocabulary of persons of different ages as follows:

Superior adult	13,500 words
Average adult	11,000 words
12 years	7,200 words
10 years	5,400 words
8 years	3,600 words

In another sense, words may be likened to fishhooks. The more hooks on a line, the more likelihood of catching fish. So, too, the more intellectual hooks that one has when dipping into a new subject, the more likelihood of pulling the known out of the unknown, thereby leaving the strange for special concentration and study.

It is true, as we have mentioned before, that age tends to become fossilized, whereas youth, with its abundant enthusiasms and energy and curiosity may be motivated more strongly to learning. But if we grant equal motivation and energy, the workman with the largest equipment of tools should turn out the best product. An average adult with 11,000 words has at least double the epuipment of the ten-year-old child. The drawback to age is the fact that it doesn't possess the exuberant energy of youth, and in hoarding its strength prefers to stick to the already learned. Men of fifty and sixty years of age can begin a new trade if they wish to do so. Their age certainly should not deter them from mentally coping with the new situations.

In summing up the influence of age upon learning, we may state that the capacity to acquire new habits seems to increase until adulthood is reached. Because of the lower energy supply and probably a lesser motivation of middle-aged persons, however, they are less inclined to change from the *status quo*, and hence are deemed much more conservative than their children. After adulthood is reached, the rate of learning

---

"We do not count a man's years until he has nothing else to count."
—Emerson

depends largely upon motivation and previous experiences or vocabulary, since the nervous system reaches its maturity during the middle teens. In the period of senescence the learning capacity wanes, probably through lack of motivation because of physiological changes in the subject's intra-cutaneous environment.

The Most Economical Methods of Learning. Many students spend literally hours on assignments that could be learned in thirty minutes by others of no greater intelligence, but possessed of superior methods of study. One of the first things to be guarded against is distraction of attention, either through daydreaming of more interesting topics, or because of noisy and fatiguing environments. The objective determinants of attention are distracters as well as attractors, depending on whether they pull one away from his task or to it.

Distraction increases fatigue even though in some experiments[24] it has been found that output does not decrease. The worker in those cases seems to muster more effort so that he not only overcomes the disturbing tendencies, but may even have a surplus. This condition, however, is detrimental to efficiency. Where concentration of effort and attention is desired, distracting forces should be eliminated in so far as possible. One way to keep a dog from chasing cats is to keep the cats away from him. In the student's room, therefore, a pile of love letters on the table, several issues of popular magazines, a phonograph or a radio, or a plate of cookies or apples certainly do not accelerate his studying. As one of our famous fiction writers recently said, "I waste more time sharpening pencils, oiling my typewriter, getting out fresh carbon sheets and doing everything else that I can think of before sitting down to creative effort, than I spend in original thinking." The same individual said he finally got around the difficulty by having his wife do every one of those tasks in ad-

---

"For every man who climbs to the top of the ladder of success, there is some woman who stays on the ground and steadies it for him."
—W. B. Garrison

vance of his entry into his study, so that he would then have no possible excuse to dally along and procrastinate.

Irregular disturbances, such as noises, are more detrimental to efficiency than are regular ones, because the sudden sounds tend to set off a fear reaction, while the regular hum or drone leads to negative adaptation on the part of the listeners. When the Air Personnel force of the Army was small, all typewriters had to be stopped whenever long-distance telephone calls came in. But the office force grew much larger with increased pressure of work so that, as Watson describes it, "it was no uncommon sight to see a man answering a long-distance telephone call with fifteen or twenty typewriters going in his immediate neighborhood and a hundred or more going in the one large room."[29]

After eliminating distraction, the matter of motivation should be kept vividly before the workers or students. In addition to the examples already cited, the use of graphs of daily output are quite effective, for they stimulate the competitive motive base in human beings. Thereafter the following methods should be applied.

(1) *Distribute the Trials.* The more the trials are distributed in point of time, up to certain limits, the faster will be the learning as measured in number of trials. Of course, if one has only half a day in which to learn to drive a machine, or master a speech, it becomes necessary to bunch the repetitions. The less time available for learning, the more trials necessary for perfection.

(2) *The Whole vs. the Part Method.* Experimental data show that the whole method of memorizing is usually superior to the part. Instead of stopping with smaller units, such as stanzas and paragraphs, the entire piece should be read through from start to finish. There are several advantages

---

"Little strokes fell great oaks."   —Benjamin Franklin

attaching to the whole method.   (a) Attention is uniformly distributed throughout.   In the customary method of learning, the first stanza is memorized; then it is repeated with the second, etc.   In this manner, the first stanza obtains much more emphasis, which partly explains why we remember first stanzas of poems we learned in grammar school, but seldom remember the last ones.   (b) Many faulty habits are eliminated.   In the part method the learner keeps returning from the last line of the first stanza to the first line again, with the result that the last line becomes tied up with the first by such associations.   This may block the later association of the last line of this stanza with the first line of the second stanza.

When the material is so long that fatigue sets in before the end is reached, or when the process of learning doesn't seem to be moving forward advantageously, it is advisable to break the material into smaller units.   By the whole method, of course, it seems longer for the student to master sentences and phrases, because of his distributed effort, but when he is able to reproduce the material, he can usually reproduce all of it.

(3) *Learn One Thing at a Time*. For the quick development of any given habit, it is well to concentrate on one habit at a time.   The experimental work of Ulrich shows that animals learning three problems simultaneously require more trials for each problem than when they learn the problems separately.   If we can use this analogy as typical of human learning it justifies the single-track mind.   Monotony, of course, may tend to appear more quickly thereby, so the teacher must keep the motivation strong.

(4) *Active vs. Passive Learning*. Active learning shortens the learning time, and renders more serviceable the material acquired.   In our previous example of the thirty in contrast to the one hundred readings of a page of verses, we found that Intention to memorize greatly speeded up the learning process.   The one hundred readings may have affected the

nervous arcs so that in an unguarded moment the reader might have recited the entire page of verses subconsciously, but he could never voluntarily and consciously recite them. Persons may see repeated demonstrations until they are positive they know all about the act in question, only to find themselves perplexed later on when they actively attempt the supposedly learned form of behavior.   In our dental, medical, and law schools we employ the case method of instruction to prevent such a catastrophe.   The tutorial system also makes use of this plan, as do examinations in courses, whether written or oral.

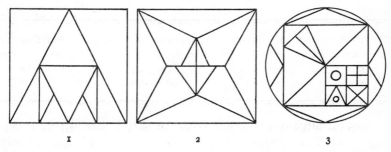

1   2   3

EXHIBIT 11.   Showing three drawings used in learning experiments described in the text.

By the drawings* shown in Exhibit 11 the writer has annually demonstrated to classes in psychology the effectiveness of frequent attempts at reproduction during the exposure period.   The third drawing is obviously the most difficult.   When it is presented to the students there is usually a groan forthcoming, but half of those same students can reproduce the drawing perfectly from memory after 20 seconds exposure to it, provided the exposure time is broken into 5-second intervals, with an attempted reproduction immediately following each exposure.   The students discard each attempted drawing when making a successive attempt, that

*The writer is indebted to Dr. Rex M. Collier for these drawings.

is, they don't simply fill in omitted parts of their first drawing until they have it correct. Each attempted reproduction
is made on a fresh sheet of paper.

Half of the students are sent from the classroom, while the
remaining half engage in the experiment. The writer then
begins the 5-second exposures, and continues until at least
fifty per cent of the subjects have a perfect reproduction.
Then the group of students previously sent from the room is
recalled and given a single exposure totaling the time taken by
the first group in 5-second doses. A comparison of the two
halves of one of my classes follows:

No. Students	No. Trials	Duration of Trial	Pct. Correct
48	4	5 seconds	50
48	1	20 seconds	0

Several advantages result from an active attempt at learning. (a) The subjects do not waste time studying already
assimilated portions of the lesson or task, but keep the focal
point of their attention always on the unknown or unassimi-
lated. This obviously results in great economy in time. (b)
By employing motor activity in response to the stimulus, they
render more permanent the effects which they do assimilate.
Two of my students a full twelve months after the experiment
just mentioned, reproduced from memory the third drawing
in Exhibit 11, with very little hesitation. (c) Rivalry usually
develops and heightens the interest or motivating force of the
strange task. This rivalry may be employed even when one
is working alone, for one is competing with one's earlier records or the clock, and sees the progress made between each
successive attempt at reproduction.

For at least fifty per cent of the university students to be
correct in their reproduction of the drawings in Exhibit 11,

requires two 5-second exposures for Drawing No. 1; three 5-second exposures for Drawing No. 2; and between four and five 5-second exposures for Drawing No. 3.

In concluding our discussion of the most economical methods of learning, it would be well to state that distractions of all sorts are generally productive of inefficiency, even though the actual output may not always be decreased. After the learner is in the most favorable environment possible it behooves him to distribute the trials unless time is at a premium, to adopt the whole method instead of the part, subject to the qualifications previously mentioned, to concentrate on one thing at a time, and especially to adopt the active method. Overlearning and frequent repetitions after the material is fully memorized also lead to greater retention.

Subconscious or Marginal Learning. It is difficult to estimate how important a part is played in our behavior by the habits which have been acquired in the second, third, and fourth Circles of Attention, as shown in Exhibit 8. The tolling of church bells, heard by the business man while he is shaving in the morning, may not have consciously been noted by him, yet the sound may set off an emotional habit that was occasioned years earlier when a similar tolling of bells became connected with the death of his mother. This emotional habit may produce a feeling of melancholy in the business man, without his ever realizing why he feels sad, and the resultant mood may lead to his decision to run down to visit his native village.

In such fashion many stimuli in the margin of our present attention-field may set off habits, the products of which are powerful enough to break into the center of our attention-field. The linkage of reflex arcs in the child's food-taking behavior occurs in much this manner, as can be witnessed in Exhibit 12. Here the reflexive stimulation by contact against the infant's cheek produces the quick turning of the youngster's head. The result of this behavior happens to be that the nipple is in physical contact with the lips of the child. This physical fact in

NON-NERVOUS LINKS
(STIMULUS)

NERVOUS LINKS
(RESPONDING MECHANISM)

CHEEK CONTACT

REFLEXIVE
TURNING OF
HEAD

NIPPLE TOUCHES
LIPS OF CHILD

REFLEXIVE
NURSING
MOVEMENTS

DROPS OF MILK
ON TONGUE

REFLEXIVE
SALIVARY
FLOW

LIQUID IN
PHARYNX

REFLEXIVE
GLOTTAL CLOSURE
AND SWALLOWING

FOOD IN OESOPHAGUS

CHAIN REFLEXES
SET UP IN THE
OESOPHAGUS

FOOD IN
STOMACH

REFLEXIVE
GASTRIC
SECRETION

EXHIBIT 12. Showing how reflexes are linked through their individual effects, the chain being called an instinct.

turn becomes the stimulus for a second reflexive form of behavior which involves his pursing his lips about the nipple and producing a partial vacuum in his mouth. The result of the vacuum is a flow of milk upon the infant's tongue. The physical presence of this foreign substance incites another reflexive arc that causes saliva to flow into the buccal cavity. Liquid, acted upon by the force of gravity, rolls down into the pharyngeal region, where it stimulates the reflexive closure of the glottis and initial swallowing action. Skipping the chain reflexes in the oesophagus which serially operate, we find the food squeezed into the stomach, where its contact incites gastric flow, etc. In this series of events, we note that the reflex arcs are not natively tied up, one to another. If they were, the simple stimulation of the infant's cheek by a pencil point which was quickly jerked away would cause the entire sequence of neural reflexes to occur. But such stimulation would not result in the hook-up shown above. Most of the reflexes bound up in instinctive action, therefore, are simply so placed, anatomically, that the product of Number 1 becomes the stimulus of Number 2.

In one of the short short stories a few years ago the hero, a young newspaper reporter, found that as he wrote at the typewriter in his study at home, he kept growing very thirsty. The desire for liquid refreshment became so strong that he had to stop writing, go to the refrigerator for ice cubes, and fix himself a glass of ice water. Within twenty minutes his thirst again broke through the attention he was concentrating upon his writing, and he was compelled to get another glass of ice water. This happened at fifteen or twenty minute intervals for an hour. He knew there was no real need for so much liquid intake, but he couldn't prevent his apparently insatiable thirst. Then he noted, across the little court and suspended in an open window, a pendant wind chime whose pieces of glass were emitting a tinkling sound resembling ice in a glass. This auditory stimulus, though in the margin of his attention-field, had been sufficient to set up an organic thirst reaction of sufficient strength to usurp the focus of his conscious attention.

To the effect of such marginal stimuli, too, belong the vague feelings of liking or dislike which we have discussed in Chapter I under the heading of feeling tone. Likewise our fondness for one type of food and nausea at the thought of another have frequently been formed without our being aware of the reasons therefor. To the four primitive gustatory stimuli have been conditioned the great variety of food likes demonstrated by the viands described in cook books and restaurant menus. Hollingworth gives the following table of likes and dislikes of infants, based on the findings of Peterson and Rainey.[25] The fondness for beefsteak, in the light of these early sensory re-

| | NUMBER SHOWING SUCH RESPONSES TO | | | |
REACTION OF INFANT	SWEET	SALT	BITTER	SOUR
Contented sucking _____747	503	31	136	
Discomfort reaction _____ 37	295	780	659	

EXHIBIT 13. Gustatory reactions of infants during the first week after birth.

sponses to the taste, can be explained only on the basis of its saline quality. But we adults like beefsteak for more reasons than that it is salty. Its odor, feel upon the tongue, and temperature are simultaneous reactions that have been acquired unwittingly, and conditioned to our general pleasant emotional state when with our parents at the table. Cod liver oil is used as a reward with a set of twin girls of my acquaintance, while the same substance is taken under force by many youngsters. Why a food tastes good or bad depends as much upon the marginal stimuli playing upon the individual at the time of first

"One should no more be affectionate in front of a child without including him than eat in front of him while he remains hungry."
                                                    —Dr. Eric Berne

encountering the food as upon its chemical reactions of sweet, sour, salt, or bitter. Tobacco, beer, and grapefruit have probably unpleasant native tastes, but they soon become conditioned to a pleasurable response.

From the standpoint of psychology, therefore, subconscious or marginal learning has today come to be regarded as of even more significance than was frequently thought. The psychoanalysts work with the habits which have been acquired unwittingly by their patients, and the advertisers depend for much of their success upon the subconscious or marginal learning of their public. The emotional coloring which attaches to many of our memories results from marginal memories or habits. Indeed, many of the likes and dislikes which we have are a consequence of marginal learning. A peculiar characteristic of marginal learning is that such memories are not under the conscious control of the possessor. Emotional memories are chiefly of this sort. The conscious utilization of marginal stimuli in child training is not even yet developed to the degree to which it should be.

The Facts About Memory Improvement. Probably ninety per cent of students and the general public feel that their memory is poor. They base their attitude on the fact that they don't remember all the experiences which they have encountered in life. As a matter of fact, it is probably fortunate that most of the stimuli which affect us do not leave permanent functional memories. We need a certain amount of perspective for distinguishing the important from the trivial, and we gain this by forgetting the unimportant.

Memory is looked upon as the physiological retention in the synapses of changes once made therein. As such, therefore, there is no way of improving memory, unless possibly through a general improvement of health. If impressions have been made, they will remain. The time when stronger impressions can be made is chiefly at the moment of exposure to the stimulus. Memory improvement, therefore, really amounts to improving our methods of learning. After the photographic film has been once exposed to light, it is too late to try to increase the clarity of the impression thereon. That should have occurred at the moment of exposure. If the image is too faint, the time of exposure should have been increased or the larger shutter opening should have been used, or both. In a similar fashion, we can increase the distinctness of the neural impression by more time spent considering the things to be remembered, or by enlarging the associations with which we connect them. If we meet Mr. Brown at a dinner, and are introduced by some one who doesn't enunciate the name distinctly to us, and if we are concerned with making the proper acknowledgement *a la* Emily Post so that we are only partly attentive to the stranger, it is no wonder we cannot recall his name two hours later, especially if we have given no thought to it in the interim. We simply used a 1/50 second exposure time and a tiny shutter opening, when the situation demanded a time exposure and a twilight shutter.

The motivation is the first step in remembering names or other items. Any intelligent man or woman could probably remember every stranger he had ever met, if he were paid $1,000 per name remembered. There is nothing esoteric about memory improvement. In the case of Mr. Brown, above, we need to get the correct stimulus to begin with. This demands actually hearing the name aright. Next comes the active use of, or response to, the name, such as, "I'm glad to meet you, Mr. Brown". Names which are spoken are much more easily remembered. The reason so many fail to recall names is because they respond to an introduction with only "How do you do", and are so self-conscious or introvertive that they are paying most of their attention to the good appearance they hope they are making, instead of to the individuals they meet. By thinking about the name, visualizing it spelled, and preferably writing it down, we help increase the effect on our synapses. Through such procedures and arbitrary associations we fulfill the two laws of learning, frequency and duration, and retain the name longer.

Unlike the camera analogy, however, human beings can keep the synapses active after the actual stimulus has disappeared, and hence can "set" the effect more surely. It was of such a situation that William James wrote when he said that "we learn to swim during the winter, and to skate during the summer".

The laws describing the four methods by which ideas and events are recalled in memory are given below. The first two relate to the temporal factor involved at the time of learning, while the last two pertain to qualities possessed by the objects themselves.

(1) *The Law of Contiguity*. If two things are experienced together in point of time frequently enough, the presence of one will lead to recall of the other. It is this law which explains the majority of memories, as can be noted from an inspection of Exhibit 14. The various conditioned habits also belong here.

(2) *The Law of Succession*. If two things are frequently experienced in immediate succession in point of time, the presence of the first one alone will tend to produce recall of the second. This law is not so easily demonstrable as the first, but it explains why one cannot recollect the third word in the first line of the poem regarding Mary and the Lamb until one has uttered or thought the first and second words.

(3) *The Law of Similarity*. If two things are similar, that is, have elements in common, the presence of one is likely to lead to recall of the other. Synonyms are of this type. In Exhibit 14 are several responses that fall under this heading.

(4) *The Law of Contrast*. The extremes or opposites tend to be associated in memory so that the presence of one leads to recall of the other. This really might be considered negative similarity, and is evident in six or seven of the most frequent associations in Exhibit 14.

STIMULI	RESPONSES			
	MOST FREQUENT	SECOND	THIRD	FOURTH
1. Table	chair (267)	wood (76)	furniture (75)	eat (63)
2. Dark	light (427)	night (221)	black (76)	color (28)
3. Music	piano (180)	sound (95)	song (68)	singing (48)
4. Sickness	health (142)	death (115)	illness (71)	doctor (62)
5. Man	woman (394)	male (99)	boy (44)	strength (32)
6. Deep	shallow (180)	water (134)	ocean (93)	sea (90)
7. Soft	hard (365)	pillow (53)	easy (34)	cotton (28)
8. Eating	food (170)	drinking (166)	bread (46)	hungry (44)
9. Mountain	high (246)	hill (184)	valley (90)	height (73)
10. House	home (103)	building (78)	barn (74)	dwelling (68)
11. Black	white (339)	dark (172)	color (129)	night (51)
12. Mutton	meat (257)	sheep (204)	lamb (121)	beef (97)
13. Comfort	ease (165)	pleasure (77)	home (63)	easy (61)
14. Hand	foot (204)	fingers (83)	arm (63)	work (49)
15. Butterfly	insect (261)	bird (64)	fly (44)	pretty (39)
16. Chair	table (191)	seat (127)	sit (107)	furniture (83)
17. Whistle	noise (173)	sound (103)	blow (95)	sing (75)
18. Wish	desire (197)	want (66)	hope (51)	thought (47)
19. River	water (393)	stream (117)	lake (65)	deep (35)
20. Beautiful	pretty (113)	nice (73)	ugly (66)	lovely (64)
21. Citizen	man (278)	person (64)	people (41)	American (35)
22. Spider	insect (276)	web (188)	fly (136)	bug (58)
23. Sleep	rest (300)	awake (94)	bed (75)	wake (60)
24. Trouble	sorrow (202)	worry (65)	sickness (47)	care (27)
25. Cabbage	vegetable (394)	plant (48)	green (44)	garden (43)

EXHIBIT 14. The four most frequent responses from 1,000 individuals to a number of common words. (Kent and Rosanoff).

Because of the different associates attaching to a list of common words, Kent and Rosanoff[20] hoped to be able to detect symptoms of mental derangement. They constructed a list of 100 common words; then gave these to 1,000 individuals from

"Men and women, like all Gaul, may be divided into three parts—the erotic, the neurotic, and the tommyrotic!" —M. H. Lichliter a wide range of intellectual, educational and business groups. In Exhibit 14 we have included twenty-five of the original stimuli, followed by the four most frequent responses. The figures in parentheses indicate the number of persons giving the response. Although these experimenters didn't find the lists to be of much practical benefit for their purposes, they do show the uniformity of response of this fairly typical group of normal men and women.

Our discussion of the facts about memory improvement, therefore, has shown that it really amounts to improvement in the learning process. The three laws of learning, coupled with motivation, attention, and the intention to remember, are the chief instruments through which an individual increases the memories available for pleasure and profit. After an impression has been made upon the synapses, this impression tends to remain. A part of memory improvement is concerned with making vivid impressions on the nervous system. Another phase of the process, however, involves the linkage of one idea with numerous associated memories so that it becomes more available to its owner. We have mentioned the four laws of association which describe the manner in which such linkages occur.

The Various Degrees of Memory. The degrees of memory correspond roughly to the regions in our attention-field where the stimuli affect us. Thus, stimuli which were in the focus of our attention-field give rise to habits that we are aware of having formed, and which we can voluntarily reinstate. We may call this *first degree memory.* The secret of improving one's memory lies primarily in getting the items to be retained into the focus of our attention-field, so that we shall have active functional memories of them which we can utilize whenever we desire.

Second degree memory is illustrated by the example previously mentioned of the man in the grocery store asking for a can of beans. Multiple choice examinations have been devised to tap this second degree memory of the student. This is called the "Age of Stimulus" method by Hunter and others, measuring a less active kind of memory from the standpoint of the subject's voluntary control.

Third degree memory is a stage farther removed. Here we not only cannot voluntarily recall, but when the stimuli are presented to us, we are not conscious of having experienced them before. We may say they are new to us, yet our behavior may not bear out our words. Often, however, we have a vague sense of familiarity with the stimulus but don't know how we obtained it. It is a hunch, or intuition. Scott[27] explains the genesis of such vague memories regarding advertising thus:

The passengers on street railways have but little to distract their attention. They go over the same road so frequently that the streets passed through cease to be interesting. Since newspapers and magazines cannot be easily read, the cards have but few rivals for attention. Even those who have but little interest in the advertisements find that they glance at the cards frequently and that the eyes rest on a single card for a considerable length of time. . . . The goods which through their advertisements have occupied our minds for long periods of time assume in our minds an importance which is often far in excess of anything which would have been anticipated by one who is not familiar with the peculiar power here described. In estimating the relative values of two competing lines of goods, I assume that my judgment is based on the goods themselves as they are presented to my reason. I am not aware of the fact that I am prejudiced in favor of the goods that have occupied my mind the longest periods of time.

Fourth degree memory is of lesser concern to us in a practical way because of its further removal from our active control. The conditioned reflexive contraction of the pupil of the eye to the sound of a bell is an instance in point. It is possible that our sense of time belongs in this category. Probably many segmental forms of behavior involving reflexes connected with

"It is a socialist idea that making profits is a vice. I consider that the real vice is making losses."   —Winston Churchill the emotions are in this class. Here we haven't even hunches or intuition, but the products of these reflexes may, like the glass wind chime's effect on the reporter, break into a more active attention-field, and affect our behavior. The psychoanalysts do their work with third degree and possibly fourth degree memories.

A psychological summary of the degrees of memory shows that they parallel closely the degrees of attention which we described hitherto. First degree memories are capable of voluntary reinstatement by their owner, while second degree memories are illustrated in multiple choice examinations. Third and fourth degree memories are far removed from the subject's attention-field, but may indirectly exert some control of his behavior. We have already explained the importance of these various degrees of memory from the advertising man's and the psychoanalyst's standpoint, and of the need for their utilization by the child psychologist and teacher. The cortical process which we call thinking is concerned primarily with first degree memories, as the following section will further demonstrate.

The Relationship of Thinking to Habit. Since words are abbreviations for actions and objects it is fairly clear that our thinking, which depends primarily on our established habits, must be concerned quite generally with words and other forms of symbolic stimuli. And as we try first one act or object, then another, in real life situations, so in mentally attempting to solve a new problem it is apparent that we go through a trial and error process with words. An excellent illustration of this is given by Watson[29] who compares the situation throughout to the trial and error physical movements of the rats in the maze.

A colleague of mine came on a visit to stay in an apartment in which I had rooms. In a passage leading from the shower bath was

"The mind grows by what it feeds upon."   —Shakespeare
"For as a man thinketh, so is he."   —The Bible

a peculiar piece of apparatus standing near a sink. The essential features were a curved shallow nickel pan about twelve inches wide by twenty inches long; at one end the pan had been bent in the form of a half circle, while at the other end the side pieces did not extend for the full width. The pan was mounted on a stand adjustable in height. Furthermore the pan itself was attached to the stand by a ball and socket joint. My friend had never seen anything like it and asked me what in the world it was. I told him I was writing a paper on thinking and pleaded with him to think his problem out aloud. He entered into the experiment in the proper spirit. I shall not record all of his false starts and returns but I will sketch a few of them. "The thing looks a little like an invalid's table, but it is not heavy, the pan is curved, it has side pieces and is attached with a ball and socket joint. It would never hold a tray full of dishes (*cul de sac*). The thing (return to starting point) looks like some of the failures of an inventor. I wonder if the landlord is an inventor. No, you told me he was a porter in one of the big banks down town. The fellow is as big as a house and looks more like a prize-fighter than a mechanician; those paws of his would never do the work demanded of an inventor" (blank wall again). This was as far as we got on the first day. On the second morning we got no nearer the solution. On the second night we talked over the way the porter and his wife lived, and the subject wondered how a man earning not more than $150 per month could live as the landlord did. I told him that the wife was a hair-dresser and earned about eight dollars per day herself. Then I asked him if he did not see the sign "Hair-Dresser" on the door as we entered. The next morning after coming from his bath he said, "I saw that infernal thing again" (original starting point). "It must be something to use in washing or weighing the baby—but they had no baby (*cul de sac* again). The thing is curved at one end so that it would just fit the neck. The woman you say is a hair-dresser and the pan goes against the neck and the hair is spread out over it." This was the correct conclusion. Upon reaching it there was a smile, a sigh and an immediate turn to something else (the equivalent of obtaining food after search).

Not only does thinking involve previous experiences or habits of the individual, but the act of thinking can become habitual. The logical manner in which debaters, lawyers, and professional reasoners attack new problems is a result of practice. Fallacious reasoning is avoided with the skill and dexterity of the fencer. The reverse of this mental agility is expressed in the statement that there can be feeble-mindedness by deprivation. This situation refers to the dulling of the curiosity by a monotonous and unstimulating milieu, so that by adulthood the individual is "set" in habits of sluggish response, even though he is surrounded thereafter by choicest gems of music, literature, and art.

William James was once asked why his family had been so brilliant, and replied that it was largely due to the free discussion in the home while he was a child. He said that his parents encouraged debate, even at the table, and the children "whetted our wits on each other's". Children can be encouraged to original thinking in many ways. Many a child in a poor home where there was no abundance of toys has utilized sticks and paper, and by use of imagination has created a wealth of playthings. True, a stick may have to represent a horse, or a walnut may stand for a pig, but this very act of symbolizing other objects with substitutes involves an additional thought process, so keeps his cortex from fossilizing. Since no one of us ever uses anywhere near his maximum mental capacity, we need have little fear of burning out a synapse.

Three types of thinking are generally differentiated. (a) Reverie. In reverie our thoughts follow spontaneously wherever fancy leads us, and we feel no sense of effort or strain. This category includes daydreaming. It is a case of free association. Animals also probably engage in this type of thinking. I have come in from the hay fields with my dog, which had been chasing rabbits all afternoon, and have observed this dog in his sleep, where he lay stretched out upon the ground, begin to grow tense, growl faintly and frequently, until he finally engaged in overt barking which became more and more excited until with a triumphant yelp he ceased, licked his chops in a relaxed and contented manner, and then subsided. During this entire process he never once opened his eyes.   If he wasn't going through a canine dream, then it will be difficult ever to determine such a thing in an infra-human animal.   Dewey suggests that reverie makes up the greater part of mental life.

(b) Routine Thinking.   This is a middle stage between reverie and reasoning.   It is demonstrated by the business man and the housewife, the scientist and the child who are concerned with meeting the demands of their positions which involve habitual responses.   Many a business executive who attains his success through original thinking finally gets much of his day's work reduced to a routine level where he can simply note that the objections raised in this morning's letters are already answered in Form Letters No. 3, No. 9, or No. 27.   We are all guilty of this "coasting" after we have attained a certain intellectual speed.

It is demonstrated every semester in my classes heavily patronized by business and professional men.   They often say that they feel mentally rusty; that it takes them almost a whole semester to get back into the swing of effective study. Such statements indicate that they have been slipping into a rut of routine thinking.   The school child probably uses his brain for reasoning activity far more than the average business and professional man, for the child is confronted with entirely new problems daily, whereas the rest of us have reached the "catalogue" state in which our already developed habits take care of almost every situation that arises, and we simply need to do the cataloguing in the morning, and our secretaries take care of the rest of the work.

(c) Reasoning.   This noble function of the human cortex is seldom if ever called into action except in times of maladjustment.   As long as there is smooth sailing we avoid expending the additional effort called forth by original thinking. It is the hungry rat which keeps running throughout the maze until he finds the reward box and food.   A rat which has been fed prior to entrance into the maze will wander around casually a little while; then lie down and go to sleep.

The contented young man likewise enjoys life with seldom a need for more than routine thinking until a wife or youngster forces him into a new situation that cannot be fully met with existing habits. Then the man buckles down to his job, perhaps takes courses in the university at night, and, much like the maladjusted rat, keeps striving until he pulls himself a few degrees higher in the financial world, when he again begins coasting. The recent economic depression in America has probably brought into activity more idle and rusty neurones than any event since the preceding one. And some men, like the obstinate rat who encountered the closure of his accustomed pathway in the maze, will keep on with the old methods and ideas, and wonder why they don't break through the red side of the ledger on to the paying side once more, while other men will quickly adjust and be in the van of business success on the economic rebound.

Reasoning is hard work, which explains why we prefer the *status quo* as soon as we are successfully adjusted to it. But there is a certain exhilaration that results from stiff mental work which can scarcely be matched in any other manner. And the more frequently we experience such a thrill of accomplishment in this fashion, the more inclined we become to the methods of creative thinking. A chronic debater actually gets homesick for a good difference of opinion, and jumps at the intimation of a test of wits as a hungry dog dives for a bone. It is this type of whetting the wits which William James had in mind.

In concluding our treatment of the relationship of thinking to habit it would be well to mention that the bulk of our thinking involves language, which in turn is composed of thousands of discrete word habits. Watson's comparison of the act of reasoning to a trial and error process involving words is especially illuminating in this regard. The three types of thinking have also been discussed, namely, reverie, routine, and reasoning. We have brought out the fact that maladjustment is the usual stimulus for reasoning, and that creative thinking may even be considered a habit in itself. The formal technique of the latter we have left for the student to acquire from a textbook of logic.

Emotional Habits. There are individuals who seem to pride themselves on the possession of a temperamental disposition. Such a disposition usually means that the parents of said individuals refrained from using the hairbrush on too many occasions. The temperamental person is usually one who has a "spoiled" child disposition. Like the child who is cruel, however, he can be changed into a sympathetic and extroverted youngster by training. The following paragraphs show the beginning of such a procedure with a four-year-old boy who had been surrounded by adults and inanimate toys all his life.[7]

. . . Four years of habitually thinking about his own desires cannot be overthrown in a night. Indeed, on the morning of the kitten's arrival Paul presents a pathetic spectacle as he vainly strives to play with Fluff.

He doesn't know how to play with a weaker living thing. At first he seizes the kitten as if it were his football and tosses it high in the air above his head. The kitten falls to the floor, bruising its mouth until the blood flows.

Paul has not meant to be cruel. He simply does not know that a living playmate must not be treated like a ball.

"Paul, dear, you have hurt Fluff," his mother protests. "How would you like to have a big man throw you up in the air and let you fall upon the sidewalk so hard you hurt your mouth?"

"He would be a bad man," Paul immediately replies. "I would not like him".

"Then you know how Fluff feels," his mother continues. "The poor little kitten has been taken away from its mother and its brothers and sisters. It has come to live with you. It likes you. But

---

"A gentleman is one who expects much from himself but little from others." —Confucius then you throw it in the air and hurt it. Do you think it will like you, if you do that again?"

Paul shakes his head soberly. This is a new thought to him. He must keep it in mind in the future. A kitten is like himself. It gets hurt when it falls. A ball is not like himself. It doesn't get hurt when it falls.

Although Paul was a brilliant child with an I. Q. of 145, he needed to be extroverted and to have analogies drawn between himself and the kitten. Fortunately, his mother kept at the job day after day until in a few weeks Paul was growing considerate of the feelings of his playmate. He had become able to identify himself with it, and to suffer pain vicariously when it was hurt. Many thoughtlessly cruel and unfeeling adults would be more considerate if they could have gone through such experiences as Paul had. Brutal tendencies can usually be eliminated without great difficulty if they are caught early in the life of the child, for the initial brutalities are quite often thoughtless actions. Thus tenderness can be inculcated and developed through training. In Chapter XIII we shall expand this subject when we consider the means of lessening the youngster's future divorce hazard.

A mother came to see Dr. H. D. Williams of our staff with the complaint that her twelve-year-old son would go into tantrums when he didn't get what he wanted, and lie on the floor, scream, kick, scratch, and in general make himself unbearable. She wanted to know how to eradicate this behavior, for she had found nothing effective hitherto. In her son we see a temperamental adult in the making.

"Well," Dr. Williams answered slowly, "I'll give you a plan which will work, I believe, if you are willing to try it, and probably work rather quickly. Just get a large pail, let the water run from a faucet until it is icy cold, fill the pail, and throw it on him." The mother consented to try the plan. The next day her son went into his usual tantrum. She followed Dr. Williams' advice to the letter, filling a large pail and approaching her boy. "Get up!" she ordered as severely as mothers can order. No action. Douse! The boy yelled, but it was an entirely different sort of yell from his tantrum cries.

The shocking change in his mother's behavior was probably as great a jolt to him as was the contact of three gallons of cold water. But the following afternoon he again went into a tantrum. Slowly, obviously, his mother procured the pail, walked into the bathroom and filled it, and returned to the living room. But her young heir was gone. Some sentimentalists may aver that the mother's behavior was brutal, but it frequently requires a revolutionary act to convince a youngster of the change in disposition of a parent on whom he has been imposing chronically. Three gallons of water is a cheap price to pay, however, for the development of a wholesome disposition in place of a temperamental one.

Self-confidence is a vastly important behavior trait which can also be developed, for confidence is a habit. The child who is given tasks beyond his ability, or who is not motivated to their performance, ends the day with failure behind him. On the morrow, when he attacks a new problem he may be influenced by his previous lack of success, and again stop short of victory or completion. If this sequence of events continues over a period of a few weeks or months, the child has a defeatism complex, and enters upon new jobs with an inferiority complex. On the contrary, the child who is given tasks which he can finish without unduly taxing his strength, and who is motivated adequately by praise, begins the new day with the exhilarated feeling of accomplishment well done, and this attitude soon becomes a habit. In adult life, therefore, when a new job comes up he attacks it without even thinking that he may not be successful. Why shouldn't he be able to do the task, he reasons, for he's done everything else he has ever tried. Shannon Fife's[10] story is especially appropriate in this connection.

"Keep company with good men and good men you'll learn to be."
—Chinese Proverb

HALF-WAY

When Hurley's wife telephoned me that he was desperately ill with pneumonia I was preparing to sail for Europe within the hour, but I dropped everything to hasten to his bedside. I had been Hurley's roommate at college and best man at his wedding, and although I had not seen him for several years the warmth of our friendship persisted.

As I taxied posthaste to the hospital I carried with me the mental picture of the same unchanging Hurley I had always known—an undersized, mild-mannered type of man, hesitant and undecided as to character, now nearing forty, and apparently reconciled to remain forever a plodding clerk.

But the moment I glimpsed him I was conscious of a startling change. Hurley had been somehow transformed into an entirely different type of person, and solely through the alchemy of a smile.

It was not the resigned smile of one reconciled to death. It was a smile of victory, of proud achievement, of triumphant success—things never even remotely associated with Hurley.

"I've won," he breathed. "I've won at last. Thank God I'm a success."

Through the delirium of intermittent unconsciousness Hurley's declaration of victory and success was repeated again and again.

The nurse, sharing my startled wonderment, whisperingly confided the details. At the time of the attending physician's diagnosis they had thought Hurley asleep, only to discover that he had overheard the tragically brief remark of the physician—a few ominous words virtually sealing Hurley's doom. And it was upon hearing these words that Hurley had first smiled his smile of success.

To add to our bewilderment we knew that Hurley wanted to live. Among many other reasons was the bond between him and his wife, a colorless, repressed little woman who moved meekly in an aura of self-obliteration, and who seemed a perfect complement to Hurley's mild negations of character. Between them was a deep love, a piteous, clinging-together type of devotion which had always been woven through the drab texture of their lives.

She was sitting there at his bedside, tremulously whispering words of endearment and encouragement to him. The pressing proximity of my sailing hour drew me reluctantly from the room. As I paused at the door for a last lingering look at my friend, there came once more Hurley's exultant tocsin:

"I've won; I'm a success."

And accompanying the words was the illuminating glory of his triumphant smile—a smile born in the same moment that he had heard the sentence of death passed upon him.

I was well out at sea when the agony of my suspenseful waiting was finally relieved by the arrival of a radiogram. I opened it tremblingly. Hurley had passed the crisis and would live! . . . .

Business kept me in Europe for more than a year. Almost immediately upon my return home a telephone message from Hurley took me to his office. If I had been amazed at the metamorphosis of the man at the hospital, I was dumbfounded now. Hurley, radiant with success, was established in a splendidly appointed office, the enthusiastic head of a flourishing brokerage business.

He immediately sensed my profound bewilderment, chuckled delightedly, settled back in his chair, and told me his story—the story of "Half-Way" Hurley.

He began with his entrance into matrimony, only half-way prepared for its responsibilities. He dwelt at length upon his half-way success as an accountant; of half-way health; of the half-paid mortgage upon his home, a home which was bereft of children because Hurley felt himself only half-way fitted for the exactions of parenthood.

"And so I drifted on and on," he explained, "always at the halfway mark in everything, until my inner mind was dominated by the psychology of defeatism, and my subconscious self labeled me 'Half-Way' Hurley.

"Finally I began to grow ashamed of myself. I thought of my wife. I began to want success. Desperately I began to plan success. I knew that I was a victim of psychology, and I knew that the laws of psychology work both ways. I reasoned that if there could be one thing in my life not done half-way that thing would serve as a psychological symbol of success.

"On the spur of the moment I selected my half-completed garden as that symbol. I worked furiously, trying to rush it to a completed condition. I badly overtaxed my strength and in a moment of lowered resistance contracted my pneumonia. I was carried to the hospital bitter with the realization that I was still 'Half-Way' Hurley—that I still lacked my symbol of success. Man, how I wanted that symbol of one thing well done. How I needed it!

"And then, suddenly, the physician who examined me gave that symbol with words never intended for my ears—words which virtually portended my death but which, ironically and whimsically enough, were to me the elixir of life; words which gave birth to my smile of achievement; words which made me resolve not only to live, but to push everything in my future life to completion and success. They were the words spoken by the doctor to the nurse when he said: 'There's nothing half-way about this case; he has DOUBLE pneumonia.'

"And there was my symbol. At last I had stopped doing things by halves."

In the silence that followed, Hurley's telephone rang and I heard him conversing with his wife. And in those few sentences was tenderly crystallized all of the love one human can bear for another.

"This time it's my wife who is in the hospital," Hurley said as he hung up. "I've got to hustle over there at once and you must come along. You see, that's the real reason I've sent for you. There's to be an addition to the family and you're to be godfather."

Enthusiastically I shouted my congratulations, and asked: "What is it—a girl or a boy?"

Hurley threw back his head with a long joyous laugh—a laugh vibrant with the pride and strength and power that comes with assured success.

"There's nothing half-way about that, either," he exulted. "It's both!"

The emotional habits which attach to music and art we shall consider in a later chapter. Suffice it to conclude by repeating that Confidence or Defeatism, Tenderness or Brutality, Culture or Ignorance, Tact or Boorishness, Courage or Cowardice, these attributes of human behavior are wholly or in part dependent upon the emotional conditioning the individual has received. His native intelligence, of course, is a factor to be considered, especially when we regard the degree to which conditioning will carry him. A person of normal mental alertness can obviously surpass a moron in cultural attainments, if given the same training, but it must also be borne in mind that a normal person exposed to boorish surroundings may be far less cultured than a high grade moron in an ideal environment of music and books, correct language and social etiquette. A high grade moron may possess the mental alertness of a twelve-year-old boy or girl, and at twelve the normal child can be speaking perfect English, can be familiar with good music and art, and can deport himself admirably in social situations, if he has been correctly trained.

REFERENCES

1 ALEXANDER, F. G., *The History of Psychiatry* (Harper & Row, 1966).
2 AM. JEWISH COMM., *Prayers & Bible Reading* (Inst. Human Rel. 1963).
3 BERG, R. H., "A Report on Hospitals" *(Look,* Feb. 3, 1959).
4 BURGESS, T. O., *Workbook in General Psychology* (Concordia, 1959).
5 CASON, H., "The Conditioned Pupillary Reaction," *(J. Exp. Psychol.,* 5, 1922).
6 CATTELL, R. B., *et al.* "The Objective Measurement of Attitudes," *(Brit. J. Psychol.,* 50, 1950).
7 CRANE, G. W., "Kiddies and Kittens Make Perfect Pals," *(Forecast,* 36, 1928).
8 CROWE, C. M., *Getting Ready for Tomorrow* (Abington, 1959).
9 CUTLER, T. H., *et. al., Analysis of Teaching Load* (U. of Denver, 1949).
10 FIFE, SHANNON, "Half-Way" (Courtesy of *Liberty,* Feb. 21, 1931).
11 FINK, H. K., *Mind and Performance* (Vantage, 1954).
12 GANNON, T. J., *Psychology – Unity of Human Behavior* (Ginn, 1954).
13 GARRISON, K. C., *Psychology of Exceptional Children* (Ronald, 1950).
14 GELDARD, F. A., *The Human Senses* (Wiley, 1953).
15 GRAY, J. S., *Psychology Applied to Human Affairs* (McGraw-Hill, 1954).
16 HOVLAND, C. I., *Communication & Persuasion* (Yale U. Press, 1955).
17 HUNTER, W. S., *Human Behavior* (U. of Chicago Press, 1928).
18 HURLOCK, E. B., "An Evaluation of Certain Incentives Used in School Work", *(J. Educ. Psychol.,* 16, 1925).
19 JANIS, I. L., *Psychological Stress* (Wiley, 1958).
20 KENT, G. H., & ROSANOFF, A. J., "A Study of Association in Insanity" *(Am. J. of Insanity,* 67, 1910).
21 LOUTTIT, C. M., *Clinical Psychology of Children's Behavior Problems* (Harper, 1947).
22 MORTENSEN, D. G., & SCHMULLER, A. M., *Guidance in Today's Schools* (Wiley, 1959).
23 MORGAN, C. T., & ELIOT, S., *Physiological Psychology* (McGraw-Hill, 1950).
24 MORGAN, J. J. B., "The Overcoming of Distraction and Other Resistances" *(Arch of Psychol.* No. 35, 1916).
25 PETERSON AND RAINEY, "The Beginnings of Mind in the New Born" *(Bulletin of the Lying-In Hospital,* N. Y., 1910).
26 POFFENBERGER, A. T., *Applied Psychology* (Appleton, 1927).
27 SCOTT, W. D., *Psychology of Advertising* (Small, Maynard, 1908).
28 STRONG, E. K., "The Effect of Size of Advertisements and Frequency of Their Presentation" *(Psychol. Rev.* 21, 1914).
29 WATSON, J. B., *Psychology* (Lippincott, 1924).
30 WALLIN, J. E. W., *Children with Mental and Physical Handicaps* (Prentice-Hall, 1949).
31 WILLIAMS, C. A., *Traffic Accidents* (Thomas, 1954).
32 WITKIN, H. A., *Personality Through Perception* (Harper, 1954).
33 WOLFFHEIM, N., *Psychology in the Nursery School* (Philos. Libr., 1955).
34 WOODWORTH & SCHLOSBERG, *Experimental Psychology* (Holt, 1955).
35 WOHL, M. G., *Long Term Illness* (Wiley, 1959).
36 YOUNG, P. T., *Motivation and Emotion* (Wiley, 1964).

CHAPTER III

INCREASING HUMAN EFFICIENCY

The matter of increasing human efficiency has been of notable importance in the industrial and commercial field where the vital ratio between output and overhead charges is a subject of constant concern. But there are other aspects of the question of broader social significance, which, though we cannot go into them here, are of recognized importance. The leisure time of the mass of our people is becoming greater. What methods of improving their capacity either to enjoy this extra time, or to employ it for personal, financial, or educational advancement are available? Are we utilizing the most efficient technique in our school system, not alone in regard to methods of presenting material to the young minds, but also as regards the choice of curricula? It is obvious that such phases of the question necessitate a careful study of the basic philosophy of society. It is not our purpose to develop this theme further, though we acknowledge the essential value of such orientation.

Efficiency Engineering. This topic covers those aspects of applied psychology in the industrial field wherein men and women are primarily endeavoring to speed up production by elimination of superfluous moves of the worker. This may involve the designing of new machinery, or a re-education process concerning the function at hand. In his analysis of the standard typewriter keyboard, Hoke[28] gives us an excellent example of what efficiency engineering can do. His proposed new keyboard is contained in Exhibit 15, and illustrates a change of the tools employed instead of a change in habits of the individual. Although the ratio of ability of the right hand to the

---

Use the "sandwich method" when offering criticism or correction. Deftly insert it between two layers of honest compliments. This avoids ill will.

	LEFT HAND				RIGHT HAND			
	FINGERS				FINGERS			
	4	3	2	1	1	2	3	4
	Y	D	M	CW	QF	V	L	K
	R	N	T	HU	S I	E	O	A
	B	P	G	JX	Z ?⁄	;	:	;
Load on above keyboard	858	888	982	1031	1098	1093	996	971
Ideal load	855	900	975	1028	1097	1097	991	968
Load on present keyboard	803	658	1492	1535	1490	640	996	296

Exhibit 15. Proposed new typewriter keyboard adjusting the loads on the various fingers more nearly to their capacity. (By Roy E. Hoke).

left is found to be as 100 : 88.87, Hoke finds the left hand carrying 47.7 per cent more load than the right, according to the present typewriter keyboard.

The Gilbreths have also done much outstanding work in this field of applied psychology. In the bricklaying trade, for example, every movement involved in picking up, mortaring, and laying the brick was carefully analyzed. By changes in the placement of materials, and in the routing of work, useless moves were eliminated until the number involved for laying each brick dropped from 18 to 4, with a resulting increase in hourly output per man from 120 to 350 bricks.

The use of the motion picture machine has been decidedly

helpful in many cases. By photographing all the processes or steps in the performance of a given task, and then carefully analyzing the films for unnecessary moves and opportunities for short cuts in the routing of work, the experimenters have effected marked economies. Even in the realm of sport this method has been employed as a means of finding ways of speeding up the runner or of reducing the "slice" of the golfer.

The matters of individual differences in working time or speed of performance have also been studied. In general, the movements of the smaller individual are faster than those of the larger. In work involving shoveling, for example, it was found that a decided increase in output resulted from adjusting the length of handle and size of the blade to the size and strength of the man. Although the smaller individuals took less per shovelful, they more than made up for this difference by their faster rate of shoveling. Not only did output increase, but the men felt less effort expended.

Wyatt reports a somewhat similar type of study undertaken by the Industrial Fatigue Research Board in England, in which the speed of the factory machine was adjusted to the reaction time of the individual worker. The investigators found that in general the machines were running too slowly for the optimum working rate of the employes. When they increased the rate, they found it possible to increase output by 18 per cent. Some employees were able to work as much as 50 per cent faster than others. In all such types of experiment, of course, it is necessary to make sure that the increased output is not made at the expense of the worker's health. The improvement must result by decreasing present inconveniences and useless expenditure of energy, not from simply increasing the worker's performance by undue motivation.

The principles involving improvement of production by mechanical adjustment of worker to machine in a more efficient

"War—what is it after all the people get? Why widows, taxes, wooden legs and debt."   —Old Proverb manner may be designated under the three major headings, Individualization, Standardization, and Specialization. As we suggested at the beginning of the chapter, although industry has held the focus of attention in regard to efficiency engineering, we can profitably bring some of these same research methods into many other phases of human endeavor. Gilbreth [24] estimates that a system of simplified spelling would save in the neighborhood of two years time for the child in his school career. In many other respects his time could also be conserved. "Counting the English units bearing the same names as our own, we have in use 4 different sizes of pints, quarts, and gallons; 3 different sizes of gills; many sizes of barrels; and untold numbers of different sizes of bushels of things in different states, such as apples, potatoes and the like; 3 kinds of ounces, drams, and pounds; 3 different sizes of hundredweight, 4 different tons, and 2 or 3 kinds of miles." The metric system, which could be learned by a child in half an hour, would greatly simplify measurements of all sorts, and relieve Uncle Sam of an estimated 300 millions of dollars annually spent unnecessarily in teaching the cumbersome system of weights and measures now in vogue.

In the realm of printed matter, for example, we could greatly improve our reading rate if some of the vowels were changed. In fine type it is difficult to distinguish such words as "minimum", "resonance", etc., because the letters "e", "a", "r", "s" or the letters "m" and "n" have the same general dimensions, and hence require closer discernment than "l" and "s". Moreover, words in which letters are of one height, as the two given above, or words printed all in upper case are much more difficult to read than those giving a more irregular word pattern. Eliminating the internal curves of the letters making up a word, and considering only the external outlines,

---

"It was found that some men and women were ill because they were not good, and that others were not good because they were ill."
—M. H. Lichliter in *The Healing of Souls*

which are incidentally quite significant reading cues, we can represent the peripheral contours of easily distinguished words in Exhibit 16.

Longfellow

applied

psychologist

shall

EXHIBIT 16. Illustration of the peripheral visual patterns of easily discriminated words.

If some of the confusing vowels and consonants which are of lower case could be changed, our reading time and inaccuracy would be reduced. There is no reason why a small triangle couldn't be used in printing instead of the letter "e", thus removing one of the chief sources of visual strain and confusion. At the University of Chicago, for example, Professor William S. Gray tested the reading speed of 664 freshmen, finding that the slowest readers covered less than two words per second, while the fastest averaged slightly over seven. This means a difference in reading materials covered that runs from 18 pages to 63 pages per hour. The fastest reader would cover a full page of print in this textbook in one minute while the slowest college reader would require 3.5 minutes. Improving the legibility of our print alphabet would undoubtedly increase the reading rate of all groups, and quite likely would lessen the gap between the extremes, since eyestrain and lack of adequate reading habits explain much of the discrepancy between rapid and slow readers in this intelligent group.

In general, therefore, anything which will eliminate a human adjustment will correspondingly reduce the time required for the performance of a given task. This holds for the housewife, the stenographer, the schoolboy, factory worker, or executive. In setting the piecework rates in factories it has been found wise to compute the number of essential moves necessary in the competition of the task; then use the normal reaction times for the muscular components of the act, thereby finding the maximum piecework items possible of production by the normal worker. With this as a standard the wage per piece is computed, so that the average worker, moving without a single useless act and not affected by fatigue might make let us say $3.50 per hour. Allowing for fatigue, however, the fast worker may seldom average over $3.00 per hour, while the slower men and women scale down accordingly. To illustrate how the method operates, let us consider the writer's signature given below. The average time required for changing

George W. Crane

the direction of the wrist movement is placed at approximately 0.00175 minutes. To find out how many signatures I can make per minute exactly like the one above, it is necessary to count the number of changes in direction of the wrist activity during the writing process, keeping in mind dots and movements down to the line below when beginning subsequent signatures. Assuming sixty such wrist changes at 0.00175 minutes per change, we find that it takes me 0.105 minutes to make my signature once. Dividing one minute by 0.105, we find that I can repeat the signature above only 9.5 times per minute. Actually, when time is called, I have nine full signatures completed, and am just writing the capital "C" on my tenth. I note, however, that

I have slurred my writing slightly in speeding; so that I have eliminated a few wrist movements originally employed in the signature above.

If I were being hired to write my signature, therefore, the basis of the piecework rate would be made on 9.5 signatures per minute. Fatigue would soon affect me, thereby reducing my output, and causing me to fall below the maximum wage.

A conclusion of this section devoted to efficiency engineering should emphasize the fact that efficiency is increased with the elimination of extra movements or thought processes entailed by the given task. The adjustment of the machine to the man, or a new course of instruction may be necessary in this process. Individualization, standardization, and specialization are the three principal ways of improving production by the adjustment of the worker to the machine. The importance of morale is significant, but will be deferred till a later point in the book.

The Effect of Drugs and Stimulants on Efficiency. Drugs of some sort have been a portion of man's chemical environment as long as history records. Alcoholic beverages may have been first, followed by narcotics; then, later, tea, coffee, and tobacco. We shall discuss them in the general chronological order of their use by mankind.

(1) *Alcohol.* Dodge and Benedict[20] have made one of the most exhaustive and controlled experiments of the influence of alcohol on the behavior reactions of man that we have on record. Contrary to the popular opinion, they found alcohol to be a depressant in all respects except the pulse, and even here there was no absolute increase. The pulse simply did not decrease gradually in the course of moderate physical and mental labor, as is true of the non-alcoholized subject. There was an increase in the latent time of the knee jerk and other re-

---

It isn't mechanical defects under the hood that cause most auto accidents but the "nut" at the steering wheel.

HANDLING STOCK SALES
OLD ROUTINE

EXHIBIT 17. An inefficient routing of work which has been much simplified in the next chart. (Courtesy of William J. Gyles).

HANDLING STOCK SALES
NEW ROUTINE

flexes. The change, converted into per cent, is tabulated in the accompanying table from Poffenberger:[3B]

	Per Cent
Increase of latent time of the knee jerk	10
Decrease in thickening of the quadriceps muscle	46
Protective eyelid reflex, latent time increased	7
Extent of eyelid movement decreased	19
Eye reactions, latent time increased	5
Speed of eye movements decreased	11
Sensitivity to electric stimulation decreased	14
Speed of finger movements (tapping) decreased	9

EXHIBIT 18. The effect of alcohol on simple motor activities.

One of the observations true of alcohol as well as of most other drugs is the fact that individuals vary greatly in their responses to such stimuli. The words of Cushny[16] probably delineate the common varieties of response that have been observed by the reader:

One person is rendered sentimental, another bellicose, while in a third there may be no appearance of excitement, the first distinct symptom being profound slumber. When drinking is indulged in in company, the excitement stage is a very common phenomenon, but if alcohol is taken without the exhilarating accompaniments of bright lights and exciting companionship, it is much less frequently seen, and the question has therefore arisen how far the environment produces the excitement in alcoholic intoxication.

The reasons for the use of alcohol are quite numerous. One takes it because he has had it in his home constantly, and it has been a habit since childhood. Another indulges because he wants to escape from a painful, humiliating, or monotonous environment, and, lacking a rich imagination by which he could have fled the present, he deadens himself to reality. The dope fiend is of this class, too. A third, who is rather timorous and shy, takes it so that he can escape these inhibitions and appear

---

When John Barleycorn gets behind the steering wheel of your automobile, the Grim Reaper is ever ready to thumb a ride! Gasoline and alcohol are becoming the initial embalming fluid for many modern motorists.

nonchalant as he makes his public speech, sales talk, or other normal appearance. A fourth indulges to set an example for his customer or companion so that the latter will be more amenable to his business or erotic desires.

Chronic alcoholics demonstrate a peculiar form of behavior known as delirium tremens, in which there are fantastic visual and tactual hallucinations. At the height of his excitement, the patient may imagine himself covered with insects or snakes, and he is constantly endeavoring to brush them off. If an interne attempts to take a blood sample, the patient shrieks, belabors the doctor, and calls him a vampire who is draining his blood vessels dry.

Because there are more feeble-minded among the alcoholics than in the general population, the opinion has grown that alcohol is conducive to feeble-mindedness. Although there is general agreement among investigators that alcohol reduces mental efficiency in the individual consuming it, we have no data to prove that it affects the germinal cells, and becomes transmissible in its effects. Perhaps a more logical explanation of the prevalence of feeble-mindedness in the alcohol group is the fact that those of subnormal mentality are more inclined to alcoholic indulgence and excess.

(2) *Opium.* This drug has a soporific effect which lasts during the early stages for the duration of the night. Vivid dreams and hallucinations are the rule, during which the patient usually revels in imaginary situations of great pleasure and beauty. Following this dream stage, the subject drops into a deep, dreamless slumber. Because of the pleasant revels through which the patient has passed, the waking world appears more drab by contrast, and it isn't long until he craves the excitement of his former dream state. Like the alcoholic, the addict is probably inclined to inferiority complexes which prevent his realizing his joys in real life; so he is psychologically disposed to a resumption of his tryst with his gorgeous-

hued Morpheus. Ultimately, the addict becomes reduced to a chaotic condition mentally, physically, and morally. He takes little nourishment and finally dies of malnutrition. Morphine differs from cocaine in that the latter is a stimulant, deferring the onset of fatigue, but a depression ultimately follows. The cocaine habit leads to even greater moral degradation, and the chance of breaking the habit is even less than the morphine habit.

(3) *Caffeine.* This is the active principle of tea and coffee. In the average cup of coffee with milk there are about 2.5 grains of this drug, and a cup of black tea contains about 1.5 grains. Because of the fact that persons develop headaches when deprived of their accustomed caffeine beverages, the drug is considered to be in the class of mild habit forming substances. The results of Rivers'[34] careful experiments in which he excluded the influence of suggestion, show a small stimulation value for caffeine, producing an increase in muscular work.

There is no question but that caffeine excites the subject who has not developed a tolerance for it. It seems to enhance the nervous condition of such an individual, rendering him sleepless. There seem to be no deleterious effects, however, if an individual does not imbibe directly before retiring. Its chief drawback is the fact that it robs individuals of a few hours of necessary slumber if taken late at night. The effect is subject considerably to the degree of tolerance of the individual in question.

(4) *Tobacco.* This substance with its effect on mental actions has been argued pro and con. Investigators have cited the fact that the non-smokers make the highest scholastic grades. Although the effect of tobacco may be a causative factor in these cases, there is also the possibility that the smoker is inclined to be more sociable than the non-smoker, and this

---

Dad and Mother sacrifice to save an extra $150 for John or Mary at college. Do they then burn up this blood money on the ends of their cigarettes?

greater fraternal tendency may be the more basic explanation for the difference in school attainment of the two.

Probably the most thoroughly controlled investigation of the effects of tobacco smoking was made by Hull.[29] His conclusions follow:

> In a final review of the various effects of tobacco enumerated above, it will be noted that only three of the twelve forms of behavior investigated reveal an unmistakable influence of smoking. Two of these (pulse and tremor) are essentially physiological. The interest of the present investigation, on the other hand, is primarily in the more strictly psychological processes. Of these, only one (Addition) shows an unmistakable effect. Several others show effects with a fair degree of reliability, however, and are entitled to consideration. Probably the two most significant tests of this intellectual group as revealing the influence of smoking on mental efficiency, are Complex Mental Addition and Rote Learning. The first, together with Reaction Time, may be presumed to give some indication of the effects of smoking upon ordinary routine thinking, which is essentially the functioning of old associative bonds. The evidence in this case is favorable to tobacco where the subject is accustomed to its use. Rote Learning, on the other hand, possibly supported by Memory Span, presumably indicates the effect that tobacco is likely to have where new associative bonds are in the process of formation, as in most school learning. The results in this case, while not so reliable, are unfavorable to tobacco. It must be remembered, of course, that the above formulations apply with strictness only to the first hour and a half after the termination of smoking. Generalizations from them must be made with extreme caution.

In summarizing the effects of drugs and stimulants on human efficiency, we can state that the general tendency of those herein described is unfavorable, although there are many, including caffeine and various medicines not treated in this chapter, which may be beneficial. Moreover, a number of drugs which have marked medicinal value or act as aids in relieving pain, may be detrimental if applied in large quantities or habitually taken. Tolerance to a drug is also of considerable im-

---

The average cigarette smoker each year sets fire to 150 one-dollar bills. That's too great an outlay for a purely individual or selfish pleasure.

portance in measuring its influence upon human efficiency. Narcotics are generally harmful, especially because of their habit-forming nature. Alcohol is less detrimental, while tobacco is probably the least injurious of the three.

The Effect of Climate and Ventilation on Efficiency. A study of the historical records of races whose habitats range from the tropics to the polar regions indicates that a moderate temperature environment and rainfall have been most conducive to progress. Physical and physiological causes underly this result. In the first place, the tropical heat is so great that physical exertion must be held to a minimum in order to keep the normal blood temperature at 98.6° Fahrenheit. Muscular exercise produces heat, and a body surrounded by external heat cannot endure too much internal combustion without showing pathological effects. Sluggishness is nature's way of protecting her children in such a situation.

The physical environment in the tropics has also conspired against civilization's advance. Because food was so easily procurable, the inhabitants found little necessity to labor and devise means of insuring a steady diet year in and year out. Clothing problems consisted chiefly in protection from insects instead of cold. In our chapter on learning we mentioned that maladjustment leads to the acquisition of new habits and progress mentally. The tropical native was fairly well adjusted from birth till death, so he lacked the goads that drove his northern neighbors.

In the polar regions, on the contrary, men were so much concerned with the struggle for physical existence that they had little time free to think of anything else. They were frequently maladjusted, but the range of situations to which they were maladjusted was very limited. They procured food from roving animals or the sea. If the animals were present, their crude weapons were adequate to procure a supply of provision. If the animals weren't present, to their primitive mental condition the situation was incapable of solution. Even a highly civilized chemist would be relatively helpless in the same circumstances. One cannot make proteins out of ice and snow.

In the temperate zones we find a climate that shows a change of seasons which are mentally stimulating, and a variety of temperatures which present varying problems to the inhabitants. Nature is therefore much more stimulating. Maladjustments are numerous but not insoluble. Aggressiveness and productivity are at the maximum in those races whose habitats show average temperatures ranging from 50° to 70° F. Changing emotional states also seem to be engendered by the seasons, as is evident from their standardized portrayal in pantomine. Spring is, moreover, the time of mating among animals, and apparently influences the thoughts of men in a similar fashion, since June is the favorite marriage month.

Ventilation seldom presents important considerations for the average individual since homes, apartments, offices, and factories have now been regulated to give a standard air content per occupant, and an appreciation of ventilation technique has become commonplace. In the description of the tragic drama enacted in the Black Hole[32] of Calcutta, however, we see clearly the necessity for an adequate ventilating system. Had these men been incarcerated at a temperature of 32° F. most of them would probably have been alive the next morning, for the two windows, even though small, would probably have supplied enough oxygen. Need of coolness, which is one of the great benefits of the moving air in well ventilated buildings, was the basic cause of a large percentage of the deaths described below.

One of the hottest of the hot nights of British India, a little more than one hundred and fifty years ago, Siraj-Uddaula, a youthful merciless ruler of Bengal, caused to be confined within a small cell in Fort William one hundred and forty-six Englishmen whom he had that day captured in a siege of the city of Calcutta. The room was large enough to house comfortably but two persons. Its heavy door

---

"Do not investigate facts by the light of arguments, but arguments by the light of facts."   —Greek Proverb was bolted; its walls were pierced by two windows barred with iron, through which little air could enter. The night slowly passed away, and with the advent of the morning death had come to all but a score of the luckless company. A survivor has left an account of the horrible happenings within the dungeon, of terrible strugglings of a steaming mass of sentient human bodies for the insufficient air. Within a few minutes after entrance every man was bathed in a wet perspiration and was searching for ways to escape from the stifling heat. Clothing was soon stripped off. Breathing became difficult. There were vain onslaughts on the windows; there were vain efforts to force the door. Thirst grew intolerable, and there were ravings for the water which the guards passed in between the bars, not from feelings of mercy but only to witness in ghoulish glee the added struggles for impossible relief. Ungovernable confusion and turmoil and riot soon reigned. Men became delirious . . . All efforts for relief were vain until at last bodily and mental agony was followed by stupor.

As soon as the moisture in the atmosphere becomes so great that evaporation from the skin and lungs is reduced, we begin to grow uncomfortable. The body has difficulty keeping its temperature from rising above the normal 98.6° F. This situation explains our discomfort on humid, sultry days when the perspiration remains on the skin without quickly evaporating. The reverse of this situation may also be true. A story has come down to us that at a certain festivity in Europe a young boy was entirely covered with gold leaf. Inside of fifteen minutes he was dead. His temperature probably dropped rapidly through increased heat radiation from his skin.

In summarizing the effects of climate and ventilation on efficiency, the keynote to our discussion lies in the fact that for human beings the healthful bodily temperature averages 98.6° Fahrenheit. Climates which make it difficult for the human being to keep his temperature at that point are detrimental to his mental progress. Hot temperatures produce partial inertia of body and mind as a safeguard against too much internal combustion, while frigid climates consume most of the person's available energy in preventing the bodily temperature from becoming lowered. The chief value of well ventilated buildings, moreover, lies in the better circulation of air with the resulting increased evaporation from the skin of the occupants. The oxygen and carbon dioxide contents of the room seldom vary enough to be a significant problem.

The Effect of Illumination and Posture on Efficiency. The most efficient lighting system is the indirect. There are several adequate reasons therefor. In the first place, indirect lighting gives a more uniform distribution over the room, pages, or work immediately before the subject. As a result, there is less tendency for the eyes to turn toward the contrast points. The native inclination of the eye to focus upon sources of light, is a second reason why direct lighting is objectionable. If one is reading, sewing or working at his desk or bench, and a low hanging light, or bridge lamp is anywhere in the field of vision, the eyes tend to turn toward the light. In order to offset this inclination, the reader must expend more energy through the contrary muscles of the eyeball. Obviously inefficiency results with additional eyestrain. Astigmatism demonstrates much the same strain upon the muscles of the eyeball that we find operative in a field unevenly illuminated, for the lens has lost its uniform curvature. Some images upon the retina are clear, while others are blurred. The eye keeps adjusting in an effort to produce uniform clarity in the fovea, and eyestrain ensues.

Habit also explains some of the inefficiency in direct lighting. We are accustomed to seeing objects in contradistinction to space, so the eye tends to focus upon the tree or house or man, instead of upon the horizon behind. Black print on white paper is superior to white print on black backgrounds, for in the latter instance we tend to regard the white spaces as the customary light horizon showing through; so we try to focus upon the black regions, as in Exhibit 19.

The great number of shadows in the field of vision under

EXHIBIT 19. Showing the difference between black and white print on the opposite background.

direct lighting, therefore, tend to operate as objects and offer counter attraction to the stimulus of the page or task at hand. Eye shades are accordingly helpful when working under direct lighting, but the under side should be covered with a light strip of paper so that the contrast between it and the environment is not so great as to call attention to the shade itself. A dark eye shade offers constant stimulation to the eye to turn and focus upon it. Individuals who wear glasses should also be careful to avoid lights and windows which reflect against the inner side of the lenses of their spectacles. This is a source of distraction seldom considered, but it can greatly increase visual fatigue.

The different fatigue effects of various colored lights is expressed in the following Exhibit 20, taken from Ferree and Rand's[22] experiments. It demonstrates the fact that the red end of the spectrum seems more efficient regarding acuity than the green, with blue running close to green, but slightly lower.

In measuring the fatigue effects of motion pictures, the

"A man without a purpose is like a ship without a rudder"   —Carlyle

"The world turns aside to let a man pass who knows where he is going."
                                                —David Starr Jordan

	PER CENT LOSS OF EFFICIENCY	FEELINGS OF DISCOMFORT APPEARED AFTER SECONDS
Unsaturated yellow	5.43	116
Reddish yellow—more saturated	7.57	94
Unsaturated yellow, with trace of red	8.29	90
Orange-yellow	8.39	90
Unsaturated yellow, with trace of green	8.48	90
Unsaturated yellow, with more green	24.00	48
Unsaturated yellowish-green	25.51	34
Unsaturated yellowish-green, with more green	33.14	25
Greenish	39.14	21
Bluish-green	54.86	14

EXHIBIT 20. Efficiency of colored lights.

same investigators, using relative scores in accurate visual perception on tests made immediately prior to, and immediately following the moving picture situation, found that there was a considerable loss of efficiency, but the loss seems to be about the same as that suffered by one who reads clear print for an equal length of time under ordinary artificial illumination. They found, moreover, that the distance from the screen had some influence on the degree of the fatigue. When the subject sat a distance of 25 feet from the screen his loss of visual efficiency was 50 per cent; at a distance of 48 feet it was approximately 40 per cent, and at a distance of 71 feet it was about 30 per cent.

The intensity of light is of less significance than its uniformity over the visual field, for the eye can make remarkable adjustments to brilliant or to faint illumination. Coming from sunlight into an artificially lighted room, the individual shifts from an intensity of approximately 10,000-foot candles of light to about 5-foot candles. Shiny objects, therefore, such as the keys of a typewriter and polished metal work on various objects in the room, reduce visual efficiency. It would be an economical move in this regard if our books were all printed on pulp or non-glossy paper and if dull finishes were given to woodwork and metal ornaments.

The matter of posture is one of the factors by which Gilbreth introduced efficiency into many of the factories which he investigated. The secret of postural change simply involves reducing the number of muscles or the number of moves involved in work. In one case, for instance, a 50 per cent increase in output was effected with girls who were sorting and filing cards, by a slight change in the height and slope of their work table. The larger the muscle employed or the more muscles utilized in an act, the greater will be the fatigue resulting from the performance of a given task. If an individual who works standing must bend over frequently, it is evident that the fatigue will be much greater than if his work is raised so that all his adjustments can be carried on without bending at the waist.

Another important consideration appropriate here is the fact that frequent periods of relaxation should be introduced. These may be brought about by occasional recesses in which the worker or student changes posture, thus relieving the strain on the set of working muscles. In the crawl stroke it is essential that the swimmer relax his arm as much as possible as he brings it over head for the down thrust, otherwise he fatigues much more quickly. Nervousness and excitement are fatiguing because the tonicity of the muscles is increased, thus producing a more rapid development of fatigue products. The worker who is contented doesn't consume as much energy as the fearful or discontented employee, and therefore he doesn't fatigue as quickly.

The effects of illumination and posture on efficiency, therefore, are explicable on the basis of the additional movements which are eliminated when the lighting is made uniform and

---

"That load becomes light which is cheerfully borne."   —Ovid indirect, and when the work bench is raised or lowered to meet the individual needs of the employees. Shadows and dark objects in the field of vision tempt the eyes to turn toward them. In order to avoid doing so, the worker must expend more energy on the opposing muscles of the eyes. The value of frequent changes of posture to avoid undue fatigue of any one set of muscles has long been appreciated in the public schools as well as in the industrial world. In recent years the understanding that a change in posture might lessen the number or size of the muscles necessary to the performance of an act has led to marked improvement in efficiency.

The Effect of Diet on Efficiency. Physiologically we are really living on the river banks of our blood vessels. The cargos which float past the colonies of cells may produce health or death. Except for the air intake by way of the lungs, we are dependent on the food intake of the mouth for our imports, and these imports are essential for existence. We know that certain drugs will quickly alter our behavior, as opium, alcohol, anaesthetics, strychnine, and bichloride of mercury. And we know that other drugs (foods) produce strength and alertness. But it has been only recently that we have appreciated the significance of such things as vitamins. Even now we don't know the chemical formulae for all the vitamins, nor just why they affect the human organism as they do, but we have gradually narrowed the field until we have cornered them in their "dens" and know they hide in lettuce, butter, cod liver oil, and many other foods.

In the Philippine Islands and adjacent countries the most energetic and alert natives often slip into a depressed and languid mental condition which leads to paralysis and death. The sailors in the Japanese Navy used to succumb in great numbers to this strange malady. It is known as beriberi, and apparently results simply from the fact that the victims have lived on an unbalanced diet of polished rice. We now know that the husk of the rice grain contains chemicals which will prevent this nervous disease.

Since the presence or absence of minute quantities of certain powerful chemicals will produce life or death, it is not surprising, therefore, that the presence or absence of certain unknown chemicals over long periods of time, as in our food, should exercise alterative effects on our behavior. Perhaps glandular deficiencies in our bodies are owing partly to improper diet over long periods of time. This field of research is one of the most promising which has ever been opened to the physician and the psychologist. In diabetes, for example, we know that clusters of cells in the human pancreas called islands of Langerhans seem to have gone on strike. We can examine these colonies of cells on a histological slide, and we can by insulin apparently inject into the blood stream of the patient the same chemical produced by the Langerhans cells. But we cannot prevail on the million or more colonies of cells to call off their strike. As long as the patient lives we have to inject the substance which these idle cells should be producing. In short, we don't act upon the islands of Langerhans with insulin and set them into functional activity once more, but we give the system the product of those cells. Why the cells went on strike in the first place we do not know. One of these days we may be able to administer a drug which will make them start activity again. It is conceivable that a dietary lack of some particular chemical may have aided in their stopping work.

From the psychological viewpoint, therefore, the diet to which an individual has been accustomed for long periods of years may hold the key to a part of the premature aging which we note in some men and women. The action of the ductless glands is still one of the new fields for medical and psychological study. The interrelationship of internal secretion and the action of external chemicals in the food which we eat may be found to have an important bearing upon much of the beha-

---

"Choose the best life, for habit will make it pleasant."   —Epictetus

A Hog Can Cross the Country Without Changing Trains—But YOU Can't!

The Chesapeake & Ohio Railway and the Nickel Plate Road are again proposing to give human beings a break!

It's hard to believe, but it's true.

If you want to ship a hog from coast to coast, he can make the entire trip without changing cars. You can't. It is impossible for you to pass through Chicago, St. Louis, or New Orleans without breaking your trip!

There is an invisible barrier down the middle of the United States which you cannot cross without inconvenience, lost time, and trouble.

560,000 Victims in 1945!

If you want to board a sleeper on one coast and ride through to the other, you must make double Pullman reservations, pack and transfer your baggage, often change stations, and wait around for connections.

It's the same sad story if you make a relatively short trip. You can't cross that mysterious line! To go from Fort Wayne to Milwaukee or from Cleveland to Des Moines, you must also stop and change trains.

Last year alone, more than 560,000 people were forced to make annoying, time-wasting stopovers at the phantom Chinese wall which splits America in half!

End the Secrecy!

Why should travel be less convenient for people than it is for pigs? Why should Americans be denied the benefits of through train service? No one has yet been able to explain it.

Canada has this service . . . with a choice of two routes. Canada isn't split down the middle. Why should we be? No reasonable answer has yet been given. Passengers still have to stop off at Chicago, St. Louis, and New Orleans—although they can ride right through other important rail centers.

It's time to pry the lid off this mystery. It's time for action to end this inconvenience to the travelling public . . . NOW!

Many railroads could cooperate to provide this needed through service. To date, the Chesapeake & Ohio and the Nickel Plate ALONE have made a public offer to do so.

How about it!

Once more we would like to go on record with this specific proposal:

The Chesapeake & Ohio, whose western passenger terminus is Cincinnati, stands ready now to join with any combination of other railroads to set up connecting transcontinental and intermediate service through Chicago and St. Louis, on practical schedules and routes.

The Nickel Plate Road, which runs to Chicago and St. Louis, also stands ready now to join with any combination of roads to set up the same kind of connecting service through these two cities.

Through railroad service can't be blocked forever. The public wants it. It's bound to come. Again, we invite the support of the public, of railroad people and railroad investors—for this vitally needed improvement in rail transportation!

Chesapeake & Ohio Railway · Nickel Plate Road
Terminal Tower, Cleveland 1, Ohio

(The late Robert R. Young, Chairman of the Chesapeake & Ohio, suggested this clever "hog" analogy. His idea was logically elaborated by Kenyon & Eckhardt, Inc. It got quick results, thus showing the power of advertising for social improvement. Courtesy of Robert R. Young and Malcolm F. Smith.)

I have used the above illustration many times before medical and dental societies to show the rest for the heart which we gain by sitting down with feet on a hassock. This posture lessens our vertical height by almost half, thus lowering our blood pressure and slowing our pulse. Remember, God figuratively places 2½ billion heart beats in our cardiac "bank" at birth. Anything that causes us to consume them prematurely shortens our life. Avoid emotional intemperance, obesity, stimulants, anxiety and unnecessary standing. And when you take a vacation, be sure your heart gets its rest!

vior of an individual. Beriberi, rickets, scurvy, and numerous other ailments which reduce the efficiency of the individual are already known to be the result of dietary deficiencies in respect to some necessary food chemical.

The Effect of Noise and Distraction on Efficiency.

The introduction of noise while subjects are working produces at first a slowing down of output. If the noise is continuous and not too intense, there follows an apparent increase in the speed of output of the workers. The explanation for the change is supposed to lie in the fact that the worker actively attempts to focus his attention more closely on the work in order to disregard the disturbance, and so he keeps up his accustomed output, but at a greater expense of effort.

The general effect of distractions of all sorts is to introduce additional muscular activity for the continued performance of the given task. Accordingly, distraction is a source of inefficiency. We have pointed out the visual distractions and their reasons for being detrimental to human productivity, as well as such psychological distractions as fear, whether it be of a dangerous machine, loss of a job, or the leaving of dependents unprotected by insurance.

The influence of distraction is, of course, more apparent in tasks which have not been reduced to routine performance. When workers are attacking problems involving a certain number of new adjustments, the presence of disturbing stimuli is more inimical to output than in the habitual manual processes. Every motorist, for instance, has felt the difference in tenseness of musculature when driving an automobile through the city, and when speeding along the country highways. Even when driving in the city, one can carry on a conversation until a traffic jam occurs or a difficult street crossing is passed. Who has not then found that he could not speak and drive simultaneously in a critical situation and so has left a sentence hanging in the middle, only to complete it a block farther down the boulevard?

Let us arbitrarily represent the total attention of an individual as 100 per cent. Distractions, as the feel of one's clothing and shoes, the temperature and vague auditory, olfactory, and other stimuli, pull some of this maximum attention total away so that we can probably muster no more than 70 per cent of our potential attention in our normal waking state, although under hypnosis we can materially increase this percentage. If it requires a minimum of 40 per cent for casual conversation and 30 per cent for driving our automobile, we can simultaneously do both. But when a critical spot appears in the driving situation, demanding perhaps 50 per cent of our controllable attention, the remaining 20 per cent is insufficient for conversation; hence, we stop that activity for the moment, and resume it only when a simpler driving condition frees at least 20 per cent of our attention for a return to speech.

Monotony is another of the important factors reducing efficiency. To be happy in a job the worker must meet enough demands on his intelligence to keep the bulk of his attention occupied. As soon as his task becomes so routine that he has considerable attention free, he begins to grow bored. The task is monotonous, irksome. He dislikes it, and dislike is similar to fear in its influence upon fatigue. In his imagination he may be able to avoid the monotony by spending time in daydreams of a pleasanter world. Some of our large factories have introduced phonograph music as a means of preventing the onset of monotony in mechanical jobs. But, lacking such escapes from the boredom of the routine task, the worker finds himself confronted day after day with the same old thing. His work has lost novelty and interest. He has to force himself to attend to those aspects of it which do demand more than habitual attention, and this forcing is comparable to the behavior of the person who forces himself to a task when noise or visual objects are constantly tempting him away.

In summarizing the effects of noise and distraction on efficiency, we can repeat that noise reduces efficiency as measured in the energy consumption of the worker even though it may occasionally show no detrimental effect upon output. Intermittent noises, however, are much more disastrous than fairly regular ones, since the worker becomes somewhat adapted to the latter. Distractions of any sort cause the utilization of more muscles or more energy than would otherwise be necessary; hence, they produce inefficiency as judged by the energy consumption of the worker. See "Noise Levels", p. 125.

The Effect of Sleep on Efficiency. The individual who has lived to the age of sixty years has spent twenty years in sleep. The temporal importance of sleep is, accordingly, quite large. Sleep has also definite physiological significance, for it is during this state that the effects of fatigue are eliminated. Our body goes on a semi-vacation for eight hours each day. We refrain from active mental and physical endeavor. Whether or not we demand eight or nine hours of sleep depends both on the amount of energy we have expended the previous day, as well as upon habit. Some individuals, like Edison and Napoleon, seem to be able to get along on half the sleep which others require. It is possible that excessive visual work with its strain upon the visual apparatus may be a factor in determining the length of sleep required. Mosso found that overfatiguing a muscle resulted in a disproportionate amount of time necessary for recovery.

Likewise, persons of a nervous disposition consume more energy than the more phlegmatic persons, and hence we see a possible logical reason for a difference in sleeping time demanded by the two. In physical exercise, moreover, persons seem to be able to get along with less sleep than under severe mental strain.

In 1925, Moss and seven associates went without sleep for a period of sixty hours, taking various mental and physical tests during the interim. Analyses of the blood and urine of the subjects then gave indications of the same conditions as are present in a mild infection, but the conditions returned to normal after a single night's sleep. The blood pressure and strength both decreased during the period of the test, and the visual and auditory apparatus reacted less sensitively. On mental tests these subjects did as well after as before the experience. The power of sustained attention after sleepless periods of long duration seems to be affected somewhat adversely, even though tasks of short duration can be effectively accomplished.

That sleep is a chemical phenomenon seems fairly well established. The blood of a fatigued dog has been transfused into the veins of a fresh animal, and shortly thereafter all the signs of fatigue have been observed in the fresh animal. The toxins of our waking metabolism are eliminated in the sleeping process. The depth of sleep is represented in Exhibit 21 taken from Kohlschutter who used the sound made by a falling ball dropped from different heights as an index of the soundness of slumber. According to his results, sleep is most profound at the end of the first hour, and by the conclusion of the third hour the sleeper can be awakened by a very light sound. If there is any relationship between the depth of sleep and the degree of detoxication going on, we might infer that three hours of sleep would be sufficient, or at least that it would be wiser to split up a six hours' slumber into two naps of three hours apiece.

The psychological onset of sleep must not be ignored. Traveling salesmen frequently kill time while riding between stops by sleeping. Incidentally, this is one of the theories for the onset of slumber. The caveman couldn't see after night, so, like the hen, he ceased activity, and found it pleasanter to endure the monotonous night in an unconscious condition. Students frequently find themselves intolerably drowsy when confronted by a difficult and uninteresting lesson, but their fatigue seems to vanish quite often when some one suggests a movie. In a similar manner the householder finds that he re-

EXHIBIT 21. Curve showing depth of sleep as measured by the intensity of
sound necessary to waken the sleeper. (After Kohlschutter).

sists the waking stimulus of his wife's insistent calls much
more strongly when they mean that a rug is to be beaten, or
the car washed. Sleep is readily conditioned by darkness.
Even in the middle of the morning when they should be quite
refreshed, medical students will fall sound asleep during a lan-
tern slide lecture, despite an interesting presentation of the
subject matter by the lecturer of the day. The darkness has
conditioned a sleep response in much the fashion of the tinkling wind chime's sound and the thirst response. Similarly,
the presence of a bed or couch in the study room is a constant
sleep suggestion, and renders study much more difficult.

The general effect of sleep upon efficiency, therefore, is beneficial, for it is during slumber that the detoxication process
goes on most advantageously. Sleep is a chemical phenomenon, although it can be conditioned by darkness, boredom,
monotony, and the hypnotist. Its greatest depth at the end of
the first hour with a very light sleep after the third hour,
coupled with Edison's apparent ability to get along successfully
on three to five hours of sleep per night, give rise to the

thought that we might be able to reduce our sleeping time by several hours.

The Influence of Age on Efficiency.   There are five age distinctions commonly recognized in science today, on the basis of which human beings can be classified. We shall list them in the following order:

(1) *Chronological Age.* This is the age determined by an individual's birth certificate, and has been the most frequent basis for age classification purposes. Our laws state that citizens must attain the age of 21 years before they are eligible to vote; they must start to school at 6 and may leave it at 16; under 5 they ride free on public carriers, and at half rates from then till 12; at 25 they may become United States Representatives; at 30 Senators, and at 35 they are eligible to reside in the White House.

(2) *Physical Age.* This is best represented in the case of girls and boys before puberty. At the age of ten years, for example, girls are physically more mature than boys, as measured by bone development, a fact which probably explains why boys' medians on intelligence tests lag behind those of girls until the middle of puberty. Even in the case of individuals of the same sex, however, all sorts of variations may occur. One man at the age of 60 is no older physically than another at the age of 40. Indeed, this variation is also found in the age of onset of puberty, which some girls reach at 10 while others do not enter until 16.

(3) *Mental Age.* This is becoming increasingly important in modern times as a means of classification of school children. It is ascertained by comparing the intellectual capacity of an individual with that possessed by average children of different chronological ages. Thus, a child aged 6 might have the mental age of normal children aged 9. This would clearly make the youngster very superior. On the other hand, at the age of 6 he might possess the mental age of normal children of 3, in

which case he would be a low grade moron. The mental age of an individual tells us little, however, until we know his chronological age, for we might have a grown man with a mental age of 8, or a grammar school boy with a mental age of 18. To express the ratio between mental age and chronological age Terman prefers the Intelligence Quotient. The I. Q. equals the mental age divided by the chronological age. For adults the chronological age is taken as 16. In the first example of the child aged 6 with a mental age of 9, the I. Q. would be 1.50; while in the second example he would have an I. Q. of 0.50. Intelligence Quotients are commonly employed without using the decimal point, the two above being stated simply as 150 and 50, respectively. There is no reason why we shouldn't also devise a Physical Quotient (P. Q.) for boys and girls, as well as men and women. It would be of more scientific value than the chronological age, and should be employed in numerous situations. The physical age would be a more accurate denominator in computing the I. Q. than is the present chronological age.

(4) *Educational Age.* This refers to the schooling level attained by the child, and is roughly employed by saying that an individual is a grammar school, high school or college graduate. If poverty and lack of educational opportunities were not involved, children of high I. Q. would of course possess the high educational attainments, but frequently men and women of brilliant intellects are met who have had little contact with the school system. A man might have a high mental age with a low educational age, but the converse is not possible.

(5) *Emotional Age.* Some of the brilliant young criminals of the past decade demonstrate cases of emotional retardation co-existent with high mental age. The emotions are closely bound up with the glandular development and functioning of the body, although training and experience also are factors. Some women at the age of 25, for example, have undergone

the gamut of passions, having experienced love and marriage twice or even thrice, with children by two or three husbands, with deaths of offspring and loved ones, or with divorce, ostracism and shame. Others reach old age with only a puppy love affair to upset the smooth course of their emotional lives, and with no social or family crises to mar the even tenor of their careers.

Prior to puberty children go through a "gang" stage in their development, when they are concerned primarily with their own sex. As they slip into puberty one after another of the gang members deserts the ranks for the greater attraction of some one of the opposite sex, until only a few of the die-hards remain to console each other for the dereliction of the majority from those sacred tenets signed in blood. This period is critical in the emotional development of the individual. If he leaves the attractions of his own sex for those of the opposite sex, his homosexual tendencies become submerged in heterosexual attachments.

The home, school, and social environments tend to prepare the child for this transition, for all around him he sees the father and mother and husband and wife matings. He expects ultimately to have a wife, or the little girl takes it as a matter of course that she will have a husband. With this heterosexual conditioning antedating puberty by a dozen years, it is quite natural to expect the majority of youngsters to encounter no stoppage in their emotional growth.

But some become unduly attached to their own sex, especially if surrounded by their own kind exclusively during the early pubertal years. Schoolgirl "crushes" are frequent, and represent simply the maturation of the sexual instinct. Some of these crushes, however, continue into adult life. The subjects are checked in their normal emotional development, and retain a more puerile emotional state throughout adulthood.

Others seem to be endowed with hypofunctioning glands, and never feel the wealth of emotional experiences which their more normal associates undergo. They may be emotionally passive and cold. On the other hand, hyperactivity of certain glands, such as the thyroid, leads to excessive excitability and emotionalism. The intimate relationship between the glands and personality is given very clearly by Beach.[4] Eventually we may be able to rate a child in grammar school in this regard, giving him an age "profile". At present our research in the field of emotions is still in its infancy.

The effect of age upon efficiency may be summarized by saying that the synapses are capable of being modified at least until definite senescence begins. With advancing years, however, the energy and emotionality of youth slip away, two factors which are extremely important for learning. Kenagy and Yoakum examined a group of superior salesmen, whose average age was 39. Almost 80 per cent of them fell between the ages of 30 to 50. In respect to mental ailments we know that dementia praecox and manic depressive psychoses usually make their incidence before the age of 35; the bulk of the cases of paresis fall between 35 and 55; while senile dementia seldom is noted prior to the three score mark.

The Relationship of Fatigue and Output.

The chemical cause of fatigue is accumulation in the blood of carbon dioxide. This is a product of muscular activity and is exhaled in the lungs. When it is produced faster than it is eliminated it tends to clog the chemical activities of muscle cells; hence we feel tired. But the individual's own judgment of his fatigued condition is not always reliable. Often a person feels tired without having done enough work to warrant any such statement, and again he may say he isn't a bit tired after he has been working steadily for two or three hours. His incentives may markedly alter his sense of fatigue.

Because of the apparent variability of the thing we call fatigue, some have advised omitting the word from our scientific

---

"Habits are first cobwebs, then cables."   —Spanish Proverb terminology, and attempting to obtain a physical or physiological standard by which to measure the actual bodily state after the duration of the working condition. The respiration calorimeter is a device by which the oxygen intake and carbon dioxide outgo are measured and the heat production resulting from muscular activity is determined. By such a device it is possible to determine the energy required for definite units of work, both physical and mental.

Because of the fact that there does not result a perfect correlation between output and expressed fatigue, we cannot use the introspective report of the worker as an absolute index of his real fatigued condition. He confuses interest with physical incapacity for work. He says, "I am tired of this job", meaning that he is bored by it, or dislikes it. Again, he says, "I am tired", and means that he is unable to work at par, at least without undue strain and abnormal incentives.

The "warming up" effect is also noted in mental and physical work. At the outset one feels quickly tired, then a "second wind" seems to arrive and one continues at a comfortable pace for a long period. This second wind has a physiological foundation, and is apparent in the output of factory workers. The typical production curve shows a low output during the first hour, with the maximum reached three or four hours after the beginning of work, and a lower output at the end of the day. Part of this reduced productivity at the two extremes of the working day is due to slowness in getting started, and premature quitting to get washed and ready to leave when the whistle blows. That workers will do as much or more work in eight hours as in the ten hour day is a matter of common knowledge. We tend to strike a congenial pace, which we make faster if we know the course is shorter. The fatigue effects of too long a working day, moreover, may carry over to the next so that the worker becomes progressively more tired.

"When you have accomplished your daily task, go to sleep in peace;
God is awake."   —Victor Hugo

In one of the war industries of England, Vernon[36] reports the output in a moderately heavy lathe operation for a period of 93 consecutive weeks. During this period there was no change whatever in the test situation save in the hours of work. After the change from 66.0 to 54.4 actual working hours there was no resultant change in production for a period of about a month. Then a rise in output from the previous figure of 108 kept up for two months until it reached 131. When the actual working time was cut down again to 47.5 hours, there was another period of no effect, followed by a second rise for a period of three months to a new level of output at 169. These data suggest the fact that it is wise in making changes in working schedules to give the new regime at least a three months' trial.

The effect of short rest periods inserted into the working day at frequent intervals has been found decidedly beneficial. The particular number and frequency vary for different occupations and should be determined by watching the production records. As long as the output keeps rising, more rest periods can be introduced. A limit will of course be reached at which the worker will not be able to profit by the warming up phenomenon before he is called off the job for another rest. This of course represents the point of diminishing returns.

In studying the working time of laborers for the Bethlehem Steel Company, Taylor[35] found it advisable to make certain changes. Prior to his changes he found that the average workman loaded 12.5 tons of pig iron daily. The usual procedure was for the men to pick up a pig of 92 pounds weight, carry it up an inclined plank, and deposit it in a railway car. Taylor had work periods interspersed with rest periods which were accurately timed by the foreman. The men all ceased work on signal, and resumed at the foreman's direction. Under this

---

When you form a partnership with God, you can let Him take over the night shift. You'll then sleep more soundly. Peptic ulcer and spastic colitis will tend to vanish. You'll also work with less fatigue, for fears will disappear and it's worry or dread which wear us out; not long hours of toil.

plan the men's output increased to 47.5 tons per day, while the men were under load only 42 per cent of the time.

From the standpoint of the psychologist, therefore, fatigue may be psychical or physical. In the former case the worker is tired without a corresponding increase in the toxins in his blood stream. His fatigue is, therefore, not real and may give way quickly to some one's invitation to go to a movie. Another striking phenomenon of fatigue is the apparent fact that it becomes cumulative. The converse of this idea, namely, that energy is also cumulative, was demonstrated in our citation from Vernon, who holds that it may require three months before a group of overworked employees react with increased output to a shortened working week. Short rest periods inserted frequently into the day's schedule are usually conducive to greater production with no apparent increase in the fatigue of the employees.

The Effect of Psychological Factors on Output. We have discussed in previous chapters some of the things that can be utilized here. The motivation by various incentives other than wages or salary is of considerable importance. Honors, promotions in rank, even with little or no money increase, are potent forces in affecting efficiency. After all a satisfied worker, like a satisfied customer, is the ultimate source of financial profit to the factory or mercantile house.

The personnel office by co-operating with the foremen and department heads can render a distinct service by avoiding placing a square peg in a round hole. We shall go into this phase of efficiency improvement at more length in Chapter IX. This task involves the recognition of intelligence levels and job specification. The man of low I. Q. can fulfill many factory functions more successfully than his more intelligent mate, for he will be more contented in them. And the worker's contentment in his niche is one of the aims of personnel administration.

This aspect of industrial improvement is becoming more apparent today than ever before. Psychology formerly was called upon chiefly as an instrument for accelerating production without increasing the overhead. The worker was looked upon too often as simply a cog in the machine. The mechanical aspects of production have now reached a high level of development. The efficiency engineer, although an excellent adjunct of the modern factory, is now sharing honors with the personnel manager. This is as it should be. The two render reciprocal services, and accomplish most by co-operation. All too often in the past the efficient methods of the applied psychologist have been met with resistance by the working man and the trades union. The attitudes of the latter have been that the management was trying to get more work out of the employees at the same wage as before.

The effect of psychological factors on output has become, therefore, an important consideration of the personnel department. A contented worker is usually a fairly efficient worker. Alteration of the machines to fit the needs of the workmen, and attention to lighting, ventilation, and other methods of reducing inefficiency may make the employee's task less fatiguing, but unless his mental attitude is wholesome, these very assets may become liabilities, for the employee will grumble at every innovation, regarding it as another indication of the employer's attempt to get more work out of him. Efficiency engineering, therefore, involves the salesmanship of new ideas and methods to the workers along with the evolution of these same improvements. Some of these psychological factors we shall discuss in later chapters under personnel administration and the development of morale.

NOISE LEVELS

In an editorial in MD, the Medical Newsmagazine for Feb., 1957, we have the following "Noise Levels", stated in decibels. A decibel is 1/10 of a bel, named in honor of Alexander Graham Bell. An increase of only 6 decibels about doubles the loudness of a sound. Hearing usually deteriorates with age. At the age of 50, some 20 decibels are lost at a frequency of 4,000 cycles.

Decibels		*Decibels*	
Threshold of hearing	0	Motor truck	80
Rustle of leaves	15	Elevated train	95
Average whisper	25	Riveter	105
Quiet street	60	Pain threshold	140
Busy traffic	70		

REFERENCES

1 ADVANCED PISTOL MARKSMANSHIP MANUAL (U. S. ARMY, 1965)
2 BAILEY, H. A., *A Matter of Life or Death* (Putnam, 1958).
3 BARTLEY, S. H., *Fatigue and Impairment in Man* (McGraw-Hill, 1947).
4 BEACH, F. A., *Hormones and Behavior* (Hoeber, 1948).
5 BERGE, C., *The Theory of Graphs* (Wiley, 1962).
6 BERGLER, E., *Tensions Can Be Reduced to Nuisances* (Collier, 1962).
7 BIDERMAN & ZIMMER, *Manipulation of Human Behavior* (Wiley, 1964).
8 BIRREN, F., *Color Psychology and Color Therapy* (McGraw-Hill, 1950).
9 BETTELHEIM, B., *Symbolic Wounds* (Free Press, 1954).
10 BRANDT, H. F., *The Psychology of Seeing* (Philosophical Library, 1945).
11 BRAY, C. W., *Psychology and Military Proficiency* (Princeton U. Press, 1948).
12 BURGESS, T. O., *Workbook in General Psychology* (Concordia, 1959).
13 CARTER, L. F., *Psychological Research on Navigator Training* (AAF Aviation Psychology Report No. 10, U. S. Printing Office, 1947).
14 CATTELL, R. B., *Personality & Motivation* (World Book, 1959).
15 CHERRY, H., "Music as an Aid in General Anesthesia," *(N. Y. J. Dent.,* Jan., 1954, pp. 78-80).
16 CUSHNY, A. R., *Pharmacology* (Lea & Febiger, 1928).
18 DAVIDSON, H. P., A Study of the Confusing Letters, B, D, P and Q," *(J. Genet. Psychol.,* 47, 1935).
19 DENNIS, W., *Trends in the Relation of Psychology to Medicine* (U. of Pittsburgh Press, 1960).
20 DODGE, R., & BENEDICT, F. C., *Psychological Effects of Alcohol* (Carnegie Institution, 1915).
21 EHRLICH, E., *Speed Reading Is The Bunk* (Sat. Eve. Post, June 9, 1962).
22 FERREE, C. E., & RAND, G., "Some Experiments on the Eye with Different Illuminants, Part II," *(Transactions of the Illuminating Engineering Society, 1919).*
23 FLOYD, W. F., and WELFORD, A. T., *Symposium on Fatigue* (London: Lewis, 1955).
24 GILBRETH, F. B., "Wealth from Standardization: A Typical Example in Simplified Spelling," *(Bulletin Soc. Industr. Engineers,* 5, 1923).
25 GRANT, V. W., *Psychology of Sexual Emotion* (Longmans, 1959).
26 GUILFORD, J. P., *Psychometric Methods* (McGraw-Hill, 1960).
27 HESS, L. W., *Do I Know How To Apply for a Job* (Test Booklet of Public School Publishers, 1949).
28 HOKE, R. E., "The Improvement of Speed and Accuracy in Typewriting," *(Johns Hopkins U. Studies in Educ.,* No. 7, 1922).
29 HULL, C. L., "The Influence of Tobacco Smoking on Mental and Motor Efficiency," (Psychol. Monographs, 33, 1924).
30 IVY, A. C., "Definition of Alcoholism" *(Listen,* Vol. 10, No. 4).
31 LAIRD & LAIRD, *Sound Ways to Sleep* (McGraw-Hill, 1959).
32 LEE, F. S., "Fresh Air," *(Popular Science Monthly,* 84, 1914).
33 POFFENBERGER, A. T., *Applied Psychology* (Appleton, 1927).
34 RIVERS, W. H. R., *Influence of Alcohol and Other Drugs on Fatigue* (Arnold, London, 1908).
35 TAYLOR, F. W., *Principles of Scientific Management* (Harper, 1934).
36 VERNON, H.M., "The Speed of Adaption of Output to Altered Hours of Work," *(Industr. Fatigue Research Bd.,* London, 1920).
37 WYATT, S., "Machine Speeds and Output," *(J. Nat. Institute Indus. Psychol.,* London, 1927).
38 WOHL, M. G., *Long Term Illness* (Wiley, 1959).
39 YOUNG, P. T., *Motivation and Emotion* (Wiley, 1964).

CHAPTER IV

INDIVIDUAL AND SEX DIFFERENCES

Although the members of the human race are so similar that we would never mistake one of them for even the nearest related form of the apes, each member of mankind is likewise distinct from all others. Thus we have difference in similarity. In any given trait, however, we fall within a rather narrow range from the median score. For example, the height of men falls at about 68 inches, plus or minus 7. This means that the bulk of all mankind lie within 7 inches of the middle score. Appreciating such narrow limits of physical variability, the clothing stores and manufacturers can afford to make up millions of suits, dresses, coats, hats and shoes without taking our individual measurements, for they know the proportions of the average American man and woman, and how far the majority deviate therefrom.

The purpose of this chapter is to consider those differences which separate two individuals from each other. We shall, of course, attempt to restrict our examination to matters of practical importance in our business, social, and educational life. One of the most fascinating as well as obvious differences in the human species is that of sex, which we shall consider first. Because of the greater intelligence of *Homo sapiens,* these differences are much more complex than the sex distinctions of any other form of animal life.

Factors Influencing the Determination of Sex. From the beginning of time man has speculated as to the reasons underlying the birth of male and female offspring. Many of them have been quite humorous as viewed in the light of our present superior knowledge of embryology. The physical and sexual vitality of mother and father, their difference in age, the positions occupied during the act of mating, and various magical potions have been used as indices of sex determination at different periods in the past, and even continue into the present generation. The modern scientific view is based on the type of sex chromosomes found in the fertilized ovum.

In 1956, a brilliant demonstration by Tjio and Levan showed that normal human cells carry 46 chromosomes instead of 48. A normal male thus has an X and Y pair, plus 22 somatic pairs, while a normal female has an XX pair, plus the 22 somatic pairs. If a male sperm (22+X) unites with the female (22+X) the result is normally a female offspring (44+X+X). But if the other male sperm (22+Y) fuses with the female (22+X), the result is a male (44+X+Y). The female has about 4% more chromosomal material so the "Y" may be slightly more motile, thus helping account for the greater number of males vs. females at birth (106:100). Sometimes a failure of chromosomes to separate may produce an XXY zygote. Mental retardation is usually the only feature of XXX and XXXX females. But an extra non-sex chromosome is linked with severe congenital defects such as mongolism, sterility, eunuchoidism, etc.

The above explanation, therefore, would seem to exclude all such factors as the influence of the environment, the time of coitus, and the relative vigor of the two parents. But in lower forms of animal life we find that diet and temperature apparently contribute to sex determination. Feeding Rotifera, minute many-celled aquatic animals, solely upon chlorophyll protozoa results in female offspring only, while a diet devoid of chlorophyll protozoa results in male progeny exclusively. Fatherless female frogs may be produced by mechanical stimulation of the unfertilized eggs. In water of normal temperature, moreover, Witchi has found that fertilized frog eggs hatch into approximately an equal number of male and female offspring, but if the water is kept at 90° F. all the eggs result in males. Of pigeon eggs laid in winter the ratio of males to females in the hatched offspring is 153:100 whereas the summer eggs hatch into males and females in the ratio of 70:100.

From his study of 10,500,000 human births, Dusing likewise found that more boys are conceived in winter than in summer, while Ploss discovered that women in high altitudes give birth to more sons than those on the plains. Perhaps all of these data are but indirect expressions of the acid-alkaline ratio existing at the time of coitus. Recent experiments in animal breeding seem to indicate that a lactic acid douche administered immediately prior to sexual mating will tend to produce an increased percentage of female progeny, whereas an alkaline douche exerts the opposite effect. Sometimes, however, the acid douche paralyzes the motility of the sperms to such an extent as to prevent conception at that coitus. Indeed, gynecologists have often found that an excessively acid vagina may be one of the causes of sterility in women. An alkaline douche will occasionally be quite sufficient to remedy this sterility.

Exhibit 22. Showing ovulation date and week of most likely conception in a woman with a 28-day menstrual cycle.

The present consensus among investigators regards the ovulation date of human females as probably the 15th day prior to the onset of the next menses. Because human physiology does not operate with clock-like precision, it is customary to allow at least three extra days on each side of this date in estimating the week of most likely conception. This is the so-called "rhythm theory". On a menstrual cycle of 21 days, the 6th would thus be the expected ovulation date. On a 35-day cycle, the 20th would apparently indicate the time when the ovum ruptures free from the ovary.

Since both sperm and ovum seem to lose their effective potency within 24 to 48 hours, or possibly even less, there is thus but a short time per month when pregnancy can occur. Dr. Elder[9] in his admirable research concerning chimpanzees,

---

A menopausal tonic: Shed the excess upholstery around your equator until you regain the classy chassis of your youth!

says that on vaginal smears taken at successive intervals after mating, he has never seen motile sperm later than three hours after insemination, and that they usually die within an hour. He states that the monkey, on a 28-day cycle, seems to ovulate about 15 days before the beginning of the next menstruation, while his series of chimpanzees, despite a week or two longer average of menstrual cycle, also appeared to ovulate about 14 days prior to the next menses.

Physical Differences Between the Sexes. Aside from the primary sexual characteristics involving the genitalia and their function, we find a number of secondary sexual factors that separate male from female. Men are heavier than women; they are taller than women; their hearts beat slower than women's; they have less fat than women; they are stronger than women not alone in proportion to their greater size but absolutely; their legs are longer; their voices are pitched lower; they have a wider distribution of hair; the development of the breasts is vestigial in men but full in women; and the erogenous areas vary in location, speed and concentration of excitability.

Many, if not all, of the behavior differences of males and females are traceable directly to these physical differences. The greater strength of males explains most of the recreational and vocational differences between the sexes. Apart from early training effects, we would probably find such differences arising again in the race if we were to segregate a group of infants from all adult influences, and let them spontaneously evolve their new civilization. Because the girls as a class would fatigue sooner and be less competent in rough activities, a cleavage would soon appear, and the weaker half of the population would begin to develop games and tasks not only more commensurate with their strength, but also enabling them to compete in a more restricted group where chances of victory would be greatly enhanced. After pregnancy and childbirth, of course, the physical cleavage would be more accentuated, the women being tied to the home site by greater inertia resulting from additional weight, as well as the emotional habits conditioned to the babies.

The lesser strength of women and girls partly explains why they are more suggestible, and also more socially minded. Having been forced to rely on wit rather than brawn to gain their ends in the contacts with their brothers and schoolboy neighbors, they tend to excel in language functions, as we shall discuss later in the chapter. Because they have repeatedly been defeated by boyhood playmates in physical contests, in womanhood they are physically less aggressive, for aggressiveness and confidence are to a considerable extent the result of habitual adaptations to situations that ended in success. Their general superiority in classroom work may, therefore, be an evidence of compensation.

Because they have formed habits of acknowledging masculine physical supremacy, even despite their later educational superiority, the more basic reactions dominate them; so they take orders from men with little resentment or resistance. Women as a class much prefer masculine employers to feminine, while men do not relish working under even intellectually superior women. The immediacy of muscle outweighs the less evident and tangible mental strength, which partly explains the sexual attractiveness of the athlete in contrast to the Phi Beta Kappa man.

One of the basic causes of behavior differences between men and women is the fact that, although both boys and girls are inferior to adults in physical strength, the boys may finally excel their mothers and equal or excel their fathers, while the daughters never can hope to excel more than their mothers. This "coming of age" situation brings the boy into a state where physically he feels the equal of anybody, and superior to half the population, whereas his sister reaches womanhood with the feeling of equality to half the population and inferiority to the masculine other half. In short, she never reaches the state of psychical adulthood attained by her brother. Throughout adulthood, therefore, she retains half of the physical inferiority outlook possessed by the child, while the man throws off almost all of his. Women have more in common with children, therefore, than do men, which partly explains why mothers seem to be more accurate interpreters than fathers of both their sons' and daughters' wishes and actions.

The differences in specific gravity of the male and female body explain why women float on water more readily than men, as well as why they do not mind cold water as do men. The fat renders them relatively lighter and warmer. The lesser clothing demanded by girls is probably founded on this basic physiological difference, despite the contradictory dictates of fashion.

Such physical differences as mentioned above apparently hold true of men and women, whether of civilized or more savage races. In his studies of Indians, for example, Hrdlicka found that the average Indian woman is only two-thirds as strong as the average Indian man despite her much greater participation in hard manual labor. Indian women are just as much shorter than Indian men as white women are shorter than white men. And the Indian man's heart beats as much slower than the Indian woman's, as the white man's heart beats slower than the white woman's. The difference in muscular strength that is true of men and women has been found to have the ratio 29:18, when weight has been the same. This means that a woman weighing 125 pounds is only 62 per cent as strong as a man of the same weight.

The difference in length of legs explains in part the preference of a woman for high heels. By elevating herself through addition of two or three inches to her pedal extremities, she not only slenderizes her ankles and gains a more shapely calf, but she attains more masculine bodily proportions and appears more slender in figure. She also looks out upon the world from an elevation of an additional inch or two. The latter effect enables her to feel more grown up; so it materially adds to her poise and self-assurance. We shall defer until later in this chapter a discussion of the effects of erogenous differences between male and female.

As regards the menstrual function and its effect upon female efficiency, we find that women take as much as three times the number of days sick leave as men in one of our governmental departments where a thorough study of the subject has been made. In almost every industrial and commercial organization where the subject has been investigated, women have far exceeded men as regards rest periods and absences on account of illness. These factors are not alone indicative of the menstrual influence, for women are usually in positions of less importance, and hence can be absent with less detriment to production. Moreover, many employed women are not free from labor when the office or factory closes, but return home to housework, cooking, etc., tasks which demand strength and often incite worry. As a general rule, the attitude toward the menstrual period has changed with the franker and more athletic views of the modern world. In Tennyson's day feminine fainting and indisposition of women for several days each month were expected of them. The psychological factors were prominent in producing her incapacity. At present a different mental attitude is also lessening the influence of menstruation on her efficiency.

In considering the physical differences between the sexes, therefore, we have brought out the importance of such things as height and weight as they affect the mental attitude of the respective sexes. The greater strength of the male explains much of the social order of all races and ages of mankind. The difference between the coming of age of the male and of the female as it affects their outlook upon their fellowmen has been emphasized. Because of this strength difference females tend to be more alert in detecting the psychological states of those around them, whereas the males are less attentive to people.

The Relationship Between Glands and Genius. In the interesting experiments of Steinach we find that the grafting of an ovary in a previously castrated male guinea pig led to the development of female secondary sexual characteristics. The mammary glands became functional, the pig nursed young, and performed in the presence of male pigs after the fashion of females. The converse of this experiment was carried out. Testes were grafted in females whose ovaries had previously been excised, and the females developed masculine behavior, courting normal females and fighting with males as pugnaciously as congenital males. Apparently, shifting the sex glands about will almost completely change the behavior, and probably the instincts, of animals. As regards instincts Thorndike believes that men and women differ in two basic ways. Men are more pugnacious than women, while women are more protective and loving in regard to their offspring. Whether or not these differences are instinctive, we know they exist in the adult, and are correlates of sexual glands. These glands, through the network of neurones of which they are a part, give rise to the motive bases on which the home and business are built up.

The difference in cultural attainments of two brothers in whom we shall grant equal innate intellectual capacities and equal opportunity to partake of educational advantages, might be explained on the basis of different glandular influences. The more sexually inclined boy would probably develop social interests, spending recreational time in dancing, parties, and heterosexual activities. Becoming adept in such matters, he might go into some phase of business in which he could capitalize upon his knowledge of human nature. We might find him in salesmanship, fiction writing, or the like. He might have

made his college letter in sport, and have graduated with a
"C" rating.

His more sexually frigid brother, on the contrary, might become a famous scientist, leaving a formula or invention behind
him to keep his memory fresh in the archives of fame. Lacking the richly developed motive bases which would make him
more receptive to sex stimuli in the form of pretty college girls,
he would not find it so difficult to sit alone in his study room
night after night. There would be less distraction that he
must overcome. And lacking the distraction of athletic endeavor and competitive sports, his attention could steer a more
placid course. His honors would be intellectual ones, and he
would be content therewith. Because of his greater time spent
in scholastic thought, he would progress much farther than his
brother in such lines, graduating with a Phi Beta Kappa key,
and a traveling fellowship. In this connection Pitkin[20] says:

"Not by chance has it happened that many eminent men have
been sexual inferiors, sexual defectives, poor family men, recluses,
ascetics and even rabidly anti-social. The explanation is so simple
that it has escaped some otherwise acute observers, who have gone
the lengths of Freud and Adler in their search for causes. Far
deeper than all compensative urges and transfers, which unquestionably come into play here and there, we find a *constitutional narrowing of competitive interests.*

"A man of weak sexuality is in luck from the point of view
demanded by achievement. For he is not distracted by blonde winks
and brunette giggles. For him none of the struggles of good St.
Anthony."

It is doubtful, however, if too weak sexual glands can be
looked upon so generally as sources of motivation to high attainment. The driving energy of the sexually mature individual is evidently a powerful force for intellectual productivity if it can be harnessed aright. Sublimation of such in-

---

"A man is in general better pleased when he has a good dinner upon
his table than when his wife speaks Greek."   —Samuel Johnson

clinations probably explains a large part of the literature, art and poetry which stands in the pre-eminent class today. The ascetics and priests of the middle ages who translated their sex energy into literary and scientific products might never have attained as high a pinnacle of excellence if they had been bereft of this powerful driving force. Castrated animals and men seem to lack the alertness and energy of the normal creatures. They grow fat, contented, and less responsive to many stimuli in their environment. If sex is so potent a source of motivation that it runs a close second to hunger, then we may reason quite logically that the stronger the sexual inclinations, the greater the possibility of tremendous intellectual attainment when they are harnessed in the interest of science and the arts. The sex glands are, therefore, bases for production as well as reproduction.

Sex Differences in Sensory Preferences. In acuteness of sensory discrimination there seem to be no valid sex differences. Women are the equal of men in regard to auditory and visual sensitivity. In reaction time they may even slightly excel men, a fact that is probably explicable on the basis of the male's greater size and weight. The passage of a nervous impulse requires time, so the longer the neural arc, the slower is the response. The eye-brain-finger pathway is shorter in the female than in the male. Moreover, the greater the weight of an organ, the greater is the inertia which it offers.

In the realm of color vision, we find a curious sex difference evident. The male is more susceptible to color blindness than is the female. This defect seems to be sex-linked, being carried by the female, and becoming apparent in her son. The incidence of this defect has been estimated as 2 to 4 per cent of males and 0.01 to 1 per cent of females.[13]

The preferences existing for colors and odors have been measured in several surveys and experiments. The following

---

"It is better to be alone than in bad company."   —Old Proverb table from Wissler[26]shows the visual likes and dislikes of the men and women in his investigation. The male preference for blue, and the female preference for red bear out the findings of Jastrow's extensive survey. These likes and dislikes probably are not so much due to intrinsic qualities of the different hues, as to childhood experience with them.

| | FRESHMEN | | WOMEN | |
	LIKE	DISLIKE	LIKE	DISLIKE
Red	22	7	42	8
Orange	5	25	8	31
Yellow	2	32	5	8
Green	7	15	9	21
Blue	42	12	9	23
Violet	19	8	19	9
White	3	1	8	0

EXHIBIT 23. The color preferences of men and women students.

When my elder son was one year old, for example, I set six colored discs against the baseboard of my study. These were red, orange, yellow, green, peacock blue, and blue—the colored discs used with the rotary color mixer for classes in general psychology. Then I placed the boy on the floor on the opposite side of the room. Immediately he began crawling toward the orange disc until he seized it, whereupon I took it away from him, escorted him out of the room, mixed the color discs so orange was at the other end of the row, and repeated the experiment. The child crawled again straight for the orange circle of cardboard. A third time I repeated the procedure, but placed the orange disc in the middle of the series. He chose it for the third successive time, but refused to continue for the fourth trial. Why did he like the orange better than the other

---

"If the eye do not admire, the heart will not desire."   —Italian Proverb

"All looks yellow to a jaundiced eye."   —Old Proverb

colored discs? Probably not because orange was intrinsically more pleasant to him, but because orange looked like the fruit with whose juice he was familiar. He had, moreover, played with an orange on the tray of his high chair on one or two occasions. Familiarity probably bred pleasure, as it usually does. This fact may be the explanation of most of the color preferences cited.

In their comprehensive survey of the color preferences of males and females from kindergarten through college, Katz and Breed[16] found blue to be the constant choice of the males, and the usual choice of the females. In Exhibit 24 appear the

GRADE	COLOR PREFERENCE OF MALE SUBJECTS						COLOR PREFERENCE OF FEMALE SUBJECTS					
	R	O	Y	G	B	V	R	O	Y	G	B	V
Kdg.	3.5	5	2	3.5	1	6	5	3.5	1	6	2	3.5
1	3	4	5.5	2	1	5.5	3	6	4	2	1	5
2	4	6	5	3	1	2	3	5.5	4	2	1	5.5
3	2	4	5	3	1	6	3	4.5	6	2	1	4.5
4	2	4	6	3	1	5	2	6	5	3	1	4
5	2	3.5	6	3.5	1	5	4	6	5	2	1	3
6	2	5.5	5.5	3	1	4	3	6	5	2	1	4
7	3	5	6	2	1	4	3	5	6	2	1	4
8	3	6	4.5	2	1	4.5	3	5	5	2	1	5
9	2.5	5.5	4	2.5	1	5.5	2	6	3.5	3.5	1	5
10	2	5.5	5.5	4	1	3	5	5	3	1	2	5
11	3	4	5.5	2	1	5.5	3.5	5	2	1	3.5	6
12	2.5	5.5	5.5	2.5	1	4	4.5	6	3	2	1	4.5
College ..	3.5	5	6	2	1	3.5	4	6	5	1	3	2

EXHIBIT 24.   Color preferences of males and females from kindergarten through college.

data for both sexes. The number of male subjects tested at each grade level ranged from 28 to 109, while with the females it stretched from 10 to 105. The median number in each case lay at around 60. They found that red was a greater favorite

"How prudently we proud men compete for nameless graves, while now and then some starveling of Fate forgets himself into immortality."
—Wendell Phillips

of the poor than of the children from well-to-do neighborhoods during their early years, and that the reverse was true of green. These differences due to social status tended to disappear as the children had longer contact with the school system.

This general markedly pleasant effect of some colors on people is obviously a phenomenon which should be given careful consideration by advertising men and others who are interested in using various color effects in their work.

As regards preferences for different odors we can cite the following table from Poffenberger[21] showing the age and sex choices between six varieties of olfactory stimuli. In this table the 3,000 subjects voted simply for the most pleasant odor, according to their own experience. Rose and Violet seem to be the least popular, while Lilac and French Bouquet are considered most pleasant.

| | YOUNG | | | | MIDDLE AGE | | | | OLD | | | |
| | MALE | | FEMALE | | MALE | | FEMALE | | MALE | | FEMALE | |
	Number of Votes	Order	Number of Votes	Order	Number of Votes	Order	Number of Votes	Order	Number of Votes	Order	Number of Votes	Order
Rose	25	5	109	6	32	4.5	79	6	1	6	11	5
Violet ...	12	6	207	5	31	6	129	4.5	5	4	13	4
Lilac	48	1	229	3	51	2.5	441	1	5	4	70	1
Jasmine .	29	3.5	261	1	51	2.5	129	4.5	5	4	10	6
French Bouquet .	31	2	213	4	59	1	162	3	7	1	21	2
Oriental Bouquet .	29	3.5	237	2	32	4.5	186	2	6	2	19	3

EXHIBIT 25. Age and sex preferences for various odors.

"Fame is the perfume of heroic deeds."   —Socrates

"Amusement is the happiness of those who cannot think."   —Pope

In concluding our discussion of sex differences in sensory preferences we may say, first of all, that males and females seem to be about the same in acuity of sensory discrimination except for the slightly greater percentage of men who are color blind. As for the preferences of the two sexes regarding color those investigators who carried on their research fifty and sixty years ago found that women definitely preferred red, whereas men were most fond of blue. In more recent studies, however, men and women both showed greatest preference for blue. As regards olfactory preferences, we shall refer the reader to the table from Poffenberger.

Sex Differences in Buying. The advent of modern transportational facilities has played a part in the increasing participation of women in retail buying. When it was more difficult to get into town, the housewife left the task of purchasing to her husband. Now she not only does her own buying, but has usurped many of his former prerogatives, probably much to the mutual pleasure of both sexes.

Another reason for the increasing female participation in retail buying has been the rising economic independence of women. With their own pay checks they feel entitled to do their own shopping. The old paternalistic home where father carried all the money and wife and daughters depended on his largess and good humor for doles is fortunately disappearing.

There is, however, a difference not only in the relative degree of participation by women in purchasing and in the range of articles that she now buys, but also in the behavior of the two sexes in their methods of buying. Women are more attentive to fashions. They will keep alert to any innovation, even though they have no money to buy at present. And they are more exacting in their demands upon the clerks. Instead of looking at two or three articles, they wish a thorough inspection of all the stock. Very few men will go into a shop just for the sake of looking around. When they enter they are purchasing bent. Women, however, will more frequently stroll through a store just to look around. As the chief buyers of the American home, it is wise that they do this, for it gives them a current knowledge of prices and qualities.

In their purchasing women resemble the professional buyers of mercantile firms more than men resemble them even though the latter are usually male. The reason lies in the fact that the wife always is buying with the husband's opinions in mind. Even though he gives her free rein, she still is not freed from his ever-present shadow when she goes shopping. She feels herself custodian of the family funds, and therefore must be sure that she gets a bargain. In her sense of responsibility to another for the wise disbursement of the pay check, she resembles the professional buyer.

In order to assure herself of adequate quality for the price she pays, she alertly scans the newspaper and magazine advertisements, which are usually written for her, anyway. She is also familiar with cloth, and means of detecting pure fabrics from imitations. Men as a rule don't know the difference between voile and crêpe de chine. On Test 8 of Army Alpha they repeatedly call "denim" a dance, and écru and beige are just names, nothing more. After men are married a few years they forget even what size of shirt they wear, and sometimes let their wives buy their shoes for them.

In discussing the woman buyer above we have had in mind the typical American housewife. It is true that a certain small and wealthy class of women buy with little heed to prices, letting father or husband take care of the bills when they arrive, but this group is small. Its purchases are frequently of a costly sort, but the total volume of business is relatively slight compared to that of the average American housewife.

In their attention to little things women also differ from men. Whether this tendency of woman to pay attention to details is instilled through habit or is a part of her original nature is immaterial, for she surpasses man in this respect. Lace and curtains, doilies and the like are really feminine items, despite the era of masculine frills in Elizabethan England. Although men appreciate the feminine environment that surrounds them, they would seldom voluntarily attempt to duplicate it if left to themselves. When left alone by their wives, they dine in the kitchen. Then they exercise unusual effort trying to figure how to eliminate an extra dish or piece of silverware, finally reducing things to a minimum. As a last resort they may even dine from the drain board of the sink, and use their fingers to avoid washing dishes.

The woman, on the other hand, likes salads. She will spend time garnishing her foods for the visual effect, and decorate her grapefruit by scalloping its edges. She has an eye for the artistic, even in culinary matters. In his physiological research Ivy has shown that there is a definite cephalic or psychological phase to the process of digestion, thus justifying all these efforts to make more appetizing the viands placed before her family. With her greater attention to such niceties of method and apparel goes her corresponding greater attention to matters of deportment and etiquette. She is more interested in persons than is the male, and desires change in her environment and clothes far more frequently.

In making a final survey of the sex differences in buying, we may state that women do the majority of the retail buying of household goods, their own and their children's clothing, and have even assumed much of their husbands' purchasing. The advertisers realize this fact and construct most of their advertising for the women. Women are also the major purchasers of magazines of a general nature. They are more difficult to please than are men, and resemble the professional buyer in that they are after bargains for they feel themselves more or less responsible to their husbands for the wise disbursement of the family funds. Buying becomes both a business and a pleasure for them, so they are ever on the alert for new styles and sales even though at the time they are not strictly shopping bent. In this regard, too, they resemble the professional buyer, for he interviews salesmen often for no other reason than to keep abreast of styles and prices.

Sex Differences in Mating. The coyness of the female is an axiom of social psychology. In human and infra-human species she must be courted, and retreats as long as pursuit is forthcoming from the more aggressive male. In the absence of such pursuit, however, she may reverse the process, as Moss[19] found true of white rats in his clever experimentation. In one of two compartments in his experiment box he placed a female in the oestrual condition. Between her and the other compartment was an electrode giving a 28 volt electrical shock. One male after another was placed in the first compartment. If it deemed its sexual gratification by the female more desirable than the pain suffered in taking the 28 volts, then it went across; otherwise it remained in the compartment where it was originally placed. Of five male rats tested, only two went across in the hour they were allowed in the test situation. The reverse of the experiment was then undertaken. The males were confined in the compartment whose door opened inward, while the females were placed across the electrode, and allowed to come to the males if they were willing to take the shock to do so. In the hour's test three females crossed over to gain access to the males.

The proverbial shyness of the girl is probably ascribable in part to the more scattered erogenous regions in her body with a resulting diffuse erotic sensation. The male is not only more localized in his sex zones, but demonstrates a correspondingly quicker and more intense excitement. It isn't until after prolonged experience that the female's neural eroticism is trained to a unified muscular response. Because of this diffusion of sensitive zones, therefore, the female enjoys the courting stage more than her mate, for it offers a heightening to her slower

---

"Sizes often are deceiving. Sometimes a woman's thumb has a man under it."   —Erma Freesman

sexual passion comparable to the psychical phase in the digestion process. The direct physical union of the two sexes is
but partially satisfactory to the female unless this imaginative,
psychical phase of love is indulged in. The usual masculine
tendency in both food and sex indulgence, however, is for directness of satisfaction.

In devious ways the sexual urge expresses itself. It may be
given indirect outlet through dancing, skating, romantic moving pictures, love stories, pornographic pictures and the burlesque show, or it may seek the more refined outlets of music,
poetry, and art. Horseback riding is a source of erotic stimulation for the equestrienne. A curious thing about this basic
motive force is the fact that individuals may seldom realize
the devious workings of their sex expression. Very often the
sex urge is at the bottom of a series of rationalized arguments
which easily obscure it from the unskilled analyst.

The following data from one of the writer's classes in social
psychology suggest a sex difference in the preference for a
male or female stepchild. The question was put as follows:
"If you were to marry a widow (widower) with a young child,
would you prefer the youngster to be a boy or a girl?" The
following apportionment of replies shows considerable uniformity among each sex voting.

	PREFER STEPSON	PREFER STEPDAUGHTER
College Men (24)	6 (25 %)	18 (75 %)
College Women (28)	20 (71.5%)	8 (28.5%)

EXHIBIT 26.   Male and female preferences regarding sex of a stepchild.

Five of the women in explaining their choices admitted they
wouldn't want a stepdaughter because the child would prob-

Modern American Family <u>Minus</u> Electricity

What would *you* do without electricity in your home? Well—you could use candles. And build fires. And entertain each other. And substitute elbow-grease for all the jobs that electricity does automatically.

You'd be surprised how much it would cost, in money, time, and trouble. In fact, it almost takes a cartoon like this one to remind us how *much* electricity does—and how *little* it costs.

In your whole family budget, electric service is about the smallest amount—and the biggest bargain. What else gives you such value in comfort, health, ease and fun—and at such low cost?

America's *business-managed, tax-paying*
ELECTRIC LIGHT AND POWER COMPANIES★
★*Names on request from this magazine*

(A unique advertisement re "specificity", as per Page 19, courtesy of the business-managed, tax-paying Electric Light and Power Companies, and N. W. Ayer & Son.)

Remember the Boston
Tea Party?

The men of colonial Boston staged their historic "Tea Party" to show George III how they felt about high taxes. These taxes were voted in England. The Colonies had no voice in the matter. It was "taxation without representation."

We Americans today are staggering under a crushing tax load. But we don't need a tea party to show how we feel. We *have* representation. But, we must wake up to the truth about taxes.

You work one day out of four to pay taxes

Three months out of the year, on the average, *you work to pay taxes.* The more you pay out in taxes, the less you have to spend for your family's welfare. The less you have to spend, the less the demand for manufactured products of all kinds. This makes it more and more difficult for business and industry to expand and to provide new jobs. And that, in turn, threatens the security of every employee, stockholder and customer of business and industry —every farmer and every professional man and woman.

What makes prices high?

You can "see" many taxes, such as income, admission, sales, luxury, etc. But consider the ones you can't see, *the hidden taxes.* Do you know that on a 15¢ loaf of bread, there are 5¢ in taxes? That on a $2,000 auto, taxes amount to about $500? Or that on a 21¢ bottle of milk, taxes approximate 8¢?

What happened to the $6,000 house that you could build before the war? Maybe the fact that on a $10,000 house, taxes of one kind or another amount today to about $3,000 might have something to do with its disappearance.

There are 197 hidden taxes on each gallon of gasoline you buy. There are 116 hidden taxes woven and cut into your new suit, Mr. America. And you, Mrs. America, will find that 150 different taxes make the cost of your new hat just that much higher. *Don't fool yourself about someone else absorbing these taxes. They're right in the price tags of everything you buy.*

What's wrong?

Reasonable taxation is right and necessary. Government must be financed by taxes paid by its citizens. But, must nearly *every* governmental problem be solved by *more spending—more taxation?*

There is one answer to this frightening problem . . . SIMPLE, SENSIBLE, DAY-BY-DAY ECONOMY. Most of us practice that kind of economy in our private lives. Isn't it time we started to practice that same kind of economy in our national, state and local governments, too?

REPUBLIC STEEL

Republic Building, Cleveland 1, Ohio

(An excellent advertisement based on a historical analogy. Courtesy Republic Steel and its agency, Meldrum and Fewsmith, Inc.)

ably remind the husband of his former wife, and they were jealous enough not to wish that. Four of the men expressed similar reasons. The others gave thirteen different reasons, yet arrived at uniformity of choice in three-fourths of the cases. Obviously, the more basic explanation is that given by the five women and the four men. The others may not have consciously faced the basic sex reason for their choices, but that reason was probably operative underneath their rationalized explanation to the extent that it controlled their decision.

The psychological phases of mating and sex behavior, therefore, reveal that males are more blunt, more easily aroused in passion, and more aggressive throughout the courtship. In the exceptions to the above statement, the female may, however, become the pursuer, as Moss has shown in his experiments with rats. The female, moreover, seems to show her characteristic interest in details by placing a premium upon the possession of rings, billets-doux, gifts, love tokens and gentle caresses. She is much more prone to keep diaries. In the limited data shown in Exhibit 26, she also seems to prefer a stepson to a stepdaughter, which is the opposite choice of the male.

The Basis of Woman's Intuition. The basis of woman's intuition is ascribable to the same environmental factors which make the younger children more intuitive than the oldest, namely, the need of utilizing wits to match superior muscular development. The physically weaker person, of necessity, must begin to watch the reactions of his fellows and learn to interpret their shades of facial expression and vocal intonation, so that he may thereby judge when to act with impunity and when to refrain.

In a survey of salesmen the writer has found that oldest and only children fall below their percentage of occurrence in the general population. Some selective factor, therefore, has operated to favor the younger sons as salesmen. That factor appears to be the greater social knowledge of the younger son, who has acquired it through adjusting his actions to the mood of his older brother, as that was written in the latter's tones and looks. A salesman must be closely attuned to the emotional and mental turmoil going on within his client or customer, and a background of thirty years of human scrutiny gives the younger brother an opportunity to diagnose symptoms mechanically.

The oldest child and only child are more accustomed to getting what they want by brute force. Why should they attempt conciliatory measures when the latter are unnecessary? As a result, we find that oldest and only children are frequently more introvertive than their younger brothers. They find it more difficult to adjust, and placate. Therefore, they tend to grow angry when selling if their customers fail to respond readily.

Like younger sons, girls grow up with the physical inferiority to their brothers. They learn to gain their ends by strategy. This is decidedly superior mental training to that of brutishness. Darwin's theory that man evolved his superior intelligence because of his physical inferiority to other animals about him is a case in point. On Moss' Social Intelligence Test women excelled men in their ability to detect the emotion of an individual from his photograph. They also were better than men in judging the mental state of a speaker from his printed words. In observations of human behavior and knowledge of the correct procedure in social situations involving tact they likewise showed their superiority. Ability in all of these items is based on a lengthy training in adjusting to a human environment.

Sherlock Holmes observed clues in every murder mystery that were unseen by other lesser detectives, even though they were a part of each tragic situation. It is adeptness in seeing these clues of emotional and mental states possessed by people, that goes under the name of intuition. After years of such tutelage, women and many men quickly learn to feel the hostility or friendliness, jealousy or dislike of those with whom they mingle. They may not be able to describe accurately the reasons for their feelings, relying on the feminine "just because", or the masculine "hunch", but there are reasons. Oftentimes they may have been conditioned to such feelings without being conscious of the stimuli in the initial learning situation.

Another characteristic of younger brothers and of women is the fact that they usually take criticism or rebuff with less hurt or discouragement than oldest and only children. Having been accustomed so long to reproof and reprimand in the childhood situation, they have become somewhat inured to it. Oldest children may whip themselves along in sales work, but rebuffs cut more deeply than in the case of their younger siblings.

In concluding this section concerning woman's intuition, we can state that women have acquired their intuition by closer study of their human milieu. It has been to their advantage to detect the slight changes in tone and expression of their male companions since their lesser physical strength has forced them to a greater reliance upon tact and cajolery. Moreover, the social restrictions which do not permit women to select their male friends with the ease and directness with which men choose their sweethearts has compelled them to become skilled in stratagems and finesse. After years of such social schooling, they find it possible to form opinions without being able to state the reasons therefor. It is this susceptibility to many slight stimuli in the total situation which we designate as woman's intuition.

Introverts vs. Extroverts. The above discussion leads us directly into a consideration of extroversion and introversion. These two types of personality are represented fairly well in Theodore Roosevelt, Sr., and Woodrow Wilson. People in any trait, as we pointed out at the opening of this chapter, tend to fall closely around the mid-point; so the mass of people are neither introvertive nor extrovertive, but both. The central category we call the ambivert group, which is where most of us will be found. In the following classification of traits taken from Laird[18] the reader may check with a plus mark the items that fit him, and with a minus sign those which distinctly do not apply, reserving a zero for cases of doubt or neutrality. Then let sister, wife, or brother check him, too, and note how close agreement exists between the self-rating and that of an intimate acquaintance. It was Dr. Carl Jung of Zurich, Switzerland, who began classifying patients as introverts and extroverts. The extroverts express their emo-

---

HOW TO TELL AN INTROVERT OR EXTROVERT

Personality signs revealed in actions:
1. The introvert blushes easily; the extrovert rarely blushes.
2. The extrovert laughs more readily than the introvert.
3. The introvert is usually outspoken; the extrovert is usually careful not to hurt the feelings of others.
4. The extrovert is a fluent talker; the introvert can prepare a report in writing easier than he can tell it in conversation.
5. The extrovert loans money and possessions more readily than the introvert.
6. The extrovert moves faster than the introvert in the routine actions of the day, such as walking, dressing, talking, etc.
7. The extrovert does not take particular care of his personal property, such as watches, clothes, etc.; the introvert is found continually oiling, polishing, and tinkering.
8. Introverts are usually reluctant about making friends with the opposite sex, while extroverts are attracted by them.
9. Introverts are easily embarrassed by having to be in front of a crowd.
10. The extrovert is a more natural public speaker.
11. The introvert likes to argue.
12. The introvert is slow about making friends.
13. The introvert rewrites his letters, inserts interlineations, adds a postcript, and corrects every mistake of the typist.

"A modest girl never pursues a man; nor does a mousetrap pursue a mouse."   —*Exchange Express*

Personality signs revealed in thinking and attitudes are:

1. The introvert worries; the extrovert has scarcely a care in the world.
2. The feelings of the introvert are easily hurt; the extrovert is not bothered by what is said about him.
3. The introvert deliberates in great detail about everything—what to wear, where to eat, etc., and usually tells one why he decided to do what he did.
4. The introvert rebels when ordered to do a thing; the extrovert accepts directions as a matter of course.
5. The introvert is urged to his best efforts by praise; the extrovert is not affected by praise.
6. The introvert is suspicious of the motives of others.
7. The introvert is usually radical in religion and politics; the extrovert—if he entertains any opinions—is usually conservative.
8. The introvert would rather struggle alone to solve a problem than ask for help.
9. The introvert would rather work alone in a room than with others.
10. Extroverts follow athletics; introverts, books and "high brow" magazines.
11. The introvert is a poor loser.
12. The introvert daydreams a great deal.
13. The introvert prefers fine, delicate work (die making, accounting), while the extrovert prefers work in which details do not bother.
14. The introvert is inclined to be moody at times.
15. The introvert is very conscientious.

(See page 757 for an Introvert-Extrovert test)

tions in motor performance and contacts with others, whereas the introverts are more self-centered and shy. Extroverts might be thought of as men of action while introverts would be the thinkers and scholars. Daydreaming is a case of introversion; an instance where the emotional expression is inward.

Salesmen and younger children tend to be more extrovertive than those persons, such as scientists and engineers, who work with tools and abstract symbols. This is well demonstrated in the following case of one of the writer's students who had been an engineer for a number of years; then changed into sales work. He says of himself:

I never realized the change in my personality after getting into sales work until the other night when I attended the opera. Arriving early, I engaged the person who sat on my right in conversation, and had an interesting chat with him before the music started. I never did such a thing in my life previously, always remaining quiet until some one else asked a question of me. It was rather surprising when I analyzed my behavior afterwards for me to recall that I had obtained the man's name, the number of his children, where they attended school, and where he lived. I knew his profession and hobbies, and his church affiliation.

The student was a salesman of an encyclopedia, which accounts for his interest in children and their place of schooling, since this encyclopedia company uses the school children as a means of initial contact for their salesmen. The student had taken the company's course in salesmanship and had been in the field only six weeks; yet his introvertive behavior had begun to undergo a marked change. As we shall observe in more detail in a subsequent chapter, we can alter the personalities of children and adults by a conscious technique. The nursery school, for example, is of great value in extroverting children.

In his tests of the socially and mechanically minded persons Freyd[10] presents a number of distinctions which we have embodied in Exhibit 27. In this classification he refers, as we have done throughout this book unless otherwise stated, to central tendencies of the majority, allowing of course for the exceptions to the rule. Moss developed his Social Intelligence Test in the hope of differentiating the salesman type from the more introvertive mechanically minded. No attempt is made here to say that salesmen enjoy life more than mechanically minded individuals, or that they contribute less to cultural and mechanical evolution. Such a debate is not within the scope of this textbook.

"Before a man can wake up and find himself famous, it is necessary that he wake up and find himself."   —Emerson

CHARACTERISTICS OF SALESMEN	CHARACTERISTICS OF THE MECHANICALLY MINDED
Credulous	Assured in beliefs and attitudes
Objective or universal in their verbal association	Subjective in verbal associations
Careless of details	Careful of details
Impulsive	Inhibited and cautious
Deficient in fine motor co-ordination	Able to make fine motor co-ordinations
Not self-conscious	Self-conscious
Not conceited	Conceited
Adaptable	Not adaptable
Persevering	Not persevering
Excitable	Calm and reserved
Self-confident	Lacking in confidence in their abilities
Open-hearted and talkative	Reticent
Quick to make friends	Slow to make friends
Present-minded	Absent-minded
Good-natured	Glum
Neat in dress	Careless in dress

EXHIBIT 27. Freyd's personality differences between salesmen and the mechanically minded.

From the standpoint of psychology, therefore, introversion and extroversion are two categories probably covering the extremes of such human traits, the majority of people falling in the ambivert group. The introvert tends to be more egocentric than the extrovert. He and his possessions are very closely linked up. The hermit and the miser are two cases of extreme introverts. Children who are alone, lacking the extrovertive influences of living playmates, whether human or animal, are likely to become self-centered and individualistic. Introversion and extroversion are therefore chiefly the products of environments which predispose to one or the other types of personality. A child with an inferiority complex, however, may become more and more introvertive as his social contacts widen, especially if some organic inferiority or physical stigmata is the cause of his complex. Cripples, therefore, tend toward introversion. The salesman is a good example of the extrovert.

Individual Differences in Perception. One of the basic causes of arguments is explained as resulting from differences of perception, which depends on the past habits of the individual. We have shown previously that words possess feeling tones, or personalities. But words and other stimuli may not give rise to the same effects in two persons. People will even argue violently over the same printed phrase or sentence, yet never lock horns because they are talking about different things and don't know it. The story of the blind men of Hindustan is quite relevant here. One fell against the elephant's side only; the second seized just his tusk; the third his knee; the fourth his ear; the fifth his trunk; and the sixth his tail. Thereafter they argued violently as to the creature bearing the name "elephant", maintaining hotly and in turn that an elephant was a *wall,* a *spear,* a *tree,* a *fan,* a *snake,* and a *rope.* Unanimity of opinion cannot result unless all the stimuli presented to various subjects give rise to similar associations and responses. The college debater's first task is a definition of the question, translating it into terms of common acceptance to the affirmative and negative sides.

But even then debate results because the various subjects have different experiences in relation to the words. Theoretically there should never be any possibility of debate when reason is employed. If all of our experiences had the objectivity of figures, as in 25 x 35, we could never develop a difference of opinion over such results as 875. Debates of all sorts, therefore, simply indicate different perceptions, and these in turn denote different learning situations on the part of the combatants.

Fortunately, the majority of men and women in the same nation, state, and city have fairly uniform experiences so that they can get along with a reasonable degree of friendliness and cooperation. But all differences of experience, resulting from defective sense organs, subnormal intelligence, differences in race and custom and creed, militate against a sense of social unity, complicating therefore such matters as government, employment management, and world peace.

The whole matter of mental testing is also complicated because of different perceptions. Even with non-language tests, such as Army Beta, where words do not enter in, it is conceivable that a Hottentot might have less experience with reference to geometrical forms than an American child who had played with toys and blocks of every conceivable type. And this same factor enters, even though slightly, in our mental test results for American girls and boys. The fact that one sex apparently excels in one mental operation while the other is superior in another is probably reducible to different motivation and training in the respective fields. We have already pointed out what appears to us an adequate explanation for feminine superiority in those phases of Moss' Social Intelligence Test that have to do with observation of human behavior.

In his extensive investigation Terman[23] found no significant sex differences in intelligence, the average intelligence of women and girls being as high as that of men and boys. When the I.Q.'s. of boys and girls were separately treated, he discovered a small but fairly constant superiority of the girls up to the age of 13, but at 14 the curve for girls dropped below that for boys. The superiority up to that year, moreover, was only 2 or 3 points in terms of I.Q. We have advanced a probable explanation for this superiority under our discussion of physical age differences.

In only a few tests were sex differences marked. Terman describes these as follows: "The boys were decidedly better in arithmetical reasoning, giving differences between a president and a king, solving the form board, making change, reversing hands of clock, finding similarities, and solving the 'induction

---

"Don't introduce me to that man! I want to go on hating him, and I can't hate a man whom I know."   —Charles Lamb test'. The girls were superior in drawing designs from memory, answering the 'comprehension questions', repeating digits and sentences, tying a bow-knot, and finding rhymes."

The reasons why gossip and rumor become so distorted are also based (to a considerable degree) on errors of interpretation. In his description of the growth and elaboration of the rumor that Belgian and French priests were committing all sorts of atrocities against German soldiers van Langenhove[24] shows this fact very clearly. In a simple form we may similarly note the changes in reports by students of the same print situation, by regarding the following horrifying description. The first student read the original version, then wrote immediately thereafter his account of what he had read. The second student in the series read the report of the first student, then wrote his remembered version of it, which in turn became the reading copy for the third. This procedure was carried out through a series of three or four students. The third or fourth versions from several classes in which the experiment was tried follow the original as described below.

(Original)

Alone, crushed beneath the fallen trunk of a cypress which had crashed during a thunderstorm, Janet Gordon lay gasping painfully for breath. There was no other human being within three miles, and the pain in her chest prevented her calling aloud.

Night fell, and with it a swarm of biting gnats and mosquitoes feasted upon her defenseless head and face. One arm was broken above the elbow; the other pinioned beneath her; so she could only turn her head from side to side in a vain attempt to frighten away the insects.

Three days later the hungry vultures descended upon the fallen tree and gradually drew closer. Finally one alighted on her chest and glared down into her staring eyes. It darted its head at her— she blinked feebly—and the vulture's beak punctured her left eyeball, tearing part of the eyelid away. . . . Her skeleton was bleached when a trapper came upon the scene a month later.

(Third version in Section A)

Alone with a fallen cypress across her chest pinioning her down Dorothy Gordon lay helpless. She could not call for help.

After 3 hours insects began to bite her and she could not ward them off because 1 arm was pinioned under the tree while the other was broken at the elbow.

After 3 days vultures circled over her and one became bold enough to perch on her body and look into her open eyes.

After 3 months her bones were all bleached.

(Third version in Section B)

A girl went into the forest and got her arm pinned under a tree. During the night she was bitten by rats and mosquitoes. Then a vulture came and ate her eyes. A month later her skeleton was found.

(Fourth version in Section C)

Alone, crushed under a cypress tree lay Janet Gordon. She was very weak. There was not a human being within three miles. Her chest was hurting her so she could not call out.

Gnats and flies were bothering her but she could not shake them off. Her head was hurting. A vulture came along but she could not open her eyes. He picked at her eyeball and took away her eyelid.

Three days later a trapper found her bleached skull and skeleton.

Under conscious endeavor to reproduce verbatim what had been read, the students in the series described above were yet guilty of numerous omissions and inclusions. If an individual of superior intelligence makes so many errors in transmitting information, it is apparent why the laymen in emotional situations may ignore some stimuli and add others not present. The writer in several experiments based on the procedure just described, but using material that did not set off strong emotional reactions, has found that many errors arise because subjects

(1) See the things which fit into their habitual backgrounds, ignoring others.

(2) Translate specific stimuli, such as "river", into more generic categories, like "water", and then at the time of repro-

duction of the material again translate the generic terms like "water" into a specific word. The latter word may be "lake" instead of the original "river", depending upon the habitual reactions of the subject. Here in Chicago, for example, students quite frequently change "river" in the original passage to "lake" in their reproduced version. And citation of cities in the original, such as Pittsburg and Philadelphia, as in the passage quoted below, become simply Pennsylvania in the reproduced version. This common memory process of placing an individual element upon its generic category not only leads to speed of logical learning, but also results in errors of fact.

(3) Shorten their reproduced version by forgetting.

(Original passage read aloud to class)

Jim Laughton, despite his six years experience as an aviator, was lost in a fog between Philadelphia and Pittsburg. Fearing a crash against the granite peaks of the Alleghenies, he pulled the stick and zoomed to an altitude of ten-thousand feet. It had been raining, so the rapid ascent froze ice on the yellow wings of his biplane. While he was attempting to level off, the Liberty motor spluttered and died.

Jim's heart sank. Below him lay an invisible landscape full of forests and rivers. He raised his goggles and looked down, but could see only a faint glow to the west. Then he threw his left leg over the fuselage and jumped. While his plane clattered earthward Jim pulled the cord that loosened the silken parachute. He landed in the top of a birch tree with only a scratch across his right cheek.

(Usual type of response written one hour later)

An aviator was lost above the mountains in Pennsylvania. A cold rain was falling and he couldn't see anything below him. He pulled the stick and rose to an altitude of 10,000 feet. Then the Liberty motor died.

He threw his leg over the side and jumped out of the plane. He pulled the cord of his silk parachute and landed in a tree with only a few scratches.

From the foregoing cases, therefore, we see that individual differences in perception are not only the causes of most arguments, but they thwart such forces in society as attempt to heighten the sense of social unity existing between people. They also explain much of the rumor and distorted gossip which one hears, and account for many of the omissions from memory of events which one witnesses. Defective sense organs and subnormal intelligence are causative factors in producing differences in perception, but even among brilliant individuals almost the same degree of difference will be found. Schools and churches are partly effective because they standardize the perceptions of the majority of the people on a number of subjects, such as patriotism and religion. The essence of differences in perception between people goes back to differences in the original learning situations as involves their intelligence, the functional state of their sense organs, the stimuli acting upon them at the time, and their interests and motivation.

The Influence of Inheritance on Behavior. The conflicting views regarding the relative influence upon the human adult of heredity versus environment have shifted from one extreme to another. It is true that an insufficient inheritance of neural equipment may prevent a child from becoming a college graduate despite the most cultural environment, and yet the nervous tissue alone is not an indication of a high I.Q., for there is the possibility of functional feeble-mindedness by deprivation of stimulating environments, as we have already discussed. As the biceps muscle depends not only on inheritance but also on the specific exercise of that particular arm, so also the quality which we call intelligence appears to be dependent on both heredity and environment.

Some psychologists, such as Watson, emphasize environment almost exclusively, claiming they can make a child into a chemist, musician, lawyer, orator, or salesman simply by complete control of the stimuli playing upon the youngster. Complete control of the stimuli is obviously impossible, but the writer doubts the result even if it were possible to manipulate the environment perfectly, unless the child possessed a normal inherited capacity. With only 100 for his I.Q., however, the child could probably be made into a genius of any sort desired, with perfect control of his milieu, since we avail ourselves of much less than our capacities. A normal boy could therefore be drilled to such an extent that he would probably far excel in ultimate attainment the child with an I.Q. of 150, assuming that the latter had not been subjected to such an ideal training system. A normal mentality with a tremendous perseverance in learning will usually far outshine the sporadic efforts of brilliance.

As regards heredity and its influence upon mankind we know that obesity and slimness of figure run in families. Longevity is another factor which appears in some families and not in others. Deafness, feeble-mindedness, color blindness, eye color, tendency to multiple pregnancy, tendency to have extra digits, such as a sixth finger or toe, and even nervous instability apparently follow hereditary paths.

Many of the defects apparent in children and ascribed to heredity, however, are more likely a result of physical or chemical factors operating on the embryo while it is in the uterus. There is a definite temporal sequence in the development of the various anatomical structures in the body. If anything interferes with the embryo at the time the limb buds are to appear, they may be stunted so that they do not form perfectly or at all. There are anomalous infants born without feet or leg, or with hands growing directly from the shoulders, no arm intervening. Remember the 1962 thalidomide scare?

The effect of the maternal environment on mammalian offspring may lead to infection of the child by a disease that the mother has while pregnant. A syphilitic mother may infect her baby before its birth. An infected mother may also give it scarlet fever or measles. The distinction between inherited and acquired factors must be kept in mind. Although the baby is born with syphilis he does not inherit this disease. He has simply caught it from his mother by proximity to her while she had it. There is no nervous connection between a pregnant mother and her child, nor do they have the same blood supply. The child has its own heart and blood system, and its own nervous mechanism. It is just about as distinct from its mother before its birth as it is after its birth while it is nursing. She is simply its food and oxygen supply. As the villi in the intestine dip into the flow of liquid food passing along them, so the villi of the placenta dip into blood sinuses of the maternal uterine wall and filter out the food required by the child. In contrast to such relationship of child to mother we have the chicken developing in the egg entirely free from contact with its mother, as in an incubator. If hen or rooster parent possessed a disease which we found appearing in the chick that had been hatched by an incubator, then we could probably say the disease was inherited.

Children of the same parents would, of course, be expected to resemble one another more closely than other children of the neighborhood. Sometimes these family physical resemblances are very marked, even in children who are not identical twins. Twins that arise from the same ovum are called identical. They always have the same sex and the same parents and share alike the chromosomal factors of both parents. Apparently they develop similar mental diseases, for we have cases of such twins, separated in childhood, who later in adult life and in different parts of the country developed the same form of insanity.

Fraternal twins, however, may be of the same or of opposite sexes. They may even have different fathers, as is true of puppies born to the same mother in the same litter. Fraternal twins have no particular reason for being any more alike than brothers and sisters born to the same mother at intervals of several years, for they develop from different ova that have been fertilized within a few weeks of each other and occupy the same uterus. They may not look at all alike, and in their intellectual attainments resemble each other only as non-twin children of the family do.

Since feeble-mindedness is heritable we may also expect a rich neural capacity to show itself in succeeding generations. Children of superior parents tend to approach the parents in the traits they possess. The aim of eugenics is to encourage the mating of superior parents for the sake of breeding a higher type of mankind. The matter of inbreeding is of interest in this connection. Although the Mosaic Law inveighed against incestuous mating, and our present statutes in most states designate that first cousins (sometimes second cousins, too) shall not wed, there is no physical nor mental deficiency resulting from such unions if both parents are of sound stock. Because many of the bodily and mental defects are recessive traits, however, an apparently normal parent may be the carrier of feeble-mindedness or deafness, and when mated to a similar person, as his cousin, may find himself with subnormal or defective children. Dunlap has recommended inbreeding, however, for the very purpose of quickly bringing out these defectives so that they can be institutionalized, and the race freed shortly from the latent defective strains.

The writer has been told of a certain family in which deafness had appeared, wherein cousins married cousins until the deafness was so accentuated that now it is almost impossible for a normal hearing infant to be born. Over a score of members of the family have attended Gallaudet College for the Deaf at Washington, D. C. It was against this result that Alexander Graham Bell tried to encourage the mating of deaf and hearing individuals so that a deaf species of the human race could not be evolved. The unfortunate situation today is that the deaf are isolated from hearing people, marry their own kind as a consequence and tend to add more deaf children in succeeding generations.

In concluding this section we ought to mention another rather obvious difference between people, namely, handedness.

Approximately 95 per cent of men and women are right-handed. Hitherto this difference has been ascribed to heredity. It is possible that the relative freedom of its two arms during the last two months of pregnancy may have a bearing on this matter which will indicate that the child's right-handedness is acquired while carried in the uterus. In his research upon this topic, however, Joteyko finds that exercise of the left hand and arm has a greater effect on heart action than does exercise of the right side, and that this result holds true for both left-handed and right-handed persons. In this event, right-handed-ness may be simply a result of natural efficiency.

In summarizing this important topic of the influence of inheritance on behavior, we may cite such valuable heritages as vitality or a tendency to longevity and resistance to disease, a rich neural equipment, physical beauty and muscular develop-ment, height and complexion as some of the factors that de-scend by way of the germ plasm. On the other hand, feeble-mindedness and a susceptibility to nervous instability and disease may descend upon children, along with certain stigmata such as deafness, color blindness, etc. In either kind of hered-ity, however, the action of the environment may greatly influence the heritage from the past. Vaccination, a well balanced diet, and an adherence to the rules of health can greatly offset the possible tendency to disease.

A rich cultural environment can stimulate both types of neural mechanism to much greater attainment and development than would likely result under a monotonous milieu. Aside from the practice of eugenics, the average person had better concentrate upon the manufacture of a favorable environment for he will thereby influence himself and his progeny to higher attainment. The average person cannot greatly alter the physical and mental inheritance of his children but he can elevate the cultural surroundings of his youngsters from a vul-gar and monotonous life to a beautiful home in which music and art and literature vie with morality and love in their uplifting influence upon the youngsters' personalities. As regards the milieu, therefore, one can theoretically make it whatever he wishes.

REFERENCES

1 ALEXANDER, F. G., *The History of Psychiatry* (Harper & Row, 1966)
2 BORLAND et al., *Psych. in Dentistry* (U. S. Dept. HEW, 1964)
3 BRANDT, H. F., *The Psychology of Seeing* (Philosophical Library, 1945)
4 BREMER, J., *Asexualization* (MacMillan, 1959)
5 BUSS, A. H, *The Psychology of Aggression* (Wiley, 1961)
6 CAMPBELL, GURIN & MILLER, *The Voter Decides* (Row, Peterson, 1954)
7 CLEETON, G. U., *Making Work Human* (Antioch Press,-1949)
8 CROWE, C. M., *Getting Ready for Tomorrow* (Abingdon, 1959)
9 ELDER, J. H., "*The Time of Ovulation in Chimpanzees,*" (Yale J. Biol. and Med., 10, 1938)
10 FREYD, M., "*The Personalities of the Socially and Mechanically Minded,*" (Psychol. Rev. Monogr., 33, 1924)
11 GARRISON, K. C., *Psychology of Exceptional Children* (Ronald, 1950).
12 GASTAUT, H., *The Epilepsies* (Thomas, 1954)
13 HOWELL, W. H., *A Textbook of Physiology* (Saunders, 1930)
14 HURLOCK, E. B., *Adolescent Development* (McGraw-Hill, 1955)
15 KENTUCKY SYMPOSIUM, *Learning Theory, Personality Theory, and Clinical Research* (Wiley, 1954)
16 KATZ, S. E. & Breed, F. S., "*The Color Preferences of Children,*" (J. Appl. Psychol., 6, 1922)
17 KRATHWOHL, W. C., "*The Persistence in College of Industrious and Indolent Work Habits,*" (J. Educ. Res., 42, 1949)
18 LAIRD, D. A., *Psychology of Selecting Men* (McGraw-Hill, 1927)
19 MOSS, F. A., "*A Study of Animal Drives,*" (J. Exp. Psychol., 7, 1924)
20 PITKIN, W. B., *Psychology of Achievement* (Simon & Schuster, 1930)
21 POFFENBERGER, A. T., *Psychology in Advertising* (Shaw, 1932)
22 SMITH, G., *Psychological Studies in Twin Differences* (Gleerup, Sweden, 1949)
23 TERMAN, L. M., *Measurement of Intelligence* (Houghton, Mifflin, 1916)
24 van LANGENHOVE, *Growth of a Legend* (1916)
25 WHITING, B. B., *Six Cultures* (Wiley, 1963)
26 WISSLER, C., "The Correlation of Mental and Physical Tests," (*Psychol. Rev. Monogr., 3, 1901*).
27 WOLFFHEIM, N., *Psychology in the Nursery School* (Philos, Libr., 1955)
28 WOODWORTH & SCHLOSBERG, *Experimental Psychology* (Holt, 1954)
29 WOHL, M. G., *Long Term Illness* (Wiley, 1959)
30 WELLER, JAC, *Weapons and Tactics* (St. Martin's, 1966)
31 WHITEHOUSE, H.L.K., *The Mechanism of Heredity* (St. Martin's, 1966)

CHAPTER V
THE EFFECT OF SUGGESTION ON BEHAVIOR

Before we consider the effects of suggestion on human behavior it would be well to lay down a rigid definition of the term, for it has been employed quite differently by several writers. The popular use of the word in the sentence, "I made a suggestion that the society table the motion", is not the one we shall employ throughout this chapter. Furthermore, we do not use the word to designate *any* stimulus that sets off a determining tendency, as Titchener employs the term, nor as a state of susceptibility to excitation by a stimulus, as Bunnerman uses it, but rather, like Gault, as a stimulus that indirectly operates (usually in the marginal fields of attention) to set off a habitual response.

The tinkling sound made by the pendant wind chime described in Chapter II fell upon the ears of the reporter engrossed in writing his story for the day, and set off an organic thirst response. It was, therefore, a suggestion. One of my students reports that as a joke on his guests he frequently offers them a coat hanger, book, or his wife's purse just as they are standing at the door putting on their wraps, and busily engaged in goodbyes. They accept whatever he hands to them, mechanically reacting to the stimulus while their major attention is devoted to their conversation. As they leave the room, this student then calls them back and asks what they mean by carrying off his books, purse, etc. The discomfiture of the guests is an occasion for laughter. In both of these examples the stimulus was applied marginally to habit systems already established in the individuals reacting.

The other kind of suggestion is that classic instance of the dilemma, "Have you stopped beating your wife?" Here an apparently innocuous visual or auditory stimulus sets up an additional thought process over and beyond the immediately obvious. This type of suggestion is often employed in advertising, as shown in the car advertisement, "136 Doctors are Members of Postl's Health Club". It is employed effectively with children who won't eat their spinach, by the father who shows his biceps to his young sons and then eagerly exclaims, "Yum, give me some more of that spinach, please, Mother!" In the famous Cream of Wheat advertisement the happy child sets up the thought in the spectator's mind, "Cream of Wheat must be good." The advertisement itself does not make that statement, yet the observer goes through that thought process by means of an indirect stimulation of the neural pattern.

Bases for Suggestibility. The instinctive and habitual neural patterns that are developed in the individual are the real bases for suggestibility. A person cannot be stimulated to a reaction which he has never previously made, without his full attention being called to the process. Only mechanical or habitual action is capable of being called out without his directing the focus of his attention to it.

Suggestions, therefore, split off segmental portions of the total experience of the individual, and cause them to function more or less independently. There is a mild form of dissociation of the personality whenever suggestions operate. Dual personalities offer extreme cases of this splitting off of the habits of a subject by the presence of suggestion. When Irene, the girl cited by Janet who nursed her mother through a lengthy illness culminating in death, was working about the house thereafter, perhaps at her sewing, some stimulus, such as a pillow made by the mother, or a book or chair always the favorite of the departed parent, would excite her retinae and set up neural processes which re-aroused mother memories so vividly as to throw Irene into somnambulistic trances.

To any one else except Irene, of course, those pillows would not have been the cause of parental memories, nor adequate to excite the emotion of grief. Irene had to possess neural patterns in connection with the pillows, etc. before they could be effective as suggestions. In a similar vein, the pecking action of a hen taking food is not an effective stimulus for corresponding behavior on the part of an ape because the latter has no habits of such a nature nor is he conditioned to her kind of food. Yet a hungry hen's pecking will cause a surfeited hen to resume eating, as Bayer[3] has shown.

The first hen was permitted to peck at a large heap of grain until she stood motionless before the food. Then Bayer introduced a second hen which was quite hungry. As the latter began pecking vigorously the first hen resumed her eating and kept on until she had consumed 60 per cent additional. She will eat still more if three hungry hens are pecking before her, showing the suggestive influences of the extra stimuli. In the converse of the above experiment Bayer began with three hens which had eaten until they were full. When he introduced a fourth hungry hen, the other three were little affected by her pecking, only occasionally striking at a grain of food. Each surfeited hen was surrounded by two non-eating hens and one eating hen. Apparently her behavior was controlled by the greater mass of suggestion operating upon her. Since the child with insufficient appetite is usually the child lacking siblings, his food habits can probably be stimulated successfully by letting him dine with other youngsters.

Bayer conducted additional experiments with hens that show the influence of suggestion. When he placed a hen which had fasted for twenty-four hours before a pile of wheat weighing 100 grams, he found that the hen would eat until she had consumed on the average 50 grams, leaving the remaining 50 grams undisturbed. If he placed a larger pile of wheat before the hungry hen, then she wouldn't stop eating at the 50 gram point but would consume 33 to 50 grams additional. Assum-

---

"Idealism increases in direct proportion to one's distance from the problem."   —John Galsworthy ing that similar suggestive influences hold true with men and women, we can better understand why people eat more when seated at a heavily loaded banquet board, with opportunity to help themselves as long as they wish. To avoid overweight, therefore, it would seem wise to keep all food off the table except the portions on the diners' plates.

A third type of experiment consisted of leaving a hungry hen before a pile of grain until she was satisfied, as judged by her motionless behavior in front of the remaining grain. Then Bayer carefully removed the food, sweeping out every grain. Immediately he replaced it. As a result, the hen invariably began eating again. When she stopped, he went through the same procedure once more, and the hen resumed pecking as soon as the food was returned. In this manner he found that many hens would consume as much as 67 per cent more food than before. The practical significance of this experiment may lead to quicker fattening of hogs and poultry through similar methods.

In summarizing our discussion of the bases of suggestibility, therefore, we may state that they coincide with the instinctive and habitual neural patterns possessed by an individual. The stimulus which is meaningless to the subject or for which he has no habits developed can not cause him to respond. Moreover, he may be acted upon by antagonistic stimuli, as in the case of Bayer's surfeited hen surrounded by two others like herself and one hungry hen, in which case the stronger suggestion determines the resulting behavior.

Suggestion vs. the Direct Stimulus. The advantage of suggestion over the direct stimulus is that action can be produced more easily. "Sales resistance" and inhibiting ideas are not so likely to be set off. The subject reacts to the suggestion in a childlike, uncritical manner. A suggestion operates like a surprise attack in a military campaign in the sense that the subject reacting is unable to marshall his thoughts to meet the issue rationally. When suggestions are employed, the subject performs as mechanically as a marionette. At the moment of reaction he has no more conscious control over the suggestion-response behavior than Irene possessed over her somnambulistic trance.

Whenever a stimulus is applied to an organism that has become habituated to it, the accustomed reaction will follow unless it is impeded by conflicting ideas or physical circumstances. The function of suggestion, therefore, is to escape the arousal of the rival ideas. In so doing, it not only leads to a quick response, but the subject, if he becomes aware of the response, feels that it is a spontaneous act of his own volition, especially as he was unaware of the external influence playing upon him. Shakespeare gives us an excellent case in which Iago indirectly produced jealousy and hatred in Othello by suggestion. A direct attack by Iago upon Cassio would probably have resulted in Othello's defense of the latter. To damn a man by innuendo avoids antagonizing his friends, yet leads to their detecting real or imagined faults in him, and they think they have done so of their own accord. The following passage is a classic example of the employment of suggestion in the interest of villainy:

IAGO: My noble Lord,—
OTHELLO: What dost thou say, Iago?
IAGO: Did Michael Cassio, when you woo'd my lady, know of
    your love?
OTHELLO: He did, from first to last: why dost thou ask?
IAGO: But for a satisfaction of my thought;
    No further harm.
OTHELLO: Why of thy thought, Iago?
IAGO: I did not think he had been acquainted with her.
OTHELLO: O, yes, and went between us very oft.
IAGO: Indeed!
OTHELLO: Indeed! Ay, indeed; discern'st thou aught in
    that? Is he not honest?
IAGO: Honest, my lord?

OTHELLO: Honest, ay, honest.

IAGO: My Lord, for aught I know.

OTHELLO: What dost thou think?

IAGO: Think, my lord?

OTHELLO: Think, my lord!
> By heaven, he echoes me
> As if there were some monster in his thought
> Too hideous to be shown. Thou dost mean something;
> I hear thee say but now, thou likes not that
> When Cassio left my wife. What didst not like?
> And when I told thee how he was in my counsel
> In my whole course of wooing, thou criedst, "Indeed!"
> And didst contract and purse thy brows together,
> As if thou hadst shut up in thy brain
> Some horrible conceit: If thou dost love me,
> Show me thy thought.

IAGO: My lord, you know I love you.

OTHELLO: I think thou dost.
> And for I know thou'rt full of love and honest
> And weigh'st thy words before thou givest them breath,
> Therefore these stops of thine fright me the more:
> For such things in a false disloyal knave
> Are tricks of custom; but in a man that's just
> They're close dilations working from the heart
> That passion cannot rule.

IAGO: For Michael Cassio
> I dare be sworn I think that he is honest.

OTHELLO: I think so too.

IAGO: Men should be what they seem;
> Or those that be not, would they might seem none!

OTHELLO: Certain; men should be what they seem.

IAGO: Why then I think Cassio's an honest man.

OTHELLO: Nay, yet there's more in this;
> I prithee, speak to me as to thy thinkings,
> As thou dost ruminate, and give thy worst of thoughts,
> The worst of words.

From the psychological standpoint, therefore, suggestion is
superior to the direct stimulus in that it avoids the arousal of

contrary ideas. When the suggested action takes place, its sponsor believes the action has been originated by himself, and is therefore much less critical of his behavior. As a consequence, he responds more easily and is more satisfied with his performance. The skilful employment of suggestion, of course, necessitates more thinking and planning than does the use of direct statements, which probably explains why it is not so frequently practiced as the latter.

Positive and Negative Suggestion. Probably the clearest delineation of positive and negative suggestion can be obtained by recalling the instance of the snail cited at the beginning of Chapter II. We noted that a bit of lettuce in front of it caused the snail to expand, to approach the stimulus, whereas at the outset the physical contact of our pencil point caused it to retract. If we assume the snail has its major attention upon some political or economic problem of the day, and then we apply the lettuce leaf, we are using a positive suggestion. The snail will advance. If we employ the pencil point, the snail retracts, and we have employed a negative suggestion.

Although stimuli which occupy our major attention are more likely to set up conflicting reactions, the marginally applied suggestions may also do the same. It is possible to have several suggestions of a rival nature operating upon sense organs of the individual simultaneously. This has been appreciated in the field of advertising, the major effect of which is in the nature of suggestion. We gaze upon cuts and copy while engaged in conversation, consciously unaware of the pictures and words which we are mechanically scanning. If we read, "Eat Red Wing Apples and Avoid the Worms," it is obvious that we have applied both a positive and a negative suggestion at the same time. The case is similar to that of the snail when we first offered him the lettuce and touched him with the pencil.

If our retraction or worm-avoidance behavior is stronger

than our desire to eat apples, we react negatively to such advertising. If the two are equal, then indecision results. The famous advertising campaign with the slogan, "Reach for a Lucky instead of a Sweet," is a case in point. Because of the danger in suggesting antagonistic responses to the individual the usual statement in previous advertisements, "Beware of Substitutes," is being rapidly omitted. To be most effective, advertisements must concentrate on a unified impression that is positive in its suggestive influence.

There are certain exceptions which appear to stand out. Not long ago the Philco advertisement depicted a driver in a predicament because of a stalled engine. The motorist exclaimed that he would never again be caught without a Philco battery. Then there was the Listerine campaign with the ugly thought of "halitosis". And Fleischmann's Yeast campaign depicting viscera and explaining that we needed vitalizing through better elimination. Just a few years ago came the astounding Razor Company's pronouncement all over the country, "We Made a Mistake." Throughout the copy we learned that as users of these razor blades we had been given inferior steel blades, but it would not happen again.

The superficial success of such advertising as the above examples may be explained on the basis of the following facts: (1) As long as enough money is spent, even on psychologically imperfect advertising, of course the volume of sales will increase. If a company spends $1,000,000 this year against $250,000 last year, we should expect an increase in its sales, but whether that increase is as large as it would be with positive suggestion advertisements is a different matter. (2) As long as the advertising commands the major attention or consciousness of the readers it is possible to use "reason why" copy, and educate the readers to the significance of the negative contents of the copy and cuts. But, also, it requires unlimited financial resources and ever changing advertisements to keep the focal circle of the average reader's attention. It cannot be done economically. The chief value of advertising is its marginal or subconscious stimulation of the readers.

"Reason why" copy is not very effective when acting upon us in the marginal rings of our attention, for reasoning involves many generic words and a greater percentage of our attention than is found out there. Consequently, after once having seen such an advertisement we lose interest in it, which means it operates thereafter in the margin of our attention. We do not heed the finer type of explanatory copy, but daily react to the slogan in bold black headlines, "We Made a Mistake." In the preceding chapter we cited similar examples of how people recall the general items and forget the details. The slogan just quoted, therefore, is inferior to "Eat Red Wing Apples and Avoid Worms," for the latter is only 50 per cent negative when operating as a suggestion.

(3) A third reason for the success of such negative advertising as the Listerine and Yeast variety is the fact that a large number of people are already afflicted with ills or think they are. They are consequently alert for relief and not only do not retract or wince at the sight of such illustrations and slogans, but actually are drawn to them instead. Once a person has lost his health or his position, he no longer feels the scorn or disgust for infection and failure, especially as it is depicted in the advertisements, but goes through a process of immediate identification, and avidly scans the copy for information as to his own cure. For this type of individual, and the success of patent medicines proves there are millions of such, the picture of a sick man, especially when the "Before and After" illustrations are employed, may even be an asset. It holds his attention because it fits in with his chronic attitude of the moment—freedom from his defect.

In repeating our stress upon positive suggestion, it is well to recall what happens during forgetting. The generic headings, such as slogans and cuts, are retained, while the minor items usually appearing in small type, drop out. In the case of the Razor Company's slogan mentioned previously, the company undoubtedly felt that the novelty of their admission would stimulate belief in the Razor Company itself, relying on the attitude that confidence is often increased in the salesman who acknowledges an occasional defect. But many, if not the majority, of this razor's users hadn't even noted any inferiority of the blades. An unnoticed defect was now carefully pointed out by the company itself, with the additional unpalatable thought that they had been selling an inferior blade to us for some time. Since no refunds were announced, the normal man felt the displeasure that results from being tricked, and no promise about future good behavior can completely erase the ego deflation of being made the "goat". This unpleasant emotional conditioning is dangerous.

Even the previous non-user of this company's blades will retain ultimately the recollection that this company made an error, which becomes shortened in memory until finally all he recalls is "Blank Razors—Defective". It seems strange that there is lack of appreciation of the fact that ingenuity can always produce an advertisement or cut which is just as good at attracting attention, just as good at holding attention, just as good at impressing the memory, and certainly far more desirable in feeling tone and positive suggestion, than any negative advertisement yet produced.

A few years ago the advertisement reproduced on the next page was sent to Professor A. J. Snow for criticism. He used it with his classes and the writer employed it in his own sections of psychology to determine the student reaction. Because of the unpleasant feeling tone noted by many of the feminine students in particular, Professor Snow voted against it, despite his realization of its uniqueness and attention attracting value. For several ensuing years in *Advertising and Selling,* the wisdom of this advertisement was still being debated. It is said, however, to have been the most successful of any used by that company.

EXHIBIT 28. One of the most debated advertisements ever run, coupling an excellent attention attracting cut with a possible unpleasant feeling tone. (Courtesy of A. Stein & Company).

(MERCIREX)

EXHIBIT 29. A good example of suggestion in advertising with the unpleasant feeling tone neutralized by the pleasant illustration. (Courtesy of The Mercirex Company).

As we shall consider more fully later, the behavior of the salesman, speaker, and leader may be either negative or positive in its results. In the example of Bayer's surfeited hen we saw that the pecking of another hungry hen incited her to action, but the restraint of two other satiated hens offset the positive suggestion of the single hungry creature. A former student of mine who was professional buyer for a Chicago organization told me about an incident which bears upon this point. A salesman of check writing machines interviewed this buyer. He presented his sales talk, and saw that the buyer was in a receptive frame of mind. "How many do you want?" asked the salesman."Thirty-five," responded the buyer.

At this point the salesman, who apparently was expecting an order for one or two machines, became so excited that he could hardly fill in the order blank, whereupon the buyer said, "But I want to think it over, so I shan't be in the market today." Later he bought of another salesman who gave no better sales presentation, but who never batted an eyelash when he found out the size of the order. The buyer, in commenting upon the first salesman said, "You know, I began to feel that he wasn't used to selling large orders, so probably his machine wasn't any good."

The psychological phases of positive versus negative suggestions, therefore, point to the greater desirability of the former. Because suggestions are indirect and consequently in the marginal circles of the attention-field, the subject on whom they are operating cannot reason with them. They produce apparently spontaneous action. If they are negative, the resulting behavior is of the avoidance or retractive sort. Since the "reason why" copy of the advertisement cannot be understood in the marginal circles of the attention-field, the subject responds only to the stimuli of the headlines, cuts, and pictures, for these can set off habit patterns from the margins of the attention-field.

Specificity in Suggestion. In our discussion of methods of motivating human beings we distinguished between the three degrees of effective stimuli, the first being the actual objects themselves; the second, specific words denoting individual objects; and the least effective being generic and nonsensory terms. Because a suggestion leads to igniting habit systems already possessed by the subject, it is apparent that the more specific the suggestion, the more readily it will set off or ignite habitual behavior.

In the old days of wall telephones, hotels found it necessary to place a memorandum pad beside the telephone in order to protect the walls, for salesmen and even fastidious ladies would soon be scribbling on the wall, making geometric patterns and hieroglyphics while they conversed. The presence of a pencil on the desk in front of the average person who is engaged in talking, either over the telephone or directly to his interviewer, is an almost irresistible suggestion to the accustomed action of writing. It is, moreover, almost impossible for boys, and even for their fathers, to walk along a stream where there are round, smooth pebbles and not pick up a handful to throw.

In the manufacture of ammonia by Germany during the World War the Haber process was adopted, which entailed the use of enormous pressures. It is reported that the employees refused to endanger their lives further by working in such an environment, particularly as many fellow employees had been killed in several previous explosions. To placate them, the management called a halt in production, and issued the statement that a new method entailing less pressure was going to be installed in the plant, and set its engineers to work for a few days. When the employees were finally recalled, they felt much reassured. Pressure dials that formerly had read, say "5000 pounds per square inch", now were only "50 pounds per square inch". But the security felt by the workers was obtained simply through the installation of new pressure gauges from which two zeros had been removed, even though a pressure of 50 pounds was sufficient to cause a fatal explosion. The absence of those two ciphers was far more effective than hours of haranguing would have been.

The story is told of a gardner who found that his neighbor's hens kept digging up his seeds and ruining his tomatoes. Protest after protest that he made to their owner was of no avail. One night the gardener placed a dozen eggs at strategic points around his garden. Next morning he nonchalantly went out with a basket, and while his neighbor's wife looked out of her window at him he gathered the eggs. His neighbor penned the chickens within his own lot before another day had passed.

It is imperative, therefore, that specificity be employed in suggestions because habits are originally formed by definite stimuli, and must be set off by the same kind of object or quality. Abstractions and generalities may be used when the focus of attention is being monopolized, but in the marginal circles of the attention-field such stimuli are relatively ineffective. As a general rule we may say that the less attention being given to a stimulus, the more specific it must be in order to produce a reaction.

Sex Differences in Suggestibility. Since women have been more accustomed to taking orders from men than have men, it follows that we should expect females to obey more mechanically than do males. They should not be so likely to consider masculine commands critically but should submit from habituation. Although we have no tests which adequately measure suggestibility of men and women as Army Alpha, for instance, will measure their intellectual abilities, empirical data would seem to indicate a slight sex difference. It must be kept in mind that by our definition of suggestion, however, the reason women may be more suggestible than men in the social environment is the fact that masculine commands are not confronted so consciously as is true of men who hear the same orders given. The male tends to make an issue out of his submission, which thereby keeps his action in the focal circle of his attention-field. The woman, by her lack of conscious attention to the orders given, is reacting to marginal stimuli.

The relationship between suggestibility and intelligence is a peculiar one. On the basis of the greater number of habits possessed by the more intelligent individual, we should say that he could be stimulated by a wider range of suggestions. The familiar stories about absent-minded professors are almost always clear examples of responses to suggestion by men whose attention-field is preoccupied with direct stimuli. On the other hand, the more intelligent person has profited from his many ludicrous automatic acts so that he is somewhat on his guard thereafter. He has developed a "suggestion resistance" comparable to "sales resistance", and this is possible through a shifting attention and critical inspection of himself. He doesn't let himself be carried away with emotional enthusiasm as does the novice, because he is more experienced in such situations, and remains on his guard.

The apparently greater suggestibility of children is not explicable on the basis of the number of habits that can be set off by marginal stimuli or indirectly aroused by focal stimuli, for the child is obviously inferior to the adult in total number of habits. The child, however, has not learned to be so self critical as the adult. He is less wary of life, and is more inclined to do a thing without realizing what he does as he does it.

In concluding our discussion of sex differences in suggestibility, we may state that women are probably more suggestible than men because they have been more accustomed to taking orders from a source of greater physical prestige, and therefore the act of submission is more mechanical. This difference is consequently traceable to the physical differences between the sexes. Children are more suggestible than adults for the same reason.

How the Subconscious Affects Our Purchases. In discussing the subconscious throughout this book we employ the term synonymously with the marginal fields of attention illustrated in Exhibit 8. Those stimuli that lie in the outer circles are subconscious or marginal. We have called them suggestions in this chapter. And those habits ignited by such stimuli constitute the subconscious or marginal behavior of the individual. We have already intimated that the chief value of advertising is produced through its effects upon the marginal fields of attention.

Manufacturers and retailers also produce buying activity by playing upon us through these marginal zones. We know that certain anatomical aspects of the eye make it more of a strain for us to look up and down than to swing our gaze horizontally. The psychological effect of this condition makes us overestimate vertical distances. In a similar manner we think that filled space is greater than empty space, as Exhibit 30 demonstrates. A number of such illusions are employed by merchants and advertisers for the purpose of increasing sales. In having his subjects rank a number of cans in order of apparent size, Starch[24] found that cans of the same cubical contents were considered of different sizes by observers. One can was uniformly voted to be more than one-quarter larger than another of the identical cubical capacity. The significance of this fact is of monetary value to concerns merchandising their products in such containers.

On many cartons and cans, moreover, contents are designated in ounces instead of pounds, especially if the net weight is exactly one pound. The statement, "Net contents 16 ounces," is often likely to create the attitude that the weight is greater than if the statement read, "Net contents one pound." This results in part from an uncritical reaction to the number "16" and the number "1". Moreover, many in-

---

"He who moves not forward, goes backward."   —Goethe

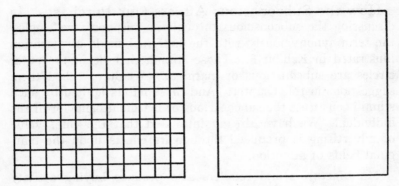

EXHIBIT 30. Showing the apparent difference in size of equal areas when one is filled space and the other empty.

dividuals may think the pound contains only 12 ounces, and hence feel they are getting 4 ounces more.

One of the writer's former students who was a radio retailer described how he used to convince his customers of the musical excellence of a radio. He would tell them in advance that good reproduction of tone on the part of a radio should enable the listener to visualize the movements of the musicians at the studio, or the throat and lip movements of the singer. Then he would have his customers sit down and close their eyes, while he tuned in. As the music issued from the radio he let them concentrate upon what they thought was occurring at the other end of the line, thus capitalizing upon their visual memories as an aid in increasing their enjoyment of an otherwise purely auditory concert. Their greater enjoyment was therefore assumed to be wholly a product of the tonal qualities of the instrument in question.

The same retailer used to enlist the co-operation of his Italian customers who wanted phonographs by always having a Caruso record in the demonstrating machine. The customer soon began to hum or sing along with Caruso, thereby rearousing memories of home and love and youth. The pleasant

emotional state of the customer was skilfully ascribed to the
excellence of reproduction of tones by the given phonograph.

Since the great majority of our opinions and decisions are
really based upon marginal stimuli, and only break into the
focus of our attention-field after the manner outlined in our
discussion of the thirst reaction of the young reporter, we shall
study more specifically these influences under the next four
sectional headings of this chapter.

Suggestive Advertising. All advertising soon slips out
of the focus of our attention, in which case its influence upon
us is by way of suggestion. But there are also certain types of
advertising that are definitely classed as suggestive, for their
effect is indirect even when they are viewed consciously. During the past decade, for example, the American public has
witnessed an era of testimonial advertising. Football heroes
and other athletes of all sorts have endorsed everything from
correspondence short story courses to cigarettes, and even
staid old American families of blue blood stock have been sub-
scribing to the merits of cold creams, beauty lotions and tooth
paste. Moving picture actors and actresses get almost as much
publicity through their photographic appearance on cartons
and cigarette billboards as from their histrionic endeavors on
the silver screen.

The purpose behind this sort of advertising is not only to
attract attention to the product, but to suggest that the reader
will also become athletic or beautiful by using the cigarettes
and cold cream. In the late summer of 1932 the breakfast
foods began to enlist moving picture stars in their advertising
campaigns, hoping thereby to increase the pulling power of
their advertisements.

But the response in other fields has also been increased by
adjusting the coupon to the type of product being merchandised. In this connection Simons[22] finds that triangular cou-

---

"The young man who has not wept is a savage, and the old man who
will not laugh is a fool."   —Santayana

pons are better when the request is for catalogues or literature, whereas a rectangular coupon is superior when free samples, goods on approval, or a trial order are being sought. When the coupon is being directed to one of the executives of a firm it is wiser to call it a "Request Form". Pointers or arrows in the body of the advertisement which are directed toward the coupon also increase the pulling power of the latter. The drawing of a man at his desk pointing to the coupon, and that of a hand holding a fountain pen with its point projecting into the coupon as if beginning to fill it out also increased the applications received.

The effectiveness of color as an attention attractor is self-evident, but that is not its only virtue in the advertisement. Color conveys an impression of richness and good quality which is impossible to portray in black and white. Unless a concern is very careful in the use of color, however, its patrons may obtain a feeling of disappointment when the dress or bedroom suite arrives. The buyers reacted not alone to the purchased article when they saw it pictured in the advertisement, but they indirectly absorbed some of the suggestions of style and trimness of the girlish figures attired in the frock in question, or of the other room furnishings in which the bedroom suite was situated. As a result, if the housewife does not have the graceful figure of the model, or if her bedroom is not the duplicate of the one seen in the advertisement, she may experience disappointment, and project her displeasure upon the concern whose product she has purchased. Even in direct retail selling the same displeasure frequently follows the purchaser's return home. While in the shop she reacted to the richness of the surroundings. Her more drab home environment doesn't contribute the pleasurable sensations which she experienced in the buying situation, and she cannot understand the apparent change in her attitude toward the hat. Like the radio and phonograph customers described above, she had unwittingly transferred many additional sensory experiences to the hat which the hat did not possess. Her brutally frank husband or relatives may also present comments concerning her appearance which are very different from those of the saleslady.

As regards the types of products that can be presented successfully through suggestive advertising, Hollingworth[10] gives the following list:

1. For all *personal* articles, the use of which is *intimate* and *private*, as toilet articles, gifts, stationery, and so forth.

2. For articles of *luxury, display,* and *adornment,* as jewelry, fancy dress goods, feathers and plumes, flowers and so on.

3. For articles enjoyed *in themselves* or *for their own sake,* rather than for remote service which they may render, as drinks, musical instruments, sweetmeats, toys.

4. For articles calculated to promote the *bodily safety* of the individual or of those dependent on him, as disinfectants, safety devices, insurance, weapons of defence.

5. For *all food products.*

6. For all clothing which tends to be ornamental rather than utilitarian in character, as ties, collars, laces, canes.

As a matter of fact, almost any product can be presented at times through the medium of suggestive advertising. Indeed, endorsements and "seals of approval" also exert an indirect effect that is suggestive. For they generate the thought, "The product MUST be good or such a renowned magazine, laboratory or bureau would not jeopardize its goodwill by letting its name be associated with the product in question." On the next page you will see a table that ran in a large ad in the New York Herald Tribune, sponsored by *Good Housekeeping.* Note that the magazines won 3 of the 4 top spots.

From the psychological viewpoint, therefore, almost all ad-

"Trifles make perfection but perfection is no trifle."   —Michelangelo

STAMPS, SEALS OR ENDORSEMENTS THOUGHT OF (FREE RESPONSE AND PROBE)	NUMBER OF CASES	WEIGHTED TOTAL 3260 % 100.0
Good Housekeeping		63.9
U.S.D.A. (Meat Stamp)		32.9
Parents' Magazine		18.3
Life		16.6
Underwriters' Laboratories		7.6
U.S.D.A. (Unspecified)		7.4
Pure Food and Drug Administration		4.5
McCall's		4.3
Better Homes and Gardens		4.0
Ladies' Home Journal		2.9
Look		2.3
Saturday Evening Post		1.3
American Medical Association		1.3
Reader's Digest		1.0

vertising sooner or later becomes suggestive in its influence, for the reader soon tires of the given advertisement and lets his conscious attention dwell upon something else even though his eyes still rest upon the cuts and headlines before him. At this moment, accordingly, the advertisement acts as suggestion unless it is strictly a copy advertisement with reason why matter throughout. Much of the advertising which falls within the visual field of the reader, however, is suggestive from the very first glance, and constitutes what is technically termed suggestive advertising. Such advertising is especially valuable for all merchandise which appeals strongly to the senses.

The Origin of Fashions. The difference between the source of clothing styles of men and women is very distinct and interesting. Women like to have clothing that is Parisian. To advertise a frock as the most popular among Berlin women, or among the feminine population of London, Brussels, or Moscow would lead to little effect in America today. But to offer the latest style creation of a Parisian modiste immediately stimulates buying. There are a number of reasons which explain this trait of American women, but probably the most basic one can be illustrated by answering the following

question. If the average American girl were to pick out a
nurse for her convalescent sweetheart, assuming that all of
the following girls spoke English and were equally pretty,
would she choose a German girl, a French girl, an English girl,
or an Italian girl? The answers of 45 college girls are listed
below.

NO. OF	PER CENT CHOOSING			
SUBJECTS	GERMAN	FRENCH	ENGLISH	ITALIAN
45	44.4	8.8	33.3	13.3

EXHIBIT 31. Showing racial preferences expressed by college girls in choosing nurses for their sweethearts.

It is of interest that two of the four girls who chose the
French nurse gave as their reason that they wanted to "test"
their sweethearts. If the men could resist the French girl,
then they would certainly be true to their wives after marriage.
It is partly because of these reactions listed above that the
French clothing is popular among our women. The most dangerous woman as regards influencing men is the one whose
methods, including clothes, are most likely to be envied and
imitated. The testimonial advertising previously mentioned
often depends on a similar appeal.

As regards men's clothing styles, however, a Parisian trade-
mark would often be a detriment instead of an asset. The
foreign source of male fashions in clothes is London. But not
all of the London styles are adopted over here. One of the
leading authorities in men's fashions in this country, John
Starbuck, says that the three most important sources of style
influence in America are (1) Yale and Princeton, (2) Wall
Street, and (3) Broadway. At these three centers the London
styles that will ultimately become popular in this country are
first adopted.

Previous to the arrival of the Prince of Wales in America in the pre-war era, manufacturers had estimated the demand for double-breasted suits at 3 per cent of their total output. Sumner[25] describes the effect of the fact that the Prince wore two double-breasted suits rather frequently. Within two years following his visit the proportion of double-breasted suits had risen in America to 45 per cent.

The shirt manufacturers had produced their new lines with scarcely a shirt like the soft blue kind with collars attached which the Prince frequently wore. The demand for this type of shirt became so great that an entire new production schedule had to be introduced at midseason, and some manufacturers suffered considerable losses in getting rid of their overstocks of white shirts. Similarly, when Clark Gable removed his shirt in the movie "It Happened One Night," thereby revealing his lack of an undershirt, the sale of men's undershirts dropped immediately.

The summer styles of men are definitely forecast in the apparel worn during January and February at Palm Beach. A number of "style detectives" follow the men around and tabulate the golf, bathing and dinner costumes, rushing off their results to New York immediately. The next summer these styles are prevalent in men's wearing apparel. If the men don't react to them at once, their wives and sweethearts soon make them conscious of the changes.

In considering the importance of the three American sources of style, we can see why these groups influence others. In the first place, styles and fashions run downhill from the financially and socially élite. The financiers and business men of America have their eyes focussed on the New York stock market and Wall Street. The incoming buyers and salesmen patronize the theaters, and night clubs, while the wealthy Princeton group of students just outside of New York City have social prestige, plus great popularity among the many women's colleges nearby.

With regard to Princeton students we may mention that they

were the first to go hatless, and to discard the garter. In 1925 they set the derby hat fashion among college men. In 1926 they adopted the suspenders, and Yale followed suit. By December, 1926, the suspenders had arrived on the campus at the University of Southern California. In January, 1927, they appeared at the University of Illinois. By June, 1927, three out of five Harvard men were wearing them, and by autumn of that year the college men all over the middle west were victims to the craze.

In general, therefore, the desire to be in fashion results from an unwillingness to be socially ostracized through too great an individual attire, especially among males. The men seek uniformity and a common denominator of dress; the women seek individuality within certain very narrow limits. The greater diversity of feminine dress is largely reducible to color and more frequent seasonal changes, for women will not attempt to alter such matters as skirt length or neck and sleeve dictates of the current styles. Their individuality of dress is obtained within the sharp delineations of fashion.

Basic determinants of fashion itself have in part been dwelt upon hitherto. The child imitates its parent—a superior individual—and mankind has followed the same general principle in its clothing. Whim, caprice, professional jealousies, and a desire to make more profit are the chief factors that cause the modistes to evolve a new type of garment. They know that the established pacemakers of both sexes will be always on the alert to maintain their reputation for style leadership. When a few princesses and actresses have appeared in the new frocks, the rest of the popularization process is similar to that of the book salesman who begins with the bankers, teachers, society leaders, and ministers and works down.

Probably no more clear-cut instance of the conscious acceptance of fashions is available than that of the young immigrant. In order to avoid being conspicuous, he quickly dons the conventional clothing of the new country, and, more slowly, its manners and customs. He attains a sense of greater social unity thereby. Back in the tenements where he lives his social prestige is likewise enhanced. His models, however, are frequently changed from touts to pugilists to aldermen as his knowledge of social distinctions develops.

In considering the origin of fashions, therefore, we must distinguish between their actual creators in the fashion marts of the world, and their popularizers, those social pacemakers who are aped by the majority of mankind. The designers and modistes of Paris, London, New York, etc., do the actual evolving of new patterns. These are then presented to the public by means of a few men and women who hold a place of preeminence in social and financial circles, for fashions are adopted in part as a means of elevating one's prestige and therefore must pass from the higher social strata to the lower. This fact is fairly well demonstrated here in the United States by viewing the three first acceptance groups for men's styles: Yale and Princeton, Wall Street, and Broadway.

The Place of Suggestion in the Sale. The more that suggestions can be employed in selling, the less likelihood there will be of objections from the customer or client. We have discussed the relative merits of positive and negative suggestions. "Take a Kodak with You" is not a suggestion as long as it is consciously reacted to, but as soon as it affects the eye or ear subconsciously it is an effective positive suggestion. The salesman, however, has more difficulty than the advertiser in employing marginal stimuli in his sale, for he cannot keep reiterating his commands until they are relegated to the fringe of attention. But the other type of suggestion—the stimulus that indirectly sets off habitual behavior from the focal region of attention—he can employ to his profit throughout the sale.

We are not decrying his use of marginal stimuli whenever he can. On the contrary, he should employ them wherever possible. We have simply indicated that he cannot use them as frequently as the direct stimulus with the indirect result. When he says, "The wives of 351 doctors are using this vacuum cleaner," he gives a direct statement which indirectly leads to the thought, "Doctor's wives would certainly want to use the vacuum that kept the floors most free from dirt and infection." The customer is led to the thought, "This vacuum cleaner picks up more dirt than others do." The salesman didn't make this statement. Therefore, the customer's tendency to doubt such an assertion is avoided, since it arises in her own mind. Thoughts that come out of our own heads we tend to believe. At least, we don't salt them so heavily.

Whenever the salesman can get his customer to evolve the selling points for his product, he profits thereby. He needs to utilize this devious method of presenting his ideas, for he encounters what is commonly spoken of as "sales resistance". This phrase is one of those generic, third degree stimuli that lead nowhere until they are torn down into their constituents. Sales resistance simply covers the fact that the buyer has no money to spend; that the buyer spent unwisely last time and is vividly recalling that chagrin; that the buyer's husband will scold if she purchases this article; that she has a similar article on hand now; that she can get a cheaper product than you offer; that she would rather have a new coat for the $75 and use a broom than have the vacuum cleaner and last year's coat; that she has an aversion to men with your type of ears or nose; that she resents your high pressure, masculine dominance; that the baby is crying for its bottle, and she hasn't heard half of your sales talk. These are only a few of the main reasons why the buyer doesn't respond. We have used the woman buyer instead of the professional male buyer in this discussion because the reasons for sales resistance are almost identical and more of the readers can identify themselves with her situation.

The suggestive value of questions should be noted here.

They are, by the way, similar in function to the fever thermometer in that they offer an outsider a means of taking a record of the customer's internal state. With some clients who refrain from speaking voluntarily and who present a stoical face, the salesman has difficulty in knowing where he stands. By means of the question he takes a reading. But there is a technique in its use which must be adhered to constantly. Since the salesman should control the interview, he must not let the conversation get away from him. In putting his queries, therefore, he should have them phrased so that the customer cannot readily respond other than in the method the salesman desires. He should employ what the lawyer calls "leading" questions. If he asks his customer, "Do you think this vacuum cleaner has a strong suction?" he leaves her with perfect freedom to answer yes or no. It is a 50:50 type of question. But because she is careful to avoid committing herself, she may either say, "I guess it has," or else "Well, it seems that Mrs. Brown's is stronger than this." By the proper intonation, however, he can make a leading question out of the 50:50 variety.

Much better than the previous query is one like, "This vacuum has a strong suction, hasn't it?" Or he may put it, "Doesn't this have a powerful suction?" Such a query we call a 60:40 type. The salesman has already steered his customer into the desired response, and a negative reply on her part demands an open revolt. Her accustomed habits of politeness force her to answer in the affirmative, or at worst, remain quiet. Her yea:nay reaction has, we shall assume, the ratio 60:40. And as long as a customer doesn't say no, the salesman can continue with the interview.

If a salesman, or a lawyer, were to put the query, "Did you see a red barn?" it would not be a leading question. But note the degrees of suggestion demonstrated by the following: "Did you see the red barn?" "Didn't you see a red barn?" "Didn't you see the red barn?" It wouldn't be long, therefore, until children would be remembering the red barn, and adults would also begin to recall it.   We tend to see what we want, or are expected, to see.   Since we have all observed red barns, it is no insurmountable task for our imagination to shift a red barn wherever we think it should be located.

The salesman must be on guard, therefore, when describing absent objects in order to avoid letting the subject's fancy run riot.   The student has probably experienced the situation when he has gone on a so-called "blind" date.   His friends have told him the girl was pretty.   Lacking her physical presence to check the flights of his imagination, he translates pretty into what he considers it—probably an unusually beautiful creature.   The contrast between his imagined picture of her and the real girl may be marked, despite the fact that she may be a normally attractive college girl.

In using adjectives describing merchandise the same danger is run.   Although the active employment of the customer's imagination may help sell the product, a good sale involves not just the name on the dotted line, but a satisfied customer.   For

GENERALITY	SPECIFICITY
Our candies are made of the best and purest ingredients selected with utmost care and combined with superlative skill.	A lemon fondant made from real fruit, freshly grated; vanilla caramel produced from pure country butter and cream; these rolled together and then covered with Norris chocolate.

EXHIBIT 32.   Showing the superiority of second degree stimuli over generalities.   (Hotchkiss).

this reason specificity is better than generality as the examples from Hotchkiss[11] plainly indicate.   Superlatives, when they do

"It is better to wear out than to rust out."   —Old Proverb lead to trains of thought, may cause too much individual interpretation on the part of the subject, and they do not suggest specific responses, either in selling or advertising. Hence, as suggestions they are ineffective.

Suggestion also is operative when "odd" prices are employed. The sales value of "odd" prices is largely owing to suggestions of bargains. As Snow[23] points out, storekeepers have been unable to sell certain merchandise at $1.50 when a change of the price tag to $1.69 caused the article to move rapidly. The latter price indirectly aroused the idea, "This is a $1.75 article," or even, "This is a $2.00 value." The figure $1.95 is really much cheaper than $2.00 in its suggestive value than the five cents would indicate. We tend to react principally to the number on the left of the decimal point. A label of $1.95 not only suggests a bargain price on a more costly article, but it suggests a much greater bargain than it really is. There is also the suggestion, as in mail order firms, that the odd figures denote close estimating and low profit for the company, thereby indicating higher value and quality for the customer.

The suggestive value of names is also important in selling. Perfumes bearing French labels can be sold much more readily than those with English names. There are cases on record where changing the English name to French and raising the price materially, have greatly speeded up the sale of the product. The French label intimates that the perfume is imported, and the word "imported" also suggests superior quality and price. A good case of negative suggestion in a name is that of "Barkeeper's Friend", a variety of polish or powder which I have seen advertised in the middle west, with the appeal directed to mothers. The name "Ivory", on the contrary, suggests richness, importation. "Camay", even without our advertising knowledge of the word, suggests a different thought than "Lifebuoy".

"All words are pegs to hang ideas on."   —H. W. Beecher

To show how a retailer can offset the effect of advertising, and change the opinion of a customer by use of suggestion I shall cite the following sale, as recounted to me two years ago by the radio dealer mentioned earlier in the chapter.

A man came into my radio shop the other evening and asked to look at the various instruments. He said he wanted a Philco, and seemed determined that no other radio would do. I told him that I didn't have a Philco (I don't handle that line) but I would be glad to get it for him. I asked him if he had any particular model in mind.

"No-o-o," he replied.

I realized then that the fellow wasn't sold on anything but the Philco name, so decided to break his fondness for that type of radio, and try to sell him one of my own. I asked him if he wouldn't care to look around at the various models in the display room, and see which he liked, meanwhile leading him to one of my most expensive brands.

After we had inspected it closely and I had pointed out some of the points of importance in examining radios, I told him that this machine we were looking at was, of course, more expensive than the Philco. I knew this would cause him to have a let-down regarding the prestige of the Philco in his mind. He would now realize that there were other radios of excellence on the market. This was all I wanted to do up to that point, namely, simply get him open-minded regarding radios.

Then I let him look inside a number of machines, meanwhile finding out what price he could afford to pay. I described the various tubes, telling him that Philco had a good tube, all right, but it had been perfected long ago. The majority of modern radios, like these models I was showing him, were all equipped with the new tube just patented this year. Of course, my emphasis on *modern* and *latest style* made him feel that Philco was an old model.

Finally, I asked him to try the real test of a radio, namely, the sound test in which he attempted to visualize the singer's lips while his eyes were closed and he was listening to the music.

When he left the shop I had sold him a Model X radio.

In demonstrating his goods the salesman may also be able to employ marginal stimuli by letting the housewife participate in the demonstration. While discussing the vacuum cleaner mentioned above he may incline the handle toward her as he stoops to insert the plug into the wall socket. The suggestion of taking hold of the handle usually is sufficient to cause the housewife to grasp it. The salesman now has his customer helping him sell her, for the pleasurable tactual and kinesthetic sensations as she later moves the shiny new machine over her rugs give rise to a desire for possession. The salesman studiously avoids taking the machine from her hand. "Just notice how easy it is for you to turn it on," he begins. "See that little lever where the handle joins the motor. You don't have to stoop, for you can just touch it with the toe of your slipper. Yes, just push it a bit harder."

In the realm of foodstuffs the offering of samples is suggestive salesmanship, for the gustatory delight resulting begins to set up appropriative reactions, and the customer wants a continuation of the pleasing stimuli. The taste qualities are operating while her attention may be focussed on the salesman's words. For a further explanation of the influence of suggestion in the sale the reader is referred to Chapter VII.

Viewed psychologically, therefore, the place of suggestion in the sale is everywhere, for the more it is employed the less likelihood of antagonizing the customer. There is no special point at which the salesman must use suggestion and then refrain from so doing elsewhere. The value of the leading question or the 60:40 query, moreover, is considerable, and demonstrates one form of suggestion. "Odd" prices, foreign trade names, samples, the minor close, and the incorporation of the customer in the demonstration—these are just a few of the other obvious ways in which suggestion operates to the advantage of the salesman. Even in his personality and method of introduction the salesman may create confidence and prestige, which thereby render his customer more liable to his suggestive salesmanship.

Securing Conviction by Suggestion. We have already mentioned that people are much less critical of ideas which apparently are a creation of their own thinking, than of ideas advanced by outsiders. Belief in a thing results from our having no contrary experiences or habits that oppose it. If an outsider presents the idea, from past experiences with salesmen and other persuaders we find ourselves cautious, doubtful. If it is evolved within us, we don't have that chronic distrust, for why should we trick ourselves?

In the sale of an automobile tire, for instance, the statement may be made that the United States mail trucks all use it. This in itself is no selling point. We must first have familiarity with the United States; we must recall that there are thousands of mail trucks, since this is a large country; we must also remember that large businesses attempt the strictest economies; therefore, the government has probably found this tire the most durable and cheap. Until we have reached this resultant thought, the initial statement means nothing. If a magazine, such as *The Reader's Digest,* advertises that "29,374 Bankers Read *The Reader's Digest*" we are unaffected until subconsciously we go through a translation process somewhat as follows: "Important men read this magazine—men who must keep posted on latest developments nationally and internationally. *The Reader's Digest* must offer a quick means to keep abreast of world affairs." The testimonial advertising involves similar marginal thinking if it is to contribute anything beyond the attention attracting value of pretty girls and women.

In the statement concerning the number of bankers reading the magazine mentioned, the reader will quickly perceive the greater convincing power of "29,374 Bankers" over "30,000 Bankers". A little introspection will reveal the fact that the former suggests an actual count that can be authenticated, if challenged, whereas the larger figure intimates a hasty generality that might be considerably over the true statement. The first connotes science and accuracy, the second denotes salesmanship and a stretching of truth for effect.

In dealing with people it will be found desirable to spend considerable time developing ways of stating selling points for a product, a personality, an idea, or a service which will avoid arousing the inhibitions attaching to direct commands. To say, "You ought to read *The Reader's Digest*. It gives you the most condensed and comprehensive survey of World News," may lead to a slangy and resentful, "Oh, yeah?"

In salesmanship, speaking, or advertising one must be careful to avoid such terms as "You ought . . . ", "You owe it to . . . ", "Common sense demands that you . . . ", "You need . . . ", "You should . . . ", or "You must . . . ". Such phrases suggest that the speaker has done your thinking for you, that he is superior to you and has found you in error. These ideas tend to arouse dislike, even open hostility on the part of the customer or audience, because the "negative protest" discussed in Chapter XIII is immediately brought into action. Americans in particular resent commands. The best logic possible may be unavailing on a person rendered bull-headed by such negative suggestions as these just described.

In persuading a person that a certain joke is funny, it is obviously ineffective to keep affirming its humor, to keep telling him that he will split his sides laughing when he hears it, that he will think it the most witty thing he has ever listened to. Why not tell him the joke itself and let him decide? Yet the number of speakers and salesmen is legion who spend good selling time telling their listeners that they will profit from the article in question, that they will save money, that they would not get along without it after they try it, that they need it in their business, etc., when they should be citing specific data, and avoiding the negative suggestions incurred by such authoritative statements about their customers' thought processes and reactions.

1 ALEXANDER, F. G., *The History of Psychiatry* (Harper & Row, 1966)
2 ANSBACHER, H. L., *Attitudes of German Prisoners of War* (Psycholog. Monogr. No. 289, 1948)
3 BAYER, E., "Beitrage zur Zweikomponententheorie des Hungers" *Zeitschrift f. Psychologie*, 112, 1929).
4 BECK, S. J., *The Rorschach Experiment* (Brunner, 1961)
5 BLOOD & WOLFE, *Husbands and Wives* (Brunner, 1961)
6 BOWMAN & MAUTNER, *Mental Retardation* (Brunner, 1961)
7 BROWN, W., *Individual and Sex Differences in Suggestibility* (U. of Calif. Publications, 1916)
8 COLLINS, W. J., *Effects of Certain Parasympathomimetic Substances on the Emotions of Normal and Psychotic Individuals* (Catholic U. Press, 1946)
9 HOKE, R. E., *How You Can Have Success Unlimited* (Psy. Service Center, Charlotte, N. C., 1956)
10 HOLLINGWORTH, H. L., *Advertising and Selling* (Appleton, 1920)
11 HOTCHKISS, G. B., *Advertising Copy* (Harper, 1924)
12 HULL, C. L., *Hypnosis and Suggestibility* (Appleton, 1933)
13 KATZ, D., (Tr. by R. Tyson) *Gestalt Psychology* (Ronald, 1950)
14 KUBIE, L. S. *Hypnotism* (Arch. Gen. Psychiatry, Jan., 1961)
15 LENNEP, D. J., *Four Picture Test* (Hague, Nijhoff, 1948)
16 LOUTTIT, C. M., *Clinical Psychology of Children's Behavior Problems* (Harper, 1947)
17 MERRIHUE, W. V., *Management by Communication* (McGraw-Hill, 1960)
18 McGILL, V. J., *Emotions and Reason* (Thomas, 1954)
19 MORTENSEN, D. G. & SCHMULLER, A. M., *Guidance in Today's Schools* (Wiley 1959)
20 OTIS, M., "*A Study of Suggestibility of Children*" (Arch. Psychol., No. 70, 1924)
21 SARTRE, J. P., *Psychology of Imagination* (Philosophical Library, 1948).
22 SIMONS, E. N., "To Increase the Pulling Power of Advertisements" *(Printers' Ink*, Dec. 15, 1921).
23 SNOW, A. J., *Psychology in Business Relations* (McGraw-Hill, 1930)
24 STARCH, D., *Principles of Advertising* (Shaw, 1923)
25 SUMNER, G. L., "The College Man—Style Mentor" *(Adv. and Selling*, June 26, 1929)
26 UHR & MILLER, *Drugs and Behavior* (Wiley, 1960)
27 VAUGHN, W. F., "An Experimental Class Demonstration of Suggestibility" *(J. Abnorm. Soc. Psychol.*, 30, 1935).
28 WALLIN, J. E. W., *Personality Maladjustments and Mental Hygiene* (McGraw-Hill, 1949)
29 WATKINS, J. G., *Hypnotherapy of War Neuroses* (Ronald, 1949)
30 WEITZENHOFFER, A. M., *Hypnotism* (Wiley, 1954)
31 WELBERG, L. R., *The Technique of Psychotherapy* (Grune, Stratton, 1954)
32 WHITAKER, C. A., *The Roots of Psychotherapy* (Blakiston, 1958)
33 WITKIN, H. A., *Personality Through Perception* (Harper, 1954)
34 WOHL, M. G., *Long Term Illness* (Wiley, 1959)
35 YOUNG, P. T., *Motivation & Emotion* (Wiley, 1964)

CHAPTER VI

THE PSYCHOLOGY OF IMPROVING YOUR PERSONALITY

The art of winning people's respect and admiration, and of gaining their friendship is one which should be understood by every individual who expects to live in a social environment. Indeed, everybody vaguely or consciously aspires to develop a personality which will be most attractive, and there is hardly a person who is not engaged in the process of "selling" his personality to his "public". Refusal to acknowledge the fact neither alters this fundamental truth, nor does it enable the individual to eliminate the flaws which appear in the sales method which he now subconsciously follows. The improvement of one's personality consists, therefore, not only in the development of virtues, but in the presentation of these talents to one's associates in a manner which will make the latter feel happier and prouder of themselves.

The employment of psychological principles in sales work has hitherto been almost wholly focussed upon the merchandise or ideas of the salesman. It is time we realized that one of the most important products which any boy or girl, man or woman has to offer the public is his or her personality. For example, here is a girl with mental talents and physical beauty who is blunt, boorish, and such an egotistical self-advertiser that people dislike her. Across the street is a girl with equal mental and physical charms, but people all love her. Boys are constantly calling for her. She isn't thought of at all as a self-advertiser, yet that is exactly how she has attained her social eminence. The difference lies in the fact that the second girl used suggestion and let her friends evolve her charms from their own thinking, whereas the first girl told them bluntly that she had travelled abroad, was a college graduate with honors, owned a costly roadster, was related to the governor, and belonged to the D. A. R. The popular girl was also known as possessing all these distinctions, but she had never told anybody—at least, no one ever remembered that she had.

The Importance of Personality Development. Every person surely has some virtues and good points. In our discussion throughout this chapter, therefore, we are only endeavoring to show how these good points can be utilized to best advantage. We do not advocate attempting to make an English sparrow into a canary, but we believe honest salesmanship of a legitimate product should have every encouragement that psychology can offer. In the quotation from President Glenn Frank we see the importance of learning this art.

THE ART OF SELLING YOURSELF

By Glenn Frank

It doesn't pay to take the old adages too seriously.

I am sure that no end of harm has been done by the time-honored theory that if you build a better mouse trap than any one else you can bury yourself in the woods and rest assured that the world will beat a path to your door and demand your superior product.

This is a very busy world we are living in. Even excellence must fight for attention. The world is sure to be waylaid by a good salesman long before it reaches your cabin in the woods. The regrettable truth is that you dare not do good work and let it go at that. Miracles do not happen even for the right. You must know how to sell as well as how to create.

I suspect that the most important man in the world is the good salesman. I do not mean simply the clerk or the commercial traveler, but the man whose whole life and work are guided by the principles of good salesmanship.

The art of civilization is largely the art of salesmanship. Nothing of permanent value has come down to us from the past save by the grace of good salesmanship on the part of somebody.

We would have no great literature to feed our spirits but for the fact that through the ages the great writers have been good salesmen. The great writers have not spent their time hawking their own wares and advertising themselves, but in the way they have thought and written they have, consciously or unconsciously, observed the few fundamental laws of salesmanship. The art of literature is the art of capturing the reader's attention and then charming his senses or convincing his mind. And that is salesmanship.

Long ago, in ancient Greece, Plato thought out most of the things that are today being hailed as progressive ideas about politics and education. But we moderns would know nothing of Plato but for the fact that, in the way he thought and wrote, Plato was a good salesman. And Socrates can still give pointers to ad writers.

The greatest statesmen have always been good salesmen. For every hour a President spends inside his study "thinking it over," he must spend two hours outside his study "putting it over." A time comes when peddler and President stand on the same footing. Both must be good salesmen.

And it may be said without irreverence that the triumph of Christianity has been, in a very real sense, a triumph of salesmanship. The Nazarene had no regiments of soldiers behind him; he employed no press agent; he controlled no syndicate of newspapers; the hillsides of Palestine were not dotted with billboards plastered with his pronouncements. By the sheer force of knowing how to teach, which is just one way of saying salesmanship, he captured and has held the attention of the planet.

The salesman is not the high priest of a sordid commercialism; the salesman is the spark plug of civilization.

We must see to it that we make ourselves and our work worth something to the world, but we must also see to it that the world's attention is called to the fact. Bullion is valuable, but it does not become currency until it is coined and stamped at the mint. Intelligent attention to the principles of salesmanship is the thing that coins the bullion of sound character and good work into the currency of success.

We must master the twin arts of creating and salesmanship.*

Young people in America vaguely realize that all is not well as regards their personalities. This fact is evident from the advertisements purporting to make the reader into an orator, a saxophone player, a magician, a pianist or violinist, an artist, a singer, or an elocutionist in the space of six or eight weeks

*Copyright by the McClure Newspaper Syndicate. Used by permission.

through the medium of correspondence courses. That such advertising can continue denotes that American youths are taking the courses. That American youths are taking the courses indicates they are not fully satisfied with their present social and economic status, but aspire to improve their positions. The development of magnetic personalities and popularity is of constant interest, at least to young people.

Even many of our social attitudes are a result of successful personality salesmanship by one individual or race, or a lack of it by another. Although the Negro has far excelled the attainments of the American Indian, the latter enjoys more prestige among the majority of citizens. The reason is probably the fact that the Indian, as portrayed by Cooper and Longfellow, is idealized, while the Negro's slave background hampers his social advancement. Nevertheless, after four hundred years of contact with white civilization the red savage has been able to make almost no adjustment, nor leave important art, literature, or music as a monument to his race, while the Negro in less than 100 years has gained wealth, education, churches, and seats in the United States House of Representatives.

An individual, moreover, not only creates positive or negative feeling tone for himself, but also for the race or nation to which he belongs. In the following table from Bogardus[1] are seen the races toward which the greatest antipathy was felt by a group of student raters after World War I. The larger the score, the greater the aversion felt for that race. In many instances, of course, these raters had had few if any personal contacts with members of some of the races, but from their vicarious contacts by way of newspapers and novels, they had developed positive or negative attitudes. Propaganda, incidentally, is the basis for many of the dislikes of American citizens for one race or another.

"An acquaintance that begins with a compliment is sure to develop into a real friendship."   —Oscar Wilde

Turk 119	Hungarian 11	Portuguese 3
Negro 79	Servian 3	English 2
Mulatto 75	Russian 8	French 2
Japanese 61	Czecho-Slovak 8	Roumanian 2
Hindu 44	Syrian 6	Spanish 2
Jew—German 42	Bulgarian 6	Swedish 2
Mexican 41	Filipino 5	Canadian 0
Jew—Russian 41	Italian 5	Dane 0
German 38	Bohemian 4	Dutch 0
Chinese 30	Finn 4	French-Canadian .. 0
Greek 19	Polish 3	Norwegian 0
Armenian 17	Irish 3	Scotch 0

EXHIBIT 33. Races against which the greatest antipathy was felt. (Bogardus).

For all those individuals who have a reasonable number of human contacts, therefore, it is necessary that tact and the art of displaying mental and physical charms be fully developed. True, some taciturn or surly individuals carry their graciousness and social charm largely in their wives' names, but this places an undue responsibility on the wives. Occasionally the reverse is the case, and we find the glum, unsociable wife with a popular husband.

Since the improvement of personality, therefore, involves not only the cultivation of talents but their presentation to one's associates, it behooves everybody to keep this two-fold process well in mind. A genius may not have an attractive personality, nor does it necessarily follow that a person who is skilled in music, art, and the sciences will be popular. On the other hand, one should endeavor to nourish one's talents so that they will furnish something worth offering to one's companions, for successful salesmanship really involves the correct presentation of a desirable and satisfactory product.

The Universality of Self-Salesmanship. In a recent campaign the Camay soap advertisements carried the heading, "You're in a BEAUTY CONTEST every minute of your life!" Not only is this statement true, but we are in perennial personality contests. When we least expect it, our associates are mentally noting faults that we possess. We do not realize the fact until later, as in a quarrel. Then watch the parade of flaws! These may be resurrected from years back. As errors are tabulated subconsciously and consciously by our fellows, so too are the virtues and graces which we possess. On a certain date some one asks us if John is neat in his attire, for he is applying for a position as floorwalker in a department store. We don't have John before us at the time we write our letter, so we go back in memory and try to resurrect some incidents which bear upon his personal neatness. Much to our surprise, for we had hardly been aware of noting these items, we recall that John wore a faded tie with soup stains on it. We recall that the cravat was loosely knotted so that it seldom fitted snugly against his throat. More memories begin to freshen, and we recall that John never was particularly careful about keeping his trousers pressed, for our picture of him is with baggy knees. And, finally, we remember the time he appeared at work with his Sunday suit but with unshined shoes which contrasted sufficiently with his neater clothing to call our attention to them.

We frequently find that our likes and aversions are founded on the basis of a few outstanding items. We dislike a certain person from childhood. Critical analysis reveals that the man threw a stone and injured our pet dog when we were just out of kindergarten. We like some one else who may never have contributed anything but friendly smiles from day to day.

Not only may we react to people with likes or dislikes, but we may be forming opinions concerning their uncouthness at the same time that we are growing fond of them. In politics it occasionally happens that a man's friends refuse to vote for him when he begins to run for an office which they feel is too high for his social standing. The writer heard a man say in a recent presidential campaign that he had always voted for one of the candidates for governor, but he wouldn't vote for him for President because he didn't possess quite the dignity and prestige that went with the higher office. When politicians want to show their fondness for the farmer they frequently permit themselves to be photographed pitching hay or running a tractor, but they are wearing white shirts with collars and ties, even though they may also be protected by overalls. The white collar shows that they really aren't farmers even though they can function as such. It is a necessary distinction. Farmers seldom send farmers to Congress, despite our class distinctions and grumbling against the rich. We may be socialists in our attitude regarding wealth and big business, but we want to be represented at Washington by men who can wear a silk hat and use a gold headed cane as if they knew how.

It is well to keep in mind, therefore, that we are really walking department stores of human characteristics and the feeling tone we develop for one trait may not be typical of the entire stock which we carry. If we become too democratic in our behavior, we lessen the dignity that we may have wished to establish. The genial secretary of a social organization frequently remains the secretary, despite the fact that all of his fellows like him very much. The overly athletic individual who is selling the public on her possession of health and vitality may also be losing the charm of the girl who depends upon the strong right arm of her escort and thereby inflates his masculine ego.

One of the writer's classmates, who has gone into executive work and holds the position of dean in an American university, is possessed of a blonde, boyish complexion and general appearance. Obviously it militates against his success as a leader. To offset this influence he consciously adopted a pipe, that badge of masculinity that ranks next to the beard so generally started by medical students of the '90's when they approached graduation. Pipes, profanity, and hirsute facial ornaments should probably be called the masculine secondary sexual characteristics of this generation. One of our pre-eminent political leaders adopted them, probably consciously, for much the same reason as that of the dean just cited.

To illustrate not only the fact that men in established positions of prestige and wealth do not cease their self-selling but that they have it reduced to a habit, the writer wishes to make the following quotation. The scene was at a banquet of a Chicago executives' organization which the writer was to address immediately after the meal on the topic which titles this chapter. The president of the organization sat on the writer's left, while a dignified director of the national organization who happened to be in the city, was seated on his right. We shall designate him as Mr. X.

The discussion which ensued took place during the 45 minutes of eating. The writer jotted it down from memory as soon as he returned home that evening. Intermittent questions which he had forgotten cause the apparent unrelated nature of many of the paragraphs. When the reader finishes the dialogue, he should try to tabulate the number of selling points which Mr. X. displayed in this short time. They are numerous and indicative of an earlier political campaign year.

"Yes, Dr. Crane, I know your president very well. You might be interested to know that he began his initial work in the applied field with our company about twenty years ago. He was a good man. I'm sorry I'm so busy these days that I don't get to see him any more."

"Mr. X, from your extensive travelling what impression have you obtained of present business conditions?" I inquired.

"No improvement whatever. In fact, I notice a slight decline in progress. We'll never be able to get out of our financial depression until we rescind the war debts. Conditions are bad here and abroad. I am in constant correspondence with continental European countries. Hardly a week passes that I don't receive a letter from Germany and England. The first nineteen years of my life were spent abroad, so you can appreciate undoubtedly that I am better able to understand the European attitude than the average American. I look to see England recover first, followed thereafter by Germany. Indeed, Germany is likely to surpass America as soon as she gets on her feet.

"I was much interested in what my friend, Prime Minister Baldwin, said to me at luncheon one day while I was in London. He turned to me and stated that England's unemployed group is identical with the number of people who have refrained from emigrating to the colonies. A quarter of a million each year used to leave England for Australia, Canada and South Africa. Since the war, this emigration has ceased.

"What we need in this country is a new conception of Business Management. The only place in the world where that is being preached is in Germany. There a young professor, Dr. F——, has been issuing a series of monographs on modern leadership which are the best in any language, and I have studied the field pretty thoroughly. As a matter of fact, I have translated one or two of these monographs so that those who could not read German might have access to them."

"I'll wager you have a weakness for books," I said.

"Oh yes, I have quite an extensive library. I wouldn't take $50,000 for my collection, and there are over two hundred etchings in my apartment that I have been gathering during the past ten years. Some of my journal files are perhaps the only complete ones in existence. The *Tailor's Journal*, for instance, asked if I would permit them to photostat some of the early numbers of their magazine, since they didn't have a complete file of their own."

"What do you think of the political situation?" I interrupted.

"Well, I'd personally like to see Al Smith in the White House. I don't drink but I'd like to cast my vote for him as a protest against intolerance. At my club in New York the other day I was talking to some of my friends on this very score. Two of them who are leading bankers in New York said they were afraid he could never be elected. I told them it was just because of people who thought he couldn't be elected that he was not now in office."

"How about Ritchie?" the president of the Chicago Club asked.

"Governor Ritchie would make a fine candidate. Surely, I know him quite well. It was only a few weeks ago that we attended a banquet together. As I was the principal speaker of the evening I turned to him before my talk and said, 'Governor, what I'm going to say is probably not news to you, so I shall not feel offended if you wish to leave early.' But he refused and remained there for three hours. At the conclusion of my address he congratulated me heartily, and in a very nice fashion.

"Yes, I was pleased to see that Hoover had enough good judgment to appoint Cardozo to the Supreme Court. Cardozo is a friend of mine. He has a brilliant mind. A graduate of my alma mater, you know."

"Mr. X, are you as methodical in your private life as in your business affairs?" asked the president.

"If you could just visit my apartment you could see for yourself. We have a suite in the hotel, for my wife is one of the responsible members of the firm, so we must be close to the office. I have set aside one room in the suite for my study, and I don't leave a thing out of place. Why, man, while out on the road, I've frequently called the office in New York and told one of my men to get the pass key to the apartment from my wife, go up to my study, look on the second shelf from the bottom in the bookcase at the left of my desk, and there, about the fifth book in, he would find such and such a volume. I seldom miss hitting the exact spot by more than one or two books.

"Yes, I give a course at ———— University. But I would not consent to offering the course until the president promised that I could shift the teaching to some of my assistants in my absence. I told him that it was a physical impossibility for me to be present in New York for thirty Monday evenings. It just couldn't be done. So the course is listed as being given by Mr. X and Associates.

"Last fall I vowed that I wouldn't give any speeches this year, but do you know, to date, I have made 51 addresses that I just couldn't get out of. And that isn't all, unfortunately. I'm to make the chief address at the national convention at S———— next month. I couldn't avoid that, for this address is to furnish direction for the whole convention.

"Then I should like to get away for a little rest and take in the international convention at Amsterdam this summer. However, I may skip that and go to Geneva instead, for I don't want to disappoint my old friend, Dr. F————, who is the chairman. But that would take about five weeks—one going, one coming, and give me only three weeks abroad.

"Really, what I feel conscience-stricken about, however, is the fact that I've promised my publishers three books, and I ought to get them out of the way. Ordway Tead met me on the street in New York just last week, and implored me to give him just an outline of my book in business management so that he could announce it in his fall catalogue, but I told him nothing doing. I knew if it were announced, there'd be nothing for me to do but to get to work on the book, for I couldn't disappoint the public in that way.

"You know, I've spent $26,000 to date just gathering data for one of my books. It's to be a doctoral dissertation at ———— University, which I had hoped to get out by 1930, but it can't see the printers before 1933. I made one oversight that cost me $6,000 and delayed the book at least a year."

"Too bad, but we all do that at times," I consoled him.

"This wasn't a careless one, however. In fact, it was because of my extensive study in the field that I was tricked. I became a victim of my own vast experience. One of my assistants, Dr. Y——, asked me if annuities entered the insurance field by 1907. I told him no. Then he asked me if they had begun to appear by 1914, or 1921. I told him not much before 1922 or 1923. Annuities are an English custom. He wanted to know if he should examine the data—I've been analyzing management in 14 of our largest insurance companies, you know—but I told him not to bother with 1907. There's where I made my error! I was too sure of myself. With all my experience in the insurance field, as you, of course, can imagine, Mr. ——, (addressing the president on my left) I didn't think I need consider 1907. But my correlations wouldn't come out; so finally I examined the data myself, and then found my error. But it cost me $6,000."

"Say, I just had a letter from Z—— yesterday," said the president.

"He's editor of ———— Magazine, Dr. Crane," Mr. X addressed me. "Z—— is a good fellow. You might be interested to know that he takes night classes at ———— University. He drops in for advice about once a month, and last week he called on me about his program for next fall for he knew I could steer him into the best courses. I know the men teaching the classes, and the personal factor is a large one, you know."

It is obvious, therefore, that self-salesmanship is not confined to young people who are desirous of making a name for themselves in the world, but pervades all ranks and social strata. This fact is so evident to the reader that he may wonder why it has been granted space in this chapter. Curiously enough, many people frown upon even the thought of a conscious technique in dealing with people and effectively and tactfully advertising themselves. Unfortunately, however, many of these same individuals are constantly trying to "sell" themselves but, having refused to focus upon their methods, are doing such a poor job that they antagonize instead of attract.

It requires great care and forethought in order to demonstrate finesse in this delicate procedure.

Tactful vs. Blunt Selling Points. We have previously commented on the advantages of suggestion in salesmanship. Direct statements of fact concerning one's products may, however, have a certain amount of influence, but they are much less effective when made about one's personal talents and abilities. A person may say, "This automobile is the most economical to operate of any on the market." The listener will probably discount such a statement considerably, but not nearly so much so as its homologue, "I am the greatest economist in the world today."

It becomes imperative, therefore, that we become adept in the use of suggestive salesmanship when we are attempting to merchandise our own personalities. The individual who attains skill in this respect can present all of his good points without danger of incurring the ill will or resentment of his associates. Like the magician, such a person keeps his public attending to the obvious while he subtly produces the changes necessary for the accomplishment of his purpose. And his public, like the magician's, obtains the effect, but has little if any knowledge of how it was produced.

"Don't you think it was sweet of Jane to give me this cute little hand painted box for my recipes?" Bill's girl innocently inquires.

The next morning at breakfast Bill's father tells him he ought to cease running around with frivolous girls and pick out one who can cook and sew and run a house.

"Say, my girl can cook fine," Bill defends, not even realizing that his sweetheart with her verbal legerdemain deftly slipped this selling point into his memory while she had him focussing upon the hand painted recipe box.

The man or woman who can continue the method of Bill's girl friend will find it possible to present the facts concerning his or her health, family tree, education, cultural attitudes, generosity, morality, love of offspring, popularity with the opposite sex, and a host of other sales points which materially strengthen one's prestige. It is on this score that my students frequently complain that psychology takes all the joy out of conversation, making them self-conscious and analytical. "I certainly wouldn't want to think that my boy friend had deliberately planned what he was going to say to me," one girl protests. "It would take all the spontaneity out of conversation."

Perhaps to a similar degree one wouldn't want to think that Stevenson wrote and rewrote his *Treasure Island* seven times before it had that simplicity and spontaneity which make it so refreshing, or that genius has aptly been defined as the exceptional capacity for taking pains. The salesman who presents the most interesting and apparently spontaneous sales demonstration, and the surgeon who shows the greatest simplicity and skill in his operative technique certainly do not rely on the inspiration of the moment. From his experience as a sales manager, the writer can truthfully state that the large commission checks go to those individuals who have most carefully planned their interviews and have previously memorized not only the outstanding selling points of their products, but have also phrased them in the most graceful and effective manner.

When one has analyzed himself for selling points and has not only formulated those advantages in the best fashion, but has memorized them, he will soon find that he can mechanically deliver them at the right time and place. Only the tyro makes himself and his public feel a lack of spontaneity in the process. In regard to memorizing a sales talk, the writer does not mean to infer that the entire speech should always be given in "1-2-3" order, with utter disregard for the exigencies of the moment. But he does insist that the "1" and the "2" and the "3" be fully memorized. They may be rearranged in the actual interview, and some may be omitted—in short, the serial order of presentation may be left to inspiration of the moment—but the phrasing of the units of the complete speech must be previously learned. When one is dealing with suggestions a single word omitted from a sentence may defeat the psychological purpose behind the statement. Precision in words must be just as great as precision in the use of a scalpel if perfection is to be attained.

The wife of one of America's foremost after-dinner humorists remarked that much of her husband's reputation for spontaneity in his sallies depended upon her. She steered the conversation so that at the proper time she could make a comment which served as the cue for him to begin, "That reminds me . . ." Most of us cannot depend on wives or husbands in such manner, but must direct the conversation tactfully so that we produce our own cues. In the student's paper* reproduced below the italicized words indicate a conversational cue or "detour" which enables the speaker to introduce sales points (5), (6), (7), and (8). The student has annotated his assignment.

(It's Friday night. They're at the dance. She is selling him now, doing most of the talking, but some of it is wasted as he is very busy taking note of how many fellows are envious of his choice of partner.)
You think I dance well? That's very chivalrous of you indeed, but of course I should be able to dance a little as I took esthetic dancing at college (1), and had the honor of leading the ballet in our spring festival (2). And I nearly died of surprise, because the ballet lead is supposed to go to the most attractive girl in the class by popular vote (3), and fancy them giving it to poor little me.

Oh, my gown? I'm glad you like it because I worked awfully hard over it. Why yes, I make my own things (4) and get a big kick out of it. *You know I made both of my costumes for that play last spring* and made up the girls in the cast besides. Why no, I had very little make-up on myself, sometimes I wish my complexion wasn't so shockingly vivid (5).

Oh, you didn't see the play then. And all the time I thought you had. Well, I took a boy's part, you know. All the slender girls had to take boy's parts (6), and besides you know I sing

*Paper written by L. J. Lutz.

contralto, so I had to be a boy (7). And you should have seen me in that riding scene with those awful old cavalry boots. Why we searched the town over, and couldn't find a pair of riding boots half small enough (8). I wear a four quadruple A, you see.

Why surely I'm going back to school. I didn't do much last semester though, just about lived in the music room at the piano and at the gym in the tank. Why yes, I adore swimming (9), but I do need a little more tutoring until I get sufficient confidence in myself. You say you will teach me? How perfectly thrilling! (10).

1. Selling prospect on her dancing ability and college training.

2. Is a leader in her set too.

3. Perhaps he hasn't noticed how attractive and popular she is with both sexes.

4. Reaching deep down with that old domestic appeal. They *all* say they can sew.

5. If her complexion is vivid, then it's different. Do not all men want their ideal just a little'different?

6. A most tactful way to sell the figure.

7. A contralto voice. Again different, rich, mellow, crooning. (Good accompaniment for a "uke" on a moonlight night.)

8. Tiny feet. The badge of aristocracy since the beginning of time.

9. Enjoys outdoor sports too—healthy.

10. The blow that slays them. Appealing through her charming feminine weakness to his rugged strength. (She could probably swim circles around him with one arm while reading her current copy of *Reader's Digest.*)

Several of the girl's comments cited above are evidences of direct self-selling instead of the more tactful suggestive method, but it is better to make direct statements than to go around tongue-tied, especially if the physical attractiveness of the speaker is sufficient to offset the resentment aroused by her words. The unpleasant reaction to direct or blunt sales statements can be materially reduced by the way in which the speaker acts at the moment. A deprecating laugh, or thumbs stuck in the armholes of one's vest while one purposely struts around as he enunciates his own honors, may lessen the resistance of his public or make them laugh. If you can make your public laugh at your antics, or if you can keep their attention focussed upon your actions, the import of your words may slip into their memories indirectly; hence, as suggestions.

Bluntly stated selling points are familiar to most readers, so we shall not devote space to a list of them. And in presenting statements which demonstrate finesse and tact, we assume temperance in their use. The woman who is chronically criticizing the orchestra, or the food, or the decorations, or the service may intimate that she has been accustomed to better, but too many intimations of the same nature begin to grow obvious. Behavior of this sort is a frequent attribute of the newly rich. Dave, a high school athlete, always "popped the question" to whichever girl he happened to be with, but it ran, "Do you like football?" That was his sole cue for launching upon a sales' monologue with his own prowess on the gridiron as the central idea. In the ensuing statements gleaned from students' papers, are a heterogeneous group of suggestive sales points. Some are not as good as others, but they all give rise to additional thoughts in the minds of the readers.

One of the biggest "kicks" I have is getting down on the floor with my nieces and nephews and playing with the toys and electrical contrivances. (Likes children—a good father type.)

I have more fun listening to the good-natured debates of Mother and Dad over the respective merits of the Virginia Penfields and the New England Brewsters. (Comes of excellent family inheritance on both sides.)

They say the good die young. If that's the case, my family is full of black sheep. (Longevity indicates health—good stock.)

I never appreciated morality until the war when I was thrown in contact with men without any whatever. (Comes from good home environment, and also served his country.)

Bill's car has the most peculiar dashboard. (I've had a date with Bill, the village hero.)

The last Derby wasn't nearly the spectacle the Preakness was. (I've attended both, so am wealthy, interested in sports, etc.)

Homecoming games always have a rejuvenating effect on me. The old spirit never seems to die out. (I'm a college person.)

One hears so much about the aged-in-the-wood variety of beauty, but believe me it's mighty good to see the Statue of Liberty after months spent in musty cities abroad. (I've travelled in Europe.)

Imagine *me* as Queen of the May with one of those ridiculous wreaths on my head! (I am the most popular girl in the crowd.)

I didn't like to think of her going that far on the street car, so I arranged a ride for her with one of the boys who goes her way. (I am considerate and generous.)

I thought the "Cuban Love Song" was an excellent picture, for it shows Cuba as it really is. (I have travelled in Cuba and know it very well.)

Our annual convention is to be in San Francisco this year. It's a nice town, but I was hoping they'd have it in New York, for there's always so much more doing there. (I'm a connoisseur of American cities and a regular delegate to the convention.)

I don't think so much of him as a critic. Personally, I see nothing in contemporary authors to compare with the power and beauty of 18th and 19th century literature. (I'm well read both in current and past literature.)

As variants of the above procedure some people find it advantageous to put such queries as, "What did you get in the exam?" The reversal of this question is expected, at which time the first speaker can say that he made an "A". Again, we hear a comment like this, "I just hate this dress. It makes me look so fat!" The girl speaking has a graceful figure, and by bringing out the contrasting thought of stoutness obtains even greater slenderness in the eyes of her listeners.

Hepner devotes a few pages to this matter of self-selling when he points out that the office worker can capture the attention of his superior by constructing charts of his own output, depicting the relationship of his task or department to that of the office as a whole. Ostensibly these graphs and curves are simply for the worker's own interest. If displayed properly, and clearly labelled, they not only call attention to the employee, but they intimate a scientific type of mind, all of

---

"He that has once done you a kindness will be more ready to do you another, than he whom you yourself have obliged."   —Franklin which are not inimical to his advancement. Some workers type a list of items to be developed and fulfilled during the current month, and post it in their office. As the work is finished they scratch off the items in red pencil.

In the preceding pages, therefore, we have gone into detail regarding the blunt versus the tactful methods of presenting our virtues and talents, showing how indispensable is the use of suggestion in this dangerous but very important field of personal salesmanship. As in the merchandising of a commercial product the salesman must first analyze his goods for their sales points and then phrase these in the most advantageous fashion, so also the one who wishes to present his personality most favorably should follow a similar technique.

The Two Essential Steps in Becoming Popular. In the preceding section we have presented part of the first phase of gaining friends, which is that of showing our merits, virtues, and capacities, for as a general rule, people like to number as friends those individuals who are important.

But only half the problem is solved when we have presented our personalities in the most favorable light, for the most excellent product cannot be merchandised successfully unless it fulfills some need or function of the public. Our personalities, therefore, must meet the public's universal desire for self-esteem. People all like to feel educated, beautiful, graceful, powerful, proud of themselves. The more their ego is inflated, the more pleased they are. And the important psychological law involved in making friends is the same which explains our likes for food. Spinach, if presented to children in a pleasurable emotional state, begins to take on part of that pleasant atmosphere, and soon is liked by the child. In the same manner, when we meet strangers and leave them feeling proud of themselves, they are in a pleasurable emotional state, which in turn attaches to us as an important part of the environment. They like us.

The secret of friendship and popularity is simply this:

Whenever you leave a person feeling more satisfied with himself as a result of his contact with you, he will like you. And love is only a heightened type of liking with an erogenous coloring. Introverts are not as popular as extroverts because they don't pay heed to the ego demands of their associates. And friends will not long remain friends if they don't keep accounts fairly even between themselves and those of their intimates. This fact is subconsciously realized by almost everybody, as demonstrated by the common statements, "We ought to entertain the Browns. They had us over for dinner last;" or, "We ought to send the Jacksons a greeting. They sent us one last year."

Complimentary remarks made to us and about us are valued, regardless of their source. A bootblack may tell his college girl customer that she is the prettiest girl he ever saw, and it certainly will not make her patronize his rival thereafter. But if Van Johnson or John Payne told her the same thing, it would have even greater effect. Thus, the weight given to our compliments depends in part upon the prestige that we ourselves enjoy. The two steps in becoming popular, therefore, consist of (1) Gaining all the prestige we can legitimately obtain in the eyes of our associates, and (2) Using this prestige to add weight to the tactfully phrased compliments we pay our associates.

A little self analysis will reveal that most of us attempt the first step, although seldom with the conscious technique described in this chapter, but too frequently forget the second step. Of the two, the latter is probably the more essential. Note the difference in the popularity which Janet gains by employing the second of the two speeches given below:

"You like my coat? Thanks, I got it at Saks and paid enough for it so it ought to be good. Yes, Jack took me to the Edgewater Beach for dinner last night. We had the best food. Jack knows Paul Whiteman, and introduced him to me. Paul played a special number just for me. Jack's taking me to dinner at the Medinah tonight, and we're going to a show afterwards."

"Do you really like it? I'm so glad, for you certainly know how to judge materials. Do you think it will wear well? I paid more for it than I should, but I remembered that your clothes always wear so much better than the cheaper things. Jack took me to the Edgewater Beach for dinner last night. It was a treat for me, but I suppose you've been there lots of times. I got to meet Paul Whiteman. Jack knows him, and introduced us. Paul even played a special number just for me! Wasn't that sweet of him? By the way, Jack's taking me to the Medinah for dinner tonight, and to a show afterwards. I'm to pick out where I want to go. You know about all the theaters, so tell me something you think I'd enjoy."

In addition to increasing the friendship of her office associate, Janet has probably created for herself in the reader's mind a much more attractive personality by her second speech than she had in the first. It is true that she employed a few more words, but as Haldeman-Julius demonstrated in lengthening his titles, she increased the good will and appeal of her personality thereby. In the following paragraphs we shall discuss more specifically these two steps in gaining popularity. The methods of fulfilling the initial step will be treated first.

(1) The physical appearance, like the show window in the shop, makes the initial impression upon our public. In our height, weight, complexion and attire we create a definite feeling tone. Some of these features are not modifiable, but many of them we can definitely improve. Aside from such well advertised flaws as halitosis, body odor, greasy skin, oily hair, twisted seams in hose, run down heels, soupy vests, frayed collars, and baggy trousers there are a number of other minor items which may detract from an otherwise admirable appearance. We have become surfeited with tooth paste advertising. But the teeth are subconsciously taken as indices of health and vitality. Decayed teeth connote an unhealthy physical condition. Dirty teeth suggest that the person may also be letting moss grow in the family bath tub. White teeth suggest

purity, as restaurants, hospitals, and soda fountains appreciate by their emphasis upon this color. Morality is denoted subconsciously by white teeth, while villains are not thought of as being good advertisements for Pepsodent.

Even international affairs have been complicated by dirty teeth, as the experience of the former king of Spain attests. When King Alfonso went to England in quest of a pretty princess who would share his throne with him, he met Princess Patricia of Connaught, niece of Edward VII. The Spanish monarch fell in love with her and, as Princess Radziwill* comments,

" . . . one evening after dinner, bluntly asked her to become his wife.

"To everybody's surprise Patricia refused him!

"The scandal, although suppressed, was the only subject of conversation in European courts and salons for weeks. The princess was severely criticized for her indifference to such a great offer of marriage. King Edward himself expressed in no veiled terms his disgust at her behavior—which was upsetting his political apple cart. But Patricia was obdurate. When she was asked to give her reasons for declining the Spanish throne, she replied that the king of Spain did not brush his teeth as well and as often as he should."

The king is probably not the only man who has failed to win his sweetheart for such a reason. In addition to teeth, however, we may cite the finger nails as important adjuncts of an attractive physical appearance. Black nails do more than connote mourning. The tendency of women, moreover, to redden their nails gives rise to a fundamental feeling tone connected with blood, despite whatever harmony of color scheme they may attain. See "Test for Sweethearts," page 765.

The clothing of individuals is also effective not only as regards its neatness and cleanliness, but in its pattern and color as well. Dark hues make one look less corpulent. Checkered and flowered fabrics make one look larger, for the reason un-

*Radziwill, Catherine, "The Woman Who Lost Her Throne," *Midweek, Chicago Daily News* (May 27, 1931), p. 4.

derlying the illusion depicted in Exhibit 30. Dark colors make one look older. A double-breasted coat makes a heavy man look thinner, and a single-breasted coat makes a slender man appear more stalwart. The reasons underlying such phenomena are contained in the discussion of illusions in any good textbook of general psychology.

(2) The honors, creations, and other assets which we possess should be thoroughly studied, just as the salesman studies the good points of his merchandise, so that we may formulate our selling talk. We have discussed in the preceding section the superiority of tactful vs. blunt sales arguments. The use of suggestion is even more imperative in personality merchandising than in that of goods. Not all of our virtues, however, require verbal treatment. Sometimes our polite and considerate actions will convey the ideas as well as language.

After we have adequately established our prestige in the manner just described, we must extrovert ourselves, like Janet, so that we can make sure that those around us feel complimented. We don't have to be blunt in telling people they are pretty, or cultured, or good cooks. The same suggestive method which we employed in building up our own prestige can also be utilized in this regard. Indeed, our compliments are more likely taken at par value when indirectly offered than when made too bluntly. But even blunt compliments have value, so we should never remain silent when speech will make our hosts and hostesses happy.

Curiously enough, even when we realize that our friends are deliberately complimenting us, we still rather like it. In the process of inflating the ego of those around us the following methods will be found of value.

(1) Ask the persons for information, advice, or direction. Janet's second speech, as given above, illustrates this point. A question is a subtle form of compliment that even the most skillful psychologists frequently fail to detect. The reason why questions are of value in this connection is the fact that

the questioner indirectly acknowledges the superiority of the questioned by coming to him for assistance. Scoldings and criticisms can often be avoided if the clever student can slip in his question before the other party can get launched into the tirade. By habit we tend to respond whenever questioned. A policeman will answer a question, much as will a child, so that the erring driver may often undermine the officer's ire by letting him dissipate his emotion through the motor activity of a number of responses to questioning.

(2) Impute knowledge and experience to your associates whether or not you know they possess it. Janet illustrated this method, too, when she said, "It was a treat for me, but I suppose you've been there lots of times." A book salesman may say, "You, of course, remember that old adage, etc." The customer feels much like the penniless actor who was approached by a pedestrian who wished a $20 bill changed, and to whom the actor replied, "I can't change it but thanks for the compliment." The public speaker frequently employs this method, as we shall develop at greater length later.

(3) Be sure to intimate that the other person has or had "it". One of the best methods of making your associates feel good is to allude to their "past", if male, or to the string of broken hearts they left when they married, if female. Most men expand and mentally preen themselves if called a Don Juan or Romeo, and seldom will a woman resent the title of Cleopatra. The surest way to incur lasting enmity is to lower a person's sex vanity. Women of sixty are just about as vulnerable to sex compliments as are those of twenty. If the compliment cannot be made of them in the present, at least it can be used with reference to their youth.

(4) Compliment the products or children of your associates, or their dogs, cats, and canaries. This is a subtle form of inflating the ego. Alexander Pope once said that the best way to compliment a man was to comment favorably on the thing in which he wanted to be proficient rather than the thing in

which he was adept. For example, the salesman who always aspired to be a writer would probably be more flattered by comments on his literary skill than upon his salesmanship. The books, clothes or ideas of people belong in this same category of objects or possessions in which the owner takes pride.

(5) Finally, make direct compliments. These are not so effective as a general rule, however, because they arouse the suspicion that you may be flattering, not sincerely praising the person.

The two essential steps in becoming popular, therefore, consist of gaining all the prestige which can legitimately be procured, and then employing this prestige to give more weight to the tactfully phrased compliments which are paid to one's associates. This simple two-stage process becomes an open sesame for the skilful person, but too many individuals don't meet success because they forget the important second step. Moreover, many fail in the first half of the problem by not using suggestion and finesse. We have recounted the two general devices for accomplishing the first step and the five ways for complimenting one's associates.

Dangers to Avoid in Self Salesmanship. We should never utilize our associates as a means of elevating our prestige at their expense. The Biblical statement, "A prophet is not without honor save in his own country and in his own house," is based on an appreciation of the thing we are decrying. The reason a man's intimate friends are so ready to use his Christian name freely after he becomes famous is evident to the careful analyst. They simply try to pull themselves up by the act of familiarity or criticism, the assumption being that the one who criticizes is of necessity superior to the one criticized. The trait is very widespread. Moreover, whenever a member of an organization, a political party, or even a department in a university becomes nationally known, many of his colleagues and former associates subtly undergo a change regarding him. Their friendship becomes less sincere, and they may ultimately begin to damn him by innuendo if not more bluntly.

When tenement women and children are taken to the circus through the generosity of settlement workers and other charitable agencies, we frequently hear them say that it is "a bum circus" or that they've had "rotten seats". When sent to neighboring farms for a week's respite from the city heat, some will complain at the station because they cannot have redcaps to carry their luggage onto the train for them. At the farms where they are guests of kindly farmers, they ask if there isn't cheese for the pie, for "We never have pie without cheese at home." The farmers have frequently asked that they be taken back, saying, "They're used to better fare than we are."

These tenement folks probably do not intend to be rude. They are simply so concerned with inflating their own egos that they minimize their associates in the process, thereby angering the latter. They criticized the circus to suggest that they were accustomed to better seats and better entertainment.

Everybody at some time or other has probably felt the resentment of having a partial stranger familiarly employ his name. Why is it that the president of our company may call us by our Christian name without irritating us, when the same action on the part of the office boy leads to intense resentment? The answer is simple. In the first case our ego is inflated by the fact that the higher officer intimates our equality by his familiar use of our name. In the latter case our ego is deflated by the fact that the office boy intimates equality with us by his familiar use of our name. In the former case we rise in prestige, while we sink in the latter instance.

Another important thing for salesmen as well as for the average person to bear in mind is this: when we are on the defensive, we feel uncomfortable. This fact explains our discomfort if salesmen call upon us. Moreover, when we recommended as a method of complimenting people that we impute knowledge and ability to them, we meant that they were not to be quizzed upon such matters, nor were we to suggest that such questioning would follow. The students well remember the nervous strain they feel when unprepared but expecting to be called upon before the class period is over.

In summing up the dangers to avoid in self-salesmanship, we should state that they arise primarily because the individual is so intent upon trying to inflate his own ego and self-esteem that he attempts to utilize his associates in the process. It is obvious that this procedure deflates the ego of each one around him, and therefore is decidedly inimical to the development of friendly relations between the self-salesman and his public. As simple as this error is, we find it illustrated among college graduates as well as among the less educated.

Why the Novice Fails in Selling Himself. The chief fault of the person who is inapt at selling himself skilfully is the fact that he fails to realize the two-fold nature of the process. He stops when he has shown off his virtues. The end of the first step is a dangerous place for him to mark time for the evident reason that we rather dislike finding our associates rising in esteem and popularity unless we partake somehow of that same elevation. If the novice will discreetly keep his associates placated by asking their opinions and complimenting their performances, he will retain their favor while he rises in general prestige.

One of the writer's girl students obtained a temporary position in an office during the absence of the stenographer. This girl was attractive in physical appearance, possessed ability and education, but was disliked by the ringleader of the office force—the stenographer—as soon as the latter returned from her vacation. The stenographer openly showed her animosity by telling the other girls in the office that the stranger would probably be let out by the ensuing Saturday. On the contrary, the new girl rapidly rose until she became secretary to the advertising manager. The stenographer continually made things unpleasant for her, however, until the new girl finally came to me for advice. Her situation, she said, was intolerable unless she could gain fairly friendly relationships with the group with whom she associated.

Since this girl could not ask advice of the ringleader without lowering her prestige in business matters, for the ringleader might then tell the advertising manager that she was really doing all the work of the new girl, there was only one short cut by which to win over the ringleader. That lay in playing to her desire to appear popular with the male sex. The ringleader prided herself on her wild parties, and general knowledge of places of amusement in the city. Here was a field in which the new girl, although more attractive than the ringleader, could nevertheless consciously humble herself to the extent of asking advice regarding places to go, shows to see, etc.

In sexual competition it is particularly difficult for a girl to take a secondary role to a rival whom she feels superior to, but the individual who can intelligently do this will often win her rival's friendship. Meanwhile she doesn't lessen her attractiveness with her own masculine friends, for they don't know anything about her office conduct, and probably wouldn't be influenced adversely by it if they did. When the new girl began to go to the ringleader for social advice, the latter underwent a change of feeling toward her. It wasn't long until she began to incorporate the stranger in her circle of friends, and eventually she became an active defender of the new girl.

Whenever people invest either money or advice in a project or person they begin to take an interest in the latter. It is frequently an advantage to allow others to do you favors because of this psychological effect. The young person, however, usually resents being under obligations to anybody, so he deliberately defeats his own ultimate good. Many an aged parent, uncle, aunt, or grandparent could be wrapped around the little fingers of the younger generation if the latter would only assume an interest in the advice coming from the older generation, and even actively court it. Many a husband, too, could hold his wife's devotion more securely if he permitted her to feel that she was important to him and his business because of her counsel and criticism. The male, however, resents what he considers lowering his dignity, especially when it involves even intimating the female's superiority, so he loses this powerful means of really becoming a surer master in his own home. This is the situation which truly involves stooping to conquer. Women, on the contrary, have no such aversion, so they frequently utilize this excellent device.

The novice fails to sell himself, therefore, either because he is not familiar with the proper technique of being his own publicity agent or because he is unwilling to undergo the process of apparently deflating his own ego in order to inflate that of his neighbor. The negative protest of young people makes them refuse to humble themselves, even when they could easily stoop to conquer if they would.

The Tactful Winning of Young People. There is one central idea which young people constantly have in mind, and that is their independence of their parents and adults in general. Age and maturity spell this freedom, while any symbol which connotes youth or childhood is a reminder of the hated serfdom out of which they have been scrambling. From his experience with Little Blue Books Haldeman-Julius says that his Juvenile Books classification proved quite unsatisfactory, and that young people don't even like to be referred to as "Young People".

Recalling Pope's advice to compliment a person on that quality in which he strives to be outstanding, we find that a safe and certain method of eliciting favorable reactions from young people is to intimate that they are grown. In the following student reports we shall observe that this principle is generally involved.

You are a senior this year? Oh, your second year. Well nobody would ever know it from the looks of you. (I look grown.)

I'm certainly glad I found a girl I don't have to be afraid to leave Jackie with. (I can be trusted—like an adult.)

Pardon me, sir (he's seventeen), but have you got a match on you? (The boy will probably carry matches the rest of his life!)

(Girl seventeen to boy of equal age, as she rubs his cheek) I don't believe you shaved tonight. You ought to be ashamed! (Does anybody think he is?)

Do you know, Mary, to hear you discussing these important matters, I'd be sure you were twenty, at least.

Boy, what big leg muscles you have! Does that come from track or basketball? (I'm strong—strength is a symbol of adulthood.)

(Older sister's beau to her younger brother) I wish I could make a radio like yours. If you could spare the time some day I wish you'd show me something about them. (I'm asked for advice by an older man—intimation being that I am his equal or superior.)

(Mary is eighteen) Gracious, Mary, you're quite an authority on Sir Walter Scott, aren't you? (Authority has always meant adulthood to the young person.)

Most women are poor drivers but here is one girl who can run rings around any man. (I'm classed better than *women,* and even superior to *men*—certainly I am grown.)

Really, it certainly is refreshing to find a girl who knows something to talk about other than the movies. (I'm more experienced than the usual girl—experience connotes age.)

One of the writer's men students remarked that he once had a date with a girl who knew and talked of nothing but movies, until he became almost nauseated. Finally he happened to learn that she could whistle, so he suggested one tune after another, praising her after each one. She reacted like Franklin to the flattery of the man with the ax, and whistled for an hour till he could discreetly make his exit.

The following student's paper* belongs in this section, but

*Paper written by Anne Filwett.

pertains to young men and women of marriageable age. We shall present it in entirety. If the girl's comments seem too obvious at times, we must bear in mind the fact that a physically attractive young woman can be much more blunt than this one, and yet have her statements discounted but slightly by the male with whom she is talking.

SCENE I. *At the Dance*—With adoring eyes directed on her subject—
> She Merely Said This: "This is a new step for me but I find it so easy to follow you, Jack. I guess you *do* dance a lot, don't you? You say you don't?"
> He Felt Thus—"Just a born dancer!"

SCENE II. *At the Wheel*—A calm glance at the speedometer and she settles back comfortably with a sigh—and
> She Merely Said This—"Seventy miles, Jim, and I'm not a bit scared—but I'd never let my brother Ed risk my life like this!"
> He Felt Thus—"She trusts my driving ability. Just a Speed Demon but a reliable one."

SCENE III. *At the Library*—Fingering the book her intelligent looking boy friend offers her—she hands it back with a sigh, but—
> She Merely Said This—" 'Stoo deep for me, Bill. I wish I could interest myself in the worth-while literature that you do. You do like the deepest books!"
> He Felt Thus—"Just a deep sea diver delving into the sea of knowledge. Crave only the best that's written! No depraved tastes here."

SCENE IV. *At Christmas*—Regarding *his* gift with *strong approval* and that Xmas Smile—
> She Merely Said—"Someone must have told you that I needed a purse! I'll bet you asked mother! You didn't? Even my brother Ed never hits it right. I guess just a *few* men are inspired."
> He Felt Thus—"Just blessed with that sense of observation with a feeling of the appropriate thrown in."

SCENE V. *On the Telephone*—Lowering her voice to a very pathetic and appealing tone—
> She Merely Said—"Tonight? Yes I'd love to see you tonight, Frank. I've so much on my mind. I can't tell the

family anything because they just laugh at me. It's so nice to have someone who understands and takes me seriously."

He Felt Thus—"So Understanding! Women know I have the type of shoulder they can cry on. Always in demand."

SCENE VI. *At the Party*—In quite an awed voice—

She Merely Said—"And you never told me before that you had a book published! If that were Ed he'd have broadcast it all over. "

He Felt Thus—"Just the 'umble type.' Brains haven't gone to *my* head."

SCENE VII. *At the Piano*—Gazing enraptured at his rhythmic fingers traversing the keys—

She Merely Said—"Do you think I could ever learn to play like that? My brother said I'm not sociable just sitting here but I'd so much rather listen than dance."

He Felt Thus—"Paderewski's only rival! A musical magnet."

SCENE VIII. *Just Outside the Parental Door*—With a little laugh—

She Merely Said—"Three o'clock, Ray? Mother angry? She never scolds when she knows I'm with you. Makes me laugh."

He Felt Thus—"Friend of American Mothers. Type to be trusted."

SCENE IX. *At Sambo's Inn*—In that surprised voice—

She Merely Said—"Do you know *everyone*, Tom? Isn't there someone who won't come over and slap you on the back? How does it feel to be so well acquainted?"

He Felt Thus—"What a popular young man I turned out to be. Just over-run with friends. No end to my followers."

SCENE X. *Any Place*—Head on a $33\frac{1}{3}$ degree angle and knowing smile—

She Merely Said—"Bobby picked out a Hart, Schaffner and Marx ad the other day and said that he looked like you. They do have such fascinating ads, don't they? If I were a man I'd want to look just like that."

He Felt Thus—"I'm a living model showing just what the well dressed man should wear. And how it wilts the feminine hearts and blows them in my direction."

The tactful winning of young people, therefore, consists principally in complimenting them upon the traits in which they aspire to excel. Since from childhood onward they have been desirous of freedom and adult privileges, it is obvious that they like to be considered grown, strong, competent, experienced, etc. Since they have been worshippers of muscular strength and sophistication for so many years, they are more influenced by persons who also possess such qualifications.

The Tactful Winning of Middle-Aged People. The usual rules for compliments hold in this age group. One must keep in mind, moreover, that such persons have now reached the stage in their mental development when they no longer resent being thought youthful. Indeed, they react very favorably to indirect and even direct comments upon their vitality, lack of gray hair and wrinkles, springy step, and schoolgirl complexions. Because they have been in business and their own homes long enough to have products of such environments, as executive positions, automobiles, pretty dwellings, and children, the intelligent observer will find a host of things by praising which he indirectly compliments their owners and creators.

The difference between such tactful compliments and those employed with young people will be apparent from an inspection of the following student reports.

Your children have such good manners, Mrs. Fox. I wish mine were half as polite. (I understand child psychology — a good mother.)

One has only to look at your wife's happy face to know what kind of a husband you are. (I am a gentleman and perfect lover.)

I sometimes wonder how you manage to stand up under the tremendous strain, with your business and practically all the work to do at the lodge. I'm afraid I'd be all worn out in two weeks if I were as active as you. (I'm virile, masculine and healthy—meaning youth.)

Really, Mrs. Brown, teaching would be a pleasure if all the boys were as alert and well trained as your Richard. (I'm a good mother.)

What kind of cold cream do you use? I've tried several kinds, but my skin never has that lively glow which is so important if one is to keep youthful looking. (I look youthful—a schoolgirl complexion.)

Don't forget to come to the country club dance on Friday night, Mrs. Miller—all the younger set will be there. (I'm still youthful enough to be included in the "younger" set.)

You and Jack certainly do look alike. I was walking in back of the two of you tonight, and I could hardly tell which was Jack. (This compliment may be taken by both father and son if the boy is not over twenty-five. It admirably illustrates the difference in attitude of father and son regarding the matter of age.)

I hope I'm not keeping you from dancing with the other girls. They've been casting pointed glances at you ever since you started talking to me. Girls do go for distinguished looking men, you know. They have so much more poise than the boys in our set. (A father-in-law cannot long maintain his objections to his son's wife, if she follows the procedure of this young diplomat, regardless of her frivolities.)

The tactful winning of middle-aged people, therefore, follows the same fundamental technique as that which we described for winning young people. They have enjoyed adulthood long enough, however, to be looking back to youth with fond memories. They want to retain as many symbols of youth as possible, included among which are, of course, health, vigor, no wrinkles, no gray hair, and sex appeal. Because they have products of their years in business or in the home, they may also be complimented on these.

The Tactful Winning of Elderly People. This group possesses many of the characteristics of the middle-aged men and women as regards the things on which they pride themselves. They still like to be considered healthy and spry, although they have relinquished the active attempt to be incorporated in younger groups. They admit they are aged, but they wish to show how little time has affected them. They have children and grandchildren concerning whom they take pride, but they are more susceptible to direct compliments about their immediate deeds and products. They are slipping into the attitudes of children in this regard. A bit of praise for their knitting or gardening seems to carry more weight than a compliment on their children. This fact probably results from the tendency of younger people to shelve their grandparents or elderly parents by taking over control of the business or household and even apportioning the furniture and heirlooms. To the man and woman past seventy, physical comforts, cushions, and easy chairs play a more significant role than in the lives of younger persons. They are also especially complimented through the question, as some of the examples below will demonstrate.

(To the man of 65 who has a wife of 55) Did you and your wife marry as a result of a school days' romance? (It would be wise to put such a question in the absence of the wife, of course!)

(To her future grandmother) Jack says he wants me to come over here and take some cooking lessons from you before we get married. (Does anybody think the grandmother will oppose this match thereafter?)

I wanted to ask your advice about buying some stock.

You can't fool me, Grandmother. I'll bet you were the life of the party before you married Grandfather.

Grandfather, tell me some of your experiences during the war?

Grandmother, you are an artist, the way you can make such beautiful rag rugs.

In the tactful winning of elderly people, therefore, one should keep in mind that the technique employed with middle-aged persons is usually effective here. However, elderly people are not so concerned with being considered youthful as they are with being younger looking than some other elderly person. The rivalry factor is now quite apparent. Because they have had some of their independence taken away from them by their children, they are interested, therefore, in being considered competent to run their homes and their businesses, and react in many ways like young people. In fact, youth looks forward to independence while age looks backward toward independence, so the same type of compliment will work with both groups.

Developing Your Social Intelligence. In this and preceding chapters we have mentioned the principal features to be considered by the person who wishes to be adept in social situations. The nursery school and the presence of playmates and siblings are quite important as early means of extroverting people. Even a few months of salesmanship is a great help, as we illustrated in the case of the young engineer cited in Chapter IV. Social intelligence can be consciously cultivated. It is not an innate characteristic of a person. To a certain extent, of course, it depends on the possession of mental alertness or abstract intelligence, for the imbecile cannot hope to become socially intelligent, but even a genius in terms of I. Q. is not socially alert unless he has been so trained by his environment. We have many brilliant men and women who are as tactless and boorish as any subnormals. In the conscious technique of acquiring social intelligence or developing it in children the following items should be considered:

(1) Recreational Habits. Learn to play the games that are conventional. Attain some knowledge and skill concerning tennis, baseball, golf, bridge, dancing, swimming and the like. Be aware of current actors and actresses, and the plays in which they appeared. Know some of the popular authors and the present best sellers in fiction. Keep up with popular music and styles. In this manner you not only direct your attention outward, but also gain a feeling of social unity with your group, and feel little shyness or hesitancy regarding the amusement plans of your social set.

(2) Etiquette. Be conversant with customary usage of language and deportment in such situations as a ballroom, a restaurant, a pullman car, or a church. Underline in red such important events as birthdays, anniversaries, and sailing dates, remembering that candy, flowers, and even a simple greeting card mean much. Quoting a few relevant lines of verse or an appropriate phrase from a popular song certainly

doesn't do any harm, especially when such quotations are complimentary to the recipient. Emily Post and Dorothy Dix can usually offer material aid in this connection.

(3) Methods of Motivating Human Beings. We have discussed this subject in Chapter I, and in the latter half of the present chapter. The art of complimenting people involves an understanding of their age and accomplishments, plus a tactful phrasing of the commendatory remarks, all of which involves extroversion of our attention. Instead of being wholly preoccupied with our own hobbies and interests, we become aware of those of our associates. It is possible to form the habit of making other people happy. The stumbling block over which most people fall is their failure to perform the second step in the two-stage process of becoming popular. They are so concerned with making a good impression that they forget the basic purpose for which that good impression is desired, namely, the weight it gives to their compliments of other individuals around them.

In conclusion, therefore, we may state that the development of social intelligence is practically synonymous with the process of extroverting an individual. It involves attention to the social habits of people and an understanding of some of the basic principles of human motivation and control. Like any other profession, the art of social diplomacy can be acquired by any intelligent person who is willing to study it diligently. It can also be taught to one's children. Because almost every business deals with people in some regard, the possession of social intelligence becomes a financial as well as social asset to the man and woman in the workaday world. See my "Formula For Being An Interesting Conversationalist" on page 760.

See my "Formula For Being An Interesting Conversationalist" on page 760.

REFERENCES

1 BOGARDUS, E. S., "Social Distance" (J. Appl. Sociol., 9, 1925)
2 CAMERON, ROD, A Dummy Goes to Africa (Missions Press, 1962)
3 CRANE, G. W., What's Your H-R Rating? (Cal Mag., Apr. 1967)
4 LICHTER et al., The Drop-Outs (Macmillan, 1962)
5 MONTGOMERY, G. H., Why People Like You (Taplinger, 1963)
6 WALGREEN, MYRTLE N., Never A Dull Day (Regnery, 1964)

CHAPTER VII

THE PSYCHOLOGY OF SELLING YOUR PRODUCT

In discussing personality development we have already treated one phase of salesmanship. The public speaker also utilizes many of the principles offered in this chapter when he convinces his hearers of the merits of his cause. The teacher should really be interested in doing the same thing, although too often the material is "dished out" to the students with little regard for the state of their intellectual appetites, or their skill in assimilating the new facts.

In the realm of business, the salesman sells products, ideas, and services. Tangible objects, of course, are easier to merchandise than are the more ephemeral ideas and services, because they have immediate sensory qualities. The customers can feel silks, or taste foods, or ride in automobiles. Insurance policies and efficiency systems cannot be experienced so directly by the sense organs; hence, they are sold with greater difficulty. Moreover, the more remote the profits in point of time, the more difficult is the sale. Animals and children, for instance, want things *now*. Even in college the students will usually prefer a half day's holiday today to a full day off next week. Future rewards, like third degree stimuli, are too vague to surpass first and second degree stimuli.

In devoting only one chapter to the psychology of salesmanship, it will be obvious that we can delineate only the important aid which psychology offers, and let supplementary volumes on the subject fill out the remainder.

The Function of Enthusiasm in Salesmanship. The majority of sales managers realize the importance of "pep" meetings. A successful salesman must be full of vigor. He cannot drag along in his walking or thinking like a foot soldier on his twentieth mile, for it is almost impossible to arouse action in a customer unless the salesman is full of enthusiasm. Lacking this quality, the salesman is likely to be convinced by his customer instead of convincing the latter. The excessive vitality demonstrated by the orchestra leader, for example, is an attempt to overcome the inertia of the audience so that they will participate in applause, laughter, or singing.

Salesmanship is one of the most difficult tasks on earth. It drains one's physical vitality and subjects one's enthusiasm to repeated deflation, for the best salesman usually meets more rebuffs than he does successes. The principal function of the sales manager is to offset the effect of the failures encountered by his men. He accomplishes this result in numerous ways, one of which is by keeping in daily contact with his road salesmen so that they obtain a morning letter of encouragement. In this letter he may cite new selling points, or enclose a record of all the salesmen so that each one is aware of what the others are doing.

Lacking this letter the salesman who has encountered rebuffs for several days, is likely to lay the blame for his failure on lack of money by his customers or the depression. When he receives records of the other men on the force, however, and finds they are selling regularly, he is more inclined to buckle down to greater effort. As a further means of increasing his enthusiasm, teams are devised so that one group of salesmen is pitted against another. Prizes may be awarded to the winning captains, who are the high point winners of the week or month.

If the salesmen are working within an hour's ride of a central office, they usually meet each morning or at least once a week for "pep" sessions. The leading salesmen give talks on how they attained their successes. The sales manager demonstrates new uses of the product or calls to his assistance one of the chemists or engineers to explain interesting processes or stages in its manufacture. The old time sales manager, like the old football coach, used to engage in fist shaking and profanity as the chief means of stimulating his men to greater accomplishment.   The new type of sales manager, although adept in the use of speech which incites his men to action and builds up their confidence and enthusiasm, nevertheless is a closer student of psychology, and adapts his methods to the individual personalities of those under him. If praise stimulates Brown while reprimand incites Smith, he modifies his speech and letters to meet the differences in his crew.

Sometimes only a few degrees difference in a man's confidence and enthusiasm will change defeat into victory, for the customer subtly feels the mental state of the salesman.   Just as enthusiasm is infectious, so doubt and uncertainty likewise are perceived by the potential clients with a resulting lack of decision on their part.   As in the realm of mental disease, the attitude of the salesman may be the basis of success or failure.   A conquering mood on his part is more likely to lead to conquest.   Every professional salesman knows that the days on which he starts out with an early sale to his credit are the days when he should work doubly hard, for the effect upon his confidence of this initial victory may bring several more sales into his order book before nightfall.   These are the times when a salesman feels invincible.   On the other hand, the sales manager often encounters his men when they are like Half-Way Hurley, described in Chapter II, and must be stimulated by some such device as the following:

Mr. Lee[25] decided that his salesmen could increase their orders for Protectographs from the 8 or 10 weekly average up to 12 or 15.   Having been a salesman himself, he challenged his force, and set the week of May 7th for the test. All challengers gave a list of their prospects, who were sent direct-mail advertising in advance.   On Monday the contest began.   No order of more than two to a customer could apply,

---

"When two men in a business always agree, one of them is unnecessary."
                                        —William Wrigley, Jr.

and all orders had to be signed that week—no hold-overs and no deferred deliveries. Mr. Lee had the agreeable surprise of selling 22 Protectographs, a record which was tied by one of his salesmen.

He thereupon made a standing offer of $100 to anybody who would exceed this mark. Shortly thereafter Mr. Johnson offered himself as a candidate, and brought in 27 orders during the week of his test. Mr. Poff raised the mark to 29 not long thereafter, to be followed during the busy week of December 15 by Du Rocher's 31. High marks like these would have been deemed impossible by the salesmen until the initial contest showed that over twenty machines could be sold in a week. This fact simply gave them confidence or belief that it could be done. In sports, too, note what happened after Roger Bannister broke the supposedly impossible 4-minute mile!

A salesman's enthusiasm, moreover, must be kept at a high level and maintained there even during unsuccessful interviews, for often it is almost impossible to gain an order on the first contact. It may require several visits on the salesman's part before he has created enough confidence in himself and has sufficiently impressed the conservative dealer with the desirability of his goods to produce favorable action. A survey by 1000 retailers who kept accurate check for six months to learn how many calls salesmen made on them before giving up the job as hopeless led to the following results[37]:

> 48.2 per cent made 1 call and quit.
> 24.4 per cent made 2 calls and quit.
> 14.7 per cent made 3 calls and quit.
> 12.7 per cent made 4 calls and quit.

Only one salesman out of every eight made as many as four calls on a new dealer, yet these same 1000 retailers discovered that the great bulk of all their buying was not made until after the third call. In short, only those men who called four or five times stood much chance of getting orders.

"Men do not FAIL; they give up TRYING."—Elihu Root.

"Nothing succeeds like success," runs an old saying which is certainly borne out in the realm of salesmanship. The salesman knows, as does his manager, that as soon as his enthusiasm wanes, his sales fall off. The records of his co-workers aid in maintaining his morale, as do inspirational speeches by his manager. Increasing his motivation, as by offers of prizes, bonuses, or positions on paper ball teams and the like have marked value. Sometimes his need of additional money, or jealousy of seeing his record topped by a rival will spur him on to greater productivity.

One of the indispensable qualities of a salesman is a constant realization of the fact that he will sell a certain percentage of his customers if he just keeps driving vigorously ahead. Unfortunately, it may be that in some cases the last day or two of the week are the only ones that result in business. For days in succession he meets deferments and rebuffs. But a knowledge of his basic percentage rate will be invaluable as a spur to his enthusiasm, and carry him through the dreary period of no sales.

A fortunate thing in the salesman's favor is the fact that he can always count on a certain number of sales for any legitimate product, if he just makes his calls. There are always some customers just ready to order his goods, and who don't need a sales talk to persuade them. Then, too, his personality will have a greater appeal to some customers than to others, for he will remind them of a relative or friend. Maybe they do not consciously realize why, but they will feel drawn to him. Unfortunately for the salesman, of course, this number is usually too few to insure him a comfortable salary without more active effort on his part.

In discussing enthusiasm one must not confuse it with so-called "high pressure" salesmanship. Although the latter involves enthusiasm, it frequently connotes an unpleasant disregard for the actual needs of the customer and a sheer physical and mental dominance by the salesman. In a certain number of persons, it is true, the salesman encounters a vacillating type of personality so that he may at times have to make up the customers' minds for them, but when he deliberately utilizes his greater skill to intimidate his clients, he is employing a figurative club. Such a method cannot lay claim to being a high grade of salesmanship. It belongs in the category of the procedure formerly in vogue whereby the salesman took his client to a risqué show and afterwards plied him with liquor until the stupefied customer allowed his hand to be steered along the dotted line.

The function of enthusiasm in salesmanship, therefore, is twofold. First, it incites the salesman himself to greater effort, and second, it infects the prospects so that they feel more interested in the merchandise and confident of its worth. The principal function of the sales manager is to keep up the enthusiasm of his men. We have recounted a few of the methods by which he accomplishes this end. Depending, of course, upon the type of merchandise and the amount of time which he can devote to the sale, the salesman should be impressed with the importance of following up one interview with later calls.

Fitting Your Product to Your Public. This problem entails some sales' prospecting, as well as a close scrutiny of the goods to be sold. It is a waste of time and energy for the salesman to call upon people who are only remotely interested in the type of article which he has to sell when he might be interviewing another class of purchaser in which he would find a ready market. If the article offers the salesman only a slight commission, he cannot devote the time for an excessively careful weeding out of prospects. On the other hand, if he is selling Cadillac automobiles or bonds he must select his clientele beforehand. Salesmanship is somewhat like fishing, for one must adapt the "bait" to the species for which one is angling. Because there are so many rival baits, one cannot expect his commissions to be large unless he first studies the habits of the species (clientele) with which he expects to deal.

"I would rather men asked why there is no statue to me than to have them ask why one was erected."   —Disraeli

Even in house-to-house canvassing, however, certain rough distinctions can be made. Homes in which there are maids offer a much greater resistance than those where the housewife herself appears at the door, and speaking through a tube in apartment buildings is enough to test the ingenuity of any salesman.

In his analysis of the problem undertaken in this section, Starch[35] offers six criteria of the consumer which are important to the salesman as well as to the advertiser.

(1) Who are the users and buyers of the article in question? Since the user is not always the buyer, it becomes important to make this distinction. Mothers are the chief buyers of their childrens' and even their husbands' clothing.

(2) Where do they live? Although this seems such a simple query as to be self-evident, it is surprising how many merchants and manufacturers are not clear as to the actual source of their purchasers. They may know, to be sure, that they live in the city or state, but it often requires an advertising firm to tell them which quarter of the city or state. The writer knows of a manufacturer, for example, with his salesmen on the road, sometimes 1000 miles away from the home plant, who made this same error. The distant salesmen lacked the advertising of the men closer home, and also missed many of the "pep" meetings. A survey of the city in which the company was situated revealed that the distant salesmen could profitably be called home and set to work within a radius of fifty miles of the manufacturing plant. Not only were their travelling expenses saved by the company, but the men were stimulated to greater enthusiasm by the frequent home contacts. Moreover, the salvaged expenses were available for more intensive local advertising purposes.

(3) How many potential buyers and users are there? In cities with large labor populations, as mining towns, one could

---

"The world belongs to the Enthusiast who keeps cool." —William McFee

Good example of importance of human interest values in art. Page 435.

1

2

3

4

(An excellent example of personality compensation, like that of the enuresis victim who becomes a chronic bully.(Reprinted from *THIS WEEK Magazine*.

6

8

DOCTOR,

WILL YOU MAKE

THIS NOSE TEST?

*SEE AT ONCE PHILIP MORRIS
ARE LESS IRRITATING.*

It is one thing to read published studies.* Quite
another to have your own personal experience
provide the proof! The PHILIP MORRIS nose test
takes but a moment. Won't you try it?

HERE IS ALL YOU DO:

1 ...light up a PHILIP MORRIS

Take a puff — DON'T INHALE. Just
s-l-o-w-l-y let the smoke come through
your nose. AND NOW

2 ...light up your present brand

Do exactly the same thing — DON'T
INHALE. Notice that bite, that sting?
Quite a difference from PHILIP MORRIS!

*With proof so conclusive, would it not be good practice
to suggest PHILIP MORRIS to your patients who smoke?*

PHILIP MORRIS

Philip Morris & Co., Ltd., Inc.
119 Fifth Avenue, New York, N. Y.

*Proc. Soc. Exp. Biol. and Med., 1934, 32, 241-245; N. Y. State Journ. Med., Vol. 35, 6-1-35, No. 11, 590-592;
Laryngoscope, Feb. 1935, Vol. XLV, No. 2, 149-154; Laryngoscope, Jan. 1937, Vol. XLVII, No. 1, 1, 58-60

(Reproduced by permission of Phillip Morris & Co., Ltd., Inc. An example of the
"parallel comparison" method in salesmanship. Contrast with P. 291, when advertisers feared to show a girl with a cigarette in her fingers lest she lose her feminine
appeal and seem masculine. These ads are about 25 years apart and show the changed
outlook toward smoking that advertisers have produced in that single generation of
time.)

not expect as wide a range of prospects for expensive automobiles or opera tickets as in a wealthy university town.

(4) How much of the goods can the buyers and users consume? This problem is of especial concern to the manufacturer and retailer, but it is also important to the salesman.

(5) How do the actual or possible users now satisfy the want which the new product is intended for? This question involves an understanding of the rival or competing goods in the field.

(6) What are the preferences with reference to the satisfaction of the need which the new commodity is to fulfill? In other words, do the people prefer one-pound or two-pound cans? Do they choose branded goods in cartons or buy them in the bulk? Which colors and styles do they like?

The last question above covers the psychological aspects of the consumer and is really the crux of the marketing problem. It offers the greatest trouble to the merchandiser and advertiser. In contrast to it the first five questions present no grave concern for they can be answered with less difficulty. One of our large mail order houses, for instance, decided to establish branch stores at numerous points throughout the country. These were located in cities and towns that usually did not exceed 25,000 to 40,000 population. A rival firm also began developing branch retail outlets, but placed its stores in larger cities. The first company has had to close most of its retail stores, whereas its rival has not been adversely affected. The second firm realized that mail order goods can be sold cheaper than when merchandised through retail outlets, and the farmer trade is interested in price. Accordingly, when it opened its retail branches, it located them in the cities, and actively began competing for new trade. The first company simply shifted much of its rural business into the county seat branches, and neglected its mail order trade. As a consequence, its customers drove to town and bought at the store, or may have continued ordering by mail from the competing firm.

The J. C. Penney Company appreciated this same desire for economy on the part of the working man when it featured overalls at $1.25 while standard overalls were selling at $2.25. It knew, of course, that overall wearers recognized differences in quality and would be willing to pay more for a better garment, *but not* 80 *per cent more*. It used the overalls as a "leader", much as sugar and nails are often employed by grocery and hardware dealers. Once the customer was in the store, he usually bought other articles, the prices of which were no lower than that of competitors. But the customer felt that he was getting bargain prices on the other articles since he used the staple as an index for comparison.

To combat Penney's method, the Oshkosh Overall Company tried to get independent merchants to buy its goods, and sell without a profit, in fact with a slight loss when overhead costs were figured in. But, as Wittmack[41] comments, the independent dealer replied, "Why should we work for you free? You get your price on overalls, and we stand the loss." The Oshkosh Company wanted to sell to the retailer at $1.70 and have him offer Oshkosh Overalls at $1.75 to $1.95.

In the process of fitting its product to the consumer the Gillette Company found that 25 per cent of its 250,000 dealers were doing 70 per cent of the selling. It found it advisable, therefore, to concentrate on these 25 per cent, making special boxes for chain drug stores, and different containers for the cigar stores. A special contest was conducted in a mid-western city with four prizes offered to the employees of a certain chain who sold the most razors in a given period of time. The Gillette Company was surprised to learn that first prize went to a cashier in one of the stores, while second prize was won by a soda fountain clerk, neither of whom had ever sold a razor in his life before. The contest brought out the

"Creditors have better memories than debtors; they are a superstitious sect, great observers of set days and times."　　—Franklin value of the cashier's desk and the marble bar as sales positions.

The psychological phases of fitting your product to your public, therefore, consist primarily of determining the preferences with reference to the satisfaction of the need which the new product is to fulfill. The other five criteria are chiefly statistical problems. We have also cited under this heading the need for a study of the methods of merchandising the product, involving an appreciation of the most efficient retail outlets as well as a knowledge of the habits of the consumer. In the following section we shall dwell upon the problems entailed by the salesman-consumer situation where they are face to face.

The Steps in the Sale. Any attempt to divide the sale situation into steps or stages must be an arbitrary process, at least if regarded from the temporal aspect. The sale may last for a few moments or it may be a product of a year of thought and planning. Snow[32] has pointed out the fact that a purchase may often be made "mentally" a number of times before the actual transfer of the article for cash takes place. In this mental prepurchasing the customer tends to think in terms of brand names and known articles, thereby indelibly impressing them in his mind. In our discussion of the sale we shall consider the following steps, beginning with the actual salesman-customer contact:

(1) Focus the customer's attention on the product. Although there are many cases where it is well to spend some time chatting about inconsequential matters and creating in the client a feeling of confidence, the writer has always found it advisable in dealing with busy men to offer the strongest appeal as quickly as possible. Then, when a motive base is aroused, the salesman can go through a verbal flash-back in which he more leisurely develops the customer's confidence in

---

"A dinner lubricates business."   —William Scott

him. There are many products for which there are no striking appeals, in which case the personality of the salesman is a deciding factor in the resulting action. In such an event, the more roundabout opening is valuable. Whether one opens with the incisive appeal followed by the flash-back, or with the circuitous approach, one should spend no unnecessary time in getting the favorable aspects of the merchandise before the customer.

(2) Arouse desire. This step involves showing the many ways in which the product will benefit the customer. In addressing a convention of salesmen some years ago Simmons urged the men to "Sell them the holes and they'll buy the augers in order to make the holes." No more pithy summary of successful salesmanship was ever made. The stress should always be placed on the *functions* of a product which enhance the pleasure or ego of the customer. An automobile's pick-up is slightly interesting unless the salesman shows you that by means of it you can beat the other cars away from a stop light, thereby intimating to your sweetheart that you are always in the lead. Its speed is a vague selling point until translated into specific situations where you can whirl past your rival on the highway, or get out of a dangerous situation more readily. The car itself is desirable not because it is a shiny four-wheel vehicle, but because it enables you to take the children into the country, or to drive to your golf club and enjoy nine holes before dark which would be impossible without the car, or to indicate your business success and financial standing to the neighbors.

Airplane advertising has aptly demonstrated this principle in recent years. To look at their posters, one would think California or Florida or Canada or Yellowstone National Park were really the sponsors of the advertisements. They show us the pleasures of wintering in Florida, then state that they can take us there most quickly and economically. This accords with the fact that the more habit patterns of a pleasing

"Don't brag; it isn't the whistle that pulls the train."   —J. H. Thompson sort which can be aroused by the salesman during the interview, the greater will be the desire for the article. It is imperative for the salesman to translate his product into its pleasing functions as regards the customer, since few articles are of interest to people in their own right, for most persons are not in the category of Silas Marner. Robinson Crusoe, for example, was astounded to find that even gold had no interest for him while he was marooned. *The value of any article depends not on the article but on the customer who regards it.* The task of the salesman, therefore, is to change the customer's attitude by successively employing his product to set off additional habit systems.

(3) Produce action. This problem is really answered almost entirely when desire is aroused, for action is the normal result of desire. In Chapter I we discussed the subject of choice or "will", showing that it is synonymous with desire, using the analogy of the scales. We pointed out that the negative weight or objections could be removed by logic, or by heaping positive weights so rapidly on the other scale pan that the customer forgot the negative ones. In the latter case desire spelled action. In the former case where the customer has time to break away from the salesman's line of thought occasionally, objections may arise. From habit, one has learned that there are many articles of the same general class, so that one should compare prices. In this type of sales situation the customer must be convinced of the superiority of the given article over all competing brands. Writers have frequently made a separate step in the sales process which they have called "Producing Conviction". The present writer looks upon this heading as comparable to the rebuttal of the college debater. If a salesman has perfectly performed his task, no formal rebuttal is necessary.

Action usually denotes signing an order blank, making out a check, or reaching into one's pocket for money. At this time the salesman usually loses some of his dominance of the customer's attention, and the latter is at liberty to do voluntary thinking. Doubts appear, and the enthusiasm of the customer frequently cools. In other words, the unanswered negative weights are suddenly called to mind, tending to restore the scales to equilibrium.

In the three steps just recounted we have outlined the essential phases of the actual sales situation. The pre-approach with its problems of fitting the product to the customer is of tremendous significance in guaranteeing a higher percentage of sales, and the matter of consumer satisfaction is also worthy of comment at this point. Even though the customer signs the order blank or pays for the goods without the necessity of a demonstration the salesman should never let him go away with his purchase without trying to present some of the functions of the product. If he does, a friend of the buyer may later say, "What on earth made you buy that kind of an automobile? You ought to have purchased a *good* car like mine." The customer finds himself at a loss to answer his friend's objections, so the friend may ultimately persuade him of the folly of his choice. When the customer meets the salesman thereafter he will think, if not actually say, "You certainly sold me a 'lemon'." On the other hand, by placing good sales points before the customer, who may not need them himself, the salesman makes another salesman out of his client. The latter may as a consequence direct additional business to the man who sold him the car.

In summarizing the psychological steps in the sale, therefore, we may state that they involve focussing the customer's attention upon the most significant aspects of the goods, arousing desire, and producing action. The salesman should never forget that the value of his merchandise depends on the attitude of his client. It becomes imperative, therefore, that he stress the functional relationship of the goods to an increase in the satisfaction of the buyer. This task involves, of course, a recognition of the customer's fundamental motive bases.

The Two Danger Zones in the Sale. Where the majority of salesmen are most guilty of error is in the opening ten sentences and in the few sentences involving the closing. In the body of the sales demonstration the exigencies of the moment can usually be met by the salesman. He doesn't need a stereotyped formula to rely upon. But in his remarks immediately following his salutation and those in which he asks for the customer's signature or cash, he needs special preparation and a memorized formula.

(1) The Opening. When the salesman first encounters his customer he needs his attention free to observe the latter's reactions. If he is mentally struggling for the right thing to say, his attention is preoccupied, and his customer can calmly survey him, having instantly gained the advantage of dominating the situation. The salesman slips into the defensive role, and his client is likely to terminate the interview quickly, or control it by his questioning.

In order to avoid this disaster, the salesman must have his initial sentences so memorized that he is free from embarrassment and can look ahead. He can, therefore, retain the offensive role throughout the interview. Take the following situation, which is one of the most critical ever confronted by the salesman. An insurance salesman has called to see a busy executive. The latter steps to the swinging gate separating the outer waiting room from the inner office. Two other salesmen are seated near by and the secretary or information girl is within hearing. The executive asks, politely but with apparent desire to get back into his office alone, "What is it you want to see me about?"

Obviously, the salesman cannot begin, "Isn't it a pleasant day, Mr. Brown? Do you play golf?" If he did the smiles of the audience would probably unnerve him, and check his speech in flushed confusion. In order to veer away from a revelation of his real purpose, he may say, "I want to discuss a little matter of private business with you," meanwhile moving as if to enter. If his suggestion of entering does not produce a favorable response from the unyielding executive, he probably receives a further question, "Well, I'm rather busy today, so if you'll tell me what it is about . . .?"

The average salesman is at a loss in this type of situation. He must now make his purpose known, since he has already indicated by his reticence, that he probably has something to sell. He feels somewhat embarrassed, of course, because other salesmen are looking on. He may bluntly say, "I wanted to see you about an accident insurance policy for your children." The reader knows the usual response.

Suppose, however, that the salesman had confidently walked over to the executive, and with no sign of embarrassment or confusion had cordially said, "Good morning, Mr. Brown. Since I was in your building I thought I'd drop in to get your advice about Betty." Here he ever so slightly turns his head to note the eavesdropping salesmen, and suggests entering by a slight forward movement of his hands to the swinging gate. Mr. Brown will usually invite him inside, for the cordial attitude of the young fellow and confident air vaguely suggest that Mr. Brown has met him before, and the mention of his college daughter by her first name increases the impression that this fellow may be a friend of hers.

If Mr. Brown is still resistant, which is rather unlikely, and asks, "What do you want to know about her?" he immediately lays himself open to having private affairs discussed before strangers. The salesman has him pretty well cornered, and the subtle compliment contained in the request for advice also conveys the intimation that Betty may be in trouble, or is contemplating marriage, or is looking for a position. Should an obdurate father put such a second question, however, the salesman can come back with, "I don't know if you are aware of it, Mr. Brown (voice now is slightly lowered), but Betty is in danger of a serious lawsuit."

From the psychological standpoint, the opening statements

of this salesman will very likely get him into Mr. Brown's office, although they may also lead to some resentment on the part of Mr. Brown unless the salesman is very competent. If the salesman intimates by word or action that he thinks he has outwitted Mr. Brown, he will quickly be escorted out of the office, but if he presents his facts in a sincere manner, showing that carefree Betty is likely to injure some one with her automobile and thereby jeopardize her freedom and her father's business, the salesman's previous remarks are made more relevant. In any case, he has passed the almost insurmountable barrier of the swinging gate, without which action his prospective sale is foredoomed to failure.

In our discussion of personality development we have already stressed the personal equation. Although it contributed part of this nonchalance and assurance of the second salesman, his confidence was partly owing to his knowledge of his opening. Regardless of whether he has to meet the secretary first or half a dozen intermediaries, he has an introduction that fits them all, and they will quickly send him to the inner office. Since he has no need for worry about the excellence of his lead-off sentences, he can calmly note the factors in the environment, including his customer, which can be utilized in his campaign. He is master of the human beings around him because he has verbally manipulated his sentences beforehand until he has a perfect arrangement. Knowing this fact, he is confident, and his confidence impresses his customers.

(2) The Close. The writer told one of his classes in applied psychology to write down ten sentences covering the actual asking for money, or the name on the dotted line, in a hypothetical sale of a vacuum cleaner to a housewife. The students could employ any type of closing they desired. Of 55 men and women who handed in the assignment *only five* actually closed the sale. And one of these ended with the nonplussed query, "Well, what do you say? Take it or leave it!" The writer offers these figures simply to show that the

salesmen themselves may tend to react like these students, and avoid the closing. As a matter of fact they often begin a recapitulation of selling points and mark time in the vicinity of the dreaded dotted line, but fail to finish their task, or else delay so long that the customer's interest has waned.

The salesman should fear the closing no more than the insurance salesman previously mentioned showed fear of his opening. In fact, the salesman should relish approaching the dotted line stage, since that means he is entering upon a mechanically perfect formula which frees his attention for keener observance of his customer. The man who shows the confidence and tact of this insurance salesman seldom excites his customer during the critical period of the close. The embarrassed and uncertain speech of the tyro salesman, however, produces uncertainty in the client.

The usual type of closing is that which involves the minor decision. The salesman tacitly assumes the sale is made, and inquires, "Would you prefer this order to be shipped by freight or express," Or else, "Would you want this vacuum cleaner in time for Saturday's cleaning, or shall we deliver it on Monday?" To illustrate the delicate approach to the crux of the sale note the importance of the word "just". It appears in almost every closing. "If you'll just sign here, we'll have this machine delivered tomorrow." That single word eliminates much of the bluntness that might otherwise attach to the closing. The salesman must avoid intimating that the customer's word is not as good as his bond. He should never say, "You have to sign this contract before the company will send you the goods." Instead, he should smilingly comment, "If you'll just O.K. this along here, we'll have the goods sent out immediately."

In concluding our discussion of the two danger zones in the sale, therefore, we can repeat that they consist of the opening few sentences and the closing. Amateur salesmen err at those two points more frequently than anywhere else in the sale sit-

uation. With an opening whose units are memorized so that
the salesman can devote the major portion of his attention
to the reactions of his client, the salesman retains his dominance of the situation and creates confidence. In a similar
fashion his assurance at the closing prevents the arousal of
negative ideas or objections in the mind of his customer.

Hitting the Bull's-eye with Your Appeals. In our
consideration of the methods of motivating human beings we
stated that stimuli must set off habits and instincts in order
to be effective. In salesmanship the chief task consists in
translating or showing the numerous facets of an article so
that it will arouse more habit systems. But we have also
previously commented on the fact that motives have both number and weight. One may be as important as several others.
The good salesman appreciates this fact, and at the outset
endeavors to show those aspects of his merchandise which
arouse the most basic neural patterns.

In a selling talk prepared for use by salesmen of a city light
and power company, the following sales arguments are presented in their apparent order of merit. The article being
merchandised is an electric, wet-proof heating pad. We shall
list only the first few arguments.

1. This new wet-proof heating pad is a new invention.
2. Here's the switch that controls the heat.
3. This pad has an all-over heating unit.
4. The cord is all silk and has 68 strands of small copper wire
   each as fine as the hair on your head.
5. The cover is eiderdown.
6. The cover can be taken off.
7. BUT THE BIGGEST THING ABOUT THIS PAD IS
   THAT IT IS GUARANTEED TO BE WET-PROOF.
8. On account of the pad being wet-proof you can use it for keeping wet packs hot.

An inspection of these eight arguments as given in chronological order in the sales talk shows that the only one that hits

the bull's-eye is number eight. All the other sales arguments are trivial matters. It doesn't make any difference to a housewife if the cord has 68 or 68000 fine copper wires in it as long as she has thus far seen no basic use for it. Every housewife, however, can appreciate having a constant heat available for headaches, rheumatism, baby's colic, etc. Even the seventh argument which apparently was deemed sufficiently valuable to warrant capitalization has no significance until the eighth is given, and we realize that the pad fits inside a wet towel, keeping the towel warm. This sales talk certainly is a good case of putting the cart before the horse. The average housewife probably would have the door shut long before Number Eight was reached.

Perspective, or the ability to distinguish fundamentals from trivialities, is one of the keynotes of successful salesmanship. Without it one may not even hit the target, let alone the center of it. We have shown in the preceding section how the insurance salesman employed his knowledge of human nature for his own profit. Others make successful entries by striking directly at the center of the situation. Here is a salesman who wishes to see the professional buyer of a large department store. The secretary insists on a card. Instead, the salesman writes on a slip of paper the following: "After the Toonerville Emporium placed one of our electric dishwashers on display, they sold 13 of the machines during the first six days and cleared $217.50 on them. Wouldn't you like to hear me explain the method they employed?" In using the example of another store, it is advisable to cite a firm from a neighboring city.

One of my former students tells me that he has found it desirable to omit carrying his brief case when he calls upon the trade, and wrap his samples in a large package, which he carries into the store when he sees the tradesman has a customer, and, laying it on the counter, says, "Go right ahead. I'm in no hurry." The shopkeeper's curiosity is stimulated. He wonders what is inside the large bundle, and is willing to talk to the salesman until it is opened, whereupon he sees the line of samples carried, and is likely to order.

In salesmanship it is also well to keep in mind the fact that we are composed of a mass of neural networks which represent our habits. Some of these habits are at variance with others. In the following paper one of the writer's former students has delineated a few of the various attitudes which she has when in one situation, then another. Since she is both motorist and pedestrian at different times, her thinking is colored principally by the role she plays at the given moment.

PROBLEM—List the groups to which you belong. How do your habits and attitudes vary according to which you are with?

FEMALE—Feel on defensive when insinuations are made that women are not as smart as men, are not able to do certain things as well as a man, etc.

(Sub-groups, I suppose they would be called.)

Brunette—Resent the well known saying, "Gentlemen prefer blondes" or other remarks to the effect that brunettes are not attractive, smart, good natured, etc. Feel pretty good when something nice or complimentary is said about a brunette.

Slender—Feel that slenderness is much to be preferred to fleshiness, have feeling would never want to be "fat", feel sorry for those who cannot eat what and as much as they want to for fear of hurting their figures, etc.

AMERICAN—Feel that United States is by far the best country to live in and that most everything we do or possess is better than any other country.

SINGLE—Have a rather pleasant reaction, for instance, when I can get a new fur coat because I have only myself to think of. On other hand, rather envy a married friend when seeing her with her baby.

FAMILY—Am inclined to "let go" of my feelings more when in the family group. Also consider them when wondering what to do on various occasions.

STUDENT—Feel a loyalty to my University, want it to be the best in the country, want it to win its football games, etc. Even when seeing a football game between two other universities, would rather see one of our "enemies" get beaten because I have developed that feeling from playing against them in our own games. Also wonder at people who are not interested in going on further with their education. Have perhaps a little superior air because I have gone a little farther than the average, though I will say I try to hide this with people who have not had the same advantages.

SORORITY—Feel a little "superior" because I was chosen by a group to be a member—though I also try not to ever let this crop out. However, would rather be a member than not organized. Am loyal to my own group as compared with other like groups and wish them to lead in every way possible. Talk college life and sorority matters when with other members that I do not talk at work, for instance.

BUSINESS—Am rather proud of our nice offices (I work for investment bankers). Enjoy all the bank holidays we get. Like working in such nice surroundings.

STOCK BUYER—Being in the atmosphere I dabble in stocks. Feel the fascination of taking the chance when buying with the hope that they will go up. (A rather forlorn one at present.) However, the gambling instinct is mingled with buying for income with possibilities of appreciation. Am interested in the quotations from day to day, hour to hour, etc. Listen to all the talk going on around me.

SECRETARY—The secretaries, especially of executives, in our office seem to be in a class by themselves. I mean there is a sort of caste, you might call it. They "rate" better than the file clerks, stenographers, multigraph operators, etc. I do not feel I am really any "better" than those who do not have as good a position, but do feel it would be congenial to have my friends among the other secretaries. While at the office I control any feelings I have of annoyance, weariness, etc., more than I would at home. I also try to keep personal affairs out of the office.

GOLFERS—I like golf as well as any sport I participate in and enjoy talking about it with anyone else who is interested in playing. When playing I try to control my feeling of annoyance when I make a poor shot. I also try not to do anything to upset my fellow players, but help them find their ball, etc.

BRIDGE CLUB—Not a very serious minded crowd, usually quite hilarious with much laughing. Thoroughly relax while with this group and act as silly as I want to. Only time anyone half-way concentrates is the little time we are actually playing. Crowd has played together for about four years and are thoroughly acquainted.

AUTOMOBILE DRIVER—When driving become very provoked with people who insist on crossing street when I have "go" signal; think all pedestrians should watch where they are going, etc.

PEDESTRIAN—When I am walking I am provoked at automobile drivers who insist on turning corner when I am trying to cross street (on correct signal), think drivers should be more careful and not tear along at such a pace, etc.

COMMUTER—Hurry to catch my train every morning and hurry to catch one ten minutes ahead of the next one at night. Am very nervous when train stops for a few minutes at some spot where it doesn't usually stop, think the service is pretty punk when I miss my train and have to wait ten or fifteen minutes for the next one, am impatient if it doesn't pull in at the moment I think it should, especially if I am afraid I will be late.

In conclusion, therefore, we may state that hitting the bull's-eye with one's appeals involves an understanding of the psychological nature of the customer and a recognition of those aspects of the merchandise which will most readily incite basic habit patterns. These factors constitute what might be termed sales perspective. In order to gain this perspective it is well to produce as detailed an analysis of the habits of the consumer as can economically be obtained.

Sensory Appeals and Salesmanship. It isn't quite so essential that the salesman employ sensory language as it is for the advertiser, since the salesman frequently has samples or the actual object to offer his client. Nevertheless, specificity produces action and sensory adjectives are next in potency to first degree stimuli. In order to illustrate the value of specificty, as well as the sections on hitting the bull's-eye and the first danger zone in the sale, we submit the following first ten sentences that a real estate salesman might offer when he enters the office of a young attorney living in an apartment and having a wife and two children. The sentences in some instances are a bit long for oral speech but could be broken into shorter units in the actual sales situation.

1. Mr. Cricks, I have been talking with Mrs. Cricks about a plan by which she can get Tom and Janice into the sunshine and fresh air of Blossomhurst, where they can romp and play with other youngsters from similarly cultured homes without always making her worry for fear of reckless automobile drivers.

2. The wives of several other successful young professional men, such as Dr. Arnold's wife, and Mrs. Alberts, wife of the district attorney, have become concerned over the need for giving their children a safe and healthful community life in which to develop, and as a result have decided to form a congenial colony at Blossomhurst.

3. With such residents as you and Mrs. Cricks, Dr. and Mrs. Arnold, and Mr. and Mrs. Alberts, we are beginning to develop a civic life through our churches, parent-teachers associations, and clubs, which in turn is leading to increased happiness and congenial friendships among the women folks, as well as desirable business and professional contacts for you men.

4. Blossomhurst has been laid out as a modern residential suburb on a gentle southern slope, 45 minutes' ride from the Loop by the Northwestern's trains, which operate on 15 minute schedule.

5. We have all improvements paid for, plus three Protestant and two Catholic churches, a new grammar school whose teachers must pass the requirements of the Chicago school system, and a specially trained kindergarten teacher for Janice.

6. There are a number of types of home from which to choose, such as Colonial and Old English, but all have deep lots and wide frontages—the smallest being 150 feet deep by 60 feet across—so that there will be ample lawn space for Tom and Janice to play in and a large plot for Mrs. Cricks' garden and flower beds.

7. In the past 18 months 187 families of the professional class have moved into Blossomhurst, and a fine civic life is developing.

8. A new 9-hole golf course is being opened next month only three miles west of Blossomhurst.

9. Property values are constantly increasing, as you are in an especially good position to know, yet the temporary lull in the real estate business enables us to give a much lower price now than would be possible a year hence when prosperity returns.

10. Since there are two homes in particular—a Colonial and an Old English—that I should like to show Mrs. Cricks and yourself next Sunday afternoon, I wonder if 2 o'clock would be the best hour for me to call for you? We can take Tom and Janice with us.

From the sales opening just presented, it will be apparent that the writer deems the safety and health of his children the strongest motive force for Mr. Cricks, and launches into it with the first sentence. Thereafter follow the usual selling points concerning property. By introducing Mrs. Cricks' name at the start, the salesman gains that confidence, or at least tolerance, which comes from knowing a mutual friend. It is always wise to utilize a mutual friend in the introduction, provided the salesman uses discretion. He should not say, unless it is really true, "Mr. Brewster told me to come over to see you."

Whenever it is possible the salesman should carry a sample of his product or a chart or prospectus containing specimen pages, if the product is a set of books. Then get the sample into the customer's hands as soon as convenient, for the sensory qualities arising help sell the client. Getting him to assist in the demonstration, or drive the automobile himself, has definite value in arousing desire. In addition, when the customer is looking at the sample, his attention is focussed thereon, and bluntly stated sales' arguments do not give rise to as much resistance. They fall upon a marginal field of his attention, so become suggestions. We have already considered the relative merits of suggestions and direct statements.

The value of sensory appeals in salesmanship, therefore, consists chiefly in the fact that more habits with pleasurable affective tone are aroused thereby, for sensory appeals are usually first or second degree stimuli. Sensory epithets cannot be combated very easily since they set off conditioned habits which are usually beyond the conscious control of the subject. Sensory appeals, as a consequence, operate as suggestions, and are accordingly invaluable aids of both the salesman and the advertiser.

When and How to Use Reason. Whenever a customer needs to be convinced, that is, whenever he is vacillating or debating with himself, it would be well for the salesman to employ reason. However, reason is ineffective unless the customer has a desire for the product. It makes little difference to me how good a violin you are selling if I don't play one. It may be imported, and twenty dollars cheaper than any other brand, and have a ten years' guarantee, etc., but I am still disinterested. The violin will never appeal to me until it is translated into a means of satisfying a habit or instinct that I possess. Once having perceived that with this violin and a few lessons, I can become the life of the party and thereby inflate my social ego, or that I can use it as an appropriate birthday gift for my musically inclined sweetheart, or that I can boast that it was once played by Kreisler, I am ready to listen to reason.

Such a desire is commonly called impulsive and is in the broadest sense the basis for almost all sales. Reasoning enters when it becomes necessary to justify our sensory preferences to ourselves and to others. It is then often designated as rationalization. In presenting the several occasions in selling where reason is demanded, we shall modify the scheme presented by Snow[32] in our following list:

(1) Reason should be used in selling to an expert.

(2) In introducing new goods reason is often valuable. In advertising we call such devices "educational copy" or "reason why" copy.

(3) When the price of a product seems too high to the customer.

(4) Whenever competition is great.

(5) Whenever the customer is of the type that prides himself on not being swayed by emotions, as in the case of professional buyers. To intimate that the client buys only on the basis of logic is a compliment in itself. Once the customer feels that you think he is logical in his choices, he is like the farmer who buys Penney's $1.25 overalls and thinks that all

---

"Have more than thou showest, speak less than thou knowest."
—Shakespeare

other prices will be equally as low. The buyer lowers his guard, as it were, and becomes susceptible to more direct compliments.

In selling as well as in advertising there are several types of evidence. First, the guarantee is probably the most effective instrument for producing belief. When an automobile tire is guaranteed for 25,000 miles of normal driving, the customer believes that the company must have tested the tire adequately before it was placed on the market, otherwise it could not afford to make such a statement. One of Chicago's largest department stores offers to refund the difference in price if any other store on the same day sells below its price. Because this offer is known to the people, they think this store gives the best bargains, and are more or less uncritical thereafter. Actually, other stores may undersell this one, but the majority never know it, and if they should, the first store might, as some occasionally demonstrate, reply to their requests for the article in question with, "Sorry, but we are all out of that size today."

The second type of evidence consists of tests. The consumer is permitted to have the article or book on trial. Or the company may conduct a public demonstration. In the realm of advertising we have noted many examples of this kind, as in Ripley's refereeing the "Blindfold Test" of Old Gold Cigarettes. The belief of the public depends largely on its confidence in the judges or the company. Occasionally, a firm may be able to cite the Bureau of Standards as its authority, or a famous auto racer who always had his car equipped with the tire being sold or the oil or gasoline in question.

The third variety of evidence consists of testimony. As a matter of fact, the reports of the Bureau of Standards could legitimately be classified here, though we generally refer to the statements of individuals. In the law courts these are called witnesses. In advertising and selling, widely known and respected persons are quoted, although the salesman in the individual case finds it even more effective to quote relatives and friends of his client. Patent medicine has been a great sponsor of the testimonial, although cold creams and cigarettes are doing the same thing nowadays. Even railroads and air lines are not averse to quoting famous passengers regarding the service or speed of their trains or airplanes.

In the use of reasons one should keep in mind the ensuing cautions:

(1) Reasons should be relevant. They should pertain definitely to the article or product at hand.

(2) Reasons should not be overstated. Excessive emphasis often defeats its own end. The understatement of a fact tends to promote belief more readily than its overstatement.

(3) Reasons should be chosen to suit the credulity of the customer. By this we mean that very unusual or surprising statements may cause disbelief, even though they are correct.

(4) Reasons should be effective sales points. To cite the great speed of a certain car which is being purchased by Mr. Brown for his daughter Betty may even detract from the ease in making the sale.

(5) Reasons should not be coercive. By this statement we mean the salesman should not elimate all choice of decision from his client. As Snow points out, it may be advisable to argue that a certain kind of automobile is the only one for the customer to buy, but he should be offered the option of several colors, styles, or models so that he feels that he has done the choosing. To rob a man of his right of choice, deflates his ego. The latter result leads to unpleasantness, which in turn defeats the sale.

(6) Reasons should be specific. The arguments in favor of a Ford must be different from the arguments for automobiles in general. True, if the customer isn't interested in automobiles as a class, he must be given "educational copy", but after he develops a liking for motor cars, he must be directed to a certain one of this type.

In the preceding discussion of when and how to use reason, therefore, we have seen that the wish for a product usually is impulsive because of the pleasure arising therefrom. The justification of the wish is one of the places where reason serves a useful purpose in the sale. We have presented five places, however, where the employment of reason is advantageous for the salesman, and have shown the six criteria of effective reasoning. The types of evidence which are available for the salesman have also been described. In the following section, however, we shall explain how reason may be short-circuited in salesmanship.

Short-circuiting Reason with Emotional Stimuli.

Suggestions are a type of stimuli that short-circuit reasoning. The clever slogan, "Say it with flowers", does not introduce a rational process. The so-called political "mud slinging" and "whispering" campaigns may undermine a very logical piece of statesmanship, or cause the defeat of its sponsor. This is one of the most frequent fallacies encountered in logic, and yet it is of tremendous power in the hands of an unscrupulous foe. It is called *ad hominem* arguing, the disparagement of a man's work or ideas by reference to his personal life, race, sex or creed. "What does a woman know about automobile motors?" a garage mechanic says disparagingly when a female driver has told him exactly what is wrong with her car. And to demonstrate the "negative protest" he examines several other things about the engine before he condescends to do what she has previously pointed out.

Woman suffrage was opposed by the Philippine Legislature and would undoubtedly have been disdained in 1931 except for the fact that one legislator short-circuited a lengthy debate on the matter by saying the United States would deem them entirely too backward a people to have self-government unless the Philippine women were given the franchise. This idea became tied up with their national spirit and undermined much of the opposition.

A piano salesman has stated that he is engaged in "merchandising heart beats and not so many pounds of ivory and wire," for he found that a poor couple wished to buy a piano in order "to make Mary a lady." One of our shaving cream manufacturers stresses the fact that the cap cannot fall off the tube, which is stressing a point of efficiency rather than the lather value of the cream. A light and power company began a campaign to sell vacuum cleaners, making its appeals to women. Although many cleaners were sold, it launched a new campaign depicting the husband in his modern office in contrast to a picture of his wife with dustpan and broom sweeping the floor and sending dust everywhere. Underneath the double cut it ran the caption "Why not equip your wife's office like your own?" The second type of advertisement sold more vacuum cleaners than the first, because it directed an appeal to the husband's love and sense of fair play. It didn't emphasize at length the virtues of the particular vacuum cleaner displayed.

In Mueller's cartoon on the next page we see how effectively emotional appeals can short-circuit a slower and more difficult logical process. In business, advertising, and public speaking these appeals are frequently employed. They usually produce action more quickly than the reasoning method. A variation of this principle is illustrated in the example of the housewife who came home from shopping, having purchased a 110-piece set of dishes. She realized, of course, that her husband might be in an irritable mood after his day at the office, and might vent his ire by choosing the opposite course of action to that which she followed. So she began the discussion in this fashion: "I'm afraid I did something rather silly today. Of course, we do entertain a great deal and our other dishes are becoming broken so that the set is hardly complete any more, but I saw a lovely style of dishes at Field's this afternoon on special sale this week and with an extra $10 discount for today only. It does seem rather silly, though, when I realize

EXHIBIT 34. A good example to show how reason can be short-circuited by emotional appeals. (Courtesy of *The Chicago Daily News, Inc.*)

that we hardly have space to put them in this apartment, even though they were an extra special bargain."

If the husband is irritated at hearing what she has done he will want to disagree with her, and almost without thinking he may launch upon a defense of the purchase of the set just because she has taken the opposite view.   An intelligent sales-man or housewife can utilize this method with great success. In salesmanship, moreover, the speaker may advance a selling point early in the interview which toward the close he ascribes

to the customer. If the point is a good one, and if the salesman is discreet, he may get the customer to believing that he
sponsored the idea.

"I agree with Mr. Brown," says the public speaker, "that
it would be a wise act on our part to defer consideration of
this motion until our next meeting." Even if Mr. Brown has
not definitely committed himself, if he isn't exactly opposed
to this action, and if he has been speaking before the group
just previously, he feels complimented that credit for an idea
has been ascribed to him, and may marshall his votes in support of the motion. He probably isn't sure of just what he
said, anyway, and gladly takes public praise in this manner.
The method is an ingenious one and frequently makes men
defenders of a cause without their knowing just how it all
came about.

From the psychological viewpoint, therefore, the task of
short-circuiting reason with emotional stimuli consists chiefly
of diverting the customer's attention by a quick portrayal of
the function of the merchandise as it affects a fundamental
motive base, particularly love, self esteem, or rivalry. Thereafter the focus of the customer's attention is kept upon the
goal attained by use of the product instead of on the product
itself. The merchandise becomes, therefore, simply a means
to an end, and the salesman keeps the attention of his customer on the end result.

Gauging the "Psychological Moment". In popular
speech the 'psychological moment' refers to that point in the
demonstration at which the customer is most desirous of the
article. It denotes, therefore, the time to close the sale. How
to determine it is a matter of considerable adeptness in selling.
There may, moreover, be several psychological moments. A
customer may want the goods, then have his enthusiasm ebb,
then find desire become strong again. If we had a psychological sales thermometer which we could insert in the customer's mouth, and which had been calibrated for such a situa-

tion, we would have no difficulty reading the degree of interest felt by the client in our merchandise.

In actuality, however, the situation is not so simple. We must note how interestedly the customer handles the article. Is he actively entering into the demonstration, or does he sit passively looking on? Does he ask questions, or is he content to let us continue our sales monologue? Does he sit in a relaxed manner, with feet crossed, or is he leaning forward with tense muscles? As one becomes actively interested in a thing, one grows tense. The experience of the audience at a prize fight or moving picture show illustrates this fact. As a general rule, therefore, the customer who is relaxed is not greatly interested, though there are exceptions.

If the customer is rather phlegmatic, the question must be employed to sound the depth of his interest. We have previously discussed the methods of phrasing the question. "Which style do you prefer?" is a suggestive or leading question, since it assumes he prefers one. "How much do you think you can use?" "How soon will you want it delivered?" "When will it be most convenient for you to take the physical examination?" These queries serve to obtain indexes of the customer's state of mind, and illustrate the "minor decision" type of closing. Some salesmen use the minor decision by asking for a trial order. The average dealer is not very loath to cooperate to this extent. But a trial order of a half-dozen lot simply indicates that the sale was not properly completed, and is a poor substitute for the real thing. The dealer and his clerks will not push the trial order goods because the stock is incomplete. Clerks will, rather, bring out the old line when customers inquire for the type of article covered by the trial order. The latter stock remains on the shelves, therefore, and becomes proof for the dealer that the goods will not move rapidly. The salesman has probably checked his opportunity for future business.

In concluding our discussion of the means by which the

salesman can gauge the psychological moment, it is well to repeat that there may be several psychological moments. If possible, however, the salesman should endeavor to close the interview when the first of these favorable moments is detected. In ascertaining its presence, he should closely observe the signs of interest and cooperation on the part of his customer, and use the leading question in taking soundings. It is advisable to close whenever possible. Additional selling points may be made after the name is on the dotted line, in case they have not been presented up to that point.

Ten Axioms for the Salesman. In numerical order we shall list ten outstanding rules whose observance will greatly increase the number of sales.

(1) *Memorize your opening and closing.* It gives you confidence and frees your attention during the two most critical stages in the sale.

(2) *Dominate the interview.* Don't slip into a defensive role. If your customer asks you a question, he is robbing you of the offensive. "Which color do you think is better?" he may inquire. If you attempt to debate the issue mentally, you become slightly detached, therefore, unobservant of him. Instead, parry his query with the 'reversible why', and ask, "Well, that depends on your tastes. How is your house decorated?" At once you have him answering, while you are interrogator. You can be planning your next step while he is thinking of a reply. The art of discreetly reversing questions can become habitual. It warrants thorough mastery by the salesman. The habitual tendency is to respond, as is demonstrated by the youngster who can hardly resist answering if he has any information whatsoever. The salesman must train himself to respond to a question with a counter question. He can then make exceptions of the few cases where he really has factual matter which should be given when requested.

In an analysis of the time spent in the sale of an article to farmers, the sales manager found that those men who received the largest commission checks spent much less time in the interview. It doesn't pay as a general rule to let the customer tell about his troubles and prolong the demonstration. If he is ready to buy, he will do so quickly. If he isn't ready, then an hour with him is unavailing.

(3) *Hit the bull's-eye with your appeals.* Don't begin with trivialities. These may be the final determinants of the sale, separating your product from competing brands, but at the start you must whet the customer's appetite for the general class of articles which you are selling.

(4) *Use samples and your pencil.* The samples not only increase the interest of your customer, and give him first degree stimuli to action, but they hold his attention so that your direct statements are reacted to with less resistance— hence, as suggestions. If you are selling a service or insurance, get your pencil out and do the figuring in front of the client. His attention is on the page, so again he reacts to your comments much as to suggestions. In figuring, go slowly so that he keeps ahead of you in the addition and subtraction. It makes him feel superior, which is a pleasant mental state. Moreover, he tends to believe the results more readily when he arrived at them ahead of you, because they seem more original to him. Then, too, he doesn't lose count and find it necessary to take your word and conclusions, both of which tend to arouse unpleasantness.

(5) *Employ specificity in words.* Don't use third degree stimuli when you can substitute second degree instead. At the restaurant the waitress asks, "What will you have for dessert, sir?" Dessert is a third degree or generic stimulus word. It doesn't make you very hungry. You counter, "Oh, I don't know. What do you have?" "Pie, cake, ice cream . . ." "I believe I'll try some pie. What kind of pie have you?" The reader will note that the word "pie" is also rather vague. "We have cherry, raspberry, custard, rhubarb, apple, and

mince." These are second degree stimuli that can make saliva flow. As a result, you find that you desire one of them.

If you have sold magazine subscriptions to 11 housewives this week, use the word "eleven". It creates a feeling of truth. If your record is so poor that you hesitate to mention it, then steer away from having to do so. Don't exaggerate, and avoid generalities and superlatives.

(6) *Keep the customer in an agreeable state of mind*. We advance or expand when we feel happy. Pleasant stimuli cause us to desire them. Unpleasant stimuli cause us to shun them. If we feel unpleasant, we are in a general state of avoidance; hence, we will not buy. Discreet compliments are invaluable in making a customer feel good. A Fuller Brush salesman of my acquaintance always jots down the eye color of the boy or girl in the home where he is now calling. A month or two later he re-calls, and asks, "Where is that little girl with those big blue eyes?" This is a compliment, obviously, and the mother feels pleased. The salesman has sold himself, so it probably will not be very difficult to dispose of his merchandise, especially if the housewife has need for brushes.

(7) *Keep the customer in an agreeing state of mind*. At frequent intervals ply him with questions. He gets used to responding affirmatively. Having said yes for ten to twenty times prior to the closing, the slight habit of affirmation renders it more difficult for him to use the negative at the finish.

(8) *Don't permit a customer to say no*. Use the leading question so that the suggestion involved produces an affirmative answer. As long as a customer doesn't say no, the salesman can keep on with his interview. If he has a good product, he may sell it before he finishes. On the other hand, if he lets the customer say no, then he finds it difficult to continue with his sales talk.

(9) *Keep closing*. Don't feel that you must deliver a good speech simply because you have it, if the customer evinces

great desire for the product. Let him sign for it on your opening sentence if he'll do so. Too many salesmen avoid the closing so long that initial interest on the part of the customer has ebbed. While keeping the customer in an agreeing state, slip in a "feeler" question to ascertain his degree of interest. Occasionally a customer needs no demonstration whatever. If he is compelled to listen to one, he may become disgruntled.

(10) *Leave an opening for a return call.* We have seen that the survey of 1,000 retailers showed that they don't buy until the fourth or fifth interview. A salesman can approach a man with whom he parted on friendly relations, and re-open the interview. He should, however, always have a new point, or an additional plan to offer his customer so that he doesn't become boresome.

The writer has gone out to interview customers who had actually thrown out previous salesmen, only to find them as friendly as one could wish. The reason is chiefly this: these men felt ashamed of their actions after the salesman had departed, and in order to "square" themselves with their consciences and the company represented by the mistreated salesmen, resolved if they ever saw them again they'd make it up to the men or their company. Parents occasionally illustrate this same behavior when they too severely criticize or chastise their children. A few hours later they begin to feel uncomfortable, and may make awkward proffers of reconciliation. Later they may overly indulge their youngsters, a form of action which is a salve to their consciences.

If the salesmen had argued with their evictors, then this reverse swing of the pendulum would not have occurred, for the latter would have felt only that they had squared accounts in a fair fight; therefore, no shame would have resulted.

Whenever the interview begins to get away from the salesman's control, he may find himself engaging in arguments. An altercation with his customer is almost always fatal. He loses a possible sale. When a man argues with his customer, he intimates that the latter is wrong, which deflates the buyer's ego and produces displeasure. This result explains our frequent dislike for those we are debating. Some people, indeed, find it almost impossible to shake hands with their verbal enemies and resume friendly relations.

A resort to humor is one of the best devices for stopping an argument for people cannot laugh together at the same time they are angry with each other. If the salesman had dominated the interview and used his applied psychology, moreover, he would never have allowed a situation to arise which would have led to debate. An argument is an indication of a double flaw in the sales talk. It shows first that the salesman erred in his presentation, and secondly, that he entered into the argument after he had permitted his client to start it.

The preceding ten psychological axioms for the salesman are intended not alone for those who sell merchandise but also for the salesmen of ideas, such as public speakers and politicians, educators and clergymen. The psychological principles underlying them have been explained in greater detail throughout the preceding chapters. The men and women who incorporate these axioms into their technique of dealing with people in the sales situation will find that they avoid many of the pitfalls besetting the uninitiated.

REFERENCES

1 ANNESS, M. E., *Song of Metamoris* (Caxton, 1966)
2 APPEL & STRECKER, *Discovering Ourselves* (Macmillan, 1964)
3 ASHBY, W. R., *Design for a Brain* (Wiley, 1964)
4 BARCLAY, G. W., *Techniques of Population Analysis* (Wiley, 1960)
5 BEASLEY, N., *Main Street Merchant* (McGraw-Hill, 1948)
6 BETTGER, F., *How I Raised Myself from Failure to Success in Selling* (Prentice-Hall, 1950)
7 BIDERMAN & ZIMMER, *Manipulation of Behavior* (Wiley, 1964)
8 BORDEN, N. H., *Advertising, Text and Cases* (Irwin, 1950)
9 CATTELL, R. B., *Personality & Motivation* (World Book, 1959)
10 CRANE, G. W., *"How To Sell Professional Services"* (Cal Dental Magazine, May, 1955)
11 DANIEL & LOUTTIT, *Professional Problems,* (Prentice-Hall, 1955)
12 DROKE, M., *How To Handle People* (Garden City, 1942)
13 EDWARDS, A. L., *Techniques of Attitude Scale Construction* (Appleton-Century-Crofts, 1957)

14 EPSTEIN, B. W., *People Are Our Business* (Lippincott, 1947)
15 FALTZ, E., *The Slogan in Modern Advertising* (N. Y. Assoc. Nat. Adv., 1949)
16 FLEMING, C. M., *Teaching* (Wiley, 1958)
17 GITTLER, J. B., *Review of Sociology* (Wiley, 1959)
18 GOODE, K. M., & ZENN, K., *Showmanship in Business* (Harper, 1947)
19 GRAY, J. S., *Psychology Applied to Human Affairs* (McGraw-Hill, 1954)
20 HARRIMAN, P. L., GREENWOOD, L. L., & SKINNER, C. E., *Psychology in Nursing Practice* (Macmillan, 1942)
21 HEPNER, H. W., *Psychology Applied to Life and Work* (Prentice-Hall, 1950)
22 HEYEL, C., *How To Create Job Enthusiasm* (McGraw-Hill, 1942)
23 JOSEY, C. C., *Psychology and Successful Living* (Scribner's, 1958)
24 KRIEGER, W. M., *Complete Funeral Management* (Prentice-Hall, 1962)
25 LEE, G. W., "Our Weekly Sales Record Was Broken Four Times" *(Printers' Ink*, Dec. 27, 1928).
26 McGEHEE & THAYER, *Training in Business & Industry* (Wiley, 1962)
27 MINNICK, W. C., *The Art of Persuasion* (Houghton-Mifflin, 1959)
28 MOLONEY, J. C., *Understanding the Japanese Mind* (Philos. Libr., 1954)
29 MOORE, T. V., *Driving Forces of Human Nature and Their Adjustment* (Greene & Stratton, 1948)
30 *Printers' Ink Sales Promotion Idea Book* (Funk & Wagnalls, 1950)
31 REMMERS, H. H., *Opinion & Attitude Measurement* (Harper, 1954)
32 SNOW, A. J., *Psychology in Business Relations* (McGraw-Hill, 1930)
33 SORENSON, H., *Psychology in Education* (McGraw-Hill, 1954)
34 SEEHAFER & LAEMMAR, *Successful Television & Radio Advertising* (McGraw-Hill, 1960)
35 STARCH, D., *Principles of Advertising* (Shaw, 1923)
36 STRAND, C. B., *Salesmanship for Vocational and Personal Use* (Gregg, 1949)
37 "The Salesman's Repeat Calls" *(Adv. & Selling*, Jan. 30, 1925).
38 TREDGOLD, R. F., *Human Relations in Modern Industry* (Intern. U. Press, 1950)
39 VISCARDI, H., *Give Us The Tools* (Eriksson-Taplinger, 1960)
40 WATKINS, J. L., *The 100 Greatest Advertisements* (Moore, 1949)
41 WITTMACK, C. E., "We Tell Our Dealers: Sell Our Goods At No Profit" (Printers' Ink, Dec. 27, 1928)
42 WILBUR, W. H., *Russian Communism - Challenge & Fraud* (Caxton, 1966)

Note the "plus value" injected into selling berries as demonstrated by the Snyder Farms in the following slip that is packed in each quart box:

TO OUR CUSTOMERS:

Strawberries must be picked by hand. We believe that strawberries must be picked by clean hands since they are, for the most part, eaten raw, except for the minimum cleansing provided by cold water.

This is to inform you that no one is ever allowed to enter the field to pick our berries unless first meeting our rigid requirements of cleansing their hands by hot water and soap.

We believe you and all other discriminating people, will appreciate this because such care is not always required by those who place strawberries on the market.

SNYDER FARMS

CHAPTER VIII

THE FIELDS AND FUNCTIONS OF ADVERTISING

Although Dr. Samuel Johnson in 1759 made the statement in his *Weekly Idler* that "the trade of advertising is now so near perfection that it is not easy to make any improvements,"* we have seen recently the utilization of art and illustration, and the employment of color in a fashion that would have dazzled the minds of earlier generations. From our newspapers and car advertisements, our magazines and billboards, sky-writing airplanes, the government postman, and our radios come announcements of some new product or a reaffirmation of the virtues of a familiar one.

Advertising may involve the whole function of selling, or it may lend itself as an aid in producing sales. The latter is its more usual purpose. In either role it has not the plasticity of the salesman, and must make general appeals to a class of buyers, without attempting to satisfy the individual differences of any single person. Although it is so widespread in its distribution and so much money is spent annually in advertising appropriations, the consumer usually has been able to obtain goods cheaper than if advertising were omitted. It may sound paradoxical, but it is true that by spending money in advertising the demand for a product can be so increased as to warrant large scale production which, in turn, brings back to the consumer the article at a lower price than he could have procured it otherwise. Seasonal fluctuations in demand can be smoothed out, as in the orange and raisin trade, with a resulting economy in distribution charges.

In some cases, as in present cigarette advertising, a market may approach the saturation point, after which one cigarette company simply launches an advertising campaign which pulls

Selling Forces (Curtis Publishing Co., Philadelphia), p. 13.

(The following typical newspaper column shows how I try to "sell" teen-agers on going to college.)

WORRY CLINIC By George W. Crane, Ph.D., M.D.

Case B-464: Don D., aged 18, is ready for college.

"But, Dr. Crane," he protested, "I don't know what courses to take.

"My father is a very succesful dentist. And I know he would like me to go to dental college.

"But I don't feel any great fondness for dentistry. However, I don't dislike it, either.

"And I don't have any great desire for any other profession, either, so what should I do? Stay home or go to college?"

IF YOU GRADUATE from a large high school with creditable grades, then that means you have an I. Q. that will permit you to carry college work.

So try to take at least one year of college, as the minimum, for Dr. Paul C. Glick, of our Census Bureau, showed that one year of college will add $25,000 to your lifetime earnings.

If you can devote only one or two years to college, then a Business College will normally give you a far better training for practical success than one or two years of Liberal Arts.

AS REGARDS liking for one subject versus another, that is largely a matter of habit.

At birth, you never liked ham or eggs or steak or bread or potatoes or any single type of food, with the exception of sugar.

Those other food preferences were learned. You were in a cheery, jolly family group at the table when Mother slipped you the first taste of potatoes or spinach.

After several repetitions on other days, you finally transferred your generalized emotional mood to the new food. It now tastes good whereas it was a neutral flavor at the outset.

MOST OF OUR college students don't know what career they will enter, even when they have spent two years in college.

So pick out the one that will permit you to render a valuable public service.

"Plant roses," as Lincoln advised, "where thistles grew before."

Then study for that career. As you become acquainted with its vocabulary and techniques, and as you make good grades therein, you will begin to like it.

Your fondness for a trade or profession will follow the very same pattern as your original development of an appetite for spinach or steak.

FURTHERMORE, ANY professional training will pay dividends all your life, even if you don't stay in that field forever.

Many dentists thus have attained eminence in politics, including the U. S. Senate.

Zane Grey was our most famous writer of tales of the Western plains, and he started out as a dentist.

Other dentists are heads of corporations, industrialists, etc., so don't feel that you cannot change, even after you obtain your doctor's degree.

But the usual reaction is to like your profession by the time you acquire reasonable proficiency thereat.

SO STUDY for something, even though you change your destination, for your education is listless and lacking motivation if it has no specific goal.

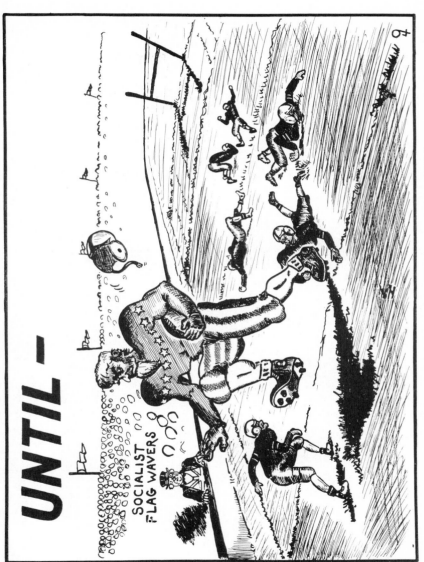

(For a fuller comprehension of this scene, see Chapter XIX.)

The Worry Clinic

Dr. George W. Crane, Ph.D., M.D.

Case N - 452: Hilda H., 43 years old, feels crushed because she says her husband has "suddenly" developed an infatuation for his secretary.

But these infatuations are usually not "sudden" affairs.

You wives just suddenly learn of them!

They have been in the making for months or even years.

Hilda's husband later confessed to me that he had been toying with the idea of this affair for five years.

For Hilda was a fat, complacent wife. She seemed to think all her husband needed to keep him snoring contentedly in his twin bed was just an extra helping of his favorite dessert at dinner.

Wives, get rid of that notion that the best way to a man's heart is via his stomach!

For it isn't in the kitchen that you lose your mates, but in your bedroom.

Thousands of divorces could thus be stopped if you wives past 40 would descend en masse on a city burlesque show and take a few lessons!

For how do you expect a fat, stodgy wife to excite a middle aged husband who associates glamor with slender figures!

And you can't feel like a sports roadster with the chassis of a truck.

Nor can you exude seductive charm if your tummy equals your bust line.

Many a wife has thrown her husband into a platonic state when she removes her girdle and he sees the waves of blubber suddenly cascade over her hips.

Girls, if you look like a waddling walrus as you jiggle down the street, you may arouse the affection accorded a "good old motherly soul" but not that generated by a siren or modern Cleopatra.

When your husband attempts to restore some of the courtship memories that have been in cold storage for maybe 20 years and thus tries to hold you on his lap, do you feel like a hippopotamus?

Or, if he steers you across the dance floor, is it like cavorting with a jumbo elephant?

Obviously, I'm needling you fat females, for you are flirting with divorce every day unless you wake up to the facts of life.

Your children usually aren't the ones who are sadly lacking in the "facts of life."

No, indeed! It is you complacent, fat wives in modern America who need to be jolted.

So get hep! Send for the booklet "How to Lose 10 Lbs. in 10 days," enclosing a stamped return envelope, plus 20c.

Use it to insure a PERMANENTLY happy marriage and thus spare your innocent children the emotional insecurity of divorced parents.

customers away from its rivals. At a later date the rivals reciprocate. Another characteristic of modern advertising is the fact that the first sponsor of a new type of goods must devote considerable money to educational copy, teaching the public the value of the new product and its many uses. Thereafter imitations may enter the field and capitalize on the first company's expenditures.

The Fields of Advertising. In viewing the things advertised we may make a four-fold classification, following the divisions listed by Moss[27]

(1) *A community.* The various business clubs in a city, such as Kiwanis, Rotary, Exchange, Lions, and the Chamber of Commerce are usually concerned to some extent in seeing that their city is gaining adequate recognition. Free land is offered new industries for the purpose not only of increasing the number of employed persons and accelerating the business turnover in the community, but of adding to the population and advertising the town. Land booms and gold rushes are evidences of the power of advertising when directed to a community. Summer and winter resorts derive their patrons largely as a consequence of advertising. In America, for example, Florida and California are rival wintering places which are actively engaged in competitive advertising for the resort trade during the cold months.

(2) *A firm or organization.* Banks have entered the field of advertising to an increasing degree in recent years, and have slowly been modifying their methods so that they now employ color. Financial advertising has been one of the most conservative types that we have. It formerly consisted of space in newspapers and magazines with only the name of the financial institution, thus illustrating what is called "good will" advertising. Now the various services rendered by banks, and their equipment and personnel are announced to

---

"The most truthful part of a newspaper is the advertisements."
—Jefferson

the public in some of the blank space that would formerly have surrounded their names only. Even religious institutions and organizations have entered the advertising field on a mild scale.

(3) *An individual.* We have already devoted a chapter to this subject. Actresses, actors, and politicians hire publicity agents to devise schemes by which the former can gain publicity write-ups in newspapers and magazines. The managers of many pugilists have a propensity for the same thing, and get occasional newspaper accounts of their proteges into the sport pages between fights. The build-up of Cassius Clay is due to newspaper accounts of him, since the majority of his followers have probably never seen him in person.

(4) *Goods and services.* Here belong the great majority of advertising appropriations. The reader is familiar with the ingenious methods and instruments by which he becomes acquainted with the merchandise with which this country teems. Advertising slogans and trademarks are far more familiar to the American boy and girl, as well as to his parents, than are Shakespeare's works or the Bible. Names of merchandise are made of nonsense syllables and thrown into the visual field so frequently that they take on meaning and he considers them a part of his regular vocabulary. A large number of Americans could not tell whether "kodak" or "camera" was the term employed in the dictionary to describe the product.

In our survey of the fields of advertising, therefore, we find that four general categories are sufficiently comprehensive to cover the various kinds of advertising commonly encountered. These include advertising a community, an organization, an individual, and goods or services.

Methods of Research in Advertising. Four general methods are usually employed in advertising research, of which the first is least valuable.

(1) *The historical method.* This one involves a study of the mortality rates among various past companies with reference to the types of advertising they employed. The inference is that those which are still in business today probably pursued a better advertising plan. So many other factors are involved, however, that we cannot depend greatly upon this method.

(2) *The statistical method.* This method involves the collection of data regarding the number of telephones, automobiles, minor children, farms, etc. in a region for purposes of adapting the advertising funds to the needs and media thereof. If a foreign element is present in considerable numbers the language factor enters in. Communities which have a high degree of illiteracy offer problems necessitating the use of simple language. A few years ago Kitson[22] made a survey of Chicago newspapers regarding the vocabulary employed and found that one Chicago newspaper had 70 per cent more words over two syllables long than did the *Chicago American.* His work led him to the conclusion that the advertiser who wished to run his advertisements in a given magazine should read the fiction in that magazine, for therein lay the key to the vocabulary level of the people who bought that magazine.

(3) *The survey.* Under this heading come those attempts to find out in advance what people will like by interviewing a sample group of the type to be solicited by the advertising. Special questionnaires are sent out to certain individuals chosen in advance, or a house-to-house canvass is made by the investigator, who questions the housewives on their preferences and buying habits regarding the given line of merchandise.

The "test run" of a certain advertisement in a try-out market is really a form of survey. Firms who do national advertising usually pick out a few centers which they call try-out markets. These must be quite similar in regard to population,

---

"Herein the only royal road to fame and fortune lies:
Put not your trust in vinegar—molasses catches flies."
—Eugene Field

class of people, number of industries, etc. There should be a variety of activities, and competing brands should not be running intensive campaigns in any of these test markets. College towns would of course not be representative. After the selection of the try-out markets, different advertisements are run, and the results are compared to determine which produced the greatest returns. The winner is then employed in the national advertising campaign.

The test run is usually considered the best method of determining the effectiveness of an advertisement, although it can be supplemented in many ways. The opinion of the salesmen may be sought, as well as the advice of a few typical customers. Sometimes the customer is asked to write the copy, or contests may be announced in which selling points are the basis of the award. Direct mail tests may also be undertaken, and the copy and cuts subjected to laboratory investigation. The fact that the test run is considered the best method at present, however, simply indicates that the subject of advertising is still in a trial and error state. If a physician had to test his medicines on a dog every time he was called upon to treat a human being, we would think he was not very well prepared for his profession.

While Dr. S. N. Stevens was teaching psychology at Northwestern, he argued this point with professional advertisers. He challenged the latter to bring out ten advertisements with whose results they were familiar, and he would rank them in their order of merit. His opponents accepted his offer, and placed ten such specimens along the wall in front of him, having mixed them in the row. Professor Stevens asked the group to which each advertisement was directed, and the purpose of the advertiser in each case. Then he went along with his pad and pencil estimating their psychological merits. He ranked them in the following order as matched by their actual pulling power: 1:2:3:4:5:6:7:8:10:9, erring only in respect to the two weakest specimens. It requires a scientific knowledge of human behavior to do this sort of thing, but that knowledge is not incapable of attainment.

(4) *The laboratory method.* There are two subheads to this form of research. (a) *Testing efficiency by returns.* In an analysis of over 3,000,000 inquiries from 2,339 advertisements during a four-year period, Starch found that the number of replies varied almost according to the size of the advertisement, although the smaller advertisements had a slight advantage. Those inserted on right-hand pages brought 14.1 per cent more replies than similar advertisements inserted on left-hand pages, while colored advertisements elicited 56.7 per cent more replies per 100,000 of the circulation than did black and white advertisements of similar size and character.

In an investigation of the advertising results during the various months of the year, Falk[12] discovered the data presented in Exhibit 35. The reciprocal number for each month has been added by Hepner to make it possible to compare advertisements. If the average for the 12 months is divided

MONTH	INDEX NUMBER	RECIPROCAL
January	184	0.543
February	157	0.637
March	107	0.934
April	77	1.300
May	67	1.490
June	65	1.540
July	76	1.316
August	92	1.087
September	95	1.052
October	92	1.087
November	89	1.123
December	99	1.010

EXHIBIT 35. Index of inquiries on one company's advertisements according to the month of insertion. (Average for 12 months = 100).

"If you don't advertise yourself you will be advertised by your loving enemies."   —Elbert Hubbard by the index number for any month, we obtain the figure listed in the column entitled "Reciprocal". Thus, an advertisement in January which produces 1,000 inquiries is not nearly as good as one in July that also elicits 1,000 responses. For example, January : July :: 0.543 : 1.316. The July advertisement is more than twice as effective as the January advertisement.

An additional interesting result of this survey is the fact that "If an ad in the *Iowa Homestead* produces three times as many inquiries when run in January as when run in June, then a *Ladies' Home Journal* ad will also produce three times as many inquiries when run in January as when run in June." The curves for the different magazines, based on their indexes of returns, are almost identical.

In order to count the returns from any single advertisement, the advertiser usually "keys" the coupon with a different box number or the name of another department of the firm. Some companies have found, moreover, that one-third of the persons who ask for free samples are children or persons who like to have mail come to them. These "rubbernecks", as the advertising men call them, can be eliminated by charging for the sample or booklet. The price, however, must be only a nominal one to cover the cost alone.

(b) *Scientific experiments.* These constitute one form of the laboratory method whose results should ultimately enable advertisers to know in advance how well an advertisement will "pull". The example of Professor Stevens shows what may be hoped for in this regard. These scientific experiments fall under several headings, and may be performed for both the copy and the cuts separately, as well as for the two when combined in the final advertisement.

(1) *The order-of-merit test.* Here a number of observers rank the illustrations or copy in regard to effectiveness in some special regard, as attention attracting value, convincingness, pleasantness, etc. The results of all such judgments are

then combined to give the consensus report. The method is similar to that employed in deciding college debates.

(2) *The recall value.* Different styles of type, copy, or illustrations may be presented to the subjects for definite brief exposures, as in a tachistoscope, and at a later date the subjects are given a memory test to determine how many of the things seen have been retained.

(3) *The recognition value.* The ease of reading various sizes of type during very short exposure times belongs here. Then, too, this heading covers a form of memory test in which the previously observed advertisements are mixed with many others, and the subject attempts to pick out the ones which he has seen before from those that are strange. This is the multiple choice, or age of stimulus method which we described in Chapter II.

(4) *The association method.* This procedure is often of value in determining the choice of a new name or trade-mark. A number of words are listed which the subject looks at and hears pronounced aloud. He is to tell what each makes him think of. These names, of course, are usually novel constructions of nonsense syllables, but some of them give rise to pleasant feelings which others do not. This method is akin to the order-of-merit procedure described above.

(5) *Eye fixation.* By noting the eye movements and the time spent by a subject on one portion of an advertisement versus another, or on one advertisement instead of another, the observer can obtain a fair indication of the relative attention attracting and holding merits of copy and illustrations, or of different colors in contrast to black and white.

One of the chief difficulties with the laboratory method is its demand for a certain amount of apparatus, and an operator who is versed in scientific technique. Another requisite is a type of subject who is comparable to the group for whom the advertisement is to be run. The language facility and extra intelligence of the college students and advertising associates who have frequently employed the laboratory method, make it unwise to generalize from their results and assume that the average American will perform similarly.

In concluding our discussion of the methods of research in advertising, therefore, we can repeat our fourfold classification, namely, the historical, the statistical, the survey, and the laboratory methods. The present superiority of the test run does not represent the ultimate goal of advertising, although it is deemed the most adequate at the present time. The laboratory method should ultimately forge into the van of advertising procedure.

The Relative Advantages of Various Advertising Media. Certain readily apparent virtues of one advertising medium over another are known to even the laymen. Newspapers are superior to magazines for local firms. Banks, department stores and other retail establishments need city advertising media. Handbills, direct-mail letters, radio skits, theater programs, church bulletins and papers, car ads, and billboards are of value to the local business house. Magazine advertisements are usually of a general nature to fit the needs of dealers and consumers all over the country, and are the manufacturers' advertising field, although manufacturers also enter into newspaper and radio advertising as well. We shall discuss radio advertising later in the chapter.

More money is spent for newspaper advertising than for any other sort. The newspaper offers several advantages not given by the magazine. In the first place, it is read by all classes of people, whereas many magazines have a definite class appeal. In this connection we might distinguish between "flat" and "standard" magazines. Those in which advertisements appear on the same page with reading matter, as in *The Saturday Evening Post,* are called "flat", while magazines of the type of *The National Geographic* are "standard". The latter are of the sandwich variety, with advertising bunched in the front and back thirds of the magazines, and reading matter massed in between.

Another superiority of the newspaper is the fact that it carries timely advertisements. If the weather forecaster predicts rain tomorrow or next day, the retailer can feature umbrellas and raincoats in tomorrow morning's paper. While newspapers seldom employ color in the way that magazines do, they can remind people more frequently and repeatedly.

In his experience with newspapers, Haldeman-Julius found that the largest returns came within one week after insertion of the advertisement. With a typical weekly magazine, such as *Liberty,* he found that an insertion would more than "pay out" in the first three weeks, although the advertisement "pulled" regularly for nearly ninety days, and then dropped to from one to five dollars' worth of orders a day for another month or so, finally dwindling to a dollar every now and then for even two years' time. A monthly magazine, as the *Review of Reviews,* pulled much more slowly than either the weekly or a newspaper. It brought orders steadily for three months, usually paying out in the first thirty days. The reason for the slower returns from magazines, especially of the monthly type, is the fact that they lie about on the table or lounge for weeks and months.

In his advertising Haldeman-Julius used the same kind of advertisement in practically all the media he employed. He stated that he was willing to spend two to two and a half cents to sell each 5-cent Little Blue Book. Concerning the difference between large and small city newspapers he says, "I can make the general statement from a wide experience that advertising a mail-order product in small-city newspapers *never* pays. Only newspapers in the larger cities—New York, Boston, Philadelphia, Baltimore, Chicago, Los Angeles, etc.—are good."[18]

Sales resistance is the triumph of mind over chatter.

We are presenting in Exhibit 36 the actual receipts which he obtained from a number of different advertising media. The reader can procure an idea therefrom of the advertising space rates, as well as the relative merits of different media carrying the same type of advertisement.

ADVERTISING MEDIA	DATE	SPACE	COST	RETURNS
New York Times Book Review...10-30-27		2 pages	$2,500	$ 4,348.89
Mid-Week Pictorial 9-15-27		2 pages	300	924.56
New York Daily News 1-30-27		1 page	1,400	2,789.49
Physical Culture .... Oct. 1927		1 page	800	1,759.19
Smart Set ....Nov. 1927		1 page	850	1,888.35
Pathfinder 4-11-25		1 page	1,000	2,763.66
Life 9-26-23		1 page	650	1,215.23
Harper's Monthly ....Oct. 1926		1 page	200	382.15
Review of Reviews.............Oct. 1925		1 page	325	642.68
Golden Book ....Oct. 1925		4 pages	800	1,927.48
Liberty 1- 9-26		2 pages	5,000	13,321.31
Chicago Tribune 2-10-26		1 page	1,300	2,884.36
The Nation 9-10-24		1 page	150	349.29
Hearst's International ....Feb. 1925		1 page	1,000	2,369.12

EXHIBIT 36. Actual receipts obtained by Mr. Haldeman-Julius from various advertising media.

In Exhibit 37 are presented the day by day returns obtained by Haldeman-Julius* from insertions in the *Chicago Tribune*, *Liberty*, and the *Review of Reviews*. These figures illustrate the comments we have previously made relating to the rapidity of returns from the different types of media.

In the field of direct-mail advertising, Maddy[26] found that the permit card was more efficient than the regular government postal card. For each of seven consecutive weeks 26,000 pieces of mail were set aside for test purposes (13,000 govern-

*All these tables are reproduced through courtesy of Mr. Haldeman-Julius.

"Men, like bullets, go farthest when they are smoothest." —J. P. Richter
"What is a cynic? A man who knows the price of everything, and the value of nothing."   —Oscar Wilde

MEDIUM AND DATE OF INSERTION	DAILY RETURNS												
	1ST DAY	2ND DAY	3RD DAY	4TH DAY	5TH DAY	6TH DAY	7TH* DAY	8TH DAY	9TH DAY	10TH DAY	11-12 DAY	13-15 DAY	FINAL TOTAL
LIBERTY Jan. 9, 1926 (1st Day 1-4)	94.86	108.47	403.83	698.57	768.65	844.81	1,222.43	356.23	526.11	612.75	920.64	802.52	(Mar. 6) 13,321.31
LIBERTY Jan. 30, 1926 (1st Day 1-25)	55.43	98.61	452.65	666.36	699.84	333.40	1,396.36	363.97	492.56	455.27	741.17	1,187.41	(Apr. 2) 12,051.46
LIBERTY Sept. 18, 1926 (1st Day 9-13)	13.74	85.01	447.38	613.07	849.06	713.48	1,042.48	319.82	429.96	344.11	412.69	904.62	(Dec. 6) 10,050.39
REVIEW OF REVIEWS, Oct. 1925 (1st Day 9-28)	10.97	4.65	12.02	8.08	17.46	11.44	7.95	14.00	14.25	9.82	22.47	33.04	(Jan. 1) 518.68
CHICAGO TRIBUNE Jan. 5, 1926 (1st Day 1-6)	14.76	350.76	448.35	332.65	295.77	53.71	153.49	98.35	81.73	141.12	54.41	105.30	(Mar. 10) 2,959.81
CHICAGO TRIBUNE Jan. 14, 1926 (1st Day 1-15)	11.31	062.08	491.67	258.32	221.54	154.23	161.19	72.10	83.55	69.56	156.81	107.56	(Mar. 10) 3,788.62
CHICAGO TRIBUNE Feb. 10, 1926 (1st Day 2-11)		202.19	391.05	177.80	408.78	118.62	210.61	198.67	100.21	74.27	135.55	361.12	(Mar. 10) 2,884.36

EXHIBIT 37. Showing the returns from a Little Blue Book advertisement which ran in three different types of medium. (Courtesy of Mr. Haldeman-(Julius) *Includes Saturday afternoon mail.

ment postal cards, and 13,000 permit cards), or a total of 91,000 of each kind over the period of seven weeks.

The government cards produced a larger gross volume of orders, but when measured in percentage of cost to sales, it was found that the permit card was 13 per cent better. When the experiment began, the incoming mail brought as high as 33 per cent of the permit cards with stamps affixed by the customer. This figure dropped to 2 per cent at the time Maddy wrote his article.

Not only do the kinds of advertising media have a bearing upon the returns obtained from advertisements, but the positions within such media as magazines also have a determining effect. There are certain preferred positions for which publishers usually charge extra. Hepner[19] offers the following list of these:

1. Upper half of page usually gains attention better than the lower half.
2. The right-hand page is better than the left-hand.
3. Outside back cover page.
4. Inside back cover page.
5. Page facing the inside back cover.
6. Inside front cover.
7. Page facing the inside front cover.
8. Page facing the first page of reading material.
9. Page at the end of main reading section.
10. The middle spread.
11. Page facing the end of the most interesting article or story.

A summary of the relative advantages of various advertising media, therefore, would indicate that the newspaper is apparently the most advantageous print medium for the local merchant, with TV, radio, direct-mail, and bus advertisements following suit. The direct-mail can be the most adaptive of all advertising media, but the cost of making it so is usually quite high. Much of the direct-mail advertising nowadays

---

"Greater things are believed of those who are absent."   —Tacitus is no more modified to meet the individuality of the recipient than are newspaper advertisements. The advent of the radio, and especially TV, have given the advertiser much of the advantage previously possessd by the personal salesman, as we shall explain in a later section.

Characteristics of Good Slogans and Trade Names. Before we enter upon a formal discussion of this heading, it would be well to mention the uses and importance of contests for slogans and trade-marks. They constitute an important form of advertising. The Bond Electric Corporation contest offered a total of $15,000 in prizes, and received over 1,000,000 inquiries and 250,000 slogans submitted. When the Camel Cigarette letter contest was held, over 2,000,000 pieces of mail were received. Of course, the actual prize money is a negligible part of the cost of such contests.

Next to their development of trade, the most frequent purpose of these consumer contests is the development of new sales and advertising ideas. This form of contest is beginning to supersede the slogan and "name" varieties, and is a consumer survey of great value. In 1915 when the Bon Ami Company held a contest over the merits of the cake versus the powder form of their product, the winner submitted 706 uses for their product. An entry of this nature would form a good encyclopedia for the advertising department when it wished to present new selling points.

Some contests in maze tracing and house naming are for the purpose of developing "sucker lists", which are then sold to various firms who wish to advertise by direct-mail and need lists of prospects. Incidentally, Mr. Haldeman-Julius paid for keeping his mailing list of 500,000 names up to date by renting it to advertisers. When Edward Bok was seeking the widest publicity for his Peace Plan, he also rented the list, sending all of his sealed and stamped letters to Girard, Kansas, by express, where the addresses were affixed and they were placed in the mail.

The importance of slogans and trade-marks is estimated in dollars and cents by many firms, as the following data reveal:[30]

```
"Coca-Cola" ......................................$ 5,000,000
"Uneeda" ..........................................  6,000,000
"Royal" (Baking powder)..........................  8,000,000
"Bull Durham" ......................$10,000,000 to 20,000,000
"Camel" ..........................................  10,000,000
"Sunkist" ..........................................  2,000,000
```

These name and trade-mark valuations have either been listed among the assets of their respective companies at the figures cited, or have been priced in sales at those amounts.

In running a contest it is well to keep in mind that the majority of the public has an inferiority complex regarding brain competitions. Moreover, within reasonable limits the amount of the prize money is secondary to the appeal of the contest task. As a general rule, the range of total prize money should lie between $2,500 and $10,000. Amounts over $10,000 do not offer much better results. In a certain annual contest run by a trade association the number of responses was doubled when it doubled the *number* of prizes but kept the total amount the same.

The government postal authorities should always be consulted before using the mails in the announcement of contests. They are very particular to guard against actual fraud, unfairness, and lottery or chance. For these reasons the contestants must not be forced to buy something. Even the fact that entry blanks must be obtained may be deemed unfair unless there are plenty of dealers, so the contest announcements often state that blanks will be mailed upon request.

Contests, however, are not always wholly beneficial in their results. Of 100,000 participants, maybe only 100 receive prizes. Despite the fact, as Slater[29] points out, that people

---

"A small debt produces a debtor; a large one, an enemy."
—Publilius Syrus

"If she undervalue me, what care I how fair she be?" —Walter Raleigh have inferiority complexes in regard to entering a contest, once they are launched upon it and mail their entries, they feel that unfairness has been evident if they do not obtain a prize. The unpleasant reaction may attach to the product being advertised, or to the name of the company, and actually militate against the purpose behind the contest. To offset this tendency impartial and well known judges should be obtained to referee the final decisions, or the public should be permitted to see the winning exhibits.

In regard to protecting his slogans after they have been obtained the advertiser must also remember that they cannot be registered as trade-marks except in a few special cases nor can they be copyrighted. His only protection, therefore, is to register them with some bureau, as *Printers' Ink,* which keeps records of slogans. This action prevents unwitting duplication and aids in establishing priority rights.

The rules governing excellence in slogans and trade names follow.

1. They should be short.
2. They should be simple.
3. They should be euphonious.
4. They should suggest selling points.
5. They should give rise to pleasant feeling tone.
6. They should lend themselves to pictorial presentation.
7. They should be flexible enough to cover additional products of the firm.
8. They should be unique.
9. They should be easily remembered—this may involve rhythm and rime, alliteration, and style of print.
10. They should be distinctive—this means they should not lend themselves to other products, nor to abbreviation.

In considering a violator of the tenth point above, we have only to cite "Eventually—why not now?" Among students, from 40 to 60 per cent associate this with a competitor of its owner, while once in a class of exactly 100 men and women I found 81 who thought it belonged to Pillsbury's Flour. The author of the above slogan and most famous sloganeer in America is G. Herb Palin, who has also given us "Safety First", "See America First", "The Thinking Fellow Calls a Yellow", and "Built on Honor to Honor Its Builder". The last one of these is typical of what Palin[28] considers a good slogan, but the writer disagrees with his views in the matter. Where there is no competitor, as in the case of "Safety First", this type of slogan is all right, but otherwise it can lend itself to any product ever produced, and becomes as inefficient as "Eventually—why not now?" Palin favors the formula, 1-2-3-3-2-1, in which he builds up a phrase, then reverses it, as in "Built on Honor to Honor Its Builder."

Probably no slogan or trade name ever devised perfectly fulfilled the ten rules listed above, but the more of those rules that do apply to the slogan, the better it will become. Keeping those rules in mind, the reader may try his skill at ranking the following slogans in order of merit. They were entered in the Hertz Driv-Ur-Self slogan contest. One of the entries won $500, the second prize was $250, and the other five, although occupying different ranks, all received $50 each. Two advertising men and a member of the Hertz Company were judges. Their decisions are given at the end of the chapter.

> A. Buy the mile—by the mile.
> B. Join the Millions.
> C. Economy and style in every mile.
> D. Drive the car you'd like to own.
> E. Economically yours.
> F. Need a car for work or play?
>   Rent a Hertz and drive away.
> G. Convenience for you—economy, too.

In comparing the pulling power of advertisements bearing

"Flowers are the sweetest things that God ever made and forgot to put a soul into."   —H. W. Beecher similar copy but containing the following headings, Lichten-berg[25]found that one of the headings "pulled really marvelous results," but the other three were failures. The reader will find the most effective title named at the conclusion of the chapter. The advertisement was of a correspondence school.

A. Afraid to Face the Facts—Then Don't Read This Page.
B. Those Who Shy at Unpleasant Facts Should Not Read This Page.
C. Men Who Know It All Are Not Invited to Read This Page.
D. Men Who Are Satisfied to Wait Ten Years for Success Will Find Nothing Interesting On This Page.

Starch holds that a heading should ordinarily be confined to one or two decks. The writer doesn't know how many decks were employed in the above headings as run in the original advertisements.

From the psychological standpoint, therefore, a good slogan or trade name should be in reciprocal relationship with the article which it advertises, or else it soon becomes valueless. It should give to a new product of the firm the prestige of previous merchandise, and should gain in return the pleasant feeling tone which should be developed by the new member of the manufacturer's family. We have outlined the ten characteristics of a good slogan, and shown how contests have often been employed by manufacturers in procuring slogans. Probably the chief value of slogans and trade names lies in their quickly gaining for a new product the prestige of familiar ones. Heinz, for instance, doesn't have to devote much advertising to a new foodstuff for the name Heinz is an official introduction thereto.

The Effect of Feeling Tone in Advertising. It will not be necessary to devote much space to a consideration of this important topic inasmuch as we have discussed the feeling

---

"In the battle of existence, Talent is the punch; Tact is the clever foot-work."   —Wilson Mizner tone of words in Chapter I, and have devoted space to it under the subject of salesmanship. Because an advertisement keeps confronting an individual repeatedly, if it is unpleasant at all, there is a cumulative effect of such repetitions which may build up an active dislike for the product, without the subject's even knowing how he developed such an aversion. On the contrary, pleasant feeling tone also is additive, and may result in a desire on the part of the observer which to him is inexplicable.

It becomes advisable, therefore, for a company to ascertain the likes and dislikes of people before running certain kinds of illustrations and copy. In South America, for instance, the pictorial example of a neat housewife scouring her pans with some brand of kitchen cleanser would be repulsive, for "ladies" don't work at such tasks. We don't have to go away from home, however, to cite similar flagrant disregard for feeling tone. One of the large coffee companies in America uses as a trade-mark the picture of what to the average citizen probably is looked upon as simply a bearded old man in turban and a flowered nightgown drinking his cup of coffee before retiring. If one regards this picture long he probably wonders only how much is dribbling into the old fellow's beard. Our rules for effective slogans and trade names are certainly violated by this case which is, unfortunately, matched by scores of others that we could cite.

In Exhibit 38 we have a converse of this type of advertisement. Even though it may be remotely relevant, it most assuredly arouses a much more pleasant feeling tone in the reader. The other advertisements which we have presented may be regarded in the light of their pleasant or unpleasant emotional significance. In the Mercirex examples, however, we must bear in mind that it is afflicted persons to whom the appeal is directed, so our possible feelings of unpleasantness will not be felt by them. Instead, they may react with delight to the pictured health which is promised them.

EXHIBIT 38.   An example of pleasant feeling tone and the sex appeal employed to increase the effectiveness of an advertisement.   (Courtesy of Lennen & Mitchell, Inc.)

In the following bit of advertising copy we have made an attempt to tap as many pleasant "warmth" memories in the reader as possible, and transfer them to the woolen sweater being advertised. Although the initial query contains the word "bug", the unpleasant connotation is probably submerged in the greater pleasure value of the childhood phrase.

"You'll be snug as a bug in a rug," Mother used to say, as she tucked in the woolly blankets, and kissed you good night. Then you snuggled into your cozy, warm nest, and drifted off into peaceful slumber.

The Snuggle Sweater also gives you that warm softness that tempts the cheek, and protects you from chill autumn winds and the damp coolness of spring evenings. As if wrapped in knitted sunshine you can play golf, or fish, or motor in the breeze with perfect safety and cozy delight.

Snuggling against your arms and throat with velvety comfort, your Snuggle Sweater offers you perfect freedom of movement. You can work or play with the same warm glow of safety that you feel at your own fireside.

Snuggle—for Sweater delight!

Doubleday & Co. recently conducted an interesting Direct Mail test in connection with their "Best in Books", a bimonthly club offering. They sent out 50,000 pieces on each part of the test below for a total mailing of 150,000. Can you rank them in their order of returns? Pick the poorest and call it 100%. Then rank the others accordingly. The correct answers appear at end of this chapter.

————(a) Accept the first book for 10¢
————(b) Accept the first book free
————(c) Accept the first book for 25¢

The Direct Mail Advertising Association comments that the word "free" used to rate tops in motivating value. But nowadays people view it with some doubt or suspicion and respond better when they pay at least a modest or "bargain" price.

The zooming effect of TV in advertising can be derived from the data on Pages 293 and 814, taken from *Advertising Age*.

Nielsen Network TV

Two Weeks Ending March 20, 1966
Copyright by A. C. Nielsen Co.
(Data on sponsor and network compiled by AA)

Nielsen Average Audience*

Rank	Program	Total Homes Reached	TV Homes Reached
1	Bonanza (Chevrolet, NBC)	18,350	34.1
2	Lucy Show (Toni, Lever Bros., CBS)	16,030	29.8
3	Batman — Thur. (Several sponsors, ABC)	15,820	29.4
4	Danny Thomas Special (U. S. Time Corp., Consolidated Cigar, NBC)	15,760	29.3
5	Red Skelton Hour (American Home Products, Philip Morris, CBS)	15,600	29.0
6	Beverly Hillbillies (Kellogg, CBS)	15,440	28.7
7	Andy Griffith Show (General Foods, CBS)	15,330	28.5
8	Bewitched (Chevrolet, Quaker Oats, ABC)	15,170	28.2
9	Gomer Pyle — U.S.M.C. (General Foods, CBS) ...	14,580	27.1
10	Green Acres (Procter & Gamble, General Foods, CBS)	14,360	26.7
11	Dick Van Dyke Show (Lorillard, Procter & Gamble, CBS)	13,880	25.8

*Households reached during the average minute of the program.

AMERICAN RESEARCH BUREAU'S COLOR TV ESTIMATES - NOV., 1965

MARKET	Color TV Homes	% of All TV	MARKET	Color TV Homes	% of All TV
Akron, O.	41,200	12	Jackson, Miss......	25,200	7
Atlanta, Ga. ...:..	71,600	9	Lexington, Ky.	10,500	6
Baltimore, Md.	138,500	7	Los Angeles	585,300	17
Bangor, Me.	7,000	4	Madison, Wis.	55,200	8
Bismarck, N. D.	3,600	3	Manchester, N. H. ..	117,700	7
Boston, Mass.	139,700	7	Minot, N. D.	1,200	2
Charlotte, N. C. ...	64,200	6	Mnucie, Ind.	23,000	15
Chicago, Ill.	249,800	10	New Orleans, La. ...	36,600	6
Cincinnati, O.	126,200	13	New York, N. Y. ...	560,300	9
Denver, Colo.	32,600	6	Pittsburgh, Pa.	122,100	8
Eugene, Ore.	23,600	10	Richmond, Va.	17,600	4
Florence, Ala.	1,000	3	St. Louis, Mo.	64,900	7
Green Bay, Wis.....	22,800	6	San Francisco	188,400	12
Hawaii	7,200	5	Selma, Ala.	1,700	5
Houston, Tex.	52,100	8	Washington, D. C. ..	120,900	7

COSMETIC PURCHASERS

(Women 15 years of age and older)

Item	Total U.S. Purchasers	Macfadden's Women's Group Unduplicated Purchasers	*MWG Percent Total U.S. Purchasers
Face Powder	4,661,000	1,624,000	34.8
Face Cream	6,165,000	2,342,000	38.0
Perfume or Cologne	4,826,000	1,833,000	38.0
Lipstick	8,320,000	2,948,000	35.4
Hand or Body Lotion	11,462,000	3,322,000	29.0
Hair Spray	10,363,000	2,851,000	27.5
Hair Coloring or Rinse	3,389,000	816,000	24.1

*Macfadden's Women's Group

One glance at the figures above shows you that the Macfadden's Women's Group audience comprises from ¼ to more than ⅓ of all American women buying the cosmetics shown. Are they buying your products?

From the standpoint of psychology, therefore, feeling tone is of very great importance in advertising. The cumulative effects of daily exposure to copy and illustrations which arouse even slight feelings of unpleasantness may become great enough to occasion definite dislike or aversion. On the other hand, the repetitive effect of pleasing cuts and copy builds desire or liking for a product. The advertiser must be acquainted with the habits of his public in order to understand which words and pictures will be pleasant and which unpleasant. In foreign advertising especially such knowledge must be carefully checked.

Advantages of Television and Radio Advertising. Radio (1922) and television (1941) are the newest outlets. They offer a widespread distribution for advertising with part of the virtue of personal salesmanship, namely, the human voice. As the silver screen came to life by means of the "talkies", so advertising has gained a third dimension through the depth of vocal intonation and expression of the radio. Advertising can now be made timely and flexible enough to meet the demands of all classes of our population.

There are several advantages possessed by these mediums which are not possessed by any others. (1) They enable the advertiser to put his public in a pleasant frame of mind by music and comedy skits at the same time that he is advertising his product. If his programs are pleasing, his product tends to be tied up with those resulting sensations of pleasure; hence, we begin to like his goods. (2) They enable the advertiser to get inside the home and do a form of personal selling at moments that are most opportune. For instance, in the morning as the housewife is doing her work, she usually has the radio turned on. The advertiser-salesman begins to talk to her about the greater convenience of vacuum cleaners even as she sweeps, or he describes the delicious foods offered by his company to tempt the appetites of husband and children. Television, though, demands "idle" time.

(3) Radio and television let advertisers capitalize upon the attention of millions that may be focussed upon an outstanding football or pugilistic contest. This aspect of advertising is similar to the policy of many moving picture producers who buy only "best sellers" among novels and published magazine stories. The public's attention has already been caught, so the producers capitalize on this previous advertising of the stories. In the same manner, various manufacturers let the sport writers of American newspapers concentrate the attention of possibly millions of men and women upon a Notre Dame-Northwestern football contest, then move their microphones and cameras to the stadium, and at little additional cost have an audience that may be 100 times as large as their usual one.

(4) Radio and television let advertisers get the attention of all the members of the family, instead of just the one or two who chance to be looking at a magazine or newspaper.

(5) They also introduce suspense and drama into advertising, and by running conversational serials of the "Amos 'n' Andy" variety, can soon educate the public to seek the adver-

tising program. Newspaper and magazine advertisements are not yet able to excite millions to the extent that they rush home to look at tonight's advertisement. Yet radio and television can do this very thing, causing men and women of all ages actively to solicit the advertiser's programs. It is a curious reversal of what has been customary with previous forms of advertising media.

(6) Radio and television help an advertiser reinforce other forms of his advertising. He can call the housewife's attention to his printed newspaper advertisement of that evening or morning, and urge her to come early to the sale and avoid the crowds.

(7) Radio and television enable advertisers to enlist the cooperation of children who are too young to read his printed statements in newspaper or magazine. By appropriate stories in which his product is prominently mentioned, and by direct commands he can induce the child to assist in "selling" his parents on a new brand of ice cream or bread. The advertiser can promise the child that a balloon or top is being given away at the grocery whenever a loaf of his bread is purchased. The young child reacts favorably, of course, whereas he might never gain this information otherwise.

(8) Radio and television add the delightful nuances of tone which attach to certain melodious voices, plus actual views of the merchandise. Occasionally one encounters persons whose voices are pleasing in their own right. Human speech, as we have already mentioned, gives depth and life to inanimate advertising. Part of the effectiveness of Amos and Andy was due to their vocal inflections and Negro dialect.

But such advertising also has its pitfalls. Just as some voices are musical and sweet, others are unpleasant and harsh. Despite the knowledge of the ineffectiveness of raucous voices, there are still too many of this type speaking to American people from their radios. Moreover, the pleasure aroused

by musical programs is partially offset by their frequent inter-
ruptions for announcements concerning the bargains which are
being offered at so and so's store. And on Sundays it is
often offensive to the habits of millions of listeners to hear
the same week-day commercial programs flooding the house.
The feeling tone created by certain musicians and entertainers
is also diminished when the advertisers have these performers
announce the selling points of the product for which the program is sponsored. It is much better to let the station announcer
handle the script which deals with the price and virtues of the
merchandise, and leave the singer or entertainer free to retain
his artistic role to the end.

The Effect of Color and Cuts in Advertising. In our
consideration of attention attractors we mentioned the significance of color as one of them. We have also commented
upon the color preferences of men and women. It might be
well to review the facts of color vision treated in general
psychology. The color spectrum is broken at the elementary
colors, which have been designated as "primary" hues in the
general psychology course, so that we have a square. The four
corners are made up of red, yellow, green, and blue, respectively, as is shown in Exhibit 42. The hues that lie between
any two points are called secondary colors, and are composed
of the two primary colors on each side of them. Colors which
are opposite each other, as blue and yellow, for example, look
richer when employed side by side in the same advertisement
than they do when next to any other color. Red and green are
complementary, as are orange and a shade of blue-green, like
peacock blue. In order to procure maximum saturation and
richness of hues, complementary colors should be used together. For an explanation of this phenomenon the reader is
recommended to consult any thorough textbook in general
psychology.

In one of its catalogues a few years ago Sears, Roebuck
and Company had two pages devoted to advertising skirts—

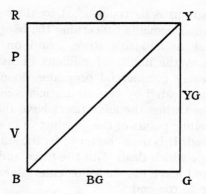

EXHIBIT 42. Showing the color square with primary colors at the corners.

one page in colors and the other in black and white. The prices were practically the same and the goods were equally desirable as regards style and quality, but the returns which came in from the colored page were ten times greater than those received from the black and white page. Part of this difference was due to the greater attention attracting value of the color page, but in addition to that fact, the colored skirts appeared richer than those depicted only in black and white. The suggestion of better quality was therefore produced by the employment of color.

When color is supplemented with the assistance of cuts, much greater pulling power is demonstrated. The nature of the cuts, of course, is a deciding factor. It is possible to hit the bull's-eye with the illustration by striking at a fundamental motive base like sex, as is demonstrated in Exhibit 38, even though the product at first thought would not seem to lend itself to such kind of picture. The reader will recall that almost all cigarette advertising is similar in this regard to Exhibit 38, while the same principle is employed to a greater or less degree by the majority of advertisements.

A Chinese proverb states that a picture is worth ten thousand words. It will be unnecessary to point out the psychological reasons underlying the partial truth of such a statement. At least, we know that cuts increase the effectiveness of an advertisement, and the result is heightened when color accompanies the cuts. Starch says that a publication can probably not carry over 15 to 20 per cent of its space in color, however, without considerably reducing the contrast effect between the colored and non-colored advertisements. In the following table from Starch[30] we see the results of color and cuts upon the returns from direct-mail advertising. In the column labelled "headings", the word "special" indicates that the regular company letterhead was supplanted by a special head originated for these letters. The same multigraphed letter was used throughout, with the addresses filled in by hand, a signature cut being used. In the letters containing cuts, the latter were always the same. Moreover, the mail was given a uniform distribution to all types of geographical areas.

LETTER NO.	QUANTITY	COLOR OF LETTER	CUTS	HEADING	RETURN ENV. COLOR	PULL PCT.
1	1,000	White	No	Yes	White	9
2	1,000	White	No	Yes	Blue	12
3	1,000	White	Yes	Special	White	18
4	1,000	White	Yes	Special	Blue	22
5	1,000	Corn	No	Special	White	14
6	1,000	Corn	Yes	Special	Blue	26
7	1,000	Green	No	Special	White	16
8	1,000	Green	Yes	Special	Blue	28
9	1,000	Gold	No	Special	White	21
10	1,000	Gold	Yes	Special	Blue	34
11	1,000	Pink	No	Special	White	26
12	1,000	Pink	Yes	Special	Blue	48

EXHIBIT 43. The effect of color and cuts in direct-mail advertising. (Starch).

In summarizing our discussion of the effectiveness of color and cuts upon returns, we can state unequivocally that both

"Don't make excuses—make good."   —Elbert Hubbard

color and illustration increase the effectiveness of advertisements. They add to the attention attracting value of the page, increase the reader's interest, explain more easily than words the nature of the merchandise, and contribute an impression of richness and quality. The value of color is somewhat lessened, however, by the inclusion of all-color advertisements in the magazine. The contrast of a black and white advertisement heightens the attractiveness of an adjacent colored page.

Humor in Advertising.

The general impression of humor as employed in advertising is that it cheapens the quality feeling tone of the product. But one needs to distinguish between wit and simple comedy of the "Mutt and Jeff" or "Jiggs" variety. Moreover, in the realm of low priced goods the sacred regard which some firms have for an article which retails at from 25 to 50 cents is ludicrous in itself. There are companies of this sort who regard their products with the hallowed deference of a Rolls Royce automobile or a Steinway grand piano, even though their goods are on sale in our quarter stores.

It is well to keep in mind that people are not so concerned with quality in the case of cheap goods as in those which are expensive. They are willing to gamble on the smaller amounts. It is true that we resent levity and attempted wit at the expense of religion, mothers, the president of the United States, and honored figures of history, such as Washington and Lincoln. But as regards insecticides, like Flit, and lesser merchandise it is questionable if the virtues of humor do not far outweigh its vices.

Humor puts the reader or listener into a pleasant mental state. It inflates his ego, and may be looked upon as an indirect compliment. He feels superior to the person who is doing the silly things depicted. Previously we have described the resulting pleasure obtained whenever our egos are inflated, and the fact that this pleasure tends to become attached to

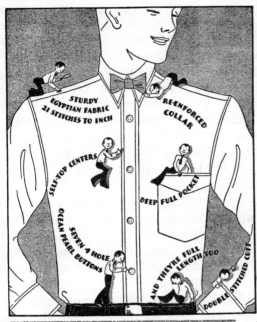

Seven Little Fellows Show You Why These

MEN'S SHIRTS

...are worth far
more than their
Sale Price of—

$1.09

On Sale
Saturday

White,
Tan,
Green, Blue.
Sizes
14 to 17

STURDY
EGYPTIAN FABRIC
21 STITCHES TO INCH

RE-ENFORCED
COLLAR

SELF TOP CENTERS

DEEP FULL POCKET

OCEAN PEARL BUTTONS
SEVEN 4 HOLE

AND THEY'RE FULL
LENGTH TOO

DOUBLE STITCHED CUFF

They're the famous KING PHILLIP brand
shirts . . . Famous for quality . . . Famous
for wear. And now we're going to make
them more famous than ever by selling
them at an unheard-of-price for merchandise
of such high calibre. Maybe you're not
interested in details — but you can't get
away from the fact that any Broadcloth
Shirt made of fine Egyptian yarn, pre-
shrunk, with full-cut armholes, full-length
square tails, full-width shoulders and self-
top full-length plaited centers—is SOME
SHIRT AT THIS PRICE!

You ought to buy a season's supply—if
you don't—don't blame us—an event like
this doesn't happen often and we don't
know if it will ever happen again.

*If You Can't Come In
Personally, this Coupon
Will Shop for You!*

NOTE: Many people will buy these
now for Christmas gifts . . . and no
wonder . . . they're REAL values!
SALE ON FIRST FLOOR

MAIL ORDER BLANK						
SIZE (14 TO 17)						
SPECIFY COLOR (TAN, BLUE, GREEN)—or WHITE						
QUANTITY						

Mail to
Ann Grey,
Care of Frank's
130 Calhoun,
Fort Wayne, Ind.

Name ....
Address ....
P. O. ....

EXHIBIT 44. A pre-war advertisement combining novelty and humor. (Courtesy of Frank Dry Goods Company.)

the thing arousing it. Accordingly, humor tends to make us like the product utilizing it as an advertising device. In conflict with this positive effect, however, is the tendency for us to feel superior to the situation portrayed, which, in turn, may lead to our minimizing the quality of the product.

In human relations we pointed out the essential nature of the two-stage process of "selling" ourselves, emphasizing first of all the need for arousing respect and admiration for our virtues before we capitalized on that respect as a means of enhancing the effectiveness of our discreet compliments. In a similar fashion, humor in an advertisement compliments us, but should be supported by factual matter to bolster the prestige of the product. If this two-fold process is carried out, there is no reason for humor's lowering the quality feeling tone in any marked degree. Chesterton's wit certainly doesn't militate against his reputation for being an educated man of the "quality" type.

In the last few years a striking change in the advertising policy of both newspapers and manufacturers has been demonstrated by the use of colored comic pages in the Sunday papers, devoted to advertising foodstuffs, beauty lotions and the like. Advertising cartoons and comic strips in even the daily papers are now in vogue.

In concluding our discussion of humor we may state that its utilization in advertising need not be detrimental to the quality feeling tone, especially of low priced goods, if other sound selling points are also displayed. This subject will soon be studied more thoroughly in the psychological laboratory by means of feeling tone analyses of advertisements which have been presented in humorous and non-humorous manners.

The Importance of the Follow-up. There are two ways of interpreting the follow-up, one of which involves the response to inquiries received from an advertisement, while the other pertains to repetitive advertising. We shall take them up in turn.

(1) Following up inquiries. In this connection Bosworth[4] cites the experience of a representative national advertiser who was selling a product whose price ran into several hundreds of dollars. The following figures are illuminating, and may be compared with the number of calls that salesmen make in order to obtain orders:

10 per cent of those who do buy, buy on the 1st follow-up.
14 per cent of those who do buy, buy on the 2nd follow-up.
22 per cent of those who do buy, buy on the 3rd follow-up.
32 per cent of those who do buy, buy on the 4th follow-up.
16 per cent of those who do buy, buy on the 5th follow-up.
6 per cent of those who do buy, buy on the 6th follow-up.

If we consider the original advertisement as the first contact with the reader, then these follow-ups should be moved forward one step, thus giving 10 per cent returns on the second consumer contact. Viewed in this light, we find that the fourth and fifth advertising contacts produced 54 per cent of the sales, a result which agrees quite well with the statement previously cited that the majority of retailers' purchases from salesmen follow the fourth and fifth contacts.

In a representative issue of a leading woman's magazine which contained 87 advertisements bearing coupons, the girls in the office answered each one. Ten of the 87 firms didn't even reply! Twenty-six responded within 10 days, of which 6 replied inside of a week. Eight took 21 days to answer, while the remaining 43 did not send a followup for over three weeks, two firms waiting for 32 days. Of these 77 firms who did respond, the following figures show the number of their letters:

52 sent 1 follow-up, then desisted.
16 sent 2 follow-ups, then desisted.
5 sent 3 follow-ups, then desisted.
2 sent 4 follow-ups, then desisted.
1 sent 5 follow-ups, then desisted.
1 sent 8 follow-ups, then desisted.

By glancing at this and at the immediately preceding table we see that 68 of these firms ceased their follow-up when 76 per cent of their sales were probably waiting for simply an additional two or three letters. After a company pays from $2,500 to $5,000 for a single magazine page, it certainly is not good business to refrain from using a few postage stamps thereafter to sell to the potential buyers who have demonstrated enough interest in the product to return a coupon.

(2) Repetitive advertising. It is a trite statement to the advertiser that advertising must be engaged in constantly, or the public soon forgets his product. Ivory soap has been on the market for years, but doesn't dare relax in its advertising program. In the first place, each year millions of young men and women are coming of age and marrying. They represent a new market which is scattered all over the United States. Then, too, other soaps would cut into Ivory's trade, for despite the conservative influence of habit we are not unchangeable.

Even though it was sold out for months ahead during the World War, the Cracker Jack Company continued advertising in order to prevent falling into oblivion and to offset the influence of new products which were trying to cut into its market. Even after its patents expired on November 15, 1921, the Gillette Company did not let competitors seize its business. Any manufacturer in the United States or abroad had the right thereafter to manufacture an exact duplicate of the Gillette razor and sell it for whatever price he chose, capitalizing on Gillette's 17 years of previous advertising.

To meet the situation, however, the Gillette Company got out a new razor which it covered with patents, and launched upon additional advertising. The following figures which Larrabee[24] offers show the revenues of the company during the two

---

"There is often as much independence in not being led as is in not being driven."   —Tryon Edwards

---

Language is the apparel in which your thoughts parade before the public. Never clothe them in vulgar or shoddy attire.

years subsequent to the expiration of its patent on the old razor:

YEAR	RAZOR SETS SOLD	DOZENS OF BLADES	NET EARNINGS*
1922	3,420,895	24,082,970	$7,602,939
1923	7,798,781	29,061,634	8,411,776

*After depreciation but before deduction of taxes.

In a certain sense, moreover, the consistency in color employed in buildings, as the red of A & P stores, the green of National Tea fronts, or the constant color of the product and equipment, as in the yellow cab, have repetitive influence. Indeed, it is almost impossible to change such factors, once they have been established, without markedly altering the reaction to the product. For example, without their beards the Smith Brothers would lose more than breast protectors.

The importance of the follow-up, therefore, has been repeatedly demonstrated in advertising as well as selling. Many firms have worked out statistical analyses of their direct-mail follow-ups of magazine and newspaper advertisements so they know the point at which diminishing returns preclude the further expense of mailing. But the data quoted from Bosworth would seem to indicate that many firms are still rather careless in this respect. The psychological significance of repetitive advertising has been proved so frequently as to warrant no further discussion here.

Display Advertising. The use of goods for advertising purposes was the original form of advertising. Since the evolution of mammoth mercantile establishments with windows which are almost as large as the stage of a theater, the problem of display advertising has become very complex. It involves not only an appreciation of the rules of art and psychological balance, but also covers the ability to write effective advertising copy, create window and show cards, and employ the principles of attention attraction which are a necessity for the print advertiser. The display advertiser must really be a jack-of-all-trades in the field of advertising. He must employ the tools of the print advertiser in much of his work, yet encounters other problems not confronted by the latter. For example, he can utilize human models, and sound. He can introduce moving objects and the real merchandise.

The popularity of the motor car has further complicated his task. Autoists move past his display in one to three seconds whereas the pedestrians take 10 to 15 seconds. As a consequence, he must concentrate on a unified exhibit whose essential features are readily apparent but whose details are interesting and numerous enough to retain the attention of the stroller.

The writer has conducted surveys of the pedestrians' reactions to displays of certain Chicago department stores, notably those of Marshall Field's and The Fair. He has found that even among the foot passers-by there is a marked difference in reaction. Those people on the outer half of the sidewalk are only slightly attentive to window displays. The men and women on the window half of the walk are the potential viewers of the advertising layout since the outer pedestrians are in more of a hurry.

Because of the counter-attractions of the city buses and mass of moving human beings on the outer side of the walk, the windows do not monopolize even the inner pedestrians' attention. In fact, they may hardly catch it at all, unless the display advertiser utilizes the principles for attracting attention which we have previously described. The best method for attracting attention is change or movement. Yet display men in the majority of cases fail to employ this principle. Since human beings on the outer side of the display man's potential public are offering movement as an attention attractor, and because people are usually more interesting than things, it becomes essential, therefore, for the display advertiser to utilize the basic attention attractor whenever he can.

Another and related problem confronting the display advertiser is that of measuring the effectiveness of his windows. Although one window may seem to him to be superior to another, how is he to make sure?   One method of answering his problem is the objective time test[11] by which he measures the degree to which the display slows the walking rate of pedestrians on the window half of the sidewalk. The writer has performed such tests with reference to some of the large Chicago department stores. It is necessary at the beginning to obtain an average walking rate for pedestrians on a crowded street but away from the distractions of window displays. The writer selected the adult woman as the subject for the time determination and found that she requires on the average 0.254 seconds per foot covered. In the data below is a comparison.

Average walking time of adult woman on
  crowded street away from windows........0.254 secs-ft.

Average woman's rate past Field's summer dresses
  display (3:30 p. m., June 6,).............. 0.385 secs-ft.

Average woman's rate past The Fair's bathing
  suit exhibit (5:30 p. m., June 6,).......... 0.330 secs-ft.

   The two windows described in the data are not comparable, however, for the reason that the test was not made on both at the same time. The pedestrian traffic is more hurried during the evening rush hour. In making such an objective time test, moreover, the observer should adhere to some such rules as the following:

   "1. Count every adult woman walking singly, taking time from the moment she approaches one end of the window until she passes beyond its other limit. In short, don't select only those women who seem to be window shopping. Take them as they come—the rapid walkers as well as the slow.

   "2. Make the count at comparable times. Don't compare a rush hour public with a mid-afternoon crowd. Preferably, conduct

---

"Nature has given to men one tongue, but two ears, that we may hear from others twice as much as we speak."   —Epictetus simultaneous experiments on different windows on the same day and hour.

"3. Don't record time in excess of 1.5 seconds per foot of window frontage. This regulation is to prevent one woman who stops for five minutes from "loading" the times of the 49 or 99 others on whom the test is based. The attention value of a window which stops ten pedestrians for five seconds apiece is better than that which stops one pedestrian for fifty seconds.

"4. Employ a stop watch and measure the window frontage ex-actly."

In the Sept. 4, 1954, issue of *Editor & Publisher* appeared an article which shows an adaptation of this objective time test. It is called "Stop-Motion Sampling", and has been developed by Alfred Politz. Still pictures are taken to stop the motion of traffic that passes outdoor advertising displays. The photos are enlarged and only the number of persons actually facing the sign during the duration, are then counted. This new method utilizes electronic photo techniques.

In concluding our discussion of display advertising, therefore, it is well to repeat that the first task of all advertising is to attract the attention. Since the display advertisement must compete with moving cars and colorfully clad persons, it should be given the benefit of that primary attention attractor, movement. The window should also be arranged in order to give a unified effect, and as a rule a wide variety of related merchandise should be present. There are some exceptions to this statement, as the large window of a firm like Field's which is chiefly concerned with creating desirable feeling tone and good will. In such a display there may be only two or three articles of merchandise. The effect of the background, moreover, should usually be devoted to focussing the gaze upon the merchandise. It should not draw attention to itself in contradistinction to the goods on display.

Answers to Hertz slogan contest: 1.E; 2.B; 3.D; 4.G; 5.A; 6.C; 7.F.
Best title to advertisement: "C".
Doubleday book replies: 160%-(a); 100%-(b); 140%-(c).

PRIZE CONTESTS

Prize contests are an excellent hobby for psychology students, since they stimulate concise thinking and forceful writing. They also offer the possibility of monetary returns. During our first year of marriage, Mrs. Crane and I entered them routinely. We won two first prizes of $1,000 each and many of smaller amounts. Several other professors are now contest "fans". Indeed, I often employ current contests as the written problems for my students when we take up the subject of Psychology in Advertising. Each year as high as $25,000,000 is awarded in prizes in this country. A number of my students have won cash and merchandise awards on the contest entries which they later submitted to official contest judges after having first submitted them as classroom assignments. (Study carefully some of the magazine references given on Page 437.)

REFERENCES

1 *Advertising & Sales Promotion Handbook* (Dartnell, 1966).
2 ASPLEY, J. C., *Short Course in Salesmanship* (Dartnell, 1966).
3 BORDEN, N. H., *Advertising, Text and Cases* (Irwin, 1950).
4 BOSWORTH, C. E., "Expensive Inquiries—Cheap Replies" *(Adv. and Selling,* April 17, 1929).
5 BRANDT, H. F., *Psychology of Seeing* (Philosophical Library, 1945).
6 BRIDGE, H. P., *Practical Advertising* (Rinehart, 1949).
7 CAMPBELL et al. *The American Voter* (Wiley, 1960).
8 CATTELL, R. B., *Personality & Motivation* (World Book, 1959).
9 CLARK, M., "Hypochondriacs at Large" *(Newsweek,* 12/8/58).
10 CROWE, C. M., *Getting Ready for Tomorrow* (Abingdon, 1959).
11 CRANE, G. W., "Practical Aspects of Display Psychology" *(Display World,* November, 1932).
12 FALK, A. T., "Analyzing Advertising Results" *(Harvard Bus. Rev.,* Jan., 1929).
13 FALTZ, E., *The Slogan In Modern Advertising* (N.Y. Assoc. Nat. Adv. 1949).
14 GANNON, T. J., *Psychology-Unit of Human Behavior* (Ginn, 1954).
15 GELDARD, F. A., *The Human Senses* (Wiley, 1953).
16 GRAY, J. S., *Psychology Applied to Human Affairs* (McGraw-Hill, 1954).
17 GUTHRIE, E. R., & POWERS, F. F., *Educational Psychology* (Ronald, 1950).
18 HALDEMAN-JULIUS, E., *The First Hundred Million* (Simon & Schuster, 1928).
19 HEPNER, H. W., *Effective Advertising* (McGraw-Hill, 1949).
20 HARSH, C. M., & SCHRICKEL, H. G., *Personality* (Ronald, 1950).
21 HENRY, O., *Writing & Selling Magazine Articles* (The Writer, 1963).
22 KITSON, H. D., *The Mind of the Buyer* (Macmillan, 1921).
23 KLEPPNER, O., *Advertising Procedure* (Prentice-Hall, 1950).
24 LARRABEE, C. B., "Expired Patents" *(Printers' Ink,* Mar. 20, 1924).
25 LICHTENBERG, B., "Test Copy on Results" *(Printers' Ink,* Nov. 8, 1928).
26 MADDY, C. D., "Big Mailing Test" *(Sales Management,* June 15, 1929).
27 MOSS, F. A., *Applications of Psychology* (Houghton Mifflin, 1929).
28 PALIN, G. H., "How Advertising Writer Works" *(Adv. and S.,* Apr. 1924).
29 SLATER, A. L., "How Well Do Consumer Contests Work?" *(Adv. and S.,* Feb. 6, 1929).
30 STARCH, D., *Principles of Advertising* (Shaw, 1923).
31 ROWSOME, F., *They Laughed When I Sat Down* (McGraw-Hill, 1960).
32 WATKINS, J. L., *The 100 Greatest Advertisements* (Moore, 1949).
33 ZIMMER & BIDERMAN, *Manipulation of Behavior* (Wiley, 1964).

CHAPTER IX

PERSONNEL ADMINISTRATION

Personnel administration as it is now regarded was not thought of in the middle ages when the condition of the worker was frequently a very drab one. He was born to a certain economic lot and trade, and so he died. It is true, of course, that our rather recent inventions were not in existence then, so the machine age with its mammoth industrial plants was not even dreamed of. The worker, as a consequence, was not required to become a "cog" in a vast manufacturing process, as has been too frequently the case in our 20th century. But his wages were mere pittances, and his social rights were ignored. Employers paid him about what they wished, and if he asked for more, they could laugh and hire his neighbor. The conditions of illumination, ventilation, and sanitation were not at all conducive to his health, nor even to his maximum output.

With the advent of the steam engine and the cotton gin the world passed through an industrial revolution of far reaching consequences. Not only have industrial concerns of the gigantic proportions of General Motors, DuPont, General Electric, and the Ford Company come into existence with a resulting growth of the urban population, but the worker is now a score of steps removed from his ultimate employer. And instead of having the varied tasks attendant upon the entire construction of his product, he now may be relegated to the monotonous duty of simply inserting a tiny screw.

With the bargaining power of the trade union the worker has attempted to meet his altered state in industry, especially in regard to working conditions, hours of employment, and wages. Management, too, in the last few decades has come to a realization that the combative relationship between itself and labor should become a cooperative one. The era of political absolution and the divine right of the foreman who "fired a few now and then to put the fear o' God in the rest of them", has become obsolete. From the point of view of efficiency alone, we have learned that the contented individual works more successfully than the one who is in constant terror of his job.

For the employee to be contented and happy in his work, however, involves not only a change from the autocratic foreman to a more understanding type of person, but also the adaptation of the worker to his job. As Scott and Clothier[39] have pointed out, personnel administration is not just the putting of a square peg into a square hole. Such a conception is too static, apparently involving the mechanical adjustment of two non-interacting entities. "There is no recognition here of the fact that men and jobs are changing in themselves, and plastic, yielding here and giving there to outside pressure. There is no acknowledgment of the common fact that with exposure to a square hole, a round peg (we are speaking of human pegs now) tends to become squarish; there is no appreciation that the square hole takes on a certain round appearance.

"This new point of view in industrial personnel differs from the square peg concept in that it recognizes that the job exercises an influence upon the worker and, conversely, that the worker exercises an influence upon the job. In fact, the job is never exactly the same job when filled by different persons, for each stamps his own impression upon it. Job A will have certain characteristics making for efficiency or inefficiency, as long as Worker M is on it; it will have other characteristics when M is replaced by N." The height of the work bench, for example, may make for efficiency when Worker M is at the task and for inefficiency when Worker N is there; on the other

---

"It is more important to know where you are going than to get there quickly. Do not mistake activity for achievement." —Mabel Newcomber hand, the speed of the machine may be too fast for Worker M to react most efficiently, but be just right for Worker N.

With this newer conception of individual differences and an emphasis upon the individual, has developed the need for tests which will adequately differentiate the behavior traits of one person from another. The man who wishes to know in what business or profession he should go, and the employer who wishes to learn which of two men he should hire, both experience an eagerness to procure some fool-proof scheme which will answer their questions most readily and satisfactorily. We shall discuss some of these devices in the ensuing sections.

Unscientific Methods of Rating Human Beings. Probably the most frequently encountered systems of unscientific rating of human beings are those twins, phrenology and physiognomy. The "bootleg" psychologist who practices one of these usually employs the other also. Phrenology is the attempted diagnosis of a person's mental characteristics by the shape of his cranium and the bumps on his skull. Physiognomy endeavors to make a similar diagnosis by using the features, such as the nose, mouth, eyes, ears, skin texture, etc. We would hesitate to devote space to such topics were it not for the fact that the skilful salesmen of these pseudo-sciences are constantly in action, and always gaining converts.

During the past semester three of my students have reported that the sales managers of their firms have not only hired phrenologists and physiognomists, but have also insisted on their salesmen's taking a course of instruction in those subjects. Apparently intelligent men and women seem to be almost as susceptible as the more patently gullible, for Charles M. Schwab wrote the introduction to one such book, and Dr. Goddard told the writer at the American Psychological Association meeting in Washington in 1924, that one of the Ohio legislators was rather hostile during the investigation of the state institution for feeble-minded because, as he afterwards learned from friends, this legislator thought Dr. Goddard should have felt the heads of all the inmates and rated their intelligence accordingly.

One of the unfortunate things about these pseudo-sciences is the fact that laymen confuse them with psychology proper. Griffitts[28] estimates that one-half of our population believe in them to a certain extent. So far as scientific data at present available indicate, it is just as illogical to estimate intelligence by the size and shape of the skull and the features, as to try to estimate the chemical content of the air inside a football from the scratches on the pigskin cover. The fallacies on which they are based will be described under the following headings:

(1) They presuppose localized character qualities, such as love, jealousy, pugnacity, generosity, perseverance, and the like, which lie in certain "spots" in the brain. Although we know that there are sensory areas for sight, hearing, etc., and motor areas from which nervous impulses go to innervate the muscles and glands, we have never found any such regions for generosity and musical talent, nor is it logical to assume that any exist. The same sensory and motor neurones may function in a great number of patterns. Neurone Number 1 may be employed in a nervous arc involved in love, in eating, in piano playing, in fighting, and in a million other character traits, just as the letter "a" may function in a vast number of words. The neurones involved in character traits lie all over the surface of the brain—not in any one spot.

(2) They assume as a corollary of their first fallacy that the cortex or gray covering of the brain thickens perceptibly in those regions where it functions most frequently. This is similar to thinking that a copper wire becomes thicker with each succeeding electrical impulse that runs through it. The error lies in failing to recognize that nerve cells and muscle

---

"Personal beauty is a greater recommendation than any letter of introduction."   —Aristotle cells are not the same. Exercise may increase the size of the biceps but not the brain, at least to any measurable degree.

(3) They assume that the brain bulges outward where it is exercised, and forces the cranium to expand. This is a sorry argument, for the brain is not in immediate contact with the skull, and if the space between the two were filled with liquid, by hydraulic pressure the whole inner surface of the cranium would get the same pressure exerted upon it; there would be no "spot" of pressure.

Daniel Webster had an unusually large skull, but his brain was of average size. Spurzheim, the famous German scientist, had a skull whose cubic capacity was exactly that of Joachim, an imbecile, but the imbecile's brain weighed 6 ounces more than the scientist's. Dr. Louis Casamajor, Professor of Neurology in the Columbia University College of Physicians and Surgeons, makes the statement that if he had a row of brains before him that had been taken from brilliant men and also from idiots, he couldn't tell by weight or shape or size which was which. [44]

(4) They generalize from a few cases where certain traits seem to be possessed by people with certain noses or skulls, and apply their generalizations to the mass of mankind. It is this tendency to remember only the coincidences which fit their ideas that make palmists, numerologists and those who use the signs of the horoscope continue to flourish along with the phrenologists and physiognomists. One of the most scientific experiments pertaining to the latter was conducted by Cleeton and Knight[12] Using the physiognomists' and phrenologists' own criteria, they took accurate skull measurements and then had their subjects judged in the traits named in the

---

"Excellence is the perfect excuse. Do it well, and it matters little what."
—Emerson

"A failure is a man who has blundered but is not able to cash in the experience." —Elbert Hubbard table below. The student subjects were rated by their sorority and fraternity mates, and then by a group of 70 judges who were business men, school superintendents, employment men, and others who were accustomed to interviewing applicants for positions. The correlation between the traits possessed by the subjects, as determined by accurate physical measurements, and the judgments of their friends and strangers will be found in Exhibit 45.

TRAIT	CLOSE ASSOCIATES AND PHYSICAL FACTORS	CASUAL OBSERVERS AND PHYSICAL FACTORS
Judgment........................	—0.005	+0.145
Intelligence	+0.027	+0.051
Frankness	+0.055	+0.155
Friendliness	—0.11	+0.195
Will Power	—0.074	+0.036
Leadership	—0.041	+0.066
Originality	+0.095	+0.079
Impulsiveness	+0.100	—0.067

EXHIBIT 45. Correlation between phrenological and physiognomic measurements and the estimates of close associates and of strangers.*

* If unfamiliar with the meaning of correlation, the student should refer to chapter xiv.

In explaining the apparent success of occasional phrenological predictions, one must also keep in mind the fact that salesmen need above all else a vast amount of confidence. If they really believe these predictions, it bolsters their confidence and sends them forth convinced of their ability to sell. This is an attitude that leads to sales, whether the attitude is based on hasty generalizations or science. Physicians since the beginning of medicine have known this same truth.

From the standpoint of psychology, therefore, such methods of rating human beings as phrenology, physiognomy, astrology and the like are considered unsound because their premises have never been demonstrated as having scientific validity. The occasional successes attained by these pseudo-sciences are capable of explanation on the basis of chance, or because of the fact that credulous persons gain increased confidence in themselves in consequence. There would be no especial objection to them if they confined themselves simply to the stimulation of confidence, but they often arbitrarily mislead and misdirect a subject. For example, when they tell a mechanic that he is in the wrong vocation, and should become an advertising man, they may cause him to become dissatisfied with the one job for which he is best fitted.

Scientific Methods of Rating Human Beings. The goal of the personnel manager and vocational counsellor in test construction would be a battery of many sub-tests, much after the fashion of Army Alpha, which they could administer to workers and students, and from which they could perfectly diagnose an individual's possibility of success in any given trade or profession. For example, let us suppose that we have 100 sub-tests. We administer the entire 100 to a large group of successful dentists, lawyers, physicians, salesmen, advertisers, *et al.* We find, let us assume, that the dentists make exceptionally high scores in tests 13, 45, 75, 91, 96, and 99. Salesmen make high scores in tests 2, 9, 54, 67, 86, and 95, and low scores on those tests in which the dentists excel. The other trades and professions likewise are distinct in the tests on which they excel. Such a battery of tests would then be ideal, for we could give it to students and applicants about whom we knew nothing, and if an individual made his admirable scores on tests 13, 45, 75, 91, 96, and 99, then we could tell him that he apparently had the qualifications that lead to success in dentistry.

Unfortunately, we have no such panacea as yet available, which explains why so many people eagerly seize upon some such simple formula as that of using the shape of the nose, or complexion, as indexes of certain abilities. The scientific differentiation of men and women regarding their abilities and talents is a slow and laborious process. It includes, moreover, many things in addition to the capacities of a person. As we shall see in a later section of this chapter, there is great overlapping of intelligence between different professions and trades. A college student has the intelligence sufficient for any profession, so we can obtain little help from Army Alpha and similar mental examinations to assist us in telling him which professional school he should prepare for.

Even his possession of extra-curricular knowledge, as in the field of mechanics, doesn't guarantee him either success or happiness in a profession such as engineering. A man may have every mental and technical qualification for a certain trade or profession, yet make a dismal failure when he enters it. If his father has been obdurate and overbearing toward the boy, the boy may hate his father's profession throughout life and always wish to escape it. He may cherish an apparently illogical desire to be a railroad conductor because his favorite uncle was one, and took him on a few of his trips. We are becoming increasingly aware of the fact that children can develop such a trade-fixation, much as they evolve mother-fixations. One of my students, a man with linguistic ability and high abstract intelligence, is at present having warfare with his parents because they have trained him for the diplomatic service, while all he aspires to do in life is act as engineer on a railroad locomotive.

A scientific method of rating human beings, therefore, involves (1) *Aptitude tests,* such as an analysis of the subject's intellectual ability. Although much overlapping occurs regarding the intelligence levels found in many different professions and trades, it is obvious that a subnormal or dull normal can never hope for success or happiness in a profession. The reversal of this conclusion is also true as a general rule. When Professor Snow was testing taxicab drivers, he frequently found Army Alpha scores to run 43, 48, 69, 57, 83, 64, 175. Instantly he guessed what was true of the "175" subject. He was a college man operating a taxicab at night to help defray his college expenses. Although this fellow could drive a cab perfectly well, he would not be happy at the task, and would desert the job as soon as circumstances permitted. As a result, he was a poor employee from the management's viewpoint, for he accelerated their labor turnover. Intelligence tests are, however, a basic type of aptitude test.

(2) *Achievement tests*. These measure the actual ability of the subject at the time of the test. In many cases, the employer wants a skilled worker. An intelligent man could probably learn the task in question, but the employer cannot afford to wait. Some of our large firms, it is true, which conduct schools for young men and women in order to train their own workers administer aptitude tests to such applicants. An examination in a school subject is an achievement test. The writer would regard Moss's Social Intelligence Test as both an aptitude as well as an achievement test, depending upon the viewpoint of the tester. As a measure of the individual's adaptation to his social environment, the test can be looked upon as measuring achievement. As an indication of the subject's probable success in salesmanship or other professions involving a knowledge of human nature, it can be considered an aptitude test.

(3) *Vocational interests test*. This type of examination attempts to find the preferences which an individual has in respect to his permanent vocation. If he possesses the aptitude and developed skill requisite for salesmanship and personnel administration, but prefers the latter, it is wise to learn this fact. A great many people, however, among the college graduates, do not have any particular preferences Aside from desiring Rockfeller's wealth and Bob Hope's or Elizabeth Taylor's fame, they have little desire for one form of productive activity instead of another. They drift into the

first type of work which offers a little ready cash and some prestige among their fellows, after which habit may grip them, and keep them in that occupation till old age arrives. College and university personnel departments may ultimately increase both the productivity as well as the happiness of their graduates by presenting them with written analyses of their vocational talents and defects. At the time of graduation this second diploma may eventually become more prized than the usual one, for it will at least be forward looking in its significance, and not a static record of the past four years' attainments.

(4) *Social attitudes test.* Industrial organizations have long appreciated the need for bonding many of their employees, realizing that their attitude might change regarding honesty. It is a very important phase of personnel work to discover the views of men and women regarding property rights, moral questions, religion, etc. Some offices prefer to avoid a mixture of religions or of races or of politics because of the possible debates and hostilities that may ensue.

(5) *Physical tests.* These involve health, examinations to determine deafness, color blindness, emotional stability, fatigue resistance, etc. In a sense, they belong under the general heading of aptitude tests except that the latter have commonly been held to apply to examinations for mental and habit patterns possessed by the subject.

In conclusion, therefore, we may state that the scientific rating of human beings involves the recognition of modern neurological and psychological laws, and the development of objective scales or tests by which to measure aptitude, achievement, vocational interests, social attitudes, and physical traits. Because of the significance of vocational interests and social attitudes in determining one's success or failure no single test or battery of tests will ever be perfectly diagnostic of one's future activity, since interests and attitudes are subject to constant social conditioning. But a careful, scientific study and measurement of men and women will be of increasing value in promoting industrial efficiency and human happiness.

Letters of Recommendation. As a partial measure of an applicant's aptitude, achievement, and social attitudes, it has been the custom to ask for a letter of recommendation. Such an instrument could have considerable merit if it were not for the fact that the applicant usually cites his friends for references, and the latter tend to give him the benefit of the doubt. Moreover, their letters are usually based on their own opinions, unsupported by objective data. The latter should consist of such items as the subject's length of service, the number of times tardy, of days absent, his rank in production as contrasted with the other salesmen, students, or employees, new ideas and improvements that he instigated, etc. The best answer to a letter of inquiry regarding a man's dependability is the reply that "He worked for us for three years without a day's absence, and was tardy only twice. He never failed to get his quota of work finished on time." Letters of this nature do not have to reiterate the worker's dependability for the specificity enables the new personnel manager to infer those things.

In answer to a letter asking my opinion "as to the character, reputation for honesty, and financial responsibility" of one of my former students, I have submitted the reply shown on the next page. The letter is still too subjective to be most effective, but a teacher who conducts lecture sections does not have an opportunity to observe his students in many situations of a sort which specifically denote honesty and financial integrity. Even concerning our most intimate friends we probably could say only "they are honest because we never saw them steal." A banker or business man might write that his messenger had carried the pay roll or daily deposits for three years without touching a penny. This would be specific, and much more objective than my final paragraph.

From the foregoing discussion, therefore, it is evident that

NORTHWESTERN UNIVERSITY

College of Liberal Arts

EVANSTON, ILLINOIS

DEPARTMENT OF PSYCHOLOGY

Mr. R. C. Bever,
333 N. Michigan Ave.,
Chicago, Illinois.

My dear Mr. Bever:

In reply to your letter asking my impression of the ability and character of Mr. Oliver B. Davison, I can offer the following data:

Mr. Davison was enrolled in my courses in Business Psychology and Advanced Business Psychology for two semesters. In the first class I administered the Army Alpha Intelligence Test, with which you are probably familiar. Mr. Davison's score thereon was 152, which means that he has a grade of "A" in mental alertness. Only four men out of every 100 are able to make over 134 on this test.

During the two years in my courses, he never missed a class, nor did he fail to hand in a single written assignment. You may be interested to learn that out of a class of fifty business and professional men, Mr. Davison was fourth high in term grades during the first semester, and second high during the last term.

As for my opinion of his moral and financial integrity, I can truthfully say that if I were in the business world I should be only too glad to place Mr. Davison on my staff.

Sincerely,

GWC-CM

Exhibit 46. Showing how objective data can improve a letter of recommendation. See "Test for Employees" in the Appendix.

letters of recommendation may be of considerable value depending upon the objectivity of the qualifications contained therein, and the honesty and prestige of the writer. Opinions unsupported by factual statements, and the use of superlatives render letters of little merit.

The Effectiveness of the Personal Interview. The frequent request for a photograph from an applicant for a position is unfortunately not always made to enable the prospective employer to judge the applicant's youth, but is often utilized for the sake of phrenological measurements. In some cases the employer today asks for both a front and side view, the latter enabling him to measure more easily the applicant's nose, eyebrows, lips, forehead and chin. If personnel management were only as simple as this, we could give a stenographer a set of spreading calipers, a sliding compass, and some steel tape, after which we could dispense with the employment manager.

To a believer in physiognomy, the personal interview is simply an additional opportunity for analyzing noses and lips. Sometimes in such interviews the employment manager actually requests his subjects to turn sidewise so that he may study their profiles! To one who is scientific in his utilization of the interview, however, the personal contact with the subject permits him to judge such things as the obvious physical proportions and presence or absence of stigmata, the general appearance and neatness in dress, the poise and carriage of the applicant, the latter's conversational ability, and social attitudes.

In addition, as Burtt[10] clearly points out, vocational preferences are more easily obtained by word of mouth than through the questionnaire, and many doubts and fears of the applicant may be allayed during the interview. His misconceptions may be corrected, and a general friendly relationship estab-

---

"A conservative is a man who is too cowardly to fight and too fat to run."   —Elbert Hubbard lished. The interviewer must be especially cautious, however, about letting his likes and dislikes obscure his clear discernment of the subject's virtues. Even the disbeliever in phrenology and physiognomy is likely to slip into a similar unscientific form of behavior by forming an instant liking or aversion for an applicant. His aversion may be based on a consciously forgotten childhood experience with a person who had the same features as the present applicant. If a fellow with a certain type of ear or chin beat him in a fist fight or stole his sweetheart from him, his resentment may carry over to all people bearing such ears and chins, and he may think they are always thieves and philanderers. Conversely, he may like and trust another individual who resembles a childhood friend or parent. Both of these reactions on the part of the interviewer may be entirely at variance with the real personalities of his callers.

As far as being able to judge the intellectual and trade capacities and abilities of applicants is concerned, the interviewer must rely on psychological tests and measurements, for his personal opinion is scarcely better than that of the schoolboy's. The most skilled interviewers will not agree on the merits of individuals, as the following data from Snow[40] clearly indicate. The Packard Motor Car Company had asked Professors D. T. Howard and A. J. Snow to help them select four or more competent salesmen of motor trucks. A large "Want Ad" had been inserted in the Chicago papers. From their letters in reply to this, the obviously unfit were eliminated, leaving twelve men ranging in ages from 29 to 46, in salaries from $3,000 to $7,000, in years of experience from 4 to 26, and in education from 8 years of grammar school to 3 years of college. Some were of native American stock, others of Norwegian, Swedish and German extraction. These twelve men were then interviewed individually by seven judges.

"The silliest woman can manage a clever man; but it needs a very clever woman to manage a fool"   —Kipling

To indicate the qualifications of the raters, we may state that interviewers A, B, and C were sales managers of automobile truck departments from three different companies. Judge D was president and general sales manager, while E was vice-president and former sales manager of two costly passenger car automobile firms. Judge F was the general sales manager of a national steel company, while G was a psychologist.

APPLICANTS	A	B	JUDGES C	D	E	F	G	TOTAL IN RANK	CONSENSUS	RANK IN TESTS
C. R. ...	1	8	4	1	2	2	4	22	1	11
C. Y. ...	7	1	7	2	5	5	1	28	2	4
B. W. ...	10	2	9	4	1	6	3	35	3	8
L. H. ...	2	9	8	9	3	4	2	41	4	5
M. R. ...	3	6	3	3	10	7	9	37	5	1
P. A. ...	4	7	1	10	8	8	5	43	6	6
B. L. ...	11	3	6	5	9	3	7	44	7	10
F. E. ...	5	5	11	6	4	11	6	48	8	2
M. M. ...	12	10	2	7	6	1	10	49	9	7
M. A. ...	6	4	10	8	7	10	8	53	10	9
S. T. ...	8	11	5	11	11	9	11	65	11	3
S. N. ...	9	12	12	12	12	12	12	81	12	12

EXHIBIT 47. Showing the difference in ranking given twelve salesmen by seven skilled interviewers, and their consensus compared with test scores. (Snow).

In concluding this section it would be well to comment on the relative effectiveness of male and female interviewers. Where men are the principal applicants, an attractive young woman of a friendly disposition may be excellent for the initial contact, but men resent having to give what they consider personal information to women. A company may engender ill will and cause many desirable applicants to stay away from its personnel office by delegating too much of the function of interviewing to female assistants. Older workers also resent having to come to dapper young men for jobs. Similarly many a physician engenders a feeling of resentment and unpleasantness in his male patients by having a nurse or young female secretary put the patient through a thorough oral cross examination.

The effectiveness of the personal interview, therefore, depends largely on the degree of cooperation between the applicant and the personnel officer. When friendly relationships can be established, the latter can correct misunderstandings and apprehensions of the prospective worker, as well as learn many things concerning his qualifications, attitudes, and interests. The applicant may even find that he does not want the vacant position, or the manager may note personal and physical defects which offset the applicant's test scores. The interview is a very desirable feature of personnel and employment work, particularly when the applicant meets a cordial official with a scientific attitude.

Psychological Tests in Employment. In order for an intelligent use of psychological tests to be made possible, it is wise to institute a job analysis. This consists of dissecting the task into its component parts so that the personnel director may know what elementary working situations are encountered in the satisfactory performance of the job. Such matters as the posture involved, the walking or standing necessitated, the use of certain tools, and the intellectual processes entailed are items contained on the job analysis sheet. When the personnel manager begins looking for workers, he follows a job specification, which simply tells what qualifications a worker must have in order to fulfill the tasks indicated on the job analysis sheet. For example, stenographers are almost invariably inefficient if they score below 60 on Army Alpha. The job specification for stenographers would, therefore, contain the intelligence score of 60 as the lower critical score. There are occasions, too, where an upper critical score is included, as our reference to the records on Army Alpha of taxicab drivers would indicate. From the viewpoint of management, a low labor turnover is to be desired, so an intelligent man in a monotonous job is a liability.

The vocational counsellor differs from the employment manager to a certain degree in his use of tests, for the former is interested primarily in learning all the capacities of an individual so that he may more adequately steer him into the right position. The employer, on the contrary, is more interested in the performance of the subject on a given test which is diagnostic for the vacant job. The employer has been but slightly concerned with the other talents and capacities of a worker if the latter fails to meet the demands of the specific task. In large industrial plants and commercial firms, however, the personnel departments now function in the role of vocational counsellors, for there are so many different kinds of work for which men and women are required that the personnel officer can utilize almost every applicant. He is interested, therefore, in all the talents and abilities of the applicant.

To show the procedure involved in applying psychology in the economical selection of workers, let us assume that a large gasoline company wished us to hire its service station operators. If 1,000 men apply and we need at the present moment but 100, how are we to select the most efficient 10 per cent of these applicants? An interview would enable us to eliminate those obviously unfitted for the tasks involved, but still we have, let us assume, 500 men who seem competent. We might select the 100 best looking men, but physical appearance is not the only asset in this business, so we may get many incompetent men whom we would be compelled to discharge after a few weeks or months. We don't want to spend the initial price of training men who will later leave us. We know that there are 100 of our 500 men who are more efficient than the remaining 400, and these are the ones we wish to discover as quickly as possible.

We decide to get an occupational description or job analysis, so we study at first hand the various phases of the work, discovering that service station men must know something about various kinds of automobiles; that they must be able to make change and do the simple arithmetic involved in their daily inventories of the accessories which they sell and leave on hand for the men on the next shift; that they should be able to talk intelligently about the relative merits of gasolines and oils and anti-freeze mixtures; that they are frequently asked directions; that they are to try to sell to various types of customers.

With these facts in mind we decide to devise a battery of several sub-tests which will enable us to give a numerical evaluation to the various applicants. Accordingly, we construct one sub-test in mathematics, following the method of Test 2 of Army Alpha. This should differentiate those who are poor at figures. Since we are in haste about hiring these men and cannot take time to train them, all of our sub-tests will incline toward the achievement type of examination. We give a short answers or multiple choice sub-test covering the mechanical parts of automobiles. Another sub-test covers technical questions regarding gasoline, anti-freeze mixtures and the various tires, tire patching equipment and other accessories sold at the station. We may include a sub-test covering important highways leading out of the city, and the best routes to neighboring states or cities. A final multiple choice sub-test should cover the salesman's knowledge of human nature—his ability to demonstrate tact in the sales situation. For example:

A woman drives up to the station in a Cadillac and says, after you have filled the tank with ethyl gasoline, "Yesterday one of your service men checked the tires and left all the valve caps off." You should

———— 1. Tell her she must be mistaken.
———— 2. Offer to replace them at once.
———— 3. Agree that he was pretty dumb.
———— 4. Tell her she can't get away with a trick like this.

Now we have five sub-tests which *a priori* reasoning leads us to believe are good. Our task is still not completed. We need to test our test. Such a procedure involves giving the test to a large group of service station operators who have been in the employment of a company for a considerable time so that their records of efficiency are well known. If the most efficient workers score highest on our test, while the poorest as judged by the company's records also get our lowest marks, then we can forthwith administer our test to the 500 applicants and select the highest 100 scorers. It may be quite possible, however, that in testing our test we find that the best workers don't make the highest scores. Then we must analyze their test papers, and see if we should "weight" the scores on certain of our sub-tests. Weighting the scores simply consists of increasing the number of items in the sub-test or in multiplying by two or whatever figure is warranted, the score made. For instance, if we had 25 items in each of our five sub-tests, the total possible score would be 125. But if we found, from studying the records of the good workers and their scores on our test, that the arithmetic sub-test was more valuable than the one pertaining to knowledge of highways, we would simply double the scores made on the arithmetic test. A perfect score in this test would now have a value of 50, and the grand total would amount to 150.

The tendency toward objectization which is demonstrated in the above tests has also appeared in our rating scales. Even the judging of college debates has gone through a "job analysis" so that we don't ask the critic simply to give us his general impression of the two teams. Instead, we tear down the job of debating into manner of delivery, constructive speech, rebuttal, poise, gesticulation and the like. In a similar manner the more intangible qualities of employees, such as cooperativeness, initiative, ability to inspire confidence, etc. have been made into headings upon graphic rating scales such as the one by Professor Delton T. Howard on the two adjacent pages. Four or five degree intervals are denoted by words along a base line. The rater checks along the line the point which he thinks indicates the position of the subject being rated. The base line is often exactly ten centimeters long so that a centimeter scale can be placed upon it for reading the checked point in terms of percentage. A check 9 centimeters from the low end of the scale would therefore mean 90 per cent proficiency in the quality designated.

In summarizing the use of psychological tests in employment we may state that they improve both the happiness of the employee and increase the efficiency of the firm, for they enable the employment manager to select workers who are suited to the tasks which they are to perform. An achievement test, for instance, will quickly indicate whether an applicant is familiar with the tools or trade in which he claims expertness, and his speed, alertness, and accuracy may be obtained within an hour's time. These characteristics are almost incapable of correct discernment in the personal interview. See my "Test For Employers," in the Appendix.

The Relationship Between Intelligence and Occupational Success. We have mentioned the fact that there are critical intelligence scores below which workers are incompetent and above which they tend to change jobs as soon as a better opening is available. In her study of 375 girl workers with an average chronological age of 16 years, Burr[9] has given tentative norms of industrial ability of various degrees of feeble-mindedness. Her criterion for success in the occupa-

---

"Genius is one per cent inspiration and ninety-nine per cent perspiration."   —Thomas A. Edison

RATING SCALE OF FURTHERANCE-HINDRANCE FACTORS AFFECTING SCHOLASTIC ACHIEVEMENT

By D. T. HOWARD

Indicate your rating in each factor by placing a check on the line where you think it ought to be.

FACTORS					
I Consider your health as affecting your studies: Is your health always good and conducive to vigorous study, or does it interfere with your work?	Excellent health, sound and vigorous.	My health is better than average.	Not especially good nor bad.	I have some cause to complain of my health.	Bad health is a serious handicap to me.
II Is the place, or places, where you do your studying ideal for the purpose, or are you distracted or interrupted to an annoying degree? Are you well satisfied, do you think that you are fairly well placed, or have you a great deal of distraction to contend with?	Ideal.	Generally favorable.	Tolerable.	Rather unsatisfactory.	Highly distracting.
III Do campus activities contribute to your success as a student, or do they engage your time and interest in such a way as to interfere seriously with your studying?	I consider my program ideal	Rather good than bad.	Neither very helpful nor very harmful.	My studies suffer some.	Very distracting and injurious to college work.
IV Are you able to arrange your time so as to provide regular hours for study? Or are you prevented from keeping to a regular schedule because of conflicts with duties and engagements that cannot be avoided?	My program can be arranged as I please.	I can always arrange for studies by giving some thought to my program.		Other matters interfere frequently to prevent me from keeping to a regular schedule of study.	I find it very difficult to provide study hours.

Question					
V Do not answer this question unless you do some work to support yourself while in college. If you work for support, does this activity promote the keenness of your scholarship, or does it operate as a serious distraction? Try to express, in terms of benefit or hindrance, the influence of such work upon your studies.	It is ideal and fits in excellently.	It is a help to me in my studies.	It makes no difference in my work.	It is annoying.	An extreme distraction and a great handicap.
VI Consider your future career and prospects. Is your general state of mind regarding your future quite unsettled so that you are restless and unable to settle down to systematic study? Or is the exact contrary the case? Or are you indifferent to such considerations?	So disposed that future prospects are a strong incentive to study.	Future prospects a help rather than a hindrance.	Indifferent to such considerations.	Could do better if I had a more settled program.	Very unsettled, and find it hard to get down to study.
VII Do you find yourself doubtful, for any reason, as to the value of your college studies? Or are you certain that they have a very high value? In this connection consider whether your present studies have or have not an important bearing on your future life and work.	I place the highest value on my studies.	Quite valuable and should be taken seriously.	At least as valuable as any other activity in which I engage.	Other campus activities are more important.	Distinctly minor importance.
VIII Do you find yourself unable to study by reason of worry, anxiety, or excessive dissatisfaction produced by causes over which you have no direct control? Or is your state of mind generally untroubled and favorable to study?	My mind is free from worries that would interfere with study.	Although I have occasional worries, these do not seriously affect my studies.	I have real troubles at times, but cannot say that they seriously hinder my studies.	I could do better work if I had less to distract my mind.	Worries are a source of real distraction to me.

EXHIBIT 48. An example of a Graphic Rating Scale.

tion was usually a period of at least three months of continuous employment at the same work. The least mental age at which it is possible for a girl to perform the given tasks with success is contained in the table below.

MINIMUM MENTAL AGE	TASKS WHICH CAN BE CREDITABLY PERFORMED
7 to 8 years..	Packing small articles not easily damaged by handling, such as powder-puffs.
8 to 9 years..	Certain operations in pencil making.
9 to 10 years..	Crude hand-sewing, such as putting buttons on cards, sewing bows on novelties; cutting and pasting in paper-box making; sewing hat linings and steaming materials used in millinery; packing and folding hair-nets.
10 to 11 years..	Stock-keeping, labeling and checking; winding cotton and wool braid, hand-sewing on garments.
11 to 12 years..	Covering buckram foundations, sewing in the wire edge and facings of women's hats.
12 to 13 years..	Sewing on labels at high speed; machine operating for straw and other millinery, for window shades, garters, powder-puffs, etc.
13 to 14 years..	Assembling of parts requiring some judgment; machine operating in sewing straight seams, bindings, etc., where threading and adjusting machines are necessary; completion of an entire garment.

In his thorough survey of the intellectual limits of various occupations, Fryer[24] amplified and corrected the data obtained by the United States Army during the war. He employed a "Business Alpha", a 20-minute intelligence test arranged and standardized for vocational and business purposes by H. D. and L. P. Fryer. The score ranges in the following table are for the most part interquartile, that is, the upper and lower

---

"A man is very apt to complain of the ingratitude of those who have risen far above him."   —Samuel Johnson quarters are omitted. It is assumed that those in the lowest quarter are having difficulty in a given occupation and those in the upper quarter are probably restless and inclined to move to a higher occupation. There are 96 occupations listed. Fryer believes an individual should have a score above the average of any profession to feel sure of being able to attain success therein.

INTEL. GROUP	SCORE AVE.	SCORE RANGE	OCCUPATION
A	161	110-183	Engineer (Civil and Mechanical)
	152	124-185	Clergyman
	137	103-155	Accountant
B	127	107-164	Physician
	122	97-148	Teacher (Public Schools)
	119	94-139	Chemist
	114	84-139	Draftsman
	111	99-163	Y. M. C. A. Secretary
	110	80-128	Dentist
	109	81-137	Executive (Minor)
C+..........	103	73-124	Stenographer and Typist
	101	77-127	Bookkeeper
	99	78-126	Nurse
	96	74-121	Clerk (Office)
	91	69-115	Clerk (Railroad)
	86	59-107	Photographer
	85	57-110	Telegrapher and Radio Operator
	83	64-106	Conductor (Railroad)
	82	57-108	Musician (Band)
	81	59-106	Artist (Sign Letterer)
	81	60-106	Clerk (Postal)
	81	57-109	Electrician
	80	62-114	Foreman (Construction)
	80	56-105	Clerk (Stock)
	78	54-102	Clerk (Receiving and Shipping)
	78	61-106	Druggist
	77	59-107	Foreman (Factory)
	75	56-105	Graphotype Operator
C	74	53- 91	Engineer (Locomotive)
	72	54- 99	Farrier
	70	46- 95	Telephone Operator
	70	44- 94	Stock Checker
	69	49- 93	Carpenter (Ship)
	69	48- 94	Handyman (General Mechanic)
	69	46- 90	Policeman and Detective

INTEL. GROUP	SCORE AVE.	SCORE RANGE	OCCUPATION
C—........	68	51- 97	Auto Assembler
	68	47- 89	Engineman (Marine)
	68	42- 86	Riveter (Hand)
	67	50- 92	Toolmaker
	66	45- 92	Auto Engine Mechanic
	66	45- 91	Laundryman
	66	49- 86	Gunsmith
	66	44- 88	Plumber
	66	44- 88	Pipefitter
	65	44- 91	Lathe Hand (Production)
	65	43- 91	Auto Mechanic (General)
	65	43- 91	Chauffeur
	65	42- 89	Tailor
	65	44- 88	Carpenter (Bridge)
	64	43- 88	Lineman
	63	40- 89	Machinist (General)
	63	46- 88	Motor Cyclist
	63	41 -86	Brakeman (Railroad)
	62	31- 94	Actor (Vaudeville)
	61	40- 85	Butcher
	61	44- 84	Fireman (Locomotive)
	61	39- 82	Blacksmith (General)
	60	38- 94	Shop Mechanic (Railroad)
	60	36- 93	Printer
	60	40- 84	Carpenter (General)
	59	40- 87	Baker
	59	39- 83	Mine Drill Runner
	59	38- 81	Painter
	58	37- 85	Concrete Worker
	58	40- 83	Farmer
	58	37- 83	Auto Truck Chauffeur
	58	37- 82	Bricklayer
	57	41- 81	Caterer
	57	39- 71	Horse Trainer
	56	38- 76	Cobbler
	55	35- 81	Engineman (Stationary)
	55	34- 78	Barber
	55	35- 77	Horse Hostler
	52	38- 96	Salesclerk
	52	33- 74	Horse Shoer
	51	31- 79	Storekeeper (Factory)
	51	26- 77	Aeroplane Worker
	51	31- 74	Boilermaker
	50	33- 75	Rigger
	50	30- 72	Teamster
	49	40- 71	Miner (General)
	48	21- 89	Station Agent (General)

INTEL. GROUP	SCORE AVE.	SCORE RANGE	OCCUPATION
C—..........	40	19- 67	Hospital Attendant
	40	19- 60	Mason
	35	18- 62	Lumberman
	35	19- 57	Shoemaker
	32	16- 59	Sailor
	31	20- 62	Structural Steel Worker
	31	19- 60	Canvas Worker
	30	16- 41	Leather Worker
	27	19- 63	Fireman (Stationary)
	27	17- 57	Cook
	26	18- 60	Textile Worker
	22	16- 46	Sheet Metal Worker
	21	13- 47	Laborer (Construction)
D	20	15- 51	Fisherman

The relationship between intelligence and occupational success is rather difficult to summarize succinctly. In general however, the demands of the job must be sufficiently complex to monopolize the attention of the worker, yet not so great as to be a strain upon his adaptive behavior. If he has either too much or too little intelligence for the given task he usually becomes dissatisfied. Such surveys as the one just cited show the intelligence ranges within a given occupation, but there is considerable overlapping, so the intelligence score of a person is not diagnostic of a single vocation. At present we shall have to be content with classifications of a general sort, such as professional, skilled, semi-skilled, and unskilled.

Adjusting the Worker to His Job. In former days the new worker was frequently made the butt of jokes and a certain amount of hazing before he was admitted into the camaraderie of his fellow workers. Nowadays he is introduced to his fellow employees, often called co-workers to avoid the idea of employee versus employer, and his foreman or supervisor gives him the necessary instructions. These are not piled upon him before he can become somewhat oriented to his new functions and environment. His first work should be rather simple, for he is in a greater or less emotional state for the first few days immediately following his placement.

The majority of companies have definite follow-up systems in order that the progress of the new workers may be observed. A representative of the personnel office a day or two later just happens to be passing, and stops beside the new worker's desk or bench for a few minutes' chat. He inquires how the latter is progressing, and lets him know that the personnel office is interested in his success. Often a second follow-up of this sort is made at the end of the week. Thereafter the worker's record is noted to see if he is making a satisfactory adjustment to the production demands of his job.

Since it is frequently true that the personnel department is given the responsibility of promotion, transfer, and discharge, it must be concerned not only with the worker's initial success, but make provision for his ultimate advancement if his capacities warrant such. Blind alley jobs must be avoided when placing the able worker, and a flexible wage scale adopted.

Regarding rates of payment, a number of plans have been devised, of which those holding for salesmen cover most of the possibilities. Of these a straight salary has been the most popular method of compensation, followed by the straight commission. Salary with a bonus is growing in popularity today. Then we have salary and commission; commission and a bonus; a combination of salary, commission, and a bonus; and a drawing account against profit on sales or bonus accumulations.

In the university personnel departments many of the same procedures are followed as in business. The students are agreeably introduced to the university life and their first year is watched very closely. Those who seem to be falling down in production (scholarship) are interviewed with the aim of finding the difficulty and removing it. New plans of study are worked out between the personnel officer and the student.

If the latter is devoting too much time to outside activities, or has lacked an adequate method of studying while in high school, the personnel worker assists in making a readjustment. Part time employment for students who are earning their way through school is a frequent function of the personnel office. Moreover, a number of students need moral guidance and friendship, especially if they are the children of divorced parents, and are struggling in emotional quicksands vainly striving for a sound anchorage. Many of the students with low grades are having emotional conflicts which make it almost impossible for them to concentrate. The personnel departments of universities, like some of the foremost ones in industry, are finding it advisable to include psychiatry within their province.

The adjustment of the worker to his job, therefore, consists largely of the establishment of friendly relations between him and his associates and superiors. Instead of adopting the critical attitude that he must disprove their suspicions of his incompetence, the modern personnel officer and supervisor endeavor to make it easy for him to do his best, and initiate him into his tasks by degrees. They have previously selected him because of his demonstrated abilities or aptitudes, so the process of adjustment is principally a social one. In college personnel work it also frequently involves teaching the student more effective habits of study.

The Causes of Discharge. A lack of skill or technical knowledge is not the chief cause of discharge, despite the findings of the army trade tests administered to 250,000 men. At that time the trade tests revealed that of those men claiming skill, only 6 per cent possessed expertness in their trades, while 24 per cent might be classed as journeymen in ability. In 40 per cent of the cases the men had only the equivalent of apprenticeship qualifications, while 30 per cent did not know anything at all about the trades in which they claimed to be expert.

In this connection the Bureau of Vocational Guidance at Harvard University made a study of the causes for discharge of employed men. In over 4,000 cases which were examined, two major categories were found to explain their leaving. These were (1) Lack of Skill or Technical Knowledge, and (2) Lack of Social Understanding. Although incompetence is the largest single cause, those items classified under the psychological heading furnished a majority of the total.

CAUSES OF DISCHARGE

	NO. CASES	PCT.
LACK OF SKILL OR TECHNICAL KNOWLEDGE:		
Incompetence	1126	25.7
Slowness	200	4.6
Physical Inadaptability	170	3.9
	1496	34.2
LACK OF SOCIAL UNDERSTANDING:		
Insubordination	486	11.1
General Unreliability	453	10.4
Absenteeism	442	10.1
Laziness	317	7.2
Trouble Making	179	4.1
Drinking	179	4.1
Violation of Rules	142	3.2
Carelessness	120	2.7
Misconduct	100	2.3
Dishonesty	91	2.1
Unclassified	321	8.5
	2830	65.8

The reader will note that slowness is placed in the same category with incompetence. O'Rourke[22] found that the slow worker is much more inaccurate than the fast worker. Taking the record of the 125 most rapid workers and contrasting it with the performance of the 125 slowest workers, he found that the slow individuals were correct in only 38 per cent of their attempts whereas the fast workers were right in 80 per

A smile is not only woman's best cosmetic but it likewise serves as a non-verbal compliment to her companion.

cent of the items undertaken. These findings are presented graphically in Exhibit 49. The college instructor has empirically observed a somewhat similar relationship with regard to students during their examinations.

ACCURACY   INACCURACY

RAPID
80%

SLOW   SLOW
38%   62%

RAPID
20%

Exhibit 49. Showing the accuracy and inaccuracy of slow and fast workers. (O'Rourke).

The causes of discharge are consequently not confined to lack of mechanical or technical skill alone, but involve in addition a number of personality traits which are strictly psychological in nature. In fact, the Harvard report, indicates that almost two-thirds of the discharged men lose their positions because of either a lack of understanding or a failure to employ psychology. The personnel department can easily eliminate the technically unfit, but it has difficulty "weeding out" the 65 per cent who are deficient in social understanding.

The Importance of the House Organ or Factory Magazine. By sponsoring a factory publication the personnel department is better able to maintain the morale and cooperation of the employees. After all, there are millions of men and women whose literary ambition would be satisfied by finding their names in print, which explains the wide popularity of the "Personals" column.

When Mr. Lee, cited in Chapter VII, endeavored to increase the sales of Protectographs, his $100 prize to the salesman breaking the previous high record was probably not as strong a motive as the fact that a picture of the winner and his family appeared in the company's magazine. These photographs, like the actress's glowing publicity write-ups, are filed away in the family archives for possibly half a century thereafter.

But there are more important aspects of the house organ than the one just mentioned. The management has an opportunity therein to present an educational program concerning the various functions of its many departments, thereby orienting the employee. The chief executives can talk *via* the printed page directly to the men whom they might never otherwise have an opportunity to meet. Explanations of the new policies introduced by the company or of the reasons for wage cuts may be made. Because they are put into the house organ, the employee's wife also gets a chance to see the management's side of the argument without being dependent solely on her husband's interpretation. In short, the house organ enables the management to speak to the wives of its employees, as well as to its workers. The house organ, however, should be in the main an employee paper apart from the dominance of the management, although two or three pages may be left weekly or monthly for information and editorials from the executives of the firm.

House organs may be simply a mimeographed page or pamphlet sent out to salesmen, or they may consist of more elaborate proportions and format. Fashions, recipes, humor, sports, editorials, children's pages—these are some of the features which make them more attractive to the entire family. It must be remembered, moreover, that thousands of families in every great industrial organization buy no magazines whatever, so the factory publication holds great potentialities, as we shall elaborate in the next section.

From the psychological standpoint, therefore, the house organ is of considerable value in the development and maintenance of morale among the employees. By enabling the management to speak directly to the wives of the latter, it not only increases the influence of the executives, but may often in consequence lessen conflicts between employer and employee. In its broader social and educational significance, the management may slowly change the attitudes of thousands of its workers and their families.

Cultural Responsibilities of Employer to Employee.

Throughout this textbook we hold to the view that the progress of civilization as it affects human beings demands that "they may have life and have it more abundantly." This has been the principle behind our public school system. With this basic philosophy of society the role of management takes on tremendous significance. Over 75% of our adult Americans are through with formal schooling forever by the age of 18. Then they enter some type of employment where they remain for their next 47 years.

The "boss" or employer really functions much as a substitute "Papa" for a group of men and women who are relatively carefree from the time they punch out on the time clock at night till they return next morning. Like typical overgrown children, millions of workers nowadays hold resentments against the boss which are simply transferred hositility from their earlier contacts with their own fathers at home.

Thus, they flaunt their disregard and often grumble at the preoccupation of the boss, failing to realize that he must wangle a constant influx of orders to maintain jobs for everybody. And the terrific energy toll of governmental red tape, confiscatory taxes and executive decisions makes the employer as irritable and short-tempered as their own fathers used to be in their childhood homes.

Nowadays, we need more of the Golden Rule on the part of both workers and management! The pendulum has swung too far in the direction of the workers, who don't seem to realize that all their jobs would vanish if management didn't assume the onerous responsibilities of leadership.

Meanwhile, of course, management should help promote sounder outlooks in various cultural fields by means of the house organ, as well as other educational aids such as the "rack service" whereby millions of helpful booklets are available to the workers.

When Hitler built up his Fascist state, he deliberately encouraged children to spy on their own parents and report the latter to his Gestapo. Alas, we have witnessed in the past decade a somewhat similar condition where workers have often been encouraged to harass the "Papa" called their "boss" and keep demanding constantly zooming "allowances" in the form of fringe benefits, without increasing proportionately their output.

Such dangerous policies are sabotaging our entire "free enterprise" system and driving us rapidly toward socialism via increasing inflation. According to Commerce Clearing House, the average taxpayer now earns about $5,000 but will pay $47,221.18 in taxes between his present age of 29 and his retirement age of 65. That's 25% of his total earnings!

REFERENCES

1 ASPLEY, J. C., *Solid Gold Hours* (Dartnell, 1966)
2 AMBERG, R. H., "*The 99 Days in St. Louis*" (Editor & Publisher, 6/6/59)
3 APPEL & STRECKER, *Discovering Ourselves* (Macmillan, 1964)
4 BERG, R. H., "*A Report on Hospitals*" (*Look*, 2/3/59)
5 BIJOU, S. W., *The Psychological Program in AAF Convalescent Hospitals* (AAF Psychology Research Report No. 15, 1947)
6 BOISEN, A. T., *Exploration of the Inner World* (Harper, 1962)
7 BRAY, C. W., *Psychology and Military Proficiency* (Princeton U. Press, 1948)
8 BRAYFIELD, A. H., *Modern Methods of Counseling* (Appleton, 1950)
9 BURR, E., "Minimum Intelligence Levels of Accomplishment in Industry" (*J. Personal Res.* 33, 1924)
10 BURTT, H. E., *Employment Psychology* (Houghton Mifflin, 1926)
11 CARTER, L. F., *Psychological Research on Navigator Training* (AAF Psychology Research Report No. 10, 1947)
12 CLEETON, G. U., & KNIGHT, F. B., "Validity of Character Judgments Based on External Criteria" (*J. Appl. Psychol.*, 8, 1924).
13 CLEETON, G. U., *Making Work Human* (Antioch Press, 1949).
14 COOK, S. W., *Psychological Research on Radar Observer Training* (AAF Psychology Research Report No. 12, 1947).
15 CRAWFORD, M. P., *Psychological Research on Operational Training in the Continental Air Forces* (AAF Psychology Research Report No. 16, 1947).
16 DAILEY, J. T., *Psychological Research on Flight Engineer Training* (AAF Psychology Research Report No. 13, 1947).
17 DAVIS, F. B., *The AAF Qualifying Examination* (AAF Psychology Research Report No. 6, 1947).

18 DEEMER, W. L., *Records, Analysis, and Test Procedures* (AAF Psychology Research Report No. 18, 1947).

19 DRIVER, H. I., *Multiple Counseling* (Monona, 1954).

20 DU BOIS, P. B., *The Classification Program* (AAF Psychology Research Report No. 2, 1947).

21 ERICKSON, C. E., *The Counseling Interview* (Prentice-Hall, 1950).

22 FILER, H. A., & O'ROURKE, L. J., "Progress in Civil Service Tests" *(J. Personnel Res.*, 1, 1923).

23 FLANAGAN, J. C., *The Aviation Psychology Research Program in the Army Air Force* (AAF Psychology Research Report No. 1, 1948).

24 FRYER, D., "Occupational-Intelligence Standards" *(School and Society*, 16, 1922).

25 FRYER, D., & HENRY, E., *Handbook of Applied Psychology* (Rinehart, 1950).

26 GIBSON, J. J., *Motion Picture Testing and Research* (AAF Psychology Research Report No. 7, 1947).

27 GORDON, E. E., "Exercise Equivalents" *(Modern Medicine*, 12/15/57).

28 GRIFFITTS, C. H., *Fundamentals of Vocational Psychology* (Macmillan, 1924).

29 GUILFORD, J. P., *Printed Classification Tests* (AAF Psychology Research Report No. 5, 1947).

30 HARBISON & MYERS, *Management in the Industrial World* (McGraw-Hill, 1960).

31 KRATHWOHL, W. C., "An Index of Industriousness for English" *(J. Educ. Psychol.*, December, 1949).

32 LAUER, A. R., *Manual of Tests for Automotive Operators* (Ames, 1934).

33 LAYTON, W. L., "Predicting Success in Dental School" *(J. Appl. Psychol.*, 1953, 37, 251-255).

34 LINK, H. C., "Workers' Reactions to Industrial Problems in a War Economy" *(J. Appl. Psychol.*, 26, 1942).

35 MAIER & HAYES, *Creative Management* (Wiley, 1962).

36 MERRIHUE, W. V., *Managing By Communication* (McGraw-Hill, 1960).

37 PRATT, C. C., *Military Psychology* (Am. Psychol. Assoc., 1941).

38 REICHARD et al., *Aging & Personality* (Wiley, 1962).

39 SCOTT, W. D., CLOTHIER, R. C., & SPIEGEL, W. R., *Personnel Management* McGraw-Hill, 1949).

40 SNOW, A. J., "An Experiment in the Validity of Judging Human Ability" *(J. Appl. Psychol.*, 8, 1924).

41 SAYLES, L. R., *Behavior of Industrial Groups* (Wiley, 1958).

42 SODEN, W. H., *Rehabilitation of the Handicapped* (Ronald, 1949).

43 STECKLE, L. C., *Problems of Human Adjustment* (Harper, 1949).

44 SUMNER, K., "You Can't Judge a Man's Mind by the Size of His Hat" *(American Magazine*, Nov., 1922).

45 TAYLOR & BARRON, *Scientific Creativity* (Wiley, 1963).

46 UHRBROCK, R. S., "Construction of a Selection Test for College Graduates" *(J. Gen. Psychol.*, 41, 1949).

47 VERNON, P. E., *Personnel Selection in the British Forces* (London, Little Paul's, 1949).

48 VISCARDI, H., *Give Us The Tools* (Eriksson-Taplinger, 1960).

49 WITTKOWER, E., *A Psychiatrist Looks at Tuberculosis* (London: Nat. Assoc. for Prevention of Tuberculosis, 1949).

50 WHITING, B. B., *Six Cultures* (Wiley, 1963).

51 WITKIN et al., *Psychological Differentiation* (Wiley, 1962).

52 YOUNG, P. T., *Motivation & Emotion* (Wiley, 1964).

CHAPTER X

THE PSYCHOLOGY OF MUSIC AND MORALE

Music is one of the least tangible products which can affect the human sense organs, yet it is also one of the most effective. Although it is fleeting, while we experience it we may be led to high resolves or passionate action. Shakespeare has said,

> The man that hath no music in himself,
> Nor is not moved with concord of sweet sounds,
> Is fit for treason, stratagems, and spoils.

Evidences of musical instruments are found among the remains of almost every early people and primitive tribe. But ancient music of the best sort was far different from that of modern times. The ancients had not learned the wonderful effect which can be obtained by simultaneously sounding several notes that "chord". They had no harmony, but produced only the melodies or simple tunes. Moreover, they knew nothing about key, failing to appreciate the facts which even the young beginner learns today. It was not until the year 1600 A.D. that the first real opera and the first oratorio came into existence, while the beginning of the eighteenth century really marks the birth of most music as we know it now.

Too many children as well as adults, however, are today developing the idea that music is the bizarre product of a gilded derby hat hung over the end of a trumpet, the mouthpiece of which is being blown by an individual who appears to qualify admirably as a contortionist. Our public schools cannot alone devote sufficient time to the musical development of the child, so his fundamental tutelage in melodic patterns should come from the home.

It is gratifying to parents and teachers to realize that musical ability, and especially musical appreciation, need not be considered as inherited talents. Aside from the necessity of having normal hearing and an extraordinary larynx if he hopes to become an outstanding vocalist, the average person can be taught good music or jazz. His tastes will be largely a result of his environment.

Conradi[8] found that even young English sparrows, when reared by canaries, developed trills and a fair imitation of canary song. In the passage below we find his observation of one of his subjects.

On September 26, when the sparrow was a little over three months old, he was for the first time observed to give a trill. It was short and musical and was given a number of times in succession. These short trills were at first only rare but they increased in frequency during the year. When he gave them he would sit still on his perch and give them one after another very modestly. Now (Dec., 1904) he gives short trills interspersed with other notes, punctuating the whole by turning complete circles and semi-circles on his perch.

None of these sparrows ever had the characteristic call note of the wild species, but by and by adopted those of the canary. They imitated the canary perfectly except that their voice did not have the musical finish.

It is interesting to speculate upon what would result if all the adult sparrows were suddenly to be annihilated, and their eggs placed in canary nests. Would the sparrow's chatter depart forever from the earth? It would seem quite possible to invest the new generation of sparrows with the language of the canary, much as the immigrants take on the speech of their new country, and drop the old. But the practical value of Conradi's work lies in the fact that if the raucous chirping of English sparrows can be moulded into melodic sweetness by the canary environment during the infancy of the former, then it seems rather logical for us to expect our far more intelligent boys and girls, men and women, to react favorably to an environment rich in good music.

"Music is the only language in which you cannot say a mean or sarcastic thing."   —John Erskine

The Place of Music in Building Morale. If we stimulate a child's imagination to noble deeds and high resolves at the same time that we expose his ears to a specific piece of music, and if we continue doing this on several subsequent occasions, the music will eventually cause him to think and act in an idealistic fashion even though we are no longer present to incite his imagination with words. This is simply the phenomenon of the conditioned reflex. We react hilariously or religiously not so much because of the tempo of the music and its particular melody, but because of the conditioned habits that have become attached to it. Indeed, in medieval times a writer of a mass would simply pick out a popular melody to which he fitted his religious utterances. Some of these melodies, such as *The Red Noses* and *Farewell, My Lover,* later gained sacred connotations. The reversal of this process is observed in the parodies of religious music which we often hear.

Parents and teachers who early capture the child's fancy in a web of melody are able to weave into the fabric of that young personality a cultural morale which will buoy up his spirit throughout all the years ahead. Indeed, the effect of music in building morale has been of marked historic significance. The Jewish nation during the captivities sustained its hope by the psalms which were sung to a musical accompaniment. The *Marseillaise* has lifted the spirits of muddy, bedraggled French legions from defeat into victory. In fact, it has inflamed the soldiers so violently that there have been times when its use has been forbidden.

In Revolutionary days *Yankee Doodle* kept the weary colonial troops in step and served as a rallying song for flagging hearts. And during the days before the Civil War the American Negro escaped the misery of his unhappy lot, in a partial degree at least, through his folk songs. Even so thorough-going a realist as Marshal Foch declared during the

World War I, "Morale is more important than material." An ancient tale of Greece corroborates this viewpoint. When Sparta, hard pressed by its enemies, sent to Athens for aid, the Athenians did not want to succor their sister state, for they were jealous of her power and hoped that she would be defeated. Fearing to refuse outright, however, they sent as their representative the poet Tyrtaeus, a man of music and not of action. Tyrtaeus, however, composed ringing martial songs under whose inspiration the Spartans gained a great victory, much to the surprise and chagrin of the Athenians.

It seems quite probable that wars could not continue without music, which serves as an auditory stimulant to the emotions and submerges psychical fatigue. Even in industrial life it serves to eliminate the ennui that results from monotonous work. Music is offered employees through the medium of amplified phonograph records and radios, with beneficial consequences. Since much industrial work becomes so routine that it does not occupy the workers' full attention, music serves as a melodic escape by which their thoughts may dwell on pleasanter things. An occupied mind is usually a contented mind; hence, music by serving as an outlet for surplus cerebral activity, lessens industrial unrest and dissatisfaction.

From the psychological standpoint, therefore, the chief functions of music in building morale consist first of all in serving as an objective stimulus for re-arousing former emotional states. As a consequence of these re-aroused emotional states, the individual usually feels more excited and energetic. The simultaneous release of adrenaline with its accompanying increase in blood sugar places the human organism on a war basis physiologically. A second value of music in morale is its capacity to occupy the unused attention of workers in industry, and thereby reduce their boredom. The third factor has national significance, for the leaders of a crowd realize that the individuals will react emotionally as they did during the learning of the music. Thus, *The Star Spangled Banner* will instantly unify in emotions and thought the listeners who have come up through the American public schools.

Jazz vs. Classical Music.   In talking about good music we refer not alone to those products of the old masters, such as Beethoven, Gounod, and Rossini, but also to many of the pieces which we hear from our better popular orchestras. After all, the criterion of musical excellence is not sheer complexity of architectural pattern, for *Old Folks at Home,* though fairly simple in this regard, holds all the essential elements of a perfect art form.   But classical music is usually of the complex kind, and is therefore considered a more "intellectual" type of music.   There are certain fairly obvious reasons for the greater "wearing" qualities of classical music.

First of all, its mechanics is not so apparent; hence, the listener's curiosity is stimulated for a longer period of time. The central theme or motif of classical music is interwoven with sub-melodies, so that it might be compared to a rail fence covered with beautiful vines, in contradistinction to a single strand of barbed wire that we shall liken to jazz.   Classical music, moreover, is akin to poetry in that it attempts to portray a number of emotions with an artistically developed climax.   Jazz is simple and adapted for the feet.   Because it usually is accompanied with verses, we are able to daydream along trains of thought set up by the romantic suggestions of the words, and consequently are less aware of the early monotony that otherwise results from the melody itself.

In the realm of poetry we are appreciative of this same difference in regard to metrical feet.   Note the greater singsong monotony of the first of the two following quotations in contradistinction to the second.

1.   Mary had a little lamb.
     Its fleece was white as snow.
2.   Strongly it bears us along on swelling and limitless billows,
     Nothing before and nothing behind but the sky and the ocean.

After a few repetitions of the first pair of lines we are tired of them. We can repeat the second set of lines two or three times as often without noting a similar degree of fatigue and ennui. Usually the dactylic hexameter is well suited for majestic compositions, which explains its use in Latin and Greek epic poetry. In this connection Gilliland and Moore performed a very interesting experiment to determine if equal boredom and dislike would result from hearing both classical and jazz music repeated twenty-five times. Four phonograph records were employed in the experiment and always played five times daily in the following order:

A. Beethoven's Fifth Symphony, First Movement.

B. Tschaikowsky's Sixth Symphony, the "Pathétique", First Movement.

C. Fox-trot—"That's It—A Fox-Trot."

D. One-step—"Umbrellas to Mend."

The complete experiment consisted of the five successive playings at five different periods, making a total of twenty-five hearings of each. The subjects were practically unacquainted with all four pieces. Only three of the college men ever remembered hearing either of the classical numbers, and only four felt that there was anything familiar about either of the two jazz pieces. At the first trial the experimenters had their subjects rate the four musical numbers on a ten-point scale of enjoyment value. At the conclusion of the whole experiment the students again rated the four pieces using the same scale. The first and last ratings are given below:

	FIRST	LAST
A.	5.88	6.09
B.	5.60	6.94
C.	5.00	4.91
D.	4.37	4.50

The experimenters' conclusions follow: "The first is that since the strongly marked rhythm of street music has such an immediate stimulating value, it is important to select as our first music for the child or the musically immature, pieces that have a strongly marked rhythm, as well as melodic, harmonic, or structural merit. It is the rhythm that will first get the child's spontaneous attention, and the other musical values will gradually unfold themselves to him as he hears the selection repeatedly. The second conclusion is that since good music apparently tends to develop interest when it is heard repeatedly with an unprejudiced mind, it is important not to inject any moral controversy into the matter of appreciating music."[18]

The chief psychological difference between jazz and classical music, therefore, lies in the fact that the latter is less monotonous because of its greater complexity, and because it usually develops a structural climax of a more imposing sort than is found in jazz. Because of the fact that verses frequently accompany the jazz melodies, the monotonous effect of the latter is not so apparent as otherwise would be true, for the listener may be reveling in daydreams set up by the sentimental words and thus pay less attention to the tune. To either type of music, however, may be conditioned habits of merriment or sorrow and gloom, dependent of course upon the emotional state of the person when he first became familiar with the given melody. Much of the Italian's pleasure in opera which he hears in America is comparable to an American's pleasure in hearing *My Country 'Tis of Thee* in Moscow, namely, its resurrected sentiments of home and parents and other loved ones. The structural merit of the music is probably of less concern to either in contrast to these conditioned emotions.

Music and Emotional Conditioning. Every reader knows that when certain musical pieces are played, he remembers old sweethearts, when others are heard, he recalls school days' experiences, while another group of songs carries him

---

"In my opinion, the great object of music is to touch the heart, and this end can never be obtained by mere noise, drumming and arpeggios. At all events not by me."   —Karl Phillip Emanual Bach back to recollections of his mother, or a church, or maybe a funeral. To the melody of one song have become attached the emotions which he felt when he first learned it, or which he underwent repeatedly as he listened to it. The reader may hum or whistle a stanza of *The Star Spangled Banner,* and find a peculiar emotional state returning which, upon analysis, may involve recall of a schoolroom, a particular teacher, flag day exercises, soldiers marching, and many other former experiences. Frequently he has forgotten the specific childhood scenes but retained only the emotions to which they gave rise. Now hum *Nearer My God to Thee,* and note the marked change in emotions. At the completion of a stanza, change to *Love's Old Sweet Song,* and follow this with *Dixie.*

One of the differences between language and music is the fact that words tend to be specific in their symbolism, whereas music is non-specific. Despite our individual differences in the conditions under which we learned "lamb chops", we are much more nearly alike in our reactions thereto than we are in reacting to *Marqueta.* Moreover, the word "beefsteak" may re-arouse our memories of "lamb chops", but *Dixie* can never re-arouse our emotional memories that have been conditioned by *Marqueta.* Emotions are not subject to recall, therefore, even though they are subject to re-arousal by their specific stimuli.

The fact that words accompany the melody aids greatly in setting the thoughts of the listener into the desired patterns. Since music is a non-specific form of symbolism, an entirely new melody leaves us rather unaffected during its initial rendition. If we can drift away into a dreamy sentimental mood because of its saccharine verses, we may begin to enjoy the piece the first time. Otherwise, our enjoyment must await the process of conditioning in which pleasant emotional states that were produced by our companions and the situation, become attached to the particular melodic pattern. This conditioning is similar to that by which a child learns to like or shun spinach, except that music tends to have more emotional experiences connected with it since we usually encounter it in exciting social situations.

Because strange music neither arouses old memories nor causes a concerted participation in its rendition, the minister who selects hymns which are unknown to a large percentage of his audience is making more uncertain his chances of influencing them by his sermon. The real function of music, from the speaker's standpoint, is to weld his audience into a unified whole and assure that similar emotions are rearoused. The sooner he can get the cooperation of action and of thought of his assembled parishioners, the easier it will be for him to give an effective address. The school teacher, chorister, and voice instructor may profitably train their subjects to sing new pieces, but the minister, public speaker, politician, and propagandist should seldom attempt this task.

In concluding our discussion of music and emotional conditioning, we might say that except for its rhythm there is probably little intrinsic pleasure in music for the child who first hears it, but it soon becomes clothed with definite emotional significance, particularly if the music is heard in the same general situation each time during the learning period. The verses which accompany much popular music help speed this emotional conditioning. Music with verses written or sung in a foreign tongue, however, as opera, is slower in winning favor with the masses.

The Educational Potentialities of Music. For too many people music is looked upon simply as something to which they can dance. Music has conditioned their feet to the actions of shuffling, but has left their minds relatively unaffected. It is largely for this type of person that jazz has been evolved.

These persons have never been taught that the notes themselves have a language of their own. They need to join the classes of alert youngsters who have been pleasantly initiated into the game of picking out the bird calls in Beethoven's *Pastoral Symphony*. We should let them hear the rumble of thunder and the sharp lightning flashes of the storm in Rossini's *Overture to William Tell*, or let them test their interpretive capacities on the tonal dialogue in *The Sorcerer's Apprentice*, Paul Dukas' adaptation of Goethe's ballad. See Page 364.

Moreover, music can become an emotional outlet of great value to the child, even before he outgrows his adolescence. Here is Larry Benson, for example, a neighbor high school lad who comes home from a basket ball defeat feeling irritable. He sits down at the piano, and the first chords which he strikes are fierce, loud, and vindictive. Martial music surges from the strings, and the listener feels that war is imminent. But after a time the music undergoes a transformation. It becomes more calm and subdued, and may finally pass over into some rollicking songs of youth.

In this instance Larry has vented his feelings *via* the music, and his emotional catharsis has cleaned out his ugly mood, leaving him in a much more friendly state of mind. His younger brother and two sisters have also been saved from probable irritable verbal attacks, for youngsters, like adults, are prone to project their ill will upon their weaker associates.

But the principal educational significance of music lies in the fact that the conditions under which we learned a piece tend to be resurrected in our memory when we later hear it. Governments rely on this fact when they get out the bands in time of war and strike up some of the stirring martial airs which they know all citizens have experienced in their grammar school days. They know that loyalty to the fatherland, a desire to protect home and mother, and a hallowed regard for the integrity of the country will be stirred into activity more quickly than if they sent skilled orators into our midst. A combination of fiery speech on top of musically inflamed emotions is almost certain to produce the desired action.

Emotions, however, can be utilized in the interest of peace

and creative enterprises. We can condition children to un-selfishness when we present certain songs to them until event-ually the music itself will suggest those same attitudes. Note the emotional reaction to "Silent Night." And because music cannot be debated verbally, it is an especially powerful weapon to employ. It is always operative as suggestion; therefore, the most intelligent people have difficulty evading its emotion-arousing action. There is only one way to combat music and that is to use music in rebuttal. We cannot argue against the mood which is resurrected when one of Sousa's marches is being played by the band. But we can set rival bands to playing, and cause an emotional impasse to result. Those in-terested in peaceful adjudication of international disputes may more profitably spend their money and vocal energy on "peace bands" and blowing the cornet than on haranguing crowds while military music is still audible on the horizon.

In yet another way, we may employ music to the profit of the individual and the race. It is not necessary that men and women be motivated to dancing behavior when music is played. They may, instead, be conditioned to thinking. Rather than indulging in sentimental "jags", they may engage in cre-ative thought. A certain prominent inventor states that he gets his cleverest ideas while reclining on a couch listening to music. Since the erotic moods may be sublimated into great poetry or art, as we have many examples to bear witness, those same moods when re-aroused by certain melodic patterns, can also, if so trained, be led into creative thinking.

The chief function of music, however, will probably always remain an emotional one. It serves as an escape from the unpleasantries of mundane existence, permitting us to flee to a make-believe world. The task of parents and teachers, therefore, consists of conditioning the child so that in this make-believe realm he does not indulge solely in emotional reveling and erotic debauchery, but diverts his emotional im-pulse into constructive channels.

In respect to the educational potentialities of music, therefore, we may conclude by stating that they pertain chiefly to the energy which is released under the revived emotions which are conditioned by the music. This energy can be sublimated into constructive thinking as well as into dancing over a ballroom floor, depending upon the previous training of the individuals. Since much of the poetry and art of the world has been evolved because of the emotional fervor of the poet and artist, it is possible to re-inflame a temporarily sluggish mind, much as the weary soldier's gait is speeded up, by appropriate melodies and thereby produce energy and incentive for creative thought. In addition to this educative potentiality of music, there is also the mental exercise occasioned in observing the portrayal of emotions by means of melody.

The Role of Music in Propaganda. Propaganda means essentially the spread of a particular doctrine without the hearers' immediate recognition of the source or motives behind the doctrine. It is apparent, therefore, that propaganda employs suggestions, for in so doing it avoids the possibilities of debate, conflict, and resistance. Whenever it can appeal to sentiments, it does so. The difference between sentiments and ideas consists chiefly in the fact that sentiments have an emotional coloring. Thus, the word "house" represents an idea whereas "home" is an example of a sentiment, for it has a host of emotional memories fastened to it, as Edgar Guest's poem so well illustrates.

We have just pointed out that music cannot be combated by words. It leads to no angry debates. The subject is practically helpless when exposed to music, for he does not realize what is going to happen to him and cannot check the revival of old emotional states when their stimulus is offered. We were not conscious of the emotional ties when they were originally being fastened to the given musical piece, so it is almost impossible for us to focus upon them now. And the average citizen does not even make the attempt.

Since the aim of propaganda is to develop or re-arouse sentiments and then suggest action, music becomes one of its best tools. It is a short cut to action, eliminating a more lengthy reasoning process. Even in a religious meeting, for example, it becomes a quicker method of increasing the offering than does speech. A man or woman who is "cold" emotionally can more quickly be aroused by an appropriate melody than otherwise.

In 1940, after Roosevelt had won his third term by "peace propaganda", we saw both music and art used on the nation for war purposes, as in World War I, when it elected Wilson in November, 1916, on the plea, "He kept us out of war," and then was eager for battle on Apr. 6, 1917. We have previously pointed out the helplessness of people before a musical attack, and the necessity for developing a counterattack with other music to which the opposite moods and tendencies to action have been attached. Since different moods may also be conditioned to the same melody, however, the propagandist must keep this fact in mind. To *The Star Spangled Banner* and military marches young men and women are usually incited to action that involves marching, cheering, and enlisting. But older women who have watched their husbands, sweethearts, and brothers leave for war to the accompaniment of these same tunes, may react with sadness, avoidance, and pain.

It is theoretically possible, therefore, for the school teachers of a nation to condition their students adversely to the military music of their country so that the adult generation would be helpless in inciting the youth to warfare by means of those military airs. Both the nationalists and the pacifists must accordingly vie for the cooperation of teachers and parents if they wish to condition the present children of the country so they will be warlike or peaceful a generation hence.

Music, therefore, becomes one of the most effective weapons of the propagandist, for it usually encounters no "sales resistance" on the part of the auditors, so it quickly arouses their emotions and renders them more ready for impulsive action. If group singing occurs, they are welded into a unified whole, ready for their leader to propose action. In the following sections we shall discuss some of the other instruments of the propagandist, particularly in the visual realm.

Propaganda vs. Advertising. The advertiser buys space for his message, and the reader knows that he is reacting to a commercial appeal. He can be on his guard, therefore, and employ reason, although suggestive advertising attempts to prevent his doing the latter. Propaganda, however, endeavors to hide its real nature at all times. It comes out as if it is educational matter with no ulterior purpose than the enlightenment of its readers or hearers. But it differs from true education in that the latter aims to present all aspects of knowledge with no hidden political or financial motives behind the process.

Probably because of its uses during the war, propaganda now has an unpleasant connotation. But propaganda may be good or evil depending upon the motive behind it. The political campaigns of a nation, the advancement of religious sects, the militarists and pacifists, these are only a few of the organizations and enterprises which employ propaganda. Indeed, the historical meaning of the word identified it with the foreign missionary work of the Catholic Church, for three centuries ago Pope Gregory XV founded the great Propaganda College to care for the interests of the Church in non-Catholic countries.

In discussing the two great social dangers in propaganda, Dodge[12] says:

The first is its concentrated power of destruction of the established order. Great destructive power in irresponsible hands is always a social menace. We have some legal safeguards against careless use

---

"Fanaticism consists in redoubling your effort when you have forgotten your aim."   —Santayana of high-powered physical explosives. Against the greater danger of destructive propaganda there seems to be little protection without imperiling the sacred principles of free speech.

The second social danger is the tendency to overload and level down every great human incentive in the pursuit of relatively trivial ends. To become *blase'* is the inevitable penalty of emotional exploitation. I believe there may well be grave penalties in store for the reckless commercialized exploitation of human emotions in the cheap sentimentalism of our moving pictures. But there are even graver penalties in store for the generation that permits itself to grow morally *blase'*. One of our social desiderata, it seems to me, is the protection of the great springs of human action from destructive exploitation for selfish, commercial, or other trivial ends.

The slow constructive process of building moral credits by systematic education lacks the picturesqueness of propaganda. It also lacks its quick results. But just as the short cut of hypnotism proved a dangerous substitute for moral training, so I believe we shall find that not only is moral education a necessary pre-condition for effective propaganda, but that in the end it is a safer and incomparably more reliable social instrument.

Propaganda and advertising employ several similar devices for effecting their ends. Cartoons, for example, are frequently a means of advancing some form of propaganda in much the manner that cuts are useful to the advertiser. Propaganda, like advertising, also appears in the newspapers and magazines, but is frequently designated as publicity. The difference between publicity and advertising is the fact that publicity attempts its purpose without having to pay space rates. The publicity stunts of actresses and actors, for instance, are aimed at gaining a few columns of newspaper space without the necessity of paying therefor. Indeed, in many cases the individuals in question do not dare pay for space, for it is deemed unethical. Publicity, of course, tends to be more effective than paid space matter for the reader is in a more credulous state of mind concerning it. He expects business firms to praise their own products as a matter of policy, but he does not expect outsiders, such as newspaper reporters, to

do so unless they are really good.   In many instances, the
advertiser himself also gains some free publicity in the medium
carrying his advertisements.   This result is especially likely
to follow if there are human interest aspects of the manufacture or sale of his product, and also if the newspaper is desirous of retaining his account.

In summarizing, therefore, we may state that propaganda
is more secretive than advertising in regard to its source and
its purpose.   Accordingly, it engenders less resistance, for the
public is seldom aware of the propaganda as such.   In consequence, propaganda is a great power for good or evil depending upon the organization and motives behind it.   As
Dodge points out, however, it may partly defeat its own end
by an excessive emotional stimulation of the public until the
latter becomes blasé.

How to Develop Propaganda.   Those organizations
which depend upon propaganda as a means of guaranteeing
their economic stability and continuance have usually created
a special department whose function is propaganda, usually
called by its less unpleasant title of publicity.   We have publicity agents for the members of the stage, for politicians, for
universities, for public utility companies and similar businesses.
Sometimes the men who function as such bear the titles,
"Public Relations Counsellor", "Manager", or "Personal Secretary".   The majority of individuals cannot afford to employ
special men or women for this task, but must rely upon their
own ingenuity in this regard.   In Chapter VI we have gone
into this phase of publicity rather thoroughly.

Whether the motives behind propaganda are laudable or
reprehensible depends upon the particular case and is not for
us to decide herein.   There are certain laws of propaganda,
however, that are fundamental.   The writer does not subscribe
to Dunlap's views that the following rules "read like a catalog
of social shame," for this presupposes that psychological laws

are evil, a tenet which we do not hold. We shall cite the six basic laws that Dunlap gives in regard to propaganda.

1. If you have an idea to put over keep presenting it incessantly. Keep talking (or printing) systematically and persistently.

2. Avoid argument, as a general thing. Do not admit there is any "other side"; and in all statements scrupulously avoid arousing reflection or associated ideas, except those which are favorable. Reserve arguments for the small class of people who depend on logical processes, or as a means of attracting the attention of those with whom you are not arguing.

3. In every possible way, connect the idea you wish to put over with the known desires of your audience. Remember that wishes are the basis of the acceptance of ideas in more cases than logic is.

4. Make your statements clear, and in such language that your audience can repeat them, in thought, without the need of transforming them.

5. Use direct statements only when you are sure that a basis for acceptance has already been laid. Otherwise, use indirect statement, innuendo, and implication. Use direct statement in such a way that the attention of the audience shall be drawn to it sufficiently to take it in, but not sufficiently to reflect upon it.

6. For the most permanent eventual results, aim your propaganda at the children; mix it in your pedagogy. Follow the example, in this respect, of Ivory Soap and Prohibition.[14]

To illustrate how propaganda is developed and utilized by industrial and commercial firms, we shall cite an authentic case. The cherry growers and canners in one of our midwestern states had a large crop and much canned goods of which they were unable to dispose. They were faced with a considerable financial loss. A newspaper man from St. Louis evolved the scheme of conducting a state cherry blossom festival, following the method of the state apple blossom festival already in existence. To this festival, which would be heralded throughout every county in the state and neighboring commonwealths, the governor and members of the state legislature would be invited, and a beauty contest would be staged

"We often excuse our own want of philanthropy by giving the name of fanaticism to the more ardent zeal of others."   —Longfellow at which time the most attractive girl present would be crowned Queen of the cherry blossom festival.

The growers and canners agreed to the newspaper man's proposal provided he could line up enough publicity men around the country for the later phase of the problem. He proved his ability by showing a long itinerary with cooperating organizations all along the route. The cherry blossom carnival was staged and it was a great success locally. The Queen was chosen. To Chicago she went, accompanied by the proper cortege. Her publicity director had already made contact with the publicity department of one of America's greatest railroads. The latter gladly cooperated in the venture since it meant opportunity for its railroad to gain some free advertising. The Queen, gracefully draped on the observation platform of a famous passenger train, would make a lovely picture, especially if the name of the train or the railroad could also show in the photograph.

Since the Cherry Queen of a neighboring state was visiting Chicago, the newspapers could be enlisted in the project. The railroad office arranged for the pictures. To make the people "cherry conscious" and also whet their appetites in that regard, some views were later shown of the girl presenting a huge cherry pie to the mayor. The railroad offered her free transportation anywhere it had a train, so she headed for New York. Another pie was presented to its mayor, after which she called upon governors, and finally even obtained an audience with the President, presenting him with one of her enormous pies. If any newspapers were hesitant about participating in the scheme, they soon became willing when they learned that some paid advertising was to follow.

Whether we are trying to motivate our fellowmen by printed or spoken words, however, we must never permit our vocabulary and histrionics to race too far ahead of the audience's present emotional state. In short, we must not "emote" or wax unduly excited before a "cold" audience. Instead, we should consciously exercise self-restraint while endeavoring to incite the crowd by specific emotion-arousing stimuli and concrete episodes. Avoid too many superlative epithets! Narration, involving nouns and verbs with but a few striking adjectives, seems to arouse an audience more successfully than a piling up of descriptive adjectives like "unjust, inequitable and un-American"[23] as in the following quoted editorial.

Mr. Hearst has written some of the most beautiful and effective prose I have ever seen in the English language, but in the editorial below he shows his personal indignation so quickly that the "cold" reader audience hasn't had the time to develop a similar incensed mood. Consequently, it reacts with surprise at the author's apparent excitement, instead of focusing its attention on the object of the latter's diatribe. Since an emotion is the psychological end result of a series of provocative episodes or stimuli, it cannot be foisted upon a cold audience like a military fiat or law. The crowd must be slowly worked up to the same emotional state by seeing or hearing the same type of specific incidents that originally inflamed the leader. To arouse an audience, therefore, employ the inductive method instead of the deductive!

INCOME TAX SYSTEM HAS BECOME GREATEST RACKET IN THE U. S.

To the Editor of The Chicago Herald and Examiner:

Please carry on sustained crusade morning, evening and Sunday against the present Bolshevist system of income taxation.

The income tax system has become the greatest racket in the United States and the government the biggest racketeer.

The system is in itself unjust, inequitable and un-American. It paralyzes enterprise and penalizes honesty.

The rich evade the tax, the poor escape it and practically the whole burden of oppressive taxation is borne by the worthy middle classes.

* * * * *

Does anybody benefit?

Yes, indeed—a standing army of snoopers, gougers, collectors, extorters, tax lawyers and dodgers, ex-government officials with a pull and incumbent officials with open minds.

To support these gentry in ease and affluence is what the tax is for.

Your fellow citizens are exploited, your business prostrated, your country plundered to encourage excessive governmental extravagance to support an unnecessary and dangerous bureaucracy, and to make a burdensome despotism out of our free democracy.

*   *   *   *   *

There are two great historic failures and political evils which this country can indelibly engrave on the blackest pages of its record.

One is the wholly ineffective and un-American policy of prohibition and the other is the inequitable, tyrannical, Bolshevistic policy of confiscatory income taxation.

The essential steps in the development of propaganda, therefore, consist of presenting the ideas in the form of suggestions, and then repeating them whenever possible. Dunlap's six rules are an excellent formula in this regard. A seventh rule should state that whenever music can be utilized, the process becomes easier. Songs may be written whose verses are propaganda itself, in which case the public will often do the repeating for months or years thereafter, and thereby help spread the propaganda at little further cost to those behind it.

How to Combat Propaganda. It is quite probable that the man who could best see through the sleight of hand tricks of a great magician like Thurston would have been Houdini. In short, the best way to see behind the illusions and pleasing display to the mechanics underlying them would be to gain a mastery of the technique involved in producing those same illusions and propaganda. Dunlap had this in mind when he dedicated his rules of propaganda not to the propagandist but to the public on whom propaganda is employed. The unfortunate situation in respect to propaganda is the fact that emotions are stimulated whenever possible, so that even the intelligent person is frequently caught off his guard, and stampeded with the less discerning. Moreover, the development of new "tricks" are likely to fool those who are skilled in detecting all the old ones.

"The fashion wears out more apparel than the man."   —Shakespeare

"Better go to heaven in rags than to hell in embroidery."   —Proverb

The Worry Clinic

George W. Crane, Ph.D., M.D.

Case W-351: Rosalie Savarino, aged 22, is a very popular music teacher in the public school at Birmingham, Mich.

She comes from a talented musical family that has included professional musicians for generations.

"Dr. Crane," Rosalie informed me, "my pupils have taken great delight in a new game called 'Musical Detectives'.

"I employ it to help teach them to be more appreciative. For example, I always select 'Little Sandy Sleighfoot' for use prior to Christmas, because it retains the essential Christmas motif. And it also has a dramatic theme that buoys up the morale of all handicapped youngsters.

"The version I prefer is Mitch Miller's arrangement with Jimmy Dean as the singer.

"When I place the record on the machine, I first ask the children to listen to the general effect a few times.

"Then I challenge them to become 'Musical Detectives' and try to identify as many different musical instruments as possible in the background.

"Most people are only subconsciously aware of the intricate blend of instruments and voices which Mitch Miller wove into the background for Jimmy Dean's clearly uttered lyrics.

"With this_ new idea in mind, my pupils have picked out the guitar notes in contrast to ukelele and celesta. Few of them are able to identify the entire melodic backdrop, for it includes:

Steel Guitar	Ukelele
Hawaiian Guitar	Celesta
String Bass	Piano
Glockenspiel	7 Voices

"My students regard 'Little Sandy Sleighfoot' as the 'dessert' item on our musical menu.

"And the inspirational value of 'Little Sandy Sleighfoot' adds so much religious idealism to this new Christmas song that it will become a permanently popular piece of Christian music, don't you agree?"

Yes, we psychologists fully agree with Rosalie and commend her deft way of introducing youngsters to the rich background effects which talented arrangers like Mitch Miller so beautifully demonstrate.

In the past generation, Irving Berlin's lovely "White Christmas" and also "Rudolph, the Red-Nosed Reindeer" have proved popular.

But they have no evident religious significance. They are purely secular, for they never mention the Bethlehem scene or Christ or anything that is rooted in the religious origin of the Christmas event.

Christmas must never lose its basic Christian nature. It is wrong to strip it bare of its traditional purpose. It is not to be construed as a midwinter Mardi Gras or just a commercial holiday on the calendar.

"Man does not live by bread alone," Jesus said, meaning that our human spirit needs regular nourishment, too.

Music thus serves as vitamins for our morale and a melodic tonic for the soul.

Employ "Little Sandy Sleighfoot" with your children to help stress the Christian nature of Christmas. It also is very appropriate to start teaching them to be "Musical Detectives". Such early training will enrich their entire future lives.

The popularity of radio, television and the 17,000 moving picture theaters in the United States shows what forces for moulding public opinion are resident therein. Prior to television 100,000,000 patrons per week went to the movies. In the schools, churches and other institutions, there are also an estimated 70,000 motion picture machines of the 16 mm. type. Even before television, Professor Ernest W. Burgess summarized the observations of 3,237 teachers of more than 100,000 school children, and concluded that 50% of the children were affected by the movies, which then ranked third in influence upon their lives, as the following order will show: (1) the home; (2) the school; (3) the movies; (4) the church.

Even the news reels may be "colored", either by means of captions, speaking, or by the selective process by which one phase of a situation is shown, and others ignored. In the war pictures that were permitted to reach the American theaters in 1917 and 1918, the doughboys were consistently pictured in happy roles, eating, playing baseball, grinning, fondling pets and French orphans, or dancing with petite French girls. The bleeding eyeless sockets of those blinded by shrapnel, the violent contortions and gasping for breath of the dying gas victim, and the rotting arms and legs and heads of boys who had been blown apart were, of course, censored.

Before the introduction of the "talkies", it was possible for the meaning of any film to be altered simply by a clever rearrangement, cutting, and rewriting of the captions and titles. Today those who write the lines spoken by the moving picture performers can also inject propaganda into the films. From general psychology we have learned the ease with which illusions can be created. If the announcer in the movie tells us to note the surly behavior of a foreign crowd when an American arrives, we have a mental "set" thereafter for anything that fits the idea of surliness, and may misconstrue innocent actions and behavior which are characteristic simply of a curious crowd. If we are told that an approaching lion is stalking its prey, we see ferociousness and cruelty in every move of the beast, even though he is a toothless pet in a California zoo, gamboling playfully after his trainer. International hatred or goodwill likewise can be materially influenced by the announcers who describe travelogue pictures. In order to show how the same print matter may be used in behalf of diametrically opposed courses of action, we shall quote a Democratic and a Republican editorial cited by Strong[40], which appeared in the presidential campaign of 1920 and are gems of Applied Psychology. The Democratic editorial said:

"Mother of America! Mother of Pennsylvania! Mother of Pittsburgh! Do you want your boy to go to war? Is the roll of battle drums sweeter in your ears than the song of his voice in the home? Would you rather have his hands in fierce grip on gun in battle's rack than have his arms in love about your neck? That is the question you must answer to your God and your fellow-man when you go into the voting booth on November 2. Do not let demagogues confuse you. The issue is plain: A vote for the league is a vote for peace; a vote against the league is a vote for war . . . Mother of an American boy! The munition makers of the world are arrayed against American participation in the League of Nations. They are snatching at your vote, because with it they may claim the body of your first-born. Mother of a Pittsburgh boy! The question comes home to you! Your boy was not born to be food for guns."

The Republican advertisement stated in part:

"Women! For your own good vote the Republican ticket . . . The American woman asks of her country: That it be a secure place for her home and for her children and that it be security with honor. That it give her children opportunity to lead their lives even better than she and her husband led theirs. That it be just in its relations with other nations, and merit the pride which the best of its citizens have in it, in its history and its ideals. A policy which has these purposes will have the support of American policy and has been Republican policy from the days of Abraham Lincoln. The Republican policy is to protect the security of the United States by preserving its

---

"Man's greatest blunder has been in trying to make peace with the skies instead of making peace with his neighbors."   —Elbert Hubbard right to make decisions regarding its action in the future as events in the future demand.   The Republican party is unwilling to pledge now that it will protect European boundary lines and to deprive Congress of the power to say in each case what the action of the United States will be . . . "

In combating propaganda we can rely in part upon its own limitations.   Professor Dodge[12] has so clearly delineated these that we shall quote him in this regard.

There are three limitations to the processes of propaganda that we have been considering.   The first is emotional recoil, the second is the exhaustion of available motive force, the third is the development of internal resistance or negativism.

The most familiar of the three is emotional recoil.   We know only too well what will happen if we tell a boy all the things that he likes to do are *"bad"* while all the things that he dislikes are *"good."*   Up to a certain point the emotional value of bad and good respectively will be transferred to the acts as we intend.   But each transfer has an emotional recoil on the concepts good and bad.   At the end a most surprising thing may happen.   The moral values may get reversed in the boy's mind.   Bad may come to represent the sum-total of the satisfactory and desirable, while good may represent the sum-total of the unsatisfactory and undesirable.   To the pained adult such a consequence is utterly inexplicable, only because he fails to realize that all mental products are developments.   There is always a kind of reciprocity in emotional transfer.   The value of the modified factor recoils to the modifying factor.

The whole mechanism of the transfer and of the recoil may best be expressed in terms of the conditioned reflex of Pavlov.   The flow of saliva in a dog is a natural consequence to the sight and smell of food.   If concurrently with the smelling of food the dog is pinched, the pinch ceases to be a matter for resentment.   By a process of emotional transfer on being pinched the dog may show the lively delight that belongs to the sight and smell of food.   Even the salivary secretions may be started by the transfigured pinch.   It was the great operating physiologist, Sherrington, who exclaimed after a visit to Pavlov that at last he understood the psychology of the martyrs.   But it is possible to so load the smell of food with pain and damage that its positive value breaks down.   Eating values may succumb to

---

"Many wearing rapiers are afraid of goose-quills."   —Shakespeare the pain values instead of the pain to the eating values. This is the prototype of the concept bad when it gets overloaded with the emotional value of the intrinsically desirable. The law of recoil seems to be a mental analogue of the physical law that action and reaction are equal and in opposite directions.

The second limitation to propaganda occurs when the reciprocal effects of transfer exhaust the available motive forces of a mind. Propaganda certainly weakens the forces that are appealed to too often. We are living just now in a world of weakened appeals. Many of the great human motives were exploited to the limit during the war. It is harder to raise money now than it was, harder to find motives for giving that are still effective. One of my former colleagues once surprised and shocked me by replying to some perfectly good propaganda in which I tried to tell him that certain action was in the line of duty, to the effect that he was tired of being told that something was his duty, and that he was resolved not to do another thing because it was his duty. There seems to be evidence that in some quarters at least, patriotism, philanthropy, and civic duty have been exploited as far as the present systems will carry. It is possible to exhaust our floating capital of social motive forces. When that occurs we face a kind of moral bankruptcy.

A final stage of resistance is reached when propaganda develops a negativistic defensive reaction. To develop such negativisms is always the aim of counter-propaganda. It calls the opposed propaganda, prejudiced, half truth, or as the Germans did, "Lies, All Lies." There is evidence that the moral collapse of Germany under the first of our paper bullets came with the conviction that they had been systematically deceived by their own propagandists.

As for legal control of propaganda, we encounter so much of the latter which is intangible and not specifically stated that it is impossible to restrain it as the *Printers' Ink* Statute curbs dishonesty in advertising. Moreover, by word of mouth it spreads rapidly, so we often are unable to ascertain the origin of the rumors and whispering campaigns which are frequently heard. When large corporations with unlimited wealth enter upon a propaganda campaign they employ experts to conduct it, and stay within the technical statement of the law. Those alert citizens who may be aware of the mechanics and motives behind the apparently innocent publicity and legislation are frequently bought off. The process of silencing an opponent is not done so blatantly as to be offensive. It may be as subtle as the propaganda campaign itself.

Suppose that Professor Brown, a specialist in the field of public utilities, is to make a report to Congress at its next session on the subject of governmental ownership. If a large holding company fears his possible censure, one of its executives is likely to take Professor Brown to dinner, and say:

"Professor Brown, we have been intensely interested in your economic research during the past few years in the field of public utilities, and feel that it would be desirable for us to have a man of your scholarly insight and scientific ability on our staff. We do not want to take you away from pedagogy, if you feel an aversion to leaving the teaching field, but should be happy to have your valuable criticisms and advice in the role of economic consultant."

No mention would be made of the future report to Congress, for the public utilities executive realizes that men will feel hesitant in reporting adversely concerning the companies from which they are receiving large retainer's fees. This method of silencing the opposition is simply a bit more subtle than the obvious gift of automobiles, stock, or cash. Some of the experts in the employment of large industrial concerns are hired to prevent rival companies from getting them, or to check their unfavorable testimony before juries and legislatures. If this method were confined only to the commercial field, it would not be so pernicious, but our universities are frequently subverted from their inherent obligation to offer both sides of a question with scientific impartiality. A public utility company or a labor union will make a "gift" of $50,000 to a university for research in its field. There are no strings attached to the bequest, so the professor conducting the investigation is theoretically free to report the facts as he finds them. Actually, however, he may go through a psychological change, and fail to observe certain things that would be detrimental to the company or union paying for his survey.

The chief safeguards, therefore, by which we may hope to obtain protection from pernicious propaganda are: (1) a thorough training of youth in honesty and morality; (2) a thorough training in the technique and laws of propaganda; (3) counter propaganda; (4) freedom of speech and of the press; (5) an endowed, impartial press and radio; (6) bureaus of information, like the U. S. Bureau of Standards.

Utilizing Advertising in the Interest of Morale.

In the last decade, the advertising in connection with Mother's Day and Father's Day, plus magazine articles and TV shows, have apparently changed even the attitude of boys and girls. For Gilbert[17] says that the earlier survey made by the Gilbert Youth Research Co., showed the favorite heroes of boys to be President Eisenhower and Elvis Presley, while the girls wanted to grow up to be like Grace Kelley, Queen Elizabeth and Marilyn Monroe. But by 1959 our American boys and girls stated the following preferences:

BOYS SAY—		GIRLS SAY—	
Father	20%	Mother	39%
Myself	8%	Princess Grace	9%
Doctor	8%	Housewife	9%
Pres. Eisenhower	7%	Myself	6%
Biochemist	6%	Mrs. Eleanor Roosevelt	5%
Other Scientist or Engineer.	4%	Teacher	4%
Dr. Jonas Salk	4%	Physical Therapist	3%
Teacher	2%	Father	1%
Uncle	2%	Other	13%
Other	18%	No Answer	11%
No Answer	21%		

You can "sugar-coat" printed advertising and coax the recipients to read every word if you weave your sales points into a "multiple choice" quiz, like that intended for heads of book stores, as shown on the next page. Always give them a set of norms so they can rate themselves thereon.

WARNING

Let all your sales force take this "Advertising Test" before you consult the answer. (See page 375).

Interpretation	Scores
Very Superior	9 - 10
Superior	6 - 8
Average	3 - 5
Uninformed	0 - 2

1. Which one of these Christmas record hits is also the name of a popular children's book?

———"Little Sandy Sleighfoot"   ———"White Christmas"

——— "Mistletoe and Holly"   ———"Let's Light the Christmas Tree"

2. According to BILLBOARD'S ratings, which one of these song hits topped all the others in popularity last season?

———"White Christmas"   ———"Let's Light the Christmas Tree"

——— "Little Sandy Sleighfoot"   ———"Rudolph, the Red-Nosed Reindeer"

3. Queen Elizabeth sent an appreciative letter on behalf of Prince Charles and Princess Anne, for which book?

——— "The Littlest Angel"   ———"Rudolph, the Red-Nosed Reindeer"

——— "The Year Without a Santa Claus" ———"Little Sandy Sleighfoot"

4. Dr. Norman Vincent Peale lauded which one of these children's books because it restores the Christmas theme to Christmas?

———"Little Sandy Sleighfoot"   ———"Rudolph, the Red-Nosed Reindeer"

———"The Littlest Angel"   ———"The Year Without a Santa Claus"

5. Richard Nixon wrote an appreciative letter about which one of these Christmas books?

——— "The Year Without a Santa Claus" ———"The Littlest Angel"

——— "Little Sandy Sleighfoot"   ———"Rudolph, the Red-Nosed Reindeer"

6. Eleanor Roosevelt devoted one of her newspaper columns to which book because it buoys up the morale of handicapped youngsters?

———"Little Sandy Sleighfoot"   ——— "The Year Without a Santa Claus"

——— "The Littlest Angel"   ———"Rudolph, the Red-Nosed Reindeer"

7. Mitch Miller, talented Maestro of COLUMBIA RECORDS, based the foremost song hit of last Christmas on which children's book?

———"Rudolph, the Red-Nosed Reindeer" ———"The Littlest Angel"

——— "The Year Without a Santa Claus" ———"Little Sandy Sleighfoot"

8. In Columbus, Ohio, which one of these books was endorsed last winter by the Board of Education and recommended to the school teachers?

_____ "The Littlest Angel"   _____ "The Year Without a Santa Claus"

_____ "Little Sandy Sleighfoot"   _____ "Rudolph, the Red-Nosed Reindeer"

9. Which one of these books was widely distributed to hospitals for crippled children last year because of its morale boosting value?

_____ "Rudolph, the Red-Nosed Reindeer"   _____ "Little Sandy Sleighfoot"

_____ "The Littlest Angel"   _____ "The Year Without a Santa Claus"

10. Bishop Raines of Indiana, Bishop Kennedy of California, and Dr. Ralph W. Sockman of New York City, all endorsed which book last Christmas?

_____ "Little Sandy Sleighfoot"   _____ "Rudolph, the Red-Nosed Reindeer"

_____ "The Littlest Angel"   _____ "The Year Without a Santa Claus"

When advertising can make people happier by its very format, as well as sell them worthy merchandise, it renders a two-fold service. By blending amusement and relaxation with logical sales arguments, print advertising more nearly matches the rival entertainment value of radio and TV. All three mediums can thus buoy up public morale.

The Relationship of Morale to Success. We have previously mentioned Marshal Foch's statement that morale is more important than materials. In maintaining a victorious army made up of various races, many of which did not even speak the same tongue, Hannibal also demonstrated his realization of the significance of morale. He instituted boxing, wrestling, and gladiatorial combats to keep up the martial spirit of his troops when they were passing through the Alps en route to Rome. In the recent World War we saw a similar appreciation of the importance of morale, and concerted effort to produce it. Moreover, the sales conventions to which manufacturers are willing to bring distant salesmen and pay their expenses are held for the sake of increasing the enthu-

"All sunshine makes a desert."   —William Dawson

siasm and confidence of the sales force. Enthusiasm, confidence, and hope are vital factors not only in war, and business, but in medicine as well. The patient who believes in his physician, or is confident that he will get well, is much more likely to do so. The man who gives up, who admits defeat, is beaten before he commences.

In London some years ago an experiment was performed with five soldiers to determine the influence of their mental state upon their physical strength. They gripped a dynamometer as hard as they could to register their maximum handgrip strength. For the five men the average was 101 pounds. Then they were hypnotized, after which they were told that they were very weak and feeble. They were again given the dynamometer and told to grasp it as strongly as possible. Their average now was only 69 pounds. Then they were given the opposite statements, namely, that they were powerful, Herculean, after which their average strength of handgrip was 140 pounds.

Several important conclusions may be drawn from this experiment. In the first place, a negative thought, such as a feeling of failure or defeatism, leads to marked lessening of physical strength. On the other hand, a positive thought leads to more than average strength. The belief that they were strong actually increased their physical strength almost 40 per cent above their normal capacity, while the belief that they were weak reduced their strength 30 per cent below their best normal record. Although we can probably never attain such a concentration of attention in the focal circle during our normal state as in the hypnotic trance, we tend to go in the direction of the 140 pounds or the 69 pounds when we are respectively confident or fearful of defeat.

The football team, the business man, and the salesman are more likely, therefore, to attain success when confident than when afraid, provided they do not ignore other necessary requirements for victory, such as adherence to training and attention to details. The overconfident football team does not go down to defeat because of this mental attitude, but because it is careless and has avoided the severe training periods as much as possible, and also because it is running against another team which is likewise confident.

Every factor which equips a boy or girl with beneficial habits is thereby eliminating just so many occasions for lack of confidence later in life. We have previously explained that confidence is in large measure a matter of habit. The story of Half-Way Hurley illustrates this point. But physical health also aids in the development of a victory morale. The weary, sick, or enfeebled persons are not sure of themselves and aggressive. They stand back to let the virile individual go ahead, and give way before the counter attacks of customers, debaters, and opponents of all sorts.

Education is also of marked value in building a winning morale. The college man and woman have the advantage over the non-trained person not only in the possession of more book knowledge but especially in the self-assurance and poise which come with knowing that they have at least been "exposed" to all the advantages and information that their associates have received. The non-college man and woman may occasionally be better educated than their collegiate neighbors but lacking the college training, they do not know that they are, so they step aside in deference to the fearless behavior of the college folks. Part of the benefit of a college training is the realization of what our opponents do not know, for we feel that as a general rule they do not possess any educational equipment which we do not also have. This attitude enables the college students to attack a new problem with the feeling that they have at least a 50-50 chance against anybody. The non-college people tend to feel that they have perhaps but a 25-75 chance.

The buoyant influence of music in building a winning morale has been treated heretofore in this chapter when we mentioned that the singing of the *Marseillaise* had at times been forbidden because of its inflammatory effect upon the soldiers. And in industry as well as in the home we find that music can produce happiness and pleasure, both of which reactions are conducive to a feeling of confidence.

Although the person with a defeatism complex may occasionally succeed because of some clever idea or a "driver" at home who forces him into the battle constantly, the man who possesses a winning morale, a confidence in himself, coupled with an intelligent appreciation of the difficulties which beset him, is far more likely to win the coveted rewards of life and ultimately leave this stage with a confident smile for whatever may lie ahead. The development of this type of spirit is one of the functions of education and a duty of parents and teachers in general.

(Answer to all questions on Advertising Test on P. 371 is—
"Little Sandy Sleighfoot".)

REFERENCES

1 ALEXANDER, F. G., *The History of Psychiatry* (Harper & Row, 1966).
2 ADLER, M. J., *Music Appreciation: An Experimental Approach to its Measurement* (Arch. Psychol., No. 110, 1929).
3 APPEL & STRECKER, *Discovering Ourselves* (Macmillan, 1964).
4 BOONE, PAT, *'Twixt Twelve and Twenty* (Prentice-Hall, 1959).
5 BRANDT, H. F., "A Scientific Approach to the Study of Magazine Readership" *(Amer. Psychologist,* 3, 1948).
6 BUCK, P. C., *Psychology for Musicians* (Oxford, 1944).
7 CHERRY, H., "Music as an aid in General Anesthesia" *(N. Y. U. J. Dent.* Jan., 1954, 78-80).
8 CONRADI, E., "Song and Call Notes of English Sparrows When Reared by Canaries" *(Amer. J. Psychol.,* 16, 1905).
9 CUVELIER, A., *La Musique et L'Homme* (U. de France Press, 1949).
10 DIETSCH, R. W., & GURNEE, H., "Cumulative Effect of a Series of Campaign Leaflets *(J. Appl. Psychol.,* 32, 1948).
11 DOCKERY, F. C., & LANE, G. G., *Psychology* (Prentice-Hall, 1950).
12 DODGE, R., "Psychology of Propaganda" *(Relig. Educ.,* 15, 1920).
13 DOOB, L. W., *Public Opinion and Propaganda* (Holt, 1948).
14 DUNLAP, K., *Social Psychology* (Williams, 1925).
15 FARNSWORTH P. R., "Sacred Cows in the Psychology of Music" *(J. Aesthet.,* 7, 1948).
16 GASTON, E. T., "Psychological Foundations for Functional Music" *(Amer. J. Occup. Ther.,* 2, 1948).
17 GILBERT, E., "Heroes Fade," *(Miami News,* 5/2/59).

18 GILLILAND, A. R. & MOORE, H. T., "The Immediate and Longtime Effects of Classical and Popular Phonograph Selections" (*J. Appl. Psychol.*, 8, '24).
19 GUILFORD, J. P., & HOLLEY, J. W., "A Factoral Approach to the Analysis of Variances in Esthetic Judgments" (*J. Exp. Psychol.*, 39, 1949).
20 GUNDLACH, R. H., "Factors Determining the Characterization of Musical Phrases" (*Amer. J. Psychol.*, 47, 1935).
21 JERSILD, A. T., & BIENSTOCK, S. F., "Development of Rhythm in Young Children" (*Child. Developm. Monogr.*, No. 22, 1935).
22 HAVIGHURST & ALBRECHT, *Older People* (Longsmans, Green, 1955).
23 HEARST, W. R., "Income Tax System Has Become Greatest Racket in U.S." (*Chicago Herald-Examiner*, Mar. 13, 1932).
24 HOKE, R. E., *How You Can Have Success Unlimited* (Psych. Service Center, Charlotte, N.C., 1956).
25 HORWICH, F. R., *The Magic of Bringing Up Your Child* (McGraw-Hill, 1960).
26 KAGAN & MOSS, *Birth to Maturity* (Wiley, 1962).
27 LARRABEE, H. A., "The Formation of Public Opinion Through Motion Pictures" (*Relig. Educ.*, 15, 1920).
28 LAWTON, G., "Mental Hygiene at Senescence" (*Ment. Hyg.*, 23, 1939).
29 LE BARRE, W., "The Psychopathology of Drinking Songs" (*Psychiatry*, 2, '39).
30 LEHMAN, H. C., "Some Examples of Creative Achievement During Later Maturity and Old Age" (*J. Soc. Psychol.*, 30, 1949).
31 LEWIS & ENGLE, *Wartime Psychiatry* (Oxford U. Press, 1954).
32 MAC DOUGALL, C. D., "The American Press's Influence on Public Opinion" (*Int. J. Opin. Attitude Res.*, 3, 1949).
33 MITCHELL, S. D., "Music in Mental Hospitals" (*Hosp. London*, 44, 1948).
34 MITCHELL, S. D., & ZANKER, A., "The Use of Music in Group Therapy" (*J. Ment. Sci.* 94, 1948).
35 MOSS, L., "Social Science and the Gallup Poll" (*Int. J. Opin. Attitude Res.*, 3, 1949).
36 RICE, S. A., *Quantitative Methods in Politics* (Knopf, 1928).
37 SEASHORE, C. E., *Psychology of Musical Talent* (Silver, 1919).
38 SHILS, E. A., & JANOWITZ, M., "Cohesion and Disintegration in the Wehrmacht in World War II" (*Publ. Opin. Quart.*, 12, 1948).
39 STRINGHAM, E. J., *Listening to Music Creatively* (Prentice-Hall, 1959).
40 STRONG, E. K., "The Control of Propaganda as a Psychological Problem" (*Sci. Monthly*, 14, 1922).
41 WEINBERG, J., "Mental Health Needs of the Aged" (*Proc. Nat. Conf. Soc. Wk.*, 16, 1949).
42 WERNER, E. M., *Work Music by Muzak* (Muzak, Corp., 1948).
43 WHARTON, D., *Shoplifting — Newest Crime Wave* (Family Weekly, March 17, 1963).
44 WHITING, B. B., *Six Cultures* (Wiley, 1963).
45 WOHL, M. G., *Long Term Illness* (Wiley, 1959).
46 ZIMMER & BIDERMAN, *Manipulation of Behavior* (Wiley, 1964).

CHAPTER XI

THE PSYCHOLOGY OF THE PUBLIC PLATFORM

Because of the widespread dissemination of information through the press, magazines, and books we tend to overlook the fact that public speakers are still the persons who teach all of our school children for at least ten years. Moreover, the clergymen of America are each week giving speeches before millions of men and women. With the advent of radio and TV it is now even possible for a single speaker to address an audience of millions, so the effectiveness of the public address is conceivably greater than ever before, and it has always been tremendous. William Jennings Bryan, an inconspicuous Congressman from Nebraska who came as simply an alternate delegate to the Democratic national convention at Chicago in 1896, stood before that great mass of delegates and, though only 36 years of age, swept them off their seats with his oratory and was immediately acclaimed their nominee for the presidency of the United States. This is one of the best examples of the power of oral speech in all history, and shows the influence of the public address in contrast to an equal exposure to print.

The person who stands before an audience either in the role of entertainer or as speaker encounters many of the same problems which are of difficulty to the salesman, and his methods of attack are also similar to the latter's in many respects. There are, however, certain differences that exist between people in a crowd and people treated singly, which warrant special consideration. We shall discuss them in the following sections of this chapter.

How to Weld a Crowd into an Audience. When the leader stands before a group, he is dealing with people who may have been thinking a thousand different thoughts. The women may be wondering if they forgot to turn off the water in the kitchen, or if the maid has started putting Johnny to bed yet, or what they are going to have for dinner the following night when guests arrive. The men may be wondering if they should not have put on the parking light when they left their automobiles, or if they locked the rear door, or what they are going to do about a business problem that is coming up for discussion the next morning. Meanwhile there is a buzzing of conversation over the auditorium, or the turning of pages of programs, hymn books, or leaflets.

Fortunately for the performer, he knows that the group has come together because of at least one common purpose, which may be the observation of a movie, the inspection of a play, or the hearing of a speech or musical program. This common bond is responsible for their being present. They are, therefore, like those persons who have returned an advertiser's coupon—they have demonstrated an interest in the performance. They form a "warm" market for his ideas or entertainment. Even before the leader addresses the group, however, there are a number of devices by which he can unify the crowd into a more wieldy audience.

(1) *The lighting.* A church, theater, or lecture room should be brightly illuminated while the audience is assembling, for the mood of the audience is more cheerful as a consequence and this mental state is beneficial to the entertainer. It is easier to sway a cheerful audience than a lugubrious one. Moreover, the members have been favorably affected even before they enter the auditorium, for a brightly lighted building suggests many people, which in turn suggests success, popularity of the idea or program. People react with a feeling that a program is good or bad partly on the basis of the number of others who are, or appear to be, present. Persons who visit a theater which is only half full when the curtain rises have already obtained the impression that the show must be a poor one. A well lighted auditorium also enables the

spectator to view the crowd surrounding him, and assists in creating the social unity which we shall explain under the second point.

In moving picture theaters and candle-lighted churches the darkened auditoriums may be a mechanical or psychological aid to the type of program being offered, but darkness has the effect of introverting people through depriving them of outside stimuli. Fear and awe are more readily developed in darkness, therefore, than in light, so programs whose aim is to frighten and thereby coerce the audience can profitably be given with reduced illumination. A seance, a Hallowe'en party, or a lodge initiation would be much less impressive if conducted under flood lights.

Since fear tends to produce introversion with a resulting awareness of ourselves, the speaker should usually avoid attempting to frighten his audience, and, instead, keep their interest and attention fully upon himself. He may reduce the illumination in the auditorium proper without unpleasant reaction if he keeps a brilliant spotlight upon himself and the other performers, or if he throws a clear picture upon the screen. In such cases, the reduced illumination in the audience is of merit in welding the crowd into a unified and stage-polarized audience, for it prevents a continuance of the distractions of page turning and is also instrumental in causing the eyes of all present to seek the source of light in front. Stage trained audiences instantly grow quiet and focus upon the front of the theater as soon as the lights grow dim. Thoughts no longer are heterogeneous, but become homogeneous. There may be such a hushed expectancy that the ticking of a watch becomes apparent. The skilful performer accentuates this tension by deferring his entrance for a few seconds.

(2) *The seating arrangement.* When people are seated in alternate chairs, or whenever there are large blocks of empty seats between individuals, the latter become more individualistic and self-conscious. They are impressed subtly or con-

sciously with their isolation, and therefore offer a more difficult problem to the speaker than the same persons would if they were rubbing elbows. As long as they are self-conscious, they feel responsible for their actions, and are more introvertive. It is more difficult for them to assent to propositions that are placed before them by the leader. They do not even laugh as readily at his attempts at wit. But when they feel themselves a part of a great throng, they gain an impression of strength and irresponsibility.

We think it makes little difference what we do if there are enough of us doing it, for we feel that a crowd cannot be punished. Therefore, we form snake dances down the boulevard, and *en masse* visit theaters and retail stores, demanding free entertainment and goods. As individuals we would never enter upon such action, for we would instantly sense our weakness and personal responsibility. Since we aspire to be strong, we like to feel the assurance that comes from numbers, which possibly explains why we do not want to vote for a candidate who has previously been defeated.

In a crowd, therefore, we can follow the dictates of a speaker or entertainer with little hesitation, for our sense of being one of a group renders us less fearful of consequences. We laugh and cheer and fight with more abandon in groups than when our sense of isolation makes us aware of our own weakness. We are less cautious; hence, we more readily act upon the words and suggestions given to us.

It is advisable for those in charge of the meeting to see that an adequate staff of ushers is available who are instructed to keep the people seated close together. Many attendants at public gatherings and church are timid about going forward to occupy the seats near the stage or chancel, and will slip into those near the door unless an usher is present to escort them farther to the front. When following in the wake of the usher, however, many people find it difficult to endure the gaze of an audience, so fail to go beyond the half-way point.

Griffith[10] investigated the effect of position within a class-room upon the grades obtained by students, and found that those in the front and rear rows made poorer grades than those in the middle section. These differences, he believes, are not due entirely to the distance from the speaker, but to the students' position with reference to the group. Those on the fringe of the crowd fail to feel that physical compactness and polarization of interest and attention which hold the attention of the majority focussed upon the speaker. In smaller classes where those on the rear rows were no farther away from the instructor than the central body of students in larger rooms, he still found the lower grades obtaining. The reason for the reduced output of the students occupying the front rows is thought to be the fact that they are so close they do not fully appreciate the group spirit of the crowd behind. Moreover, their attention is likely to be caught by irrelevant details of the speaker's manner of delivery, his dress, or minor characteristics of the apparatus on the platform.

(3) *The auditorium.* Everything in the meeting hall that causes a feeling of isolation or separation of sub-groups and individuals from the speaker and the other members of the audience will tend to render the group less suggestible and therefore more difficult to weld into a polarized whole. The persons sitting on the aisles do not feel the sense of social solidarity which others react to who are seated in the middle of the section. Moreover, those people who happen to be unable to see the speaker because of intervening pillars or the large hats or heads of persons seated immediately in front of them, are inclined to become restless and inattentive. A number of such persons scattered through an auditorium reduce the degree of concentration upon the stage of others who are seated in their vicinity.

A room with a low ceiling is, moreover, conducive to a

"It is better to have a lion at the head of an army of sheep, than a sheep at the head of an army of lions."   —Defoe greater feeling of compactness and informality. People will laugh more easily therein than when placed in an auditorium with a high vaulted dome. The speaker consequently finds it necessary to be more direct in his delivery. Flights of oratory are not only more difficult for him to make, but are not accepted so readily by his hearers. People expect talks of less majestic sweep in such rooms, and do not look for the pompous manners and oratory of the loftier type. Although a skilful speaker may captivate their attention and ultimately lead them into imagery of the latter variety, he does it at a greater effort for the suggestive influences around them do not contribute to this end.

The clergyman who has utilized a theater in holding noon Lenten meetings not only senses the change in feeling tone and the effect of the environment, but his auditors are also vaguely aware of the difference. A large part of this result is traceable to the habit of hearing religious themes discussed in churches instead of commercial auditoriums, but the suggestive effects of crucifixes, choir lofts, painted windows, and hymn books are also lost in the theater setting. It requires a better speaker to influence a group religiously when outside of a church than when inside. Indeed, many clergymen when they grow older and less inclined to do the difficult work of planning and preparing an effective address are disposed to rely on more painted windows, carvings, crucifixes, music, candles, black clerical vestments and semi-darkness as aids in impressing their hearers, and consequently let the excellence of their sermons degenerate. They do not fully appreciate this fact until they give an address in a radio studio where they are deprived of all these crutches, or chance to deliver a sermon in some bare little chapel at a summer resort.

Chautauqua lecturers found that crowds housed in a large tent were rather easy to influence, especially in regard to political, educational, and entertainment programs. There is a general feeling of pleasure and good cheer prevalent in such a gathering. Perhaps the transitory nature of the canvas auditorium contributes largely to this result, for we know that people are more carefree when their surroundings suggest instability. The social revolts during the years subsequent to the World War are traceable to a similar effect, while the converse of this type of influence is demonstrated in the massive stone fronts of our banks and financial institutions. Tents are conducive to a feeling of social solidarity and a chummy attitude. The differences in caste system are considerably eliminated therein, for rich and poor are thrown into closer physical contact.

(4) *The ritual*. Whenever people begin to act together they are vividly impressed with a sense of social unity. These two factors, a sense of social unity and a community of interest, are the basic axioms of crowd psychology. Our discussion of lighting, seating, and auditoriums has been chiefly directed to showing how the social solidarity of the group can be increased through attention to these factors. The use of ritual advances a step farther in the polarization process, for it involves common motor responses. By ritual we refer to other than just fraternal rites. The hymns and liturgy of the church, the national anthem and other songs used to begin a political meeting, and the singing of popular verses thrown on the screen in the moving picture theater may be looked upon as ritual. Even the cheering and applause following humorous initial sallies of the speaker or chairman may be so regarded. Cheering and applause are of especial value in welding a crowd into a unified whole, for they audibly convince each member that he is surrounded by many others with the same community of interests and feelings.

(5) *The speech or performance*. The person who strikes at fundamental issues, hitting the bull's-eye with his appeals, is obviously going to rivet the attention of his hearers upon himself. The slow, roundabout opening will seldom polarize an audience. Description alone, without a previously created

suspense and conflict, is usually monotonous.   If the speaker is not going to attempt a humorous beginning, but intends launching upon his address immediately, he should be sure first to catch the attention of his group by some such devices as those to be recounted in later sections of this chapter.

The Psychological Functions of the Chairman.
The chairman of a meeting is not supposed to employ his position as a means of advertising his own virtues.   The example of the politician who spent almost all of Bryan's time between trains discussing his own political prowess and haranguing the audience on his own desirability for re-election is the antithesis of a good chairman.   Instead, the chairman must perform the following functions:

(1) *Polarize the audience.*   This may involve telling a few humorous stories, especially if the main speaker has a serious subject which renders it difficult for him to preface his remarks with levity.   In all cases, however, the chairman should remember that he should perform his function as quickly as possible so that the main speaker may begin his address.   It is better to have no chairman at all than one who leaves the audience restless, bored, and fatigued when the principal speaker stands up to address it. As a rule the chairman should confer with the speaker who is to follow, so that he may learn the nature of the latter's remarks.   As a result, he can make his comments relevant and pave the way for the main address. Some chairmen carry the audience in the wrong direction during the few minutes in which they stand before it, thereby placing an additional burden upon the speaker or performer.

(2) *The chairman should build up the prestige of the speaker or performer.*   We have previously discussed the influence of prestige in rendering people suggestible.   If a man is an authority and has written books or has occupied exalted executive and political positions, he experiences less difficulty in persuading his public when the latter knows these qualifications.   The chairman, therefore, should act as a publicity agent

for the principal speaker, for he can tell all of the prestige-building facts about the speaker without making the listeners antagonistic.

(3) *The chairman should act as buffer when audience and speaker are known to hold opposing views.* In such delicate situations the chairman, by his dignified and fair-minded comments and behavior, can produce greater courtesy and open-mindedness on the part of the audience. By discreetly praising the auditors upon their scientific attitude, which involves hearing both sides of every proposition, he can force the audience into politeness by causing each one to feel intellectually complimented as long as he renders courteous attention to his opponent's remarks.

(4) *In parliamentary and executive meetings the chairman should expedite the passage of worthy measures before the group.* To do so he must studiously avoid irrelevant discussion and keep away from demagoguery. The emotional behavior of various members must be curbed in so far as possible by a dignified manner on the chairman's part, and by occasional humorous sallies that relieve the tension. The chairman should not degenerate into simply giving recognition to one speaker after another, as a switchboard operator, but should exercise directive influence upon the course of discussion.

One of our most successful business leaders, who functions constantly in one directors' meeting after another in the role of chairman, explains his rare ability to expedite the business before the group by saying: "Whenever a man proposes a motion which I feel is irrelevant or unwise I do not criticize the motion at that time, for its propounder is so definitely tied up with his proposal that my comments would be taken as a personal affront, and an emotional conflict would result, with his friends on one side and mine on the other. Instead, I tell the group that the new proposal certainly warrants a full consideration and ask that a committee be appointed to look into it more fully. During the intervening weeks or months until the ensuing meeting, I see that the fallacy of the proposal is understood. When the committee reports adversely upon the measure, therefore, its authorship is practically forgotten, and an emotional conflict is avoided. Indeed, the author of the motion may be glad that his name has tactfully been omitted when he hears an impartial listing of the pros and cons."

Professor Lew Sarett recommends another skilful maneuver for producing the action desired by the chairman. It consists of an appreciation of the fact that there are usually a certain number of neutral voters in every group who have little preference one way or the other. They are, however, entitled to cast their ballots. They will be influenced by what they think is the consensus of the group, and are inclined to vote on the first question put by the chairman. It is wise, therefore, for the chairman to see that the motion is propounded so that the first vote taken is on the side which is more desirable. If necessary his friends may be discreetly "planted" in the group, and by having them respond vigorously when the question is put to the crowd, he can capture the bulk of the disinterested voters. In most of our national elections a shift of not more than 5 percentage points in vote caused defeat or victory of the Republican party during the past three-quarters of a century. In a group of 100 voters arranged equally on the two sides of a proposition, we must keep in mind that a shift of only 17 votes will give one side a two-thirds majority.

When the vote is by a show of hands the chairman can further aid the desirable cause by a vigorous and positive upward thrust of his own hand as he calls for the vote. Crowds respond to suggestion more easily than individuals. A class of students will react to the movement of their instructor's hands rather than to his words. If he tells them that at a given signal they are to drop their uplifted hands upon their desks, he may produce the desired action without giving the signal simply by dropping his own hand vigorously. Certain children's games have been based on this phenomenon.

Sometimes, too, the chairman may anticipate proposals by the opposition and have one of his friends make the opposing motion first but in such a way that it demands later amendments because of objectionable features contained therein. If the objectionable features are then attacked by the chairman's friends in a telling manner, he may discredit the opposition so greatly that the neutral group swings to him. A candidate for political office may occasionally do good for his conservative cause by secretly aiding the radical opposition. If the latter's fanaticism and emotional rantings become too intense, they drive all of the conservative element and even many liberals to the polls to vote for the conservative cause.

In the preceding paragraphs we have been showing how the chairman can influence the proceedings of his group. But individual members of the organization may utilize many of these same principles, even without the knowledge or cooperation of the chairman. They may obtain recognition from the presiding officer and put a motion which is just the opposite of what they want enacted. Realizing that the conservative element is against anything proposed by radical members, one of the latter may make a dangerously phrased motion of the sort which, if it were worded a bit differently, would have been offered by the conservative element itself. Some of the conservatives who are sluggish in their reactions may vote against the measure just because of its radical sponsorship. Others who realize that the motion is fundamentally of the sort which they want enacted, may try to amend it so that it is acceptable. There is always likelihood of dissension among the conservative ranks as a consequence.

Holding the Attention by Stage Materials. There are a number of devices by which the speaker can keep the curiosity of his public aroused, apart from the actual contents of his talk itself. These should be relevant, of course, and not so dramatic as to detract from the effect which he endeavors to produce by his address.   Charts, graphs, curves, and pictures which he places around the platform or hangs upon the blackboard or wall behind him all serve as attention holding instruments, at least until he has explained them. Even some long columns of numbers exercise a charm over the uninitiated listeners and spectators, although the latter may be averse to mathematics itself.   Until we know what those figures mean, they hold our attention.   Because the speaker placed them in front of us, we assume they must have some relationship to his address.   It is this uncertainty that makes us interested.   As soon as we learn that those figures are simply thermometer readings at different points around the United States on a certain July day, they have no suspense value and we may be no longer interested in them.

The chemist and physicist know how much better attention they receive during lectures when apparatus is on the platform, than when the students see nothing that holds promise of a demonstration.   The use of living models or real objects and merchandise likewise helps the speaker.   The fact that a stereopticon or motion picture machine is set up in the auditorium suggests a "show", so the crowd is in suspense and more attentive to the speaker's words.   If costumes are worn by the performer, or queer utensils and weapons are on a table within view, the spectators are also more interested.

Indeed, the simple act of picking up a piece of chalk from the tray beneath a blackboard will instantly heighten the interest of the audience.   The speaker may stand beside the blackboard as if just about ready to illustrate his words, and the crowd will wait expectantly.   If he fails to justify their hope, but wanders away to the front of the platform, they may begin to grow less interested.   He can immediately regain their attention by stepping back to the blackboard. It is possible for a speaker to employ this crude device throughout an entire lecture with definite aid in heightening the attention of his group, and yet never make a mark upon the blackboard. His auditors, of course, grow less responsive to the trick as it becomes repeated several times, but they never fail to react in a partial degree. If the speaker does not enlighten them at the end with a drawing, formula, or phrase they may feel disgruntled, it is true, but they will have heeded his words just the same.

Such stage tricks and materials as we have mentioned above are usually resorted to by the speaker who has not evolved a speech which is interesting in its own right. They are also almost indispensible aids to the expositional speaker. In educational addresses it is more difficult to employ emotional and rhetorical material than in the popular oration. The subject matter is often of such a nature that it does not lend itself to poetical utterances and majestic flights of fancy. Talks about bricks and automobile tires are not as intrinsically thrilling as ardent appeals to arms in defense of liberty, or as breath-taking glimpses into eternity where eons of time are treated as lightly as an hour, and space is limitless.

A word of caution should also be sounded regarding certain actions on the part of a speaker which lessen the interest of his group. Whenever he looks at his watch, a goodly number of his listeners react to the suggestion and do likewise. Although many of these may not heed the time, reacting mechanically throughout, some of the listeners will become aware of it, and thoughts which have been conditioned to 8:45 P. M., or whatever the time may be, will instantly come to mind. The women may begin to wonder about their young children and the men about the parking lights on their automobiles. Even the initial deliberate unfastening of his watch from its chain and the placing of it upon the table in front of him, partially de-polarizes the speaker's audience.

Moreover, whenever the speaker coughs he utters a stimulus which is likely to cause similar coughing responses throughout the crowd. Sometimes an epidemic of such behavior passes over the audience. Even the harsh, rasping tones of a speaker with a sore throat, or the labored utterance in a semi-whisper of the laryngitic patient will act as suggestions for the arousal of throat tickle in the members of the audience, much as a yawn will often lead to a multitude of open mouths.

Holding the Attention by the Manner of Delivery. Since the advent of radio speeches it has become imperative that the orator spend more time studying this phase of public speaking. Over the radio, for instance, he cannot utilize the stage materials mentioned in the previous section, so he is confined to the vocal delivery of his talk and its contents as the sole methods of heightening the interest of his listeners. The matter of increasing the pleasing qualities of the voice is a subject in which we have done very little. Many of the graduates of American schools of speech go forth with voices that are loud enough to reach the listeners on the rear rows of seats, and enunciate clearly, but have very little music in their speech. There is a flat, metallic sameness to their utterances which tends to become exceedingly monotonous, and sounds "artificial".

An interesting voice is one which can hold our attention even when it is speaking an unknown language. Alexander Moissi, the German actor, is a genius in this regard. Indeed, vocal intonation and inflection constitute one of the best ways to hold attention and stimulate interest. The trouble with most of us Americans is that we have schooled ourselves in restraint of our emotions until we are scarcely capable of demonstrating them by the nuances of our speech. Tyro actors and actresses show their amateurishness more quickly through their lack of tonal inflections than in any other quality. When told to portray hatred, they may exclaim, "I hate you!" in tones which are no different from those employed in saying, "I will not go!" When the director orders them to put more expression into their voices, they simply increase the intensity of their utterance, especially of the second word,

"I *hate* you!" Again it sounds almost exactly as "I *will* not go!" They fail to realize that tonal inflection is what the director wants, not variations in intensity. This same error is made by radio performers every day. When the story teller during the children's hour wishes to speak as Bunny Rabbit and then as Mr. Possum, he alters the intensity of his speech but his tonal inflection is almost the same in both instances.

The average American, if he were confined to nonsense syllables or an extinct language, could hardly show us whether he was angry, excited, frightened, or in pain, for he has almost lost the art of expressing feelings by means of nuances of tone. When we wish to express condolence for a friend we say, "I am sorry for you." If it were not for the word "sorry" in our sentence, he would scarcely know it, for our tonal inflection does not convey much to him. A good speaker should be able to say, "Ro ro roro ro ro," and thereby show his feeling of sympathy. If a person cannot inject his emotions and personality into his oral speech, then his utterances have little more effect than if they were on a printed sheet.

The children of this country, therefore, should be encouraged to play with their voices and mimic sounds. They should be praised in their efforts to portray a happy child through the *sound* of their voices; they should be stimulated to do the same in respect to an eager child, a crying child, a brave child, a sleepy child, a grateful child. After an intensive training of this sort they will later be able to utter with adequate expressiveness soft verbal caresses, friendly condolences, tender solace, rollicking gayeties, sober admonition, and caustic diatribe.

At the present time we hear speakers and singers over the radio who may be technically perfect in their enunciation and song, but who do not arouse interest. Then a girl begins singing in a voice which may lack the power and tonal range of the dozen other singers we have just "tuned out", but who possesses what is commonly called a "sweet" voice. We hear her entire repertoire with pleasure. There is more "expression" in her voice, by which we mean the overtones and nuances of inflection are more abundant and pleasing. When she sings or says, "I love you," we are emotionally stimulated. When a dozen others say, "I love you," no responsive chord is struck within us. Voices, like people, may be drab and colorless, or rich and fascinating.

Some people are endowed with vocal organs which are superior to others for speaking and singing purposes. A tenor voice, for example, cannot show the power and ruggedness of the bass. But all voices are capable of modification and improvement. It is said that Tiberius Gracchus, the great Roman orator, kept a slave behind the stage with a pitch pipe which he sounded whenever his master's voice rose too high. During an enthusiastic presentation of his address, the speaker invariably elevates his pitch. A skilful orator can, thereby, introduce suspense and a climax into his oration by means of his delivery, even though his speech has no logical climax. A perfect arrangement, however, consists of a speech which is technically built up to a climax in thought and which is delivered so that the vocal climax coincides with it.

The performer who confronts his audience face to face may also use gesture as an aid in holding the attention of his hearers. The graceful use of his hands may be of considerable importance not only in holding attention through their frequent movements, but also in depicting scenes and in emphasizing his points. The lifted arm in the peroration is a vivid symbol of the suspense of the moment, and almost hypnotizes the audience while it awaits the final movement. The performer, however, must guard against the development of peculiarities of diction and of gesture, for such things may detract from his effectiveness by calling attention to themselves instead of to the ideas for whose increased emphasis or elucidation they have been employed.

Holding the Attention by the Speech Itself. Although we have devoted several pages to the two preceding methods of holding attention, the speech itself should be so constructed that it hits the bull's-eye in its appeal to the hearers. A man may have a non-musical voice and no arms at all, yet he can captivate my attention by telling me that my house is on fire, my children kidnaped, that I have won an automobile, that my stock has gained five points, or that my advice is being sought in the sales or advertising departments of some large company. Pleasing utterance, graceful gestures, and curiosity-provoking stage materials are all desirable aids in public speaking, of course, but a man should have something to say or else all this forensic machinery produces nothing fundamentally valuable.

It is well for the speaker to model his behavior upon that of the salesman who changed his attitude from one of thinking, "How can I sell my product to these people?" to that of, "Why should these people buy my product?" It will be of decided value to the speaker or entertainer to think, "Why should these people spend an hour of their time listening to me?" They do not do it to pay the speaker's salary or flatter his ego. He stands before them to procure these rewards, but they sit before him in order to get what? Upon his correct diagnosis of the answer to this question will depend how accurately he can shoot his verbal shafts at the bull's-eye. He may have other purposes in mind which he expects them to support, but he must constantly keep aware of their basic desires or he will fail to enlist their cooperation.

When an audience begins to go to sleep, the speaker should not censure it for being unappreciative and ignorant. As a speaker it is his task to find out in advance the level of education, the interests, aversions, ages, sex, vocations, and hobbies of his hearers so that he may adapt his address to them in an interesting manner. If he is normally polysyllabic, he should either avoid a monosyllabic crowd, or learn how to readjust to its level of vocabulary and comprehension. He is socially maladjusted when he cannot do so. It is a good motto for every one who aspires to influence people in groups to remember that "An inattentive crowd means an inefficient speaker." There are occasional exceptions, perhaps, but the speaker must not bolster his ego with this thought.

A sleeping audience is usually an indication that the speaker has been employing third degree stimuli in his language, or has failed to show the relationship between what he has to say and the immediate needs of his people. The subject of "bricks" is of no particular interest to me, but it could be made so by showing that a new invention renders possible the production or laying of bricks at only one tenth their present cost, so the city tax rate for civic building could be lowered to the degree that I would save $1.13 on my fall tax bill.

The Psychology of Persuasion. In Chapter I we pointed out that it is generally better to coax than to whip people into the desired course of action, and the same principle holds for men and women in crowds. The speaker who verbally fights his listeners almost instantly antagonizes them. When we are hostile to an individual we will scarcely take even his logical advice, and his prestige is so lowered that we react but slightly to suggestions from him. Another axiom to remember in connection with persuasion is that a feeling of fear, pain, or unpleasantness usually results in withdrawal behavior on the part of the subject, while a pleasant emotional state causes expansive or approach reactions.

The speaker, therefore, should endeavor to get the crowd into a pleasant mood, and link it to himself as securely as possible. He should diligently refrain from using the pronouns "you" and "I", replacing them by the editorial "we". If he attempts to criticize, he should by all means include himself with his crowd so that there is no intimation of the "judge" versus the "judged", no "holier than thou" inference.

In joining himself and the crowd he must not throw all formality and decorum to the winds but, like the farmer-politician, should retain his white collar and tie behind his overalls.

This is clearly demonstrated in Paul's defense of himself before the Jewish mob which was attempting to kill him. Although he was both Jew and Roman, Paul skilfully emphasizes his Jewish antecedents and training, and also indicates his importance in social rank among the Jews by reference to the high priest:

Men, brethren, and fathers, hear ye my defence which I make now unto you.

(And when they heard that he spake in the Hebrew tongue to them, they kept the more silence: and he saith,)

I am verily a man which am a Jew, born in Tarsus, a city in Cilicia, yet brought up in this city at the feet of Gamaliel, and taught according to the perfect manner of the law of the fathers, and was zealous toward God, as ye all are this day.

And I persecuted this way unto the death, binding and delivering into prisons both men and women.

As also the high priest doth bear me witness, and all the estate of the elders: from whom also I received letters unto the brethren and went to Damascus, to bring them which were there bound unto Jerusalem, for to be punished.

Realizing, moreover, that his listeners think in images, and images are always concrete, the speaker must employ specificity—second degree stimuli. He should also capitalize upon the emotional habits of his group, employing words with emotional color like "home" instead of "house". In this connection Scott[19] has the following to say:

The orator who has welded his audience into a homogenous crowd should never be guilty of attempting to reason with them, for, by the very process of forming them into such a crowd, he has deprived them of the power of critical thinking. He should affirm reasonable things and affirm conclusions which he has come to by processes of

"A great memory does not make a philosopher, any more than a dictionary can be called a grammar."   —Cardinal Newman reasoning, but he should not presume to conduct the crowd through such a process.

Not only do crowds think in images, but a very striking characteristic is the part played by the emotions in awakening the images and the peculiar emotional tone which accompanies them. This might have been anticipated from a study of emotions. Human emotions are always awakened by strong forms of imagery. Logical processes of thought are practically devoid of emotional coloring, while the conclusions reached by primitive man and by crowds are the results of feeling rather than of reasoning.

We have previously discussed the ways by which action is produced. The selling points may be made to outweigh the objections either by shattering the latter through reasoning, or by so concentrating the attention of the group upon the desired course of action that it is temporarily oblivious of the inhibiting ideas. Affirmation and re-affirmation of the "battle cry" or strongest appeals are not only effective in collegiate debate but also in more emotional types of audience. Both methods of producing action, however can be employed simultaneously. Opposing ideas may discreetly be demolished as the desired behavior is praised.

In striking at the fundamental motive bases of the audience, the speaker must vividly keep in mind that self-preservation (covering, food, health, shelter, and money) and sex are scarcely stronger than the desire for ascendance. The audience's ego or vanity is always to be inflated, just as the individual's requires expansion in order for him to be friendly and cooperative. Recalling the statement of Pope that the way to please a man is to compliment him upon the subject in which he wishes to be considered proficient, the reader will appreciate the strategy in Paul's opening words to Agrippa:

I think myself happy, king Agrippa, because I shall answer for myself this day before thee touching all the things whereof I am accused of the Jews:

Especially because I know thee to be expert in all customs and questions which are among the Jews: wherefore I beseech thee to hear me patiently.

How the Radio Tests a Speech. Too often speakers get into the habit of depending upon the predisposing influences of the church or other auditorium, and therefore allow their addresses to deteriorate. Before a radio microphone, however, the matter of speaking is reduced to a straightforward presentation of appeals through the words and the orator's tonal inflections. A shallow, emotional address is not only fully brought to its author's attention, but with equal force is made apparent to the thousands of listeners in armchairs scattered around the city and state. If the speech does not ring true and strike directly at the radio listeners' primary interests, they tune out the speaker. Since they are emotionally cold as compared with the crowd which has been wrought up to an emotional level by interstimulation and the physical presence of the speaker, the radio address must be of a superior type.

After a listener's attention has been caught, however, and if he hears the applause of a real audience, often "planted" in the studio, he may become so interested that he reacts almost as if he were present in the amphitheater. He does not entirely lose himself in the speech, nevertheless, for he seldom applauds or joins in the singing and cheering. Aside from a more dramatic opening which strikes at some basic interest of the listener, the radio speech may proceed much like the one administered face to face. The speaker should unite himself and his public and rely upon all the prestige he can muster as a means of increasing the suggestive value of his words. He must, however, curb his emotionalism for radio listeners may be tuning in at any moment in the address, in which case he may appear ridiculous. He can sincerely employ sentiment, but he must be extremely cautious not to slip over the line into sentimentality. The danger of the latter is much more grave in radio speaking than in the direct address.

The Anecdotal Address. The use of anecdotes and suspense in the speech itself is a common factor of almost every address. Illustrations not only make printed and oral material more interesting but they also clarify the more general abstract enunciations. In our quotation from Scott we read that the audience is more like primitive people in that it thinks in a succession of images. As a consequence, the audience enjoys a series of stories. These should be carefully selected, of course, so they may be relevant and capable of advancing the speaker's thought a bit further toward the conclusion.

The clergyman, for example, not only reads his text but usually a passage from the Bible which is narrative in nature. Thereafter he constantly refers to this narrative and reinterprets it throughout his address. The original creation of the parables was undoubtedly in order to heighten the listeners' interest, clearly to demonstrate the more abstract ideas of justice and virtue, and to leave the people with tales which they could easily remember and with whose repetition the underlying principles would again be brought to mind.

The politician employs the same method when he recounts familiar stories about a few of our famous historical leaders. These tales are known to probably every member of the audience, but we adults sit there in almost the same degree of rapt attention demonstrated by our youngsters who are listening to the nth repetition of The Three Bears. Like the children, we apparently are waiting to see if the story unfolds as we have always heard it before, or if some new twist is introduced by the narrator. The new twist is never forthcoming but we seem to be possessed of perennial hope.

For the past decade the writer has been analyzing public speeches with reference to the anecdotal type of address and has encountered two men who have built up entire speeches out of anecdotes. These were dovetailed very neatly into a unified structure with simply a few transitional sentences interspersed between each pair. One of these two men was elected a bishop, and his successor, who practised the same method, packed the church auditorium so early that the writer missed hearing him for three Sundays. The people who formed the audience were of the upper class socially, financially, and educationally, so this form of address is apparently quite popular.

It entails considerable reading, of course, and a logical arrangement of the stories so that they form a well-knit structure, but a speech of this kind is easy to deliver, for a few story titles are all that the speaker has to hold in mind. As a general rule, however, it is probably more effective to employ fewer stories and insert more affirmation of basic truths by the speaker. The average audience must be interested and entertained, but it also must be impressed by the speaker's erudition and forensic ability. It craves a few minutes of elevated style and imaginative flights of fancy coupled with some awe-inspiring denunciatory thunder. After it is convinced thereby of the speaker's capacity, he may give them straightforward talking and somewhat less formal subject matter.

In employing anecdotes the speaker may whet the interest of his group by saying, "On the street yesterday I met one of our foremost citizens—I shan't mention his name, for many of you know him quite well—and he told me this curious thing about one of our leading merchants, etc." The use of the subject's name would lessen the curiosity value of the story even though it may prevent many of the listeners from going off on independent trains of thought involving the possible identification of the unnamed person. On the other hand, the giving of the right name of the hero, if the story about him is not derogatory, inflates his ego and therefore tends to make him an ardent admirer of the "new preacher". Next to seeing ourselves mentioned in print we probably desire public recognition of this kind. A speaker who tactfully introduces his parishioners' names into his weekly addresses is ingratiating himself with his constituency at no loss in the effectiveness of his sermons.

How to Manage a Hostile Audience.

One of the quickest ways in which to quiet an audience which is already hooting the speaker is for him to lean upon the edge of the speaker's stand and smilingly begin speaking to the people on the front row, narrating some humorous story in a conversational tone as if entirely oblivious of the yelling crowd. Almost invariably those in front begin listening, partly because of their admiration for his lack of concern about his hooting enemies and partly because they do not want to miss anything. This circle of listeners instantly begins to widen. If a few of those in front begin to laugh, then he quickly gains the crowd's temporary attention for the rest of the audience wants to know what is happening and what it has missed.

With apparent unconcern he can slowly increase the intensity of his voice and lead the group gracefully along until he may have so captured it that he can mould it to his own wishes. Nothing angers a badgering crowd more than to be verbally chastised for being unsportsmanlike and ignorant, ill-bred and rowdy. In short, it cannot be clubbed into a courteous attitude although it can be coaxed into one.

If the speaker cannot think of anything humorous to say, he may quiet the crowd, though more slowly, simply by standing nonchalantly and grinning around at his audience. Fighting cannot long continue unless active opposition is encountered. We feel foolish when our rival smiles good-naturedly at us. And those on the front row lack the coercive action of the crowd for they are meeting the speaker face to face where he can recognize them later if he sees them on the street. They feel more individualistic in their reaction to him, therefore, and can seldom retain open hostility very long. A socially intelligent speaker can always depend upon his front rows for listeners, and a nucleus is all he needs in order to quiet his audience.

If the crowd is not yet openly hostile, then the speaker can begin his address at once but should follow practically the same procedure as that outlined above. He should open with either some good humor, and deport himself with dignified nonchalance, or else commend the crowd on its good sportsmanship and scientific attitude in wishing to hear both sides of the question. Since both humor and compliments inflate the egos of the listeners, it does not make much difference which opening he employs. What he is after in both cases is quickly to make the audience feel pleasant and more intelligent. After he has established rapport with the group by a continuation of his compliments and an affirmation of basic beliefs common to himself and his audience, he can slowly begin to turn about in the direction of his talk and head for his real destination. At the outset he goes with the crowd until it feels a sense of social unity with him and drops its intellectual guard, after which he leads the group where he wishes. By employing suggestion he can get his audience to thinking certain ideas without ever putting them into words, thereby freeing himself from possible censure. One way of absolving himself from blame, yet fully presenting his ideas, is the familiar device that follows: "I am not here to try to prove that the prohibition party has given the workingman's wife an auto in place of a scrub board, nor is it my purpose to show that babies in the tenement districts are now drinking milk whereas they used to have only a little sweetened water. I do not come before this intelligent audience of thinking men and women to repeat those old chestnuts about the workingmen who left their pay checks at the saloon and reeled into the voting booths to reelect the brewery candidates who refused to close the saloons to children. No, nor is it my purpose to say a word against those millionaire brewers who laughed at the social worker's requests for funds with which to open milk stations for the babies of the very men whose pay checks they got on Saturday night, etc." In his eulogy of Caesar we see the same technique employed by Mark Antony. Although not permitted to say anything against Brutus and Cassius, he obtained his desired action by suggestions.

Ant. Friends, Romans, countrymen, lend me your ears;
　　I come to bury Caesar, not to praise him.
　　The evil that men do lives after them,
　　The good is oft interred with their bones;
　　So let it be with Caesar. The noble Brutus
　　Hath told you, Caesar was ambitious;
　　If it were so, it was a grievous fault,
　　And grievously hath Caesar answer'd it.
　　Here, under leave of Brutus and the rest,
　　(For Brutus is an honorable man,
　　So are they all honorable men),
　　Come I to speak in Caesar's funeral.
　　He was my friend, faithful and just to me:
　　But Brutus says, he was ambitious;
　　And Brutus is an honorable man.
　　He hath brought many captives home to Rome,
　　Whose ransoms did the general coffers fill.
　　Did this in Caesar seem ambitious?
　　When the poor have cried, Caesar hath wept;
　　Ambition should be made of sterner stuff;
　　Yet Brutus says, he was ambitious;
　　And Brutus is an honorable man.
　　You all did see that on the Lupercal
　　I thrice presented him a kingly crown,
　　Which he did thrice refuse. Was that ambition?
　　Yet Brutus says, he was ambitious;
　　And, sure, he is an honorable man.
　　I speak not to disprove what Brutus spoke,
　　But here I am to speak what I do know,
　　You all did love him once, not without cause;
　　What cause withholds you, then, to mourn for him?
　　O judgment! thou art fled to brutish beasts,
　　And men have lost their reason.—Bear with me;
　　My heart is in the coffin there with Caesar,
　　And I must pause till it come back to me.

First Cit. Methinks there is much reason in his sayings.
Second Cit. If thou consider rightly of the matter,
  Caesar hath had great wrong.
Third Cit. Has he, masters?
  I fear, there will a worse come in his place.
Fourth Cit. Mark'd ye his words? He would not take the crown.
  Therefore 'tis certain, he was not ambitious.
First Cit. If it be found so, some will dear abide it.
Second Cit. Poor soul, his eyes are red as fire with weeping.
Third Cit. There's not a nobler man in Rome than Anthony.
Fourth Cit. Now mark him; he begins again to speak.
Ant. But yesterday, the word of Caesar might
  Have stood against the world; now, lies he there,
  And none so poor to do him reverence.
  O masters! If I were dispos'd to stir
  Your hearts and minds to mutiny and rage,
  I should do Brutus wrong, and Cassius wrong,
  Who, you all know, are honorable men.
  I will not do them wrong; I rather choose
  To wrong the dead, to wrong myself, and you,
  Than I will wrong such honorable men, etc.

The Psychological Formula for an Effective Speech. A truly effective speech must rest upon the bed rock of a polarized, crowd-conscious group which has accepted the speaker as a friend. The address itself must contain ideas that are presented with a wealth of sensory qualities by which the hearers can develop concrete imagery. These ideas must also be vital; they must be related to the fundamental motive bases of the listeners. They should be phrased in simple language and illustrated by references which are familiar to the crowd. Shakespeare is relatively unknown to the average citizen today, so references to his characters give rise to few intelligent responses. Accordingly, the speaker loses many of his hearers for the few seconds during which the strange material is cited, and some other stimulus may attract their attention. The speaker should never let his hearers slip away from his control if he can help it. The speaker should be as despotic in his domination of the audience's attention as the hypnotist is in monopolizing his subject's thinking. In the list below we have offered some of the salient principles which the speaker should employ in order to obtain the maximum effect. We are presupposing that the auditorium, lighting, and seating have already been attended to.

(1) *Compliment the audience.* This method entails humor as well as direct statements containing praise. A disgruntled, offended, or "ugly" audience cannot be moulded by the speaker until he gets it into a pleasant, friendly frame of mind. Criticisms, denunciation, and badgering by the speaker are usually disastrous. If he does attempt to point out flaws, he should always identify himself with the group being reprimanded.

(2) *Link yourself to the audience.* Employ "we", "our", and "us" whenever possible. As a general rule never utter the word "you" or "your", and seldom say "I", "my", or "mine". Let the audience know that you were born on a farm, if the group is rural, or that you attended Yale if the crowd is from New Haven. By so doing you more quickly enable your listeners to identify themselves with you, and realize that you are a friend. This result is necessary for people will not take advice or criticism from an enemy.

(3) *Use specificity.* Memories and emotions are originally developed by specific sensory stimuli and must be aroused by the same. Since images are definite in their structure, the speaker must use sensory adjectives and specific nouns so that his hearers have the elements for constructing mental pictures. We have discussed this subject in greater detail in previous chapters.

(4) *Strike at fundamental motive bases.* Keep in mind that the crowd is only interested in your address as it fits into the basic habitual patterns of the crowd. What does it procure from your talk that meets its basic cravings and desires?

(5) *Keep your speech moving steadily toward its climax.* A judicious admixture of description, exposition, and narration is desirable, but do not mark time in a forensic eddy nor

get lost on a conversational tangent. There should be a recurrence of emphasis upon the central idea, much as the refrain in music and verse, but the speech should march steadily onward. A speech, like a musical composition, should be an artistically balanced affair in which all the components point toward the finale.

(6) *Rise to a majestic note as you approach the climax.* We are not very easily thrilled nor inspired by petty things, but massiveness, eons of time, eternity, and infinity are breathtaking. A truly effective address should carry its listeners to an emotional peak where for at least a few moments their scalps will tighten and they will feel a shivery, awed sensation in which they forget selfishness and mundane things. This peculiar effect should coincide with the vocal climax in the manner of delivery.

(7) *Enter the climax in rhythm.* The majority of the most thrilling speeches to which the writer has listened have used verse to gain that emotional peak described in the preceding paragraph. Poetry which is relevant, which contains the final idea to complete the superstructure of the oration, will make the difference between a good speech and a great speech. Since we are more emotionally conditioned to rhythm than to prose, verse and music suggest idealism, while prose is more matter of fact.

In conclusion, we should sound a warning regarding emotionalism and the public address. The speaker should select his words with such care that they will develop the desired feelings in the audience apart from his gesticulation, intonation, and pantomime. If he endeavors to make a shallow speech into an emotionally thrilling oration, his hearers are likely to become aware of his efforts to produce an effect, but miss the effect itself. Ideally, a good speech should be one which is also so effective when in print, that it will incite its reader to the lofty feelings of its author. Too much weeping and wailing, denunciation and shaking of fists may even become ridiculous and provoke laughter in the audience unless the speech itself has warmed them in advance. In fact, a truly effective speaker can stand with his hands in his pockets and speak in a harsh voice, yet depict pathetic scenes in such well chosen words as to force tears from the eyes of his listeners. By refraining from an undue show of his own emotions, moreover, the speaker avoids the criticism of sentimentalism, even though he may be causing a lacrimal shower from his audience.

REFERENCES

1 ASPLEY, J. C., *Power of Enthusiasm in Selling* (Dartnell, 1966).
2 BOONE, PAT, *'Twixt Twelve and Twenty* (Prentice-Hall, 1959).
3 BRIELAND, D. M., "Speech and Personality Factors in the Education of the Blind" *(Amer. Psychologist*, 4, 1949).
4 BRINGS, L. M., *The Master Guide for Speakers* (Denison, 1960).
5 CARHART, R., "A Method of Using the Gault Teletactor to Teach Speech Rhythms" *(Amer. Ann. Deaf*, 80, 1935).
6 CRANE, G. W., *Worry Clinic* (Daily Newspaper Column, 1967).
7 DIETZE, G., *In Defense of Property* (Regnery, 1963).
8 FLESCH, R., *The Art of Plain Talk* (Harper, 1950).
9 GRAY, J. S., *Psychology Applied to Human Affairs* (McGraw-Hill, 1954).
10 GRIFFITH C. R., "A Comment Upon the Psychology of the Audience" *(Psychol. Monogr.*, 30, 1921).
11 HANNA, H., *Public Speaking Without Fear* (Macmillan, 1959).
12 HENNEKE, B. G., *The Radio Announcer's Handbook* (Rinehart, 1958).
13 MONTGOMERY, G. H., *Why People Like You* (Taplinger, 1963).
14 O'NEIL, P., "Star Attorney For The Defense" *(Life*, 6/22/59).
15 PRICE, S., *How to Speak With Power* (McGraw-Hill, 1960).
16 PROCHNOW, H. V., *The Public Speaker's Treasure Chest* (Harper, 1960).
17 ROBINSON, O. P., & ROBINSON, C. H., *Successful Retail Salesmanship* (Prentice-Hall, 1950).
18 SARETT, L. & FOSTER, W. T., *Basic Principles of Speech* (Houghton, 1946).
19 SCOTT, W. D., *The Psychology of Public Speaking* (Noble, 1926).
20 VAUGHAN, W. F., *Social Psychology* (Odyssey, 1948).
21 WEBB, E. T., & MORGAN, J. B., *Strategy in Handling People* (Halcyon, 1948).
22 WHITING, P., *How to Speak and Write With Humor* (McGraw-Hill, 1960).
23 YOUNG, P. T., *Motivation & Emotion* (Wiley, 1964).

Edward B. Williams[14], famous Jesuit-trained criminal lawyer, tells how to handle a witness:

"You must never explore or experiment during cross-examination. You must never ask a question if you do not already know the answer. If you do know it and the witness refuses to say what you know, you can slaughter him. Otherwise, he may slaughter you. Never attack points that are unassailable. And if you hit a telling shot, try not to let the witness know it. Keep quiet and go on. The time to dramatize it to the jury is during your closing argument."

CHAPTER XII
THE PSYCHOLOGY OF WRITING AND OF ART

The prevalence of magazines and newspapers in the modern age has led to the development of the literary profession. No longer are verses and prose penned by only a few wealthy gentlemen who dabble in fiction writing as a hobby, but tens of thousands of men and women are earning their livelihood to-day by playing on the keys of their "ink pianos". As newspaper reporters, magazine writers and correspondents, free lance business writers, advertising copy writers, publicists, literary contestants, poets, and authors they are devoting their entire working time to placing print symbols on paper so that readers will later be able to obtain enjoyment, education, and profit from the habitual responses set off by those same ink stimuli.

Despite many newspaper mergers in recent years, there are still 1,751 daily newspapers in the United States, plus 98 in Canada. And the Ayer Directory lists 9,396 U.S. non-dailies, of which 9,025 publish once per week. Meanwhile, several hundred book publishers keep swelling the book totals steadily, as shown below. Many of these publishers each year edit over 100 books. The following list shows the output of a few of the largest firms.

The Macmillan Company	750 titles yearly
Doubleday, Doran & Co.	300 titles yearly
Harper & Brothers	250 titles yearly
Oxford University Press	250 titles yearly
Appleton & Co.	225 titles yearly
Dutton & Co.	200 titles yearly
Houghton Mifflin Co.	200 titles yearly
Longmans, Green & Co.	200 titles yearly
Scribner's Sons	200 titles yearly

"No man but a blockhead ever wrote except for money."
—Samuel Johnson

In the realm of magazines, the *Author and Journalist* carries a quarterly market list of over 700 weeklies and monthlies which pay for the material they use. In addition, there are numerous scientific or technical journals which do not reimburse their contributors. Notice the wide variety of cash literary markets in the following tabulation of magazines published in this country:

MAGAZINES

List A _____ 137

(General periodicals, standard, literary, household, popular and non-technical, which ordinarily pay on acceptance at rates of about 1 cent a word or better.)

List B _____ 145

(General periodicals which ordinarily pay less than 1 cent a word, or pay on publication, or which are chronically overstocked, or which offer a very limited market, or concerning which no definite information has been obtainable.)

List C _____ 378

(Trade, technical, religious, agricultural, business, educational, and other class publications.)

Agriculture, Farming, Livestock 14
Art and Photography 2
Automobile, Aviation, Boating, Transportation, Highways 13
Business, Advertising, Salesmanship 23
Building, Architecture, Landscaping, Home Decorating.. 11
Educational 8
Health, Hygiene 6
Musical 8
Religious 21
Scientific, Technical, Radio, Mechanics 17
Sporting, Outdoor, Hunting, Fishing 18
Theatrical, Motion Picture, Radio, "Fan" Magazines.... 18
Trade Journals, Miscellaneous 219

List D _____ 82

(Juvenile and Young People's Publications.)

In addition to the print media already mentioned we could cite as the products of writers house organs and advertising brochures, as well as all the copy that confronts the reader in newspaper and magazine advertisements. In order to give a sparkle to your business correspondence, avoid hackneyed terms used in letters as reported by The New York Life Insurance Company in a recent issue of *Popular Science Monthly:*

Don't Say	*Do Say*
attached (or enclosed) please find....	here's
acknowledge receipt of	got; received
at an early date	soon
at this writing	now
(a check) in the amount of	for
beg to advise that	(omit it entirely)
beg to remain	(omit it entirely)
take the liberty of	(omit it entirely)
pursuant to our conversation	as we agreed

The Psychological Basis of Suspense. Suspense is simply the observer's expectancy that a suggested act will be performed, plus uncertainty as to the actual outcome. We noted in the preceding chapter that a speaker could heighten the interest of a crowd simply by taking a piece of chalk from the tray of a blackboard behind him. The suspense results because the students are accustomed to seeing a man write when he stands before the blackboard with crayon in his hand. If they were Hottentots, his behavior would not occasion suspense, unless the savages might expect him to throw it at them, in which case we would still find the teacher's simple action fraught with suspense.

When a baby picks up a straight edged razor, of course there is suspense, for we know from previous experience that the infant can wave its arms about and that razors are exceedingly sharp. These two facts serve as suggestions for the idea that he will cut himself, and our likelihood of witnessing the act is called suspense. When a drunken man is pictured staggering along a steel girder on the 77th floor of a skyscraper,

"It's strange that so many smart people work for such ignorant bosses."
—H. V. Prochnow

we also undergo expectancy. Whenever an attractive young man and young woman are together, we likewise have suspense. The statement that a thief is in the crowd, or a hostile submarine in the sea, immediately creates suspense. The thief and the submarine are simply stimuli that serve as suggestions for the thought that some one will be robbed or the ship sunk.

It is evident, therefore, that suspense depends upon our habitual background and the suggestions playing upon us. If we know nothing of submarine warfare, we do not care if a dozen hostile submarines are all around our vessel. And though we may know the dangers of modern naval methods, we are likewise undisturbed until we are aware of the possible presence of the submarine. The four factors, therefore, which are indispensable for suspense are (1) the possession of habits with reference to the given situation; (2) suggestions which can set off these habits and lead to expected future action; (3) the actual operation of these suggestions upon the subject; (4) the possibility that the future action may not occur. In terms of the submarine example, we must not only be familiar with the danger of submarines, and submarines must be present, but we must be aware of or reactive to those submarines. The presence of submarines, however, may not be a matter of fact but only a belief. We do not need to have seen them as long as somebody else has told us he has seen them.

When a youngster toddles over to place its hand upon the glistening head of a coiled rattlesnake we observers certainly undergo suspense but the child does not, for he has had no experience with reference to the situation. In a movie the hero who reaches into a box for an aspirin tablet is entirely calm about the procedure for he does not know what we have seen, namely, that his enemy has substituted bichloride of mercury tablets for the aspirin. In other words, the third indispensable factor for suspense is lacking in his case. The suggestion that would lead to his thinkng of death is present but inoperative upon him.

Another critical thing for the writer to bear in mind is the fact that it is not our thought of the death of the toddler mentioned above or of the movie hero which causes us agony of suspense, but the waiting for it to happen or not to happen. It is the *expectancy* of a serious consequence with the possibility that it may be avoided. Some writers fail to make this distinction and slay their characters on every page but still cannot command the reader's interest. They have filled their stories with blood and thunder in response to an editor's request for more action. What the editor probably meant was more suspense. The simple physical action of the villain in dropping one bichloride of mercury tablet into the aspirin box belonging to the handsome young hero can fill the feminine spectators with terrible suspense, and keep the masculine onlookers in almost equal perturbation.

Another significant factor in considering suspense is the fact that there are degrees of it. That a robin is hopping near a fishworm creates little suspense for me. That a tiger is stalking a Boston terrier is more emotionally arousing, and if the terrier is a pet in my household, I am quite excited. This suspense is trivial, however, compared to what I feel if I am watching the jungle beast approach my own child. Similarly, if a bucket of sand is lowered over a cliff by a rope that is becoming frayed, I may be only mildly concerned. If a valuable animal is being lowered I grow more interested, and become frantic when I learn that a human being is below. As the rope becomes increasingly worn against the rocky edge of the cliff, I become a wildman on learning that one of my own loved ones is suspended in the cage that swings above the abyss.

The fundamental motive bases, therefore, must be aroused before we react with a maximum of suspense. Threatened curtailment of food, drink, wealth, health, loved ones, or prestige immediately produces suspense. The writer must aim at the bull's-eye just as necessarily as the speaker and the salesman.

Why Suspense Depends on Characterization.

In the examples just mentioned we found that the danger threatening an unknown terrier did not produce as much suspense in us as that which imperiled our family pet. The reason therefor lies in the fact that we identify ourselves and the pet dog. He is a part of us, and gives rise to memories and emotions that are pleasant to us. It is characteristic of human beings to resent the loss of that which produces gratification and pleasure. No such identification occurs in the case of the bucket of sand. The animal produces a noticeable suspense, however, because it has some attributes which we also possess, notably the capacity to suffer pain, hunger, thirst, and cold. We can identify ourselves with animals, and do so the longer we are in direct association with them. With a fellow human being, the possibility for identification is correspondingly greater. It reaches its climax in our own kin.

In characterization the writer simply endeavors to portray his hero or heroine so that the reader quickly identifies himself with them. We cannot enjoy fiction or the movies unless this identification is made. It is imperative, therefore, for the writer to employ specificity in delineating his characters for we link ourselves only with those who do the specific things which we do and in the same way as we perform them. In the previous chapter we emphasized the necessity for the speaker to facilitate this identification process. The reason why we take sides in a debate is because we note the identity in beliefs of one speaker or the other with our own.

The necessity for good characterization is brought out in the following statement of F. E. Blackwell, editor of several magazines belonging to the Street and Smith group.[13]

"No race can prosper till it learns that there is as much dignity in tilling a field as in writing a poem."　— Booker T. Washington

Recently I have been able to sum up writing in this way: Interest in a story is in proportion to interest in the characters in the story. Of course, in a detective story it's a good thing, almost a needful thing, to have a novel method of killing, stealing, etc.—something that one would remember to tell a friend—but this doesn't *make* the story. You must become interested in the characters, and the more you are interested in the characters, the better you'll like the story. Thus: I recently complained to an author that I didn't think his story had much suspense in it. This remark brought a violent protest from the author. He said that on the first page he had killed a gentleman; on the second page he'd abducted a young woman, and on and on through the story, violent action had been taken against the characters. How absurd, he said, that there could be no suspense in such a story. But I told him I didn't care about the death of the gentleman on the first page, nor did I give a rap about the abducted lady. Had he written well enough, all he would have had to do, to move me to tears, would be to have had the gentleman spill a drop of ink on his new spring suit, and the lady come down stairs to meet an admiring caller without first powdering her nose . . .

The chief difference between a novice and a literary master like Wilbur Daniel Steele is partly reducible to the latter's excellent characterization. The reader easily finds himself portrayed in the characters and therefore undergoes all the emotional crises and suspense which they experience. The tyro, on the contrary, quickly turns out his characters with the essential qualities of man in general, but not of man in the particular. These characters have no more distinguishing marks than a factory made dining room chair in contrast to an Italian hand carved piece of furniture. The reader, therefore, sees but little of himself in the person about whom he is reading.

Amateur writers and introverts in general fail to perceive the fine distinctions in behavior and character which make living personalities of their paper heroes and heroines. The latter may sometimes be so unreal and artificial that they appear comical when they are supposed to be playing serious roles. The following quotation from Daisy Ashford is a striking case in point. This girl was only nine years old when she wrote her novel, so she warrants praise instead of criticism. Her narrative, nevertheless, is a good example of the point just mentioned, for many college students in the sentimental mood of midnight write love scenes scarcely more true to life than this one. The narrative quoted begins at the point where the two lovers had decided to go for a day's outing. The punctuation and spelling are retained as in the child's own version. [2]

They arrived at Windsor very hot from the jorney and Bernard at once hired a boat to row his beloved up the river. Ethel could not row but she much enjoyed seeing the tough sunburnt arms of Bernard tugging at the oars as she lay among the rich cushons of the dainty boat. She had a rarther lazy nature but Bernard did not know of this. However he soon got dog tired and suggested lunch by the mossy bank.

Oh yes said Ethel quickly opening the sparkling champaigne.

Dont spill any cried Bernard as he carved some chicken.

They eat and drank deeply of the charming viands ending up with merangs and choclates.

Let us now bask under the spreading trees said Bernard in a passiunate tone.

Oh yes lets said Ethel and she opened her dainty parasole and sank down upon the long green grass. She closed her eyes but she was far from asleep. Bernard sat beside her in profound silence gazing at her pink face and long wavy eye lashes. He puffed at his pipe for some moments while the larks gaily caroled in the blue sky. Then he edged a trifle closer to Ethels form.

Ethel he murmured in a trembly voice.

Oh what is it said Ethel hastily sitting up.

Words fail me ejaculated Bernard horsly my passion for you is intense he added fervently. It has grown day and night since I first beheld you.

Oh said Ethel in supprise I am not prepared for this and she lent back against the trunk of the tree.

Bernard placed one arm tightly round her. When will you marry me Ethel he uttered you must be my wife it has come to that I love you so intensely that if you say no I shall perforce dash my body to the brink of yon muddy river he panted wildly.

"A short letter to a distant friend is, in my opinion, an insult like that of a slight bow or cursory salutation."   —Samuel Johnson

Oh dont do that implored Ethel breathing rarther hard.

Then say you love me he cried.

Oh Bernard she sighed fervently I certainly love you madly you are to me like a Heathen god she cried looking at his manly form and handsome flashing face I will indeed marry you.

How soon gasped Bernard gazing at her intensly.

As soon as possible said Ethel gently closing her eyes.

My Darling whispered Bernard and he seiezed her in his arms we will be marrid next week.

Oh Bernard muttered Ethel this is so sudden.

No no cried Bernard and taking the bull by both horns he kissed her violently on her dainty face. My bride to be he murmured several times.

Ethel trembled with joy as she heard the mistick words.

Oh Bernard she said little did I ever dream of such as this and she suddenly fainted into his out stretched arms.

"Pitching" Your Opening. When a writer begins his literary composition he should usually "key" it in the opening paragraphs so that the mood typical of the story or chapter is set. It is difficult to create a single mood for such a lengthy string of situations as we find in a novel, but shorter literary works can usually employ this technique with profit. If the story is to be an artistically constructed episode with a central motif, the opening words should sound the appropriate note. A tale of horror or a rollicking narrative of carefree youth should obviously open in different keys. Observe the contrasting feeling tone embodied in the following two paragraphs:

Like gaunt wolves slinking out of their mountain den in search of unsuspecting prey, a dozen gray-black clouds slid off the jagged peaks guarding the lone entrance to the Devil's Corral and darted across the leaden sky. Old Jed Blanton cursed beneath his breath at the ill luck which had steered him into this ominous valley with his two comely daughters. He had hoped to get through Hell County the day before, but the Evil Eye of the valley had noted the radiant beauty of Jed's older girl.

It was an ideal spring day—just the sort which Janet had hoped for to make the picnic a success. Against the blue sky she could see many fluffy white cloudlets drifting along like so many fleecy lambs. The warm sun was taking fragrant thank offerings from woods and flowers and freshly plowed fields. Even the birds seemed on a holiday. When Bob's blue roadster swooped up the drive and stopped before the white pillared veranda, Janet was so happy she gave her mother two extra kisses before she ran down the steps.

We must also remember that young people are more energetic than their parents and grandparents, so they desire faster action. The slow tempo and lengthy descriptions of Henry James are especially unsuited to youth. Young people are in the fox trot mood. They can enjoy waltzes when they are tired or grow older. Quick, incisive characterizations with plenty of suspense resulting from muscular and love conflicts make them happy. The love interest is most effective when tied up with athletics, warfare and similar forms of competition necessitating the expenditure of much energy. Roughly speaking, the gridiron is a popular locale for the creation of a love story for youth, while the golf links are a more appropriate setting for romance among the older generation.

The psychological explanation for these two preferences is rather simple. Whenever we become interested in the hero or heroine we, of course, identify ourselves with them. If we are in ill health, or lack energy and vitality, we must, however, hoard our strength. The combats in which our heroes engage tend to deplete our store of energy, and therefore lead to fatigue and unpleasantness. This depletion of energy is similar to that which follows when we witness a boxing match or a football game. We tense our muscles and implicitly undergo all the action which we see or about which we read. It follows, therefore, that we tend to avoid those tales in which the performances of the leading characters are too vigorous for our vicarious participation. It is conceivable that a suitable objective test might show differences between the people of Florida or Alabama and those of Michigan and Maine in respect to this question, for we know the warmer southern climate produces a slower tempo of living.

How to Increase the Attention Value of the Page.

Yellow journalism relies upon the attention attracting value of photographs, pictures, and headlines. An intimation of sex situations in the latter holds the attention, and produces the sale of the paper. We have cited in Chapter I the experience of Haldeman-Julius regarding the value of headlines and titles. The conservative writer, however, can utilize many psychological facts for whetting the reader's interest without blatantly employing the sex appeal. We shall list some of the more obvious ones as follows:

(1) *Use short paragraphs.* From habit we have associated short paragraphs with conversation, and conversation denotes human beings. We are more interested in persons than in things. It is this fact which explains why many readers skip much of the descriptive matter and follow the dialogues. Young people are prone to do so. The writer has tested children in regard to paragraph lengths and has found that they invariably will choose a page broken into short paragraphs in preference to one where the paragraphs are long.

The short paragraphs also suggest short sentences, with a resulting ease in comprehension. Magazines and novels usually have much shorter paragraphs than textbooks, so the short paragraphs connote suspense. Indeed, we have become so accustomed to associating long paragraphs with polysyllables and educational treatises that the college reader a generation ago would hardly respect a textbook which did not have paragraphs covering half of a page, and whose style was not cumbersome. William James' works were a novelty in the scientific field, therefore, because he had an interesting style and illustrated his laws with concrete cases.

Short paragraphs are also easier upon the eyes, for they produce more half lines. The last line of a paragraph usually does not extend the full width of the page, so the eye muscles do not have to do as much work. Moreover, these broken lines break the monotonous appearance of the page.

(2) *Use quotation marks.* These attract attention not only because of their upper case position in the line, but also because they denote human repartee with possible conflict and suspense. In a one-second exposure to a page the reader will usually observe almost all of the quotation marks. They have interest value far above that possessed by any letters of the alphabet or other punctuation marks. As a rule, the writer should change indirect discourse into direct, for the page is made more attractive to the reader in consequence. Economy of space may be violated thereby, but the material gains in interest value.

(3) *Use illustrations.* Many an article is sold to an editor because it contains photographs or pen sketches. Pictures attract us much more quickly than do words and they greatly simplify our comprehension of an idea. Of two stories in a magazine with equally attractive titles, the average reader will choose the one which contains an illustration. There are some qualifications to this statement, however, for a few years ago when modernistic art was in its heydey, the freakish appearance of the hero and heroine in the sketch accompanying the story repulsed many would-be readers, causing them to search for an equally promising story title with a normal type of pictured heroine or else none at all. It is frequently more pleasant for the reader to construct his own image of the leading characters from their verbal description alone than to have a sketch which violates his sense of beauty.

Advertisers have long realized the importance of cuts in selling merchandise. They have statistically proved their superiority to the straight copy advertisement. Accordingly, the modern newspapers fill their sheets with cartoons and photographs. The widespread popularity of the Sunday comic pages and the daily cartoon strips is also ample evidence of the effectiveness of pictures.

In scientific treatises a similar heightening of interests is obtained by the employment of curves, charts, and graphs. We have already pointed out the effectiveness of such material in public speaking. The trouble with many charts and curves, however, is the fact that they are not self-explanatory. To be truly effective, of course, they should readily reveal their significance. Even quoted material from which quotation marks have been omitted is often attention attracting if it is printed in a smaller size of type than the body of the treatise or article.

(4) *Open your paragraphs with dynamic and attention holding words.* Although it has been customary to consider the end of the sentence as the place of greatest emphasis and importance, modern advertising procedure tends to reverse positions, and begin with the most dramatic word in the sentence. In running down the page with our initial glance the opening words of the successive paragraphs are first focussed upon. The value of striking words at the start of the first sentence of each paragraph is shown in the following cases.

Womanlike, she decided that her next action . . .
Shrieking like a madman he raced onward . . .
Terrified by what had happened, she . . .
Attacked without warning, they resolutely . . .
Helpless in the face of the oncoming . . .
Love being now impossible after what she . . .

Whether the reader will like the material contained within the paragraphs depends upon other things than the attractive first impression which he gains from a quick survey of the page, but a dramatic plot can be made to appear uninteresting by lack of attention to these details. A dull or poorly written narrative cannot become a best seller simply by attention to the mechanics of the page any more than a drab and colorless personality can be made the life of the party by Listerine,

Lifebuoy soap, and a new suit of clothes, but an interesting framework should at least assist in rendering a story more attractive.

How to Make Your Style More Interesting. When asked for a definition of literary style Dean Swift replied that it is simply "proper words in proper places." The task of putting proper words into proper places, however, is a very difficult one, involving a thorough knowledge of human motivation and control, as well as the technical and less important factors such as punctuation and diction. One of the greatest masters of English style, Stevenson, writes: "From the arrangement of according letters, which is altogether arabesque and sensual, up to the architecture of the elegant and pregnant sentence, which is a vigorous act of the pure intellect, there is scarce a faculty in man but has been exercised. We need not wonder, then, if perfect sentences are rare, and perfect pages rarer."

When the young poet Racine wrote to Boileau for criticism and advice, he said of himself, "I ought to tell you that I write with great facility." Boileau's response was, "I hope to teach you to write with great difficulty." In a similar vein Byron is reputed to have once said, "Easy writing's damned hard reading."

Fundamentally, therefore, it is not agility in bandying words about which makes us skilful writers, but the structural patterns in which those words are arranged. A mason could lay bricks with great facility without ever knowing anything about architecture. It is not the bricks themselves, therefore, which make a great cathedral but their arrangement. The same brick might be employed with equal ease in the construction of a dog kennel, a garage, or a house. In like manner the facile speech of the college major in English does not enable him to write interesting stories. In fact, one of the most successful story writers in America knows very little about grammar or punctuation. He simply scribbles his tale with entire disregard for the English language and its rules of usage. A college girl in the editorial office of the magazine rewrites this author's stuff as soon as it arrives. The curious thing about the situation is the fact that the college girl with a superior knowledge of English cannot create the story itself. She may contribute the vocabulary but the man fills his plot with its drama and suspense. See the terse "triangle" plot, page 437.

We have presented this example to show that the psychological appreciation of human nature is the principal factor in effective writing. Any intelligent person with a few years' study of Webster and an English grammar has the verbal "bricks" for literary masonry, but few can thereupon duplicate Conrad's psychological technique in laying these "bricks" so they produce a dramatic structure.

Dean Swift's definition of literary style includes both the basic understanding of human nature plus the knowledge of the mechanics of the writing process. Often, however, the meaning of literary style tends to be associated with the melodious combination of words, involving the avoidance of redundancy and tautology. As a matter of fact, it is about as difficult to separate literary style from literary content as for the cartoonist to separate the black lines which delineate his pen characters from the characters so circumscribed. Whether he uses a fine black line or a heavy one is of relatively slight importance as long as his characters themselves are interesting.

There are a few general comments, however, which we shall make concerning the mechanics of style in contradistinction to the content of the literary product. We shall present them in the following paragraphs.

(1) *Avoid repetition of the same words and sounds whenever possible.* This simply involves the employment of synonyms, and is advisable in order to eliminate monotony.

(2) *Avoid redundancy or the use of superfluous words,* as in "Raise up the window."

(3) *Avoid tautology or the needless repetition of the same idea in different words,* as in "audible to the ear."

(4) *Avoid triteness in words and analogies.* This admonition covers not only the hackneyed words and phrases which have become so overworked that they possess little intrinsic interest, but also those proverbs, similes, and metaphors which are equally threadbare. Writers who scintillate in their literary style are seldom guilty of such phrases as "marble brow", "iron willed", "ship of state", "in the blink of an eye", and "like water off a duck's back."

In trying to be different, however, the writer must be discreet, for it is possible to re-phrase so many old ideas and analogies that the reader becomes more conscious of the writer's attempt at cleverness than of the cleverness itself. Three or four new twists to old phraseology in a single short story will usually be sufficient to impress the reader with the freshness of the author's style.

(5) *Maintain a consistent feeling tone whenever possible.* For example, it is not wise, as a general rule, to mix slang and colloquialisms with elegant diction. Colloquialisms may be unknown in another region of the country; hence, the readers there will react as if blank spaces were in the sentences. The writer, like the public speaker, should endeavor to hold his public throughout his entire contact with it. It is also advisable to let others read your writings before they go to press, for words which are quite proper and pleasant according to your own environment and experience may have unpleasant connotations for persons not similarly trained. The subject of feeling tone has been treated more exhaustively in earlier chapters.

(6) *Read your work aloud in order to catch phonetic harshness and unmusical combinations of vowels and consonants.* A story or article which reads easily aloud, will flow along well when read silently.

(7) *Use specificity in your description.* Sensory qualities enrich any object, making it appear less barren and uninteresting. In fact, the reason old phrases and apothegms are threadbare is simply because their sensory qualities have "worn off" as stimuli to our conscious attention. The word "Ivory" connotes richness, African elephant tusks, Steinway piano keys, importation, and luxury, but it is now almost threadbare of such qualities in the phrase "Ivory Soap". We have simply employed it so frequently that the muscular (kinesthetic) quality of the word far overshadows its other sensory attributes, and it is no longer attended to consciously.

In shunning hackneyed epithets, we must create new ones which still possess sensory attributes over and above the kinesthetic qualities involved in their pronunciation. Accordingly, these adjectives will create mental images, for they will lie in the focal circle of our attention. Three years ago the writer read the following sentence which is possibly not a verbatim reproduction, but at least closely approximates the original, "The wind in the pines sounded like a cello in a gloomy temple." This simile is specific and novel. The fact that it has remained in memory when the story containing it has faded, augurs well for it.

How to Write Interesting Exposition.
Descriptive or informative material is uninteresting until it is tied up to some fundamental motive base of the human being. The art of making the educational process interesting, therefore, is principally one of showing the relationship of the new object or idea to a basic need of the reader. Boys are not much interested in social etiquette until they are to take their best girls to a formal party. Then they may become omnivorous readers of Emily Post.

The reason that Emily Post's writings then become popular with them is simply the fact that they have become acutely aware of the functional relationship of her advice to their immediate needs. They desire to be considered sophisticated and retain the respect of their sweethearts. Formerly uninteresting rules of etiquette may now transcend the sport page in interest value.

It is well to crystallize the attention of the readers upon the subject to be explained, by means of an effective headline or a question. Both of these should strike at the bull's-eye by arousing basic habit patterns possessed by the reader. Correspondence schools have employed the question method in much of their advertising. "When are you going to sit behind a mahogany desk?" "Are you prepared for the bigger job?" "Where will you be ten years from now?"

After the initial appeal to a fundamental desire of the reader, the writer should quickly state how his measure or idea enables the reader to satisfy his want. This may consist of no more than a blunt affirmation of the practical value of the measure. Then a parade of exposition may follow. Such a procedure introduces suspense into the situation. The reader has been told that he will profit greatly by the new product or idea. He awaits with interest the further details.

All the previously mentioned devices of the writer may then be utilized. Cleverness of style, the inclusion of narration, and the numerous methods of increasing the interest value of the page help sustain attention. Always, however, the intimate connection between the idea and the reader's basic need must be kept fresh in his mind. The teacher who fails to emphasize this connection finds that her students are less interested than those of another instructor who does make the tie-up between education and life's needs.

Much of the spectator's attention during a moving picture show is really taken up with exposition. The suspense is first created by showing us the hero, the heroine, and the villain. Thereafter we watch with considerable interest the machinations of the latter. The same type of thing is shown upon the pages of a novel. After the development of suspense, the writer inserts description—pages of it. We follow the heroine through the routine affairs of her life for perhaps an entire chapter before she and the hero or the villain are again brought together. But we are willing to read description because of the underlying suspense. The writer of exposition, therefore, must also develop suspense if he is going to hold his readers until the end of his article.

Writing Effective Advertising Copy. Advertising copy is chiefly expositional. It contains descriptions of a piece of merchandise, and a cataloguing of its uses. But it can retain the reader's interest by the same methods which we have described in the previous section. It must first of all strike at a fundamental need. Utility is the first asset of any product. The merchandise must serve some want, and the more basic the need, the more we are capable of becoming interested in it. Listerine advertisements illustrated an appreciation of this fact by making their appeal to the sex vanity and business ambition of people.

In order to illustrate the importance of making the tie-up between the need and the product, as well as to point out once more the absolute necessity of being definite, concrete, in motivating human beings, we shall cite the case of a young man who built a large garage featuring the mechanical department and the overhauling of cars. He sent out a neat form letter saying that he employed only competent mechanics, and that he would be open for business on the first of the week. Not ten letters were received in reply. His direct-mail venture was an advertising failure. But one of his few patrons, an advertising man, had received a copy of the letter. He came to the young garage owner and offered to write him another one. His offer was accepted, and here is what went out on the second direct-mail attempt:

"We make an interesting offer. When repairing your car we invite you to come around and see how it is done. Allow us to explain some of the mysteries of the inside of that power plant.

"There are parts of your car that you know little about. There are intricacies that mean trouble on the road. We will gladly explain these points to you and initiate you into some of the little-known engine problems."[19]

This letter brought 70 per cent of replies and the garage was quickly booked with work throughout the entire winter. The letter was effective because it corroborated the garage owner's statement that he had only competent mechanics. It acted much as a guarantee, for he offered his patrons a chance to watch his men work. Men who knew gasoline motors could therefore see if his mechanics were skilled. Moreover, many patrons, particularly women, would be pleased to be taught some of the mechanical details concerning their own automobiles. His letter met the need of these women for information.

We have already explained the method by which a public speaker can profitably disclaim his intention of criticizing his opponent or of trying to influence his hearers to his own cause. It can also be employed in writing advertising copy, as the following first paragraph of one such letter well indicates.

Dear Friend:

There's no use trying. I've tried and tried to tell people about my fish. But I wasn't rigged out to be a letter writer, and I can't do it. I can close-haul a sail with the best of them. I know how to pick out the best fish of the catch, I know just which fish will make the tastiest mouthfuls, but I'll never learn the knack of writing a letter that will tell people why my kind of fish—fresh-caught prime-grades, right off the fishing boats with the deep-sea tang still in it— is lots better than the ordinary store kind.

An attention to feeling tone is also imperative in writing advertising copy. Our copy concerning the Snuggle Sweater, which appeared in Chapter VIII, demonstrates the influence of specific sensory adjectives in creating pleasant feeling tone. It is just as essential for the writer as for the salesman to

---

"Where the press is free, and every man able to read, all is safe."
—Jefferson

UNION PACIFIC SYSTEM

The Overland Route

J. P. CUMMINS
GENERAL PASSENGER AGENT

DEPARTMENT OF TRAFFIC
OMAHA, NEBRASKA

Mark Twain
writes of his
disappointment

when his first balloon ride revealed that the States were all the same color. He had always believed, from a study of maps, that Ohio was red and Indiana was blue.

Just one of the great humorist's many witticisms, to be sure. But you and I know that there are regions, especially in the West, where Nature has been most generous in conferring her treasures of form and color. There is a region in Southern Utah and Northern Arizona called Zion, Bryce Canyon and Grand Canyon—three national parks—so colorful that it almost defies description.

Then there are other regions of colorful beauty, such as Yellowstone, Rocky Mountain-Estes, Yosemite, Rainier and a host of others, any one of which offers a delightful vacation in the out-of-doors. Possibly you have visited some of these places, but since railroad fares will be lower this summer than ever before, why not plan to see more of our national playgrounds?

Perhaps California, the scene of the Tenth Olympiad, will be your goal this summer, as it will be the goal of thousands of others. President Hoover will officially open the Olympic Games in Los Angeles on July 30. Athletes of fifty nations, led by their national colors, will take part in the great "Parade of Nations". What a colorful and never to be forgotten spectacle that will be!

No matter what part of the West you plan to visit, the Union Pacific can take you, for it serves more of the West than any other railroad. Along its lines are located the finest dude ranches in the West. An easy and inexpensive side trip en route to or from California will take you to Hoover (Boulder) Dam, where operations are now on in full swing.

We will gladly give you complete information and literature about the trip you have in mind. There is real economy in planning your trip well in advance, and that is just the service you can receive by returning the enclosed card. We invite you to do so.

Cordially yours,

J. P. CUMMINS

EXHIBIT 51. A good direct-mail piece of advertising. Note how it "sells them the holes" as per Chapter VII. Observe the opening words of the paragraphs. They are a bit weak in dramatic value.

remember that habits are developed because of definite stimuli in the environment, and consequently they must be re-aroused by specific stimuli, either actual or symbolic.

The advertiser may also frequently inject suspense into his copy to increase its interest value. In the following part of one of the Grinnell Company's advertisements we have annotated the copy, and appended explanatory footnotes below it.

"Oh, that's the same old idea you sprang five years ago, Tom," said the president[1] as he laid a friendly hand on the old[2] engineer's shoulder. "I'm sorry, but the prize money[3] for coal-saving suggestions *must* go to those whose ideas are more practical."

"But[4]—" the old man started falteringly[5] to explain, when the production manager cut in with, "Why, that idea came from his boy the year he was getting through Tech. That waste heat would not generate an ounce of steam. The boy himself would laugh at it today."

"But my boy[6] . . . " began the old man again.

"What was the college boy's idea?"[7] interrupted the consulting engineer, who had consented to help in awarding the prize money.[8]

1. President versus employee, therefore conflict indicated.

2. Employee is an *old* engineer, therefore probably the under dog as regards the young president, so we side with him.

3. Prize money increases the suspense by denoting competition, conflict.

4. The conjunction "but" denotes the old engineer is still battling.

5. "Falteringly" shows another bid to gain our sympathy for the under dog.

6. Another indication that the old man is still fighting and not for himself alone but for his son, also.

7. At last! Somebody is at least impartial enough to give him a hearing.

8. Aha! This last interrogator is one of the judges who award the prize money, too. Maybe we'll see justice win out after all.

How to Write Credit Letters That Collect. The need for the use of applied psychology in credit work is being realized more fully today than ever before. Credit managers must be familiar with the methods of motivating human beings, and must appreciate that people can be coaxed into the desired payment of their bills more successfully than they can be clubbed. We do not imprison men in America, as was done in England a century ago, for their business debts, although they are still incarcerated for lack of alimony payments.

An intimation in a collection letter that the writer needs the money owed him to meet his own obligations nearly always gets a check out of the debtor, provided the latter is solvent. When a credit manager threatens his debtors, however, they grow hostile. A characteristic of hostility is the fact that cooperation between the warring factions is reduced to nil. "Let him go to court, if he wants to," we say or think, even though we may finally grudgingly meet his demands. And if we cannot pay all of our outstanding obligations, we prefer to remit to those who have been fair and considerate of us, leaving the bills of our enemies on the bottom of the pile.

Many times some unusual device will make a credit letter stand out from the "please remit by return mail" variety, and it is often far superior to the "we shall be forced to turn the account over for collection" kind of missive. A very effective type of credit letter which has been cited by McCuaig[14] is the one following:

"When I was a kid my mother taught me to remember things by tying a piece of string around my thumb. This worked fine.

"I am enclosing a piece of the kind she used, of proper length for you, and I am going to ask you as a favor just to tie it around the

---

"You write with ease to show your breeding,

But easy writing's curst hard reading."   —Sheridan

middle of the thumb on your right hand. You will soon see how conveniently and reliably it operates.

"Presently your bookkeeper will come in about some other matter. You will take the paper which he gives you in your right hand. You will at once see the string! Then you will say: 'Oh, yes, Smith, I wish you would make out a check for the Packard Electric Company and let me sign it right away. There is a balance overdue.'

"You will be glad to have the matter settled. We will much appreciate getting the money to pass along to the people *we* owe. The string you can keep and use again for all sorts of things—possibly to remind you to send your next order our way."

The reader will observe that the final sentence in the above letter attempts to take any sting out of the credit manager's words by showing that the debtor's friendship and continued patronage is desired and hoped for. There is no intimation that a conflict or legal suit is at all contemplated. It also dispels the possible thought in the recipient's mind that the credit manager is unpleasantly sarcastic. That one sentence just goes to show the importance of "proper words in proper places."

Sometimes, of course, credit men may have to write very straightforward letters. But they should never stoop to emotionalism. It is always a good thing to leave an opening so that a later reconciliation is not too difficult, nor too demeaning to the pride of the present debtor. One large firm manufacturing mattresses let a certain dealer act as its representative in a large mid-western city. The dealer did not push this company's goods and was very slow about remitting, being six months in arrears. The company finally wrote him a very honest letter stating that they felt he was not doing their line of mattresses justice, and that they thought he was not treating them fairly in regard to prompt payment of bills.

On the return mail they obtained an angry letter in which the dealer told them they could take their old mattresses out of his store, for he did not want to have anything more to do with them. The credit manager, however, sent another letter in which he stated that they did not wish to discontinue business with him, but simply wanted a fairer treatment in regard to settlement of bills. He further stated that it would be unpleasant for the mattress company as well as for the dealer if a change were made. If the company turned their account to another dealer in his city they would feel compelled to tell the new dealer the full facts. They would have to say that the present dealer was careless about keeping up a first class credit rating, that he fell six months in arrears, and that he did not push the line of goods which he was supposed to sell. The mattress company did not want to make any such statements because they would lower his standing among his fellow merchants and would be an admission that the mattress company had misjudged their man originally. Moreover, their goods had long been advertised as being on sale in his store, and they would lose some trade if the change were made. However, they left it up to his good judgment, being entirely willing to continue amicable relationships if he would change his methods in their regard.

In a week a letter came from their dealer in which he apologized, and paid up his accounts. Thenceforth he vigorously pushed their line of merchandise. They never had any more trouble with this man. The reader will have observed the credit manager's clever stimulation of fundamental motive bases possessed by the dealer. The latter had to acknowledge that the company was right, that they had treated him more than fairly, and *that he would lose in social prestige as well as financial standing* if the company changed their account to one of his rivals. Since the credit manager had not become emotional and made it impossible for the dealer to restore friendly relationships without a tremendous cost to his self-esteem and pride, the retailer came back. The credit manager had left the door open for just this possibility.

The Psychological Aspects of Art. Such problems as balancing objects upon the page are not solved by simply using a ruler and a compass and geometrically bisecting the space. The psychological center of the page, for instance, is above the geometrical center. A line crossing at a point approximately 60 per cent of the distance from the bottom of the page (the golden section) appears to divide the space into equal parts. Perspective as employed in art depends on habit. Indeed, space perception in general is developed by the infant through his experiences with his environment. He reaches for the moon, not realizing the differences in the distance of objects surrounding him. He therefore lacks perspective and could not appreciate landscapes portrayed in the art galleries. Only as he gains the power of self locomotion does he fully realize those psychological elements which enable accurate spacial perception. He then finally becomes aware of the fact that in general the less distinct an object appears, the farther it is from him; that the seemingly smaller of two like objects is farther away; that the object which he sees in entirety is between himself and the object which it overshadows. These and other visual habits have already been fully presented to the student in his course in general psychology.

Without having been conscious of the learning process underlying the phenomenon, we have become conditioned to the fact that the more strain upon the rectus medialis muscle of each eyeball, the nearer is the object upon which we are focussing. Vertical distances appear greater than equal horzontal ones because of the greater strain upon the superior rectus muscles. In short, we project into our environment as distances those sensations of effort entailed by the muscles of the eyeball. In a similar manner we project upon a stone more weight than upon a feather, when our bases for such comparisons really lie in the greater strain in the arm muscles while lifting the stone. This is psychological weight in contrast to physical weight as measured by specific gravities.

The balance of a picture depends upon both its physical measurements and its psychological attributes. A little dog pictured on one side of the middle of the page overbalances many times his actual area on the other side providing the latter space is filled with a boulder or other less attractive object. Our interest in a thing renders it psychologically heavier. In advertising, for example, a cut more than balances an equal area devoted to copy. A very striking headline for the copy may help offset this difference, and the whole situation is also influenced by the interest value of the scene depicted in the illustration.

An unbalanced scene is vaguely unpleasant because we either identify ourselves with the pictured characters and feel implicit muscle strains arising in consequence, or else the prolonged suspense resulting from our expectancy that an object will fall, becomes fatiguing. The suggestive value of unbalanced figures, however, is utilized in denoting movement, as in the case of the winged Mercury. The human figure itself may be represented in an unbalanced posture to create the illusion of running, but the entire piece of sculpture retains a balanced effect by having streamers extend behind the runner, or by some object in the hand behind him which is of interest value.

The employment of color also involves psychological factors, dependent largely upon our early experiences. Blue is considered cool, probably because water has often had this appearance. Red, being the color of fire, denotes warmth, and yellow-orange is cheery because of its association with sunlight. Green, being the principal hue of all vegetation, suggests those qualities that are experienced in the outdoors, namely, relaxation and relief. It is therefore regarded as a restful color. White denotes both coolness, cleanliness, and purity, for reasons that are self-evident. It also conveys a suggestion of spaciousness, which partly explains the fact that light colored clothing enhances its wearer's appearance of corpulence.

White paint makes a house or other building appear larger. The ceilings of rooms are usually lighter than the walls in order to increase the apparent size of the room. A black or dark brown ceiling makes a room seem small and oppressive. Black and very dark blues are forbidding colors because of their association with storms and nightfall. Fear lurks in darkness, not in brightly lighted regions. Light shades and tints, and bright hues like yellow, tend to be extrovertive in their influence, whereas dark colors tend to produce introversion.

We have previously discussed such matters as the color preferences of males and of females, and have pointed out the resultant effects of simultaneous color contrasts, and the fact that complementary hues increase each other's apparent richness. In addition to colors, moreover, we find that certain distinctive feeling tones attach to lines. Hollingworth states that delicacy of texture is denoted by the fine gray line, while the fine black line suggests precision and hardness. Homeliness and solidity are connoted by a broad rough line.

Beauty and grace are so dependent on psychological interpretation, however, that it is almost impossible to define them arbitrarily. A beautiful female figure in one generation may be too fat or too slender to be so considered by another generation or a different race. Since such mechanics as line, color, and perspective are so dependent upon the previous conditioning to environments of both artist and critic, it is little wonder that the more fundamental aspects of the subject are so frequently debated. The items which we have just been discussing are comparable to the popular interpretation of literary style, namely, the mechanics of putting the material into lasting shape. There are thousands of artists who understand these facts, but they still do not become famous. They are like the college majors in English who possess the

---

"Architecture is frozen music."   —Goethe

knowledge of vocabulary, punctuation, and grammar, but cannot write an effective short story.

Why Some Artists Succeed While Others Fail.

Although many artists and sculptors fail financially because they have not attained sufficient knowledge of the mechanics of their craft, the majority of them never rise above mediocrity because they do not choose scenes and themes which have dramatic value. They may be hired by Gutzon Borglum or Lorado Taft to do much of the work of the latter but they themselves lack the ability to conceive ideas which are of interest or suspense value when crystallized in marble or bronze. They may be skilful enough in laying the "bricks" as long as some artistic genius creates the blue prints for them.

To illustrate this point more clearly, we may mention the cases of two young people starting out on a pleasure trip, each equipped with a camera and plenty of films. One of them "snaps" everything that has any appeal whatever to him. The other waits until he sees especially intriguing combinations of wood and sea and sky. Both persons have the same technical equipment, namely, their cameras and films, but one has the ability to select scenes which will interest the folks back home, whereas the other's prints will scarcely hold the glance of any but himself. The one can probably sell some of his photographs to travel magazines because the scenes have general interest. The other may not be able to give his away.

The psychological test of a promising young artist would be his skill in the use of a camera. If he could not bring back photographs of human interest value, then he certainly could hope for little success on the end of a paint brush, for he would not be greater than his technical ability, whereas a great artist, like the writer, depends on a combination of technique and interesting subject matter. In the realm of cartooning, for instance, many of the skilled technicians depend upon other people for ideas. They can illustrate your mental picture provided you tell them just what you have in mind. They are simply pen photographers. Too many artists are of the same class. They can paint well enough if they can be given a thrilling scene. After all, a great artist, sculptor, speaker, writer, salesman and advertising man have much in common, namely, an understanding of human motivation.

A pastoral scene, especially a landscape, is about as interesting as its homologue in the literary field, namely, exposition. The artist's technique may be very good and he may at times inject a reasonable amount of suspense, but he cannot hope to compete in interest value with the painting which, like the short story, strikes at more fundamental motive bases of human behavior. Since human beings are usually more interesting than trees, other things being equal we shall look at and purchase scenes depicting men and women, girls and boys, in preference to the technically clever, but less interesting inanimate objects. The skilful artist, like the understanding writer, of course, can intertwine description and exposition with conflict and suspense.

A final comment concerning financial success in art involves the matter of salesmanship, not only of the producer's creations but also of himself. It has not been an exceptional thing for a great artist, musician, or writer to live in poverty for years until some society leader, connoisseur, or social pacemaker "discovered" him, whereupon work which he had done years before suddenly becomes great. Critics who would not look at it previously, now proclaim it remarkable. Even Michelangelo deliberately tinted one of his paintings to give it the impression of an antique after which it was sold at a large sum to Raffaelle Riario, cardinal di San Giorgio. Additional methods by which the artist can increase his prestige may be found in Chapter VI.

We may conclude by stating that the reason why some artists succeed while others fail is owing to the fact that the successful persons have acquired not only the mechanical technique of their craft, but also a basic understanding of human nature so they can select scenes and situations which have greater human interest value. In addition to these two necessary qualifications, the artist who hopes to earn a livelihood needs to be a good salesman or else enlist the cooperation of some one who will care for the publicity and merchandising of his products.

TERSE TRIANGLE PLOT
(Business Man's Notebook, 1964 adaptation, N. Y. World Telegram).

April 3—Advertisement for stenographer ....$ 1.50	
April 5—Violets for new stenographer 2.50	
April 8—Week's salary for stenographer 45.00	
April 11—Roses for stenographer 9.00	
April 15—Candy for wife 1.75	
April 19—Lunch with stenographer 15.00	
April 25—Stenographer's salary 75.00	
April 25—Dinner and theatre with stenographer..... 30.00	
April 26—Fur coat for wife 1150.00	
April 26—Advertisement for stenographer 1.50	

REFERENCES

1 ALEXANDER, F. G., *The History of Psychiatry* (Harper & Row, 1966).
2 ASHFORD,DAISY, *The Young Visitors* (Doubleday, 1919).
3 *Author & Journalist* (Monthly, 1964, Topeka, Kans.).
4 ARCHER, J., *I Sell What I Write* (Fell, 1956).
5 BERNSTEIN, T. M., *The Careful Writer* (1966).
6 BURACK, A. S., *Writing Detective and Mystery Fiction* (Writer, 1945).
7 *Contest Magazine* (Monthly, 25¢, Upland, Indiana).
8 COUSINS, N., *Writing for Love or Money* (Longman's, 1949).
9 EDEL, L.J., *The Psychological Novel* Lippincott, 1960).
10 GASSNER, JOHN, *Masters of the Drama* (Dover, 1954).
11 HENRY, O., *Writing & Selling Magazine Articles* (The Writer, 1963).
12 KING, H., *Prize Contests* (Freese, Upland, Indiana, 1950).
13 LICHTBLAU, J., " 'Pet Peeves' of Editors" (*Author and Journalist*, July, 1932).
14 MC CUAIG, C. B., "The Human Interest Angle the Credit Man Needs" (*Printers' Ink*, June 17, 1920).
15 MEIER, N. C., "Studies in Psychology of Art" (*Psychol. Monog.*, 18, 1934).
16 MC GURDY, H. G., *The Personality of Shakespeare* (Yale U. Press, 1953).
17 NEAL, M. B., *Writing and Selling Fact and Fiction* (Funk, 1949).
18 ORVIS, M. B., *The Art of Writing Fiction* (Prentice-Hall, 1949).
19 *Printers' Ink* (Dec. 15, 1921).
20 REYNOLDS, P. R., *The Writing Trade* (Writer, 1949).
21 *The Writer* (Monthly, 25¢, Boston, Mass.).
22. VAN O'CONNOR, W., *Forms of Modern Fiction* (Colwell, 1948).
23 WHITING, P., *How To Speak & Write With Humor* (McGraw-Hill, 1960).
24 *Writer's Digest* (Monthly, 1967, Cincinnati, O.).
25 *Writer's Monthly* (Monthly, 1967, Springfield, Mass.).

CHAPTER XIII

CHILD PSYCHOLOGY

The modern trend in child psychology is to look to the environment of the youngster instead of to his heredity for those determining factors which will make him good or bad, introvertive or extrovertive, confident or afraid. If a choice were to be made between heredity and environment, the latter would be the more dynamic selection since it enables people to build personalities of the sort which they desire, whereas their own heredity is beyond their control.

A complete discussion of the child must, nevertheless, involve his inherited traits as well as the environment in which those traits are being expressed. A good environment somewhat offsets a poor inheritance, while a poor environment stunts to some degree the talents of a rich inheritance. Ideally, the optimum heritable traits in the most favorable milieu would produce the best results. In stating that a favorable environment partly offsets a meager inheritance, one must not forget that there are limitations to the interaction of heredity and environment. A moron cannot become a college graduate despite a wealth of music, books, and tutors with which he may be surrounded. Indeed, the parable of the talents may fittingly be applied to human inheritance. Some children receive five mental talents, whereas others receive only two or but one.

This fact is illustrated indirectly by Hollingworth[18] in the following table. The reader will note the earlier maturity of those children who possess high intelligence quotients, and the significant delay in walking and talking of the subnormal youngsters. Throughout the remainder of this chapter, however,

---

"I don't know who my grandfather was; I am much more concerned to know what his grandson will be." —Abraham Lincoln we shall emphasize chiefly the influence of the child's environment upon him.

INTELLIGENCE LEVEL	AVERAGE AGE AND MEASURES OF VARIABILITY	
	WALKING	TALKING
Gifted (600 Cases)	12.8 months S. D. 2.5 mo.	11.2 months S. D. 2.8 mo.
Normal, or somewhat higher (50 Cases)	13.9 months A. D. 1.6 mo.	15.3 months A. D. 3.0 mo.
Feeble-minded (144 Cases)	25.1 months A. D. 9.6 mo.	38.5 months A. D. 16.8 mo.

EXHIBIT 52. The different average ages of walking and talking of superior, normal, and subnormal children.

The Child's Struggle for Individuality.

In order to imagine more accurately the attitude of children regarding their adult surroundings, it is well to remember that chairs, tables, and other items of furniture are almost all built for persons who are giants in the eyes of their youngsters. We can comprehend this fact more readily if we suppose as adults we were placed in a world where all those who arbitrarily commanded us were at least 10 feet tall, weighed 400 pounds, and mysteriously possessed the ability to know what we were doing in their absence. The pre-kindergarten youngster, for instance, may have a father who is twice his height, and five times as heavy.

During childhood, therefore, the boy and girl are vividly aware of their dependence. "Don'ts" and "mustn'ts" are frequently heard, each of which deflates the child's ego. For twelve to fifteen years he does the will of his parents and teachers, with only occasional revolts. As he enters puberty, however, the size difference between himself and his parents has become lessened. He may even be as tall as his mother and the school teacher. He begins to taste some of those choice pleasures that follow partial independence. He goes to the scout camp alone, and has his own friends.

Meanwhile, in order to bolster his sense of importance he tries to impress his playmates in various ways, one of which is the creation of secret societies. Maybe these are for his own sex alone, girls being entirely taboo, although often they are heterosexual in personnel. By such a method he arbitrarily separates himself from the *hoi polloi* and with elaborate ceremonies as well as the use of the blackball he indirectly inflates his own ego. The following college girl's paper describes a fairly typical instance of this sort.*

The ROYAL ORDER OF WHAT we called it, and our pins were gold question-marks. Ours was a very exclusive organization, since it would not admit anyone under twelve years of age and then only on the very highest recommendation and after a rigid examination. Those who did not belong to our club delighted us by asking the name of the club. "We belong to the royal order," we'd respond. That was their cue for "The royal order of what?" Then we would beam with the snappy comeback: "That's just it—THE ROYAL ORDER OF WHAT?" So great was the curiosity of those not admitted to our club that those under twelve counted the days to their twelfth birthday, and those over twelve but not admitted formed counter-organizations of their own. These, however, never attained the status of our club and were not very long lived.

Both boys and girls belonged to our club, and nationality was something we never thought of   Most of us went to the same church, but there was no connection between the club and the church, except that we found Sunday School a very fertile field for seeds of curiosity, on which we fed with relish.

Because so much eagerness to join was displayed by the initiates, we made the initiation quite difficult, "a test of character" we called it. Each initiate was subjected to three tests: the mock initiation, which consisted of the usual pranks and foolishnesses, but perhaps a little more foolish; the intelligence test, which consisted of answers to as many questions as we could think of, with a good deal of our

*Paper by Mary Campbell.

own homework thrown in; and, finally, the solemn initiation, which we all attended in our long black robes and masks. At the solemn initiation, the constitution was read by candle light, and every initiate had to sign it in blood, a rather severe test and somewhat of a shock. We never experienced any difficulty, however, in getting the victims to conform with the requirements.

The election of officers was also a serious business surrounded with a great deal of formality. The most coveted office was that of "High Monkey-Monk." He was assisted by numerous royal officers, so that almost everyone had some fancy title. The vote was by secret ballot, in keeping with the spirit of the Royal Order.

However, the high position was usually held by the same boy every time. This is not hard to understand as he was an extremely capable leader with a powerful imagination, of which most of our ritual was a product, and he wore his ceremonial robes with a majesty which suited us all. In addition, he was a great diplomat, with a gift for eloquence which kept everybody happy.

At his suggestion, we held our most important meetings in his attic, which he furnished to suit the majesty of the occasions. However, we considered our homes good enough for ordinary meetings and took turns as hosts. Although everyone knew when and where the meetings were to be held, we had a Grand Scribe whose duty it was to send mysterious notices to the members.

Although the secretiveness formed a very important part of our activities, we were primarily a social group. Parties, picnics, beach parties, and grand tournaments (with much ceremony) helped to make us a self-satisfied organization.

However, this was not to last forever. One day the minister of our church, probably on the theory that too much self-satisfaction is bad for the soul, told our High Monkey-Monk that we really should be more democratic and let any young people of the church join our club. At the next meeting an atmosphere of tragedy prevailed, for we were to decide how to reply to the minister's request. We finally decided on "Give us liberty or give us death," and so as a club we broke up, but many long friendships have grown out of the old ROYAL ORDER OF WHAT.

I should like to tell WHAT it was THE ROYAL ORDER OF, but I promised I wouldn't and signed my name in blood!

The badges or pins of secret organizations are invaluable insignia without which the parent societies would probably disintegrate, for a part of the ego inflation of their members results from the envy of those with whom they associate. Other insignia prized by the child are those items of apparel or profession which pertain to adults. Thus children like to dress like their fathers or mothers. Long trousers, silk stockings, the father's old pocketknife, or the mother's discarded purse—these are cherished possessions of youngsters. Indeed, games in which they "play house" and assume parental roles are quite popular even with tots.

The child's struggle for individuality, therefore, consists of an attempt to throw off the bonds of serfdom and gain the social freedom of adults. His ego is deflated so constantly by his subservient position that he prizes anything which will bolster his individuality. In Chapter VI, for example, we pointed out how the tactful winning of young people presupposes a realization of this powerful motive base. The intelligent parent and teacher endeavors to give the child a reasonable amount of ego inflation by granting him possessions and praise and by making him class monitor, a juvenile traffic policeman, a member of the boy or girl scouts, or disburser of his own money. Those children who do not receive such treatment, moreover, are usually the ones who get into trouble when they go to college or otherwise attain independence. Many adults go through life always struggling to make up for a childhood which was too repressed. They form the nuclei for the "anti" groups in society and compensate so far that their behavior becomes almost atypical. We shall develop this topic more fully in the ensuing section.

Why We Sympathize with the Under Dog. Because the child himself has been the under dog for almost a score of years it is easier for him to identify himself with those who are being victimized or abused than with their tyrants and taskmasters. Even after the child reaches adulthood he still reacts with feelings of sympathy for the weaker party. It is possible that the maternal instinct, if there is one, explains in part the sympathy of women for the unfortunate folks around them, but the former explanation alone is adequate.

The successful person is envied by all and imitated by many, but is seldom sympathized with, for success and superiority have so long been identified with adulthood that it is difficult for us grown men and women to avoid slipping into the childhood attitude of resentment toward such persons. Other things being equal, the challenger has more friends among the spectators than does the champion, and the independent grocer gains sympathy in contrast to the chain store, even though people may patronize the latter.

Such behavior illustrates not only our identification with the weaker individual or business organization, but demonstrates the "negative protest" of youth. It is this protest against authority which explains in part the desirability of avoiding direct statements in salesmanship and the effectiveness of suggestion. The popular belief that youth must have its fling expresses an appreciation of the tendency toward radicalism on the part of young people and their desire to break conventions and restrictions. Some of those children who have been ordered about most autocratically during childhood become the violators of laws and conventions when they do have their fling. We have mentioned in the previous section the chronic "antis". For fifty years of adult life these individuals may continue their protest against those forces and ideas connected with the adults who robbed them so completely of their youthful self-respect. That college men and women often flaunt the religious tenets of their parents, and choose any vocation except that of their fathers, show evidences of simply a negative protest which has not expended itself.

For the average adult, however, the pendulum ultimately swings nearer the vertical, although few persons ever lose their sympathy for the under dog, since memories and attitudes of childhood are so lasting and dominant. The typical plot for a story or novel accordingly carries the hero or heroine along in an under dog role until the final chapter. Villains must be in the dominant position or be actively attempting to hold such authority. Even Cinderella would not elicit much interest if she were always a princess. But as a scullion who was ordered about by her cruel stepmother and stepsisters she obtains our support, for although we may not have been scullions we can readily identify phases of our childhood with her subservient position. If human beings sprang, like Athena, fully developed from their parents, it is quite likely they would feel less sympathy for the under dog, so the appeal of much current popular fiction would be considerably reduced.

From the psychological aspect, therefore, the adult's sympathy for the oppressed individual results from his ready identification with the latter, an identification which is a direct outgrowth of his many years of childhood wherein he himself was dependent and weak. In the following section we shall see how the child's intellectual immaturity leads to his belief in the supernatural and mysterious.

Why Children Believe in Magic. The child differs from the adult not only in his more limited experiences with life but also in his nervous immaturity which renders him incapable of the involved thought processes of the intelligent grown person. A little girl asks, "I bet you can't guess who drove the horses this morning?" An older girl replies bluntly, "You did." The younger child then inquires in mingled wonder and disappointment, "How did you know?"

In a similar manner the child who has been left at home alone by his parent and who knocks over the fish bowl or breaks a window, may reply to his mother's accusation, that he did not commit these errors. When his parent punishes him, he is nonplussed at her psychic power. How did she know he did it, for she was not there at the time? The "little bird" which tells mothers such things amounts to simply the five or ten years of additional mental age which the mothers possess beyond that of their children.

The child cannot reason, as does his parent, that inasmuch as he was the only occupant of the room or dwelling during her absence he is the one who must be responsible for any changes occurring therein. Because he sees evidences of apparent omniscience on the part of his father and mother, therefore, he is inclined to believe in magic.

Among the phantom creatures with which he peoples his childhood milieu are, of course, giants and ogres, but his usual favorite is the elf or fairy, for the latter is a little fellow who can defeat a big fellow. He can identify himself with the fairy on the basis of size and apparent inability to defend himself against superiors. The success of the tiny magical creature becomes his own success, experienced vicariously. The elf or fairy shares the hero or heroine role with little boys and girls in childrens' tales, and helps the latter out of difficulties.

In conclusion, therefore, we may state that the youngster's predilection for fairy tales results from his contact with adult reactions which are magical to him. Since his parents are apparently psychic, he finds no difficulty in granting reality to additional supernatural phenomena. His faith in fairies is not dispelled simply because he is unable to see them, for he cannot see how his mother knows his actions in her absence, but he must admit that she knows them. When his memory span and ability to handle longer and more involved ideas become greater, he can understand those mysterious inferences which his parents now make. His belief in fairies and a Santa Claus will then wane.

The Effect of Siblings on the Child's Personality. Because children are born of the same parents, develop in the same home, and have the tutelage of the same school teachers, people are inclined to state that their environment is the same. But such is not the case. The first child, for example, monopolizes the attention of both parents, and maybe the grandparents. His whims are the laws of the household. The people with whom he mingles are all adults. He finds that he is on the receiving end of almost all the parent-child reactions which ensue. He is the center of attention and occupies the spotlight on his domestic stage.

Then a younger brother or sister arrives, and for the first time in his life he becomes aware of real competition. His parents may hardly realize the shift in their interest to the newborn, but the older child instantly feels the change, and resents it. He dislikes the newcomer, and wishes for its removal. Since it cannot be removed, he must readjust his outlook upon life and try to effect a fairly satisfactory compromise. As the younger child grows older, the pleasure which the older youngster obtains from games in which the two engage begins to offset the dislike and antagonism which previously existed. But the elder child is inclined to be more domineering and blunt, relying upon his superior strength to procure the toys which he desires. However, his introvertive tendencies which developed prior to the second child's birth are somewhat modified by the extrovertive influences of the latter's presence, and his parents' insistence that he share his pleasures and property with the baby.

As for the second child's environment, we may begin by stating that he does not monopolize the family stage at any time, even though for the first few weeks he obtains the major portion of the parental attention. As soon as he is old enough to take note of his surroundings, he sees another youngster present, much like himself but stronger. Thenceforth he finds himself in competition with the older child, and is compelled to rely on his wits to satisfy his wants, since he is physically weaker than the first-born. He starts out in life with a tendency to extroversion, therefore, and soon begins to utilize his mother as a defense against his older sibling. He quickly learns that if he cries, the mother on general principles will assume that the older child has taken something away from him, and especially if she is weary or ill she will be inclined to make the elder youngster surrender any desired possession to the baby. When they are out of her sight, however, the stronger child usually regains his toys.

Another difference is the fact that the first child obtains new playthings, new clothes, new books, while the younger sibling frequently has only secondhand toys, "made-over" clothes, and used schoolbooks. The second child, moreover, tends to be more bold and irresponsible than the older, for he always feels that he can rely on the greater strength of his elder brother or sister, and his tendency toward extroversion renders him more socially curious and explorative. In previous chapters we have mentioned in this connection how the intuition of women tends to develop because they are physically weaker than their masculine playmates, and how younger children seem to be relatively more prevalent than first-borns among salesmen.

Let us suppose, moreover, that a third child enters the family. The effect upon the oldest youngster is not very great, since he must share with simply an additional sibling. But note the dilemma in which the second child finds himself. He neither has the prerogatives of the first-born with the consolation of probably being his grandparents' favorite, nor can he maintain his former special rights which belonged to being the baby. He finds himself confronted with the difficult situation of using his wits to deal with his stronger elder sibling, and using his greater muscular power in taking what he desires away from the new baby, which in its turn soon learns to utilize its lungs in gaining its mother's favor and partiality. The middle child, therefore, is in an environment which is most conducive to extroversion, while the youngest probably is next most extrovertive, whereas the first-born still tends toward introversion. The introvertive tendency of the eldest comes chiefly from the fact that he was an only child for a while. The manner in which introvertive personalities militate against successful social adjustments is brought out in the next section.

We may conclude our survey of the effect of siblings upon the child's personality, therefore, by saying that additional brothers and sisters tend to extrovert him. If only a year or two separate the ages of the first-born and the next youngster, this extrovertive influence has a greater effect upon the elder child's personality. If the latter is five or ten years old before the younger sibling arrives, he more nearly resembles the only child in his tendencies toward introversion.

How to Lessen the Child's Divorce Hazard.   It is well to keep in mind that the majority of factors which occasion divorce do not develop only within the duration of the couple's marriage, but antedate it by almost a score of years, for they originate in the childhood experiences and training to which the husband and wife have been subjected. Such essential social virtues as a spirit of fair play, a willingness to compromise, an appreciation of the feelings and interests of others, and a realization that money is simply minted energy, these and many others are taught the child who develops in an auspicious milieu, or are lacking to the youngster in a less favorable environment.

Despite certain sentimentalists who emotionally look upon youth as "that sweet period of irresponsibility and earthly paradise," and who aver that it is wrong to "shackle the life of a carefree child with the fetters of adult society," we know that the youngster develops wholesome character only by grappling with the problems of his own little world as they arise. Experience is the bedrock on which the young as well as old construct personalities which will withstand the temporary squalls of emotional discord. And for later social contacts, particularly of the strenuous sort involved in marriage, the child deserves all the intelligent training and preparation which parents and teachers can offer him.

A child in a totally carefree environment cannot be expected to blossom into a responsible and responsive husband or wife through the magic ritual of a marriage ceremony. But the youngster who has grown up with a sense of some responsibilities intermixed with his play, and with the extrovertive influences of other children to produce unselfishness in him, will be a good marriage risk. In the preceding section we have discussed the different types of personality which tend to develop in siblings from such similar surroundings as the same home. In the following exhibit we shall show the divorce hazards of husbands and wives who came from homes in which they grew up as the only child, the oldest, the middle, or the youngest. By "middle" child we refer simply to a youngster who has at least one older and one younger sibling. These data are based on 2634 divorced men and their 2634 divorced wives, the family histories of whom were procured from college students who knew the participants in the divorces.

HUSBANDS		WIVES			
		Only	Oldest	Middle	Youngest
	(%)				
Only _____	754 (28.6)	191	236	147	180
Oldest _____	655 (24.9)	153	158	176	168
Middle _____	638 (24.2)	132	155	207	144
Youngest _____	587 (22.3)	74	158	181	174
Totals _____	2,634	550	707	711	666
(%)		(20.9)	(26.8)	(27.0)	(25.3)

EXHIBIT 53. Showing the percentage of various types of children who as adults procure divorces.

To fully understand the significance of children's order of position in the family and its relationship to their divorce hazard, we must obtain an index of the percentage of only children, oldest, youngest, and middle children among the adult population. Since the United States Census Bureau has informed the writer that no such tabulation has been made heretofore, he selected at random 100 families with children. Since the majority of the participants in divorces listed in the above table were from 20 to 40 years of age, the writer chose his 100 families so that the offspring thereof would now be within the age range mentioned. In these 100 families were 16 only children, 84 oldest, 84 youngest, and 132 middle children, making a total of 316. On the basis of these figures, therefore, there are in the present adult population falling between 20 and 40 years of age the following percentages: Only children, 5.0%; oldest, 26.6%; youngest, 26.6%; and middle, 41.8%. The exhibit below will show the difference between the percentages of various types of child in the adult population and the incidence of divorce in such groups.

TYPES OF CHILDREN	% IN ADULT POPULATION	% DIVORCED HUSBANDS	% DIVORCED WIVES	HUSBANDS' HAZARD	WIVES' HAZARD
Only	5.0	28.6	20.9	5.72	4.18
Oldest	26.6	24.9	26.8	.94	1.01
Youngest	26.6	22.3	25.3	.84	.95
Middle	41.8	24.2	27.0	.58	.65

EXHIBIT 54. Showing the divorce hazards of men and women occupying different positions in the sequence of children. Hazards are computed by dividing divorce percentage by the percentage in adult population.

From the above hazards it will be seen that an only child of the male sex has 5.72 times as great a likelihood of divorce as should be warranted by the percentage of only children in the adult population, and for only children of the female sex the ratio is 4.18. The middle child, with his greater extroversion which we have previously mentioned, is the best marriage risk for both sexes. Indeed, among men an only child is approximately ten times as likely to enter divorce as is a middle child.

Such ostensible causes for divorce as differences between

husband and wife in race, religion, education, and social position, or the effects of alcohol and sexual maladjustment are probably spread uniformly throughout the various classifications of children, for there seems no *a priori* reason why only children should be especially prone to cross religious or racial lines, or be any more addicted to liquor than oldest, youngest, or middle children.

Since in these 5,268 cases the only child is such a great divorce hazard in contrast to children who have grown up with at least one sibling, it behooves educators and parents to adopt every ameliorative measure which will reduce his danger of marital unhappiness. Among such instruments we can cite the presence of living playmates in the home, such as kittens or puppies, in case the parents are resistant to having an additional youngster. In a preceding chapter we showed how sympathy and tenderness can be inculcated in the only child by such playmates.

Moreover, the early contact of the only child with human companions of approximately his own age will help reduce his hazard. The nursery school is especially valuable in this regard. Indeed, it might be wise to reduce the age of entrance to kindergarten to three years instead of the present five years. Such a change would seem to be advisable, since the increasing economic competition is reducing the size of families, and as the number of one-child families increases, it seems probable that the incidence of divorce will correspondingly be accelerated. There seems to be a marked negative correlation, therefore, between the size of the average American family and the divorce rate.

In subsequent sections of this chapter we shall describe additional methods of lessening the child's divorce hazard. It is sufficient to conclude here that the chief method of insuring children a later marital happiness lies in extroverting the youngsters by means of such available instruments as animal playmates, other children either of the neighborhood or of the nursery school, and, as we shall later discuss, by developing self-reliance in them. Since the integrity of the home is one of the principal bulwarks of the nation, and since the divorce rate in the United States is now about one to six, it is apparent that the divorce problem is of national as well as of moral significance.

The "Reversible Why" in Child Training.

Everybody who has dealt with young children is familiar with the incessant barrage of questions which they can fire upon the adults in their vicinity. Many of these queries are rather profound, or at least demand a keener insight into science and religion than the average person possesses. And because of their constant recurrence many parents become irritated at the child and send him forth to play.

As a matter of fact, it is quite likely that the more questions a child asks, the more intelligence he possesses. Since his queries are mental hooks with which the youngster goes fishing for information about the mysterious universe in which he finds himself, it is wise for parents and teachers to satisfy his curiosity as long as their patience will last. In so doing, however, they must not only phrase their replies in language which the youngster can understand, always remembering that his mental age is far below the adult level, but they should also recall that active learning is superior to passive. They should, therefore, endeavor to reverse the child's query so that he utilizes all his present fund of knowledge in regard to his own question. Then if he cannot evolve a solution, they must add their comments.

The "reversible why" is an excellent habit for adults to acquire, as we have previously mentioned in our discussion of salesmanship, for it quickly places the mental effort upon the other party, thereby freeing its propounder for a moment's respite in which to collect his thoughts or survey his comrade. In dealing with children the teacher and parent can also profitably employ it, thereby keeping on the offensive and giving the youngster more cerebral exercise. The following excerpt will demonstrate the method more clearly, although in dealing with adults a little more finesse should be shown in reversing their queries.

"Why do you put that white stuff on your face?" Junior asked on the first morning of my visit, while I was going through the drudgery of my daily shave.

"Why do you think I put this on my face?" I countered.

He stopped for a moment, probably dumbfounded at this sudden offensive on my part.

"I don't know," he replied, but I refused to let him off with such an easy answer.

"What does it look like?" I continued, glad of the chance to keep on the offensive.

"Like cream when Mother whips it," came his immediate response.

"All right," I agreed, "but what else does it look like—something you use when you take your bath?"

"Oh, I know. It's soap."

"Righto," I answered. "Now why do you think I am putting soap on my face?"

"So you can wash it."

"But I'm not putting it all over my face. I rub it just on the hairs on my chin and jaws. Why do I do that?"

"So they'll get clean," he replied.

"All right," I said, "but how does your hair feel when Mother puts soap on it and gives you a shampoo? Is it soft or is it hard?"

"It's soft and wet," he answered.

"That's the way my beard is. The soap makes it soft and it's easier to cut the hairs when they are soft. They don't pull so much and hurt me while I am shaving."

"Then why doesn't the barber put soap on my hair? He didn't do it when I got my hair cut."

Fortunately his mother called us to breakfast and I deemed this an opportune moment to drop the conversation.[10]

A few years ago the writer tested this method with five children ranging in ages from four to seven. They were with

---

"Infancy is the perpetual Messiah, which comes into the arms of fallen men, and pleads with them to return to paradise."   —Emerson him at various times and of course wanted to know this and that. The writer made notations of the first forty questions each child asked. In the first twenty of these he made a careful reply, which was entered upon his data sheet. On the second twenty questions of each child, the writer employed the reversible why, holding the youngster to his query until he had answered it himself in as complete a fashion as he could, after which, if he was not then successful, the correct information was given to him.

Ten days later the writer took each of the youngsters in turn and put to him the same forty questions which the child had previously asked. On the twenty questions which the writer had carefully answered as soon as the child had originally asked them, the five youngsters averaged twelve correct replies each, but on the twenty where the reversible why had been employed, they averaged eighteen correct responses apiece. In this experiment, therefore, the reversible why apparently led to a 50 per cent greater retention of the information which was presented to them. This occurred not because the writer had not fully replied to their first twenty inquiries on the initial day of the test, but because the answers to the second set of queries made a deeper impression upon them, due in part to the fact that they themselves had helped work them out.

From the psychological standpoint, therefore, the reversible why enables the adult to remain on the offensive and compels the child to cerebrate in response to his own question. Since he takes an active role in evolving the solution to his query, he is much more likely to retain the information thus arrived at. The reader will recall the statement from William James regarding the fact that children whet their wits on each other's. In the employment of the reversible why, moreover, the child has an opportunity to whet his wits upon problems turned back upon him by the skilful adult interrogator. The net result of this procedure is beneficial to the youngster both in respect to the greater retention of material which he encounters, and also in the mental exercise engendered in the process.

How Children Educate Children. We have previously mentioned the extrovertive influence which children have upon each other, and the value of such training as it relates to their later marriage risks. But there are other aspects to this problem which should be noted. The first-born, for example, tends to be slower in his development of speech than do his younger siblings, owing largely to the lack of oral stimuli with which he is surrounded. Adults may think that they converse freely with the only child, but they do not equal the talkativeness of an equal number of youngsters.

Playmates are stimulating in other respects, moreover, than simply the acquisition of oral language, for they bring to bear upon each other the combined knowledge of all members of the group. Probably no one parent takes the time to answer all his son's queries, or to explain every aspect of a new situation or object. But if each of a dozen parents gives his child one different idea regarding the operation of a toy or machine, when these twelve youngsters get together they soon gain eleven additional viewpoints, and go home to lunch with twelve ideas instead of the original one.

This result is especially true in the realm of sex where, despite the franker discussion of the subject by parents and teachers of the present generation, the youngsters still gain most of their knowledge from their playmates. Just one of the latter who possesses some first-hand information may enlighten the children of the entire neighborhood or school. The avoidance of sex topics by some parents of course whets their children's curiosity, rendering them more ready listeners to their playmates' ideas on the topic. In the quotation which follows the reader will see how Professor Katz's older son casually discussed the matter of human births with his mother, and then probably dismissed it from his mind. The reader may be interested to know that the child, named Theodor, had

a chronological age of not quite five years and two months
at the time of this conversation. His parents have obviously
already enlightened him concerning the origin of human infants.

Conversation: December 29th. Evening, in bed.

T. "Why did you stay in Berlin and not go back to that school?
(A school in which Mother had been a teacher.)

M. "The war came, so I couldn't go back again."

T. "Why couldn't you go back?"

M. "The railways were being used by the soldiers, so I couldn't
get a train."

T. "Was there a lot to eat then?"

M. "No, there wasn't much to eat."

T. "But Papa had enough to eat, didn't he?"

M. "Yes, Papa was a soldier and the soldiers had enough to eat."

T. "Why did the soldiers have enough to eat?"

M. "If the soldiers hadn't had enough to eat, they couldn't have
fought."

T. "And the other people didn't have enough to eat?"

M. "No, they were all hungry, even the little children."

T. "Mama, the little babies who hadn't been born yet had the
best of it, didn't they? They were lying nice and warm inside their mamas."

M. "Yes."

T. "Mama, when the babies crawl out, have they anything on?"

M. "No, they are naked."

T. "Aren't they cold, when they're naked?"

M. "No, because they're dressed immediately."

T. "Why don't the children come out together?"

M. "What do you mean?"

T. "I mean, why didn't Baby and I come together?"

M. "Babies do sometimes. Then we call them twins."

T. "Then they would have to be smaller, or else they couldn't
come out easily."[23]

The above conversation also illustrates the fact that children
cannot be looked upon as simply the uncritical recipients of

"The proper time to influence the character of a child is about a hundred years before he is born."   —Dean Inge

information, but have the capacity to do some original or creative thinking. It is partly because of the latter function that they educate one another. As a consequence, it is well that they be given correct advice at the outset, else they may later develop resentment toward the parent or teacher who misinformed them, particularly when some other child in the neighborhood challenges their statements, and proves them in error.

The methods by which children educate children consist primarily, therefore, in their extroversion of one another, but they also serve as stimulants to each other's thinking by means of their frequent challenges of one another's statements, thereby whetting their wits after the fashion described by William James. They also bring to bear upon a given problem their combined knowledge and consequently play respectively the roles of teacher as well as pupil. Since the formulation of ideas for their presentation to others is likewise beneficial to the instructor, these youngsters not only gain information from each other, but they obtain the profit which results from organizing facts. The older children, moreover, repeat the admonitions of parents and instructors to their younger siblings and serve as models after whom the younger children can pattern their behavior. Both of these functions relieve adults of a part of their teaching load, yet further increase the enlightenment of the children. In the next section we shall consider an additional important educational function of youngsters.

How Children Educate Adults. The classic instance in literature of the remarkable transformation in Silas Marner when he became the guardian of a child demonstrates one of the principal educative effects of children upon men and women. Childless adults tend to grow more and more introvertive with age. Indeed, all adults approach extreme introversion at senescence but the presence of children and grandchildren greatly retards the process. At the age of sixty people could probably be classified in four general groups as regards their degree of introversion; first, the bachelor or spinster; second, the childless married person; third, the married person with children; fourth, the married person with children and grandchildren.

Parents are usually compelled to become somewhat conversant with current educational methods, at least as long as their youngsters are of school age. They even follow the athletic successes of the teams representing their children's school or university. In fact, vicariously they gain many of the advantages of a college education through the letters and oral descriptions of their offspring, often possessing information concerning campus matters which is unknown to the professors at the university.

With current amusements of young people they also are in touch, and become attentive to styles and fashions in the apparel of youth. Their active participation in religious affairs is frequently a direct result of their desire to set an example to their youngsters, and they are usually active sponsors of the boy and girl scout organizations, and similar societies which will exert wholesome influences upon their progeny.

After a quarter of a century they again go through a part of this extrovertive process when their grandchildren are born. They do not follow the school curricula so closely, nor are they in such daily contact with the children, but they find many more outside interests than other elderly persons who lack the interrogations of youngsters.

But the extrovertive influence of children is not their only means of benefiting the adults in their environment. The frequent queries of the youngsters force their parents into cerebral activity, often of a sort which is severe. Moreover, the candor and naivetè of children is often refreshing as well as informative. To answer the demands made upon them by their offspring, many adults find it necessary to engage in more reading and study. Parent teacher organizations and books on child psychology become popular with mothers. Several magazines in the United States are maintained chiefly by parents who wish advice concerning the rearing of boys and girls.

Parents also become aware of the need for better pictures and music with which to stimulate their children's imagination. Encyclopedias and reference volumes of different sorts also begin to make their appearance in the home, and are used by the adults as well as the children. Meanwhile the fathers and mothers find themselves going through a change of attitude regarding international politics, for those who have several sons are not so prone to telegraph their senators at Washington to vote for war.

The principal educative value of children upon adults, therefore, consists of the extroversion of the latter with its attendant advantages of keeping the adults in touch with current phases of business, science, and the arts. Additional benefits which accrue to parents are their increased participation in worthy school, civic, and religious activities as well as their greater patronage of music and literature. Such activities also are frequently of value to the community as a whole so that the state gains a more responsible type of citizenry thereby. The adults themselves profit by the wider range of interests which they develop and their greater capacity for social enjoyment.

Developing Self-reliance in the Child.   Whether or not the child will be able to face the responsibilities and defeats of adulthood will depend very largely on the training which his parents give him. If they constantly act as buffers between him and the hard knocks of life he will find adult problems too fierce or rigorous for his temperament, and may lean upon his parents for comfort and assistance as long as they live. Every reader is doubtless familiar with many such individuals who may have remained bachelors and spinsters because of mother- and father-fixations, coupled with an inability to fend for themselves. Others may attempt marriage and economic independence only to make miserable failures of both, after which they return to the parental roof.

In our discussion of the development of confidence and aggressiveness in the child we pointed out the fact that the tasks assigned to him must not be too great for his capacity, nor must they be permitted to remain unfinished, else he develops a defeatism complex similar to that illustrated by Half-Way Hurley. Since confidence is really the habit of success, parents and teachers must be careful to motivate the youngster adequately, and adjust his duties to fit his present capacities.

Since life cannot satisfactorily be met by an individual who is always carefree, it becomes advisable to temper the youngster's play with a judicious admixture of tasks or "chores". These may begin as soon as he is old enough to walk. He should learn to put his playthings away after he is through with them, and thereafter should be taught the various responsibilities which he is supposed to assume in life.

In this connection it is well for him to gain an impression of the meaning of money, for when he realizes that it stands not only for ice cream sodas and candy but also for human energy expended in its acquisition, he is able to disburse his funds wisely. Children who are dependent upon coaxing and cajolery and their parents' largess in order to have spending money are losing one of the best means of gaining self-reliance, namely, the earning of their own nickels, dimes and quarters. When a child earns his money his ego is inflated, for he feels more independent and competent. In order to illustrate an ingenious method by which a father not only changed his twelve-year-old boy's attitude concerning mathematics, but also made him much more self-reliant, we shall offer the following paragraphs[11].

_____

"The darkest hour in any man's life is when he sits down to plan how to get money without earning it."	—Horace Greeley

"He told the lad that he might act as purchasing agent for the family's groceries. Under the new arrangement the boy bought at cash and carry stores, whereas formerly the father had patronized a store nearer home from which goods had been delivered. The prices had been slightly higher at the latter store, and these prices were used as the basis on which the youth was permitted to operate.

"If, for instance, he purchased butter at fifty-two cents a pound at the cash and carry store, when the other grocer was charging fifty-four, the boy received two cents for his foresightedness and effort in carrying the goods home. Soon he became so interested in this financial game that the page of the evening paper to which he turned first was that on which the grocers' advertisements were displayed. Arithmetical figures no longer remained only stupid black marks to be juggled according to some stereotyped rule, but were changed into useful tools. Without being aware of what had brought about his new attitude, the boy presently found himself taking an interest in arithmetic, and soon he was the most proficient mathematician in his class.

"His parents had not scolded him. He had, therefore, been saved from developing a defense reaction. And by the father's tactful plan he had also been brought to the forefront of his class, and hence developed a liking for mathematics."

In the public schools it is not unusual to find projects undertaken in which the pupils build a miniature store, and go through the actions of buying and selling. Such procedures are not only of educational value, but they are pleasant to the youngsters, who feel more grown up in consequence.

Another very good method for increasing the child's self-reliance is that of letting him assume the responsibility of some living thing, such as an animal, or potted plants, a garden, or the goldfish. He attains, therefore, the feeling that some weaker being is dependent upon him, and as a result not only is complimented but also is extroverted by his duties with reference to these living objects.

In the child's play, moreover, he finds an additional opportunity to develop his self-reliance, for he discovers that compromises are a necessity if he is to retain the friendship of his mates. It is not difficult to diagnose the environmental background of the youngster who is of the I'll-take-my-ball-and-go-home-if-I-can't-be-captain type. Until puberty, however, the child is rather uncoöperative and individualistic. But as he enters the teens he begins to like group games and will acquire a spirit of coöperation and fair play if he is situated in the proper environment. It is illuminating in this connection to note the words of Dr. H. D. Williams' son who, while visiting a summer camp of juvenile delinquents, entered a ball game being played between two teams of young offenders. Later he remarked to his father, "Those kids don't know how to play. They stand there and argue and fight, and hold up the game so there's no fun in it."

There is no more tragic sight among children than a youngster who wants to be included in the games of others but who has been deprived of human playmates for several years so that he is ignorant of the rules of their games, or is so awkward and inept that the other boys ignore him. When sides are being chosen for a ball game, he stands up hopefully, thinking that he may be selected next by one of the respective captains only to find that the last member of each team has been chosen without his name being called. "Aw, we don't want him on our side," his associates may remark with the brutal frankness of youth, "for he can't hit the ball." If the child is very intelligent and sensitive a few such public humiliations may send him to the sidelines for the remainder of his youth, and perhaps his entire life. Thereafter he may retain his interest in social groups, but always stay on the outskirts of the crowd. "Wallflowerism" is a category which covers his social inferiority complex.

On the other hand, this disappointed child may become a misanthrope, or engage in atypical behavior in order to attain some social recognition and envy. He frequently becomes the scholar so that he can compensate intellectually for his physical inability. If, however, a child has physical strength and dexterity but lacks brilliance or polite manners, he may compensate by becoming the bully of the crowd, or the "bad" child in the school. He finds that he can gain thereby a certain awed admiration and notoriety even if he cannot attain fame by the more onerous plan of study and scholastic preeminence.

Neither of the two types of reaction just mentioned is expressive of a well integrated personality. Because both youngsters feel their lack of self-reliance, they have adopted a compensatory form of reaction, and to explain their apparent inefficiency in the quality wherein they are inept, adopt a "sour grapes" attitude. Although it is true that some of the great works of art and of literature, of music and of science have come down to us as the fruits of compensation, as probably demonstrated by Beethoven, Byron, and Steinmetz, they have been produced at the cost of social maladjustment. Although society occasionally may profit thereby, from the standpoint of psychology such compensations as those of the two boys mentioned above are unwholesome.

As for the matter of emotional development and its relationship to the self-reliance of the child, we may state that many of the fears and doubts and emotional stresses which trouble the adult have their roots in childhood experiences. We shall treat this subject more fully in Chapter XV. Although Watson believes there are only the three primitive emotions—fear, rage, and love—these three may, like the four primary taste qualities, become so tied up with thousands of situations and stimuli as to affect a large portion of the individual's reactions. The difference between the coward and the brave man, for example, is often simply the fact that the coward is afraid, while the courageous man is afraid of being afraid.

In concluding our discussion of the development of self-reliance in the child, we should state that the aim of parents and teachers should be to add to the sum of the child's wholesome habits. The child with 1,000 habits is obviously less self-reliant than the youngster with 10,000 habits, other things being equal. Accordingly, it is imperative for adults to see that the child knows how to play the games of his age and sex, how to earn and spend money, how to care for his wants and make the mechanical and social adjustments expected of him because of the type of environment to which he will be exposed. Confidence and assurance follow the youngster who is sufficiently equipped with methods of reaction to the stimuli of his milieu so that he can make satisfactory adjustments thereto. No one is continuously successful, so the child must be schooled to meet the stimulus of defeat and know how to react successfully to it. This reaction does not involve running home to mother, or the development of a sour grapes attitude, but a close scrutiny of his own performance so that he can detect the flaws therein and avoid their repetition.

Sculpturing in Human Clay. When a Michelangelo stands before a block of marble he may sculpture a "Moses" or a group of "slaves", but in either case his product is insignificant compared to the human personality which can be produced by intelligent parents and teachers out of eight pounds of animate human clay. If the child possesses normal intellectual endowment and sensory acuity, he can be moulded into an outstanding surgeon, lawyer, artist, musician, poet, philosopher, orator, or writer. His parents, by the proper control of the stimuli playing upon him, can direct him into any one of these professions. The difficult task which they confront, however, is twofold, consisting of an understanding of what are the kinds of stimuli to employ to sculpture the child's personality, and how to procure or utilize those stimuli after they are known.

The first of these two problems is usually the more frequent cause for failure, since the intelligent parent and teacher do not need million dollar equipment and tools for the training of their Lincolns, as the following quotation from Dorothy Dix's column demonstrates.

(By Courtesy of the Philadelphia Public Ledger.)

"I know now that when I was a child we were very poor. I had so few clothes that my mother used to wash at night the little shirt that I wore to school the next day, but I was always clean and neat. I had to begin earning money almost as soon as I could walk, and I delivered papers when I was so little I could hardly reach a bellpull. We had such plain food that it was a gala day to be remembered for weeks when we had pie for dinner.

"But I never knew that I was poor because I never remember to have heard the subject mentioned in our family. My mother never whined and complained about what she couldn't have or because she wasn't as well off as other women or because she couldn't give us children the advantages that rich parents could give their children. She was always cheerful and made our home the happiest place in the world, and if we didn't have anything but stew and bread for supper we ate it to the accompaniment of so much laughter and good cheer that it made it a feast.

"My mother never let us be sorry for ourselves. She never inoculated us with the virus of self-pity, as so many poor mothers do their children. She never let us feel that it was hard luck that we had to work when other children played. She managed somehow to make us feel that we were superior to the poor little rich children who had to ask their parents for pennies, because we were clever enough to earn money ourselves. She made us feel that we were men and women while they were still children. I can remember being actually sorry for the little boys who didn't have newspaper routes and had nothing to do but to play marbles, while I was a responsible individual with what I considered an important job.

"My mother never deplored the fact that she couldn't give us college educations and that our father didn't have a bank that he could take us into as soon as we were grown. She never even intimated that poverty was a handicap to a boy.

"On the contrary, she talked to us continually about the poor boys who had become millionaires, about the boys who had no schooling, but who had educated themselves by reading and study; about the boys who had gone from behind plows and the towpaths of canals, from the humblest places, to the President's chair. The names of great doctors, lawyers, merchants, men of affairs who had been poor boys were always on her lips, and it was just bred into us that we could be like them if we were man enough to do it.

"I often think of my mother and other poor mothers that I have known since—mothers who make failures of their children in their very cradles by bringing them up in an atmosphere of gloom that chokes out every hope and aspiration and makes them feel that they are the victims of a malign destiny against which it is no use to struggle.

"Mothers who break down their children's morale and weaken them by weeping over them because they have to work. Haven't you seen such mothers, time and again, wringing their hands and shedding tears because their poor little Tommies had to punch the time-clock in a factory every morning instead of lying abed or because their darling Mamies had to stand behind a counter or pound a typewriter instead of going to pink teas?

"And, of course, that made Tommy and Mamie feel that they were poor, persecuted martyrs when they should have been rejoicing that they had brains enough to hold down a job and were independent, self-supporting men and women who could look the world in the eye and tell it where to go."

In summarizing this matter of sculpturing in human clay, it is evident that a thorough understanding of human motivation and control must be possessed by the sculptor if he wishes to mould his clay into the desired form. In addition, he must be cognizant of the great responsibility which devolves upon him after he has attained this knowledge. The majority of parents and teachers do not wish to be held accountable for pre-determining the child's future vocation, but are content if they can only equip him adequately for whatever demands life may make of him. That goal in itself is sufficiently difficult to test the ingenuity of adult intelligence, and should occupy the attention of those who have the opportunity to sculpture in human clay.

Since such tremendous potentialities reside in the child, it is no wonder, therefore, that many parents and teachers are awed by the responsibilities which are theirs. And if an artist or sculptor in marble feels that he must spend many years mixing paints and learning the technique of wielding a chisel, how much more imperative must be the need for men and women who deal with youngsters to acquire adeptness in manipulating verbal stimuli and the physical elements of the milieu. Consult my "Tests for Parents" on page 777.

REFERENCES

1 ALEXANDER, F. G., *The History of Psychiatry* (Harper & Row, 1966).
2 BARRON & TAYLOR, *Scientific Creativity* (Wiley, 1963).
3 BIDERMAN & ZIMMER, *The Manipulation of Human Behavior* (Wiley, 1964).
4 BOONE, PAT, *'Twixt Twelve and Twenty* (Prentice-Hall, 1959).
5 BUSS, A. H., *The Psychology of Aggression* (Wiley, 1961).
6 CATTELL, R. B., *Personality & Motivation* (World Book, 1959).
7 CHURCHMAN & RATOOSH, *Measurement* (Wiley, 1960).
8 COLE, L., *Psychology of Adolescence* (Rinehart, 1954).
9 COLEMAN, J. S., *The Adolescent Society* (Macmillan, 1962).
10. CRANE, G. W., "The Reversible Why" *(Child Welfare*, 26, 1931).
11 CRANE, G. W., "Tact and Child Education" *(Forecast*, 35, 1928).
12 CRANE, P. M., *The Democrat's Dilemma* (Regnery, 1964).
13 DUFFY, E., *Activation & Behavior* (Wiley, 1962).
14 FINK, H. K., *Mind & Performance* (Vantage Press, 1954).
15 GETZELS & JACKSON, *Creativity & Intelligence* (Wiley, 1962).
16 GRINKER, R. R., *Psychosomatic Case Book* (Blakiston, 1958).
17 HARMS, E., *Essentials of Abnormal Child Psychology* (Julian, 1954).
18 HOLLINGWORTH, H. L., *Mental Growth and Decline* (Appleton, 1927).
19 HOPKINS, P., *Gone Up in Smoke* (Highland Press, 1948).
20 HORWICH, F. R., *The Magic of Bringing Up Your Child* (McGraw-Hill, 1960).
21 HARGER, R. N., "Pharmacology & Toxicology of Alcohol" *(J.A.M.A.* 8/30/58).
22 KAGAN & MOSS, *Birth to Maturity* (Wiley, 1962).
23 KATZ, D., *The Vibratory Sense and Other Lectures* (U. of Maine Studies, No. 14, 1930).
24 KUNST, M. S., *A Study of Thumb- and Finger-Sucking in Infants* (Psychol. Monog., No. 290, 1948).
25 LICHTER et al., *The Drop-Outs* (Macmillan, 1962).
26 LLOYD, F., *Educating the Subnormal Child* (Philos. Libr., 1954).
27 MAURER, D. W., *Narcotics and Narcotic Addiction* (Thomas, 1954).
28 MYKLEBUST, H. R., *Your Deaf Child* (Thomas, 1954).
29 NEWTON, NILES, *Family Book of Child Care* (Harper, 1957).
30 PALMER, F., *And Four To Grow On* (Rinehart, 1958).
31 SARASON et al., *Anxiety in Elementary Children* (Wiley, 1960).
32 SKODAK, M., & SKEELS, H. M., "A Final Follow-Up Study of One Hundred Adopted Children" *(J. Genet. Psychol.*, 75, 1949).
33 SMITH, H. P., *Psychology in Teaching* (Prentice-Hall, 1954).
34 STOLZ, L. M., *Father Relations of War-Born Children* (Stanford U. Press, '54).
35 VISCARDI, H., *A Letter to Jimmy* (Eriksson, 1962).
36 WHITEHOUSE, H. L. K., *The Mechanism of Heredity* (St. Martin's, 1966).

CHAPTER XIV

PSYCHOLOGY APPLIED IN EDUCATION

The relationship between psychology and education has been a very close and cordial one. Each has profited by the data and principles of the other. The first practical applications of psychology of a systematic type were made in the field of education, where today many of the individual and group methods of the laboratory are employed under the heading, "experimental pedagogy". Indeed, both the methods of teaching and the content of the curriculum have been altered in accordance with progress made in psychology.

At an early period education was directed toward "training the mind" in which the mind was conceived of as a distinct entity which was more or less independent of the environment but could grow stronger or more powerful by contact with external stimuli. The difficulty with this conception was the confusion between intellectual development and muscular development. In the latter the same dumb-bell is just as effective in increasing the size and strength of the right biceps as are 100 equally heavy dumb-bells, so the subject needs but one to become a second Samson. In mental development, however, the very reverse of this rule holds true, for twenty years spent upon the study of Latin declensions will never stimulate mental growth like one year devoted to each of twenty different subjects.

Even yet this fallacy is not wholly understood. We send our children to high school and teach them geometry, for which the great majority will never have a single use later in life, yet fail to train them in applied psychology which is fundamental to their social and economic success. The former belief that geometry exercised the reasoning "faculty" more than salesmanship or accounting is now known to be false. A young fellow can obtain as much mental exercise trying to develop a successful campaign by which to win a girl who shows no interest in him, as he can in working any of the theorems presented to him in high school, and the relevancy of the former to his life's problems is obviously much greater. Thorndike[59] has the following to say regarding the relative disciplinary values of various school subjects:

By any reasonable interpretation of the results, the intellectual values of studies should be determined largely by the special information, habits, interests, attitudes, and ideals which they demonstrably produce. The expectation of any large differences in general improvement of the mind from one study rather than another seems doomed to disappointment. The chief reason why good thinkers seem superficially to have been made such by having taken certain school studies, is that good thinkers have taken such studies, becoming better by the inherent tendency of the good to gain more than the poor from any study. When the good thinkers studied Greek and Latin, these studies seemed to make good thinkers. Now that the good thinkers study Physics and Trigonometry, these seem to make good thinkers. If the abler pupils should all study Physical Education and Dramatic Art, these subjects would seem to make good thinkers. These were, indeed, a large fraction of the program of studies for the best thinkers the world has produced, the Athenian Greeks.

Since reasoning is resorted to in the solution of any problem it makes little difference where the problem is encountered, for the effect upon the subject's thought processes, if the problems are the same in difficulty, will be equally beneficial. As a result, the choice of the curricula for schools and colleges can be made more profitably on the basis of the practical value of various subjects as related to the child's needs. This modern viewpoint is especially significant when one realizes that millions of children never finish high school and thus need practical, vocational training to become self-sufficient.

"The man who has nothing to boast of but his illustrious ancestors is like a potato—the only good belonging to him is underground."
—Thomas Overbury

1964 PUBLIC SCHOOL ENROLLMENTS

Population 5 to 19 years_____	54,958,000
Elementary enrollment _____	26,221,705
Secondary enrollment _____	15,194,584
All Higher Institutions _____	5,320,294
First-time college entrants _____	1,234,806

Universities, Liberal Arts and Technical Colleges numbered 2,183 in 1964, not to mention over 1,000 splendid Business Colleges.

In addition to producing changes in the curriculum, however, psychology has been of considerable value to pedagogy in bringing out the definite fact of intellectual differences between pupils. Heretofore, the teacher has attempted to deal with varying degrees of mental age within her class, even though the children were all of the same chronological age. Her task has been somewhat like that of a teamster with a dozen spans of horses among which there were Arabian thoroughbreds coupled with large draft horses. As the thoroughbreds would leap at the command to go and chafe at the sluggishness of the slower animals, so the teacher's bright pupils quickly grasp the new problems, and are irked at the repetitions thereof which she must perform with the slower children.

In consequence, the more alert youngsters must be given additional material which their mates do not receive, or they may divert their idle energy into destructive channels. Some of the most brilliant of her pupils may be promoted ahead of their classmates until they get into a group more nearly matching their intellectual level, but the majority of them do not "skip" grades. By means of the intelligence tests to be described in succeeding sections it is possible to sort the youngsters who are of a given chronological age into groups with comparable intellectual endowment. For example, in one large city school where the fourth grades were divided in three sections, called "A", "B", and "C", on the basis of their mental age, it was found that the "A" class covered 225 pages in reading during the term against 150 pages covered by the "B" group, and 95 pages by the least alert section.

Numerous advantages result from such a preliminary selective process. In the first place, the most alert youngsters can be given new material as fast as they can assimilate it, and they will all advance at about the same rate. Competition therefore becomes keener, so the children do not "coast" throughout grammar and high school on the basis of their superior intellectual heritage, and then "flunk" out of college during their freshman year because of faulty habits of study. In the colleges, of course, the student is confronted with a very intelligent group, so he does not surpass his mates as he may have done in high school and especially in grammar school. He is compelled, therefore, to study diligently, for his fellow students are just as alert as he. If he lacks adequate habits of study, he is likely to be left behind.

Even in the least alert section of school children, moreover, there is a marked advantage because of the uniformity of ability demonstrated by the children. They no longer need feel an inferiority complex about competing with their classmates, since they all are of about equal ability. Rivalry is more fruitful of productivity since they are now more willing to compete inasmuch as they have a chance to win. The other advantages, of such a mental age classification of school children, particularly in regard to simplifying the teacher's problems, we shall not be able to consider here because of space limitations.

Intelligence and Intelligence Tests. We have previously remarked upon the intimate relationship between heredity and environment as they pertain to intelligence. Since it is impossible in the light of present scientific advancement to separate the two, as might conceivably be done by calling the number of synapses the inherited intelligence, and the number of functional synaptic linkages the acquired intelligence, the reader will understand why there has been so much difficulty in defining intelligence. Probably the most widely accepted definition is that one given by the German psychologist Stern, who says that intelligence is the ability to meet and solve novel situations.

Although people had long recognized intellectual differences between individuals there was no systematic and objective test for separating children or adults into groups with definite mental ages until the French psychologist Alfred Binet was commissioned in 1904 to survey the schools of Paris for the purpose of detecting feeble-minded pupils. With the cooperation of Theodore Simon, Binet set to work developing a scale of tests for the mental alertness of youngsters of various chronological ages. In 1905 the Binet-Simon test was first published.

Almost immediately the Binet scale established itself as the most reliable method of measuring general intellectual ability then in existence. But there were many defects in the original scale, some of which Binet himself attempted to remedy, while others were modified in America by such experimenters as Kuhlmann, Goddard, Terman, and Yerkes. Of these the latter two have made the most significant alterations, and Terman's *Stanford Revision of the Binet-Simon Intelligence Scale* is now the standard intelligence test in this country for school children.

The actual standardization of the test was as follows. First a representative group of children was obtained. Let us assume there are 100 three-year-olds, 100 four-year-olds, etc. The experimenter then administers various items of the scale to each youngster. Suppose he inquires, "Are you a little boy or a little girl?" He finds that maybe 20 per cent of two-year-olds can answer correctly; that 77 per cent of three-year-olds are correct; and that 98 per cent of four-year-olds give the proper answer. As a result, he places the ability to

give one's sex as an item which should be characteristic of the normal three-year-old, using the attainment of 75 per cent of the children at any given age as the standard. If, however, 95 per cent of three-year-olds could give their right sex, this question would not be a desirable one for any age group. Not only must 75 per cent be able to answer the query correctly, but not much over 75 per cent must be able to do so.

Following such a plan Terman re-standardized Binet's scale upon American children. Some of the items for different ages will be found below.

THREE YEARS

Points to nose, eyes, and mouth.
Enumerates objects in a picture.
Gives family name.
Repeats a sentence of six syllables.

FOUR YEARS

Compares lines regarding length.
Counts four pennies.
Copies a square.
Repeats four digits.

SIX YEARS

Distinguishes between right and left.
Counts thirteen pennies.
Names missing parts of mutilated pictures.
Distinguishes between morning and afternoon.

When the scale is actually administered to a child, the psychologist first endeavors to establish friendly relations and gain the cooperation of the youngster, after which the test items are regarded as a game. The highest age at which the child passes all tests is termed his basal age. For example, a four-year-old youngster might be able to answer all the items under the THREE YEAR test above, but not perform but three items under FOUR YEARS. His basal age would therefore be three years, or thirty-six months. For each of the items under FOUR YEARS he gets a credit of three months, if it is correctly answered. The child receives a total of nine months from the FOUR YEARS category, and is able to pass one item under FIVE YEARS, for which he obtains an additional three months. His total mental age is 36 plus 9 plus 3 months, or 48 months. Since his chronological age was stated as being four years, or 48 months, the child is normal and has an intelligence quotient of 100. We have previously discussed the fact that Terman, following the idea of Stern, has introduced the I. Q. or Intelligence Quotient as a means of expressing the relationship between a child's mental and chronological ages. The I. Q. equals the mental age divided by the chronological age.

The Intelligence Quotient is fairly constant, varying scarcely at all when the child remains in the same type of environment throughout his development to maturity. Thus, the youngster who at the age of four is given a Binet test which shows him to have an I. Q. of 120, will also be found to have approximately 120 for an I. Q. when he is tested at ten or fifteen years of age. If, however, he has visual or hearing defects at the age of four, or if he is undernourished or convalescing from a protracted illness, his decreased energy and lessened sensory acuity may cause him to obtain a lower I. Q. than he will later demonstrate when these errors are corrected.

The I. Q. has also been found to change somewhat when children are adopted into homes where the educational influences are more pronounced than in the child's orphanage or tenement environment. Freeman has shown that the greater the change in the conditions of the home. the more likely will be the alteration in I. Q. In a few cases, after several years' exposure to the superior milieu children gained as many as fifteen to twenty points. In this connection Terman states that children of the same native ability but located in superior and inferior homes may show a difference of about ten points in favor of the youngsters from the better type of environment.

In addition to the Binet test, the Army Alpha examination is another famous mental scale noted for its widespread use in measuring the intellectual differences of adults. During World War I this examination was devised by a group of psychologists appointed by the American Psychological Association and administered to 1,750,000 men. Since then it has been used extensively in colleges and the business world, although a number of somewhat similar examinations superseded it during World War II.

The Army Alpha is a battery of eight sub-tests, of which the first is intended to measure the subject's ability to follow oral instructions and contains twelve items. The second sub-test consists of 20 problems in arithmetic running from very simple addition to rather complex problems. The third sub-test of 16 problems endeavors to measure common sense, and is of the multiple choice type with three answers given to each question. The fourth is a synonym-antonym test in which the student determines whether two words mean the same or the opposite. There are 40 such pairs in the list. The fifth sub-test consists of disarranged sentences which must be mentally re-arranged into sensible statements, and then answered with the words "true" or "false". It contains 24 items.

The sixth sub-test consists of 20 sequences of numbers which must be completed, as 2 2 4 4 6 6 — —. The seventh sub-test involves a somewhat similar recognition of logical relationships among words, as Hand : Arm : : Foot : -- EAR TRUNK LEG HEAD. The student underlines one of the four capitalized words which has the same relationship to "foot" as "arm" has to "hand". There are 40 items in this sub-test, and 40 in the eighth, which is a range of information test. In the latter the student completes a sentence by un-

derlining one of four words, as BRIDGE is played with
RACKETS PINS CARDS MARBLES.

The total score possible is 212 which is practically impossible of attainment, while that made by the average person
is probably around 70. In Chapter IX the reader will find
the average scores made by members of 96 business, professional, and labor groups. The median score for college students falls at 150, and practical experience has shown that
those who make below 110 are not very likely to succeed in
college. In this connection it is well to remember that the
possession of a high I. Q. or a remarkable score on Army
Alpha is not an invariable prognosis of business or scholastic
success, for studious habits and the adequate motivation for
hard work are also important correlates. A person with a
low I. Q. cannot graduate from college, but one having a high
I. Q. may not do so, either.

The Army Beta was developed at the same time as Army
Alpha but for use with those recruits who were either illiterate
or non-English readers. It is a non-language examination
and is akin to the usual performance tests except that it involves the use of pencil and paper, and was employed chiefly
with adults. Performance tests were given considerable impetus by Pintner and Paterson, who had to perfect some scale
for testing the alertness of deaf children. They employed
fifteen tests derived from various sources, among which the
following three are representative.

(1) *The Seguin-Goddard form board* which has also been
extensively used by Sylvester with children of various ages.
In this test the task confronting the child consists of laying
a wooden block in the form of a cross, a square, a circle, a
triangle, etc. into its appropriate indented place in the form
board, in a minimal time and with no errors. The time limit
for placing the ten blocks in their proper positions is five
minutes. A common error of the feeble-minded youngster is
his attempt to place a triangular block into the indenture for

the star, or the rectangular block into the space for the square. Even normal youngsters of limited years are liable to the same confusions.

(2) *Healy's pictorial-completion test,* in which the child is to complete a picture by inserting the proper cut-out portions. This test is somewhat similar to many games sold on the market except that here the child has a great many choices from which to select the appropriate cut-out pieces, and is scored on the basis of the relevancy of each insert.

(3) *The Knox cube test.* There are five of these small cubes of which four are placed in a row before the child while the fifth is held by the experimenter. The latter then taps the other cubes with the one which he holds, varying the order to form a more difficult sequence on succeeding trials, as 1-2-3-4, 1-2-3-4-3, 1-3-2-4-3. At the conclusion of each series the experimenter hands the cube to the child who is told to tap likewise. A definite, unchanged series of numbers is used with all subjects tested. Pintner and Paterson offer tables based on the extensive examinations made by themselves and other researchers. In them one finds that both the time consumed and the errors made in the test decrease with the increasing age of the subject examined.

In summarizing our discussion of intelligence and intelligence tests, we may state that Stern's conception of intelligence as the ability to meet and solve novel situations furnished the incentive for an attempt to create an objective scale for measuring this capacity. Such scales involve a number of sub-tests on which measures are taken, the sum of which constitutes the person's score. Some of the sub-tests may be weighted, as numbers 4, 7, and 8 on Army Alpha where there are 40 items each, instead of 12, 16, 20, or 24 as in the other sub-tests of that scale. The matter of weighting sub-tests has been discussed in a previous chapter. As for the types of mental tests developed, there is the Binet-Simon for children, the Army Alpha for literate adults, the Army Beta for illiterate adults and children, and the performance scales usually for children. Among these tests the Binet-Simon is strictly an individual examination wherein the administrator takes but one child at a time. The same procedure is true of most of the performance scales, but Army Alpha is a group test, being given to as many as a hundred or more simultaneously. Other intelligence tests are usually based on these general principles, and employ a number of sub-tests, the sum of whose scores becomes the subject's final index. In order to interpret the latter, of course, norms or the known performances of large groups of persons must be available. A score of 106 is only half the possible score on Army Alpha, but it is decidedly above the median for the American population, for only about 20 per cent can attain it.

The Uses of Intelligence Tests. During the years immediately following the World War psychological tests were employed more or less indiscriminately in the hope that a panacea of industrial and educational problems had been obtained. But mental and vocational testing requires a rigid technique and a scientific training for the adequate interpretation of the records procured. Many persons were lacking in at least one of these respects, so their results were often disappointing. Moreover, there are usually so many additional factors involved in both scholarship and industrial ability that the intelligence test score must be supplemented by other data. When rightly used and modified by additional measures, intelligence tests are of marked value in the following fields:

(1) *The classification of pupils in the schools.* In addition to the uses in sorting pupils of the same school grade into different groups, these tests may show those who warrant immediate promotion or demotion, and are of assistance in rating the ability of children who transfer to a new school. The personnel director of the university or the teacher may watch the performance in classroom work and note whenever it falls below the standard which should be maintained accord-

ing to the student's mental abilities. He may then interview the student at once in order to correct the factors which are interfering with the latter's optimum output. The intelligence score of a person is, accordingly, the best single measure of his ability, and forms a quick means of gaining an idea of his possible future development.

(2) *Selection of college entrants.* Particularly in the privately endowed colleges and universities intelligence tests have been employed as a means of selecting the most alert applicants. When such educational institutions have two or three times the number of applicants for which they have available space and equipment, it becomes advisable to choose those high school graduates who hold the most promise of profiting richly by the college training. Other things being equal, the more intelligent men and women are of this type. Because of the lack of uniformity in standards of grading students from one school to another, a high school average of 93 from one institution may not mean the same as one of 93 from another. The intelligence test is usually a method by which inside of an hour the university director of admissions can gauge the intellectual capacity of all the applicants. Instead of using the numerical or letter grades which high school graduates cite, moreover, he is more interested in their relative standing within their graduating class, for the latter measure is now considered a more nearly accurate basis for comparison.

(3) *Personnel administration.* The vocational counselor usually wishes to know first of all the intellectual capacity of his student. Although the public school system is a rough intelligence scale in itself, since most subnormals never are graduated from grammar school, and most normal children never matriculate at college, still a special mental test is even more nearly accurate. In employment, moreover, the intelligence score is also revealing, both as to the lower and upper critical limits. We have previously discussed this topic when

we mentioned how Dr. Snow used to encounter Army Alpha scores like 45, 67, 83, 56, and 175, among the taxicab drivers, and soon found that the 175 men were college students working their way through school.

The principal uses of intelligence tests, therefore, have to do with the sorting and classification of school children, the selection of college entrants, the guidance of young people into phases of industry in which they are intellectually capable, and the selection of employees who will be most satisfactory. In the following section we shall consider the intellectual strata in modern society.

Intellectual Levels of the Population. From the data procured by Army Alpha and Binet examinations Terman[58] has presented the following apportionment of Intelligence Quotients:

I. Q.	CLASSIFICATION
140- up	"Near" genius or genius
120-140	Very superior intelligence
110-120	Superior
90-110	Normal or average
80- 90	Dull, rarely classifiable as feeble-minded
70- 80	Border-line deficiency, sometimes classifiable as dullness, often as feeble-mindedness
0- 70	Definitely feeble-minded

Among the definitely feeble-minded, morons are usually considered to have Intelligence Quotients from 50 to 70, with imbeciles falling between 20 and 50, and idiots lying between 0 and 20. The adult idiot's mental age is under three, with the adult imbecile having the maturity of normal children of three to seven years, and the grown moron having a rating of

---

"The United States never lost a war or won a conference."
—Will Rogers

"Schoolhouses are the republican line of fortifications." —Horace Mann from seven to twelve years. Terman presents the percentage of the population possessing various I. Q.'s in the following table:

OF 1,000 UNSELECTED SCHOOL CHILDREN

The lowest 1 % go to 70 or below; the highest 1 % reach 130 or above
The lowest 2 % go to 73 or below; the highest 2 % reach 128 or above
The lowest 3 % go to 76 or below; the highest 3 % reach 125 or above
The lowest 5 % go to 78 or below; the highest 5 % reach 122 or above
The lowest 10 % go to 85 or below; the highest 10 % reach 116 or above
The lowest 15 % go to 88 or below; the highest 15 % reach 113 or above
The lowest 20 % go to 91 or below; the highest 20 % reach 110 or above
The lowest 25 % go to 92 or below; the highest 25 % reach 108 or above
The lowest 33⅓% go to 95 or below; the highest 33⅓% reach 106 or above

Since nowadays 10 per cent of students enter college and these are usually of the very superior type, it will be apparent that an I. Q. of about 115 is probably the lower level of college intelligence. Terman states that an I. Q. of 75 might even be considered the upper limit for the category of feeble-mindedness, in which case there would be almost 4,000,000 such persons in the United States. This figure is in fairly close agreement with Dr. Goddard's[25] report of 2 per cent of feeble-minded among 2,000 public school children in New York City, and slightly in excess of the 1.5 per cent of feeble-minded found among the 12,000 pupils in the Toronto public schools in the survey under the direction of the Canadian National Committee of Mental Hygiene in 1919. Because in the latter survey a number of retarded children were absent from school during the time of the investigation, Professor W. G. Smith of the University of Toronto believes the total number of feeble-minded would also be about 2 per cent.

To illustrate an extreme case of intellectual brilliance in a child the reader's attention is called to the following comparison as given by Hollingworth *et al*[33]:

"I care little who makes a nation's laws if I have the making of its ballads.   —Andrew Fletcher

"A university is a place where pebbles are polished and diamonds are dimmed."   —Robert Ingersoll

SUBJECT: Edward Rochie Hardy, Jr.   BORN: June 17, 1908.

NOVEMBER 4, 1916	EDWARD	NORM*
Height -----------------------	54.3 inches	49.5 inches
Weight -----------------------	89.3 lbs.	54.2 lbs.
Intellectual status -------------	I. Q. 187	I. Q. 100
	(Stanford-Binet)	(Stanford-Binet)
School status ------------------	6th grade	3rd grade*

SEPTEMBER 29, 1921		
Height -----------------------	64.2 inches	58.2 inches
Weight -----------------------	166 lbs.	89.5 lbs.
	(light clothing)	
Intellectual status -------------	194 points	47 points (Alpha)
	(Alpha, Form 5)	
School status ------------------	4th semester college	8th grade*

*Norms for height, weight, and school status are taken from Bird T. Baldwin, as established on children from Horace Mann School, Francis Parker School, and the High Schools of the University of Chicago, where the children are above average (for population at large) in intelligence.

In 1920 Edward took the Thorndike Mental Tests for freshmen for entrance to Columbia College and was second highest out of the 483 entering the college. Edward was then 12 years and 0 months of age, while the median age of the others was about 18 years. On the day cited in the table above Edward not only made 194 on Form 5 of Army Alpha, but a little later in the afternoon he took Form 6 and scored 201 thereon.

An I. Q. of 187 is obviously phenomenal. In our discussion of physical age, however, we mentioned that children mature at different rates, and as a consequence I. Q.'s would be more nearly accurate if we had norms for physical development so that we could insert physical age for chronological age in the formula by which I. Q.'s are obtained. From Edward's height and weight it would seem very likely that he is precocious in his physical maturity as well as in his mental alertness. His I. Q. would as a result be considerably less than 187 when he is matched with children of equal bone and muscular development. Even so, however, a score of 194 on Army Alpha puts him in the upper 1 per cent of Terman's classification, granting him a minimum I. Q. of 130.

In concluding our survey of the intellectual levels of the population, therefore, we may state that the average mental age of the adult is considered to be 16 years, although that of the principal sample of the white draft, when transmuted from Alpha and Beta examinations into terms of mental age, was placed at 13.08 years, a figure which is deemed a bit low. Hollingworth[34] has placed the average mental age at 14 years, and includes 50 per cent of the American population in that category, with the other 50 per cent equally distributed above and below that point. The number of feeble-minded persons in the population is usually estimated at from 1 to 3 per cent. In the light of these intellectual differences in children, consequently, it is not difficult to imagine the struggles of the school teacher who has hitherto obtained her pupils chiefly on the basis of their chronological age alone.

The Relationship Between Health and Intelligence. The proverbial curiosity of youth is largely a function of an abundance of physical energy and vitality. As age advances, this surplus diminishes so that the average person curbs his desire for intellectual exploration in order to horde his strength. The parent has frequently noted the striking curtailment in his child's curiosity when the latter was suffering from sickness or was undergoing convalescence. Nature inhibits cortical activity when the vegetative functions of the body demand all the youngster's strength and energy. A partial measure of the child's return to health is accordingly his greater interest in his milieu.

"Labor to keep alive in your breast that little spark of celestial fire, conscience."   —George Washington

Since a violent attack of disease will so markedly lower the curiosity of a youngster as to render him relatively oblivious to the stimuli in his environment, it is not difficult to understand the dulling effect of undernourishment and infection of a slower sort. The Army Alpha records from the war show a noticeable difference in the intelligence scores of white recruits infected by hookworm and a group of the same race not so infected.

In this connection the psychological examiners urge, "It is important, however, to guard against the assumption that data of this kind prove the existence of a causal relationship between hookworm disease and mental inferiority. Low native ability may induce such conditions of living as to induce hookworm infection, or poor environmental conditions may be responsible for both the disease and the low test record."

In this particular instance it may be granted that hookworm disease is not the sole cause of low native ability, but it is probably a safe conclusion *a priori* that hookworm disease and other long continued infections are causes of a mental dullness which may be as serious in its effect upon the behavior adjustments of the individual as feeble-mindedness itself. Moreover, as Gault[24] points out, "by way of social inheritance, the dulling effect of this and other diseases may be passed on to succeeding generations; for the dull head of a family, from whatever cause he may be dull, creates an atmosphere in his home in which his children live and grow . . . until fixed dispositions are built up in them."

It is quite probable that part of the greater alertness of children from better homes is to be explained on the basis of their greater energy and vitality with its attendant increase of the children's curiosity. We know, for example, that the onset of the menses in girls from poorer homes tends to be later than in those from better environments, and malnutri-

"God made mothers because he couldn't be everywhere himself."
—Old Hebrew Proverb

tion is detrimental to scholarship; so anything which would lower the health reserve of a youngster should also begin to curb his curiosity.

It is consequently imperative for parents not only to remedy any visual and auditory defects of their children which can be corrected, but also to keep the youngsters in robust health, since the latter supplies the basis for intellectual activity. A listless child is likely to become an uninteresting and uninterested adult.

The Most Critical Stage in the Child's School Career. The first years of contact with the school system are the most important of all those spent in classrooms, for it is then that the youngster is likely to develop his liking for, or aversion to, education. After he grows older his experience with a teacher whom he dislikes is not so critical, for then he is more likely to realize that she is just the exception to the rule. At the ages of six or eight years, however, an antagonism for a certain teacher is often transferred to the whole educational system, after which the child loses interest and falls in scholarship. As his marks drop, his aversion to education tends to increase, and the youngster may dread coming to school.

Indeed, it is possible for a dyspeptic teacher of the early grades to alter the enthusiasm and delight of forty youngsters so that they become prejudiced against her and all that she stands for, namely, education. The fault in this kind of situation is not wholly the teacher's, for her ill health or increasing age may render her less patient and interested in youngsters, especially when they have not yet been fully "broken in" to the regulations of the classroom.

The advisability of having young teachers in the early grades is therefore apparent, for they are more inclined to have enough energy and patience to submit agreeably to the demands of a roomful of six-year-olds. It would probably be a good thing if teachers moved along toward the upper grades as they advanced in years. Instead of letting women 60 years of age deal with beginners, it would probably be advantageous to both the youngsters and the teacher if she moved along toward the eighth grade, and let younger women take her place in the kindergarten. The average woman of 60 has not enough energy to keep up with the demands of 20 to 40 youngsters, so she is more inclined to resort to the ruler as a means of holding her young charges in check. The more fatigued she becomes, the greater is her use of the stick, and therefore the less likely she will increase the children's fondness for school.

Because the young teacher is only a score of years removed from her own kindergarten age, and since she has the exuberance of health and vitality to cope with the demands of the early grades, she is much more likely to coax her youngsters into the desirable form of behavior, and consequently her influence is of lasting benefit. She is less inclined to be autocratic, and her recent graduation from normal college where she imbibed some of the idealism and social responsibilities entailed in teaching enables her to regard her youngsters as something more than just a monotonous method of earning her pay check. All too frequently old teachers lose sight of the ultimate goals of education, and they seldom grow tearful over their inability to deal successfully with a problem child. "Oh, you will get over that after you have been here as long as we have," they remark to the young teacher. Unfortunately, they are correct, which leads us to the opinion that young teachers should enter the educational system in the same manner as they first encountered it, namely, *via* the kindergarten and first grade.

The Nursery School and Its Future. Because of the diminished size of the average American family, and the fact that apartment dwellers cannot let their youngsters run out to play as readily as used to be the case, there is a growing need for some means of enabling the only child to have social contacts with other youngsters of about his own age. In fact, at the present time many children of pre-kindergarten age seldom get outside except when with an adult.

In the previous chapter we explained the detrimental effect upon the child of a lack of siblings and playmates, yet many parents today seem little able to remedy matters owing to their limited financial resources. Except for his thirty minutes or so in Sunday school, their child is almost as closely confined to the apartment as the spinster's cat.

The nursery school offers an excellent partial remedy. By admitting tots who are old enough to walk, it socializes and extroverts these probably introverted children. In fact, it is frequently possible to pick out the nursery school child from others not so favored simply by its greater cooperation in the play group. It seems not unreasonable to assume that a lowering of the entrance age for kindergarten would be a distinct advantage not only to children, but indirectly to the state itself through its tendency to lessen the divorce rate of these same youngsters. Since over 40% of teen-agers do not go onward for any type of college training whatsoever, then it behooves our elementary and secondary schools to practicalize the curriculum as Business Colleges do.

The church school might be impressed to offer such a service to the community, for there are churches in every village and city which stand more or less unused between Sundays. And there are many idle young women of good education and altruistic interests who would be rendering children and the state a great service by conducting daily nursery schools therein. Many city parents would be delighted to pay a nominal fee for an opportunity to place their youngsters in such a beneficial environment. As a method for the "ladies aid" and similar women's religious organizations to earn money for the church, nursery schools hold great promise. If necessary the women could alternate, or spend only half a day a week in the work, so it would not be burdensome to any and should, in fact, be almost as stimulating to these young matrons as to the tiny tots.

The future of the nursery school seems, therefore, to be very bright, although it appears that private organizations will be its chief sponsors, at least for several years to come. Eventually, however, the state may find it desirable to assume the instruction of children at a lower entrance age than the present five or six years.

The Qualifications of a Good Teacher. In discussing the factors which make a good teacher Dean Ashbaugh[2] says, "The evidence of a great teacher is not that his students know the material he has taught but that they come from his courses with an insatiable desire to know more and more of his field." In order for this result to occur the teacher must usually possess enthusiasm. We have previously commented upon the salesman's need for enthusiasm if he wishes to be a success. After all, the teacher should also consider himself a salesman of education. Too many men and women, however, take the attitude that they are being paid their salaries simply to deliver a fifty minute lecture three times a week, and if the students do not get anything out of the address that is their bad luck. A good teacher, on the contrary, should be so interested in his own subject that, like the missionary, he cannot be content until he has converted his listeners.

In the second place, a good teacher should also possess intellectual perspective. He should be fairly well oriented in the field of education, so that he can relate the specific material within his own province to other fields, and his social intelligence should be such that he knows the current interests and humor of the group to which he speaks. Just because he is a member of Phi Beta Kappa and has held a fellowship for research is no positive indication that he is fitted for

---

"The secret of education lies in respecting the pupil."   —Emerson pedagogy. Indeed, it is this misconception concerning the cardinal purpose of teaching which explains in large part the students' ennui during lectures and the presence of Morpheus in so many classrooms. The fact that they wander "through courses in the Greek thought of the Fourth Century or the social institutions of Medieval Spain . . . somnolent and pathetic" cannot be gainsaid, for how can we expect a zestful interest on the part of youth in subjects which are often presented with a dyspeptic lack of enthusiasm by an instructor whose chief forensic virtue qualifies him for the degree Doctor of Somnolence?

Nor does it follow that because a professor spends years of research on the cultural significance of the castanet in medieval Spain and hopes to advance himself professionally through an article or two containing the results of his investigations, that his students will become enraptured listeners to the same subject. Since teaching is salesmanship, the instructor must remember the axioms of the salesman and strike at fundamental motive bases. As a public speaker, moreover, he should consider himself at fault if he cannot keep his students awake.

Aside from his enthusiasm and perspective, the teacher should bear in mind that his students also obtain ideas concerning politics and morality from him. They will go back to their respective communities and states with social attitudes colored by their contacts with him. It is important for the instructor to remember that these same students may be sending their children to him a generation later if he has given them sound advice both as to his specific field and also as to morality, statesmanship, and religion. In the latter connection it should be evident that it does not become any young Ph. D. to ridicule the religious tenets of the 18-year-olds who sit in his classes and who lack the forensic training to defend themselves and their beliefs.

As regards the teacher's own scholastic and research background, Dr. Martin L. Reymert* has constructed with the cooperation of 42 psychologists a scale by which to evaluate such qualifications. Although it was intended primarily for rating psychologists, it may easily apply to teachers in other

I. TRAINING	POINTS	
Ph.D.	4.9	
Sc.D.	4.6	
M.A.	1.8	
M.S.	1.8	
A.B.	.6	
A. DEGREES		4.9
Professor	4.5	
Associate Professor	3.1	
Assistant Professor	1.8	
Instructor	.8	
Assistant	.3	
B. Present Academic Position		4.5
Fellowships	1.3	
Scholarships	.3	
Assistantships	.8	
C. Appointments		2.4
D. Amount and Quality of Laboratory Training		3.4
E. Other Training in Psychology		2.6
Other Sciences	1.9	
Philosophy	.5	
Mathematics	1.2	
Statistics	1.1	
F. Training in background subjects		4.7
Attending University	.4	
Research	.9	
Travel	.3	
G. Training in vacation period		1.6
TOTAL		24.1

*Quoted by permission of Dr. Martin L. Reymert. This survey is published in the *Psychological Bulletin*.

II. LENGTH OF EXPERIENCE IN YEARS

0- 2	1.7
3- 4	2.9
5- 6	4.5
7- 9	5.9
10-14	7.2
15-19	7.0
20-24	6.4
25-29	5.6
30 and over	5.1

A. Years in psychology _____   7.2

Under 5 years	.2
Over 5 years	1.1

B. No. of years in present position ___   1.3

TOTAL _____   8.5

III. PUBLICATIONS

A. Books	8.6
B. General articles (no experimental) _	4.6
C. Experimental studies	10.3
D. Editorial Service	3.1
E. Review and Abstract Service	2.5

TOTAL _____   29.1

IV. RECOGNIZED CONTRIBUTIONS

A. New Apparatus	3.9
B. Improvement of Technique and Method	10.0
C. Statistical devices (formulae)	4.9
D. Contributions to Systematic Psychology	8.8

TOTAL _____   27.6

V. MEMBERSHIP RANK

A. Associate	2.2
B. Member	5.6
C. Fellow	8.1
D. Officer	10.7
E. Promoter	7.5

TOTAL _____   10.7

branches of knowledge. There are five general headings which are subdivided as in the preceding chart.

The training of teachers should also be such that their knowledge of statistics and grading methods is fairly uniform. Even at the present time there is considerable variation among teachers in the manner of scoring examination papers. Starch and Elliot[54] for example, took Question X from a final examination paper in geometry by a pupil in one of the largest high schools in Wisconsin. Plates of this answer paper were made and several hundred copies were printed upon foolscap, thus exactly reproducing the original in every detail.

A set of questions and a copy of the answer paper were sent to about 180 high schools in the North Central Association with the request that the principal teacher in mathematics grade this paper according to the practice and standards of the school. In the following Exhibit will be found the results. The teachers' marks varied from 39 to 88.

In the night schools of two large urban universities the

EXHIBIT 55. Passing grade 75. 75 schools. Median 70. Probable error 7.2.

following grade distribution shows a lack of uniformity somewhat comparable to that demonstrated in the grading of the mathematics paper mentioned above. The reader will note

---

"The probability that we may fail in the struggle ought not to deter us from the support of a cause we believe to be just."   —Lincoln that a student in School B has a greater chance of making an "A" than in School A. It is this lack of uniformity among schools which has led the directors of admission in American universities to place more reliance upon a high school graduate's relative position in his graduating class than upon his actual grades. The "Normal" has been included in the table

	% A	% B	% C	% D	% E&F
School A _____	15	38	34	8	5
School B _____	21	46	23	7	3
"Normal" _____	5	20	50	20	5

to show a distribution which would form what is called a normal distribution curve if plotted. The other two would form "skewed" curves, that is, there is an overloading of "A" and "B" grades for a five point scale, with a marked diminution in "D" and "E" percentages.

At this point it would be well to mention a few statistical terms. The *mean* or *average* is a measure of central tendency which is found by dividing the sum of all the individual scores by the number of cases. It is laborious to compute when there are a large number of cases, and when there are few cases it may give a distorted view of the data because of a few extreme scores. For example, let us assume that five persons contributed to a campaign fund the following amounts: $1,000,000; $100; $100; $100; and $100. The mean contribution would, therefore, be $200,080, which makes it appear that all the individuals gave large sums.

The *median* is the middle score in the series, and is not only easier to compute than the mean, but is not influenced by extreme cases. In the five contributions just mentioned the median is the third measure, or $100. In a normal distribution of scores based on a large number of cases the median, the mean, and the mode fall at the same place, which is the highest point on the distribution curve when plotted. In the event of an even number of cases, the median is the point above and below which 50 per cent of the scores fall.

The *mode* by common usage refers to the score or measure at which the most cases fall. In Exhibit 55 the mode is 75 while the median is 70.

The *inter-quartile range* is the spread of scores of the middle fifty per cent of the cases when the latter have been previously arranged in order from highest to lowest. Because it eliminates the highest and the lowest fourths of the group it is less influenced by extreme cases than is the total range. In Chapter IX the range of Army Alpha scores for various occupations was inter-quartile.

The *average deviation* or *mean variation* is the average deviation from the mean or average score. The formula given below simply calls for the sum of the individual deviations from the mean score, divided by the number of cases. In this formula Σ stands for the sum, while d represents the

$$\text{A.D. (or M.V.)} = \frac{\Sigma d}{N}$$

deviations from the mean, and N denotes the number of cases. An average deviation of 10 from a mean of 75 represents much less relative variability than an average deviation of 10 from a mean of 35.

The *standard deviation* is usually more useful and more frequently encountered than the simpler average deviation, and is designated by σ, as shown in the next formula, where the other symbols have already been defined above. If after the scores are arranged in ascending or descending order a

$$\sigma = \sqrt{\frac{\Sigma d^2}{N}}$$

distance equal to the standard deviation is laid off on each side of the mean score, then 68.26 per cent of the scores or measures will be included in this range.

The *coefficient of correlation* is a statistical measure of the degree of similarity or dissimilarity existing between two series of scores from the same persons. There are several methods of obtaining it, but we shall illustrate only Spearman's rank-differences method. With any of the methods, however, the coefficient will range from +1.00 to —1.00. If with a class of 40 children we compared their proficiency in spelling with their excellence in reading and found that the best speller was also the best reader, that the second best speller was also the second best reader, and so forth, the correlation would be +1.00. On the other hand, if the best speller was the poorest reader, the second best speller was the next poorest reader, and so on until the worst speller was the best reader, then we would have a perfect negative correlation which would result in a coefficient of —1.00. If some of the best spellers were the best readers, but some were also the poorest readers and so on, we would find a correlation in the neighborhood of 0.00, which denotes a chance and non-significant relationship.

In the rank-differences method the raw scores must first be changed into ranks, as will be evident from the following comparison between the Army Alpha scores and the final examination marks of 25 students selected from one of the writer's classes in applied psychology. In case of ties, the ranks involved are added, then divided by the number of identical scores. In Army Alpha, subjects "G.F." and "R.H." are tied for 6th place, so we add 6 and 7, divide by 2, and award each a rank of 6.5. There will be no 6th or 7th ranks thereafter.

STUDENT	ARMY ALPHA	EXAM.	RANK IN ALPHA	RANK IN EXAM.	DIFFER- ENCE	DIFFER- ENCE SQUARED
J. A. _____	122	22	21	23	2	4
V. B. _____	133	89	18	6	12	144
N. B. _____	150	79	13	9	4	16
B. B. _____	156	67	11	15	4	16
E. B. _____	137	115	16	2	14	196
J. B. _____	194	91	1	4	3	9
J. C. _____	193	90	2	5	3	9
E. C. _____	143	118	15	1	14	196
L. C. _____	146	87	14	7	7	49
R. D. _____	127	45	20	19	1	1
E. F. _____	179	71	4	11.5	7.5	56.25
G. F. _____	164	68	6.5	14	7.5	56.25
F. G. _____	157	69	10	13	3	9
P. G. _____	109	19	25	25	0	0
C. G. _____	173	55	5	18	13	169
R. H. _____	164	66	6.5	16	9.5	90.25
W. H. _____	163	71	8	11.5	3.5	12.25
G. H. _____	135	56	17	17	0	0
J. K. _____	110	32	24	20	4	16
M. K. _____	162	84	9	8	1	1
J. L. _____	113	29	23	21	2	4
R. L. _____	129	21	19	24	5	25
R. M. _____	121	25	22	22	0	0
A. M. _____	180	93	3	3	0	0
L. S. _____	151	78	12	10	2	4
						1083

The rank-differences formula is as follows:

$$Q = 1 - \frac{6 \, \Sigma \, D^2}{N \, (N^2 - 1)},$$

in which Q stands for the coefficient of correlation; D, the difference in rank in the two tests; and N, the number of paired measurements, which in this particular instance equals 25. After substitution, we find:

$$Q = 1 - \frac{6 \, (1083)}{25 \, (625 - 1)} = 1 - 0.416 = 0.584$$

The correlation is positive; therefore, it shows a definite tendency toward similarity in ranks between the two tests. Before we can rely fully on the correlation, however, it is wise to determine its probable error. Some mathematicians maintain that to be dependable the coefficient of correlation must be three times its probable error, while others say four times. By the formula below we are able to determine the probable error of Q.

$$\text{P.E.}_q = 0.706 \; \frac{1 - Q^2}{\sqrt{N}} = 0.706 \; \frac{1 - (.584)^2}{\sqrt{25}} = 0.092$$

Our coefficient is accordingly six times its probable error, so we may state that the 25 college students showed a significant tendency to rank in examination grades according to their rank in Army Alpha.

In concluding our discussion of the various qualifications of a good teacher, therefore, we may repeat that they consist of an enthusiasm for the subject and its presentation to others, an intellectual perspective or orientation, the possession of social intelligence in order the better to understand the pupils, an adequate appreciation of moral values, and experience in the field of teaching, including as it does an elementary knowledge of statistical methods. The instructor who possesses these assets will find that pedagogy is intensely interesting, and will engender the gratitude of the alumni. In the following section we shall discuss one of the methods by which the teacher can improve his classroom effectiveness.

The Case Method in Education. In Chapter II we mentioned the superiority of active over passive learning. The case method in education is valuable, therefore, because it enables the student to apply some of the principles to which he has been listening and thereby find out if he has fully acquired a mastery of them. In medicine, law, and dentistry the case method has been used for generations, but other branches of learning have adopted it more slowly. In recent years economics has availed itself of the case book, and the project method is gaining favor in public school education. In abnormal and clinical psychology, too, the students encounter living cases. The writer has noted a difference in their interest even in psychology classes when personality cases of the following sort are a part of the weekly assignments.

PERSONALITY CASE No. 4.

John Randall—aged 60; with the Blackburn Company 35 years fifteen of which he had been manager of a branch office; salary $75.00 a week; always on the job, even when so ill he could hardly stand; drank, smoked, and talked of his wilder youth but disapproved of his employes gambling, drinking, or running around nights —objected to letting his employes be promoted, saying, "I have a good office force together now and don't want it disturbed." Randall's immediate superior started with the Blackburn Company ten years after Randall did. Randall disliked him and said he got his promotion through lies and cheating This superior placed Vernon Jenness in Randall's office. Jenness was a good worker, but drank a bit, and ran around nights. Jenness came up for promotions but Randall wouldn't let him go. Jenness had now spent five years in the office.

Jim Morton, department head in Randall's office but lacking initiative, often went to Jenness for advice. Randall once asked Jenness, "Doesn't he know anything? Do you have to do his work for him?"

Ed Wheaton, another employe, rather surly to customers and inefficient, continually pestered Morton with childish pranks, causing Morton to lose his temper on numerous occasions.

With the depression Randall laid off one of his employes. Was it Morton, Jenness, or Wheaton? Give full reasons for your judgment, assuming that all three had equal numbers of dependents.

From the psychological standpoint, therefore, the case method is valuable because it enables the student to apply his knowledge and find out what he does not know, thereby granting him the opportunity to concentrate further on the unknown. In Chapter II we explained that certain geometric figures were quickly memorized when the students had 5-second exposures followed by an attempted reproduction, because they were always concentrating upon the unknown elements. In addition, by working with actual cases the student is more vividly impressed with the practical value of his studies and his interest is accordingly heightened.

Education and Politics. The teacher should not attempt to inject bias and partisanship into his discussion of educational matters. He should, on the contrary, endeavor to encourage the scientific attitude regarding political questions, and minimize the employment of emotionalism in discussing international relations. Political impartiality is difficult to obtain, however, because so many politicians purposely stimulate the suprarenal glands of their hearers, and thereby incite them to emotional responses. Justice should be conceived of as emotionless, but even our law courts and juries are often led astray by propaganda, pretty complexions, and silk hosiery. Indeed, the peculiar nature of mankind makes individuals susceptible to appeals which short-circuit reason with emotion.

One of the functions of a good teacher, however, is the instruction of youth in the fallacies of reasoning until emotional appeals are so thoroughly understood that the commonly encountered ones are mentally tabulated by the student whenever he hears them. In so doing, he frees himself in part from their likelihood of inciting his own emotions, for a rational attitude is inimical to emotionalism, and renders its hearer partial immunity.

Public school teachers, therefore, by bringing before their students the commonly encountered emotional appeals, can condition the students to an intellectual process instead of an emotional one. The average adult not only never heard of *ad hominem* as a fallacy in reasoning, but he is not aware of the situation in real life to which that phrase belongs. After he has been taught the type of situation which warrants the *ad hominem* epithet, he is largely free of its dominance. This is the principle which is so commonly employed in psychoanalysis, namely, make the patient conscious of his previously unconscious slavery to a habit, and he thereafter becomes free. By using the case method and grading the student upon his recognition of emotional appeals, the teacher can build up in him a critical attitude whenever he encounters printed or oral speeches.

It is true that the average schoolboy and also the adult will be unable to ascertain the subtleties of much of the propaganda with which they are surrounded, but there is too much obvious emotionalism which could be nullified by the proper training of children. If a large fish by bumping into the glass partition separating him from minnows in an adjacent portion of the aquarium can be taught to ignore the minnows, even when the glass partition is removed and they are swimming around him, then it is not too much to hope for that intelligent human beings can be schooled to refrain from certain responses to which they now are addicted.

In fact, the writer has trained some teen age youths in the analysis of public speeches until they are quite adept in spotting the emotional appeals and fallacies of reasoning. When this habit becomes a part of the personality of the average citizen, then we can look for a more sensible and logical analysis of political problems by the politicians who stand before us, and political campaigns will be much freer of hatreds, "mud slinging", and emotional ranting.

From the teacher, therefore, must come the training in detecting fallacies and resisting emotional appeals. Until the educators of America point out these fallacies and stereotyped incentives to emotionalism, the graduates of our public schools should not be criticized severely for submitting thereto. Until an elementary course in logic and applied psychology is introduced into the public school system, two-thirds of the citizens will continue to graduate with little protection against the illogical reasoning of emotional demagogues.

The Teacher's Opportunity to Elevate Civilization. Teachers should give their students not only a knowledge of spelling, arithmetic, reading, and geography, but also an appreciation of many virtues not specifically designated in the curriculum. Much of the child's spirit of fair play and honesty, his morality and confidence, his liking for education and music and art come from the teacher. These subjects are not designated when she is appointed to a definite classroom, but she finds them a part of her duties nevertheless, especially if she would be an excellent teacher.

The habits of brushing their teeth, of personal cleanliness, and of health are gained by many students almost wholly from their teachers. The latter even encourage the children to eat vegetables, and to retire at a certain hour each night. They also interpret literature and art and religion for their youngsters, and develop tenderness and kindliness in boys and girls who might be thoughtlessly cruel without such object lessons as are given to them. The teachers are chiefly responsible for the children's knowledge of American history and the relationships of this nation to foreign powers.

With ten years of contact with the children of America the public school teachers have almost unlimited opportunities for social, moral, and intellectual improvement of the coming generations. Sometimes the entire future of a child is altered by the understanding sympathy of a good teacher. Foreign children are Americanized largely through the teacher's influence, and their home environments are often greatly improved because of her advice and interest.

The teachers in institutions of higher learning, of course, do not deal with more than 10 per cent of the youth of America, but these 10 per cent are destined to become the principal leaders in business, science, and the arts, as well as in the civic and domestic affairs of their respective communities. It behooves the instructor who wishes to be most effective to remember the fundamental purpose for which he is teaching. Latin should not be taught for the sake of Latin, but for the sake of the student, and the same is true of all other branches of learning. Too often this mistake in emphasis reduces the effectiveness of the teacher as well as of his subject matter. Pedagogy must never be looked upon as a parroting of information, but rather as an interpretation and evaluation of the mental heritage of mankind in the interest of more satisfactory adjustments of the student to his environment.

REFERENCES

1 ANNESS, M. E., *Song of Metamoris* (Caxton, 1966)
2 ASHBAUGH, E. J., "Qualifications of Good Teachers" *(School and Society,* 30, 1929).
3 BARCLAY, G. W., *Techniques of Population Analysis* (Wiley, 1960).
4 BARRON & TAYLOR, *Scientific Creativity* (Wiley, 1963).
5 BERNARD, H. W., *Psychology of Learning & Teaching* (McGraw-Hill, 1954).
6 BRANDT, H. F., *The Psychology of Seeing* (Philosophical, 1945).
7 BLUM, G. S., *A Model of the Mind* (Wiley, 1961).
8 BREDOW, MIRIAM, *The Medical Assistant* (McGraw-Hill, 1958).
9 BROWN, J. S., *Theory & Research in Motivation* (U. of Nebr., 1955).
10 BURGESS, T. O., *Workbook in General Psychology* (Concordia, 1959).
11 CAMERON, ROD, *A Dummy Goes to Africa* (Missions Press, 1962).
12 COLEMAN, J. S., *The Adolescent Society* (Macmillan, 1962).
13 COMMINS & FAGIN, *Educational Psychology* (Ronald, 1954).
14 CRANE, P. M., *The Democrat's Dilemma* (Regnery, 1964).
15 CUTLER, T. H., *et. al. Analysis of Teaching Load* (U. of Denver, 1949).
16 DANIEL & LOUTTIT, *Professional Problems* (Prentice-Hall, 1955).
17 DRIVER, H. I., *Multiple Counseling* (Monona, 1954).
18 EDWARDS, A. L., *Techniques of Attitude Scale Construction* (Appleton-C-C, 1957).
19 EHRLICH, E., "Speed Reading is the Bunk" (Sat. Eve. Post, June 6, 1962).
20 FEDER, D. D., "An Evaluation of Some Problems in the Prediction of Achievement at the College Level" *(J. Educ. Psychol.,* 26, 1935).
21 FREEMAN, L., *So You Want To Be Psychoanalyzed* (Holt, 1958).
22 GARRISON, K. C., *Psychology of Exceptional Children* (Ronald, 1950).
23 GATES, A. I., *Educational Psychology* (Macmillan, 1948).
24 GAULT, R. H., *Social Psychology* (Holt, 1932).
25 GODDARD, H. H., *Feeblemindedness, Its Causes and Consequences* (Macmillan, 1926).
26 GODDARD, H. H., *How to Rear Children in the Atomic Age* (Hopkins, 1948).
27 GRINKER, R. R., *Psychosomatic Case Book* (Blakiston, 1958).
28 GUILFORD, J. P., *Psychometric Methods* (McGraw-Hill, 1960).
29 GUILFORD, J. P., *et. al. Fields of Psychology* (Van Nostrand, 1950).
30 HARRIS, I. D., *Emotional Blocks to Learning* (Brunner, 1962).

31 HERZBERG et al., *The Motivation to Work* (Wiley, 1964).
32 HESS, L. W., *Parents* and *Vocational Guidance* (Ft. Wayne, 1950).
33 HOLLINGWORTH, GARRISON, & BURKE, "Subsequent History of E-; Five Years After the Initial Report" *(J. Appl. Psychol.*, 6, 1922).
34 HOLLINGWORTH, H. L., *Mental Growth and Decline* (Appleton, 1927).
35 HORWICH, F. R., *The Magic of Bringing Up Your Child* (McGraw-Hill, 1960).
36 JANIS, I. L., *Psychological Stress* (Wiley, 1958).
37 JEFFREYS, R. J., *God Is My Landlord* (Van Kampen, 1947).
38 KELLER, W., *The Bible as History* (Morrow, 1956).
39 KRATHWOHL, W. C., "Effects of Industrious and Indolent Work Habits on Grade Prediction in College Mathematics" *(J. Educ. Res.*, 43, 1949).
40 KROUT, M. H., *Introduction to Social Psychology* (Harper, 1942).
41 LAURITSEN, MARNE, "And the Deaf Shall Speak" *(J. Expr.*, 2, 1928).
42 LINDGREN, H. C., *Mental Health in Education* (Holt, 1954).
43 LICHTER et al., *The Drop-Outs* (Macmillan, 1962).
44 MENNINGER, K., *Theory of Psychoanalytic Technique* (Basic. 1960)
45 NEWTON, NILES, *Family Book of Child Care* (Harper, 1957).
46 PERRY, J., *17 Million Jobs* (McGraw-Hill, 1960).
47 ROE, A., *The Psychology of Occupations* (Wiley, 1958).
48 SADLER, W. S. *A Doctor Talks to Teen-Agers* (Mosby, 1948).
49 SALZER, K., *13 Ways To Break The Smoking Habit* (Sterling, 1960).
50 SEGEL, D., *Intellectual Abilities in the Adolescent Period* (Fed. Secur. Agency Bulletin No. 6, 1948).
51 SMITH, G., *Psychological Studies in Twin Differences* (Gleerup, Sweden, '49).
52 SODEN, W. H., *Rehabilitation of the Handicapped* (Ronald, 1949).
53 SIMON, B., *Psychology in the Soviet Union* (Stan. U. Pr., 1957).
54 STARCH, D., & ELLIOT, E. C., "Reliability of Grading Work in Mathematics" *(School Review*, 21, 1913).
55 STOLZ, L. M., *Father Relations of War-Born Children* (Stanford U. Press '54).
56 STONE, C. P., *Case Histories in Abnormal Psychology* (Stanford U. Press, '49).
57 TAYLOR, W. S., *Dynamics & Abnormal Psychology* (Am. Book, 1954).
58 TERMAN, L. M., *The Measurement of Intelligence* (Houghton, 1916).
59 THORNDIKE, E. L., "Mental Discipline in High School Subjects" *(J. Educ. Psychol.* 15, 1924).
60 VISCARDI, HENRY, *A Letter to Jimmy* (Eriksson, 1962).
61 VISCARDI, HENRY, *Give Us The Tools* (Eriksson-Taplinger, 1960).
62 WALGREEN, MYRTLE N., *Never a Dull Day* (Regnery, 1963).
63 WOLFFHEIM, N., *Psychology in the Nursery School* (Philos. Libr., 1954).
64 WHITEHOUSE, H. L. K., *The Mechanism of Heredity* (St. Martin's, 1966).

Socrates (469-399 B.C.) Said:

"The children now love luxury; they have bad manners, contempt for authority; they show disrespect for elders, and love to chatter in place of exercise. Children are now tyrants, not the servants of their households. They no longer rise when their elders enter the room. They contradict their parents, chatter before company, gobble up the dainties at the table, cross their legs and tyrannize over their teachers."

CHAPTER XV

PSYCHIATRY AND MENTAL HYGIENE

Mental illness is the greatest medical problem in the 1960's. A recent bulletin issued by the National Association for Mental Health tells us that almost 1 out of every 10 persons (17 million) has some form of mental or emotional disorder requiring treatment. Each year, about 1,220,000 persons are given psychiatric care in mental hospitals or in psychiatric wards of general hospitals. Approximately 750,000 patients are under mental hospital care on any one day of the year, which equals ALL the other types of hospital patients, combined!

About 500,000 persons will be admitted during each year for psychiatric treatment, of which 100,000 will be re-admissions. And psychiatric complications are cited as important factors in 50% to 70% of the medical cases treated by physicians. There are now about 10,000 psychiatrists in the U.S.A., or only one for each 19,000 persons. We need 13,000 more: About 3 billion dollars is spent annually on care and treatment of the mentally and emotionally ill, of which 1.7 billions come from tax funds. And 11,500 youths are admitted to public mental hospitals each year, of which 1,500 are under 15 and the rest between 15 and 24 years of age.

The diagnosis and approximate ages of new admissions to our state hospitals are: *Schizophrenia*—about 23% of admissions, mainly 16 to 35 years of age. Since they often remain for long periods of time, they make up half the mental hospital population. *Senile psychosis and cerebral arteriosclerosis*—about 21%, mainly 60 years and older. They make up about 13% of resident hospital population because of high death rates. *Involutional psychosis*—about 6%, usually between 45 and 60. *Manicdepressive psychosis*—about 5%, mainly 35 to 50 years. *Severe alcoholism*—about 13.7%, chiefly between 25 and 55. *Personality disorders other than alcoholism*—about 6%, mainly between 15 and 35 years.

Psychoneuroses—9% of admissions, chiefly between 25 and 45. *Mental deficiency*—2.3%, usually between 15 and 45. Other disorders comprise the rest of admissions.

In considering mental diseases from the historic viewpoint we find that abnormalities in behavior were originally ascribed to demons. The insane were simply those persons afflcted with devils. This attitude regarding mental abnormality greatly retarded the advancement of its scientific study so it has remained for the modern age to point out the organic bases for many types of anomalous mental functioning. Indeed, of the two groups of mental disorders now recognized, namely, the *organic* and the *functional*, the influence of the former seems to be advancing at the expense of the latter. With continued increase in scientific knowledge regarding infections of the brain and its membranes, the toxins in the body, and the functional interrelationship of the glands of internal secretion, it appears that several more of the present functional types of insanity may be shown to have an organic basis.

Even when organic defects may be cited as the cause of many mental abnormalities, however, the psychiatrist today realizes that the behavior reactions of two persons having apparently identical organic defects, may be quite different. There are marked individual variations not only to drugs, but also to diseases, as we shall elaborate more fully in the last chapter of this book. A moron, for instance, may be an honest, law-abiding citizen or he may be a chronic offender. His subnormal intelligence cannot be cited therefore as the sole basis of his atypical behavior when we find him breaking the law. In a similar fashion, organic defects probably function along with social maladjustments to produce abnormality. Lacking a strain upon their adaptive capacity many persons are regarded as entirely normal, and lead useful lives until in times of stress, such as of war, death of loved ones, or sexual maladjustment, they "go to pieces", and may even require institu-

"The eternal stars shine out as soon as it is dark enough."   —Carlyle tional treatment. These psychically unstable persons are more numerous in the population than are the feeble-minded. In the next section we shall consider some of the acquired behavior patterns which may lead to behavior maladjustments.

Subconscious Learning and Maladjustment. In Chapter II, we have already mentioned how marginal learning takes place. Not only may habits like the pupillary reflex be conditioned to external stimuli, and operate entirely beyond the person's knowledge, but many other experiences of the individual may either have occurred in the margin of his attention-field, or else have been ostensibly forgotten, yet still continue to influence his adult behavior.

The reader may already have observed this type of phenomenon in his neighbors or even himself, for almost every one has fears and compulsions which are difficult to explain but which are nevertheless potent determinants of behavior. Bagby, for instance, cites the case of a man who was constantly fearful of being seized from behind. He always occupied a seat in the rear row, and even preferred sitting with his back to the wall. In his own home he was likewise nervous and fearful unless his chair was against a solid object, such as a partition or wall.

This peculiarity was so pronounced that the man's neighbors and acquaintances considered him queer as a consequence, and he himself was at a loss to explain what made him afraid. Even though he knew that there was nothing to fear, he could not escape this obsession. When he was middle-aged, he happened to return to the village of his birth and there met the old grocer past whose store he had always gone en route to school. The grocer laughingly reminded him of how he had always taken peanuts from a barrel in front of the store, and how the grocer finally hid in preparation for him. When the boy next reached for peanuts the grocer yelled and seized him from behind. The boy fainted from fright. Here was the origin of the strange fear which later dominated his adulthood. Lacking a knowledge of where it came from, the grown man was unable to escape its baneful influence.

The writer noticed that his older boy at the age of twentysix months would go into a spasm and scream in terror whenever a stranger touched him or spoke to him. No verbal reassurance from his parents appeared to have the slightest influence upon the boy, nor did he seem to be wholly aware of his surroundings after he once launched upon his screaming. The writer was at a loss to comprehend what caused the attack. Spanking and reprimands had not the slightest effect, yet the emotional shock of the muscle spasm was too great to permit its continuance. Thereafter, of course, attempts were made to condition the child favorably to strangers, although he had never previously shown any fear of them.

For a period of nearly a month, however, the favorable conditioning was not sufficient to offset the boy's entering upon one of his attacks of screaming. By means of the favorable conditioning, however, the child was eventually led to a normal reaction to strangers. The writer then remembered that the boy had gone to the grocery with his mother about a month earlier, and had followed another woman out of the store. After walking for a block he suddenly realized that he was with a stranger, and lost from his mother. He began screaming in terror and sat down upon the sidewalk where he mechanically beat upon the cement with the doll which he had been carrying, although the stranger had attempted to lead him back. His mother found him a few minutes later still so terrified that he hardly recognized her, and with the doll's head crushed to bits. She finally quieted him, and thought no more about the incident, but it had apparently left a marked effect upon the child, for several weeks later the touch or speech of a stranger was sufficient to re-induce the terror response.

This case has been cited to show how indelibly a childhood

experience may affect a youngster's nervous system, and how it might continue into adulthood if it were not treated early. The previous instance of the child and the peanut barrel shows the permanence of such influences when uncorrected. There are literally thousands of particular objects or situations that engender fears even in adulthood. Some people are terrified at the thought of being alone in a large open space (Agoraphobia), while others will not ride in subway trains and elevators or go into closed places, at least unless the windows are open (Claustrophobia). Some are afflicted with a fear of contagion and are incessantly washing their hands, while others are afraid of running water, and cannot endure the sound from a faucet which is turned on. Some are terrified by darkness while others feel frightened by crowds. A further cataloguing of such phobias and their explanations will be found in the references appended to this chapter.

Since Watson's research indicates that the only two ways by which fear can be demonstrated in the infant are by loss of support or falling and by loud noises, it is evident that the fear of the dark or of any other situation or object is acquired by an individual because of his contact with his environment. When the child is too young to recognize how he has acquired these fears, it becomes essential that his parents or teachers uncondition him so that he will not continue until adulthood a victim of injurious emotional habits.

When a young couple at Madison came home to their three-year-old son one evening they found that he was afraid of the wardrobe closet in the front hall. They later learned that the maid had told him about a spook in this closet which would get him if he was not a good boy. The parents immediately played hide-and-seek with the child, the father hiding first in the living room, then in the hall with the light on, then in the closet with the light on, then in the closet with the light turned off. Soon the child wanted to hide and let his parents search for him. It was not long until the boy also hid in the closet. His fear had been overcome by a greater amount of pleasure which attached to the closet in consequence of the game.

In the conditioning of children it must be remembered that the greater of two rival influences will likely mask or cover the lesser. If the unpleasant is stronger than the good in its emotional effect, then it will make him dislike the good with which it is associated and conversely. In the above example the pleasure engendered by the game of hide-and-seek which he was playing with his parents, and his delight in discovering his Daddy in the closet, overcame the fear of the closet. If his parents had allowed the child to continue in his fear, he would have developed a habit of fright in connection with the closet, which would later have been much more difficult to eradicate.

With adults it is usually sufficient simply to point out the original situation in which the fear reaction occurred, and they can free themselves from its dominance thereafter. In some cases their lifetime slavery to a fear may be destroyed in a few days. Until they can be shown how they obtained their fears, however, it is difficult for them to become free.

Freud's View of Repression and the Censor. Freud and the psychoanalysts look upon the mind as a stage upon which ideas are the actors. Some of the latter which violate our sense of justice, virtue, and modesty may be forbidden the right to perform upon the stage. The Censor who does this forbidding is the ego, which pushes the unpleasant ideas out of consciousness and submerges them in the realm of the unconscious. In explaining this process Freud[11] speaks as follows:

Suppose that here in this hall and in this audience . . . there is an individual who is creating a disturbance, and by his ill-bred laughing, talking, by scraping his feet, distracts my attention from my task.

Nostalgia is the most prevalent ailment on college campuses and one of the chief contributors to low school marks.

I explain that I cannot go on with my lecture under these conditions, and thereupon several strong men among you get up and after a short struggle, eject the disturber of the peace from the hall. He is now "repressed" and I can continue my lecture. But in order that the disturbance may not be repeated, in case the man who has just been thrown out attempts to force his way back into the room, the gentlemen who have executed my suggestion take their chairs to the door and establish themselves there as a "resistance" to keep up the repression. Now if you transfer both locations to the psyche, calling this "consciousness" and the outside the "unconscious" you have a tolerably good illustration of the process of repression.

This quotation is typical of the attitude of the Freudians and confuses the student greatly, for the entire concept of repression intimates a repressor as a distinct entity or force which bodily "pushes" or "submerges" the so-called repressed idea. The analogy is fraught with connotations of spacial changes and muscular effort involved in the repressing. As a matter of fact, the entire idea of repression should be dispensed with. We do not "push" ideas out of our minds, but simply pursue trains of thought which keep away from the unpleasant ideas as the rat does not push the cat from his field of vision, but follows a course which will avoid his feline enemy.

Whenever a neural impulse leaves a sensory cell and enters the cortex, it seems to involve both an activation of specific conditioned reflex pathways as well as a partial arousal of many neural paths which function in associated habits. The course which it takes is the one of least resistance. If the person in question is hostile to ideas pertaining to sex and friendly to those having to do with virtue, this mental "set" facilitates an association process in the realm of honor and virtue because such associated habits are more active than the opposing ones.

During sleep, of course, the individual is less likely to try to facilitate one train of thought in preference to another, so the neural impulse still follows the line of least resistance, which now probably lies along the neural network of a fundamental motive base. Freud's view that during slumber the Censor no longer represses submerged ideas is a confusing analogy. If he must resort to analogies, however, it would be more in accordance with our present knowledge of neural action if he said simply that the "facilitator" was no longer operating. In the following section we shall discuss further the course of neural currents during sleep.

The Significance of Dreams. Dreams in olden times were looked upon as having prophetic value, as the reader will recall from the story of Joseph who rose from a prison cell to become ruler of Egypt because of his skill in interpreting the symbolism of Pharaoh's double dream. At the beginning of this century dreams had fallen into disrepute in the scientific world, although many rural families had a dictionary of dreams on the shelf and consulted it each morning to learn the significance of money, travel, death in the family, marriages, and other events about which they had dreamed the previous night.

With the development of psychoanalysis, dreams have been restored to a position of some scientific value, and are one of the chief data employed by the psychoanalyst. The origin of dreams is the same as the origin of any thought process, namely, the stimulation of some sense organ with the resulting entrance into the cortex of a nervous impulse. The dreamer's feet may be projecting from beneath the covers on a cold winter night, in which case the cold receptors are activated, and neural currents begin to bombard the cortex. The sleeper may in consequence dream that he is with Commander Byrd on a new polar expedition, or that he is wading through the snow barefooted.

Visceral discomfort resulting from indigestion, the sunlight upon his face, the sound of an alarm clock, and a host of other stimuli may cause the thought process to arise in the sleeper's cortex. The peculiar linkage of ideas which constitutes the dream will be a result of the previous habits of the slumberer, of his instincts and internal chemical environment, as well as of the external stimuli affecting him at the moment. If he has been without food for several meals, the internal chemical condition of his body will facilitate a train of thought pertaining to food. If he went to sleep thirsty, then his dream will probably have to do with cool springs of water. If his sexual appetite is whetted but unsatisfied, he will likely dream of the opposite sex. If he is obsessed by some constant fear, as of ill health or detection for having committed a crime, or if he has been puzzling over a problem of some sort, then these topics will probably be the center of his dream. If his feet are cold, or mosquitoes are biting him, he may construct dreams built around the stimuli of cold or pain.

Freud believes that dreams become expressions of unfulfilled wishes. They may commence in any one of the sense organs, but the free association chain of ideas ultimately leads to the subject of most interest to the sleeper. Freud admits that hunger is the chief motive force in life, but hunger does not present great difficulties to the average man and woman. They normally retire with no unsatisfied craving for food, so they consequently are not likely to dream of tempting viands. On the other hand, they may often go to bed at night with their sexual natures sensitized by romantic fiction and moving picture plays to which they have been exposed within a few hours before retiring, or by social contact with members of the opposite sex. This psychological sensitization to ideas concerning sex may be further reinforced by the sleepers' physiological condition. If it is spring, or if for any other reason they possess an abundance of sexual energy, they are ready in mind and body for dreams of a sexual nature.

It will be obvious that this type of dream would occur more frequently in the unmarried than in the married. The latter no longer find sex of so much curiosity value, nor are they likely to have the abundance of undissipated sexual energy. Since they are older and with interests centered more on their work, or the home and their children, the latter subjects are very likely to appear in their dreams. As a consequence, Freud's extreme emphasis upon the sexual basis for dreams may be valid for youths from fifteen to twenty-five years of age, and for mismated and sexually unsatisfied adults, but these two groups probably form a minority of human beings.

That dreams are generally wish-fulfilling is probably true, for even little ones are prone to dream of the things which they desire. Very young children, moreover, do not always make a distinction between their dreams during sleep and their waking thoughts. When four-year-old Paul, mentioned in a previous chapter, had learned that he might become the owner of a kitten, he came downstairs the following morning and said, "Mother, there was a kitty in my room." His mother expressed surprise, for she realized that the doors had been locked and the windows were screened. "Yes it was," her son maintained. "It jumped up on my bed and said, 'Hello, Paul', and then it jumped down and went out the door and that was all."

Before we conclude this section it would be well to state that many dreams are full of symbolism. If the sleeper has been reared in a moral environment where he has been taught not to think about sexual matters, and if in the dream world he dwells upon them nevertheless, he may attempt to avoid an emotional conflict by representing the sexual situation in a disguised form. There is nothing unusual in this performance, for it is conventional to avoid painful things, as in the representation of death by use of such euphemisms as: "He passed away"; "He went west"; "He crossed the great divide"; "He went to his rest". Freud has presented a long list of the conventional symbols which denote the two sexes, and cites numerous dreams to illustrate them. The writer, however,

will offer two from his own files which are so evident in their
symbolism as to warrant no explanation.

NUMBER ONE

Mary (eighteen and a stenographer):   I dreamed about you last
    night.

Her Young Employer: That's interesting.   What did you dream?

Mary: Oh, we were quarreling.

H. Y. E.:   Quarreling?   What about?

Mary: It was about a letter which I had just received. You wanted
    to open it and I wouldn't let you.

H. Y. E.:   Well, how did we settle it?

Mary: Oh, I finally gave it to you and you opened it.

NUMBER TWO

A college girl dreamed that she and her male escort were riding
in the rumble seat of an automobile with another couple inside the
car and driving. In a park along the lake the car upset. Only she
and her escort rolled out and down into a wooded ravine. She then
discovered that she had a hole in her head and was trying to shake
her escort into sensibility, but he seemed to remain unconscious of
her attempts to awaken him.

In concluding our discussion of dreams, therefore, we may
repeat that they are always initiated by some sensory process,
but after they are started they tend to develop around the
subject of greatest interest to the dreamer, whether it be
appetitive, vocational, recreational, or fearful. The dreams
may be symbolic, and their parts may be illogical and impossible as viewed in the light of the next day. Persons long since
deceased are present with the living and enjoying life with no
intimation that they had ever departed from this world. This
unreality of the dream is not evident to the dreamer, however,
until after he wakens, for during sleep portions of his cortex
are relatively inactive, thereby rendering inoperative many
ideas which would inhibit the fantastic elements of the dream.

Emotional Conflicts. The reason why human beings are
not coldly analytical persons reacting with the mechanical

detachment of automatons is owing to their possession of an autonomic nervous system which innervates the visceral regions, producing thereby the emotional states of fear, love, rage, and the like. Human life accordingly does not proceed with mathematical monotony, but is made both pleasantly changing and often unpleasantly inefficient by means of emotional squalls. In the chapter devoted to salesmanship we have already discussed the manner in which emotional appeals can be used to short-circuit reason.

In almost every phase of human affairs emotion creeps in, and complicates matters by producing conflicts. The mother, for example, finds that her child soon reaches the age where it is ready to transfer its interest to a sweetheart. In fact, at the time of its marriage both parents usually feel somewhat jealous of the newcomer who has been able to dominate the affection of their offspring. The average mother and father accept the situation, however, as one of the inevitables, and attempt to make a harmonious adjustment. Too many of them, though, inject bitterness and hatred into the situation, thereby definitely widening the breach to a point where it may never be remedied. Children are cut off in their parents' wills, or they are upbraided or else completely ignored simply because they wished to marry whom they chose.

The reader is probably familiar with the innumerable emotional conflicts of human beings, so we shall forego a tabulation of them, and confine ourselves to a discussion of the Psychological Diagnostic Chart in Exhibit 56, which is a modification of Menninger's[25] adjustment diagram. The "Personality" encounters a "Situation" such as the winning of a sweetheart, and goes through a period of attempted adjustment, ending possibly in success and marriage. On the other hand, if failure results, the Personality is still maladjusted, as represented by the circle and rectangle in juxtaposition.

"The winning of friends is truly the deepest concern of the world today."
                                        —Dr. Henry C. Link

EXHIBIT 56. A diagnostic chart showing the various types of adjustments possible when emotional conflicts are encountered.

The Personality may be able to effect a successful compromise so that the emotional tension is reduced through sublimation, as in the case of the disappointed girl who goes into a convent, or becomes a settlement worker or missionary.

Again, the Situation may be too powerful for the Personality, in which case the Personality may crack. For instance, one of the writer's former students who had been a boyhood sweetheart and classmate of a girl who lived a few houses down the street, learned the week before their graduation from high school that she had betrothed herself to another senior and was to be married shortly. The disappointed youth fled the situation immediately after commencement by entraining for California where he remained so alcoholized for three months that he did not know when the date arrived for the marriage. The reverse of this response may take place where the disappointed person breaks the Situation by murdering his rival or even his sweetheart.

In the case of the student just cited, however, he did not remain permanently in the Broken Personality category, but effected a Constructive Compromise, aided materially, of course, by the exuberance of youth. The reader's attention is called to the dashed lines running between the Constructive Compromise and both of the broken figures. The double arrows indicate that a Broken Personality, barring suicide, can often be salvaged and attain the Constructive Compromise category. On the other hand, an individual who has effected a Constructive Compromise may find that a change in his internal or external environments may cause him to slip into the Broken Personality or the Broken Situation categories. A young man who flees his native town because of disappointment in love may settle down to constructive work in a neighboring metropolis and be apparently readjusted until he encounters his former sweetheart on the street and learns that she and her husband have also moved to the same city.

The cases of Steinmetz and Stevenson are probably indicative of compensations and constructive compromises regarding childhood situations of physical deformity and ill health. Possibly the prevalence of slender pipe smokers among authors and newspaper reporters is similar in explanation. Napoleon, Byron, Kant, Demosthenes, and perhaps even Lincoln represent cases of constructive compromises to unfavorable physical and social elements in their childhood. Bernarr Macfadden, the sick little boy, and Theodore Roosevelt, Sr., demonstrate the category of successful adjustment to similar childhood frailty. In their cases they overcame the ill health itself, whereas in some of the former instances, notably Stevenson's, the health factor was unchanged but the individuals became powerful in other realms.

In concluding our discussion of emotional conflicts, therefore, we may state that they are a constant factor in human relationships. The child is jealous of his father's dominance of the mother, and to a greater or less extent the converse is true. The daughter likewise wants all of her father's affection and the mother may be somewhat jealous. When younger siblings arrive, new compromises must be made if wholesome personalities are to develop. As we shall point out in a later section, the secret of emotional stability and a wholesome personality lies in making a satisfactory adjustment to each situation as it arises. This response must not be the permanent or temporary assumption of oblivion through suicide, alcohol, or narcotics, nor the atypical behavior of the radical or anarchist, but a compromise which adequately dissipates the emotional tension through constructive activity. An intelligent person can steer his course of behavior accordingly, and assist in the creation of stable personalities in his children by realizing that emotional crises can be adjusted by intelligent action, not by sitting still.

The Normal vs. the Abnormal. There is no sharp line of demarcation between the normal and the abnormal. They both have probably the same traits but with a slightly different degree of synthesis thereof. The normal person possesses a social perspective and rapport which enables him to react with only a nominal amount of friction and emotional conflict, whereas the abnormal has lost much of his social perspective through organic or functional brain defects. Sometimes a paranoiac may discuss a subject quite intelligently so that at the moment the listener is unaware of his abnormal mental condition, but the conversation will soon veer around until he strikes his obsession, when it becomes apparent that he is not normal. The case of the guide at the asylum who took the visitors through the institution and explained the types of abnormality evident in the inmates is an example. When the guide came to the last inmate he said, "That poor fellow has a delusion of grandeur. He thinks he's Napoleon. But he isn't for *I'm Napoleon.*"

The abnormal is usually considered as the individual who once was normal but has deviated therefrom, while the subnormal is looked upon as an individual who never fell heir to an Intelligence Quotient of 100. In fact, the subnormal is now regarded as being the feeble-minded, with a maximum I. Q. of about 75. The abnormal may also have a low I. Q. because of the destruction of brain tissue, as in paresis, but he probably possessed a higher I. Q. at a former time. Feeble-minded persons, however, can become insane and abnormal. A destruction of brain tissue in a moron may render him insane and leave him an intelligence level of the idiot or imbecile.

One of the commonest methods of determining abnormality is to find whether or not the patient can support himself in society, providing of course that he is not too aged for work. If he can maintain his economic existence without conflict with law and the policeman, he is usually deemed within the category of normality, despite his possible eccentricities and queerness. If, however, he persistently comes into conflict with his superiors or believes himself persecuted or is so deluded as to be a menace to society, then he becomes a fit subject for an institution. We shall quote cases 4 and 22 from the Presseys* to show instances of normality and abnormality, and to illustrate a common method of history taking.

CASE NO. 4

Name: Marion R. *Age*: 34. *Sex*: Female. *Race*: White. *Birthplace*: Massachusetts. Married, 3 children. *Sources of information*: "patient," father, aunt, family doctor, husband.

I. History of the Family.
- A. Medical—Mother's father and two uncles on mother's side chronic alcoholics, and several times in state hospital for the insane. Uncle on father's side a dementia praecox case, was brilliant but eccentric; an inventor whose inventions paid him enough to support him and his wife for the rest of their lives. Another uncle very eccentric. One cousin feeble-minded. Mother died at patient's birth. Father died of a shock.
- B. Social—Harmonious family. Strict discipline.
- C. Educational—Father and the two brothers all have college education.
- D. Economic—Father was high school principal, one brother lawyer, the other a doctor.

II. History of the individual.
- A. Medical—Sick from infancy with poor digestion. Had very mild attack of infantile paralysis when two years old. Suffered also probably from rickets. Had insomnia; subject to nightmares when able to get to sleep. Has had attacks of a somewhat undefined character when she had to be held down on the bed and fed forcibly. Was too sick to attend school regularly.
- B. Social—Stole all sorts of small objects. Was almost never caught. Always played with boys. Began having sex experiences at 7 years and continued until adolescence. Lied in preference to telling the truth, just to "fool people." Had terrific outbursts of temper in which she would break any-

*Pressey, S. L., and L. C., *Mental Abnormality and Deficiency* (The Macmillan Company, New York), pp. 102-103; 178-179. Reprinted by permission of and by arrangement with the publishers.

thing she could get her hands on. Was noisy, boisterous, and destructive. Once set fire to a barn. Was expelled from school for stealing.

C. Educational—Went through college although never very well. Graduated with honors.

D. Economic—Became successful professional woman. Has married and has three healthy children.

III. History of the Present Crisis—None.

IV. Present Condition.

A. Physical.
General Condition—In good condition, vigorous, but still has weak digestion.
Special Defects—None.

B. Appearance and Behavior—Somewhat overactive. Has several pronounced tics. Talks rapidly and a great deal. Gestures frequent and vivid.

C. Intellectual Condition.
General Level—Very high. Learns with great speed and retains remarkably. Once learned a three page poem in two readings and could repeat it eight years later.
Special Functional Disorders—Nothing.

D. Emotional Condition.
General Emotional Tone—Somewhat excitable and irritable; no marked pecularities.
Special Emotional Trends—Nothing.
Emotional conflicts—Nothing.

V. Summary and Conclusion.

A. Summary—A family containing many unusually capable and also many very eccentric individuals. Bad start physically in childhood. Many childhood delinquencies, possibly due to physical condition. Superior ability.

B. Conclusion—Normal woman, with considerable early physical handicap, probably due primarily to childhood diseases.

CASE NO. 22

Name: Charles M. *Age*: 60. *Sex*: Male. Born in rural Indiana. Widower. *Sources of information*: the man himself, son, neighbors.

I. History of the Family.
A. Medical—Normal.

    B. Social—Normal.
    C. Educational—Illiterate.
    D. Economic—Were modestly successful farmers.
II. History of the Individual.
    A. Medical—Normal.
    B. Social—Has always been extremely religious. Is a Catholic. Has covered the walls of his house with "holy" portraits, crucifixes, etc. Had an altar built in his living-room. When he was about forty, he conceived the idea that he would be a great man, if he could only get to some city where he would be appreciated. He rented his farm, left his wife and boy with relatives and went to Chicago, feeling that he was fulfilling a "call". Five years later he returned, convinced that everyone in the city was plotting against him. He believes that the time will come when everyone will realize his greatness. For about the last ten years, has occasionally, after much praying and fasting, heard a voice calling him to become a follower of Christ. Since his wife's death, about five years ago, he has given his farm to his son and has moved into a near-by city to retire into a holy life. He spends most of his time in the Cathedral at prayers. He says that he has the power to communicate with any dead person; claims that he sits on the right hand of God and that the angels will do his bidding. Says he can hear angels sing and that he can see Christ on the cross. Spends most of his day in prayer and devotion.
    C. Educational—Had a grammar school education.
    D. Economic—Owned a large farm and became moderately wealthy. Before he retired he bought the house he now lives in, and is living on his income.
III. History of the Present Crisis—None.
IV. Present Condition.
    A. Physical.
    General Condition—He shows some signs of senility, white hair, tottering gait, and partial deafness. Is rather stooped and thin from constant fasting. Bears scars of self-inflicted torture.
    Special Defects—Partial deafness.
    B. Appearance and Behavior—Spends most of the time praying. Walks about with arms folded across his chest in the sign of the cross. Talks considerably, but always on re-

ligious matters. Has a pompous air and important manner. Talks as if he were giving commands. Is stiff and domineering.

C. Intellectual Condition.

General Level—Probably about average.
Special Functional Disorders—Judgment—completely dominated by religious ideas and delusions. Attention—excellent where anything religious is concerned, but impossible to distract from this channel. Memory—unimpaired. Association—normal. Intake—occasional experiences of an apparently hallucinatory nature.

D. Emotional Condition.

General Tone—Over-emotional and sentimental.
Special Emotional Trends—Dominated by religious fervor. Fanatic.
Emotional Conflicts—None determined.

V. Summary and Conclusions.

A. Summary—Approaching old age; underweight, gradual development (through "paranoid" period) of religious fanaticism. Now complete domination by religious ideas; religious delusions. Questionable hallucinations. Deports himself in a pompous manner that he thinks is fitting for one of his high position.

B. Diagnosis—Paranoia.

In general, therefore, abnormality refers to a reduced abstract intelligence or a lowered social intelligence as a result of organic or functional disease. The abnormal person finds it difficult to make the social adjustments demonstrated by the majority of the population. In paranoia, however, the patient may show little if any reduction in abstract intelligence, although his delusions soon reveal his warped social perspective, as we shall discuss in a later section. In the following paragraphs we shall describe the methods by which the normal person avoids emotional conflicts.

Normal Ways Out of Emotional Conflicts. The normal person during the numerous emotional conflicts which he experiences endeavors to protect himself against deflation of his vanity or ego. We have previously mentioned the widespread tendency to think well of ourselves, and our constant efforts to avoid social pain, involving as it usually does a wounding of our vanity through some humiliating and therefore ego-deflating episode. The reader may note this basic tendency to guard the ego in the normal emotional outlets which we shall describe below.

(1) *Reverie.* When an individual finds himself in a difficult and unpleasant situation from which he cannot readily extricate himself, he very often flees from his dilemma *via* his thoughts. He daydreams of the "good old days" when he was young and handsome, or affluent and popular, or a famous football hero or actor. He treasures his newspaper clippings and press notices to give tangible assistance to his reverie. He delights in recounting his war experiences, in part because then he wore a uniform which eliminated many social distinctions between himself and his more sophisticated "buddies", and enabled him to gain attentions which he never could receive when dressed in civilian attire.

Ideas of heaven and a future reward for virtuous living sustain many persons who are having an unfortunate time of the present life. Indeed, reverie is an excellent means of maintaining morale providing it is used judiciously. The poor boy who dreams of the day when he will be a millionaire and return home to make life easier for his mother finds that his incentive is kept fresh before him by use of the imagination, and he is stimulated to renewed endeavor. However, there are cases in which the individual obtains so much pleasure out of the act of dreaming that he fails to work diligently in order to attain his goal.

As a general rule the more intelligent the person, the more capable he is of maintaining his morale by use of the imagination. The dullard finds it more difficult to deal in the rich ideas and complex memories which permit escape from present monotony and pain, so he flees the situation by alcohol and drugs or by the adoption of a nomadic life.

(2) *Inactivity*. In many emotional situations a person cannot make up his mind what to do, so he decides to wait for chance to settle the question for him, and thereafter remains passive. This attitude is well illustrated in Macbeth's conflict between his sense of loyalty to the king and his desire for the throne, as shown in his words:

"If chance will have me king, why, chance may crown me
 Without my stir."

When this reaction occurs it becomes especially pernicious if the individual has a tendency to refrain from mingling with other persons. And since many unsolved problems have to do with people, it frequently happens that the passive individual remains aloof and dwells upon his own troubles. The etiology of functional insanity shows that such behavior frequently precedes the onset of the disease. As a general procedure in mental hygiene, therefore, it is well to keep trying to make some sort of adjustment.

(3) *Flight*. A common characteristic of frustration in love is the desire of the jilted and disappointed suitor to get away from the region in which his sorrow occurred. He wishes to flee to the city, or travel afar. New scenes and experiences will help keep his mind occupied and also keep him away from people who are aware of his ego-deflation. Many workers, moreover, look to California, Chicago, or some other distant point as a place where they feel sure they can succeed. When they reach California, for example, they may then try to browbeat the natives and bolster their own self-esteem by taking the attitude that California is not what it is advertised to be, and that, conversely, the East or the Middle West is far superior. Failing in Caifornia, they return home with a rationalized explanation, and thereafter bemoan their fate in not being back in California, meanwhile minimizing the good points of their home state and city.

(4) *Sour Grapes*. This category of responses is often resorted to in an effort to bolster one's hurt pride. When defeated or jilted, one is very likely to go through a psychological process in which one minimizes the talents and desirability of the previously sought object. "Oh, well, I would
rather be popular with the crowd than win a Phi Beta Kappa
key," says one. In this procedure the individual attempts
to render the stimulus inoperative upon himself so that he can
thereafter meet it without so much suffering and social pain.
In psychoanalysis, for example, it is necessary at the conclusion of the treatment to break the patient's attachment to
the analyst. The patient ultimately finds himself dreaming
the analyst is a repulsive individual when theretofore his
dreams had always been most flattering to the latter.

(5) *Dissociation*. In this case the person refuses to acknowledge the incompatability of conflicting methods of response, and becomes a Dr. Jekyll and Mr. Hyde personality.
He acts as if he had logic-tight compartments in which he
segregates opposing habit systems. He may be the saint on
Sunday and the sinner on week days, or he may be gracious
in company and a selfish brute inside his own domicile.

(6) *Compensation*. This is one of the most common emotional outlets, and takes various forms. As a rule, the com-
pensator is an extremist. The physical weakling, for example,
may become overly intellectual or develop into a health faddist.
In fact, many of the world's strong men have begun life as
sickly children. Bernarr Macfadden is an excellent instance
in point. Another illustration of compensation is the case of
a certain newspaper editor, hunchbacked and weighing about
95 pounds, who is a reckless automobile driver. He made a
parachute leap from an airplane which was passing over the
center of the city and tried to alight on the top of a certain
building on the main street. At another time when he learned
that an automobile had swerved into a stone quarry in midwinter, and had sunk, he sprang into his automobile although

attired only in his bath robe, drove out to the deserted quarry, and dived time and again into the icy water in an effort to locate the sunken automobile. He also spends far more money than he can afford on liquor, which he always indulges in, and is an inveterate pipe smoker. Although this editor is a Harvard graduate, he is so intent on trying to prove to the world that he is a regular "he-man", that he has lost perspective in his compensation.

Compensation is unfortunately often engaged in without the person's consciousness of his action, and is therefore frequently a detriment. If it is knowingly entered upon, and if the form which it takes is such that a creditable type of behavior develops, then compensation is a desirable emotional outlet. The chief danger, therefore, comes when the person selects a form of compensation which is detrimental to his own best interests, or when he fails despite his utmost efforts. In the one event he creates antagonism, and in the other he falls into despair.

(7) *Projection.* A curious characteristic of human beings from infancy onward is their tendency to blame the environment for their errors, thereby avoiding deflation of their self-esteem. The child bumps his shin against a chair and immediately blames the chair, often giving it a vicious retaliatory kick. In an automobile accident it is almost always the other fellow's fault. The husband blames his wife because he cannot find his tie or collar, and the wife blames the husband and children because she cannot keep her home neat. There is occasionally a certain amount of truth in the accusation, at least enough to draw the critic's attention to the particular flaw which he thereupon magnifies.

A good instance of projection is demonstrated by the reaction of a slightly inebriated passenger whom the writer recently steered onto the right train, in which they later occupied the same seat. The drunken man was rather soiled in clothing, with trousers and coat which did not match, with patches on the knees of his trousers, and with a white shirt which was not very clean. He realized his unkempt condition and volubly explained that he had just come in from Detroit the night before, and was headed for Wilmette where he would be able to don other clothes. He apologized for his appearance for a period of ten minutes or so, while the writer meanwhile attempted to read. Receiving no attention, the drunken fellow finally surveyed the writer critically, then said: "Say, you look more near the end of your rope than I do! Gee, man, you look bad!" After this single resentful bit of projection, he lapsed into a different mood during which he said he would always be sympathetic whenever he met a fellow in the future who was drunk or down and out.

(8) *Identification.* This device explains our pleasure in fiction and movies, where we identify ourselves with the hero or heroine. Parents do the same regarding their children. Indeed, a person identifies himself to a greater or less extent with his possessions. A good example of identification is mentioned by Frink[12] who tells of a young woman who came to him complaining of insomnia and a depression which had lasted for two years. During her second visit she mentioned that she had dreamed the previous night of Evelyn Nesbit Thaw. When asked what she thought of Mrs. Thaw, she began a vigorous and passionate defense of her. Because her emotion concerning Mrs. Thaw, whom she had never seen, was so excessive, Dr. Frink concluded that his patient must be identifying herself with that well known character, and inasmuch as her defense had pertained entirely to the question of sexual temptations to which Mrs. Thaw had been said to have succumbed, he decided that his patient must have yielded to some temptations of that nature. This proved to be true.

Advice to menopausal neurotics: You can't feel like a sports roadster with the chassis of a truck!

Her defense of Mrs. Thaw, therefore, was simply a defense of herself.

(9) *Rationalization.* This is one of the most frequently employed methods of eliminating an emotional conflict. The person acts impulsively; then manufactures what appear to be very logical reasons why he has done so. His reasons are more often excuses, a distinction which it is well for every applied psychologist to recognize. A student confronted by a few hours of difficult study grows very sleepy, so he decides he really ought to get some sleep, arguing that one cannot profit very much from studying while in half a doze. Then the telephone rings, and he is invited to a party or to the theatre. Now he decides that it was not sleep which he needed so much as recreation, and falls back upon the adage that "all work and no play makes Jack a dull boy." His conscience does not trouble him, thanks to the adage, but the reader can readily see the fallacy in his reasoning.

As Robinson ably points out, thousands of argumentative works have been produced in order to vent a grudge, and despite the stateliness of the reasoning, it may be chiefly rationalization. "A history of philosophy and theology could be written in terms of grouches, wounded pride, and aversions, and it would be far more instructive than the usual treatment of these themes." John Dewey has already reached the conclusion that philosophy is mainly rationalization; Veblen and others have revealed a similar condition concerning many of the presuppositions of traditional political economy, and the Italian sociologist, Pareto, believes that the social sciences rest upon a bedrock of rationalized customs and beliefs which are the heritage of the middle ages.

(10) *Substitute responses.* In our description of the Psychological Diagnostic Chart earlier in the chapter we showed

---

"We dress the wound; God heals it." A motto over the fireplace in the Medical Room of the Harvard Club at Boston.

the many possible responses to an emotional situation. *Sublimation* is one form, which on the chart was represented by the constructive compromise. A poet translates his sex cravings into beautiful verse, and his confrere in the field of music writes melodies. The artist paints portraits, and the average person labors in the industrial or commercial world. The sexual energy created by social contacts among young people also often finds a legitimate outlet through dancing, hiking, picnics, swimming and the like.

As long as the emotional outlets lead into constructive compromises, the person is normal. When, however, they lead into the broken personality or the broken situation category, the person is approaching the abnormal type. Mental hygiene, therefore, consists of training the individual to sublimate, or substitute a legitimate and beneficial response for one which is injurious to his personality. In the following section we shall study the mentally unhealthful and abnormal responses to emotional difficulties.

Abnormal Ways Out of Emotional Conflicts. In discussing the atypical reactions of individuals to emotional conflicts we shall employ a two-fold category as follows:

(1) *Insanity.* There are various subdivisions of insanity within the organic and functional types, and common characteristics are the presence of hallucinations, delusions, and a deterioration of intelligence. With the possible exception of paranoia the mental disorders show an impairment of memory and a lack of orientation on the part of the patient. On intelligence tests the scores tend to decrease when the patient is examined from time to time. Insane patients are frequently victims of hallucinations in which they hear voices advising or threatening them. They will carry on conversations with imaginary figures and often go to extreme lengths to free themselves from their visionary enemies, in many cases slaying friends and relatives who have been mistaken for evil spirits.

As for the delusions of the insane, they are false beliefs tenaciously held in the face of obvious evidence to the contrary. The patient is apparently impervious to logic or evidence, looking out upon the world with preconceptions which are unalterable. Of the commonly encountered delusions we shall briefly describe the following general classifications:

(a) *Delusions of Melancholia.* In this type of delusion the patient is usually characterized by an abnormal inhibition of mental and bodily activity, being relatively passive and unresistant. He monotonously repeats his delusion and makes no attempt to remedy his unfortunate condition. In this category falls the belief that one has committed the unforgivable sin. The patient may not be able to designate what this is, but he knows that he has committed it. Again, he may possess a delusion of negation in which he believes that his leg is missing or that he has no stomach, and the fact that his leg is not severed does not disturb his belief to the contrary. Furthermore, he may think that his arm is made of glass and caution attendants to take care lest they shatter it.

(b) *Delusions of Grandeur.* When afflicted with this type of delusion the patient identifies himself with some famous personage of the present or the past. He imagines that he is the King of England or the President of the United States. Again, his fancy runs to literature and he becomes Shakespeare or Goethe. The patients may often endeavor to dress the parts which they play. A General Grant constantly smoked cigars and discussed the campaigns around Richmond with the detail and familiarity which would have surprised the original Grant himself. Patients may call themselves Mohammed or God, and seem undisturbed by the fact that their assumed omnipotence is oddly at variance with their present confinement in the institution.

(c) *Delusions of Persecution.* Unlike the patient who has a delusion of melancholia and admits that he has committed the unforgivable sin, the patient who believes himself persecuted usually strikes back by actively declaring his innocence and frequently attacking his enemies. Here is a workman, for example, who lost his position because of his incompetence. To defend himself to his wife he demonstrated the common defense reaction of projection, and blamed his employer for having it in for him. His wife does not censure her husband, therefore, but vents her indignation upon the "boss". The husband gains sympathy and encouragement instead of reprimand. From subsequent positions he also is discharged, so he repeats his accusation and elaborates his story by telling that his former employers have blacklisted him, and are reporting against him to all the factory employment offices in the city. Later he begins to note hostile reactions from groups of citizens gathered on the street corners and overhears whispering which he knows is directed against him. Ultimately he may even link his wife and family with his foes, and when he comes to the asylum he fears to taste his food lest his enemies have slipped poison into it.

Delusions of persecution have a tendency to remain permanently and to grow worse with the passage of time. They are also the most dangerous from the point of view of the general public, for they are nearly always the basis of murders committed by the insane.

(2) *Subconscious Malingering.* There are many people who are afflicted with ailments which are apparently so critical as to thwart their remaining at work, yet which are entirely figments of the imagination. They are not conscious malingerers for they are not deliberately feigning illness. The whole process of developing the illness has occurred in the margin of the patient's attention-field so he is not consciously aware of what has happened even though the ailment relieves him from some very painful situation.

Shell shock was usually a physical illness which resulted when no other method seemed capable of preventing the emotional impasse resulting from the fear of battle and the fear of fleeing from it. In the "cannot fight, cannot run" dilemma an imaginary ailment invalided the soldier to a base hospital where he seldom recovered until after the armistice. Many soldiers developed blindness, often in just one eye, which then happened to be the "sighting" eye for their rifles. Physical deafness and paralysis also were frequently resultants of shell shock.

It is not so difficult to realize how shell shock develops when one considers what happens when an individual is struck by an automobile. Let us suppose that he gets up immediately, brushes off his clothing, and goes on his way. When he gets home and his family or neighbors hear of the accident, they tell him he should have sued the motorist. How does he know, they argue, that he is not injured internally? They are sure to tell of some case within their knowledge in which the effects of internal bruises and hemorrhages did not appear until months later. The accident victim begins to analyze his sensations, and also realizes that if he fails to sue within a certain period of time, he will have difficulty convincing the jury that he actually suffered his injury from the automobile accident. He decides that he does feel a bit sore and pained in the visceral region, especially as the bruises of his muscles are more evident the following day.

"I told you so," his neighbors exclaim with emphatic nods, and he begins to feel worse. Two or three days later if he is not walking on crutches he may be bedridden, where he remains until the case is satisfactorily settled or else carried to the Supreme Court. It has been a common characteristic of railroad and automobile accident victims that the patient makes a remarkable improvement after his case is settled unequivocally. Even if he obtains no redress, he usually regains better health after he finds there is no further possibility of a financial settlement.

In subconscious malingering, therefore, it is evident that various "faith" cures are effective. A mental or functional ailment is often susceptible to mental treatment. And since specialists in internal medicine have stated that 60 to 70 per cent of all patients coming to them are simply mental cases, it is easy to understand why certain religious sects can cite thousands of records of faith cures. In the final chapter of the book we shall elaborate this topic more fully.

We may conclude our discussion of the abnormal ways out of emotional conflicts by stating that they fall into two general classes, the insanities, and subconscious malingering. The latter classification is less dangerous inasmuch as patients therein can more frequently be restored to normal life by psychiatric treatment. Except for the strictly organic insanities, moreover, the application of the laws of mental hygiene early in the career of the patient is of great prophylactic value, often thwarting the tendency toward an abnormal way out of emotional conflicts.

Stuttering and Stammering. Stuttering pertains to the repetition of a syllable in an endeavor to enunciate, as in "M-m-may I have some more cake?" and usually appears at the beginning of a sentence or clause, after which the stutterer proceeds fairly fluently to the end of the thought. In stammering, the speaker stops in the middle of a thought, as in "May I have . . . some cake?" The two speech defects may appear in the same individual.

The etiology of the two varieties of defect is usually the same, although stuttering occasionally arises from a malformed denture, a tongue which is unwieldy, or incorrect habits of articulation. Stuttering may also be acquired by children through imitation of some confirmed stutterer in the home or the neighborhood. In this case it may pass away when the child moves to a different milieu. Again, the child may be laughed at by his schoolmates and rendered so self-conscious concerning his imitative stuttering that the habit fastens itself upon him permanently. Brain injury may also be a factor explaining both kinds of disorder.

But the majority of cases of stuttering and stammering are a result of fear, and are therefore functional defects subject to correction. Shell shock may give rise to these speech abnormalities, but most of the functional instances of stuttering and stammering go back to instances of actual or threatened social humiliation and punishment. The child who masturbates, or who is in terror of a brutal parent, or who is introvertive and ill at ease among other people, or who has been ridiculed in a social situation like the classroom when he has attempted to speak—these youngsters often develop speech defects of the kind just mentioned. They usually suffer from a social inferiority complex.

Stuttering and stammering, therefore, result because the muscles of the larynx have been conditioned to abnormal reactions when their owner finds himself in a situation comparable to the one in which he developed his fear. Why the laryngeal muscles react atypically instead of the biceps is because they are the principle "social" muscles of the body and hence are likely to be affected by painful social conditioning. Because they are reacting overtly or implicitly all day long in the speech and thought of their owner and because they are therefore the chief functioning muscles in the situation where the fear originally arises, they become tied up with the fear reaction.

To show more clearly how this tie-up takes place, let us consider a somewhat similar situation in which the writer burned his tongue on some scalding hot coffee and spilled part of the contents of the cup because of the quick retractive jerk of his wrist. Thereafter whenever he brought a cup of coffee within three or four inches of his mouth his hand would immediately begin trembling to such an extent that some of the coffee was spilled. This reaction demonstrates a subconsciously acquired habit where the muscles functioning at the moment the pain was received became conditioned to trembling in the "sipping" situation. Had the writer not directed his conscious attention to this peculiar reaction, he might have become a slave to it, but by realizing its origin and by deliberately going through the motions of raising a cup to his lips, he freed himself from it.

In the case of the stutterer and stammerer the laryngeal muscles have likewise become conditioned to "trembling" in the social situation of speaking, and their owners are victims of these subconsciously acquired muscle spasms. Their cures consist of their becoming cognizant of the origin of their trouble and of becoming the masters instead of the slaves of their laryngeal muscles.

Common characteristics of functional stuttering and stammering are an ability to converse normally with dogs and other infrahuman creatures, as well as the capacity to sing or read without trouble. The stutterer and stammerer can also pitch their voices higher or lower than normally and then speak without difficulty. A curious case which came to the writer's attention was that of an Englishman, a graduate of Oxford. His stuttering was so painful that he refused to talk over the telephone. But when his French sweetheart called him, he would converse with her in French with the facility of the native Parisian. In short, he stuttered in his native tongue but was a fluent speaker in a foreign language.

The cure for stuttering and stammering consists of a realization of the cause of the speech defect, plus a deliberate attempt to regain the mastery of the laryngeal muscles. In the public schools we often send the stutterers and stammerers to a special teacher, who encourages them to relax in all their musculature. Army cots may be at hand on which the children stretch out. Then they may be given a book from which to read aloud. In a modulated voice the teacher asks questions. As soon as the child's laryngeal muscles begin to tighten she again urges the youngster to relax. After half an hour or so the child is sent back to his own classroom with the injunction that whenever the regular room teacher calls upon him to recite he must first think of his relaxed condition in the speech room and try to regain the same kinesthetic sensations.

The advantages attaching to this advice are obvious. First, the child's tendency to focus his thought upon the speech room instantly renders him oblivious of his classmates and the social situation in which he stands. The chief stimulus for his laryngeal spasm is therefore inoperative. The attempt to regain the same muscle sensations which he felt while stretched upon the army cot also draws his attention away from his present audience. His resulting calmness is similar to that of the public-speaker who begins his address in a state of nervous tension and knee-trembling, but becomes poised as soon as he forgets his audience in his concentration upon the thoughts which he wishes to present. As soon as a stutterer or stammerer has demonstrated his ability to speak fluently in a group his inferiority complex is dissipated. The Oxford graduate just mentioned was completely cured of his stuttering inside of a fortnight.

In concluding our discussion of stuttering and stammering, therefore, we may repeat that the great majority of such cases are functional, and therefore can be cured, sometimes in a few weeks. The patient must be shown the psychological causes for his defect, and be given a means of forgetting his audience until his facile speech restores his confidence in himself. Until he understands the true nature of his defect he may go through life like the man who possessed the peculiar fear of being seized from behind, always a slave to a subconsciously acquired habit. Introverts and socially fearful youngsters are more likely to become addicted to these speech disorders than are extroverts.

Hypnosis and Its Significance. Hypnosis is characterized by a dissociation of the personality in which the normally adequate sensory stimuli operate only at the command of the hypnotist. Persons can seldom be hypnotized against their will, and they normally awaken from their trance in a few minutes even though the hypnotist forgets to rouse them. In case it is late at night and they are fatigued, they may sleep on throughout the night, if the hypnotist does not waken them, their temporary trance simply merging into normal slumber.

The hypnotic sleep is very similar to that of a young mother who goes to bed at night with the welfare of her baby uppermost in her mind. She remains constantly attuned to any whimper of the infant even though she may be oblivious to many other stimuli of a louder nature. She may even sleep through the ringing of the alarm clock. In a similar manner, the hypnotic patient must enter the trance with the idea in mind that he will be attentive to the hypnotist. During the trance which ensues he is alert to the commands of the hypnotist but does not heed other stimuli. He will perform the commands of the hypnotist but show no sign of hearing the shouted words of others who may order him about.

At the command of the hypnotist he may forget upon waking everything which occurred during the trance, but when re-hypnotized he regains functional control of the memories concerning his actions in the previous hypnotic state. By means of post hypnotic suggestions, the subject may perform duties the following day which the hypnotist ordered during his previous trance, yet be unable to account for his behavior. He does not realize or remember that the hypnotist ordered him to carry out the idea now in mind, but he feels a compulsion to do so. The act, however, must not be at great variance with his normal behavior. Even under hypnosis, moreover, the patient will not break his established habit systems. Unless he is a gangster, he will not attempt murder even at the command of the hypnotist.

Münsterberg employed post hypnotic suggestion in tapering off the dope fiend's doses on successive days, and also cured chronic seasickness in this manner. Indeed, wherever functional disorders are encountered, hypnosis may be of aid, particularly in plumbing forgotten memories. Persons who are suffering from amnesia and cannot remember even their own names are often able to tell this information to the hypnotist. Inasmuch as hypnosis is characterized by a high degree of suggestibility on the part of the patient in respect to stimuli emanating from the hypnotist, and because the patient is freed from distracting stimuli, he is capable of focussing a greater degree of attention upon the problem before him. He may perform feats of strength which he cannot duplicate when in the normal waking state. We have previously contrasted the strength of handgrip of patients in the waking state with their strength when under hypnosis. In a similar manner he may concentrate his attention upon past events and resurrect memories which are too faint or too greatly inhibited by conflicting ideas to be available in the waking state.

In concluding our discussion of hypnosis, it is well to repeat that the patient's dissociation from extraneous sensory stimulation with its resulting increase in his utilizable attention, renders him able to bring forth memories and submerged fears which he has consciously forgotten. He accepts stimuli from the hypnotist uncritically, morever, and frankly recounts information which normally he could not or would not divulge. Feeling tones regarding certain objects may be implanted by the hypnotist and ideas for future action may be offered to the patient which in the later waking state he reacts to or carries out without knowing why he feels the compulsion to do so. His dissociation under hypnosis, moreover, may be so great that he fails to react to pain and can undergo a surgical operation without an additional anaesthetic. However, the principal use of hypnosis lies in the field of the psychoanalyst.

Psychoanalysis. The chief functions of psychoanalysis consist of an attempt to bring to the subject's conscious attention the previous experiences which bear upon his emotional conflict, and then effect a constructive and conscious compromise through re-education and sublimation. We have already described several instances of childhood fears which fettered the adult life of the persons in question. The man who was always in dread of being seized from behind, the functional stutterer and stammerer, the patient addicted to phobias and compulsions are cases for the psychoanalyst.

In his endeavor to learn the disturbing causes for adult maladjustment the psychoanalyst tries to tap the experience of adolescence and the ostensibly forgotten wishes of childhood. In order to procure the information which he desires he resorts to the following procedures:

(1) *Free association of ideas.* When he comes to the office of the psychoanalyst the patient reclines upon a couch and begins thinking aloud. He talks in rambling fashion passing from one idea to another according to the laws of association which we described in Chapter II. Despite the fact that he may be paying the psychoanalyst a high fee for discovering the etiology of the patient's emotional conflict, the latter usually avoids the very data which is most significant. His train of association will reach an impasse. This "blocking" as it is called is indicative of the fact that the patient is approaching the group of ideas which form his "complex"—a term employed to designate the related ideas and memories clustering around a central emotional situation often taboo. After hours and weeks of such rambling conversation the patient may finally exclaim, "I cannot think of another idea." Then the analyst will probably retort, "But you have not even begun to tell me about your trouble." The patient's speech has thus far been a camouflage to hide from the analyst as well as from himself the real cause of his conflict.

In explaining more clearly the significance of the conversational impasses or "blocking", we should recall that the normal individual who has a grave but unsolved problem relating to business or social life finds that he cannot refrain from thinking about it for any lengthy period of time. Wives know when their husbands are perturbed because of their repeated return to the same topic of conversation. In the realm of emotional conflicts the patients also tend to return to the complex which disturbs them, but they stop short at the threshold.

The psychoanalyst may stimulate them with a new word by asking, "What does 'storm' make you think of?" The patient pursues his train of thought until he will go no farther, at which point the analyst gives him a new starting word. Frequently these trains of thought lead, like the spokes from the tire of a wheel, into a central hub which is the complex. The patient may block out the thresholds of his complex by means of the ideas which ended each fresh thought sally. The skilful analyst soon guesses what is troubling his patient.

(2) *Controlled word associations.* In this method the analyst asks his patient to reply with the first thought or word which comes to mind as the analyst presents a series of verbal stimuli. This method follows the procedure described in Chapter II, where we presented some of the words and the most frequent responses thereto which Kent and Rosanoff had employed. The Pressey X-O test is also an attempt to plumb the emotional reactions of individuals by having them cross out from a list of words designating objects over which they have worried or which they dislike. By following the crossed out words, the analyst can make a fairly accurate guess concerning the complex or complexes of his patient.

(3) *The interpretation of dreams.* The patient keeps a little notebook at the head of his bed and is instructed to write down every dream as soon as he awakens, whether it be in the middle of the night or in the morning. Psychoanalysts believe that chance neural currents soon lead to the complex and the tabooed thoughts. If these do not appear directly in the resulting dream, then they appear in symbolic guise, as we have already explained in an earlier section of this chapter.

(4) *Purposive accidents.* Many of the errors in speech and

action are traceable to basic wishes or desires which are not in the forefront of the person's attention-field. Faulty memories belong in this same category, for people tend to forget the things which are unpleasant or distasteful to them. The writer whose opus has been severely criticized by some reviewer may find that he cannot recall the name of the latter a short time later. Slips of the tongue or fingers also often reveal underlying motives. Menninger cites the case of a stenographer patient of his who possessed a fear of syphilis, syphiliophobia, and had spells of great irritability. While copying a railroad case concerning a conductor who revealed the onset of syphilitic infection of the brain by his intense irritability, she wrote "Me. A." in two places instead of "Mr. A." Thus she identified herself with the patient whose nervousness was of the same origin as she thought her own to be.

The limitations of space prevent our further discussion of other technical words which constitute a part of the psychoanalytic terminology. We may conclude our discussion by saying that psychoanalysis has been one of the most wholesome influences which has ever affected the scientific study of human behavior. Freud and his disciples have emphasized the fact that no response occurs without a stimulus, that no behavior reaction occurs without a cause. Thus the importance of taking note of minor experiences of the patient is made more apparent. Psychoanalysis has also pointed out the relationship of emotional thwartings to functional diseases, and has given great impetus to child psychology.

On the other hand, psychoanalysis has not been entirely free from criticism. We have already discussed the confusion which is engendered by the idea of a Censor and of repression. Because the Freudians have emphasized the sexual side of emotional conflicts rather exclusively heretofore, psychoanalysis has been criticized severely. The beneficial results obtained by the psychoanalysts cannot be controverted, but the unscientific concepts and analogies employed in explaining how these results occurred are the causes of debate and censure.

The student should remember that there is no Censor which "submerges" or "pushes" ideas out of the focal circle of the attention-field, nor is there a crude vital force called the "libido" which operates independent of the neural patterns of the individual. Lashley[20] has aptly diagnosed the situation as follows:

> Instead of employing the available and pertinent facts of neurophysiology the writers (Freudians) are content with a crude mechanics which seems to have been derived from analogy with the simplest physical forces. The mental mechanisms of the psychoanalysts resemble more closely the behavior of liquids under pressure than they do any physiological processes and, indeed, the similarity is so exact that we might justly call the Freudian dynamics a system of psychohydraulics.

The importance of understanding psychoanalysis is becoming imperative in the field of medicine, as we shall discuss more fully in the next chapter. The physician of tomorrow must know not only how to write pharmaceutical prescriptions and wield a scalpel, but he must also be familiar with the psychoanalytic technique. This fact is already being realized in our medical schools where psychiatry is becoming an important part of the curriculum.

REFERENCES

1 ALEXANDER, F. G., The History of Psychiatry (Harper & Row, 1966).
2 APPEL & STRECKER, Discovering Ourselves (Macmillan, 1964).
3 BLANTON, M. G., "What is the Problem of Stuttering" (J. Abn. Psychol., 13, 1919).
4 BURGESS, T. O., "Hypnotherapy in Obstetrics" A chapter in LeCron's Hypotherapy (Grune & Stratton, 1950).
5 BUSS, A. H., The Psychology of Aggression (Wiley, 1961).
6 CASON, H., "The Nightmare Dream" (Psychol. Monog., 46, 1935).
7 COOK, S. W., "The Production of 'Experimental Neurosis' in the White Rat" (Psychosom. Med., 1, 1939).
8 CREAK, M. & GUTTMANN, E., "Chorea, Tics and Compulsive Utterances" (J. Ment. Sci., 81, 1935).
9 DODGE, R., "The Problem of Inhibition" (Psychol. Rev. 33, 1926).
10 FARRELL, G., "Mental Hygiene for the Blind" (Ment. Hyg., 23, 1939).
11 FREUD, S., "The Origin and Development of Psychoanalysis" (Amer. J. Psychol., April, 1910).

12 FRINK, H. W., *Morbid Fears and Compulsions* (Dodd, Mead, 1921).
13 FRENCH, T. M., *Integrative Process in Dreams* (U. of Chicago Press, 1954).
14 HALL, C. S., *Primer of Freudian Psychology* (World, 1954).
15 HEITH, R. G., *Studies in Schizophrenia* (Harvard U. Press, 1954).
16 HOCH & ZUBIN, *Psychiatry & the Law* (Grune, Stratton, 1954).
17 JENNESS, A. & WIBLE, C. L., "Electrocardiograms During Sleep and Hypnosis" *(J. Psychol.,* 1, 1936).
18 KANT, F., *Treatment of the Alcoholic* (Thomas, 1954).
19 KUEHNER, G. F., "The Role and Scope of Psychosomatic Dentistry" *(J. Am. Soc. Psychosom. Dent.,* July, 1954, 7-11).
20 LASHLEY, K. S., "Physiological Analysis of the Libido" *(Psychol. Rev., 31, 1924).*
21 LEWIS & ENGLE, *Wartime Psychiatry* (Oxford U. Press, 1954).
22 MANDLER & KESSEN, *The Language of Psychology* (Wiley, 1959).
23 MASSERMAN & MORENO, *Techniques of Psychotherapy* (Saunders, 1960).
24 MAYER, J. E., *Jewish-Gentile Courtships* (Macmillan, 1962).
25 MENNINGER, K. A., *The Human Mind* (Knopf, 1930).
26 MENNINGER, K., *Theory of Psychoanalytic Technique* (Basic, 1960).
27 NEWTON, NILES, *Family Book of Child Care* (Harper, 1957).
28 POLING, D. A., *Mine Eyes Have Seen* (McGraw-Hill, 1960).
29 SCHAFER, R., *Psychoanalytic Interpretation in Rorschach Testing* (Grune, Stratton, 1954).
30 TAYLOR, W. S., "Behavior under Hypnoanalysis, and the Mechanisms of the Neurosis" *(J. Abnorm. Psychol.,* 18, 1923).
31 TORGERSON, W. S., *Theories & Methods of Scaling* (Wiley, 1958).
32 WALLIN, J. E. W., *Personality Maladjustments and Mental Hygiene* (McGraw-Hill, 1949).
33 WATKINS, J. G., *Hypnotherapy of War Neuroses* (Ronald, 1949).
34 WEITZENHOFFER, A. M., *Hypnotism* (Wiley, 1954).
35 WELCH, L., "The Space and Time of Induced Hypnotic Dreams" *(J. Psychol.,* 1, 1936).
36 WELLS, W. R., "Experiments in Waking Hypnosis for Instructional Purposes" *(J. Abnorm. Psychol.,* 18, 1924).
37 WEPMAN, J. M., *Recovery from Aphasia* (Ronald, 1951).
38 WHITING, B. B., *Six Cultures* (Wiley, 1963).
39 WOHL, M. G., *Long Term Illness* (Wiley, 1959).
40 ZIMMER & BIDERMAN, *Manipulation of Behavior* (Wiley, 1964).

HYPNOSIS VS. NUISANCE HABITS

Munsterberg at Harvard used to employ post-hypnotic suggestion to help offset seasickness, the tobacco habit, etc. Nowadays hundreds of dentists and physicians are banded together in professional hypnotherapeutic societies. And post-hypnotic suggestions help kill the pleasing taste of food, cigarets, alcohol, dope, etc. very successfully. An obese woman may thus fill her plate but then be unable to swallow more than a bite or two of any food item.

CHAPTER XVI

PSYCHOLOGY APPLIED IN THE PROFESSIONS

In such professions as advertising, salesmanship, and public speaking it has long been recognized that a knowledge of human motivation and control is requisite for success. In the fields of dentistry, medicine, and law, however, the emphasis has heretofore been upon the acquisition of specific techniques and precedents with but slight regard for a psychological understanding of the patients and clients. Accordingly, many a brilliant physician or law student has graduated from his alma mater without later attaining a success commensurate with the excellence of his training and ability. Classmates of these brilliant students who barely passed their courses may soon become eminently successful. Probably the same social traits which led to their low grades in college produced their rise in their profession after graduation.

With increasing knowledge of the importance of a favorable environment and of a wholesome morale upon the later health and moral integrity of men and women, the modern medical, dental, and law schools are beginning to give more time to courses devoted to a study of psychology and psychiatry. Since the human being is regarded as a unity of all of his habit systems and organs, a surgeon does not operate upon the foot or appendix but upon the patient. It becomes necessary, therefore, not only to know the anatomy and physiology of the foot and the appendix, but also to understand the mental condition of the person to whom these organs belong. Indeed, the skilled pediatrician of the modern age knows that when he operates upon a youngster's body he likewise operates upon the child's mind and also, vicariously, upon the minds of the parents. And the success with which he relieves the fears and inspires the confidence of his immediate patient and the latter's relatives and friends will influence the rapidity of the patient's physiological recuperation.

Fear not only delays the patient's recovery by robbing him of relaxation and refreshing slumber, and by upsetting his appetite, but in extreme cases it seems able to produce death. It is well known that fright can produce fainting and unconsciousness, and there are many instances on record in which death has followed extreme emotional shock. In fact, surgical shock is not infrequently given as a cause of death, and it undoubtedly has a marked psychical phase.

In our emphasis throughout the first half of this chapter upon the psychological aspects of medicine we do not wish to minimize for the student the organic bases of disease, nor are we sympathetic with those sects which deny the presence and effect of micro-organisms and toxins just because they cannot see or finger them. The hyperope does not deny the presence of printed words on this page simply because he is so farsighted that he cannot see them, for his spectacles will quickly supplement the flattened lenses of his eyes and enable him to read. Similarly, the scientist supplements the lenses of his eyes with his laboratory spectacles (the microscope) and then he sees blood corpuscles and bacteria which were previously invisible.

In the preceding chapter we mentioned that even organic insanities are influenced by the previous habit systems of the patient prior to the onset of the brain deterioration. So, too, the particular pathological state of an organ in the human body interacts with the previously acquired disposition or personality of the patient to produce various effects. The same type of infection, therefore, will not always produce identical results in persons who have the same physiological susceptibility to the disease, nor will the stimulation of equal numbers of free nerve endings in two persons necessarily give rise to the same behavior responses. The pregnant Indian woman at parturition, for example, reacts differently than the pampered white woman, and apparently suffers less pain although her cortex is probably receiving an equal number of incoming nerve currents from the stimulation of free nerve endings in the parturient canal. We shall treat the psychological aspects of pain at more length in a later section. For the present we shall begin with a discussion of the assistance which psychology renders preventive medicine.

Psychological Aspects of Preventive Medicine. In medicine as well as dentistry and law the emphasis today is upon prophylactic measures which will preclude a later disastrous pathological condition. A dentist can easily preserve a molar if the patient comes to him early, and the physician can likewise effect cures for such dangerous maladies as cancer if the sufferer therefrom will only consult the medical expert at the beginning of his attack. The principal difficulties encountered in educating people to protect their health are as follows:

(1) *Lacking immediate pain, they procrastinate or forget.* The average person with a toothache will fail to visit his dentist if the pain subsides before he gets started to the office. This lapse of memory is explicable on the basis of our discussion in the preceding chapter, since we tend to forget what is painful or distasteful. It is because people lack the goad of actual pain that experimental health centers have usually been unsuccessful. Even though the latter are supported chiefly by private funds and call for but a slight fee from the individual, they find it difficult to get him to come in for a health examination. The person who is well feels that it is a waste of time and money to receive a physical examination. The average person, moreover, does not realize that disease may be undermining the margin of safety in various of his organs even though he feels no pain until his condition becomes acute.

It is because of this human tendency for a person to feel that he is the exception, that disease and poverty may attack everybody else but himself, that life insurance salesmen used to encounter so much difficulty, and finally evolved annuities, paid up insurance, and other plans by which they could more readily interest their prospective clients.

(2) *They fear disease.* On first glance we might think that this argument should send people to their physician for diagnosis, but it does not function in this manner. Because they dread disease, they refuse to dwell upon it in their thinking, and forget or procrastinate as we mentioned in the previous paragraphs. The failure to make a will or purchase a burial plot is also based in part upon the same tendency. People will often prefer to remain in ignorance and be contented than to incur worry and unhappiness from a physical examination which may reveal disease. In fact, like the psychoanalytic patient, even after they have consulted a physician and are paying him a goodly fee, they will frequently withhold facts which would enable the physician to treat them much more successfully.

Here is a woman, for instance, whose physician sent her to the hospital for a determination of her basal metabolic rate, warning her to eat nothing on the morning of the test. Her rate was high, and the chief interne asked her if she had eaten any breakfast that morning. She replied in the negative. A little later a second interne came along and in a casual tone asked, "What did you have for breakfast this morning?" The woman replied to this positive suggestion by saying, "Oh, just a cup of coffee." Then the interne continued, "What did you have with the coffee, toast or rolls?" The woman replied that she had eaten "only two slices of buttered toast," and the interne also learned that "just an egg" had accompanied the toast. Her own doctor had found her basal metabolic rate high, so he had sent her to the hospital for a second test. She informed her present interrogator that she had also "had a few bites of food and a little coffee" before her own physician had tested her. This kind of case is so frequently encountered that the average physician suspects breakfast whenever he finds a high basal metabolic rate in a non-hospitalized patient. We are citing it to show the lack of cooperation which the physician finds in too many patients.

(3) *They become conscious of minor ailments and magnify these disproportionately.* Although it is wise for people to have health examinations at frequent periods, there is also the danger that many suggestible individuals will have their attention drawn to minor aches and pains which they will magnify until they take to their beds. We mentioned in the previous chapter how accident victims tend to develop critical symptoms through excessive introspection, and the student has undoubtedly met persons who could be caused to leave the office and go home simply by a prearranged plot on the part of their associates who would keep remarking, "My, you look ill! What's the matter?" There are thousands of such persons in every large community who are semi-invalids because of their mental attitude. This is the type of person who benefits from mental treatment and becomes an ardent follower of certain sects which practice faith healing.

The functions of psychology in preventive medicine, therefore, consist chiefly of overcoming the inertia, ignorance, and fears of people and educating them to a sane attitude concerning mental and physical health. The task is partly one of advertising and selling. The work of certain large insurance companies, such as the Metropolitan, has been and is of great assistance in bringing health information before the masses of the population. Insurance companies are also beginning to sponsor the free annual physical examination of their large policy holders, a procedure which is profitable to both the company and the client. Some of the advertisements of commercial products have also enlightened the public regarding vitamins at the same time that they have increased sales; e. g., the orange growers and cod liver oil manufacturers. Tooth paste companies have also been reiterating before millions of readers and listeners the advisability of regular visits to the dentist, and the paid advertisements of certain non-profit making city clinics in social diseases are of distinct educational value. In the schools the teachers are endeavoring to educate the coming generation to correct habits of health by stimulating attention to diet, sleep, and personal hygiene, functions which we have described in Chapter XIV, while the psychological clinics are of definite assistance in correcting emotional maladjustments of children.

Since good digestion is also one of the basic principles of physical and mental health, we shall devote the next section to a description of the various psychological aspects of alimentary function.

The Psychological Phase of Digestion. In Chapter II, where we presented Exhibit 12, the student saw how elementary reflexes become linked into a chain through the mediation of the physical and physiological consequences of each separate reflex arc. At the beginning the tactual stimulus on the infant's cheek had no effect upon his salivary glands nor did it stimulate the gastric glands to secretion, unless a series of intervening reflexes produced milk from the nipple caught between the baby's lips. After sufficient repetitions of the entire sequence of reflexes, a point is reached where the tactual stimulation alone, without the seizure of the nipple and the resulting flow of milk, will innervate the entire chain. Saliva will flow and the mucosal glands of the stomach will begin functioning.

Pavlov clearly demonstrated this phenomenon by employing dogs with esophageal fistulas. If the esophagus is divided and the two ends sutured to the skin, the dog will continue to eat with great relish but his chewed food will keep dropping from the lower end of his throat where his esophagus comes to the surface at the point of suture. No food enters his stomach, therefore. If the sight, odor, or chewing of food will occasion an increased flow of gastric juice thereafter, it must do so through conditioned neural pathways. This sham feeding does produce gastric secretion. Even the sound of a bell to which the dog has been previously conditioned during the food-taking situation will also incite the glands of the stomach to activity.

In a similar fashion we become conditioned to odors, temperatures, and tastes. The aroma from coffee or the odor of frying meat will stimulate the salivary and gastric glands of adults whereas they will not do so the first time a person encounters them in infancy or childhood. We have previously mentioned that oral or printed words will do the same because they have functioned in the original food-taking situation until they become symbolic or substitute stimuli.

But many other factors than the odor and sight of the food are operative in affecting digestion. The surroundings, including the room and table, exert an influence. One's appetite would be less if one were to dine in a bedroom, and greasy knives, forks, spoons, and a soiled tablecloth are inimical to gastric secretion because of the negative cephalic effect. A fly in the soup will kill the appetite of many an adult although it will not disturb a child, while a honeybee will have less unfavorable effect than the fly. Barren walls and an atmosphere of gloom will retard the flow of saliva and gastric juice, as will various emotional states, as of fear and anger. In the latter emotions the body tends to be placed upon a war basis emotionally, which means that there is a relatively greater portion of blood in the skeletal muscles, and a less amount in the walls of the stomach and intestines. Even the effect of music is often detrimental to good digestion, especially if it produces a melancholy state or a condition of muscular tension and nervous excitement.

The person's previous experience with foods will also affect his present appetite. If he has an especial dislike for fish, garlic, onions, cabbage or any other odorous food, he may not fully enjoy his beefsteak as long as the menu or the fishy odor are affecting his eyes or nostrils. Strange foods also do not stimulate digestions as do old favorites. There are various degrees of fondness and dislike for certain foods, depending upon the individual experience of each person, but many attitudes are fairly well standardized by common factors in the environment. A college group of men and women were asked to express their order of preference for the following meats: dog, cat, horse, snake, monkey. They were very uniform in their decisions, arranging these five kinds of flesh in the order given at the end of this chapter. Young children who have not been influenced by adult reactions have little preference between horse or cow meat, and would probably as soon eat snakes as frogs or shrimps.

Not only are the viands and the service of significance in affecting digestion, but more remote factors also enter in. If one is visiting a hospital for the first time, or an institution for the feeble-minded, the insane, the orphaned, or the criminal, one often lacks appetite. If one has heard that a cook in a certain restaurant is diseased, or if a housewife is untidy and careless, one likewise does not relish the food prepared by these individuals.

The reverse of this process occurs when a foreigner visits a restaurant in which his native dishes are served. The familiar food, like the songs of the fatherland, resurrect thoughts and emotions of pleasure and happiness experienced in the homeland.

Because of a recognition of these facts and the realization that people carry over from childhood the intimate relationship between pain and chastisement, modern hospitals are beginning to be equipped and decorated to avoid the coldness and austerity which formerly made them seem like jails and places of punishment. The presence of other colors than the chilly white or gray walls of the past, and the employment of bright curtains, radios, pictures, and the use of a menu card from which the convalescent can select his favorite foods, are helping to create a different feeling tone regarding hospitals and surgical operations. To the degree to which the former fears and dreads of hospitals and surgery can be removed, the patient's recovery will be facilitated. A happy outlook on life and a confidence in the physician treating him are almost as valuable (in many cases more valuable) to the patient as are the medicines which he receives.

The psychological phase of digestion, therefore, is what the physiologists call the cephalic phase. It involves the multitude of conditioned reactions to food over and above the four fundamental taste qualities which it possesses. Some of these conditioned habits facilitate an abundant flow of digestive juices while others are distinctly inhibitory. Among the latter are fears and emotional tensions as well as specific unpleasant stimuli, such as flies, filth, surgical odors and instruments, strangeness in objects and surroundings, and foods which have sickened the individual at some previous time. The proper attention to diet involves not only a study of the vitamins and a healthful balance between proteins, carbohydrates, and fats, but an understanding of the importance of the cephalic phase of digestion. As we have already discussed in Chapter VI, the suggestive value of companions is also a significant factor in stimulating the appetite because throughout youth we have been accustomed to dining in the family, so associates tend to set off the former pleasurable reactions. In the next section we shall discuss other psychological aids to the physician.

How the Physician Utilizes Psychology. Physicians have realized probably since the age of Hippocrates that many patients recover because of their belief in the physician and his medicines instead of because the pills and prescriptions are intrinsically of benefit. Indeed, the medicines may often be administered for their psychological instead of physiological value. A large part of every physician's effectiveness is psychological. Many times a parent consults his physician because his youngster is feverish and ill. The parent fears the unknown, for he does not know which of a half a dozen serious diseases the child may have. The pediatrician does almost as much good in the community, therefore, by relieving parental fears as by healing his child patients. The dread and uncertainty about the causes of their own ailments may also be great depressants to the morale of adults. It is not difficult to imagine the relief of the young woman who for weeks and months has been afraid she had a cancer, when her physician pronounces the lump on her breast an innocent fatty tumor. Dr. Campbell[12] has so excellently described these problems of the physician that we shall quote him in this regard:

> It is better to think of the physician as a man whose business it is to treat not symptoms or diseases, but sick people . . . The patient is more than a group of symptoms, more than a collection of interesting juices; he is a living individual with a most complicated pattern of reactions, and the physician who overlooks this pattern may find the symptoms intractable, the disease unintelligible. Headache may be a reaction to eye strain, but it may be a reaction to a mother-in-law; pain in the back is sometimes explained by an X-ray plate, but sometimes by unwillingness to work; indigestion may be more closely related to troubled conscience than to poor cooking; palpitation is not always an indication of organic heart disease—it may be the expression of the romance of life gone astray. Not that the situation is always simple; the patient with organic heart trouble may have romantic longings; a bad cook may conspire with a troubled conscience to ruin the digestion. The extent to which a man is disabled depends partly on the nature of his disease, but perhaps more on the way he reacts to it.

At the beginning of the chapter we compared the reactions of the Indian mother in childbirth to that of the pampered Caucasian woman. In a similar degree we see differences between two men who have pains in the lower right abdomen. One goes on about his business, and enjoys life about as usual,

---

"Keep your fears to yourself but share your courage with others."
—Robert Louis Stevenson

whereas the other is bedridden, hospitalized, makes his will, and enters the operating room with the priest beside him. The first of these two should probably be a little more cautious, and the second much less so. The physician encounters both types among his patients and must understand when to arouse the concern of the one and when to allay the fears of the other.

There are also patients who wish to know the causes of their disease and the details regarding their treatment. They resent evasive replies and an attempt to keep them in ignorance lest they become unduly fearful. Then there are other patients who do not care to know anything further than the directions on the bottle and who would become hysterical if they thought they were as seriously ill as the physician knows them to be.

As a general rule, however, it is not wise to ridicule the fears and anxieties of the patient, even though to the physician they may be groundless and often ludicrous, for to the patient they are very important. The average patient, moreover, wants to have a justification for his ailment in order to win sympathy from relatives and friends. He also wants the assurance that he will certainly recover by following the doctor's orders. There is an elation in feeling that one is so ruggedly and basically healthy that one can recover from a serious disease, whereas it does not flatter one's ego particularly to recuperate from a trivial illness. People like to boast about the fact that everybody gave up hope concerning their recovery and then they pulled through the dangerous period in spite of everything. In fact, children are not the only ones who enter into debates as to who was the more sick of the two individuals now arguing.

Physicians have long understood the psychological value of not minimizing too greatly the danger of the patient's ailment, but this very fact has sometimes aided the faith healers. A patient whose physician has agreed that he is in a serious condition may be cured by a practitioner of some sect, a fact which reflects against the physician and to the credit of the practitioner, who will thereafter state that "Dr. Brown gave up Mr. X as hopeless and I cured him."

Other psychological functions and dangers which confront the physician we shall describe briefly in the following section where we discuss his relationship to the female patient. We have selected her because women make up the greater number of patients of the medical profession and because they present some difficult psychological problems.

The Father Fixation and the Female Patient. Because of the childhood tendency to regard illness as punishment and to associate punishment with parents, particularly the father, the close connection between the physician and the male parent is not difficult to understand. Moreover, the fact that the physician holds the position of confidant, and soon obtains information concerning the patient of an intimate and personal nature again assists the latter to identify the physician with the father. And because of the girl's erotic attachment to her father (the Electra Complex), when she makes the transference to her physician she often becomes emotionally attached to the latter in the same subconscious manner as she regards her male parent.

It is also a psychological characteristic of people that when they share their secrets with another person, not only do they obtain a partial emotional release from their tensions, but the person who knows their secrets becomes identified with those confidences and thereafter is a symbol of them to the patient. The student is probably aware of the fact that he tends to avoid the man from whom he has borrowed money, and shuns those who know of his humiliation or shame. On the other hand, the girl or boy who has shared pleasant erotic experiences with us, becomes henceforth a desired companion.

In a somewhat similar manner the woman patient who reveals confidential and intimate information about herself, some of which is often sexual in nature, thereafter feels more closely attached to her physician than before she divulged her secrets to him. Through the centuries the physician has encountered this transference to himself with a consequent fixation. It has remained for the psychiatrist, however, to offer the technical terminology and the full explanation for this type of behavior.

It is a usual event during psychoanalytic treatment for the patient to realize the nature of her transference and fixation, after which the psychiatrist no longer appears in her dreams in a favorable light, but is transformed into a despised creature. In ordinary medical practice a somewhat similar reaction often takes place. Patients who keep running to the doctor's office at frequent intervals and return feeling in good spirits even though they have received little if any medicine, eventually may find that their subconscious ideas and wishes become conscious. They may then be shocked or shamed by their own feelings toward the physician, and begin developing a negative transference, as is denoted in the familiar lines:

> "I do not love thee, Doctor Fell,
> The reason why I cannot tell;
> But this alone I know full well,
> I do not love thee, Doctor Fell."

The writer has encountered a number of previously chronic medical patients who now will have nothing to do with medicines or physicians, and have gone into certain sects of faith healers chiefly because of this phenomenon of negative transference. They are, for the most part, female patients. In many instances it is necessary for the physician deliberately to break the fixation of his chronic patients for the good of all concerned. He also finds it advisable to keep a nurse as his assistant in order to protect himself from calumny and litigation because of patients who project upon him attitudes

---

"The disease of an evil conscience is beyond the practice of all the physicians of all the countries in the world." —Gladstone and behavior of which he is innocent. The following quotation of a similar case is taken from Frink[19].

"A young woman student had at various times a number of attacks which invariably began with her becoming attracted by one of her professors. She would for a time talk a great deal about him, of how able and attractive he was, but without intimating that she was falling in love with him. Then she would begin to think that he was falling in love with her. This would seem to please and amuse her at first, but soon she would get the notion that he was hypnotizing her, and her pleasure would be succeeded by anger. She would complain that through hypnotic influence he was putting into her mind all sorts of erotic fancies about him, that by telepathic suggestion he gave her impulses to come to his apartment, etc., all of which would get her into a state of great rage and excitement and she would have to abandon her studies. Thereupon the attack would gradually subside, only to be repeated in connection with some other teacher when she resumed her work.

"It is apparent that this patient's delusional ideas were nothing but a projection of her own erotic interests in her teachers. What she felt as a hypnotic or telepathic influence brought to bear upon her from without was simply an externalization of her own desires. Her anger against the teachers represented her pathological resistances against these desires. Presumably had she been able to regard her sexuality in a normal way, as something perfectly legitimate and wholesome, what appeared as delusional attacks would otherwise have been ordinary love affairs."

From the standpoint of psychology, therefore, the father fixation renders the female patient more suggestible and amenable to medical treatment by her physician, but in its occasional abnormal degree complicates the duties of the physician. If he finds it necessary to break the subconscious emotional attachment of the patient to himself he may create a negative transference thereby which completely alienates his patient. There are times, of course, when this extremity is wise.

How the Physician Wins His Public. There is no type of worker who more greatly needs to understand the art of improving his personality and "selling" himself to the public than does the professional man. After graduating from his professional school the physician, as well as the dentist and lawyer, may enter a city where he is comparatively unknown. The ethics of his profession forbid his advertising for patients in any of the usual media. He can run an announcement that he has opened his office, or has moved to a new address, and can send out direct-mail letters containing cards with similar information upon them, but thereafter he must rely upon the social contacts through various civic, religious, commercial, and fraternal organizations. If he is without any "pull" it may be necessary for him to devote his spare time to Boy Scout work as a means of breaking into the newspapers. In Chapter VI we described at some length many of the principles which he must follow in order to increase the number of his friends. In the socialization process, however, he must constantly keep in mind that a physician should retain a certain amount of dignity and fatherliness.

There are physicians, for example, whose physical presence is so peaceful and inspiring of confidence that the patient feels half cured when the doctor enters the room. Other physicians of a nervous temperament and fidgety manner do not irradiate the same positive suggestions of competence and health. The temperamental genius may become successful in a specialized field, but in general practice where the personal contact is especially great the kindly, confident man with dignity and social intelligence usually far excels him.

Although this is an age where relatively young men are presidents of large corporations, the general public still wants to look upon the physician in a filial manner, regarding him as a father. It is wise, therefore, for the physician to develop those personality traits which the average person associates with fathers. An impression of maturity is one important asset, a fact which was fully understood by the young medical graduates of a generation ago who started letting their beards grow during their senior year so they could gain in apparent age.

The physician should be jovial but not too informal. He

should extrovert himself so that he is interested in those around him and in the smaller towns should be able to slap a fellow citizen cordially on the back and call him by his first name, but he should not have cultivated a personality which warrants the fellow citizen calling the physician by the latter's Christian name. We made this distinction in a previous chapter when we mentioned that the politician in the hay field retains his collar and tie even though he wears overalls.

In his sociability, therefore, the young physician must not fail to maintain some badge of dignity, whether it be the wearing of a coat while others are in their shirt sleeves, the refrainment from participation in youthful sports particularly when older people are among the spectators, or the carrying of his black satchel. The public has a mental stereotype of a physician, and it is not profitable for the young doctor to enter upon a radical change of the stereotype. In fact, the latter is like a well advertised trade-mark or slogan; so he should capitalize upon it by selling his services under this professional label. To disregard a well advertised slogan or a familiar stereotype is poor business, especially when a person can avail himself of either at no financial outlay.

In concluding our discussion of the relationship between psychology and medicine, it is well to point out that the successful physician of the next generation will have to possess an even greater social intelligence than has been true in the past, for the field of psychiatry and mental hygiene is growing rapidly. In previous years physicians have developed a fair knowledge of human behavior traits from experience after they left the medical school, so that many of them became remarkably good applied psychologists. It is more economical, however, for the young medical student to obtain his knowledge of psychology in the classroom.

The dentist has practically the same problems as the physician except that he usually does not enter into such confidential relationships with his patients. He is much less likely to have them develop father fixations, and his youthful appearance is not quite so inimical to his professional success.

In the following address I have summarized a few of the salient principles of applied psychology of especial interest to dentists, but quite applicable to lawyers and physicians as well.

THE USES OF PSYCHOLOGY IN DENTAL PRACTICE*
George W. Crane, Ph. D., M. D.

Although many modern dentists as well as physicians realize that we do not operate on the patient's tooth or appendix but upon the entire patient, many of us have doubtless failed to analyze thoroughly the full effect of our professional contact with the entire personality of the subject who calls at our office.

Indeed, it is rather surprising that we practice as much social psychology in our professions as we do, for the great majority of men and women who go into these professions have been compelled by college requirements to concentrate upon chemistry and physics, zoology and bacteriology, anatomy and physiology.

In most of those fields we study either inert substances or else non-human entities. As a result of this rigid ten-year attention to everything else except people, we are usually not good salesmen of our professional skills when we suddenly are thrown upon the community in which we elect to set up an office.

In brief, our entire technical education has been devoted heretofore to preparation for work upon teeth or appendices, yet as soon as we leave our professional school and pass the state board examinations, we find ourselves dealing with people. Our financial success depends largely upon how well we can sell ourselves to the public.

Is it any wonder, therefore, that many of us fail to become outstanding in the community when we have had no education in the art of tactful self-advertising; in the delicate job of manipulating people and making them like us; in the psychological task of inspiring confidence in our abilities and capacities?

Most of us leave the university as introverts; that is, as persons who are more interested in things than in people. We aren't glib conversationalists, nor are we carefree playboys around town with plenty of money to join the wealthy clubs. We cannot dance or

*Read before the Wisconsin State Dental Economics Group.

sing and after ten years in college we aren't rivals of Bobby Jones on the golf links.

We are proud of our technical training and frame our diplomas to show off the fact that we are competent. But to the average layman what does a diploma mean? Many a patient who comes to every one of us hardly knows we must pass a state board examination and have many years of college training.

Probably half of the general public look upon physicians and dentists as just "docs". They assume we must be all right or we wouldn't be in business, and even after they come to our office they judge us not by our Phi Beta Kappa and scientific keys, but by many little characteristics which we often overlook entirely.

On the evening of September 23rd, I met my class in Applied Psychology on our Northwestern Campus in Chicago. It was our first meeting for the fall semester. Exactly fifty men and women were present, ranging in ages from 20 to 45. A number of them were married, and almost all were employed during the day in Chicago stores, offices and schools.

They represent a college group who are employed during the day. Their intelligence and educational advantages are obviously much above the average. So I decided to give them a brief questionnaire regarding dentists and dentistry. They willingly cooperated.

"What prompted you to visit a dentist the last time you went to one?" I asked, and they wrote their reasons. I shall tabulate them herewith:

	No. persons
Pain, aching tooth, or abscess	13
Had noted a cavity, by tongue or mirror	9
Just for a general dental check-up	6
To have teeth cleaned	5
Routine semi-annual visit	5
Routine annual visit	4
Dentist phoned or wrote them to come in	3
Swollen gums—not painful	2
Broken tooth—traumatic	1
Pink toothbrush	1
Oculist urged it	1
Total	50

"Why did you select the particular dentist you visited?" I next asked.

	No. persons
Parents, or other relatives recommended him	16
Friends of patient recommended him	12
Dentist was a relative of the patient	5

Dentist was a friend of the patient _____ 4
Dentist's office was nearby _____ 4
Dentist was a high school classmate _____ 2
Dentist belonged to same business club _____ 2
Dentist was father of his sweetheart _____ 1
Dentist took care of her employer _____ 1
Recommended by an Extractor _____ 1
Recommended by a physician _____ 1
Xmas eve and only available man _____ 1

Total _____ 50

(Note that the first 28 calls above represent referred business; only 22 calls represent primary or original contact business.)

"If you have visited more than one dentist, select the one you deem the best and write down the specific reasons for your choice," was my third query. Some replied with several reasons, others with none.

                                                          No. choices
Dentist was cheerful, friendly, congenial _____ 7
Inspired me with confidence in his ability _____ 6
Dentist's charges were reasonable _____ 6
Dentist's work was painless _____ 4
Dentist was quick but gentle in his work _____ 3
Dentist had new, clean, modern offices _____ 3
Dentist was on State Board of Registration _____ 2
He answered my questions honestly _____ 2
More interested in me than in my money _____ 2
He was careful to do a good job, unhurried _____ 2
His tools looked shiny and new _____ 1
He did a minimum amount of drilling _____ 1
Dentist seemed "knowing" _____ 1
He treats the tooth instead of pulling it _____ 1
His work lasted well—fillings didn't come out _____ 1
He does research in dentistry _____ 1
He was very fastidious in his dress _____ 1
He was quiet—didn't talk my head off _____ 1
He was out of school but a few years, so modern _____ 1
He did very artistic work _____ 1
Many of my neighbors went to him _____ 1
He was president of the Rotary club _____ 1
He was steady and was thorough _____ 1
I heard no complaints about his work holding up _____ 1

If you practicing dentists will simply scan the above reasons cited by intelligent adults as to why they thought a given dentist was the best of those they had consulted, you will find that 80 per cent of the replies are of a definitely psychological nature.

Did these people mention the university from which the dentist graduated? Did they consider what college grades the dentist had made? No mention of scientific honor fraternities the dentist belonged to, or of his membership in scientific organizations!

But much weight was placed on his personality, pleasantness, clean modern office equipment, fastidiousness in dress, and his ability to appear "knowing" or inspire confidence. The "shiny tools" he used got more credit than his diploma! And from university people! The above data came from 41 of the students. Nine had never gone to more than one dentist.

Specificity is the basis of proof as well as of scientific progress, so I shall quote some of the exact statements of these men and women regarding the dentist they consider best:

"I consider my present dentist best because he treats a tooth instead of pulling it immediately." (Female)

* * *

"Dr. Blank was the better because he was reasonable in his charges and I liked him personally." (Female)

* * *

"I think my present dentist is best because he seems more intelligent, answers my questions honestly, and does considerable research and study in his field. Also, of primary importance, his office and work-rooms are always immaculately clean." (Female)

* * *

"My second dentist was best, because he was more honest, told the truth, tried to see my viewpoint and on several occasions suggested means of saving money without injury to my teeth, such as silver in place of gold, etc." (Male)

* * *

"The dentist I considered best was the last one to which I went as he has some harmless hypodermics that make the drilling painless." (Female)

* * *

"I believe the dentist I now patronize is the best I have ever visited because he is in a new, thoroughly modern office, is a most fastidious person in dress and cleanliness, and seems so very 'knowing' when explaining the conditions of the teeth and gums. I know, too, that many of the persons in our town have been giving him their trade." (Female)

* * *

"My first dentist was best because he took the least time to do his work, and he held the drilling down to a minimum," (Male)

* * *

"The dentist I now go to is the one I like best because of his carefulness and painstaking work. He never hurries and won't be rushed. The job must be done right." (Male)

* * *

"My last dentist was the best because his professional bearing and his office equipment seemed of a higher standard than the preceding ones. He was several years out of school but young enough to be thoroughly up-to-date." (Female)

"I tried another dentist for experiment once, on recommendation of a friend, and promptly returned to the family dentist as several fillings had to be replaced that the second dentist had put in." (Female)

* * *

"I have gone to four dentists, and the third and fourth are my choice, for they are both cheerful and seem to be interested in me and my work. I go to the fourth because his office is more convenient for me." (Male)

* * *

"I prefer our family dentist because he is very friendly, jolly and as painless as possible." (Female)

* * *

"Of the four dentists I have gone to, I liked the third best. This was because of reports from the neighbors as to his ability and I went back several times because he deadened the nerves of the tooth he was working on, thereby eliminating all pain!" (Female)

* * *

"I think my last dentist is best because he is more popular in the town, and he is a member of the State Board of Registration." (Male)

As you dentists can readily perceive, many of these so-called reasons are not logical nor based on the dentist's technical skill, but represent emotional reactions of the patient toward him. Some differences of opinion exist as between the two men one of whom thought speed was a criterion of excellence, whereas the other was pleased by the slow but thorough work of his dentist.

In carrying further this "consumer survey", as we would call it in applied psychology, I asked my fifty students to report which dentist they considered the worst or least competent and their reasons are tabulated as follows:

	No. choices
His fillings fell out	5
His fillings were rough and hurt my tongue	3
He was old—too long out of school	3
He was too talkative	2
He'd rather pull than save with a filling	2
He tried to scare me into having work done	2
His office was very untidy	2
He smoked cigarettes and failed to wash afterwards	1
He was a very sloppy worker	1
He had dirty eyeglasses with specks on them	1
His hair was full of dandruff	1
His breath smelled of alcohol	1
His breath smelled of tobacco, which sickens me	1
The dentist had decayed teeth	1
His fingernails weren't clean	1
He was careless about sterilizing his instruments	1
He argued and browbeat his assistant	1
He belittled me for showing pain	1

He did too much drilling --- 1
His office was poorly lighted ------------------------------------- 1
He overlooked a cavity and later pulled the tooth ---------------- 1
My teeth decayed underneath the filling ------------------------ 1
He overpacked a tooth and gave me a toothache ----------------- 1
He wasn't punctual -- 1
He was haphazard with his appointments ----------------------- 1
His breath was terrible --- 1
He was more interested in my money than my teeth ------------- 1
He didn't tell me the truth ------------------------------------- 1

As unrelated as many of these trivial factors are to the dentist's skill and scientific standing, they nevertheless resulted in the loss of patients and the development to this extent of unfavorable publicity in the community.

It may appear like facetiousness when I say it, but it would seem that halitosis, body odor, dirty fingernails, dandruff, and carelessness regarding personal appearance are responsible for the loss of more business than defective dental workmanship.

It may be of interest to list a few quotations from these papers which were handed in to me:

"I don't think a dentist should recommend yanking teeth unless he has an absolute reason for it. More than one person I know has run away from one dentist to another because of a threatened extraction. Ladies don't like it!" (Female)

* * *

"The previous dentist seemed the worse because he seemed more concerned with making money than with serving me." (Male)

* * *

"Because he did too much drilling, I think the second was worst. Most of it seemed unnecessary. My teeth were well looked after before I even consulted him." (Male)

* * *

"The first and our 'family' dentist was the worst. He was rough and didn't seem to be up-to-date on his methods." (Female)

* * *

"I have gone to four dentists. The first was the worst because his work was roughly done and didn't prove satisfactory." (Male)

* * *

"The first one I consulted in Chicago I consider the worst. He told me I had to have seven teeth filled—at a stiff price. He sold me and then pushed a drill through my jaw instead of the tooth. That might have been an accident but he said it was *my* fault because I jumped." (Male—salesmanager of large firm)

* * *

"I've been going to my brother-in-law, but once I went with a friend of mine to her dentist and I didn't like him. He tried to scare me. I didn't intend to continue with him, anyway, but went just to see what he would say. My brother-in-law later contradicted what the other dentist said when I told him about it." (Male)

"The next to the last was the poorest dentist because of his mental attitude. He belittles his patients, and scoffs when they wince at the pain, and does everything but call them cowards." (Female)

* * *

"I thought the first dentist was worse because he pulled my tooth without seeming to care whether I was in pain, and made me feel like I was merely a case and not a person," (Female)

* * *

"Poor light in his work room and his personal uncleanliness cause me to vote the second dentist the worst." (Male)

* * *

"My worst dentist? One who smoked cigarettes while waiting for the fillings to harden—and was not very careful about washing his hands before resuming work." (Female)

* * *

"I considered the last one inefficient because his eyeglasses were covered with spots and when he drilled into a cavity his hand shook. He was also far behind in modern dentistry." (Male)

* * *

"The one I considered the worst wasted too much time and talked excessively." (Male)

* * *

"I didn't like the third dentist because he had very unpleasant breath and his own teeth were decayed." (Female)

* * *

"I was very much dissatisfied with my first dentist as he had no business principles, no conception of arranging his appointments for his customers. I also noticed that his office was untidy, and his work has not proved satisfactory. I had two fillings done by him and within a short time I was compelled to have the work done all over again." (Female)

* * *

"The one I think was the worst overlooked a cavity in my tooth and then pulled the tooth out on my next visit." (Female)

* * *

"I consider our family dentist the worst because he usually left me with the rubber dam on and a nerve exposed while he argued with his wife, who assisted him in the office." (Female)

* * *

"I liked my brother-in-law least of the dentists I have visited because he was always careless with his instruments and tended to put work off." (Female)

* * *

The worst dentist, in my estimation, was the one who found too much to talk about. Perhaps he was only intending to make me feel at ease, but it made me feel that his work was not as good as it might have been had he tended strictly to business." (Female)

* * *

"I consider my first dentist the worst. I don't think his work was well done, and in addition, he was unusually slow. One had to spend an average of 2½ hours at his office for a single visit." (Male)

"Dr. Crane, would you have faith in a dentist who had just finished $75 worth of work about 6 months ago for you—and then when you go for a regular check-up, he finds five new cavities and wants to replace another dentist's inlay? I checked about the new cavities with three other dentists, who told me that absolutely there were no cavities present." (Female)

Patients certainly seem to exercise their critical capacity regarding the work of professional men, even though they lack adequate technical training themselves. And they notice many things about dentists as well as physicians, which we professional men scarcely realize are true. A good critical examination of the sort we have just presented is invaluable to every professional man who wishes to be most successful in practice.

In fact, this market research or consumer survey method is being widely recommended by psychologists. Business men, manufacturers, advertisers and salesmen, and even newspaper editors are beginning to sound out the wishes and desires of their clients with the aim of more accurately fitting their merchandise to suit consumer demands.

We need to do a searching analysis of ourselves with the aim of finding out just how we can impress our patients with the fact that we are competent, modern, up-to-date, and well trained. Patients seldom read the diplomas on the wall, so how can we intimate skillfully that we are "expert", for that is what the public wishes? I don't mean that they want specialists, solely, but they do like to feel that their physicians and dentists are expert.

Good dental work is one of the best sales arguments, but it isn't enough of itself, for many excellent dentists are hardly earning enough to live, and yet they can do admirable work. Why don't people come to their offices?

Both medicine and dentistry are surrounded by a high board fence called professional ethics. We dare not shout our own virtues by means of newspaper advertising, billboards, or the radio. We must be dignified and conservative.

But there are many ways by which we can plow much closer to this high board fence than we are now plowing and still be quite within the confines of current dental or medical ethics.

To put it bluntly, how are we to advertise ourselves and put our virtues before our public, yet not be criticized for unethical behavior or crude self-advertising? How can we toot our own horn, and yet tactfully appear to be modest, unassuming scientists? In short, how can we extrovert ourselves and utilize many of the methods of advertising, yet remain apparently diffident, research men?

This is a grave but very essential problem for all professional men to attack, since their financial future depends upon the degree to which they can cleverly answer those questions.

Some successful practitioners have developed from experience a mass of psychological principles whereby they have made a success. But such a trial and error plan requires too much time, and is fraught with considerable danger. We need more courses in applied psychology in both our dental, as well as our medical, law and engineering schools, for despite a few courses here and yon, psychology isn't yet taught adequately in professional schools.

Yet it certainly represents a good half of a man's later success. But he hears a few cursory talks upon the subject, at best, before he leaves college and meets the public in his own office. We have an unbalanced curriculum at present throughout the entire land.

It is folly to educate a tyro aviator in the principles of gasoline motors and wind resistances; then send him aloft without a bit of training in flying an airplane. The same fallacy, however, is evident in almost all of our technical schools. We are well grounded in the mechanical side of our science, yet are sent out with almost no advice regarding the social and intensely practical aspect of it.

But to return to specificity, how can a dentist advertise himself discreetly and ethically? Here are some devices which have already proved their worth in actual use:

First, a young professional man must go to the public since the public does not come to him immediately. How? By joining various organizations, such as the Lions, Rotary, Kiwanis, the Elks, the Masonic Order, the Knights of Columbus, the local church of his own denomination, the YMCA and sundry civic groups.

A socially minded wife is also of excellent assistance to every man whose living comes from the general public. Everybody remembers the graciousness and charm of Mrs. Coolidge, and what a tremendous help it was to the President. An introvertive scientist can often "get by" in society, thanks to the tact and diplomacy of an extrovertive wife.

Many a good wife is largely responsible today for the professional clientele of her dentist husband, even though the husband may be so introverted that he doesn't recognize the fact.

At a bridge party or other social gatherings a dentist's clean, well manicured hands are always noted, even though subconsciously. So are the other items of his general appearance, such as dandruff, his eye glasses, the press in his trousers, and shine on his shoes, his dignified but friendly bearing.

And remember this, the general public does *not* lose respect for a professional man because he refrains from smoking or drinking liquor. Some young professional men get the erroneous idea that they will be thought prudish and unsociable if they do not accept drinks from their associates.

Many a social comrade at a party, who slaps you on your back and likes to call you by your first name, will nevertheless send his wife and children to the dentist across the street who is not nearly so convivial, and who is known to be a teetotaler.

Seneca once gave some excellent advice regarding how a young man should deal with a girl in courtship. "Take a lesson from the archer," he said, "and observe how he handles the bow. With one hand he pushes it away, and with the other he draws it back again."

That isn't a bad motto for a professional man. It doesn't pay to become too intimate and informal with one's clientele. It may delight them to know us so well they can use our nicknames, but that very familiarity will breed contempt, or, at least, a lack of adequate appreciation for our talents, so in a crisis they will patronize our more aloof neighbor. Keep them at arm's length as regards intimacy, but be cordial and friendly with all.

I have seen men progress in their profession very rapidly because of some hobby. A certain physician I know became almost famous in the community because he was a very clever magician, and soon people began to say, "Oh, Dr. X, isn't he the doctor who pulls a rabbit out of your hat?" And his popularity with child patients was phenomenal.

Others organize hiking or skiing clubs among the younger crowd, or get an "in" with certain groups in the community by means of their skill with water colors, or a musical instrument. Perhaps they sing well, or are amateur cartoonists. Indeed, hobbies are worth a great deal of money to the young man starting forth into practice.

But after a client comes into the office, a dentist also can do a great deal to build up his own prestige. You will recall the comments about dingy offices versus modern, well equipped quarters. What do clients mean by modern offices? They seldom can recognize modern technical instruments, except by their "shine". Instead, they "size up" the office in respect to its cleanliness, its modern chairs and lamps, its recent issues of fashionable magazines, the pictures on the walls, the drapes or curtains at the windows, a radio in the waiting room.

Patients are likewise not nearly so fearful of young dentists any more. In fact, you will remember several comments from my students about old dentists who had been out of school a long time and were not up-to-date. Today the young professional man has a greater advantage than ever existed before. His very recency in professional school is now converted into an asset, for it indicates that he has the latest scientific tools and methods. Scientific progress has been so phenomenal in the last few decades that we want 1965 models in our automobiles before 1964 is hardly half over, and this same tendency shows itself in the ready acceptance of young dentists in the community.

I was surprised by the number of my students who have been educated to semi-annual or annual routine visits to their dentist. I hope this tendency is very widespread. And I was quite interested in the fact that some of the dentists notified their clients by telephone or by postal card of the approaching date for the semi-annual visit.

In the reception room of the dentist a client often sits for several minutes until his turn or appointment hour arrives. Furthermore, relatives or friends occasionally accompany the patient and wait until the dental treatment is completed.

An advertising man would say that those valuable minutes while customers or prospective customers are in your office, ought to be utilized for advertising your wares. My personal viewpoint as a psychologist is that clients should see something tangible as evidence of the fact that your office is a dental office.

I admit that many professional men furnish their reception rooms in an attractive and artistic fashion so that one scarcely knows whether he is at home in the parlor, or in a downtown office. But unless there is some distinguishing mark to indicate that your office belongs to a dentist, you have lost an excellent advertising opportunity.

Some men install a neat little x-ray box in one corner of the room and place a dental x-ray on the frosted glass pane, with a little placard saying, "Pull the cord and turn on the light. You will see a good x-ray of an abscessed third molar". An arrow on the x-ray points to the pathology.

Such a device indicates several things. It intimates that you are a modern, scientific dentist. It shows that you are interested in revealing scientific knowledge to your clients, and are not like a quack who deals in secrets which he jealously guards from the layman.

You would be surprised at the number of patrons who will turn on the light. Even if it means little or nothing to them, they go away from your office tooting your horn.

You become the dentist where one can actually see an x-ray of one's teeth. Women will repeat that fact at bridge tables long after they have departed from your office.

Remember this important psychological fact! People like to show their fragmentary scientific knowledge. It makes a woman or a man feel more important if he can tell somebody else a new joke or a new scientific fact. Therefore, he will tell about the x-ray. In so doing he mentions your name. Thus starts the "talk up" which becomes your publicity.

Some of you austere members of the old school may scoff at such devices and say that good work is the only way to advertise. Don't make such a grave mistake. Plenty of men today can do very good work but they don't get a chance until they have hypertension and grandchildren, because the public doesn't hear about them.

I can cite you numerous examples from the medical field where young men are going out and taking their share of business the first year in practice simply because they are selling themselves as modern, scientific physicians. For example, one Chicago obstetrician who teaches in a leading medical school, found that he gained 13 new pregnancy cases in one year by simply lengthening the rubber tubing to his stethoscope and letting the husband and wife both listen to the fetal heart tones.

In fact, he said the first time he tried it, the couple were very pleased. The next time the woman came in for a prenatal visit she had two neighbor ladies who also "wanted to hear the baby's heart beats." You can readily see how this man became known as the doctor who would let you listen to your baby's heart beats. Publicity? Certainly, and good publicity. Profitable, too! Thirteen new obstetrical cases in the first year from that extra six inches of rubber tubing on the stethoscope!

Other young physicians let their patients look at a red or a white blood corpuscle under the microscope. Or they make a urine analysis with the patient standing by. The news spreads, and these doctors not only get mentioned widely but they are associated with microscopes, the modern badge of a scientific physician.

In fact, one branch of the American Medical Association today is planning a series of moving pictures for adults only, which are to be run in the local theaters, with tickets being issued only by physicians to their own patients. The medical association finances the movies as a form of group advertising for the local physicians.

Perhaps your dental society might find it profitable to do the same thing.

Another psychological point of interest: people like to see what they pay for. Let them use your dental mirror and look on the back side of the molar you have filled before they leave your office. They will feel better satisfied with your work and with the fee. And it inflates their ego somewhat because they get to hold your dental instruments. This sounds foolish, perhaps, but it is very true.

If you have any printed matter or dental charts which you can give away, hand them to patients. Chewing gum and lollypops work magic on youngsters, and may place a much more pleasant memory "halo" over their first contacts with the dental profession.

Physicians have now partly educated the pregnant women to make frequent prenatal calls for check-up. We need more of such education regarding their visits to dentists.

Before I close I want to emphasize the fact that in motivating people, you must use language they understand. Remember that your technical terms, while a-b-c stuff to you, are x, y, and z to the layman, even of college level.

When I was an interne, I was standing with one of our leading Chicago obstetricians talking to a man whose wife was six months pregnant, but whose high blood pressure and kidney damage necessitated a Caesarian operation.

"I think we'll do a low cervical section on your wife tomorrow," the physician said, and moved on. The husband had nodded, as if understandingly, but he soon turned to me and naively asked, "Are they going to operate on my wife?" He hadn't understood a word that was said!

So I told him in simple terms what was going to be done. This case illustrates the important fact that you cannot expect people to advertise you professionally unless you let them know what you do and how you do it. You must give them specific sales points.

And, finally, learn the magic art of complimenting people. A tactful compliment to a woman about her frock will cause her to forget a twinge of pain or a little roughness on your part. Mention that you saw she was elected president of the club, or had entertained at bridge for some distinguished guests. Mention the fact that you noticed her house was newly painted, or that she had won a prize at the county fair for her jellies.

Even a technically poor dentist can almost make a success if he is adept at complimenting. Most scientists are so introverted, however, that they seldom think to pass a verbal bouquet either to their wives or to patients.

In conclusion, I don't want you professional men to think for one moment that I decry a most thorough and intensive scientific preparation for dentistry. What I am trying to convey is simply the fact that we need salesmanship after we are out of college in order to sell even superior dentistry today. And the lessons in such salesmanship should be taught more fully in the dental colleges themselves before young men are thrown out into the active practice of dentistry.

Professional men should be taught more principles of applied psychology as related to normal human beings, not just a few lectures on abnormal psychology and psychotic patients.

Osteopathic physicians, optometrists, morticians, chiropractors, nurses and chiropodists likewise must be adept at the Applied Psychology mentioned above. The same is true of accountants and engineers, but lawyers also succeed or fail largely due to their "H-R" score (Human Relations). Excessive library work required for our degrees tends to make us introverts, so deliberately try to extrovert yourself in professional practice.

Psychology and the Law. Since law consists of the codified social habits of mankind it is closely related to psychology. Because the social habits of men and women vary somewhat with the changes in their environment produced by inventors, educators, and scientists, it follows that law is not a static instrument for human regulation and control, but a dynamic, changing code. Like all large systems, of course, it possesses inertia and tends to lag behind new changes in social relations, while it carries over in its momentum many obsolete concepts and statutes.

The regulation of human behavior by law was instituted for the protection of society, and because of the primitive ethical and moral ideas of ancient days punishment was meted out for the purpose of vengeance or retribution. "An eye for an eye, and a tooth for a tooth," reads the Mosaic code. Society sought relief from crime by setting up guardians who protected it by means of sabers and guns. Its intention was to repress the criminal by scaring him through public hangings, by torturing him in foul prisons, and by annihilating him with guillotines, wild beasts, or bullets.

At the present time the emphasis has shifted to the prevention of crime. Psychology is closely related to this phase of the evolution of law, because the prevention of crime entails a consideration of the individual and his motives to action. With this newer viewpoint has come a recognition of the great differences between the child and the adult as regards intelligence and experience. The juvenile court and homes for delinquents have been evolved to take care of the youthful violators of codified precedent. Moreover, the male and the female differences are now taken into consideration, and distinctions are made between first offenders and recidivists. Criminal acts have been classified into different degrees of heinousness so that thieves are no longer hanged in civilized countries and debtors, except of the alimony type, are not imprisoned for their financial incompetence. By means of the indeterminate sentence, the parole, and the suspended sentence the judge is able to modify punishment according to the individual case instead of according to the crime committed.

This attention to the nature of the individual offender should also be carried over to all persons involved in the administration of justice. The selection of twelve good men and true should include a number of other considerations than their virtue and veracity. Their acuity of sensory discrimination, their intelligence quotients, their familiarity with logical concepts and fallacies of reasoning, their emotional biases and complexes—these are very important characteristics. When our jury system was instituted, our forefathers had never heard of morons and imbeciles, and the important findings of psychoanalysis and psychiatry were unthought of.

Indeed, it would seem time to institute a psychological "job analysis" for jurymen and prepare a "job specification" in order to save effort and money. In one case cited by Suther-land, for instance, 4821 persons were examined and $13,000 was spent for jury fees before 12 were accepted for jury duty. If two personnel directors or employment managers could not concur on the qualifications of but 12 applicants out of 4821 who were considered for a position it would indicate that either the judges or the judged were of a very inferior quality in respect to the function or task at hand.

Since acceptable jurors seem so difficult to find it might even be well to train a group for such service, as we train the judges of our courts, and list jury service among the professions open to college graduates. Justice might be better served thereby, and perhaps much of the emotionalism injected into present jury trials might be avoided.

In our discussion of criminals in succeeding sections of this chapter we are speaking of those who have been caught. It is difficult to estimate the number of lawbreakers who are free in the population. They are perhaps more clever and intelligent or more wealthy than the men and women who are apprehended. We shall begin with a consideration of those predisposing factors which produce crime.

The Causes of Crime.   Crime should be regarded as a habit, for children are not "born criminals". Even feeble-mindedness is not an immediate cause of crime despite the high percentage of morons in various institutions of correction. Goddard[20] found as many as 52 out of 56 inmates of a girls' reformatory to be mentally defective. The following percentages of feeble-mindedness were found among the inmates of various juvenile houses of correction, as per Exhibit 57.

In penitentiaries the percentage of mentally defective inmates is considerably less than the above figures, and varies for the different types of crime. A "confidence man", for

---

"Wise men, though all laws were abolished, would lead the same lives."
—Aristophanes

INSTITUTION	PER CENT DEFECTIVE
St. Cloud, Minnesota, Reformatory	54
Bedford, New York, Reformatory	80
Lancaster, Massachusetts, Girls' Reformatory	60
Lancaster, Massachusetts, Paroled Girls	82
Westboro, Massachusetts, Lyman School for Boys	28
Pentonville, Illinois, Juveniles	40
Massachusetts Reformatory, Concord	52
Newark, New Jersey, Juvenile Court	66
Elmira, New York, Reformatory	70
Geneva, Illinois	89
Ohio Boys' School	70
Ohio Girls' School	70
Virginia, three Reformatories	79
New Jersey State Home for Girls	75
Glenn Mills Schools, Pennsylvania, Girls	72

EXHIBIT 57. Showing the percentage of feeble-minded among the inmates of various state institutions of correction.

example, would ordinarily rank above the average in intelligence. From various estimates of feeble-mindedness among the criminal population a conservative figure would lie between 20 and 30 per cent.

In stating that feeble-mindedness is not an immediate cause for crime, we should remind the reader that there are probably a score of honest feeble-minded individuals outside of prisons and reformatories for each one inside. The possession of mental defect is a *predisposing* factor in crime but not an *immediate* one. The person with subnormal intelligence is less likely to see the future consequences of his actions, so he lacks many of the inhibitions possessed by the normal individual, but a wholesome environment and training will make him a law-abiding citizen. Dogs, cats, and even fish can be conditioned to refrain from actions which are native to them, so the mentally subnormal specimens of the human race need not be arbitrarily labelled as criminalistic.

Among the various predisposing factors in crime might also

be cited mental disease, drug addiction, emotional instability, and a paucity of habits relating to honesty and morality. Victims of certain types of insanity, especially those in which the patient develops delusions of persecution as in paranoia and dementia praecox, may often perform criminal acts. The drug addict when he is deprived of his dope may commit both robbery and murder. Crimes of passion may occur in entire disregard of intelligence quotients. Jealousy, hatred, rage, and fear may lead to sudden violations of the most serious sort, and love is directly or indirectly the basis of many crimes ranging from robbery to assault and murder. Emotional instability may be owing to an abnormal glandular condition in the subject, to a lack of inhibiting habits, or to a combination of both.

As regards the paucity of habits relating to honesty and morality, we may mention the evils of bad neighborhoods and faulty training of children. A few weeks ago a mother came to the writer for advice because she feared her five-year-old son was headed for a criminalistic career. She had noted a commotion in the back yard after their trip to the city that morning, and looking out of the window she saw her young heir displaying candy and trinkets before the envious eyes of neighbor children. The mother interviewed her son at once and found that he had filled his pockets at a drug store while she was making a purchase. She threatened him with jail and bread and water. She told him the police would get him if he ever stole things again, and then escorted him back to the drug store where his crime had been committed. Tearfully he apologized to the druggist and restored his possessions, but when the mother stopped at the stationery shop next door her son filled his pockets with Northwestern University stickers and also managed to get a few erasers and some crayons stowed away before they left. When his mother found out about the second case of thievery, she decided her boy was destined to become a kleptomaniac.

During her tearful recital the writer learned that the boy was accustomed to taking money out of his mother's purse whenever he wanted to buy candy or ice cream cones. The parents had thought his action cute. He had also brought home toys belonging to other children. It was just his Scotch ancestry breaking out, his father laughingly told her. At the drug store he appropriated candy and gum. That was kleptomania! The tragic part about the case is not that his parents are moronic in intellectual heritage, for they are college graduates, but they certainly demonstrate a moronic understanding of child psychology.

Under the heading of inadequate training in habits of honesty and fair play we might also cite the unfavorableness of newspaper publicity which portrays the criminal nattily dressed and bejeweled, or smilingly displaying silk chiffon hosiery. The suggestive influence of newspaper accounts of notorious crimes leads to many imitations of the offense, and the tendency to depict gangsters as Robin Hoods and to cast a glamour of romance about villainy is detrimental to both our native and immigrant youths.

In describing the immediate causes of crime we may classify them as those sensory stimuli in the environment which incite nervous patterns that are peculiarly susceptible to stimulation. The hungry man is more likely to steal unguarded foodstuff than is the well fed individual, and the man whose sweetheart is shifting her affections to a wealthier suitor is more likely to be receptive to money. Crimes of passion are usually an outgrowth of the immediate stimuli acting upon the individual. In Chapter I we described an excellent case of the effect of immediate stimuli upon a normally moral young matron.

In summarizing the causes of crime, therefore, we may repeat that they consist of predisposing factors and the stimuli of the immediate situation. The interaction of these two may produce atypical behavior. If the motives are greater for lawful than for criminalistic reactions, then we are good and upright; if the reverse is true, we transgress. Our wrong-doing may occur in spite of an excellent background provided, as in the case of the young matron described in Chapter I, our inhibitory ideas are not aroused.

Methods of Detecting Crime. The methods by which crime is detected have remained fairly constant throughout the years, except that the products of science have lately been called into play, as in the case of the "lie detector", chemical analyses of poisons, fabrics, and ashes, finger prints, and the use of the microscope. In listing the principal methods we shall proceed from the actual discovery of the crime itself.

(1) *Scientific Analyses.* These pertain not only to the firearms employed and the peculiar scratches on the bullets, but also to the factors just mentioned. After a suspect is apprehended, science has heretofore been limited in its ability to determine his guilt. Even today it has not attained per-fection. The use of controlled word associations has been of-fered as a possible method of detecting the suspect's guilt. By this method a list of words is read to the subject who is to respond to each as quickly as possible with the first thought which arises in his mind. Among the stimulus words read to him are inserted "critical" or "key" words which pertain directly to the crime. The assumption is that the real culprit will hesitate longer than usual when he hears these key words, or else will make responses which indicate his guilt. Because the suspect may refuse to cooperate with the experimenter, and because it is possible to outwit the test in other ways which we shall not take time to describe here, this method is not infallible. The "lie detector" operates similarly as re-gards the oral stimuli from the experimenter, but instead of noting the length of time the suspect requires to respond to questions, his blood pressure and respiration rate are auto-matically recorded. The experimenter then asks him ques-tions concerning the crime he is supposed to have committed.

If he begins to prevaricate, his automatic nervous system affects his heart beat and respiration rate. Excellent results have been obtained thus far with the "lie detector". Its findings are not admitted as evidence, but they lead to confessions on the part of guilty individuals.

(2) *Analysis of Motives.* This time honored method is still one of the most successful in limiting the number of suspects, and in finally leading to the culprit. "Cherchez la femme!" is an illustration of this principle. While the finger prints are being examined and the revolver is being analyzed, the detectives are busy constructing their picture of the crime and its cause. If they can discover the motive, it is seldom difficult to decide who is responsible. Even so, they still must apprehend the culprit.

(3) *Stool Pigeons.* Almost every police department and detective bureau have informants among the denizens of the underworld who receive pay or favors of other sorts for bringing back information about crimes which have been committed. Because of jealousies and hatreds of one another, the criminals are often trapped as follows: A robbery committed by several members of a gang involves the loss of perhaps $20,000. In describing the event in the newspapers, however, the amount lost is given as $30,000 or even a larger sum. Some member of the gang reads an account of his crime and decides that his leader who had agreed to divide the spoils equally must have "held out" on him. Friction ensues, or the disgruntled thief talks to his intimate friends. Sooner or later the stool pigeon hears about the affair. Although this device of raising the amount of money stolen for the sake of the newspaper report is an ancient one, it still works. Some subnormal thief is sure to "bite" on this old bait.

A variation of the above plan is to instill jealousy in the sweethearts of some of the members of the underworld who are suspects. These women may become so enraged that they will forget discretion and loose their tongues. If the police do not receive their information directly, the stool pigeon may relay it to them. After the suspects are rounded up the following methods are frequently practiced.

(4) *The Third-Degree.* In the past it was the custom to torture the suspects until they confessed. Even innocent men were willing to swear to any sort of crime by the time their shin bones were cracking on the "wheel" or their feet began to sizzle against red-hot irons. These extremities of torture have been reduced in the modern age, but the suspects are still starved and prevented from falling asleep until they become willing to confess. Many a modern crime has been cleared up by such inquisitorial methods, and many an innocent man has likewise confessed in order to get to sleep or free himself from other torture.

Before we conclude this section it would be well to cite a method by which another variety of law breaking may be settled through the aid of psychology. In trade name infringements the courts have frequently made arbitrary rulings concerning what constituted infringement and what was an instance of non-infringement. Paynter[35] conducted an investigation in which he employed a psychological technique in determining how much confusion existed between certain names on which the courts had already made rulings. In Exhibit 58, next page, the per cent of confusion means the per cent of his subjects who confused the imitation and the original from their appearance and sound.

The methods of detecting crime, therefore, consist of an examination of the crime itself and the implements and evidence pertaining thereto, supplemented by an analysis of the motives. Thereafter the aid of stool pigeons assists in bringing in the guilty or the suspects, after which jealousies may be aroused, or a culprit may be made to feel that his pal

"He who sells what isn't his'n, must buy it back or go to prison."
—Daniel Drew

"He who brings not up his son to some trade makes him a thief."
—Proverb

ORIGINAL	IMITATION	PER CENT CONFUSION	LEGAL DECISION
Sozodont	Kalodont	28	Non-infringement
Nox-all	Non-X-Ell	28	Infringement
Club	Chancellor Club	35	Infringement
Bestyette	Veribest	35	Non-infringement
Mother's	Grandma's	38	Non-infringement
Au-to-do	Autola	40	Infringement
Peptenzyme	Pinozyme	43	Non-infringement
Green River	Green Ribbon	50	Infringement
Ceresota	Cressota	63	Infringement

EXHIBIT 58. Showing the various degrees of confusion between trade-marks and the court's ruling thereon.

"squealed" on him and accused him of doing all of the crime. In his weakened condition from the third degree inquisition to which he has submitted, he may believe the statement and try to "square" himself by showing how he did only part of the crime and his pal pulled the trigger. In the realm of evidence involving the memory, as in the case of trade-mark confusions, psychological tests are an excellent aid in determining guilt or innocence. The peculiarities of memory have already been discussed in Chapter II. Try Exhibit 59.

The Deterrent Effect of Punishment. This topic has been debated pro and con for many years. Those opposed to drastic punishment cite the hangings of pickpockets in England which were supposed to be an object lesson to these petty thieves, but which instead produced a large crowd of witnesses whose purses were filched even as they watched the trap sprung and the luckless thief plunged to his death.

On the other hand, the defenders of punishment cite the fewer crimes in Canada in support of their contention that punishment is a marked deterrent. It is unquestionably true that punishment does have an influence, although the fact that many crimes are a consequence of passion precludes it noticeable effect thereon. When people are in the mood of the young woman described in Chapter I, their inhibitions to illegal behavior are not operative, at least for the few moments or hours of the crime itself. Punishment, therefore, does not affect their actions. But many acts are subconsciously if not consciously contemplated in advance. It is during the weeks and months of such preparation for the crime that the effect of punishment exercises its wholesome influence.

Hollingworth[23] used twenty-five men and twenty-five women students as the basis of an order of merit method in which he endeavored to measure the deterrent effects of various amounts of punishment coupled with various degrees of certainty of detection. He found that extremes either of penalty or of certainty of detection had the greatest deterrent effect on his group. The most deterrent arrangement was the one in which, although there would be only 10 convictions out of every 1,000 cases, a life imprisonment followed conviction. Second in its deterrent effect was the arrangement wherein 30 convictions occurred in every 1,000 cases, but a penalty of 16 years followed each conviction. The third most deterrent combination consisted of 1,000 convictions in every 1,000 cases, with a penalty of 10 days attached to each.

It would seem that the certainty of trial and conviction would greatly influence our crime rate, despite the fact that the prevention of crime goes back to the basic factors which we have described in a previous section of this chapter. The numerous delays and prolongations of criminal cases does tend to permit emotional hatreds to become allayed, but it likewise lessens the efficient administration of punishment. In this connection the following description by Paine[34] of the cumbersomeness and inefficiency of the jury trial is very apt:

The Police Department may arrest a criminal, or it may fail to catch him. It may prepare and present the evidence properly, or it may fail to do so. If the Police Department does not catch the

"Lord, make me an instrument of thy peace; Where there is hatred, let us sow love; Where there is doubt, faith; Where there is despair, hope; Where there is darkness, light; And where there is sadness, joy."
—St. Francis of Assisi

Exhibit 59. Would You Make a Reliable Witness? Study this picture carefully for three minutes ... then turn the page over and answer the questions listed on the reverse side.

What Kind of a Witness Would You Make?

If you had been a witness to the accident pictured on the other side of this sheet, and were being cross-questioned by the lawyers, how accurate a story could you tell? After studying the picture for three minutes, then answer the questions below.

1. What time of the day was it?
2. What day of the week?
3. What season of the year?
4. Was the automobile a closed car?
5. What was the name of the town?
6. Was the automobile headed for the east, west, north or south?
7. Did the auto driver have a hat or cap?
8. Was the boy bareheaded?
9. What was in the window with the clock?
10. Which direction was the trolley car going?
11. On which street was the grocery?
12. Exclusive of the motorman, how many people were in the trolley car?
13. How many others saw the accident?
14. How many people were in the whole picture?
15. Was there a mailbox on the corner?
16. What was the license number of the auto?
17. How many animals were shown?
18. Was the man in the postoffice bareheaded?
19. Who had the right of way?
20. What was the price of the bananas?
21. How many children were visible?
22. What was the name of the grocery store?
23. On which street was the hardware store?
24. What was the name of the hardware store?
25. What was the number of the trolley car?

Exhibit 59. *Reader's Digest* ran this test in one of its summer issues. But Dean John H. Wigmore, world authority on legal evidence, had used it on thousands of his students and at legal conventions. A score of 21-25 is Very Superior; 16-20 is Superior; 11-15 is Average; while 1-10 is Below Average.

criminal, of course the matter ends. If the Police Department catches the criminal and properly presents the evidence before the Police Court, the Police Judge, or City Judge, binds him over to the Grand Jury. If the City Judge binds over to the Grand Jury, then the Grand Jury may indict or return a not true bill. If the Grand Jury fails to return an indictment, that usually ends the case, and two members of the Grand Jury can prevent an indictment. If the Grand Jury indicts, the Prosecuting Attorney usually reviews the evidence and the facts, and sometimes nolle prosses the indictment. If he recommends such procedure, that usually ends the case. If the case goes to trial in the Criminal Court, a jury of twelve men must first be selected, with the attendant delays, if it be a case of major importance. After our best citizens have either disqualified themselves, or been disqualified by reason of our antiquated jury system, the trial is had in the Criminal Court, and one man out of twelve on the jury can cause a mistrial, bringing about the usual delay, scattering of witnesses, etc., all of which operates for the benefit of the criminal. Attorneys for the defense interpose all manner of objections in the effort to get the court in error. If the jury finds the defendant not guilty, that, of course, absolutely ends the case. If the mistrial is had, then on a second trial, it is even more difficult to obtain a conviction. If, however, the defendant is found guilty, and, as is the case usually in this county, a minimum sentence is imposed, it goes to the Supreme Court for review. It there passes completely out of the hands of local officials and the State Attorney General presents the case before the Supreme Court, examines the record, and, if errors of procedure appear, the case will be returned for a new trial in the local criminal court with its attendant delays and disadvantages. If, however, the Supreme Court affirms the decision of the usual minimum penalty, the convicted person immediately starts about to get a pardon. His family and friends bring all pressure to bear upon the Governor and the Pardon Board, and if the criminal is pardoned, of course the whole procedure goes for naught.

Psychological Prophylaxes for Crime.

From the viewpoint of psychology the criminal response is no different from any other action of the individual. It consists of an interplay of motives for socially approved action against other incentives to responses which are socially taboo. Which course is chosen depends upon the four factors, described in Chapter I, which influence human behavior, to wit, the inherited mechanisms of the human organism, its previous experiences, its intra-cutaneous chemical condition at the moment, and the external influences affecting the sense organs.

Eugenics can affect the first of these, but eugenics will be slow in altering human inheritance. In regard to the previous experiences and habits of the human being we may look for our principal aid in preventing crime. When we can teach morons and normal children a wholesome attitude toward property and people, and can extrovert the only children into a spirit of fair play and unselfishness we will have stabilized them considerably. Emotional ballast can also be guaranteed them through the proper childhood milieu. Child psychology and an effective instructional staff in the schools and homes is the best safeguard which psychology can offer to prevent the development of crime. This involves religious as well as civic and secular education.

As for the internal chemical environment of the individual, it will be necessary to eliminate the emotional tensions and fears through the common understanding and practice of psychiatry. Gnawing stomachs and starving minds must be adequately satisfied with the appropriate stimuli. Sublimation of the sexual energy through heterosexual games, amusements and sports must be encouraged. Organic diseases must be remedied along with the correction of functional disorders.

In respect to the external environment it will be necessary to change slums and sweat shops into more pleasant places for residence and labor. The growing leisure of the masses must be diverted into outlets which will round out the thin places in the personalities of our citizens. The gangster and the villain must not be pictured before our youth in a glamorous light, but a premium must be placed on honesty, unselfishness, and morality.

The psychological prophylaxes for crime therefore, consist of removing those elements in the milieu which build neural patterns predisposing to atypical behavior and replacing them with stimuli which develop desirable habits of thought and of action. In attaining this goal it is necessary to enlist the cooperation of educators and psychiatrists, employers and physicians, dentists and ministers. In treating physical ailments the physician realizes that the whole system is ill, not just the kidney or liver, although these organs may be the foci of infection. In treating a social ailment like crime. therefore, it is likewise indispensable to realize that the whole social body is feeling the effects of the various foci of criminal infection, and the function of psychology is to re-orient and re-educate the social body through the medium of the individuals of which it is composed.

REFERENCES

1 ADVANCED PISTOL MARKSMANSHIP INSTRUCTOR'S MANUAL, Vol. II, 1965.
2 ALBUM, M. M., *Dentistry for the Handicapped* (Nat. Soc. Handicapped, 1960).
3 BARRON & TAYLOR, *Scientific Creativity* (Wiley, 1963).
4 BERG, R. H., "A Report on Hospitals" *(Look, 2/3/59)*.
5 BIRREN, F., *Color Psychology and Color Therapy* (McGraw-Hill, 1950).
6 BIDDLE, W. E., *Integration of Religion & Psychiatry* (Collier, 1962).
7 BOISEN, A. T., *Exploration of the Inner World* (Harper, 1962).
8 BONNELL, J. S., *Psychology for Pastors and People* (Harper, 1948).
9 BREDOW, MIRIAM, *The Medical Assistant* (McGraw-Hill, 1958).
10 BUCKLEY, W. F. Jr., *The Committee & Its Critics* (Regnery, 1963).
11 BUSS, A. H., *The Psychology of Aggression* (Wiley, 1961).
12 CAMPBELL, C. M., "The Minimum of Medical Insight Required by Social Workers with Delinquents" *(Mental Hyg.,* 4, 1920).
13 CRANE, G. W., "Symbiosis in the Professions" *(CAL Mag., 2/1/60)*.
14 CURRAN, C. A., *Counseling in Catholic Life & Education* (Macmillan, 1952).
15 DANIEL & LOUTTIT, *Professional Problems* (Prentice-Hall, 1955).
16 DONIGER, S., *Religion & Human Behavior* (Assoc. Press, 1954)
17 ERICKSON, C. E., *The Counseling Interview* (Prentice-Hall, 1950).
18 FINK, H. K., *Long Journey* (Julian, 1954).
19 FRINK, H. W., *Morbid Fears and Compulsions* (Moffat, 1921).
20 GODDARD, H. H., *Feeblemindedness: Its Causes and Consequences* (Macmillan, 1914).
21 GARMA, A., *Peptic Ulcer & Psychoanalysis* (Brunner, 1960).
22 HOKE, R. E., *How You Can Have Success Unlimited* (Psych. Service Center, Charlotte, N. C., 1956).
23 HOLLINGSWORTH, H. L., & POFFENBERGER, A. T., *Applied Psychology* Appleton, 1923).
24 KARNOSH, L. J., "Neurology and Human Emotions" *(J.A.M.A.,* 147, 1951).
25 KANT, F., *Treatment of the Alcoholic* (Thomas, 1954).
26 KRIEGER, W. M., *Complete Funeral Management* (Prentice-Hall, 1962).
27 KUTNER, LUIS, *I, the Lawyer* (Dodd, Mead, 1966)

28 LOCHAPELLE, FATHER PAUL, *Psychiatry for the Priest* (Catholic Truth Society, 1945).
29 MAYER, J. E., *Jewish-Gentile Courtships* (Macmillan, 1962).
30 MUSCIO, B., "The Influence of the Form of a Question" *(Brit. J. Psychol., 8, 1916).
31 MECHANIC, D., *Students Under Stress* (Macmillan, 1962).
32 MYKLEBUST, H. R., *Your Deaf Child* (Thomas, 1954).
33 NOVECK, S., *Judaism & Psychiatry* (Nat. Acad. Jewish Studies, 1960).
34 PAINE, R., "Crime Prevention" (Report of Dept. of Health, City of Memphis).
35 PAYNTER, R. H., "A Psychological Study of Confusions Between Word Trade Marks" *(Bull. U. S. Trade Mark Assoc.*, May, 1915).
36 PEALE, N. V., *Stay Alive All Your Life* (Prentice-Hall, 1960).
37 PEARSON, G. H. J., *Adolescence & Conflict of Generations* (Basic, 1960).
38 SLOAN, R. P., *Today's Hospital* (Harper & Row, 1966).
39 SPARER, P. J., *Personality Stress & Tuberculosis* (Intern. U. Press, 1966)
40 VARNEY, A., *Psychology of Flight* (Van Nostrand, 1950).
41 VEDDER, C. B., *The Juvenile Offender* (Doubleday, 1954).
42 VISCARDI, H., *Give Us The Tools* (Eriksson-Taplinger, 1960).
43 VOSS, E. H., *Nuclear Ambush* (Regnery, 1963).
44 WALGREEN, MYRTLE N., *Never a Dull Day* (Regnery, 1963).
45 WEEKSLER, A. N., *Incentive Management* (Lincoln Electric Co., 1966).
46 ZIMMER & BIDERMAN, *Manipulation of Behavior* (Wiley, 1964).

(College students' preferences for meats listed: 1. Horse; 2. Dog; 3. Monkey; 4. Cat; 5. Snake.)

THE REAL "CONSUMERS" OF TEXTBOOKS

Dryden Press recently warned would-be authors of college texts to remember that the real "consumers" thereof are students, aged about 18 to 21. It urged writers to employ terse, shorter words instead of polysyllables to impress their own Ph.D. colleagues! I have tried to steer a middle course and wish to express my thanks for the loyal support of the following eminent teachers who have used my textbook:

L. M. Sullivan (New Bedford Tech.)
E. M. Swan (Lincoln Chiropractic)
Jewell Levy (SW. Louisiana Inst.)
R. V. Phillips (Pa. Coll. Optometry)
G. B. Walker (Detroit Tech.)
R. W. Erickson (Miss. St. Women)
J. C. Shepard (U. of N. Carolina)
H. Moldenhauer (Spokane Conserv.)
R. Perreault (W. Carolina Teachers)
E. W. Shaffer (Denver Central)
William C. Fisher (Curry)
Beatrice Denton (Benton Harbor)
Joseph Sutherland (Pontiac Inst.)
Helen T. Daniel (Whitworth)
Lee A. Wheeler, Jr. (Webber)
Mrs. Preston Sawyer (Phillips)
Dr. T. Howard Winters (Bliss)
Frances J. Hounshell (Steed)
Dr. Leroy J. Garrett (MacMurray)

John A. Flanagan (Regis)
E. J. Parry (I.B.M.)
E. N. Foster (Washington)
S. F. Collins (Lincoln U.)
Harold Parker (Cazenovia)
Keith A. Bell (Cascade)
Boleslaw Wysocki (Alliance)
Robert C. Fife (Milligan)
John Leach (Goldey Beacom)
Augustus Fenn (Curry)
H. W. Harshman (Muskegon)
L. E. Kaupp (Itasca)
Richard Williams (Mankato)
Dorothy Matthews (Bennett)
Arthur E. Jones (L. Columbia)
W. H. Hossick (Northland)
Kenneth C. Buchanan (Cecil's)
Dr. Z. Marchant (W. Tex. St.)
Pres. H. G. Green (Phillips)

CHAPTER XVII

HOW PSYCHOLOGY PROMOTES HAPPY HOMES

It usually requires two good women to produce a good husband! The first of these should be his mother. If she permits her son to grow up as a selfish, temper-tantrum brat, then even an angel from heaven might not be able to make a success of marriage to him. All too many modern mothers fail to housebreak their sons for later happy matrimony. By sins of omission, if not of actual commission, they predispose their children for later divorce. And many fathers are equally guilty, for they spoil their daughters until the latter make poor managers of homes of their own.

Beware of grown men who say: "Mother is my best sweetheart." And use caution in selecting a girl who makes a similar declaration about "my Daddy." For such cases often indicate an undue parental influence over the children. These parents have taught their youngsters to rely upon them too much for solace and affection. And subconsciously such parents may hold an excessive jealousy of any younger rival for the affections of that son or daughter.

Here's a good example in point. A widow had two sons. She showered not only the usual maternal affection upon the boys, but unwittingly lavished on them the love that would normally have gone to her husband, had he been living. They were a fusion of husband and son. So, having invested doubly of her affection in the boys, she was doubly interested in them. Jesus stated, "For where your treasure is, there will your heart be also." But "treasure" includes anything belonging to us which we invest either in other people or organizations. Thus, the giving of advice or affection will thereafter fasten us to the recipient thereof just as our investing of money. And the more we put into a business or personality, the more fearful we become of losing our control thereof.

This mother managed to tie her two sons to her apron strings, at least till the elder was 27. Then he ran away with an attractive girl from his home town. His mother was very indignant at first, but after they returned from the honeymoon, she nominally accepted the situation, and even went out of her way to be too helpful. In fact, she arranged that they live in one of her houses just three doors down the street! But secretly she resented the younger woman who had won first place in the heart of her older son. Though she was sugary sweet in public, she kept planting poisonous darts in his mind.

"Alice had company today," the mother would inform her married son as he dropped in to say "Hello" on his way home from work. "Alice said he was a magazine salesman, but he seemed to stay a very long time!"

By means of these nasty insinuations, the mother finally caused her son to get a divorce within two years. And though she professed to be so sympathetic about the break-up of that home and seemed so genuinely sorrowful for "My poor boy," she was secretly elated. Meanwhile, her younger son never married. And his mother would tell her friends in a mildly reproving manner that it was because he always insisted she was his best sweetheart. This was a wonderful tonic to her ego, causing her to forgive him for any faults.

And faults he had, for he caused three young women in his town to bear children out of wedlock before he finally ducked out by joining the Army. But he was too mollycoddled to stay away from his doting mamma, so he went A.W.O.L. several times and finally reached the psychiatrists, who diagnosed him as a psychopathic personality.

In selecting a mate, therefore, be sure you let your brain be your Captain and never permit your emotions to mutiny against it. For you act as proxy for your unborn children when you select their other parent, so look far ahead. Moonlight and "moonshine" are both intoxicating! Don't permit an infatuation based on sex appeal, liquor and romantic Luna to stampede you into an unwise marriage.

How to Vaccinate Newlyweds Against Divorce.

The greatest contribution of medicine to public welfare has been vaccination. But vaccination involves letting the body actually confront a small dose of attenuated bacteria or toxins of the dangerous disease, long in advance of actual exposure to an epidemic.

Applied to marriage, therefore, vaccination becomes largely a psychological inoculation and consists of exposing the newlyweds to specific problems that often lead to later divorce. These problems are best presented by the Case Method and the solutions thereto should be memorized in advance, just as are the axioms in geometry. "Forewarned is forearmed," runs a maxim quite true in this regard.

(1) The prospective wedding couple should select wisely at the outset. You pay full price when you marry, so get A-1 matrimonial merchandise instead of seconds, culls or defective material. Rate your prospective mate by the "Sweethearts Tests" on pp. 765-772 in order to gain a more objective attitude. For when you are intoxicated with romance, you should welcome the advice of parents and friends about your choice to help add sober, impartial judgments to your own somewhat biased viewpoint.

(2) Be married by a clergyman instead of a justice of the peace, for the wedding ceremony is more than a civil contract, and should be consummated in an atmosphere of idealism and religion, rather than in a shoddy environment where smoking cigar butts are fouling up the air and cuspidors stand in the corner. This does not mean that you should insist on an elaborate church wedding, for you can quietly be married by your priest or clergyman at the altar with only a few close friends in attendance.

(3) Verbalize your love for each other every day. It isn't enough that a husband stay home nights and always hand over his pay check. For women want words! Especially sweet compliments, and that applies almost equally true of men.

So make it a rule to pay your mate at least one honest compliment every day. And never permit yourselves to go to sleep in a quarrelsome, hostile mood. Always make up, though you have to grit your teeth to force an apology across them! For an unresolved quarrel can become more diffcult to break with each new day that passes. Square accounts each night before you fall asleep.

(4) Become active together in a local church. It is a comparative rarity for two such people to seek a divorce. Most of those who finally become embroiled in Courts of Domestic Relations are either non-church attendants, or else only one goes to church. And even then, this one is not likely to be very active in the work of the church. Too many so-called church members are passive and rather irregular in their attendance. In our largest placement center for adopted children, namely, Kansas City, the prospective parents must both be ACTIVE church members or they are not given a youngster.

(5) Formally revive your courtship emotions at least once per week, by having a date with your mate. Remember, motions are the precursors of emotions. You can't control the latter directly but only through your choice of motions or actions. This means, in brief, that you should have a romantic date with your mate at least once per week, exclusive of your attendance together on Sunday at church. Go to a movie or a dance. Allow for this night out when you make up your budget. And when your children arrive, don't grow so stodgy or so parental that you forget this vital need to exercise your romantic emotions via indulgence in the proper motions.

The wedding ceremony contains a beautiful bit of idealism when it asks the bride and groom to pledge their love until death do them part. But it is not possible to pledge emotions for future delivery with any sure expectation of said delivery! For emotions are not directly subject to our will. We can, however, pledge motions, such as that weekly date with our mate.

Suppose you were to promise me that tomorrow at exactly noon, you would be frothing at the mouth with rage or shedding tears of grief or terrified with fear. You might be very sincere in your pledge, and even set an alarm clock to be sure you were aware at noon of that previous vow. But you would not be raging or grief-stricken or fearful when that alarm sounded! No, your emotions would have to be re-aroused or resurrected by stimuli in your immediate environment tomorrow noon or you would not be able to experience those pledged feelings.

In like manner, love must be evoked afresh every day. We dare not coast on our plighted troth at the original wedding ceremony. And it is futile, as thousands of wives have done, to protest: "My husband is running around with a young secretary in his office only half his age. But I love him so how can he do such a thing? Don't a man's promises mean anything, for when we were married he pledged that he would love me all his life?"

To avoid this all too common tragedy in previously happy homes, become aware of the true psychological facts. Go through the proper motions each day and you'll soon begin to feel the corresponding emotions! Just be sure you and your mate go through those motions of dates and kisses, the phrasing of sincere daily compliments, plus the many other little courtesies, and you need not worry about the emotion of love. You can't "act" devoted for very long without feeling devoted.

(6) Use horse sense in the business conduct of your domestic corporation. Operate your home on a budget, as explained more fully in a later section of this chapter. Modern husbands find that it is usually wise to let the wife act as treasurer, for then their male friends can't borrow so readily from them. "Say, pal, can you lend me a five-spot till payday?"

"Many a man in love with a dimple makes the mistake of marrying the whole girl."   —Stephen Leacock.

the average man may be asked by some of his co-workers. If he has the money, it is embarrassing to refuse the request, even though he is dubious about ever being repaid the loan. "Sorry, but my wife is treasurer of our family and handles all the money," you can reply, knowing well that the would-be borrower will rarely ask your wife for a loan.

Young people must remember, too, that the ownership of a little cottage, plus an automobile and a television set, represents the end result of 25 years of frugal efforts by their parents. So don't think you newlyweds can have these same luxuries the first year of wedlock. You have lived on the fruits of your parents' thrift so long that you may find it difficult to economize adequately.

If the young wife works for a time after marriage, make it a rule NEVER to apply her earnings to the upkeep of the household, such as food or rent bills. Invest her money in purchasing a home or in buying major furniture items, but learn to live on one salary alone for the actual operation of your home. Otherwise, it will be very difficult for the wife to stop and have any children, for the two-salary living standard will become so entrenched, the young couple will grow irritated at each other in trying to cut back to a single salary.

(7) Allow for the sexual disparity between males and females. God Almighty made women and men so that they experience marked quantitative differences in their two major appetites. Thus, the wife is able to live contentedly on 2,500 calories of food per day when her husband may need 3,500. In the erotic realm, too, an even greater difference exists. Males of the major mammalian species, such as the horse, the cow, the dog and man, are basically created for having herds or flocks or harems. But monogamy is superior to polygamy on many counts, both psychological and economic.

Most divorces start in the bedroom, therefore, because the average wife has not been taught that she must feign ardor

---

"Faults are thick where love is thin."   —Danish Proverb.

on many occasions to satisfy her husband's natural erotic hunger. A successful wife is one who functions as a one-wife harem, being sweetheart and wife, as well as mother, cook and playmate for her husband, as the following section will elaborate more fully.

The Five Basic Hungers in Normal Marriage. For simplification, we shall list the first basic hunger as the gastric, though we include the other self-preservation factors thereunder, such as clothing, shelter and health, plus their conventional modern symbol, namely, money.

Although the gastric hunger (including self-preservation) is regarded by psychologists as the most powerful human tendency, in luxurious America and most of the other civilized nations of the world, it is not a very significant factor in causing divorces. Our bountiful economic system furnishes us with too much food, rather than not enough. "Americans dig their graves with their teeth," is an adage not far from the truth, medically speaking. But immediately after World War II, hunger did exercise an influence on certain foreign nations, where wives were tempted into unfaithfulness by a chocolate bar or a loaf of bread.

Obesity is far more prevalent in America than starvation. But obesity has a definite marital disadvantage, over and beyond its predisposition medically to high blood pressure, diabetes and even cancer. For the usual male has associated romance with slender women. On his wedding day, therefore, his bride may weigh 115, but at the age of forty her poundage may have reached the 150 or 175 mark. When her husband then hugs her or tries to hold her on his lap, she feels somewhat elephantine. Even the artist knows that the simplest way to depict a matronly figure versus that of a coed is to add more girth to the former.

Because the middle-aged married person, whether husband or wife, so often has become rather portly, part of the stimulus

Always be true to your teeth or they'll be false to you!

for the courtship emotions has now vanished. Unless the corpulent married folks have meanwhile developed compensating charms, which is quite possible, of course, there is danger that their former stimulating value will drop noticeably. Indeed, after dieting and regaining a more youthful figure, many a wife reports that her husband's ardor has zoomed markedly. If space permitted, I could cite many cases from my own office practice to corroborate this point in dramatic fashion. One of the best menopausal tonics, therefore, is to regain the slender figure of one's college days.

The second fundamental hunger that needs to be satisfied adequately for permanently happy marriage is the erotic or love appetite. And in modern society this seems to be the most critical of all as regards divorce. "Mental cruelty" and incompatibility are cited as the conventional causes of divorce, but they usually are superficial symptoms far out on the periphery of a more basic maladjustment in the core of marriage, namely, sexual adjustment. I have previously commented that most divorces start in the bedroom, for the erotic hunger is usually the one that is not properly understood even in modern marriage.

When an animal is hungry in the gastric realm, he may even snarl and claw at his own loved ones. At the zoo, therefore, a hungry lion or tiger may snap at its mate and even bat its cubs half way across the cage. Just give that carnivore a few pounds of raw beef, however, and it will be almost as docile as a housecat. Its cubs can then clamber all over it and even nip its ears without causing an angry reaction.

In much the same manner, a food hungry male or a husband with a gnawing peptic ulcer may be snarlish until his stomach is full. Most wives soon learn the strategy of feeding their husband a good dinner before showing him the monthly bills or telling about junior's breaking of a window. But brides have not been briefed in advance about this irritability of a love-hungry male. Nor have they been taught that their husband has much more erotic desire, as a rule, than does the average wife.

In past generations, such wives have often accused their mates of being selfish in the latter's desire for marital relations and have tried to limit the husband to the same input of "erotic calories," so to speak, as they themselves craved. But God made man to have a much greater demand for food and for physical affection, than woman. Thus, patriarchal Jacob had two wives, plus two concubines. Such plurality of wives is not permitted nowadays, though it may have served a vital purpose in the earlier history of the human race when wars and animal foes cut down the male population drastically.

So a successful modern wife must see that her husband is completely satisfied in his erotic hunger or else suffer the consequences of his caustic criticism, fault-finding and bitterness. When men begin to belittle their wives and quarrel, or when, after several years of apparently happy marriage, they suddenly become tavern habitues, you can be suspicious that they are deflated in their sexual ego and are growing panicky about premature erotic senility.

Oddly enough, a man doesn't object to his wife's stopping with 2,500 calories at the table though he demands 3,500, but he feels offended if she doesn't at least affect an ardor and appetite equal to his own in the erotic realm! Smart wives soon discover this fact and become actresses in their own boudoir. Then their husbands will remain devoted to them through their Golden Wedding Anniversary.

The third basic hunger is the parental. This includes the desire to fondle and care for some weaker defenseless creature. If husband and wife cannot have children of their own, they should try to adopt some, preferably in pairs so the youngsters can socialize each other. If that isn't feasible immediately, then adopt an entire Sunday school class or Boy and Girl Scout Troop. You can thus stake out a claim to the developing personality of youngsters of other parents and often be more of an inspiration to these children than are their own fathers and mothers.

Indeed, some of the best parents in the world are of this foster type, as represented by the devoted teachers in the schools and the unselfish Catholic sisters. Remember, the average teacher during the typical school week, may stand in front of her children more hours per day than the actual parents of those same youngsters. The teachers thus are glorified parents before their children.

If you adopt a child, remind him that you deliberately chose him whereas other parents have no choice but must take what they get. And as a further solace to his ego, remind him that you and his mother are of no blood kinship whatever. You selected her from among total strangers because you loved her and she reciprocated your feelings. And after marriage, you feel more closely knit to her than to your own flesh-and-blood brothers or sisters. In like manner, when you wanted a son, you chose him because you loved him. There is no blood kinship between you, but neither is there any between you and his mother. All three of you are thus bound together by the strongest bonds on this earth, namely, love or voluntary affection. This will help banish the child's later belief that he doesn't exactly "belong" or that he isn't quite a member of the inner sanctum. Instead, he will recognize that everybody is on the same footing in the family team, and that each must try to keep up the good name of the entire family unit.

This parental hunger is sublimated constructively in child welfare agencies, fund drives for hospitals, the polio campaigns, and all such extensions of the maternal urge, for women are the major custodians of culture and morality, love and child education. In spinsters, we see similar outgrowths of this same hunger in their desire to cuddle cats or dogs, goldfish and even their flowers.

"The thing that impresses me most about America is the way the parents obey their children!"   —Duke of Windsor.

Fourth among the basic hungers is a desire for friends and social esteem. Sometimes jealous husbands refuse to permit their mates even to attend church. Or they will not let them go to the grocery alone or even to a party of their girl friends or former sorority sisters. It is surprising how many men are victims of this green-eyed monster, jealousy. And many women are likewise its prey. But jealousy usually indicates an inferiority complex. This is often sexual in nature, and, in my consulting experience, usually based on misconceptions rather than organic deficiency. When a wife removes the underlying cause, her mate not only may blossom out as a jolly trusting individual, but may change dramatically from a penny-pincher to a generous person. Miserliness in a husband is often a final attempt to dominate a wife when his erotic inferiority complex makes him fearful that he can't hold her by love.

The fifth and final basic hunger is for religion and its cultural offshoots, such as music and education. Every normal person seems to have a divine spark implanted in his rather mechanical physiological make-up. Descartes called these sparks the contact between man and God. If it were not for such potential divinity, then we would not react to lofty poetry and music. We would not feel a lump in our throats and a tug or dull ache in the region of our hearts when we hear a great sermon or the climax of an uplifting play.

When a steel magnet passes close to iron filings, the latter quiver and finally jump across the intervening gap. But before they leap across, if they were sentient, they might experience somewhat comparable feelings to our lump in the throat phenomenon. God's tug on human beings is thus comparable to a spiritual magnet being brought close to us. But without those initial divine ideas or sparks in our human personality, there would be no more response to noble ideas or sentiments than a wolf or tiger demonstrates.

How to Live Happily on a Budget. There is an old adage to the effect that "Love flies out the window when poverty stalks in the door." When a young couple have over extended themselves by the installment buying of furniture, plus an automobile and many unnecessary luxuries, they may soon find themselves hounded with bill collectors. This is a very deflating experience, especially if some of their furniture is finally repossessed by the finance company.

The fear of losing caste among their neighbors, plus the worry and headaches of trying to keep up their payments, will ultimately cause the young couple to quarrel and argue. So it behooves every family to operate on a rigid budget. But money management is one of the blind spots in our educational system. Very few children obtain any specific tutelage therein, except the boys and girls who work as newspaper carriers. They operate on what is called the "small merchant" plan and thus acquire a broad view of our economic machine.

Insurance premiums are about the only savings that the average family possesses. Every intelligent man who is emotionally mature thus tries to protect his wife and future children via life insurance. Term insurance is cheapest for emergencies, but my favorite policy is the "family income" type, which pays 1% of the face value each month for 20 years after issuance, if death snatches the husband and father away from that home.

A $10,000 policy of this nature thus pays the wife $100 per month. At the end of the 20-year period, she also gets the full $10,000 in addition! And the cost is but slightly more than for straight life insurance. For a slight additional premium, too, the policy pays double for accidental death, so in that event she'd obtain $20,000 at the end of the 20 years. This amount can also be paid to her in monthly installments, so she and the children are guaranteed a modest regular income. A "family income" policy thus permits a man to reach back from the Great Beyond and place his protective arms around his loved ones, buoying them up until the youngsters are at least through high school.

Home ownership is another great stabilizer of happy families. It isn't much cheaper to own a home than to rent, but many psychological advantages accrue to the home owner. First, he becomes a more intelligent citizen, for he pays closer attention to civic matters and the local tax rate. Second, he and his whole family feel safely anchored, so they don't live under the vague worry of being dispossessed, as in times of housing shortages.

Third, his children will be able to stay in the same school without being shunted in and out of several different school districts while first contacting important subjects like arithmetic. This frequent changing of schools often causes a child to drop in his grades. Finally, the children learn to be more careful of property when they occupy their own home. Tenants, on the contrary, are more destructive because they feel no such pride of ownership. A home is thus good insurance against divorce.

But in purchasing a house, Dr. E. F. Donaldson[10] recommends a down payment that will equal from 20% to 25% of the total cost. And that total buying price should not run more than $1\frac{1}{2}$ to $2\frac{1}{2}$ times the annual income of the purchaser. Thus, if your salary now averages $5,000 per year, Dr. Donaldson says you should not pay more than $12,500 for your home.

Another method for determining the maximum price you can afford to pay for a house is to compute the total carrying charge for the property after the initial down payment has been made. This carrying charge involves installment payments, interest, taxes, repairs and insurance, but not depreciation or interest on that down payment. And this total carrying charge should not exceed one-third of the buyer's annual income. With a down payment of 25%, the carrying charges will run at least 10% of the cost of the property. So a couple with an income of $5,000 you should thus not pay more than $1,666 per year for housing.

If the in-laws wish to help the newlyweds, they may very profitably make a down payment for them on a cottage of their own. Indeed, it would be very beneficial if more parents with reasonable financial means would pay $1,000 to $5,000 on a new home for the young couple than to hold that money for 25 years and then bequeath it to them via a will. For a down payment NOW of $2,500 will do the couple more good than $10,000 some 25 years later, when the young couple have reached middle age themselves. The parents-in-law might very properly pay the medical expenses, too, for the birth of their grandchildren, for this philanthropy will guarantee them more grandchildren.

But cash gifts, applied to the weekly budget of a family, are usually unwise, for such a "dole" then is used for current expenses and simply cultivates a more luxurious standard of living that isn't warranted. The down payments on a cottage or on the new babies are perfectly proper for such expenses are capital investment. In pioneer days, young married couples were helped to build their log cabin and get launched into marriage with furniture. We should revive this excellent plan in our competitive modern age whenever the in-laws can afford to do so.

How to Lose 10 Pounds in 10 Days. In dieting, it is always well to remember that the body has plenty of sugar and fat stored away but not protein, so the latter must be ingested afresh each day. The dieter should thus include 400 to 600 calories in protein foods in his daily menu. Protein has another advantage for it is the only type of foodstuff which loses 15% of its caloric value in the process of assimilation, due to what is called in physiology the "specific dynamic action" of protein. Thus, 100 calories of protein in the mouth furnish only about 85 calories when absorbed from the intestinal wall. Sugar, carbohydrates and fats, however, go through into the blood stream at approximately face value.

Dieting is also economically wise, for each pound of surplus

FAMILY BUDGET CHART

Monthly Income	$75	$100	$125	$150	$175	$200	$250	$300	$350	$400
Food	31	35	41	44	48	51	55	61	70	75
Wearing Apparel (clothing, hats, shoes, dry cleaning, sewing supplies, etc.)..	9	12	17	20	26	29	35	40	45	50
Rent	20	25	30	35	40	43	50	60	65	75
Operating Expense (taxes, fire insurance, union dues, telephone, fuel, gas, light, water, ice, wages to maid, cook laundress, etc.)...	8	15	18	22	25	30	40	50	65	73
Education and Recreation (newspaper, magazines, books, music, movies, social dues, etc.)......	2	4	6	9	10	15	20	28	30	32
Health (medicines, tooth paste, eye glasses, doctor, etc.)	2	3	4	5	7	8	10	12	15	20
Savings (life insurance premiums, saving deposits, etc.)	2	4	6	10	12	15	25	32	40	50
Benevolences (Church and Sunday school, Community Chest, Red Cross, Salvation Army, etc.)..,	1	2	3	5	7	9	15	17	20	25

The BUDGET CHART reproduced above is based on take-home pay, after income taxes and Social Security deductions have already been made. It represents the net wage or salary available to the intelligent housewife for budgeting purposes. If your net income does not coincide exactly with any one of these, then employ the same percentage distribution as that income on the chart which is nearest your own.

This BUDGET CHART has been prepared from a psychological and medical angle, as well as the financial viewpoint. Many budgets seem to be based too much on the desire to present an adequate savings each month for deposit and hence don't always stress many of the social needs or psychological hungers of mankind. The Bible says a man does not live by bread alone!

fat represents from $2.50 to $5.00 of groceries at the current prices. If you temporarily live off your excess fat, therefore, you save money meanwhile. But the medical advantages of dieting are far more significant. The body must sprout 3 miles of extra blood vessels for each 5 pounds of additional fat! Thus, a man who is 25 pounds overweight must maintain blood pressure in an extra 15 miles of blood vessels! But this demands more pressure in the pumping station, so his blood pressure rises. It is not uncommon for an obese man or woman to lose one point in blood pressure per pound lost in dieting.

A foster aunt of mine weighed 212 pounds and had a blood pressure of 220. I finally got her dieted down to 160 pounds and her blood pressure meanwhile fell to 155, which meant that the weight reduction of 52 pounds lowered her blood pressure 65 millimeters of mercury. In addition to the financial and health advantages in slenderness, many people have reported to me the remarkable change in their romantic appeal when they streamlined their figures. My daily psychology feature in the newspapers pulls 1,000 letters per day, among which I have often received the following type of report:

"Dr. Crane, I've been married for 15 years. But for a long time something has been missing from our marriage. My husband has remained dutiful and kind, but he hasn't been very ardent or romantic. For he kisses me more or less as a father would kiss his child. So I had begun to worry lest we were becoming platonic and middle-aged, though I am only 35 and he's just 37.

"Then I read your article about the dampening effect of obesity on romance. Right then and there I vowed I would launch upon your diet by which you promised we could lose 10 pounds in 10 days, for I had increased from 118 on my wedding day to 148.

"Well, your diet worked a miracle. I was down the 10 pounds on schedule. It was exhilarating, too, for then I was able to slip into a size 16 frock again. And my husband apparently sensed the difference, too, for he began to come out into the kitchen to kiss me as soon as he arrived home from the office. That was a delightful novelty because he had previously just shouted 'Hello, honey,' to let me know of his homecoming.

"But I didn't stop with those first 10 pounds. I kept right on till now I am down to 122. And what you psychologists say about our regaining our romantic moods is very true. Why, I feel 10 years younger and I'm not nearly as tired when I go shopping all day or do the week-end housecleaning or laundry.

"Best of all, however, my husband has changed from an unromantic though kindly man into an ardent suitor who spontaneously suggests a movie date without my prodding him as I used to have to do. His kisses, too, are now of the sweetheart variety. And he even hangs around the kitchen while I am getting dinner, whereas he used to sit in the living room reading the paper or listening to the radio till I called him to the table."

It is really more difficult to diet than to stop the liquor or tobacco habits. For the dieter can't make a dramatic and complete elimination of his former temptation. He simply tapers off but still goes through the old habit of dining two or three times daily, though on smaller amounts. But, as William James ably pointed out, it is easier to break off completely than to taper off.

Dieters, too, must beware of alcoholic beverages, for alcohol ranks next to butter in fattening or caloric value. Besides, the irritation of the mucosal lining of esophagus and stomach stimulates a gnawing that resembles hunger. One gram of sugar is the equivalent of 4 calories. One gram of starch counts 4 calories. One gram of protein also produces 4 calories, but when ingested, please remember the 15% loss because of that specific dynamic action of protein. But one gram of pure alcohol counts 7 calories in contrast to one gram of pure fat which has the top value of 9 calories.

FRUIT   CALORIES

1 prune (stewed)	25
1 peach (raw)	50
1 pear (raw)	50
1 tangerine	50
1 peach (2 halves canned)....	75
1 slice pineapple (canned).....	75
1 apple (raw)	100
1 banana	100
1 cantaloupe (5 inch size)....	100
1 orange (medium)	100
1 cup applesauce (sweetened)..	150
1 cup grape juice	150

SOUPS

1 cup bouillon	25
1 cup consomme	25
1 cup chicken	100
1 cup clear tomato..........	100
1 cup vegetable	100
1 cup creamed asparagus......	200
1 cup cream of tomato........	200
1 cup oyster stew............	200
1 cup split pea	200

BREADSTUFF

1 piece Ry-krisp	25
1 soda cracker (2 inch).......	25
1 slice baker's bread..........	50
1 cookies (3 inch)	100
1 biscuit (baking powder).....	100
1 muffin	100
1 hard roll (French)..........	100
1 doughnut	200
1 sweet roll	200

VEGETABLES

1 beet (2 inch)	25
1 carrot (large)	25
1 onion (raw)	25
1 cup green beans............	50
1 cup cabbage (raw).........	50
1 cucumber (7 inch).........	50
1 head of lettuce.............	50
1 cup sauerkraut	50
1 cup spinach	50
1 cup tomatoes	50
20 stalks asparagus	100
1 cauliflower (small head).....	100
30 stalks celery	100
1 cup peas (cooked)	100
1 potato (medium)...........	100
1 cup turnips	100
1 cup squash (unseasoned)....	150
1 cup beans (cooked)	200
1 sweet potato (large)	200
1 cup mashed or fried potatoes	200

PROTEINS   CALORIES

1 piece bacon (crisp).........	25
1 frankfurter (small)	100
1 hamburger patty (2½ inch).	100
1 egg (large)................	100
1 lamb chop (medium)	100
1 slice steak (2x2x½ inch)....	100
1 slice roast beef or lamb (Size of slice of bread but ¼ inch thick)	100
1 piece veal or pork (half size of slice of bread and ¼ inch thick)	100
1 serving liver	100
1 serving fish	100
1 cup cottage cheese	200
1 cup salmon (canned)	200
1 chicken breast (large)	250
1 chicken drumstick (large)...	250
1 liverwurst sandwich (rye)...	250
1 cup stuffing (dressing)	600

DESSERTS

1 teaspoon sugar	25
1 teaspoon honey	25
1 teaspoon jelly	25
1 teaspoon molasses	25
1 cup jello	200
1 cup junket	250
1 piece apple pie (1/6 pie)....	250
1 piece cream pie (1/6 pie)....	350
1 cup tapioca cream pudding..	300
1 cup baked custard	300
1 iced cup cake	300
1 cup ice cream (½ pint).....	400
1 cup rice pudding...........	500
1 cup chocolate pudding......	500

BEVERAGES

1 glass buttermilk	100
1 glass gingerale	100
1 glass whole milk...........	150
1 glass chocolate milk	200
1 glass Ovaltine	200
1 glass chocolate milk shake...	400

MISCELLANEOUS

1 serving butter	50
1 tablespoon cream	50
1 cup cornflakes	75
1 tablespoon French dressing	75
1 tablespoon Mayonnaise	100
6 English walnuts	100
1 tablespoon peanut butter....	100
1 Shredded wheat biscuit	100
1 cup cooked Farina..........	150
1 cup cooked oatmeal........	150
1 cup cooked rice	150
1 cup whole wheat (cooked)..	150

In cold weather you can follow my dehydration diet, which should lop off at least 10 pounds in 10 days. Women should limit themselves to 800 calories of food input per day while men may have 1,200. On the first day, however, restrict your total fluid input to one full glass (8 ounces). You may move up to two glasses the second day and three on the third. Continue with three glasses per day through the 10th day.

This low fluid input not only seems to dry up your saliva and make your mouth cottony, but it apparently does likewise as regards gastric juice. Peptic ulcer patients have reported that this dehydration quickly checks their ulcer pains. And you become more concerned about fluids than food, so you can thus stay on your lowered caloric intake without much effort. You actually don't feel very hungry. I've personally tried this dieting plan on three different occasions and I can attest to its effectiveness in killing hunger.

Follow the accompanying Caloric Chart, and shop around as you wish, for this dieting plan doesn't require elaborate menus. Since caffeine drinks apparently stimulate gastric secretion, which, in turn, creates hunger, you better go slow on such beverages while dieting. After you conclude the 10-day diet, if you still wish to lose more weight, then shift to a caloric input of 1,200 calories per day for women and 1,600 for men, with normal fluid consumption. On this more liberal input, you should lose from 1 to 2 pounds per week until you attain your goal.

How to Answer a Child's Frank Questions. There is an admirable psychological strategy in connection with meeting questions, whether these come from children, from customers or from the lecture audience during an open forum period. It has three distinct parts. First, smile. Second, pause and praise the acumen of the questioner or the timeliness of his query, its relevancy to the problem, etc. Lastly, employ the "Reversible Why" (See p. 452), and tactfully let the propounder of the question try to answer it himself.

"Daddy, where does the sun go at night?" a 7-year-old boy asked his weary father, who was a physician friend of mine. The latter tried to collect his wits and phrase his reply in simple language. But the boy had shot nearly 20 more queries at his dad before the latter finally delivered his studied answer to the first.

"And, Dr. Crane," protested my friend, "I don't think he paid any attention to my answer when I finally did give it to him. So what do you psychologists suggest in such a dilemma?"

By use of the 3-part formula mentioned above, the father should smile approvingly; then pause and praise, and reverse the query, as follows: "Junior, that is an excellent question you have asked. In fact, you might be interested in knowing that even the school teachers didn't know the answer to it at the time of Christopher Columbus. So here's what I'll do. I'll give you two guesses as to where YOU think the sun goes at night."

Obviously, this technique inflates the child's ego, for he feels proud of himself, for he has asked a question that even the school teachers didn't know in years past. His attention has meanwhile been held by that first question so he hasn't shot 20 more queries at his dad, and thus half-forgotten the first. Moreover, it is stimulating to him to use his own wits in trying to derive an answer. Perhaps he has a few fragments of information that bear upon his question. Maybe, therefore, he can contribute 25% or even 50% to the solution. His father can then add the balance for a complete answer.

The psychological merits of this plan are rather evident. First, the child feels happy about the question, since his ego has been inflated. Second, he stops thereat and thus doesn't race ahead with many irrelevant intervening queries. This permits the answer to be hooked upon the query to which it pertains. Third, he helps derive the solution, so becomes a

"Character is what you are in the dark."   —Dwight L. Moody.

partner in this educational process. Fourth, this "pause & praise" strategy lets the father, teacher, salesman or public speaker collect his wits, in case he may have been wool gathering at the moment. It lets us tactfully stall for time.

When children ask their frank queries about where they came from, parents should realize that they aren't salacious in their desires. Nor do they lie awake at night dwelling on the sexual nature of the answer if their parents have given them straight replies without tittering or raised eyebrows and other carryovers of adult prudery from preceding generations. In thousands of interviews with patients, as well as by an open challenge issued several times on a coast to coast basis in my daily syndicated newspaper column, I have never found one individual who criticized his parents, teachers or Scout Master, for having given him too much scientific sexual counsel or for having offered it too early.

On the contrary, however, I have in my files hundreds of records of grown men and women, possibly sterile because of venereal infection contracted during their exploration of the sexual realm because nobody had given them the simple facts. They still blame their parents for failing to enlighten them properly. I have thus come to the conclusion that it is far better to give youngsters too much scientific advice and to give it too early than to err in the other direction. They absorb only what they are interested in at the moment and the rest is disregarded, if it is beyond their primary concern at the moment.

"Where did I come from, Mother?" a toddler may inquire, for in the pre-school years our children begin to wonder about origins. This query should not be sidestepped. If the child is adopted, the parents should use strategy outlined earlier in this chapter. For the longer the information is deferred, the more difficult it is to handle the problem. Meanwhile, the child may have lost confidence in his parents, so he may never voluntarily bring up the question again. He may rely on other youngsters or "alley" instructors thereafter, and thus obtain much misinformation with a salacious instead of a scientific slant.

"You came out of Mother's tummy," is a very successful answer to the query of that 4-year-old. Actually, the baby is carried in the uterus, but that is too technical for the toddler, so "tummy" is a close approximation. There are several other related questions that adults would usually assume the child might ask next, such as "How did I get out of your tummy?" and "How did I get in there?" But children often are content with that first query and may not raise the others till several years later.

On the Binet Scale children can copy a square long before they are able to trace a diamond. This same variation seems to be true regarding their sex queries. They first inquire, "Where did I come from?" and the logical follow-up queries may not occur for a year or more later. If they don't ask the additional questions, you may wait until later when they do inquire, or give them the information voluntarily. In my experience, I find that children do not absorb it till they are ready, so it apparently does no harm to offer them more sound sex education than they ask for.

To that query, "How did I get out?" you can tactfully reply, "There are several ways. In one of them (Caesarian birth), the physician puts Mother to sleep so she can't feel anything, and then he cuts a little door in the tummy wall and thus lets the baby out. Then he sews it up again, much as the Little Red Hen did the cloth sack of the Fox after she had placed the stone in it following her escape. Don't you remember that story about the Little Red Hen?"

The latter query diverts the child, in case you are surrounded by other people and prefer not to go further with the normal process of birth. But make it a rule to answer the

child when he asks! Don't stall him off! And if he later
inquires, "How did I get in your tummy?" which is usually
the third question in the sequence, you can reply:

"God put some tiny eggs in every little girl. When she
grows up and marries, then one of these eggs may turn into
a baby."

In dealing with some of these delicate situations in child
training, it is well to memorize your answers, as a star salesman does his canned sales talk, for you can't depend on the
inspiration of the moment. Remember, too, that the child is
purely scientific at the outset so his queries about his origin
are no different in his mind than a similar question about
where the sun goes at night. Unprepared adults, who blush
or giggle self-consciously, are generally responsible for making
children salacious in their attitude about such matters.

Merits of "Earned" vs. "Gift" Money for Children.
The aim of child education is to prepare youngsters for the
problems of real life. But life makes no allowances for anybody. The pay-off is based primarily on accomplishment. So
in dealing with children, it is wiser to let them earn their own
spending money than to place them on a family "dole", popularly called an allowance.

By working for the nickels and dimes, they soon begin to
realize that money represents minted human life. It symbolizes
the many hours of sweat and toil that went into its acquisition.
Earned money is thus spent far more carefully than gift money.
"Easy come; easy go," is the proverb that explains why
Prodigal Sons and other recipients of gift money let it slip
through their hands so readily.

In every household there are plenty of special or "pay"
tasks that can be assigned to children of various age levels.
The rate of pay should be based on output, and the prevailing
wage scale in the neighborhood should be adhered to. It is
thus very unwise for a thoughtless parent or fond relative to

offer $1.00 for a task that normally rates only 50c in the neighborhood. Such lavish pay does more harm than good, for it discourages the morale of the entire group of children up and down the block.

Boys may be paid for cleaning windows at a piecework rate of 5c or 10c per window. If they do as good a job as an adult, pay the same rate, even though they may require far longer to accomplish the same task. Other special pay jobs might be tending the furnace, cleaning out the ashes, mowing the lawn, washing the auto or even simonizing it. They can also polish their dad's shoes or give him a scalp massage. Girls can likewise perform many of these tasks, plus the Saturday housecleaning, or ironing the flat work, washing the dishes, vacuuming the rugs, making the beds, etc. They may have their routine chores to perform, over and beyond these special pay tasks.

All children should be taught the three major parts to our national economy. The first consists of the creation of goods, as by manufacturing, mining, fishing, farming, etc. The second is called merchandising, which covers advertising and selling. Lastly, we have the credit field, which includes not only the individual credit man in a store or office, but also finance companies and lending agencies such as banks. Operating a newspaper route gives children the best all-around training in these different phases.

Newspaper carriers purchase their papers at wholesale prices. Then they must merchandise them to customers. In this process they learn to smile and be reasonably diplomatic. They must be faithful to duty and careful not to break a window pane when they sail a folded newspaper upon the porch. If a customer is irate, they must try to placate him. If he cancels his subscription or is a newcomer to the neighborhood, they try to sell him on becoming a permanent subscriber. Finally, they must handle their own collections, so they obtain the credit training in business. Occasionally they lose 70c or more when a deadbeat moves without paying his paper bill.

Because of this wide perspective, newspaper boys and girls are probably better trained in our American economic system than even the usual college student. They should make good marriage material as viewed from the angle of living on a budget, and I recommend them especially to personnel managers and colleges for jobs or scholarships. Carrying a newspaper route ranks in the same category as membership in the Boy Scouts in its character building functions.

A permanently happy home must be a solvent home, so we must stress the proper training of children in earning and handling money. Parents should encourage the youngsters to budget their funds and set aside their own contributions for Red Cross and the church.

"Dad, will you match whatever I give to the Red Cross?" our youngsters would ask, while they were in grammar school, and I always assented, for they wanted to raise as much as possible, since each room was competing with the others for the largest contribution. Sometimes they'd tax me 50c or $1.00 and sometimes several dollars, if it was a Thanksgiving fund for poor families. But they made the decision as to how much they could afford to give, and I simply agreed to match it. This kind of "gift" money is beneficial in its effect. Furthermore, occasional cash gifts to children, as for birthdays, are quite in order, but the regular cash dole in the form of an allowance is psychologically inferior to the pay-for-work plan.

Sex Worries That Complicate Happy Marriage.
In the past decade alone, I have handled more than 1,000,000 letters from fellow Americans which dealt with psychological dilemmas and marital or sexual problems. Other Consulting Psychologists and Professors in their personal counseling, have experienced the same type of cases. Indeed, most of the private consultations with the clergy also revolve around

similar maladjustments where sex is either the direct or indirect cause of the victim's seeking a personal interview. So we shall list the following typical sex worries.

(1) Organic Sexual Inferiority Complexes. These may often seem trivial but actually they fetter the happiness of thousands of adults. Here may be included such worries among women as the fact their busts are too flat or they have hairs on their breasts or a slight overgrowth of hair on their face or their legs, or they may have lost a breast or an ovary through surgery. In the case of males, the worries are often of an opposite type with a complex based on lack of adequate beard or hair on the man's chest, or loss of a gonad via surgery, or fretting about the size of the genitalia. Most of these dreads are unnecessary and simply indicate too much attention to one's own anatomy. The remedy lies in part in getting the true facts and then in extroverting one's attention.

For example, the human body is constructed so there is a good margin of safety with reference to many of its organs. Thus, we have two eyes and two ears, with one being a "spare tire," so to speak. We can likewise get along on one-half of one kidney and one-half of one lung, and about one-eighth of the liver tissue. One gonadal gland, too, is entirely adequate for vigorous sexual development and parenthood. The loss of one ovary and one Fallopian tube, therefore, does not prevent a woman from becoming a mother.

The hair on a man's chest, or its absence, is a familial trait and not an indication of sexual vigor or potency. Some women likewise have a greater hair growth on the legs, but this is also no serious cause for worry. A fuzz on their chin or upper lip, as well as hairs on the breast, are likewise very common, and unless of such an extreme nature as to qualify them for the bearded lady of the circus, usually have no medical disadvantages. Bearded ladies of the circus type, however, may have a masculinizing tumor of the ovary.

Furthermore, a flat bust may be even more functional in

later motherhood than the fuller breasts of a beauty queen, for the thing that counts in lactation is the amount of secretory mammary glands, and the full breast often is deficient in this tissue. Size of the male genitalia likewise has no more bearing on sexual vigor than does the size of the skull on the I.Q within it (See p. 314).

(2) Pregnancy Complexes. Many expectant mothers still fret about "marking" their babies because of shock or dreadful emotional experiences. They also think that pica, which is strong craving for some special food, such as strawberries will mark the baby with a strawberry blotch on the skin if their hunger isn't satisfied. There is no medical or psychological evidence to support this superstition. The umbilical cord is the only anatomical connection between mother and child prior to its birth, and it contains no nerves whatsoever. No thoughts or emotions of the expectant mother can thus go across to the unborn baby. She can't influence it by her mental attitude before birth any more than she can the day after its birth while it is nursing at her breast.

Many husbands become relatively impotent and sometimes engage in clandestine affairs at this critical time, partly because their wives are viewed as medically abnormal. Or the husband may become so protective and respectful that he cannot wax ardent with his wife. She becomes associated with hospitals and a vague emotional inhibition may ultimately make him entirely passive in the erotic realm. In his resulting worry and dread of impotence, he may start drinking and may unintentionally become unfaithful during his drunken spree. Wise wives should anticipate this dangerous possibility and never lose their sweetheart appeal just because they are expecting a baby. Pregnancy is a normal physiological process and not incompatible with marital relations.

(3) Complexes of the Climacteric. From time immemorial women of all races have often become neurotic, crying, frus-

trated and afflicted with many other menopausal symptoms after the age of 40. In most cases, these are based on a mistaken notion that the uterus is a primary sexual organ, which it is not. A young wife with fibroids may suffer the surgical removal of her womb (hysterectomy), or a wife of 45 may have it cease its regular function due to age, yet both wives can still be thrilling and thrillable in the marital relation. In fact, the uterus has scarcely any more effect on a wife's marital charm than does the vermiform appendix on her digestive efficiency.

Women can remain seductive and thrilling as long as they live, for it is not the uterus but the tactile nerve endings in the genitalia that count. And as they are linked with the central nervous system, they bear no terminal date line. Like the tastebuds of the tongue or the rods and cones of the retina, these sensitive receptor cells don't suddenly drop from 100% efficiency to zero! Possibly as we grow older we lose 5% or more of our general sensitivity, but we don't dramatically drop to nothing just because we have passed the age of 40 or 45. In some cases, glandular extracts are indicated for such patients, but in my extensive experience, I find that normal saline is just about as effective for the great majority of them, since their trouble lies chiefly in their mind.

Men often go into similar emotional upheaval at this time which we call the "Ponce de Leon Complex." They suddenly imagine they are losing their erotic vigor. A defeatism complex soon develops which actually produces what they have dreaded, yet the entire process may be above the eyes, namely, mental. Then they may become caustic and bitter, criticizing their wives and insulting the latter by saying they never loved them, even on their wedding day. They may also start drinking heavily or gambling or staying out at lodge meetings and other real or manufactured engagements, for they are afraid to face their wives lest the latter wonder why they are no longer affectionate. The men are panicky lest their wives suspect the real truth, so if they come home drunk, they subconsciously realize this will divert the wife's attention from the man's impotence.

Many of these men go emotionally berserk when they finally have a clandestine date with some slender young thing, possibly half their age, and then discover that their romantic emotions, in psychological cold storage for many years, are now suddenly aflame once more. They become intoxicated with love rather than with their paramour. A wise wife should prevent this tragic event by waxing more ardent and aggressive in her boudoir so she will banish her husband's secret dread long before it leads to such devastating consequences. God intended marriages to be permanently happy affairs, but He expects us to use scientific techniques to accomplish this goal.

Psychosomatic Medicine and Hypnotherapy.

Psychosomatic medicine is zooming in its importance, for we are learning of the tremendous effect of the mind on bodily health. It pertains to those bodily ailments which are rooted in psychic, emotional or mental causation. Notice the following current case of a prominent newspaper executive, who was a college graduate, married and the father of two youngsters.

Because he had been troubled with a cough for a few days, he stopped to see a doctor. The latter gave him a cursory examination; then asked, "Joe, don't you have night sweats?" Joe said he never had. "Well, you ought to," affirmed the doctor, "for one of your lungs is entirely destroyed by tuberculosis. You are through with journalism as of now—3 o'clock this afternoon. I'm making a reservation for you at my private sanitarium for 9 o'clock tomorrow morning, and you'll be there not just a day or a week or a month, but at least a year and maybe more."

Joe's morale was devastated. He had no financial reserves, so he didn't know how he was going to support his family, let alone pay for the sanitarium treatment. As he approached his home, his wife looked out the window and saw him. She decided something terrible must have happened, so she rushed to the door to greet him. He told her the dire news. She indignantly informed him that he did NOT have tuberculosis, and that if he did, she wouldn't believe it till he consulted a reputable M.D. who was a specialist in chest medicine and who confirmed the diagnosis with x-rays. Then she called the other man who had made the original diagnosis and cancelled her husband's appointment at his sanitarium.

She gave her husband a good dinner and tried to buoy up his morale. They went to bed at 10 P.M., but at 2 A.M. her husband awakened just drenched in a severe night sweat. Perspiration streamed off him as if he were in a Turkish bath. His wife had to give him dry pajamas because he was so wet. Joe was now sure he was dying, but he finally drifted off to sleep again. Shortly after 4 o'clock, however, he awaked again just oozing perspiration at every pore. It stood out in drops on his brow. His wife again had to give him dry pajamas and also was forced to change both the upper as well as the lower sheets on the bed because they were so soaked with Joe's night sweat.

Next morning Joe consulted a bona fide M.D. who examined him thoroughly, including the taking of x-rays. The physician finally conluded by saying, "Joe, there isn't a single sign of tuberculosis in your chest. You are as sound as a dollar." But when Joe still looked gloomy, the medic inquired, "What's the matter, man? You should feel good."

"Well, doctor," said Joe, "I don't want to seem disrespectful but I can't believe your diagnosis." So the physician then made a final delicate test called the sputum test, which involves injecting some of the patient's sputum into a guinea pig. Later, the lymph glands of the pig are sliced and stained; then examined under a microscope. If any possible tubercle bacilli are present, they will almost inevitably show up. But Joe was again negative. He insisted in a re-test, however, before he grudgingly admitted he must be O.K.

"Dr. Crane," Joe confided in me, "I went back for three

more years to have those sputum tests performed before I finally felt secure, and even now—25 years later—if I get a cough I think to myself, 'Joe, maybe you're coming down with T.B.'."

Joe's negative thinking sprouted such an organic symptom as severe night sweats. The latter are, admittedly, often a symptom of tuberculosis, though not always so. That quack had implanted this negative thought in Joe's mind. It percolated in his subconscious until it short-circuited across into his autonomic nervous system and thus stimulated his sweat glands. By the strongest act of voluntary thought, you and I can't make sweat suddenly stand out upon our brow. Yet Joe did so, even when sound asleep! So you can see why thoughts and fears experienced in the central nervous system, can provide a wide variety of psychosomatic symptoms.

In this connection, Dr. Thomas O. Burgess has been doing pioneer work with members of the American Dental Association in the use of hypnotherapy as a therapeutic agent for reducing fears and tensions in dental patients. What he has done for dentistry is comparable to the recent progress in obstetrics by which expectant mothers have been able to go through childbirth with little or no anesthesia, all because of previous psychotherapy.

Millions of people are hypochondriacs largely because they have concentrated so long upon their "innards" that they have become hypersensitive. They actually feel pain which the normal, extroverted individual never notices. In an interesting experiment a few years ago, Dr. A. C. Ivy, eminent physiologist, swallowed a small deflated balloon. Then it was inflated and he was asked to tell where he thought it was located—esophagus, stomach, duodenum, jejunum, etc. At the outset, he was very vague in his judgments, for normally we are not aware of peristaltic movements or tactile sensation in the gastro-intestinal tract. But with continued practice, Dr. Ivy became very accurate. After each guess, an x-ray was taken to double check. His experience shows that we can apparently become hypersensitive to abdominal sensations by long continued attention to our anatomy.

How to Prevent Nervous Breakdowns and Insanity.

We have an axiom in psychology to the effect that human beings always like to return to the person or place where they have previously been happy. A corollary states that people flee from, or withdraw from, situations which seem cold or cruel and forbidding. Tersely stated, if an environment inflates our ego, we like it and approach. If it hurts us, either physically or psychologically, we cringe and shrink from further contacts.

Insanity is often a flight from reality. Some deranged states do develop from organic causes, such as syphilitic infection of the nervous system with a resulting paresis, as well as arteriosclerotic changes and those traceable to alcohol and metallic poisons. But the most serious type of insanity, schizophrenia, seems to be functional and is being treated with considerable success by such great psychiatrists as the famous Menninger brothers (Drs. Karl and Will).

They are setting the pace in the psychiatric world by their return of approximately 80% of patients in the Topeka State Hospital to useful lives on the outside. And their secret is not primarily based on drugs, electro-shock therapy, surgery or other conventional methods but is contained in the word "love." By affection, kindliness and gentleness, these patients are being re-conditioned to look upon external reality as something pleasant, so they no longer wish to withdraw from it. "Our patients are simply people who have bumped up against a tough outside world," says Dr. Karl Menninger, "so they come away with the feeling of being rejected and unloved. They withdraw from reality."

It behooves parents and teachers, therefore, to help build up a child's fondness for external reality so he will have so many pleasures and valued possessions and friends and loved ones therein, that his imaginary world can't compete therewith. Children also need to see their parents kiss and go on dates regularly just to be sure that love exists between them, for thousands of youngsters are unnecessarily worried lest their parents may become divorced.

Children need more praise and less caustic criticism from their parents, too, for they hear family quarrels and receive deflating reprimands so often that they frequently believe they aren't loved. This feeling of emotional insecurity is a most devastating influence on children. Parents and teachers should all join the "Compliment Club" and pay a minimum of three sincere compliments every day. And school teachers should smile freely, especially in the early grades.

Nervous breakdowns are not to be confused with a psychosis. They indicate long continued frustration or conflict between two strongly opposing forces which produce physical exhaustion. Fear and sexual guilt often are at the bottom of these breakdowns. The victim may flee into an exaggerated activity and simply burn up energy for 18 hours per day in his attempt to hide from his inner torment. Like Jonah, he runs away from the issues as long as possible, only to be engulfed in a storm and finally tossed overboard. Facing each issue is good insurance against nervous breakdowns. Obtain all the scientific counsel possible, especially from a psychologist and clergyman. Then resolutely do your duty. Teaming up with God is also the best antidote as will be explained more fully in Chapter XVIII.

How to Break the Tobacco and Liquor Habits. In law there is a distinction made between small crimes and larger ones, as indicated by petty larceny versus grand larceny. In the realm of our bad habits, this same type of distinction can be made, for obesity, vulgar speech, emotional intem-

---

"Tact is the ability to describe others as they see themselves."
—Abraham Lincoln.

perance, smoking, and drinking might be placed in a psychological hierarchy.

Tobacco costs the cigaret smoker approximately $115 per year, so it is economically unwise. Medically, it has many hazards, too, so it is smart to avoid this nuisance habit or to break it, if you are now its victim. In our hectic modern age, the muscular behavior involved in searching for a cigaret, shaking one out of the pack, lighting it and then waving the arm back and forth at regular intervals in the act of smoking, drains off nervous energy. It seems to lower the electrical potential in the central nervous system so the smoker feels less like "blowing his top."

In breaking this habit, therefore, it is wise to muster up great emotional fervor. Then stop all at once; don't try to taper off. Meanwhile, give your hand and arm a chance to function in the familiar smoker's pattern, as by carrying candy coated gum in the usual pocket. You can then reach in, shake out a chiclet, place it in your mouth and chew vigorously for 15 to 30 minutes. Whenever you feel nervous again and wish an outlet, repeat the process with your candy coated gum.

The alcoholic habit is bad because it subverts human intelligence and predisposes to accidents on the highways and in the factories. One of its greatest dangers is the fact it slows down one's reaction time but he doesn't realize this fact so fails to make allowances for it. The fine organization called Alcoholics Anonymous has developed a number of our standard psychological axioms into their famous "12 Steps." They have learned that nothing can be done to help a drunkard who doesn't sincerely want to free himself from his slavery to John Barleycorn.

They also find that the victim who glibly says, "Sure, I can quit whenever I want to," is not likely to be a good prospect. They also stress quick victories. For example, they don't ask an addict to quit liquor forever, or even focus on a 3-months' dry period. No, they work only on a 24-hour plan! The

"People do not lack strength; they lack will."   —Victor Hugo drunkard tries to avoid liquor "just for today." Next morning he repeats this same 24-hour plan. It inflates his ego to win these small battles.

Meanwhile he is made the protege of a big brother who has been a drunkard every bit as depraved as himself, but who has stayed dry for several months. These big brothers are most generous in their donation of time and money to help their protege. Moreover, they don't criticize nor stress the negative, but ignore lapses and are very liberal with praise for all good behavior. They schedule regular city-wide meetings, too, at which several members confess their own drunken past. The beginners thus don't feel that they are surrounded by saints who are simply taking a patronizing attitude. Then the city organization divides into small groups for cottage meetings each week, much like the old fashioned prayer meetings, wherein everybody gives his "testimony." The help of God Almighty is always invoked for God is the Biggest Brother of all in this admirable organization.

Since the heavy drinker is usually a victim of vitamin deficiency, especially of the Vitamin "B" complex, he needs a nourishing menu and nerve stimulants to carry him along during the first few weeks. Like the epileptic, however, who soon learns to utilize his "aura" as a preceding symptom of a convulsion, the alcoholic must also detect his dangerous premonitory symptoms of frustration, fear, loneliness or shame and instead of going on a binge, immediately launch in the opposite direction as vigorously as possible, knowing he is allergic to liquor. If he is an A.A. member, he should contact his sponsor or big brother at once.

The very best way to break the liquor habit, however, is to avoid taking the first drink. That's the one, moreover, which members of Alcoholics Anonymous try to shun. We need student chapters of A.A. on hundreds of campuses. Here are the 12 essential steps in the creed of A.A. The first 3 are intended to deal with intellectual humility. The next 6 are the "housecleaning" steps, while the final 3 furnish the A.A.

program for maintaining sobriety. They are psychologically quite sound.

(1) We admitted we were powerless over alcohol—that our lives had become unmanageable.

(2) Came to believe that a Power greater than ourselves could restore us to sanity.

(3) Made a decision to turn our will and our lives over to the care of God as we understood Him.

(4) Made a searching and fearless moral inventory of ourselves.

(5) Admitted to God, to ourselves, and to another human being the exact nature of our wrongs.

(6) Were entirely ready to have God remove all these defects of character.

(7) Humbly asked Him to remove our shortcomings.

(8) Made a list of all persons we had harmed, and became willing to make amends to them all.

(9) Made direct amends to such people wherever possible, except when to do so would injure them or others.

(10) Continued to take personal inventory and when we were wrong promptly admitted it.

(11) Sought through prayer and meditation to improve our conscious contact with God as we understood Him praying only for knowledge of His will for us and the power to carry that out.

(12) Having had a spiritual experience as the result of these steps, we tried to carry this message to alcoholics, and to practice these principles in all our affairs.

REFERENCES

1 AHMANN, M., Race: Challange to Religion (Regnery, 1963).
2 ALEXANDER, F. G., The History of Psychiatry (Harper & Row, 1966)
3 APPEL & STRECKER, Discovering Ourselves (Macmillan, 1964)
4 BERGLER, E., Tensions Can Be Reduced to Nuisances (Collier, 1962).
5 BLOOD & WOLFE, Husbands and Wives (Brunner, 1962).

6 BURKE, F., *God is for Real, Man* (Association Press, 1966).

7 BURGESS, T. O., "Hypnotherapy" *(Cal Dental Magazine,* Oct.-Nov., 1950).

8 BUSS, A. H., *The Psychology of Aggression* (Wiley, 1961).

9 CRANE, P. M., *The Democrat's Dilemma* (Regnery, 1964).

10 DONALDSON, E. F., *Personal Finance* (Ronald, 1948).

11 DUCKER, E. N., *Christian Therapy for a Neurotic World* (Taplinger, 1963).

13 FRANK, J. D., *Persuasion and Healing* (Brunner, 1962).

14 FURBAY, J. H., *Workbook Manual for Marriage and the Family* (Appleton, 1949).

15 GESELL, A., & ILG, F. L., *The Child From Five to Ten* (Harper, 1946).

16 GODDARD, H. H., *How to Rear Children in the Atomic Age* (Hopkins, 1948).

17 HARRIS, I. D., *Emotional Blocks to Learning* (Brunner, 1962).

18 HEARN, C. A., *What About Smoking* (Irwin, 1950).

19 HOKE, R. E., *How You Can Have Success Unlimited* (Psych. Service Center, Charlotte, N. C., 1956).

20 HOPKINS, P., *Gone Up in Smoke* (Highland Press, 1948).

21 HURLOCK, E. B., *Child Growth & Development* (McGraw-Hill, 1955).

23 KELLER, W., *The Bible as History* (Morrow, 1956).

24 LATZ, L. J., *The Rhythm of Fertility and Sterility in Women* (Latz Found., 1947).

25 MAYER, J. E., *Jewish-Gentile Courtships* (Macmillan, 1962).

26 MYKLEBUST, H. R., *Your Deaf Child* (Thomas, 1954).

27 NEWTON, NILES, *Family Care of Child Care* (Harper, 1957).

28 PERRY, J., *17 Million Jobs* (McGraw-Hill, 1960).

29 PEARSON, G. H. J., *Adolescence & Conflict of Generations* (Basic, 1960).

30 RYNEARSON, E. H., *Obesity* (Thomas, 1954).

31 SHULTZ, G. D., *Letters to Jane* (Lippincott, 1948).

32 STOLZ, L. M., *Father Relations of War-Born Children* (Stanford U. Pr., 1954).

33 STONE & STONE, *A Marriage Manual* (Simon & Schuster, 1960).

34 WYLIE, P., "Encourage Young Marriages" *(Family Weekly,* 6/7/59).

35 YOUNG, P. T., *Motivation & Emotion* (Wiley, 1964).

LET WIVES OF STRIKERS VOTE

Wives are the chief sufferers in unwise labor disputes, for their frugal habits and bank accounts become sabotaged quickly. Thus, they lose incentive for saving money in the future. Arbitration needs to replace the present costly labor deadlocks. And all wives of workers should be granted equal suffrage re strikes. *Editor & Publisher* (6/20/59) reports the end of a strike deadlock of 123 days by the stereotypers at the San Jose newspaper. The weekly pay gains ranged from $3.50 to $5.50. But the top workers lost 17 weeks pay at $137 per week, so it will take 423 weeks (over 8 full years) at the new scale before they will be even! Pity the poor wives!

CHAPTER XVIII

PSYCHOLOGY GOES TO CHURCH

Civilization, which is represented by progress in arts, science and statecraft, must never be confused with Christianization. These two terms are definitely not synonymous. At the outbreak of World War II, Germany and Italy were certainly rated as civilized nations. Japan, too, was included in this category. For these nations had as good art as did America. Their chemists and physicists were just as advanced as ours, and their science of government was excellent. Yet they browbeat smaller nations and advocated superiority of one race over another. They finally resorted to barbaric mass murders.

Without the moral influence of the churches to humanize man's relations with his fellows, we would still be as brutish as the denizens of the jungle. "Might makes right" is the rule of all mammals below mankind. Even our domesticated dogs and cats, or pet pigs on the farm, have no unselfishness whatever for their own brothers and sisters. If a sow has a litter of pigs and one of the litter is stunted or a runt, do the sturdier brother and sister pigs stand back from the swill trough and say: "Brother Runt, you are more in need of food than I, so you may drink first"? You know they don't! In fact, they shoulder him away and gorge themselves till they are about to burst.

Even then, they don't let him taste the dregs, for they jump into the trough and lie down lengthwise, or at least used to do so until smart farmers learned to put crossbars at stipulated intervals to prevent their spilling the remaining swill upon the ground. And what is thus true of pigs, is equally true of puppies or kittens in your own home. Animals have no sympathy for, nor unselfishness towards, their own siblings, or even their parents.

Human babies likewise are selfish at the start. And they would apparently stay selfish all their lives if it were not for the moral instruction which they receive from parents, clergymen, Scout leaders and other religious teachers. Just because modern boys and girls are surrounded by television and movies, bath tubs and other evidences of civilization, doesn't mean they will also be unselfish and Christian. Our leading gangsters live in modern apartments, too, but modern plumbing doesn't make morality.

Nor do the latest household conveniences teach unselfishness! Changing tenement hovels into modern housing projects still doesn't alter personality in regard to ethical rules! No, we must be taught specific moral precepts or we'll be wolfish despite the latest scientific inventions and luxurious conveniences in our homes. Civilization actually makes mankind far more destructive than he was in the Stone Age, unless he has meanwhile been Christianized, for H-Bombs and other modern weapons simply expand his lethal influence.

Our churches are fortunately availing themselves of the latest psychological techniques for helping spread constructive moral instruction. And that is very proper, for Jesus was the foremost Applied Psychologist of all time. Just read the four gospels, Matthew, Mark, Luke and John, from this angle and you will be astounded at Christ's consummate skill in handling people, whether in crowds or during private interviews.

Jesus—The World's Greatest Applied Psychologist. The tremendous influence which Jesus exerted over people was not due to their belief that he was the Son of God. Why, even his 12 Apostles were not clear in their own minds on that point on the very day of the crucifixion, or they would never have deserted him. And they couldn't believe it was the Messiah who later stood before them as they huddled, fearful and downcast, in that famous Upper Room.

No, Jesus attracted huge crowds chiefly because he was a

past master of Applied Psychology and thus knew how to handle an audience with perfect ease. Moreover, Christ did not talk in a timid, weak voice! How do we know? Because he addressed outdoor audiences that numbered 5,000 men, not to mention the women and children. Since women and children almost invariably have outnumbered men in all churches, whether in pagan temples during the ages before Christ, or in modern cathedrals, it is logical to assume that he spoke to at least 10,000 people at one time in the great outdoors. Remember, too, he had no modern amplifying system! His powerful voice must have been far superior even to that of the great William Jennings Bryan. No wonder Matthew and Mark both exclaimed: "He taught them as one having authority, and not as the scribes." Christ's powerful voice and positive statements must have been largely accountable for his "authority," since the people didn't yet believe that Jesus was the Son of God.

Jesus also employed the anecdotal or episodic formula by which he strung together a series of parables or relevant stories to amplify his major ethical principles. This always makes an interesting type of speech, for we never lose our delight in actual cases and narratives. Alas, many devout clergymen haven't yet profited from this forensic formula.

Jesus employed the "reversible why" to sidestep the dangerous 2-horned dilemmas that his enemies used to entrap him. Remember his classical retort about rendering tribute to Caesar (Matthew 22:17)? Or his oral contract with his critics who wanted to know whence came his power? When they declined to answer his query first, he used a very interesting retort: "Neither do I tell you." (Mark 11:33). He didn't say he couldn't tell!

Christ invariably preached a positive gospel. He was not an ecclesiastical "detective" seeking to catch people in sins, whether big or little. No, he stressed eternal projects like brotherhood and the Golden Rule. To demonstrate lack of prejudice, he employed a Samaritan (the most despised of all races in the eyes of the Hebrews) as the hero of his Good Samaritan Story. And then to prove that he wasn't simply theorizing, he fraternized with the Samaritan woman at the well, and even asked her for a drink of water (John 4: 4-26). Jesus likewise did not believe in choking out basic moral truths by an excessive adherence to petty ritual. Thus, when his disciples were criticized for not washing their hands before eating, Christ retorted, "Not that which goeth into the mouth defileth a man; but that which cometh out of the mouth, this defileth a man." (Matthew 15:11).

Moreover, when his disciples began to pluck the wheat and eat it as they journeyed through the fields on the Sabbath, the Pharisees criticized them. Jesus quickly defended his disciples and, like a modern college debater, first went back into history to show a precedent for similar behavior on the part of David and his men. Then Christ delivered what was really an ecclesiastical knockout punch. For the highly ritualized religion of his day was predicated on a slavish deference to the Sabbath. That was one of its main foundation pillars. Jesus indicted their abject serfdom to ritual by exclaiming, "The Sabbath was made for man, and not man for the Sabbath." (Mark 2:27).

Christ was also fond of fun and dinner parties. He liked to spend week-ends at the home of Mary, Martha and Lazarus. But such visiting obviously involved good meals. His first miracle was not at a funeral or military parade but at a wedding feast. He started the first church picnic when he fed the 5,000. He said farewell to his Apostles at the Last Supper. And upon his resurrection, he broke bread with the two travelers with whom he had walked en route to Emmaus. On another occasion after his resurrection he called to some of his Apostles who were fishing and asked: "Children, have ye any meat?" (John 21:5). When they reached shore, Jesus had a fire of coals ready with fish laid thereon and bread, and invited them to dine. This is unique in that Jesus served as the host to this breakfast party, whereas he had always previously been entertained as the distinguished guest. Strong's *Concordance* lists 38 references where Jesus is associated with meat, plus 107 more allusions to eating.

Since Christ was possessed of an athletic physical body, and since he was not afflicted with the fears that beset his disciples, who were never certain when they might be arrested or their ship might founder, Jesus probably reacted with normal hunger. He was never neurotic, tense or afflicted with spastic colitis, as they may have been. Though they might be scared until they had forgotten food or weren't interested in dining, I believe that Jesus with the regularity of clockwork, would ask, "Isn't it dinner time?" Certainly this is a very logical psychological deduction. And I mention it because it explains a very strange request that Jesus made in the Upper Room. For, after his resurrection, when his Apostles couldn't believe that Jesus really stood before them, he asked, "Have ye here any meat?" (Luke 24:41-43). "And they gave him a piece of a broiled fish, and of an honeycomb. And he took it and did eat before them." Then they knew him! Why?

Did Jesus request that food just to prove that he wasn't a wraith or apparition, which is, of course, quite plausible? Or had his hearty appetite and keen enjoyment of meals become so linked with his personality that his Apostles may even have teased him good-naturedly about always being ready to dine, though they were often too terrified or apprehensive to feel the pangs of hunger? So now, when logic couldn't make them understand that Christ was before them, and when the sight of his wounded hands and feet wouldn't banish their disbelief, might not Jesus have fallen back on the one sure method of clinching his identity, namely, his familiar request: "Have you anything to eat?" If you will read your Bible from a psychological slant, you will be re-thrilled with a new concept of Christ.

"Men must be governed by God or they will be ruled by tyrants."
—William Penn

In this connection, you will therefore find that Jesus believed in advertising, for he sent the 70 ahead of him, two by two, to prepare and recruit the crowds for his own arrival later on (Luke 10:1). He knew they'd be more courageous in pairs! Moreover, Christ likewise engaged in consumer surveys and polls of public opinion (Matthew 16: 13). It is also quite possible that Jesus was only feigning sleep during the storm at sea (Mark 4:37-39) just so he could observe how his Apostles would react. He may have been simply making a psychological "sounding" as it were as to the depth of their faith after all those months in his company.

Jesus also understood the fickleness of crowds, for when great mobs trailed him after he had fed the 5,000, he told them, "Ye seek me, not because ye saw the miracles, but because ye did eat of the loaves and were filled." Of the 10 lepers whom he healed, only one (10%) returned even to say "Thank you." Despite the many thousands whom he had healed and fed, only Peter had the courage to draw near during the trial, and he was so scared that mob psychology stampeded him into a triple denial. Despite all the mistreatment Jesus received from the very people he was helping, he still didn't lose faith in them but resolutely went on to the crucifixion to fulfill his destiny! That's a marvelous characteristic of Christ.

During World War II, a Hebrew soldier was heard to ask, "What could any future Messiah have on Jesus? So what are we waiting for?" That question has intrigued me during the intervening few years. Can you describe even one thing which might be added to Jesus that would qualify him more fully for the Messiah? Or can you suggest the elimination of any trait or action attributed to Christ by either Matthew, Mark, Luke or John, which detracts from his being the Son of God? For example, don't you want your Messiah to smile and attract children until they climb into his lap? Don't you wish a Christ to heal the sick, feed the hungry, give hope to the despondent and preach the absence of prejudice, as well as intolerance? Don't you prefer a Messiah who stresses fundamentals instead of trivialities? And who is voluntarily so forgiving that he would say of his murderers, "Father, forgive them; for they know not what they do"? If this is what you really want, then what are you waiting for? Better put your shoulder behind the constructive wheel of the church and help push it along. That's why I have missed church but 3 times in the past 30 years. For it requires more than tacit assent to make this world better. It requires action. "Faith, if it hath not works, is dead." (James 2:17).

Why Partnership With God Promotes Better Health. One reason for the alarming increase in nervous breakdowns and other types of mental illness, is a feeling of emotional insecurity. During World War II approximately 2,000,000 men and women were either rejected by their examining boards, or later discharged, because of mental and nervous ailments. This high incidence of psychological casualties occurred while our government was attempting to develop a military force that finally totalled 11,608,000 by 1945.

The general public is meanwhile becoming so neurotic that one eminent psychiatrist recently said half the American people would be in sanitariums in another generation, with the other half required to wait upon them! While that was probably intended as hyperbole, it does indicate a serious trend. And here is one of the basic causes for it. As children, we lean upon our parents. They seem omniscient and omnipotent to our childish minds. Later we realize they are only human beings, too, but as long as they live we still tend to feel a sloughing off of responsibility when we return to our old homesteads and let our parents take over.

Many high pressure business executives and factory heads, possibly 50 years of age themselves and directing thousands

---

"Sometimes an open mind is too porous to hold a conviction."
                                                                —*Banking*

of employees, will thus grow weary of such weighty responsibilities. So they may drive back to their old home town for a week-end visit with their aged parents. The latter then assert their former parental prerogatives and even order these "big shot" sons to wear their overshoes if it happens to rain. Or an elderly mother may send the noted offspring to the neighborhood store for groceries, and he meekly follows orders. In fact, he subconsciously relishes the childlike role which he now re-enacts, for he can let his parents boss him around as of yore and make the decisions. This is a mental rest for him. After a few days, however, he may again return to his hectic executive post back in the city and carry on with his executive duties.

But the time ultimately arrives when his father and mother pass onward to their reward. He now finds himself the oldest of the line. Vaguely he senses the fact that he is looked to by his wife and children, as well as his employees, for advice, direction, or support. But from time to time he still wishes for a chance to "go back home" himself and be a child again. He yearns for a release temporarily from responsibility with its burdens of making decisions. But his parents are no longer there at the old homestead to give him his childhood relaxation.

Eventually, therefore, the tension produces peptic ulcer or spastic colitis or hypertension and many other psychosomatic manifestations. He finds it difficult to sleep soundly, for insomnia hounds his slumber. During the day, he may resort to liquor and become a chain smoker. At night he may rely on sleeping tablets. Since he now knows he is trying to solve his problems all alone, he may grow unduly fearful about his health and become a hypochondriac, who shops around from one physician to another, more for sympathy than for medicine. The physicians are thus glorified "parents" to millions of distraught patients who simply crave comfort and reassurance.

However, if such a man links up with God Almighty in an

active daily partnership, he can throw off his tension at night and, in effect, say a prayer somewhat as follows: "Oh, Heavenly Father, we are partners, but now I need sleep, so please take over the night shift for me!" This vivid realization that one has a Heavenly Father to fall back upon, will produce remarkable medical benefits. It lessens the tension, so one's peptic ulcer is not so likely to start gnawing, for the hydrochloric acid secretion is then diminished. Blood pressure will also drop, for fear elevates blood pressure, while peace and confidence reduce it.

At the start of World War II, a retired Army Colonel consulted me about his blood pressure. His private physician had taken it at 135, but the army doctor caught it the same day at 219. The latter realized the Colonel was apprehensive and suggested that he come back for a second test a week later. The Colonel told me he had a complex about military doctors, for he could always feel himself grow tense and panicky whenever a medic in military uniform approached him. Well, the Colonel consulted two more physicians in private practice during the next few days. They tabulated his systolic pressure at 136 and 138. But when the army doctor again tested him, his blood pressure was 223. That remarkable increase was obviously on an emotional basis. Now the reverse tends to occur when one falls asleep unafraid and relaxed. God lowers our blood pressure!

Alas, we still have in the United States nearly 68,000,000 religious "orphans" or non-church people. They are vainly struggling to carry all of their burdens alone. But that is too great a strain on people in this hectic modern age. So— when deprived of their parents or loved ones, either by death, or by absence from home on a distant college campus, or while in military service—they may undergo a nervous breakdown. The very best kind of insurance against such a state of maladjustment, therefore, is to team up with God and

---

"Nations of drunkards are nations of slaves."
                                        —Thomas G. Masaryk,
                                Former President of Czechoslovakia

become active each week in the work of your neighborhood church.

Contributions Of the Bible To Modern Society.

Astute Dr. Robert M. Hutchins (now of the Ford Foundation) has long been stressing the importance of our reading certain great books, and he deserves much commendation in this respect. But all the other great books combined have had but a trivial influence on modern society when compared with the Bible. Just look around you today and see the offshoots of the Bible.

For example, most of our colleges and universities have been founded by churches, which are really Bible societies. Our Y.M.C.A., Y.W.C.A., and C.Y.O. Halls are due to the Bible. So, too, are most of our hospitals, plus the Red Cross and the Salvation Army. Where do the Boy Scouts and Girl Scouts meet on Friday nights? In churches! Where do you find edifices on the Sabbath that are crowded with people at their very best?

Why, the churches, of course, for there people are not only scrubbed behind their ears and generally clean in body, but they are dressed as spotlessly as possible and entertaining lofty ideas, as well as noble sentiments. Human beings may react like animals at other times, or grow pugnacious while witnessing a prize fight, or salacious and drunken in taverns, but in church they are usually more nearly divine than àt any other hour or place during the week. Incidentally, think of the billions of dollars in valuable real estate sites now occupied by churches, which are Bible outgrowths. Are any other great books so memorialized in modern society?

For instance, do you know of any contemporary Aristotle University? Ever hear of a Socrates College? Or an Archimedes Youth Hall? Has Shakespeare caused the erection of any hospitals? Do the Boy and Girl Scouts meet in Victor Hugo Halls? Is there any Salvation Army or Red Cross rooted in Goethe's writings? Why, even our merchants defer two months out of the year in their advertising to events depicted in just one great book—the Bible. For they use the Christmas theme almost before Thanksgiving is over, and in the spring they employ the Easter motif in window displays and newspaper advertisements. Most of the great music and art, too, are of direct or indirect Bible origin, so every person should read it as an intellectual tribute to its tremendous social influence, apart from its great moral values.

At least, you should study the first four gospels of the New Testament, namely, Matthew, Mark, Luke and John. I started reading the Bible at the age of seven, beginning with Genesis and continuing on through Revelation. I had read it through in its entirety 6 times before I finished high school and twice more during college years. General MacArthur had read it 6 times before he graduated at the head of his class from West Point. It was Abraham Lincoln's source of beautiful English prose, as exemplified in his Gettysburg Address. Shakespeare quoted it liberally.[9]

The Bible portrays the ethical evolution of mankind. Certain ancient people had a "corner," as it were, on contributions to man's cultural progress. Thus, the Phoenicians developed navigation and trade. The Greeks were noted for philosophy; the Romans for law; the Egyptians for astronomy. But the Hebrews were custodians of ethics. They were more than 1,000 years ahead of other contemporary civilized nations in their attitude toward God. Indeed, at the birth of Christ, Rome and Greece still worshiped a multiplicity of deities.

The King James version of the Bible contains 66 books, divided into the two major sections called the Old Testament and the New Testament. To recall how many books are in each of these two major divisions, use the "derivative" instead of the "rote memory" strategy. Thus, count the number of letters in "Old," which gives you 3. Do the same for "Testament" which totals 9. So there you have derived the 39 books of the Old Testament. Then multiply the 3 times 9 and you get 27, which is the number of books in the New Testament. According to Stimpson[43] there are 773,692 words in the King James version of the Bible. Of this total, 592,439 are in the Old Testament and 181,253 in the New Testament. Of the latter number, 36,450 are attributed to Jesus. To appreciate the terse style of writing in the Bible, notice that its 773,692 words contain a total of 3,566,480 letters, or an average of less than 5 letters per word! Advertising copy writers might well study its admirable compression of ideas and succinct exposition.

Why I Have Missed Church But 3 Times In 30 Years. Originally I was started to church by the wise teaching and diligent example of a Christian mother. But later I became aware of certain definite psychological reasons why every intelligent person should be a regular church attendant.

(1) It's a tonic for one's morale since it serves as spiritual calisthenics for one's good emotions. Psychologists realize that emotions, as well as muscles and glands, must be exercised regularly to be at their peak. And church attendance stimulates the good emotions linked with love and unselfishness and charity, instead of fear and anger and hatred.

(2) It permits you to exert a constructive reciprocal influence on the other church goers. Despite Thoreau's talk about worshiping God in the outdoors, that is not a substitute for church going. For human beings stimulate other human beings! Your presence at church thus buoys up my morale and vice versa. The good prophet Elijah once asked Jehovah to kill him because he grew so disheartened at not seeing other people at church. He cried out: "O Lord, take away my life. I, even I only, am left." But God told him there were still 7,000 other faithful souls in Israel who hadn't bowed the knee to the idol Baal. But they hadn't been at church with Elijah, apparently, so this reciprocal effect was lacking. And that's why you can't

---

"He who waits to do a great deal of good at once, will never do any."
—Dr. Samuel Johnson

worship God as well when you are away from church, for your personality will not cause a reciprocal improvement in the trees or fish or golf clubs with which you may be surrounded on Sunday morning in the great outdoors!

(3) It encourages you to make positive commitments of a laudable sort at the peak of your exalted mood, such as teaching a Sunday school class or visiting the sick or leading a Scout Troop or even doubling your contribution to foreign missions. And, having made such a pledge before your fellowmen, your pride then compels you to fulfill it. Incidentally, did you ever hear of a religious transformation of personality during a Sunday fishing trip or golf game or even a hike or picnic?

(4) It places you in contact with human beings who for at least that hour are at their very best in thought and deed.

(5) It serves as a token payment of the interest you owe on your debt to devout loved ones in previous generations who have helped make religious liberty an established fact, and who have surrounded you with the cultural benefits of Christian colleges, hospitals, the Red Cross, etc.

Why Tithing Needs To Be Revived By Churches. The ancient Hebrews were urged to pay God a tithe or 10% of their crops and herds. Many Catholic and Protestant church members nowadays have adopted this admirable custom. In fact, Uncle Sam even permits a 30% deduction for religious, charitable and educational organizations before income taxes are computed. I was reared to tithe all my earnings and have continued to do so to this day. Indeed, my mother taught us children that we weren't being generous until we went beyond that 10%.

A very unique modern experiment described by Jeffreys[28] deals with the famous "Biblical Wheat" tithing venture of a Michigan miller named Perry Hayden who planted exactly one cubic inch of wheat on a little plot of ground 4 feet wide by 8 feet long. At harvest time, Mr. Hayden deducted 10% of the crop as a tithe and gave it to the church, after which he planted the remainder the following season. A tithe of each new crop always went to the church. During the sixth and final year, the wheat fields covered 2,666 acres of land from which 72,150 bushels were harvested. Henry Ford cooperated in this remarkable venture. Since I was asked to furnish the title of the book describing this "Biblical Wheat" experiment, I recommended *God Is My Landlord* and as a consequence was asked to address the final concluding rally at the fair grounds at Adrian, Michigan.

Many people nowadays protest that they can't afford to tithe their income and give 10% to church or charitable causes. The curious fact that many people on $100 per month can still give 10% to the church, while others on $250 or more per month can't make ends meet, is partly explained by the fact that the tither has learned how to budget money wisely. Besides, God seems to cooperate well with those who team up with him, for I have never heard of a tither who starved or was without a roof over his head!

The Steward Secretary of a large church denomination recently informed me that he and his wife felt they couldn't afford to pay their 10% tithe any longer so they quit doing so. But they were always broke meanwhile and everlastingly in debt. So they finally decided to take out God's 10% of their income first, and give it to the church or other worthy causes. Then they'd try to live on the remaining 90%.

"Strange to say, Dr. Crane," this clergyman informed me, "we now live better on the 90% than we did on the entire 100% of my salary. And we are less harassed by unpaid bills and financial worries."

The Mormon Church[41] likewise makes tithing an integral part of its ritual, and the Mormons are noted for not having had people on relief during the last depression! Besides, tithers always have money available for good causes. They make the most regular contributors to churches. Their financial envelopes are always on the collection plate each Sunday. It has been found in church surveys, moreover, that the church people who make a financial pledge and then use the envelope system actually give about four times as much to churches as those who are sporadic or spur-of-the-moment cash donors.

Vital Importance Of Church Camps For Teen-Agers.

Mrs. Crane and I have sent each of our five children to a one-week summer church camp during their late grammar and high school years. I attended such camps twice during my own teen-age period and have spoken to many such gatherings of youth in the intervening decades. After a careful study of the matter I feel that it would be a great boon to both the churches and our youth if every young person could thus spend at least one week per summer at a church camp. Here are the psychological reasons why:

(1) The leaders of such camps are usually specially trained and talented in dealing with young people. Many clergymen of the home church, however, may not possess the skill in motivating adolescents and making them enthusiastic about humanitarian causes. Although such clerics may be excellent in dealing with the parent age group or with the elderly population in their parish, they may lack the specific techniques needed for swaying adolescents.

(2) The camp leaders also have a stratified audience, polarized in many of its basic attitudes and interests, instead of a heterogeneous crowd of all ages. Thus, they can utilize crowd psychology to stampede young people toward moral goals instead of toward cigarets or liquor.

(3) Church camps are the recruiting spot for religious leadership. There seems to be a natural stage of hero worship and spiritual idealism during adolescence which, if properly evoked

---

"War leaves 3 armies in its wake—an army of cripples, an army of mourners, and an army of thieves."　　—German Proverb and rightly channeled, can furnish the religious motive force for all one's future years. This is the age when high resolves and noble ideals produce that unique phenomenon described earlier in which there is a lump in the throat and a peculiar ache around the heart, plus a yearning to do great deeds for humanity. Nurses, missionaries and clergymen are recruited at this time in life. In former decades, such transformations in outlook were called "conversion." It is almost imperative that young people obtain this lofty moment of high resolve and spiritual commitment, or they may remain morally inert and cynical in their later adult life. During the peroration of a great speech or sermon, or the climax of an outstanding musical number, we adults may experience a resurrection of this same exhilarating mood which we underwent in the teens. But if we never experienced such a unique feeling at that time, we have nothing to be revived or re-incited.

(4) These attendants at church camps go back home to serve as sparkplugs in the machinery of the youth organizations of their local churches and thus pass along some of their religious enthusiasm and broadened outlook.

(5) The camp experience helps wean young people away from their mamma's apron strings, and thus fortifies youth against the dangerous nostalgia which still overcomes thousands on college campuses during the fall quarter of their freshman year.

How To Pep Up Church Attendance. In time of war the churches are usually crowded, partly because parents hope thereby to gain God's protection over their sons or daughters in the battle zone. They might fittingly be termed "foul weather" friends of the Almighty. Anxiety and terror stimulate them. But people should not be driven to church by fear! Religion is supposed to be a POSITIVE force that attracts because of its constructive appeal, rather than through a coercive or negative influence. In accordance with the "coaxing" vs. "clubbing" techniques (p. 15), note the following methods by which laymen can assist their priest, rabbi or minister in making the church a more effective force in the community.

(1) Employ the "block system." In politics a city block or section of farm land may be delegated to a specific worker whose job is to interview all the residents therein and find out their specific political affiliation. He sees that those of his party, plus the neutral voters, are encouraged to register. On election day, he makes sure they get to the polls, even if he must take his own car and deliver them in person, especially the feeble and semi-invalids. Many churches have utilized this block system to wonderful advantage. The young people may be paired off, two by two, as Jesus sent out his 70, and then allotted a residential section. They take a complete inventory.

"We are making a religious survey of this area," they can smilingly introduce themselves, "and wonder if you belong to any church?" If the householder is a church member but of a different denomination, the callers add, "We are trying to stimulate better church attendance for all churches, so it will raise our score if you will attend your own church next Sunday. We are in a contest, and thus obtain points for everybody who goes to church. We shall call again from week to week to keep our records up to date, so we hope you will not mind our ringing your doorbell again next week?" The latter should be said with a smile and the questioning inflection of the voice.

If the householder is already a member of your church, urge him to appear next Sunday. If he is a non-church member, politely extend a cordial invitation for him to attend, and offer to call for him the next Sunday so you can sponsor him and thus make him feel at home. Non-church folks are usually shy about going to a meeting where they are strangers and thus don't know people. This offer to call for them, ranks at the top in prodding inert citizens into actually being at your church next Sunday.

Remember, too, that every church member should regard himself as a salesman for his church. And one of the cardinal rules of salesmanship is that you must first sell yourself before you can sell your wares. Christian missionaries to China labored in vain for a long time, trying to show by logic the superior merits of Christianity over Confucianism, Buddhism, etc. It was only when they began healing the dying babies and feeding the starving children, however, that the Chinese finally accepted them as true friends. Then, and only then, did the Chinese heed the advice or religious sales talk of those same Christian missionaries. So an effective church salesman must smile freely and pay genuine compliments. He must toot the other fellow's horn. "Whenever you lay your hand upon a child's head, you place it on that mother's heart," runs a truism very appropriate for church salesmen.

(2) Assign several couples to stand at the door and serve as hosts and hostesses for that given Sunday. They should also be encouraged during the preceding week to mail out postal cards or make telephone calls to their friends and absentee church members urging them to be present on this day to help their own batting average as official hosts. Posting the attendance records from week to week injects a little wholesome competition between the different weekly sets of hosts. The latter's names should be included in the printed church bulletin, too. Enough couples should be recruited for this job so no one need be required to function more often than once per month or even once every six months.

(3) Assign volunteer couples the job of inviting strangers at church to take dinner with them on Sunday. A newspaper executive in St. Louis now has a group of married couples who do this every Sunday. It has proved a boon to the church, both in stimulating attendance and also in promoting closer friendly ties among the people therein. In our large cities, this hospitality to strangers is a critical need. Such a gracious act certainly comes under the heading of admirable home missionary activity.

(4) Arrange to have a simple dinner immediately following the 11 o'clock service, at which all are invited to attend. Box lunches or sandwiches, plus pie and coffee or milk laid out in self-serve fashion, can be made available in the church basement at a modest cost. But this "breaking of bread" together emphasizes the fact that all are spiritual kinfolk dining together much after the fashion of an individual family reunion. This innovation is beginning to appear in many city churches. It helps banish the loneliness and tension of thousands of timid folks who feel that nobody cares for them. In my daily mail input via my syndicated newspaper column, this heart cry that "Nobody cares" is becoming increasingly evident.

(5) Schedule a "family night" on Sunday evening to avoid closing up your church. In a Hoosier village of 500 population I recently saw a good example of this "family night" innovation. The attendance at the Sunday evening service had averaged between 15 and 20 people, all being of the older generation and faithful wheelhorses of that little church. This enterprising clergyman, however, decided to pep up the attendance, so he announced that wholesome games would be scheduled the next Sunday evening at 5:30 in the basement. Everybody was welcome—children and their parents. Supper would then be served at 6:30. At 7:30 they would all go upstairs into the sanctuary for a 45 minute religious service, which would include singing and a 20-minute talk or a popular religious movie. Then, at 8:15, they'd all go back to the basement for more games.

Although there had been 72 at the morning church service, there were actually 85 people present for that first "family night." It is very unusual for churches to have a larger evening congregation than at their morning service. This 85 contrasted with 17 who had been in attendance the preceding Sunday evening. The recreation was adapted for both children and adults. It included box hockey, shuffle board, and similar action games. Our younger children, then in grammar school, actually scolded Mrs. Crane and me about not getting started to church soon enough that evening, for they didn't want to miss playing box hockey with their pals. It was the first time in our experience where our children had actually prodded us parents into being at church on a Sunday night!

A year later, another clergyman succeeded this one who had initiated the "family night," but the newcomer vetoed games in the church on Sunday evening, As a result, his audience dwindled right back to a mere handful and children were no longer interested in prodding their parents to attend Sunday night services. "By their fruits ye shall know them," Jesus once stated, and it seems to me that innocent games, plus a light Sunday night supper, are good psychological techniques for helping fill the churches and for thus combatting the objectionable appeal of taverns, night clubs, dance halls and commercial movies. Alas, many churches are actually closing up altogether on Sunday night, which is a complete surrender to the enemy. A little Applied Psychology could reopen their doors and make them popular centers for Christian fellowship.

How A Livewire In The Pulpit Electrifies A Congregation.

There is an old adage that you must first fill the pulpit before you can fill the church. The implication of that maxim is simply that it takes a good public speaker or sermonizer in order to make the members of the congregation feel that their time has been well spent. And this is well demonstrated in all churches. Some clergymen are the foremost orators of the land, whereas others put a congregation to sleep by their expositional instead of narrative forensic formulae.

Since the use of one's voice in public speaking is an integral part of the professional duties of all clergymen, certainly they should never fall lower than "good" in their addresses, even on an "off" day. And they should then rise to "better" or occasionally "best." In Chapter XI, we have already discussed

---

"Moral indignation is jealousy with a halo."   —H. G. Wells the psychology of the public platform. Christ employed the narrative or parable formula. It consists of stringing a number of relevant stories, like beads, on the central motif or sermon text. Each episode should be relevant and advance the thought steadily toward its climax.

The importance of using actual cases and narratives is well borne out in publisher DeWitt Wallace's prescription for a *Reader's Digest* essay, which contains three parts: (a) Start out with a striking statement or text; (b) Document it with two cases from real life that are both narrative and dramatic; (c) Tie the wheat in the sack with a punchy terminal paragraph. A clergyman may need to add a few extra examples in making a longer talk than the usual brief *Reader's Digest* article, but that formula is basic to vital sermonizing. In a pre-Easter sermon, for example, I once heard Dr. Roy L. Smith include 12 stories as illustrative material during his 35-minute address and he is one of North America's foremost orators.

A clergyman should also be very liberal with compliments for his assistants, including the musicians and ushers. Moreover, if he will mention a few of the members of the audience in his discourse, in a relevant and complimentary way, that very fact will help keep the whole congregation awake and more alert. Besides, each person so named then feels that the sermon has been better than usual, for we adults react just like youngsters. Thus, after one of my regular Sunday school talks to an adult group, my daughter Judy, then about 9 years of age, said: "Daddy, your speech was much better today than it was last Sunday." I thanked her for the compliment but inquired why she thought it was superior to the preceding Sunday's address. "Oh, you talked about Danny and David and me," she nonchalantly added. Adults don't always admit such things as naively as Judy did, but when we are favorably named in a good speech, we become psychological partners of

---

"Eloquence is logic on fire."   —Lyman Beecher

the clergyman, so we naturally think his address is then superior.

A livewire clergyman should also have an editorial group which puts out a little mimeographed paper each week of at least 3 or 4 pages. Be sure you name as many parishioners as possible therein. People look first to see if they are mentioned in such a weekly newspaper. The secret of human interest is wrapped up in a person's own epidermis. Every inch that you move away from there in space and every minute you get away from the present in time, you will find his interest consequently waning. Every human being, regardless of how old or successful he may be, should thus be visualized as bearing an indelible tattoo across his chest which reads, "I want to feel important." To finance this weekly mimeographed newspaper, ask for voluntary contributions, and then list the names of the donors.

In this connection, a clergyman will find that parishioners are very generous if their thinking can be steered toward definite gifts which they can make to the local church, especially as dynamic memorials to their departed loved ones. Stress the greater value of such "dynamic" memorials in contrast to "static" monuments such as tombstones or even elaborate mausoleums. The dynamic memorial continues to render helpful service to mankind.

It would be well if the clergymen had a "Memorial Committee" which would prepare a catalogue of gifts fitted to the varying amounts which parishioners might feel like donating. These could range from $5 worth of song books for the children's department and continue with $100 for some new chairs, or $250 for a television set for the Young People's Society, up to $750 for a chimes and loud speaker system, or even upward to $50,000 for a recreation room, etc. Prospective donors like to shop through such a catalogue of suggested gifts. Moreover, the specific recommendations will help plant the idea

---

"Everything will perish save love and music."   —Scottish Proverb which later materializes in an appropriate church donation.

Every church should also have remembrance cards or "get well" greetings available so that interested members could immediately put their good resolves into action. Many a time, for example, I have heard the announcement made in church that somebody was ill. I have planned to send a greeting when I got home, but I forgot. So some donor could profitably invest a few dollars in post cards or greetings and have them available in the church, stamped and ready to be addressed. It would certainly bring much joy to the sick and sorrowful, for our kindly resolves would then be harnessed at once.

Clergymen should also operate Marriage Clinics routinely. Many denominations have been doing this for several years. The Roman Catholic church is thus famous for its very helpful and popular Cana Conferences. During 1949, moreover, nearly 7,500 engaged folks enrolled for the pre-Cana conferences in Chicago alone, under the able leadership of the Rev. John Egan. He launched another series of 27 such conferences in late July, 1950. I had the pleasure of cooperating with the Rev. R. J. Kinnavey of St. Ambrose College when he was preparing material for a seminar for priests who were to organize such helpful marital and pre-marital church conferences.

Many other progressive clergymen, such as Dr. Roy Burkhart of Columbus, Ohio, Rabbi G. George Fox of Chicago, and Dr. Norman Vincent Peale, of New York, annually pioneered similar marriage and psychological clinics under church supervision. Since clergymen have better rapport with engaged couples than the average physician, I feel the clergy should give prospective newlyweds a full briefing in advance on marriage situations, including the sexual adjustments. The clergy can then refer these young couples to local physicians, too, for a double tutelage on the latter score.

A livewire clergyman should also regard funerals as his golden opportunity for evangelism. Many non-church members may then be back in the familiar pews where they used to sit as children. On such an occasion, the congregation is already meditative and philosophical. So the thinking of the audience is already polarized and just ripe for the leadership of a talented clergyman. The latter in 15 minutes should take that audience up to the mountain top and give it a momentary glimpse into heaven itself. This brief panorama of eternal verities should transfigure members of the audience until their faces almost glow, like that of Moses when he saw God. A funeral permits a talented clergyman to electrify his listeners and recruit backsliders into regular church attendance once more.

Psychology Applied To Church Music. The primary function of the church music is to revive or resurrect those high resolves and noble aspirations typical of our teen-age idealism. This means that unfamiliar hymns do not aid the clergyman very much, for they are not linked with the appropriate emotional states which he wishes to arouse in his congregation.

At the outset, a child has no associated memories or emotions when he first contacts a strange piece of music. But he later becomes "conditioned" to it so that it symbolizes very definite moods or memories. In dealing with youngsters of Sunday school age, therefore, new hymns can very properly be introduced, always associated with beautiful stories and lofty idealism so the two will become synonymous. After a lengthy tutelage in this manner, the music will later resurrect those vague, suffuse emotions of love and mother and childhood ideals linked with church and God.

So it behooves the choir director to think of the over-all purpose of music and fit it into the clergyman's desire to polarize the audience, incite it to high resolves, and thus deliver it to the clergyman just ripe for a stirring verbal message. Some choirs become so interested in showing off their own melodic "pyrotechnics" that they overlook that fundamental point. There are times, too, when sheer volume is more vital than technical skill. Thus, at the start of a church service, lusty singing advertises the fact that a large crowd is present and the program is already under way. These intimations help recruit people from outside and encourage them to drop into the back of the sanctuary.

With an average American audience, it is often a negative approach to suggest that "Everybody sing his part. You sopranos and altos be sure you stick to your parts, and you tenors and basses do likewise!" That warning makes the average person uncomfortable for he usually can't sing anything but the soprano melody. So he shuts up to avoid revealing his ignorance. But this fact reduces the audience participation. And the less audience participation, the more difficult it is for the clergyman to influence that congregation. Hearty singing that almost bursts out the windows, thus encourages wider audience participation, since the average person then feels that his voice will be drowned in the sheer volume of harmony.

There is also a universal disadvantage in a song leader's asking the congregation to sing softly, for the usual adult male cannot carry a tune when his volume is greatly reduced. His vocal cords require a certain minimum amount of exhaled breath to function smoothly. The advice to "sing softly" thus "freezes out" many of the male voices. Such subdued singing may fit into the prayerful mood, as at the climax of a great sermon, but it meanwhile robs the men of an adequate chance to raise their voices in lusty singing. Listen to a man in the bathroom while he is bathing or getting ready to shave and you'll find the volume that men delight in! It certainly isn't a soft tone, is it? Billy Sunday's remarkable influence over his vast audiences was due in no small part to the musical psychology previously employed by his great song leader—Homer

"Music washes away from the soul the dust of everyday life."
—Auerbach

Rodeheaver. Mr. Rodeheaver avoided feeble, half-hearted singing.

Personnel Strategy Needed In Every Local Church. Clergymen are already so swamped with duties that they need to be twins or triplets to meet the present demands upon their time. So every church ought to have a personnel manager who would volunteer to help take inventory of the various needs in the parish, as well as assay the abilities and talents of all the members. Ideally, he should develop a card index system containing the psychological "profile" of every member. Indeed, the potential talent in every church is really astounding! It includes not only skill in music and oratory, banking and sales promotion, advertising and vocational counseling, but in hosts of other fields. Some of the personnel strategy every livewire church should demonstrate would involve the following major functions:

(1) An employment service should be maintained so that every unemployed church member would be apprised of jobs available by firms owned or operated by other members of that same church. Simple typewritten announcements on the bulletin board would often suffice for the local church. But a weekly or monthly mimeographed list should be available throughout the entire area or conference or diocese. For unemployed church members can't very well marry and start new Christian homes! They can't even make financial contributions to the local church. So it is plain "horse sense" for us to operate an employment service under church direction.

(2) Vocational Guidance Clinics should likewise be sponsored, plus personal clinical counseling with distraught members. Dr. Norman Vincent Peale thus has Dr. Smiley Blanton and a corps of other trained psychologists and psychiatrists cooperating with him in New York City, while many other leading priests and clergymen are doing the same thing elsewhere.

(3) Weekday nursery schools should be operated by local

churches, both to socialize the growing number of "only" children, and also to free their harassed mothers for a few hours each morning. Besides, many non-church parents are led to become active members through first having sent their youngsters to such a daily nursery school. And the Women's Society in the local church can obtain revenue from their operation of such nursery schools, thus helping the church budget.

(4) Churches should operate Scientific Dating Bureaus. About 2,500 priests, rabbis and ministers now are serving as Counsellors for the interfaith, nationwide Scientific Marriage Foundation[2] at Mellott, Indiana, which is introducing 20,000 certified and congenial folks per year via the IBM machine. The Applicants are usually far above average in pulchritude, morality, education and cultural idealism. They definitely are not culls or matrimonial "seconds" but include nurses, secretaries, physicians, attorneys, dentists, teachers and advertising executives. Why, I have lost four private secretaries in the last few years to such men who have simply written me in care of my daily syndicated column, "The Worry Clinic." One of my secretaries thus married a professor in a medical school. Another chose a patent attorney. A third picked a scientific farmer, and the fourth is now happily married to a biology teacher.

Many people either defer marriage to help a widowed mother rear the rest of the children. Or they remain at home to nurse an elderly parent. At the age of 28 to 35, maybe they finally become free to think about marriage. But by then most of the eligibles in their village or neighborhood are already taken. Lacking the time and money to tour the country like a playboy seeking romance, these faithful young men and women must stick to their jobs. If the churches pooled their efforts in this vital field, we could probably add 100,000 more marriages each year to our total. And they would usually be happy marriages, too! Besides, in 5 years they'd add almost 250,000 youngsters to our Sunday schools, for their churchgoing parents would take care of that without further effort by the churches themselves. Dating Bureaus already operate in a modest way on many college campuses. They should be widened in scope, for they serve as an admirable type of home missionary activity for churches.

(5) The Personnel Director in every church should function much as the executive vice president in a business firm. He should thus organize and coordinate many active committees. If possible, he should maintain a select squad of volunteer "Minute Men & Women" who are ready at a moment's notice to render helpful service, such as picking up elderly parishioners by automobile on inclement days and bringing them to church. These volunteers can also conduct nursery schools for toddlers on Sunday while the latter's parents are attending the main church service. And these "Minute Men & Women" should be on call for baby sitting jobs. Many young people can thus donate one evening per week at baby sitting and let the church receive the fee as their contribution to its Christian work.

Newcomers to church should be acknowledged within the next 72 hours by the helpful clerical assistance of these "Minute Men & Women," who should send off cards and make personal calls. The sick and hospitalized should likewise be remembered every week. These "Minute Men & Women" should function like the Big Brothers in Alcoholics Anonymous, who are always ready, day or night, to rush to the aid of their proteges. Our churches need to operate 16 hours per day with helpful service to their community, for there is a growing rumble of criticism against the tax free nature of church property. In 1960, our daily newspapers again carried some critical articles demanding that churches be taxed. This had been a recurring refrain for several years and seems to be growing stronger with the increasing tax rates borne by individuals and private business firms.

One of the very best ways to combat this complaint, is to

"An expert is simply a person who is 25 miles from home."
—Dr. John W. Holland

make the church so productive of good that it is always above criticism. It should literally function 16 hours per day and 7 days per week, as not only the moral but the cultural and recreational center of the community. In this respect, it should offer Marriage Clinics and popular courses on any constructive topic, whether that be Applied Psychology, Public Speaking, Choral Singing or the technique of preparing popular "true-false" or "multiple choice" quiz games, either for pencil and paper use, or as ammunition for mechanical quiz machines like Quiz-Master.

Incidentally, the main secret in using intellectual quiz material for group entertainment, is to protect the ego of the individual. Most people are very much afraid of being shown up as dumb. That is especially true if a person is trying to make a good impression on some member of the opposite sex who is likewise in the group. If quiz material is thus offered to a crowd for individual competition, the general reaction is boredom by possibly 95%, for only the 5% of brilliant or Phi Beta Kappa variety are willing to compete. But if you will divide the group into teams, then each person's ego is protected. For even if he loses, he is with enough other people so that the stigma is thinned down greatly, and he can laugh it off. Even with Sunday school tests, therefore, if the children are getting into the dating age bracket, it is wiser to let the students form teams and compete in groups, instead of as individuals.

Editors and radio managers should be praised liberally for all aid to moral causes! Space will not permit a more exhaustive list of specific projects for the "Minute Men & Women." But with 76,000,000 Americans not members of any church whatsoever, there is a fruitful field for the use of sound Applied Psychology in helping the church function more nearly at its optimum level. So let psychology go to church! It's a remarkable ally, whether in the pulpit or the choir, in the finance committee or the Sunday school!

1 APPEL & STRECKER, *Discovering Ourselves* (Macmillan, 1964).
2 ARNOLD, O., *"Maker of Happy Marriages"* (Reader's Digest, Feb., 1960).
3 BAKER, S., *Visual Persuasion* (McGraw-Hill, 1962).
4 BERGLER, E., *Tensions Can Be Reduced to Nuisances* (Collier, 1962).
5 BRANDT, H. F., *"A Study of Motivation, Involving Self Announced Goals" (J. Soc. Psychol.*, Vol. 10, 1939).
6 BRAUER, O. L., *"College Students Want Alcohol Education" (Listen*, Vol. 3, Sept., 1950).
7 BUCKWALTER, J. A., *"Washington State Penitentiary Survey" (Listen*, Vol. 3, Sept., 1950).
8 BURGESS, T. O., *"Hypnotherapy in Obstetrics"* (A chapter in L. M. LeCron's *Hypnotherapy*, Greene & Stratton, 1950).
9 BURGESS, W., *The Bible in Shakespeare* (Winona Publishing Co., 1903).
10 BURKE, C. F., *God is for Real, Man* (Association Press, 1966).
11 CAMERON, ROD, *A Dummy Goes to Africa* (Missions Press, 1962).
12 CRANE, G. W., *Guidebook for Counselling* (Hopkins, 1966).
13 CURRAN, C. A., *Counseling in Catholic Life & Education* (Macmillan, 1952).
14 DICKS, R. L., *Pastoral Work & Personal Counseling* (Macmillan, 1955).
15 DONIGER, S., *Religion & Human Behavior* (Assoc. Press, 1954).
16 DOUGLAS, L. C., *The Robe* (Houghton Mifflin, 1942), and *The Big Fisherman* (1948).
17 ELSON, E. L. R., *America's Spiritual Recovery* (Revell, 1954).
18 ERICKSON, C. E., *The Counseling Interview* (Prentice-Hall, 1950).
19 FOX, G. G., *An American Jew Speaks* (Falcon Press, 1946).
20 FOX, G. G., *Abraham Lincoln's Religion* (Exposition, 1960).
21 GODDARD, H. H., *How to Rear Children in the Atomic Age* (Hopkins, 1948).
22 HAGEDORN, H., *Prophet in the Wilderness* (Macmillan, 1947).
23 HAHN, M. E., and MacLEAN, M. S., *General Clinical Counseling* (McGraw-Hill, 1950).
24 HEARN, C. A., *What About Smoking* (Irwin, 1950).
25 HEPNER, H. W., *Psychology Applied to Life and Work* (Prentice-Hall, 1950).
26 HOLLAND, J. W., *The World's Greatest Prayer* (Elgin Press, 1947).
27 IKIN, A. G., *Life, Faith & Prayer* (Oxf. U. Pr., 1954).
28 JEFFREYS, R. J., *God Is My Landlord* (Van Kampen Press, 1947).
29 KELLER, W., *The Bible As History* (Morrow, 1956).
30 KIN, REV. U ON, *Are We All Gamblers* (Thu Dhama Wadi Press, Rangoon, 1949).
31 KRIEGER, W. M., *Complete Funeral Service* (Prentice-Hall, 1962).
32 NOLL, BISHOP, J. F., *Father Smith Instructs Jackson* (Our Sunday Visitor Press, 1950).
33 NOVECK, S., *Judaism & Psychiatry* (Nat. Acad. Jewish Studies, 1960).
34 OLT, R., *The Psychology of Religion* (Christopher, 1948).
35 OUTLER, A. C., *Psychotherapy & The Christian Message* (Harper, 1959).
36 PEALE, N. V., *Stay Alive All Your Life* (Prentice-Hall, 1960).
37 RODEHEAVER, H., *20 Years With Billy Sunday* (Rodeheaver Press, 1936).
38 SCHLICHENMAIER, A. W., *Six Foolish Drivers* (Manual Arts, 1941).
39 SMITH, E. A., *Men Called Him Master* (Westminister, 1948).
40 SMITH, E. S., *Facts About the Bible* (Miami Post, 1945).
41 SMITH, JOSEPH, *The Book of Mormon* (Grant, Salt Lake City, 1920).
42 SOCKMAN, R. W., *The Unemployed Carpenter* (Harper, 1933).
43 STIMPSON, G., *A Book About the Bible* (Harper, 1945).
44 TULLIS, D. D., *God's Garage (Dorrance, 1948).*
45 VAN LOON, H., *The Story of the Bible* (Garden City, 1941).
46 VOSS, E. H., *Nuclear Ambush* (Regnery, 1963).
47 WALGREEN, MYRTLE N., *Never a Dull Day* (Regnery, 1963).
48 WILBUR, W. H., *Russian Communism – Challenge & Fraud* (Caxton, 1966).

MORAL "SPARKPLUGS" IN PSYCHOLOGY

A false notion has become widespread in America to the effect that psychologists are usually atheists or anti-Christian. That is actually the antithesis of the true facts. In any profession there may be a few iconoclasts, but the vast majority of professors of psychology are outstanding leaders in moral and civic progress. Among these, I wish especially to salute these prominent teachers who have adopted *"Psychology Applied"*:

H. M. Sorkin (St. Louis U.)
Peter Ciklic (Loyola of L.A.)
W. J. Wilson (Central Seminary)
Wendell Stearns (N. E. Theol.)
Howard Hayes (Minn. Bible)
Andrew Leitch (Bethany)
Ivan L. Foster (N. Okla.)
Paul S. Campbell (Tenn. Temple)
J. M. Ackerman (So. Missionary)
L. A. Marsh (Abilene Christian)
J. M. White (Wheeler)
R. H. Watkins (Decatur Baptist)
Roy G. Boger (W. Tex. St.)
Ileta V. Rohde (Prospect Hall)
Dorothy Amundson (NW. Bible)
K. S. Bennion (L.D.S. Bus.)
E. R. Naylor (Emory & Henry)
Don Briggs (W. Tex. St.)
V. G. Rasemaret (Huron)
S. H. Adamson (Tenn. Temple)
R. W. Frick (Robinson)
Elizabeth Brandon (Garfield)
Frederick S. Kring (Grove City)
K. E. Gillming (London Bible)
Donald F. Tweedie (Endicott)
Edward T. Sheehan (McIntosh)
Sister Mary Amatora (St. Francis)
M. J. Boylan (Xavier)
D. T. Johnson (Ky. Christian)
Dean F. F. McCallum (Owosso)
Walter L. Spratt (Ozark Bible)
Rae Tennant (Bliss)
J. E. Eggleton (Ky. Christian)
B. M. Canup (Steed Tech.)
Robert E. Stevens (Lee)
F. P. Moss (Schreiner Inst.)
Z. T. Huff (Howard Payne)
Bill M. Holbert (Howard)
E. K. Shroyer (Beckley)
Lloyd Dryer (Kans. St. T.)
D. A. Hiles (Skagit)
Richard H. Renner (Sullins)
Gordon Silas (Roanoke)
T. H. Durham (Howard)
Bess Blackman (Robinson)
E. C. Christenbury (Lee)
Kathryn Crumbaker (Eugene)
John Capp (Grove City)
V. Odell (Eugene)
R. F. Estes (Denver Central)
H. C. Bennion (Ricks)
W. C. Muck, Jr. (Huntington)
W. Bartlette (Davenport Inst.)
C. J. Ettinger (Great Lakes)
W. E. Baldwin (E.N.Mex. U.)
W. J. Fewkes (Cambridge)
F. L. Johnson (Columbus B.U.)
H. L. Woll (Devil's Lake)

R. L. Herren (N. Okla.)
E. G. Anderson (Hammel B.U.)
H. E. Ryan (New Kensington)
Donald W. Sydow (Black Hills)
C. J. Gaston (Briggs)
Kenneth Piety (David Lipscomb)
Hugh E. Williams (S-D Massey)
E. N. Cullum (David Lipscomb)
H. H. Hohn (E. N. Mex. U.)
M. M. Black (Okla. Sch. Acct.)
H. L. Rasmussen (Emmanuel Miss.)
N. S. Metfessel (Compton)
D. E. Buzby (Beaver College)
Charles Jackson (N. C. Presbyt.)
A. E. Jones (Lower Columbia)
Ruth Haycock (Bapt. Bible Sem.)
R. C. Nickeson (St. Louis U.)
R. D. Andrews (Scottsbluff)
R. R. Ullman (Lenoir Rhyne)
Ronald F. Keeler (Minn. Bible)
John T. Carter (Clarke)
F. L. Dryer (Joplin)
W. W. Garver (Bismarck)
D. H. Markle (Ohio N.U.)
Gilbert Driscoll (Bliss)
Earl Edmondson (Col. B.U.)
H. Everett Pope, Jr. (Okla.)
Ida D. Henton (Black Hills)
A. D. Bell (Howard Payne)
L. E. Megredy (McLains)
Carl T. Vance, Jr. (Sullins)
Leslie E. Church (Northland)
Gordon Nelson (Black Hills)
John B. Van Dyke (Beckley)
B. F. Ezell (Stetson)
Mary Anderson (U. of Ala.)
R. V. Hamilton (U. of Wichita)
Homer Townsend (Tusculum)
T. C. Irwin (Summers)
C. D. Anderson (U. of Portland)
R. B. Mease (Culver-Stockton)
Mary Gassaway (Sanford-Brown)
C. Prewett (E. Car. St.)
A. C. Steinback (Tiffin)
J. T. Zebrowski (Robert Morris)
Ronald E. Lee (Fla. Central)
H. F. Sewell (Goldey Beacom)
J. L. Logsdon (Pacific Bible)
V. W. Maves (Evansville)
L. H. Mendenhall (Wm. Penn)
R. E. Wood (Jacksonville U.)
Norman Hilden (Madison)
George R. Hoff (Compton)
Edna Winters (Manatee)
G. H. Kramer (Del Mar)
C. T. Leaf (U. of Dubuque)
W. F. Vaughan (Boston U.)
L. C. Ward, Jr. (U. of Georgia)

CHAPTER XIX

PSYCHOLOGY GOES TO THE POLLS

We psychologists have just as much claim to politics as a branch of Applied Psychology as we do to advertising or personnel administration.

From the time of William James, we have stressed the vital importance of building self-reliance into human personality. We have tried to train youth to be independent, self-supporting, well integrated, and free from undue dependence upon mama's apron strings. For the past generation, however, an opposing ideology has swept this nation in which people deliberately have been encouraged not to think for themselves but to let a glorified "mama" called Uncle Sam do their thinking and tend to their medical as well as economic welfare. "Santa Claus" has become a synonym for "Uncle Sam", and childish wishful thinking typifies millions of voters. That ideology is unAmerican.

Uncle Sam's Debt To Salesmen And Advertisers. There is a familiar story to the effect that if you wish to be seen, stand up. If you wish to be heard, speak up. But if you wish to be appreciated, shut up! Too long, however, American business and professional men, including the teachers and clergy, have allowed themselves to be deluded by that final admonition, "Shut up". They have modestly believed that their effective contribution to our welfare and economic stability would be self-evident and appreciated by all mankind. Alas, this has not been the case, for at present we harbor possibly millions of alien indoctrinated people, albeit of American birth, who are preaching the vast superiority of Socialism and Communism. They have even reached the impertinent stage nowadays where they actually sneer at our "free enterprise" system and call it a relic of the "horse and buggy days".

Actually, however, our American salesmen and advertisers have been the sparkplugs of civilization. They were largely responsible for our success in both World War I, and World War II, as well as in the Korean conflict. With all due respect to the bravery of our American soldiery, we can't claim that our enemies were cowardly. When the Japanese suicidal planes were flown against the side of American battleships, that was bravery in any man's language. And it wasn't that our generals or admirals so far outmaneuvered the enemy, either, for German tacticians were brilliant, too, on land and sea and in the air. Nor did we have any tremendous superiority in population. No, the determining factor that tipped the war scales in our favor was our productive and mechanical superiority. It was ordnance that beat our foes! It was tanks and airplanes and bulldozers and jeeps and guns and ships and foodstuffs. The Russian troops that finally routed Hitler's forces in World War II rode triumphantly into the Balkans on American manufactured tanks and trucks!

How did our salesmen and advertisers enable us to equip almost 12,000,000 American troops in World War II, and meanwhile furnish much ordnance to Great Britain and Russia? By their go-getter American business tempo in the peace time years prior to the wars! For our salesmen and advertisers took the products of cloistered scientists, such as Edison and Marconi, and made them standard equipment in American homes until our average citizens nowadays live like royalty abroad. They literally punched doorbells and sold our people on a superior standard of living.

By their diligent efforts, they zoomed the civilian demand for goods in the peace time years to such mammoth proportions that great corporations like the Ford Company, General Motors, U. S. Steel, DuPont, General Electric, Boeing Aircraft, IBM and countless others, had to build or expand their factories to meet that demand. Then, after war finally came, it was comparatively simple to convert those industrial plants to the making of war goods or ordnance. Historians of the future should thus pay a long overdue debt to our salesmen and advertisers, instead of glorifying a few generals and admirals, as has been the usual procedure in the past. American salesmen and advertisers seem to be the world champions in their fields. It is high time we began applying some of their unique talent to selling our very type of government and economic system to our home folks. Let's begin with our Republic.

Why The U.S.A. Is A Republic And Not A Democracy. On a recent lecture tour of the South, I was scheduled for a noon talk before the Civitan Club at Knoxville, Tennessee. Like many of these admirable service men's organizations, the members opened with singing of our national anthem, plus the pledge of allegiance to the flag. So we all joined in reciting: "I pledge allegiance to the flag of the United States of America and to the Republic for which it stands . . ." After we had seated ourselves a young businessman asked, "Dr. Crane, why do we pledge to the Republic instead of to the Democracy? Almost everybody nowadays calls this a democracy." Well, suppose you readers had been asked that question. Could you have neatly delineated the difference between our Republic and a democracy?

Although I had been born and reared in this country and had spent 11 years as an undergraduate and graduate student at Northwestern and Yale in obtaining my five earned degrees, I regretfully confess that nobody in any of my classes, whether in history, political science, philosophy, economics, medicine, or even psychology, had ever explained the nature of the government in which we live! Apparently, everybody seemed to take it for granted that everybody else knew. Yet when I have recently quizzed cultured men and women, including distinguished attorneys, they haven't known how to differentiate between the two types of political system. Like me, they had been using the word democracy as a synonym for our Republic.

When I returned to Chicago, therefore, I decided to in-

"In our Republic, the government should fear the people; not the people, the government."   —Frank E. Gannett vestigate the matter. In reading some of former democratic Congressman Samuel B. Pettengill's writings, and he is an authority on government, I found that even the American Army Manual expressly explained that our government is NOT a democracy but is a Republic! So I decided to go back to the works of John Marshall, most famous Chief Justice of our United States Supreme Court, where he presided for 34 years and was called "the second maker of the Constitution." Chief Justice Marshall writes: "Between a balanced Republic and a democracy, the difference is like that between order and chaos." Well, "order" and "chaos" certainly aren't synonyms! Instead, they are direct opposites or antonyms! They are **antithetical terms!**

Then I read further and found that the word "democracy" doesn't appear in the Declaration of Independence, the Constitution of the United States, Washington's famous Farewell Address, Jefferson's First Inaugural, the Monroe Doctrine or the Gettysburg Address. Instead, the terms "Republic" and "republican" are always used! Our wise forefathers, including astute Thomas Jefferson, were well acquainted with all types of government, including limited monarchies, absolute monarchies or dictatorships, communistic states, democracies and republics. It was thus by deliberate intent that they set up our Republic. Now, in a nutshell, I shall delineate what our Republic means and why the term democracy is an alien word not warranted in the U.S.A.

In a democracy the majority rules, quickly and unrestrainedly. Great Britain is now a democracy. Its House of Commons is its supreme law making body. Oh, its House of Lords has the token power to slow down the House of Commons by veto, in which case a bill cannot become a law for one year. Until 1950, the House of Lords could hold up a measure that had been passed by the House of Commons, for two full years, but the House of Commons suddenly changed that, and may at any future time hamstring the House of Lords entirely, for the latter is not an equal member of the British

Parliament, as our U.S. Senate compares with our House of Representatives.

In England, the House of Commons is the supreme dictator of British governmental policy. Thus, on the whim of a majority vote it nationalized the mines and railroads. But it can likewise establish complete communism and then eliminate the private holding of property, for in a democracy the will of the majority prevails. Democracy simply means mobocracy! It can destroy minorities or disfranchise them, as the House of Commons has almost totally disfranchised the House of Lords. It can confiscate property of any minority race or religion.

That's why Chief Justice John Marshall said a democracy differs from our Republic as chaos differs from orderly government. And don't let anybody delude you by saying this is a "representative" democracy instead of a "true" democracy. That distinction simply means caviling with words. A representative democracy is simply one with so many people therein that they can't all meet under one roof to vote directly on bills. So they must then elect representatives to the House of Commons or some other legislative assembly. But the quick rule of the majority prevails in both a true and a representative democracy! So they are equally dangerous.

In our Republic, however, the last bill passed by both houses of our Congress is still not necessarily the final law of the land. For we have a written Constitution which contains certain guarantees of inalienable rights retained for minority citizens EVEN AGAINST THE MAJORITY VOTE OF CONGRESS! And to prevent any invasion of these written guarantees, we also have nine watchdogs called Supreme Court Justices, who are very jealous of that Constitution. They can invalidate bills passed by Congress!

Knowing that even entire legislative bodies can be stampeded, our founding fathers also provided that two-thirds of the members of the U. S. Senate shall not come up for election in any given national election? Of our 100 Senators, 67 carry over. This majority of the higher house of our Congress thus helps resist any nation-wide hysteria that might temporarily clean out the entire 435 Representatives in the lower house. For a classical example of why democracy is mobocracy, just remember that a young Hebrew named Jesus was brought before a Roman judge, who was supposed to operate his court-room under the high principles of the Roman Republic.

But Judge Pontius Pilate was a cheap politician, who wished to curry favor with the populace. A politician is defined as one who thinks of the next election whereas a statesman thinks of the next generation. So Pilate changed his courtroom into the most perfect democracy ever described in history, for he apparently let men, women and children all vote. They were to decide whether he should release the arch criminal Barabbas, or the innocent Christ, whom Pilate had personally interviewed and declared to be entirely innocent.

That democratic courtroom voted 100% wrongly, and thus consigned an innocent man to a cruel death on a cross! That's the "chaos" which John Marshall says is typical of a democracy, for a democracy lets the changing whims of mob majority determine what is right, instead of logic or legal evidence or scientific facts. So Jesus was crucified by a democracy! That word is thus alien to our entire American history. It has been confused with the extension of voting to wider population groups, as in Georgia's lowering the voting age to 18. But it is not the "number" of voters which is so vital as the guarantee of inalienable rights in a written Con-stitution! "Our peculiar security," said Thomas Jefferson, "is in the possession of a written Constitution."

It is thus no compliment to call a man democratic, since that means he operates on a "might makes right" basis, and the weaker groups around him are then at his mercy. Remember, too, that we are all members of minority groups in America.

"Always look a mob in the face."   —Wesley

The largest religious sect in the U.S.A. is the Roman Catholic, yet even it is greatly in the minority. So, too, is every racial group, whether Irish, French, Jewish, English, German, Polish, Italian, Negro or Scandinavian. No trade or profession is a majority group, either, so if it weren't for our Republic with its written constitutional guarantees, we'd all be living under a political sword of Damocles, as democratic Britain now is. So hereafter, when you pledge allegiance to the Stars and Stripes, speak up forcefully as you say "and to the REPUBLIC for which it stands . . . ."

Why "Free Enterprise" Zooms Scientific Discoveries.

The white settlers in North America had been here for more than 150 years before the Boston Tea Party in 1773 brought to a head the difference between American business methods and those of Europe. The Americans had fled from Europe essentially for freedom from unwarranted governmental interference, not only regarding their desire to worship and speak as they pleased, but also their right to establish private business ventures and hold property without unfair taxation or unwarranted search and seizure. They had evolved a distinctive politico-economic "game", as it were, which was just as truly American as basketball or football.

We call this "game" a Republic and it is played under the "free enterprise" system. Our forefathers relished this "game" so well, they wanted to pass it on to their progeny, so they formulated what might be termed a "rule book" (the U.S. Constitution) which provided that Uncle Sam should be the referee or umpire. He was to stay on the sidelines of that gridiron and make sure that the game was played according to the rules. He could penalize commercial "offsides" and industrial "clipping", as well as other infractions. He was even permitted to alter the rules (by Amendments) in the interest of a better game for all concerned. So he levied tariffs to protect the American worker against goods produced at 5c or 10c per day wages in foreign countries. These tariff rules enabled us to erect our great industrial plants, which have been our major protection in time of war.

Uncle Sam likewise passed the pure food laws, interstate commerce regulations, anti-trust legislation, etc. In brief, he opened up the American politico-economic game, much as our football rules have also been changed since 1895 to permit lateral passing and less of the bone crusher (trust) methods. All the while, however, Uncle Sam was to stimulate better playing by the freely competitive teams. Banker could thus be arrayed against banker, oil dealer vs. oil dealer, doctor against doctor, grocer against grocer, etc., as shown on Page 272-B. During his role of impartial referee, America flourished as no other land in all the history of the world.

We attained the highest standard of living on earth. Pettengill says that our workmen, even at their lowest wage scale, obtained a higher "take home pay", when converted into its equivalent buying power in bread and meat and clothing, than any other worker of a foreign nation under the latter's highest wage scale! We were thus the Mecca for liberty loving folks from all over the earth. And in times of war, as well as in the post-war periods, where did the world look for military aid and billions of dollars? Did you ever hear of Socialism or Communism forking over billions to Uncle Sam? Not on your life! But we have been milked consistently for billions in Marshall Plan funds to bolster Socialistic Britain and even Communistic Russia, plus many of her satellites!

Then a tragedy hit America's famous politico-economic game. For in 1910, Uncle Sam flagrantly violated the intention of our founding fathers by seizing the ball and rushing out upon the gridiron to compete with the very "free enterprise" players over whom he was supposed to be the impartial referee. He became a player-referee, which is an intolerable thing. This occurred when he launched the Postal Savings System in 1910, operated by every local post office in the land. For thereby he started competing with every life insurance company and private bank.

"But didn't the Postal Savings System encourage many poor people to save money?" somebody may inquire. Yes, it undoubtedly did. But if encouragement was needed for any new type of small banking organization, Uncle Sam should have subsidized the latter, as he did the air lines and merchant marine, but let private "players" operate it. Thus, he might very properly have created a Bureau of Banking, like his Bureau of Standards, to release relevant data impartially to help small bankers on both competing teams, but Uncle Sam should have stayed off the gridiron! By taking the ball, he instituted Socialism, which is the half-way point on the highway to Communism. When he owns the stadium seats, he will finally be communistic!

Even before 1910, however, Uncle Sam had engaged in some socialistic and even communistic behavior, for the operation of the post office is a form of socialism, and the fact that military personnel often live in government quarters, is a communistic characteristic. It may even be expedient that some major ventures, such as a Hoover Dam or other tremendous projects, be sponsored by the government, especially if private capital cannot be attracted to do so because of the indefiniteness of the returns thereon or their long deferred nature. But our forefathers expected Uncle Sam to stay on the sidelines WHENEVER POSSIBLE and act as an impartial referee, letting the players have the zest of actually competing. This lack of zest in Socialism is perfectly depicted by Joseph S. Lawrence[16], vice-president of the Empire Trust Company of New York, when he analyzed the British system. In 1948, Freddie Mills, British boxer, refused to accept a battle for the title because John Bull would permit him to retain only 10c out of every $4 paid to him for thus risking a concussion or fractured jaw in defense of his championship. When pugilists will quit fighting because there is not an adequate financial incentive, just think what happens to business men and inven-

---

"A nation may lose its liberties in a day, and not miss them in a century."   —Montesquieu tors, scientists and other professional groups! Mr. Lawrence further cited the alarming fact that in 1948, only 70 Britons had incomes of over $24,000 per year after taxes had been deducted.

To the man on the street, even in America, that $24,000 seems a large sum. So the Communists constantly agitate to confiscate the possessions of such men, as well as those who have automobiles and other evidences of private capital. But without wealthy men to furnish leadership and offer wide employment via their factories, even the average American would suffer. Andrew Carnegie gave away most of his wealth, as in endowing thousands of public libraries. Rockefeller donated millions to research and charity, in addition to more than $76,000,000 to the University of Chicago, where much of the research for the Atomic Bomb took place. Our colleges have similarly been endowed by men who earned big incomes.

If our government took away everything from the worker except enough to buy his rationed goods each week, as in Russia, what then? Have such European governments given their people better living standards than ours? Which country has a vast majority of all the automobiles? Or the telephones? Electric toasters? Radios and television sets? Or college students? Why are there more college students in the U.S.A. with only 195,000,000 people than in all the rest of the world, with over two billion people? Because incentive has been the keynote of American progress and it thrives best under our "free enterprise" system. Socialism and Communism simply kill the goose that lays the golden eggs! Woodrow Wilson said all we ask in America is a free field and no favors!

How To Select Candidates Who Will Win An Election. Prior to the 1964 campaign, I addressed a banquet meeting of a Southern Executives Club on this very topic. During my remarks, I mentioned that winning an election is primarily a "selling" job. "When you business men want to move your wares from the factory to the consumer," I began, "you don't choose your corporation lawyer for the job, do you? Nor do you assign that critical task to your factory superintendent or to any of his engineers. The treasurer of your company is likewise not the man. No, you delegate the job to your sales-manager. Well, the man to head a political ticket also needs to be a star political salesman, for his job is to sell the voters and win their 'deposit' on that sale via their ballot which is deposited in the local balloting box."

During the open forum following my address, a Nashville dentist asked this hypothetical question: "Dr. Crane, for sake of argument, let's assume you were nominated to head the ticket. Whom would you want for your vice presidential running mate?" And I replied, "John Roosevelt." The audience laughed, but I explained that I wasn't joking. When either party has long been in power and has begun to use the federal treasury indirectly as a means of buying votes, the opposing party is hard pressed to combat such expenditures. In this regard, the Dunn Survey (Greenwich, Connecticut) has shown that every federal office holder controls four votes for the party in power! At the beginning of 1964, the civilian (not military) employment in the executive branch of the federal government was well over 2,500,000 or a potential "bought" vote for the party in power of over 10,000,000. Shefferman[27] says of all U.S. employed workers, over 10 per cent draw their pay from the Local or Federal Government. The "Average American" now works 3 full months to pay his taxes (25% of his total income).

The total federal budget expenditures of the United States even in these peace time years now approximate $100 billions. You might wonder what hope the party out of power would have with a mere three or four millions of dollars of campaign funds against that $100 billion but it does have a good chance if it staffs its ticket with familiar names like Roosevelt which are nationally popular and have previously obtained millions of dollars worth of effective advertising.

Suppose, moreover, that other talented young people of good habits and widespread previous "build-up" were to be drafted for a ticket, such as Billy Graham, Bob Richards, Pat Boone, Bing Crosby, Bob Hope, and the like. Ronald Reagan and George Murphy had millions of dollars worth of free publicity from the movies, the radio, the newspapers, magazines, television and other sources, which the Republican Party then tapped at little extra cost. When such men are capable of adequately handling a given political job, wouldn't it be good sense to use such candidates instead of comparatively unknown entries? This is specially true if we wish to win the young voters.

For we must remember that a great crowd of new voters come of age between national presidential elections. For example, the total high school enrollment alone in the U.S.A. is over 12,000,000. Every four years, therefore, the new crop of potential first-time voters totals at least 12,000,000. This is usually an enthusiastic group, too, for young people consider it a mark of adulthood to cast their first ballot. They very properly regard this patriotic duty as a serious responsibility. President J. F. Kennedy won the 1960 election by only 118,550 votes (including 406,176 by the New York Liberal Party) so Nixon actually defeated him on straight party ballots. Knowing he would be called a bigot unless he "beat them to the draw", Kennedy outfoxed the Protestants. Many Protestant clergy thus ran paid ads saying they were voting for Kennedy to prove they were NOT bigots! They forgot to read Webster! At his heyday in 1936, President Franklin D. Roosevelt won 68% of the voters of the age group from 21 to 29 years. This had dropped by 1944 to 58%. During the 1944 election, however, Gallup points out that the per cent of potential voters in the Armed Forces who actually cast their ballots was only 35% as against a figure of 57% for the civilian population.

In 1940, when F. D. Roosevelt was violating the precedent against a third term, the extra outpouring of voters still totalled only 63% of the potential voting population in the U. S. A. This contrasted with 75% in the year 1900. In that 1940 outpouring of votes, the following table will show the percentage of potential voters who actually cast their ballots in the 5 heaviest voting states, vs. similar figures on the 5 lowest voting states:

Heaviest Voting States		Lowest Voting States	
Utah	83%	Alabama	19%
West Virginia	83%	Arkansas	18%
Illinois	82%	Georgia	18%
South Dakota	82%	Mississippi	15%
Indiana	81%	South Carolina	10%

The foregoing figures also demonstrate the advantage in having a vigorous two-party system, for the apathy shown in those five southern states was due to the lack of well organized Republican opposition. By 1964, however, the southern voting percentages more nearly matched those of the northern states.

Why Big City Machines Can Easily Intimidate Voters. Thomas Jefferson regarded big cities as one of the gravest threats to the future integrity of our American Republic. In this connection, he stated: "When we get piled upon one another in large cities, as in Europe, we shall become corrupt as in Europe, and go to eating one another as they do there. . . . The mobs of great cities add just so much to the support of pure government as sores do to the strength of the human body." He again inveighed against the mob reaction which is inherent in massed populations, when he added, "It is not too soon to provide by every possible means that as few as possible shall be without a little portion of land. The small land-owners are the most precious part of the state."

It is an axiom of public platform psychology that vacant seats and all other vague indications of isolation, retard the cooperation of that audience with its leader or speaker. The more closely packed the listeners, the easier it is to sway them with oratory. When their arms are almost imprisoned against their sides by jamming the room full, they are deprived of a sense of independence, so they stampede more readily. Members of mobs and lynching parties thus lose their sense of indi-

---

"An empty stomach is not a good political adviser."   —Einstein vidual responsibility and become semi-automatons. They apparently regress to the weaker childlike state, where they are more uncritical of statements made to them, and hence they follow suggestions, as well as direct orders, much as children do. Congested populations thus aid mobocracy and mass intimidation. It was the British farm vote that finally returned Churchill's party to power on Oct. 25, 1951. In 1963, U.S. farmers first cracked Kennedy's dynasty via the wheat referendum.

In the large cities, moreover, people do not actually produce food or dig coal or catch fish. No, they work for symbols called money. Thus, 10,000 men may look to possibly a single paymaster for their weekly pay checks. This habit of looking to one person for their living, instead of relying more fully on their own independent efforts, not only is another throw-back to their childhood attitude of taking orders from "papa," but it thus renders them more susceptible to direction from any powerful center of influence. Furthermore, many naturalized Americans are still so imbued with submission to symbols of authority that even the police squad cars which parade up and down the streets on election day, help coerce them to vote for the party in power. And every uniformed policeman at the polling places likewise exerts a similar subconscious coercive effect on their balloting.

Corruption is thus far easier to accomplish in the big cities where people often don't even know their neighbors in the same block, so "chain voting" is still a prevalent practice. The "machine" stations a man at a tavern close to the polling place. He is given a ballot marked for his party. Then he hands this marked ballot to one of the "bought" voters, who hides it in his pocket and heads for the polling place. This voter accepts a blank ballot from the official in charge. He then steps into a screened voting booth, and folds the blank ballot, after which he puts it into his pocket. Next, he removes the already marked ballot and walks over to the box where he deposits it therein. Now he goes right back to the saloon to deliver his fresh, unmarked ballot and get his free stein of beer or other repayment. The process can then be repeated till the polls close.

Political corruption even exceeds the realm of common sense, too, for in Kansas City during the Pendergast expose, one of my friends was an agent of the F.B.I. sent there to investigate that mess. He told me of a certain precinct with 300 registered voters in it. The crooked judge of that polling place was so sure of himself that he marked up all 300 votes for Roosevelt, not even leaving a single Republican ballot to allow for any Republican who might later swear an affidavit that he had voted at that particular polling place. But this precinct official went even further and also marked up 300 additional votes for Roosevelt, thus certifying to 600 votes when only 300 were registered in his entire precinct! Later, he laughed in the face of this F.B.I. agent, saying that nobody could convict him, for the Kansas City judges were all elected by the Pendergast machine and would support everybody clear down to the local precinct worker. This apparently wasn't a far-fetched boast, so outside judges were finally brought in to hear the case, and the F.B.I. evidence then proved effective.

Several psychological measures should be adopted to prevent or at least partially counteract the "machine" pressure on city voters. (1) Plain clothesmen instead of uniformed policemen should be on duty at polling places, to avoid the subconscious intimidation exerted by the uniformed officer of the city government. (2) Voting machines should replace the Australian ballot whenever possible. (3) The initialing of ballots should be done with different colored pencils, changed every 15 minutes, to avoid the chain voting from a near-by tavern or "machine" hang-out, as aforementioned.

(4) An independent Better Government Organization should be formed in every precinct, which should place competent watchers at every polling place on election day. It should previously check on every registered voter to make sure that "tombstone" names are not being registered and then voted by paid stooges of the "machine" who routinely go from precinct to precinct to claim their ballot in the names of these dead or

---

"When you see a wrong, hit it."   —Lincoln

phoney voters. (5) Members of Boy or Girl Scout troops in each precinct should be encouraged to help prod laggard but bona fide voters into getting to the polls to help raise the percentage of votes cast by eligible citizens. The Scouts might be granted credit toward Merit Badges in the field of Civics, for this patriotic service. Incidentally, the voting turnout in Italy was 89%; in France 81%, and in Great Britain 76% to our high point of 63%. In Australia, the turnout was well over 90%, but voting there is compulsory. Since the furnishing of information to our U.S. Census Takers is likewise a compulsory duty of Americans, it might be well to add some similar penalties for inexcusable failure to vote.

(6) The American Legion and other patriotic organizations should stress the fact that men have died to grant Americans the privilege of the ballot, so the laying of a wreath on a soldier's grave on Memorial Day is not nearly as intelligent a tribute to those sacrificial dead as to vote at every election for the continuation of this Republic and its "free enterprise" system, which they died to preserve for us. (7) All legitimate encouragement should be given to citizens to buy property, for real estate owners are a more critical type of voters than tenants and especially than the relief clients of the city or state.

Propaganda Techniques Used in Politics.   These techniques are varied and apply not only to local politics and national contests, but even to the international field. Some of the major techniques are as follows: (1) The *ad hominem* fallacy. This consists of sidestepping the logic of an opponent and then attempting to divert attention from the main issue by some "red herring" method such as personal villification of the opponent's character. Thus, when Col. Charles A. Lindbergh caustically reported before the Pearl Harbor incident that we were wholly unprepared in our military aviation, the president characterized him as a liar, and one of his mouthpieces, a senator from Florida, immediately termed Lindbergh a 5th columnist, citing among other evidences for this emotional charge that Lindbergh had once been decorated by the

Germans. When I pointed out this *ad hominem* fallacy of the Florida Senator in my daily syndicated quiz column called "Test Your Horse Sense," several newspapers immediately canceled my column. This tendency of the government to label its critics as "liars" is not only an indelicate strategy but has often boomeranged, as in the repeated slandering of such columnists as Drew Pearson. Whispering campaigns and mudslinging also fall under this general heading.

(2) The financial strategy. This may involve promising government contracts to a firm in repayment for campaign contributions. It may even involve deferring anti-trust suits, as in the case of the "loan" of $196,000 requested by one of the Roosevelt sons from the head of a large chain grocery store. It may involve placing men on the payroll at a retainer's fee as technical consultants. It may indirectly be evident in federal aid to schools. It may consist of giving airline franchises or radio licenses, for services or money to the party.

(3) The coining of labels of opprobrium or approval, as in the "Me, too" for Dewey, the "Slave Labor Law" to designate the Taft-Hartley bill, the "Isolationist" epithet, the "One Worlders," and the "Welfare State." Positive slogans also fall here, as Wilson's famous "Make the World Safe for Democracy" and "He kept us out of war." McKinley's "Full dinner pail" was another, and LBJ's "Great Society."

(4) Licensing of radio or television stations brings intimidation of various sorts, and the similar dependence of certain foreign newspapers on governmental O.K., as in Argentina, also is a propaganda technique. (5) Studious indoctrination of school children through both direct and indirect methods. No better example of this can be cited than Publisher John S. Knight's trenchant report of the parade of German youth in Russia's Berlin sphere of influence. Here it is, by the gracious permission of Mr. Knight and his Chicago *Daily News*, which ran it on May 29, 1950:

Hate in Red Berlin,
Auto Show in West

BY JOHN S. KNIGHT

Editor and Publisher, Chicago Daily News

Berlin—This might be called the tale of two cities—East and West Berlin.

Early Sunday morning, armed with proper credentials from the East Berlin authorities, I walked through the famous Brandenburg Gate and on down Unter Den Linden to witness a sight I shall never forget.

Here were massed columns of the Free German Youth Organization carrying wooden hammers, paper sickles and banners denouncing the capitalism and "imperialism" of the Western world.

Gen. Maxwell Taylor, flying overhead in a helicopter, estimated that about 370,000 young Germans assembled from various sections of Eastern Germany participated in the demonstration.

The boys were clad in shorts and blue shirts, the girls in skirts and blue blouses. Ages of the paraders ranged from 8 to 25 years.

The girls were of the stocky Teutonic type, mostly with blond hair. The boys and young men looked grim, older than their years, and their faces generally were pale in comparison to American or British youngsters of the same age.

The procession lasted until the cold and dreary mid-afternoon. The marchers were well drilled and sang the words of songs played over a series of loudspeakers strung through the line of march.

The singing was interspersed with handclapping in unison and music from drum corps units.

Along the avenue at intervals were huge posters flaying the "capitalistic warmongers" and carrying slogans urging "Strength Through Peace."

In conjunction with a somewhat faded British society picture portraying some elderly dowagers and men wearing grey toppers appeared the question: "Do you want to fight for these ladies and gentlemen?"

Other posters accused Winston Churchill and Foreign Minister Bevin of England as "tools of Wall Street." The picture of the American singer, Paul Robeson, was displayed prominently as a friend of the "democratic peoples" of the world.

Also included in this category were all of the prominent Communist leaders of Europe.

When American helicopters appeared over the area the demonstrators waved and shouted, "Americans, go home."

* * *

The parade was orderly and I saw no incidents of any sort. East German police had roped off the streets so onlookers could not crowd beyond the curb. The spectators applauded certain units from time to time but there was no wild enthusiasm.

None of the spectators took any particular interest in the American and British newspapermen who covered the area. In the several hours in which I watched the parade I did not rate even a single glance of curiosity.

At no time was there any possibility of a clash between the youth of East and West Berlin. The Western youth simply didn't appear near the scene. And East Berlin police threw up a blockade that prevented youngsters from the Soviet zone from straying over into the Allied sectors.

The entire affair brought back recollections of the Hitler youth movement in the 1930s. Here it was again, the same tactics, the same appeals to emotionalism and idealism of the young.

It was frightening in its potential aspects; impressive as an example of how young minds can be distorted through clever propaganda and efficient methods of organization.

Furthermore, no one who witnessed this tremendous outpouring of youngsters living in the Soviet zone of Germany could ever be convinced that we are not at war with Russia except that for the time being neither side is doing any shooting.

In the late afternoon I saw quite a different sort of exhibition in Western Berlin. This, oddly enough, was an auto show that drew huge crowds throughout the day.

Here were on display all of the American makes as well as German, French and British cars. It was almost impossible to see some of the new models because of the throngs of curious West Berliners who wanted to see the latest automotive creations.

This interest was all the more remarkable since few of these people have the means to purchase the cars in which they were so absorbed.

* * *

In Western Berlin, capitalism seems to be very much alive. In East Berlin where the Russians are condemning all aspects of commercial business and trade, capitalism is one of the Soviets' main targets for destruction.

The propaganda war, intended to capture the minds and hearts of the German people, is being waged in Berlin at a furious rate.

On the side of the Western German republic are 11 newspapers and the radio station RIAS.

In East Berlin under Soviet control there are also 11 newspapers, spewing their propaganda against the Western world.

The Russians also have Radio Berlin from which Lord Haw-Haw made his daily broadcasts during the war. Ironically this Russian station lies within the British sector.

* * *

Russian objectives in the "Battle of Berlin" are to break the morale of the West Berliners and to attack the American pocketbook by making our presence here as costly as possible.

American withdrawal from Berlin would leave about 2,000,000 residents of West Berlin at the complete mercy of the Russians.

It is quite impossible to remain in Berlin for more than a few hours without realizing the intensity of the cold war in this area.

Then, when one sees 370,000 young Germans parading with banners that thank Joe Stalin for the privilege of holding such a youth conclave in Soviet Berlin, the realization is clear that Russia has made remarkable strides in indoctrinating the young minds of Eastern Germany with the Communist ideologies.

* * *

I could conclude only that any hope for a United Germany along the ideas of Western freedom and liberty is not even a remote possibility now or in the future.

It seemed also quite apparent that without strong Allied support for Western Germany, this country would be dominated by the Russians within a matter of months.

The Social Frankenstein Producing The Socialism Trend. In our civilized nations we are now witnessing a reversal of the age-old rule about the survival of the fit. Instead, the unfit are beginning to overpopulate us. A century ago, the good stock produced large families, as the feebleminded still do. Suppose your great great grandfather had 8 children, like the feebleminded Kallikak family in the same neighborhood. Both families may have suffered typhoid and diphtheria, scarlet fever and the other children's diseases. But because the intelligent family was a bit more provident and better fed, let's assume that only 3 of its 8 children died before adulthood, while 4 of the Kallikaks succumbed. In this situation, your great great grandfather thus saw 5 of his offspring mature against 4 for the Kallikaks. The survival of the fit was still in evidence.

But limitation of the size of the families has become more apparent in the civilized nations nowadays, especially among the better educated and more intelligent stock. This has reached such an extreme state that our college population today often doesn't even reproduce itself, although the subnormals continue to breed like guinea pigs. Because we now vaccinate and inoculate the feebleminded children, furnish them free food and shelter as relief wards of the state, and even screen them out by psychological tests so they can't go to war, they actually lead a coddled, sheltered existence unheard of in all previous history. They can't die from epidemics or starvation or battle injuries! So the subnormals are becoming a unique social Frankenstein, supported by the normal stock whose taxes keep increasing meanwhile until the size of the normal family is further reduced.

Politically, too, this is becoming a grave condition, for the subnormals can vote, even if they can make only an "X" on a ballot and are unable to sign their own names. Suppose we start out with two American couples and carry them through 100 years. One is of sound intelligent stock whom we'll call "Normal." The other is "Subnormal." We'll allow a breeding cycle of 25 years, although the feebleminded actually start mating in the teens, with or without benefit of marriage. Even incest is no great deterrent to them. Our juvenile homes are full of such pregnant girls, many of whom are bearing offspring to their own brothers or fathers. We'll be ultra conservative, too, and limit the family of the "Subnormal" to 4 children. The "Normal" will have 2 children per generation. Assume, too, that all offspring live to adulthood and reproduce their own kind. Now examine the data and see how the "Subnormal" offspring will be outvoting your "Normal" stock. The two couples marry in 1965 when they offset each other's votes in a ratio of 1:1.

	Subnormal Couple	Normal Couple	Voting Ratio
1967	2	2	1 : 1
1992	4	2	2 : 1
2017	16	4	4 : 1
2042	64	8	8 : 1
2067	256	16	16 : 1

In one generation of 25 years, therefore, the children of the 3,500,000 college students in the U.S.A. are snowed under at the polls in a 2:1 ratio by the offspring of an equal group of 3,500,000 subnormals who have far outbred them! No wonder demagogues can win elections with beautiful promises of giving impossible pensions and more free medicine, or even a free automobile to every poor couple! The subnormals forget readily, so even if these pre-election promises are not fully kept, their votes can be won the next time simply by varying the nature of the promised rewards. Subnormals naturally want something for nothing. They will even sell out the future heritage of their children, as the Indians traded Manhattan for a few dime store beads (anachronism) and some firewater. For even the top level of the feebleminded (moron group) has only 11-year-old mental ability. It lives for today and seldom thinks ahead of the next meal.

When Benjamin Franklin was eagerly asked what kind of government we were to have, he replied, "You have a republic, if you can keep it." He recognized the precarious nature of

"All that is necessary for the triumph of evil, is that good men do nothing."
—Edmund Burke

this remarkable political system, for he understood how easily mobs can be seduced against their own ultimate good. Hitler and Mussolini and other European dictators subconsciously sensed this same dangerous trend and resorted to Fascism to control the masses without letting them have a free vote. In Russia, the Communist party is also really an oligarchy for it restricts voting to its few million members out of the total population of approximately 200,000,000 Russians, The Roman Republic rotted internally because of the degeneration of intelligence and morality, for the populace began to sell its votes for wheat and thus lazily waited for the highest bidder. Politicians have lately begun to express bewilderment at their inability to predict the outcome of elections. They need to recognize this Frankenstein that has doubled in size in the last generation. The churches, too, must realize that ethics depend on high intelligence, as do trigonometry and other refined cerebral functions, so the zooming percentages of subnormals will be a serious religious threat. For stupid mobs not only can be incited to lynch a man, but they can also be agitated against the churches and especially the tax-free nature of church property. Everybody is thus in danger when demagogues can appeal to subnormals to win elections. Socialism came as a surprise to Britain, too, for the rapidly mounting subnormal voting population can turn on any benevolent economic system that has nurtured it, and then actually destroy its benefactor as Frankenstein killed his highly intelligent creator.

Efficiency Engineering Applied To Government. Since the budget of the U.S.A. is the largest annual appropriation of any government or mammoth private corporation on earth, Uncle Sam thus operates the world's foremost business organization. Accordingly, it behooves him to follow the old slogan, "More business in government; less government in business." If we applied our psychology to government, here are a few of the major improvements that should be instituted: (1) The Cabinet Members should be chosen to function like

---

"A mob is a monster with many hands and no brain." —Old Proverb executive vice-presidents in private business. Every year the President should urge each cabinet member to lower the operational costs of his department, yet increase the service and efficiency meanwhile.

Instead, Cabinet Members now get jealous of each other's prerogatives and actually try to gain BIGGER appropriations and LARGER staffs of employees each year to highhat the other Cabinet Members. For the more money and the more employees they can control, the more social importance they feel. In the summer of 1950, I addressed the national sales convention of Motorola, Incorporated. Its talented president, Paul V. Galvin, announced that within the last year the price of its most expensive radio-television outfit had been dropped from $800 to $575. Meanwhile, the instrument had been improved in quality until Motorola had won the Fashion Academy Award for its 1951 models. Motorola typifies the methods of private business in our "free enterprise" system, where competition constantly promotes better goods or services and at lower prices.

As a contrast, in the spring of 1950, the United States Post Office Department, which is a socialistic and non competitive organization, lowered efficiency by reducing mail deliveries from two to only one per day. In 1963, it increased first class postal rates 25%, added "zip" numbers, and then was demanding that Congress further subsidize it with larger appropriations.

(2) People deriving their living from the government should be disfranchised meanwhile. Our forefathers intended that this be true, which is why the residents of the District of Columbia were so long deprived of the ballot. It was deemed imprudent to let government job holders vote themselves into continued office. But such federal employees are now scattered throughout the various states. In keeping with the intent of our forefathers, therefore, they should not be permitted to vote nor should the families on relief. This regulation would immediately increase governmental efficiency. Instead of adding thousands of unnecessary job holders to the federal payroll

in election years, as an indirect means of buying votes, the party in power would then be inclined to discharge workers so they could cast their ballots. Thus, our tax rate would be proportionately reduced.

(3) The President should be limited to a single 6-year term so he would not spend time on supposed "inspection tours" trying to campaign for his own re-election during much of his fourth year in office. He could be more of a statesman and think in terms of the ultimate good of the nation, rather than degenerating into a politician who is primarily interested in his own re-election.

(4) United States Senators and Representatives should be limited to a total of 12 years service each. At present they often exercise a lifetime tenure. U. S. Representatives should have 4-year terms, staggered so half are to be elected every 2 years.

(5) The national Capital should be moved to a more central location, and one more defensible in time of war. Omaha, Kansas City and Denver have been suggested. For historical purposes, the present buildings could be maintained in Washington. But a new White House and Capitol, plus a modern Library of Congress, should be erected possibly near Denver. This would help make sure that all of our copyrighted books would not be destroyed at once, as in case of fire or bomb attack. At present, a $4 fee and the deposit of 2 copies of any newly-to-be copyrighted book must be made with the Register of Copyrights, Library of Congress, Washington, D.C. Publishers wouldn't mind depositing four copies in the future —2 at Washington and 2 at the new Capitol, such as Denver.

(6) The Hoover Commission's report on governmental reorganization should be adopted to reduce inefficiency and duplication, red tape and petty harrassment of citizens, even down to the antiquated requirement of a 25c notary fee and the waste of 30 minutes of a citizen's time in trying to get an auto license application notarized. Uncle Sam obviously needs a financial "transfusion" every year, but why not use the

"One man with courage makes a majority."   —Andrew Jackson "horse sense" of the medical profession in so doing? If you donate a pint of blood, 100 different physicians don't extract a few drops here, a teaspoonful there, another dozen drops some place else, etc. and then present 100 different fees for the job. No, we let one doctor take out the full pint. The job is performed as painlessly and cheaply as possible. Our taxes should be raised in the same way. Moreover, the less paper work required by the citizens to compute their taxes, the less preemption of their valuable time, which is a hidden tax nowadays not even showing on their income tax sheets.

(7) Panels of trained jurors should be available to all of our courts. Instead of picking Tom, Dick and Harry off the street, with no regard to their lack of training in logic or the various fallacies thereof, we should have men and women who had been given at least a rudimentary course in how to sift facts from emotionalism. Too many jurors nowadays are enamoured of a nylon clad knee with a skirt pulled well above it, so when the accused sheds her artificial tears, these jurors forget legal evidence and acquit her.

(8) When taxpayers are indicted by the government, the government should pay all defense costs. At present citizens must contribute taxes to prosecute themselves, which is a financial violation of the 5th Amendment!

(9) Radio and television stations, once they are licensed, should thereafter be as free from government regulation as the newspapers. They should never be coerced under veiled threat of revocation of their permits. At present, that sword of Damocles hangs over all of them.

How To Safeguard Our Republic By Audio-Visual Education. The vast majority of Americans never enter college, even for one semester. They leave school forever by the time they are 18. Metropolitan Life Insurance statistics show that they live on an average to be approximately 70. So for those final 52 adult years, who will educate and inform, as well as entertain and lead, them in their thinking?

Well, about 63% belong to churches, yet only about 25%

of our total population are very regular in their church attendance. A small percentage belong to literary and forum groups, such as the Town Hall, Lyceum, and the like. But we know that the majority follow their newspapers, the radio and, more recently, television. In a former address before the New York State Newspaper Editors Association, I mentioned that the newspaper and radio are the Siamese Twins of Adult Education. We might very properly add TV and magazines, thus forming the "Quadruplets" for quick influence of public opinion.

Daily newspaper circulations in the United States have now reached a record high of 61,000,000, according to *Editor & Publisher*. This includes both morning and evening dailies. Advertising men claim about 3½ readers for every newspaper subscriber, which would total more than our entire 1965 population. But millions of people buy both a morning and an evening daily, which helps clear up this apparent discrepancy. In my personal experience, I find that my daily psychology column attracts an input of letters from readers which runs between 3% and 5% of the total circulation figure annually. In a few cases, such as the Columbus *Citizen*, the Akron *Beacon Journal* and the St. Louis *Globe Democrat*, the mail has run above the 7% figure. Thus, if a newspaper's circulation is 100,000, I normally receive 3,000 to 5,000 letters from its readers each year. Among the professional groups, the three that send me the most mail are dentists, clergy and school teachers or administrators. My annual letter input for these three groups now exceeds 2,000 from dentists, 1,500 from clergy, and 1,200 from school officials.

In the fields of American Radio and TV, the 1966 *World Almanac* listed total U. S. home radios at 114,000,000 and TV sets at 70,000,000. There were also 47,000,000 auto radios and over 18,000,000 in business places, barns and on farm tractors. Surveys show that 1.3% of farm tractors are radio equipped, while 11.8% of all trucks and 19.8% of all barns likewise are equipped with radios. In one of its national surveys, the American Research Bureau made a breakdown of the time devoted to various educational media. The data showed that the average person gives a daily time of 108 minutes to radio; 43 minutes to TV; 34 minutes to newspapers, and 18 minutes to magazines. The corresponding figures for the average farm adult were 189 minutes to radio; 33 to TV; 31 to newspapers, and 26 to magazines. Since farmers eat at home, they often listen to radio at meal time. They have an early bedtime curfew, too, which may explain why they devote fewer minutes per day to TV programs.

When my daily transcribed radio talks on practical psychology were issuing from the 50,000-watt WGN station in Chicago, at 11:45 A.M., I was surprised to find a liberal input of mail from men. One morning, for example, I personally opened exactly 200 letters taken at random, and found that 69 were from men. So I had a count made of the next 3,000 letters and men accounted for 32.7% or almost one letter from a man for every two from women. Puzzled at this high input from men, I read further and found a surprising number of clergymen, physicians, and salesmen who were tuning in via automobile radios. Other men, like tailors and barbers, apparently listen while they work, for their duties are not interfered with by the radio. A third group consisted of men on the night shift who were having "brunch" about 11:45 in the morning.

Since advertising is really an instance of adult education, paid for by commercial and industrial firms, it can often perform a dual job of stressing its own commodities while informing the general public on social problems. Some of the striking advertisements reproduced in this textbook show how our Republic with its "free enterprise" economic system can thus be aided through the mass enlightenment made possible by patriotic American advertisers. But printed matter demands literate citizens. In the summer of 1959, the NEA released data it had compiled on 16-year-old high school sophomores who were asked to write the Pledge of Allegiance to the Flag. And following are commonest words that confuse college students:

High School Students	Errors of College Students	
I plage of lieglion	their	believe
I plege allenaige	they're	choose
I pleadge a leision	there	chose
I pledge a leasor	too	principle
I plege alginyence	two	principal
I pleage allenciss	to	professor
I pleague the Leaguence	occur	success
I pledge a leiguch	separate	necessary
(Yet in 5 years these	its	it's
students will be voters!)	personal	personnel

George Washington said "The mass of citizens of the United States mean well and I firmly believe will always act well when they can obtain a right understanding of matters." Through audio-visual media we can thus reach the 85% of people who do not attend college. But we must employ simple, dramatic presentations of our profound ideas both to catch their attention and persuade them to the right viewpoint. For example, in a survey after World War II, it was found that 72% of the public thought industry's profits totaled MORE than industry's wages. Actually, even in the boom year of 1948, the profits were only one-sixth[27] of wages. It would thus be better to publish company earnings in terms of %, as 5% or 8%, rather than as a lump sum like $50,000,000.

Better Use of Radio & Television for Social Improvement. In 1950, many radio station managers were afraid that the new TV spelled the end of radio. But this terror was premature. Television simply forced radio to improve its programming policies. There are several inherent advantages which radio holds over television and vice versa. Television demands "idle" time whereas busy housewives and many men working at routine mechanical duties can still listen to radio. Their ears are free but not their eyes! The idlers around the house are usually watching television while the real spender of the family pay check, namely, the housewife, is elsewhere doing the dishes or attending to other household chores. Since the advertiser, who supports both television and radio, is primarily concerned with the housewives, radio thus will probably always be tops during the daytime and can hold its own as night entertainment if it will develop a strong programming policy.

Radio needs to focus more particularly at adults and leave the kids as TV's idle market. Both radio and television should also use the following psychological strategy: (1) They should avoid program monotony, for even Hollywood stars grow boresome after excessive repetition. A good Program Director not only tries to diversify his around-the-clock radio log, but should select programs which in themselves will vary from day to day in their own 15-minute time slot. In my own daily radio transcribed series, for instance, I thus alternate between Child Problems, Love and Marriage, Personality Improvement, Mental Health, and Business or Professional cases dealing with Applied Psychology. I use the "Radio Smorgasbord" format!

(2) Radio and television should increase their "curative" rather than their "sedative" or merely entertaining programs. They should have a healing pill inside the sugar coating of light entertainment. The usual music and humor programs entertain, but they don't help the public avoid divorce, win friends, raise a child's low school marks, or banish the needless anxiety about mental aches and pains that afflicts millions of American hypochondriacs. When it is possible to rate just as high on the Nielsen survey as sheer entertainment, but ALSO leave a wholesome residue of human betterment, the smart Program Director should always choose the latter course.

(3) Radio and television need to cultivate more acceptance from the prestige sources in their area, such as clergy, other professional men and teachers, Parent-Teacher-Associations, Women's Clubs, etc. It isn't necessary to be dull or deadly to qualify as a constructive, cultural program. In many cases old-time advertising men are dominating radio and television

---

"I felt sorry for myself because I had no shoes until I saw a man who had no feet."   —Proverb policy. They need to wake up to modern Applied Psychology. (4) Radio and television should quickly tap the ready-made audiences of eminently respected leaders who, in addition to their own fame, are also talented public platform artists.

Dr. E. B. Hurlock[12], one of our leading authorities in Adolescent Psychology, gives these tips to parents regarding a child's time spent with TV: (1) Don't ban television, but apportion the youngster's time therewith. (2) Help your child select appropriate programs and explain fully why you veto others. (3) Whenever possible, watch the programs with your youngster. Later, discuss their merits and faults. (4) Look on his television as a form of education, as well as amusement. (5) Encourage him in outdoor play that will throw him in contact with other children. (6) Let watching television be a reward for good deeds or acceptable school marks. (7) Don't grow unduly alarmed about the craze over television, for its novelty will wear off somewhat.

Many generous persons have presented television sets to churches and schools, YMCA and CYO groups, which is quite commendable. But there is room for even wider employment of both radio, television, sound slide films and movies, especially among youth. Mercer Francisco, who has long been one of America's top producers of training films and advertising pictures, informs me that over 25,000 schools, especially of the high school level, have 16 mm. moving picture machines and are eager for films that are both colorful, entertaining and instructive.

He is now concentrating upon the problem of getting some films developed showing the difference between a democracy and this great Republic, with its "free enterprise" system. He also believes we should stress the importance of our house key as a symbol of the sanctuary we enjoy in our own homes in contrast to the insecurity in many foreign countries where secret police can break open the door and seize the householder without due process of law or a previously procured warrant. Our house key vividly symbolizes all of our other freedoms in America.

We must employ consummate psychological skill with all of our educational agencies, including newspapers, magazines, radio, TV, the movies and sound slide films, to preserve our cultural, economic, and moral leadership. Our 200 million people are surrounded by over 3 billions of mainly envious, spiteful or actually hostile neighbors. Our Republic with its "free enterprise" system is an island surrounded by the raging seas of alien ideologies. We should be reasonably generous but never permit anybody, at home or abroad, to poison and kill the goose that lays these wonderful golden eggs. Beware; only 32 of the 104 members of the U. N. grant habeas corpus to their people!

REFERENCES

1 ABRAHAMSEN, D., *The Psychology of Crime* (Brunner, 1962).
2 BAILEY, S. D., *The Secretariat of the U. N.* (Taplinger, 1962).
3 BRIDGE, D. U., *Men and Methods of Newspaper Advertising* (Arco, 1947)
4 CAMPBELL et al., *The American Voter* (Wiley, 1960).
5 CRANE, G. W., *"The Worry Clinic"* (Daily Newspaper Column, 1967).
6 CRANE, P. M., *The Democrat's Dilemma* (Regnery, 1964).
7 FLYNN, J. T., *The Road Ahead* (Devin-Adair, 1949).
8 GALLUP, G., "Newspaper Polls" (Am. Inst. Pub. Op., 1960).
9 GUILFORD, J. P., *Psychometric Methods* (McGraw-Hill, 1960).
10 HOCH & ZUBIN, *Psychiatry & the Law* (Grune, Stratton, 1954).
11 HOVLAND, C. I., *Communication & Persuasion* (Yale U. Pr., 1955).
12 HURLOCK, E. B., "Television Tips for Parents *(Today's Health, June, 1950)*.
13 KING, W. I., *The Keys to Prosperity* (Constitution Found., 1948).
14 KUTNER, LUIS, *World Habeas Corpus* (Oceana, 1962).
15 KOTTMEYER & LAMBADOR, *New Goals in Spelling* (Webster, 1960).
16 LAWRENCE, J. S., "Socialism Weakens England" *(Empire Trust Letter,* 9/8/49).
17 LARRABEE & MEYERSON, *Mass Leisure* (Macmillan, 1962).
18 LEWIS & ENGLE, *Wartime Psychiatry* (Oxf. U. Pr., 1954).
19 LINCOLN, J. F., "Is Labor Riding for a Fall" *(American Mag.,* June, 1950).
20 LIFTON, W. M., *Working With Groups* (Wiley, 1964).
21 MINNICK, W. C., *The Art of Persuasion* (Houghton, Mifflin, 1959).
22 NORTON, T. J., *The Constitution of the United States* (World, 1940).
23 PALYI, M., *Compulsory Medical Care and the Welfare State* (Nat. Inst. Prof. Services, 1950).
24 PETTENGILL, S. B., *Jefferson; the Forgotten Man* (America's Future, 1940).
25 PETTENGILL, S. B., *Smoke Screen* (Southern Publishers, 1940).
26 POLING, D. R., *Mine Eyes Have Seen* (McGraw-Hill, 1959).
27 SHEFFERMAN, N. W., *Labor's Stake in Capitalism* (Lab. Rel. Assoc., 1954).
28 VISCARDI, H., *Give Us The Tools* (Eriksson-Taplinger, 1960).
29 VOSS, E. H., *Nuclear Ambush* (Regnery, 1963).
30 WILBUR, W. H., *Russian Communism — Challenge & Fraud* (Caxton, 1966).

CHAPTER XX

PSYCHOLOGY GOES TO WORK

Applied Psychology offers business and industry their greatest opportunity to forge ahead of their rivals. It is difficult for any manufacturer to beat his competitors significantly in the tensile strength of his steel or the quality of his plastics or rubber or even his gasoline. In life insurance, too, the premium rates on comparable policies are very similar as between one company and another. Mechanical engineering has thus reached such a standardized level that Company "A" may be lucky if it can cite even a one per cent superiority in the quality of its merchandise over similar goods from Company "B."

But psychology is such a young science that many firms aren't as cognizant of all its useful contributions to advertising, selling, personnel administration, public relations and credit. As a result, it is still possible for one corporation to be 100% ahead of its competitors in its psychological strategy. The formula for success in this modern competitive age consists of topnotch merchandise or professional services, linked with equally superlative psychological strategy.

Psychology Counts At Least 50% Towards Success. Dr. R. S. Uhrbrock[33], a famous industrial psychologist, compared the earnings of engineering graduates of Purdue University 5 years after they were out of college. The brilliant or Phi Beta Kappa boys averaged about $150 more per year than their classmates who just barely managed to skim through with a passing average. But when he contrasted the men who had rated high in personality traits—popular, well liked by their classmates— with those rated low in such traits while on the campus, he found that the popular men were obtaining nearly $1,000 more in annual salary.

Dr. A. H. Edgerton[8] discovered fairly comparable results in his extensive surveys. In one group of 3,607 employees who had lost their jobs, the data showed that 77% were fired for purely psychological ineptness, such as bad manners, irritability, tactlessness, etc. He also found that the highest third in intelligence were earning $139 more annually than the lowest third, while the upper third in personality were paid $842 more annually than the bottom third in such traits. In this connection, you may recall the Harvard report (p. 338) where approximately 66% of discharged workers were fired because of lack of psychological understanding.

When I addressed the Brooklyn Dental Society in 1938, its president informed me that over 200 dentists in just that one section of New York City were then actually on relief. They were finally paid $25 per week to do routine checking of children's teeth in the schools, although stenographers in the relief offices were paid $30 a week. "And, Dr. Crane," said this dental leader, "there are more physicians on relief than dentists!" Those professional men were often brilliant students who had won honors. They had also passed their State Board Exams with flying colors. They were thus technically trained, at least in their fingers. But their tongues had not been educated in skillful psychological strategy. They didn't know how to win friends and develop prestige in the eyes of patients.

During the past 25 years I have addressed state dental conventions from coast to coast, and my opening sentence is this: "Gentlemen, as we psychologists view your profession, your greatest problem is not how to fill a patient's tooth but how to fill your dental chair!" They always applaud vigorously at this point, for medical and dental colleges have too long ignored the vital importance of Applied Psychology. They intimate to their students that practicing superlative medicine or dentistry from the mechanical angle, is all that is needed. But that is

---

"Cold" sweat is essential to success for it proves you've left your previous *status quo*.

only about 50% of the problem. The other half is a keen understanding of human nature, including how to motivate patients or customers or clients or parishioners successfully.

The Importance Of Vocational Counseling. In medicine it is now the trend for patients to want a physician to do ALL the curing of them, failing to realize that the body must heal itself. There is thus a growing tendency for people to impute almost magical powers to their doctors, whether in medicine or psychology. Vocational Counseling is a rapidly expanding and exceedingly important field of Applied Psychology, but, as Dr. Joseph V. Hanna[14] so expertly points out, there is likely to be an over-confidence in tests and an over-dependence on test results. He lists the following reasons for this threat to the constructive use of tests in guidance: (1) the insecurity of the individual; (2) the prominence given tests in general publicity and social agencies; (3) failure of staff counselors to orient the client regarding the proper use of tests in a counseling service. Dr. Hanna thus is simply advocating a little more "horse sense" in this vital field.

A Jewish merchant in Baltimore once gave me an excellent practical rule for vocational guidance. "Take the best job you can get at the moment," he said. "Perform it to the best of your ability. But keep on the lookout for better openings up ahead." We Applied Psychologists often encounter college graduates who hang around the house, possibly smoking cigarets which they have mooched from hard working Dad or an indulgent sister, but refusing to take a job because they argue, "There's no future in that job."

Actually, there's no future in ANY job! The future always lies in the person who holds that job. For jobs are just rungs on the ladder to success. Rungs, however, don't move upward. They are stationary. It's the man or woman who steps on those rungs who can climb to the top. Whether you start out

---

"Never give a man up until he has failed at something he likes."
—Lewis E. Lawes

as a dishwasher at a restaurant, or a carrier of newspapers, an errand boy or a baby sitter, if you have normal intelligence and physical ability, you may be stimulated to reach the top in any of dozens of fields. Look at WHO'S WHO and you'll be surprised at the menial tasks that served as the initial stepping stones for those promiment Americans.

There is no magic to vocational guidance. It is a laborious scientific task for a psychologist to make a full inventory of all the factors involved, since intelligence, personality, health, education, vocational likes or dislikes, perseverance, honesty and many other qualities are involved. Even when the Vocational Counselor has selected several positions for which you are adapted, don't imagine you will fall so in love with any job that you write love ballads to it, and can't wait to punch a time clock each morning!

Success is predicated in a large degree on elbow grease and the routine performance of "chores" which you complete because they are simply inescapable steps towards the success or fame or salary you really do crave. We psychologists don't want you to evaluate jobs solely on the basis of their salary tags, either, for you should abhor subversive work which fails to give customers a fair exchange for their money. The liquor salesman, though he gets a higher income to assuage his twinges of conscience, has little to rejoice about when he surveys the damage he has wrought in society, such as broken homes, cheated children, auto accidents and immorality.

A New Vocational Guidance Chart. The accompanying Vocational Guidance Chart is offered as a rough model which you can polish up and amplify. It attempts to classify jobs on the basis of the minimum amount of schooling usually demanded for success therein, plus the personal outlook of the individual as regards his introversion or extroversion of interests. If the goal you have in life is not specifically named, try to find a job that is closely related to it. This will enable you to place your "dream" position in its approximate location.

Happiness is never a destination but a way of traveling.

VOCATIONAL GUIDANCE CHART

Minimum Education	Introvert	Intro-ambivert	Ambivert	Extro-ambivert	Extrovert
COLLEGE	Accountant Architect Chemist Engineer Pharmacist Statistician Forester Surveyor	Dentist Lawyer-Corp. Optometrist Physiothera- pist Veterinarian Surgeon	Clergyman Lawyer-Crim. Missionary Nurse Physician Teacher YMCA Sec'y YWCA Sec'y	Athletic director Executive— Sales Football— coach Osteopath	Congressman Public Rela- tion official Senator Campaign Manager
HIGH SCHOOL or some COLLEGE	Air Pilot Poet Radio Operator	Ad Writer Author Banker Contractor Editorial writer Librarian Mortician Private Secre- tary (Bus.) Singer	Governess Personnel director Reporter Retailer Stewardess	Bond salesman Chiropractor Insurance salesman Private Sec'y Sales Mgr. Sales Engineer Social worker	Lesser politician Scout Master Sec. Chamber of Commerce
HIGH SCHOOL	Draftsman Motion Picture Operator Railway Engineer Railway mail clerk Telegrapher	Actor Artist Bank Cashier Bank Clerk Credit Mgr. Designer— fashion Florist Musician Photographer Stenographer	Garage owner Manufacturer Minor Executive Office Mgr. Policeman Public Stenographer Radio announcer	Filling station operator Beauty Shop operator Small retailer	Retail sales clerk Information clerk
GRAMMAR or some HIGH SCHOOL	Adding ma- chine oper. Bookkeeper Designer—tool Farmer File Clerk Mechanic Printer Typesetter Window trimmer	Conductor Dressmaker Electrician Milliner Plumber Postman Typist	Barber Cashier-retail Detective General office clerk Masseur Telephone operator Ticket seller	Factory foreman Floorwalker Usher	House-to-house salesman Clown Waiter Waitress
GRAMMAR SCHOOL	Baker Brakeman Cabinet Maker Cobbler Fisherman Gardener Machinist Mason	Carpenter Cook Elevator man Factory worker House painter Paperhanger Tailor	Butcher Maid Chauffeur Soldier	Sailor Taxi Driver	Vendor

It is possible for an extreme introvert to make a success in such a distinctly extrovertive field as house-to-house selling. One of my clients was a high school chemistry teacher who insisted on trying out as a magazine salesman. He led not only his own crew but the entire national sales force within 6 weeks. But he was exhausted each night until he couldn't even eat a full meal. The rebuffs and tension took a greater toll of his nervous energy than they did of the relatively callous extrovert who could shrug his shoulders when a door was slammed in his face.

As a rule, therefore, we Applied Psychologists play the batting averages and try to steer a definite introvert into a position which introverts usually like and in which they get along fairly well. Inanimate objects, whether ledger sheets, musical instruments, machine tools, chemicals or farm implements, are the usual desire of extreme introverts. Extroverts, on the contrary, generally dislike details and fine movements. They seem to prefer "talking" jobs which involve dealing with people. The first born child is often more introvertive than his next sibling. Remember the Prodigal Son and his elder brother?

The Personnel Strategy Of Big Business Firms. All intelligent young people nowadays should certainly try to obtain their high school diploma and then take at least a year of college work, just as job insurance. Suppose, for example, a certain corporation advertises that it needs 10 workers. Perhaps 100 apply. How does the company find which 10 it prefers? "How many of you are high school graduates?" is a familiar opening query. Let's assume 40 have their diplomas. That leaves 60 who don't. "Sorry, but we have nothing for you at the moment," the company may tell the non-graduates, "but we'll keep your names on file and if anything opens up later on, we'll be glad to contact you."

That is a polite run-around, as a general rule, so the 60 who failed to finish high school are out of luck. This first screening process has possibly reduced the number of applicants from 100 to 40. So the next question is often this: "How many of you are college men?" The employer doesn't always ask if you are a 4-year graduate, but just if you have had some college training. Suppose 20 fall in that elite category. These then run the "gantlet" of various tests, and finally may go through a short oral examination during which their physical appearance, poise, and total personality effect may be rated.

If applicants are to write letters seeking jobs, the Specimen Letter of Application on Page 759 should be helpful. In such an event, it is preferable to find out in advance the actual name of the Personnel Director and thus address him accordingly, instead of using the vague, "Dear Sir." Remember, too, that your letter is not supposed to land you a job but just to procure a personal interview. So don't fill your missive with too many details. Stick to one typewritten page. And use a fresh typewriter ribbon with well cleaned type. Avoid anemic old ribbons in dust-clogged typewriters. Then sign your name in a bold, firm hand, if you are a man, employing dark ink instead of the pale blue or more "sissy" colors.

For the actual interview, dress conservatively. Don't look kiddish or collegiate. You men should wear a collar and tie, instead of a T-shirt, and avoid sideburns, as well as ultra long hair. Don't talk too much. Let the prospective employer do most of the speaking. Girls should not dress in a flashy manner with an excess of rouge and lipstick, mascara or glaring red fingernails. Blondes tend to appear more youthful than their years, especially during the late teens or early twenties, so try to look and act older than your years. It may make a difference of several dollars per week in your starting salary. Many firms have a sliding scale for opening salaries. You can thus boost your wages more during that initial interview, if you make the proper impression, than you may be able to raise them in the entire next year.

Running The "Gantlet" Of Psychological Tests. In Chapter IX you read the psychological background of various aptitude and achievement tests. This field of Applied Psychology had made great progress during the years between World War I and World War II. During the latter conflagration, however, American industry operated on a "cost, plus" basis. Manpower was also difficult to get in adequate quantities. So the facetious remark was then made that all the employer asked concerning prospective workers was: "Is the body warm and still breathing? If so, put it on the payroll!" Regardless of the limited output of such an employee, the government paid the cost, plus a standard profit. The individual employer didn't care too much if he got stuck with a "lemon", for if the latter's weekly wage ran to $90, that was included in Uncle Sam's ultimate bill, plus possibly a 10% gross profit charge. So the inefficient worker still brought the manufacturer a good profit in those days.

With the return to normal competitive business, it again became imperative that good workers be culled from the inefficient applicants. Tests again came back into popularity. The usual employer who is hiring applicants for specific jobs, such as that of an office girl or stenographer, thus employs a few specific tests, like the Thurstone Test for Clerical Workers, plus maybe an intelligence test. But a personal interview is usually the final decisive event, for tests are simply aids to this end. Unlike the lengthy testing to which college freshmen are put during their first few days on the campus, the applicant for a job seldom has to run a very lengthy "gantlet." But if he is seeking a complete analysis of his personality, one of our talented Consulting Psychologists will then give him a wide range of tests and prepare a "Personality Profile" which lists his major strengths and weaknesses in great detail.

"Around-The-Clock" Or 24-Hour Personnel Policy.
When Dr. T. H. Cutler invited me to Mare Island Naval Yards during World War II, he took me on a full tour of that vast enterprise. Some of the top management informed me that it wasn't the workers' problems ON the job which caused them

as much inefficiency as their troubles OFF the job. Our Personnel Directors have now reached a fairly high level of proficiency in the interviewing of applicants, as well as in testing and screening them, plus job placement, wage incentives, factory magazines or house organs, and similar on-the-job measures. But they are now expanding their horizon to include those 16 hours the workers are not in the factory or shop. The marital adjustments of the employees, as well as their recreational opportunities, and their rapport with their children, as well as their health and even their budgeting skill with their pay checks—all these are now vital factors included in the 24-hour personnel strategy.

For a man who fears lest his wife will leave him or have an affair with somebody else while he is away from home, or who is worried about his child's school progress or the youngster's need for hospitalization, obviously can't focus with 100% efficiency on his job, even though the personnel procedures are perfect during his 8-hour shift. The latest trend in personnel psychology is thus to release marital bulletins to workers, as well as information on child psychology and social adjustments. Banking services are often operated by the firm for its employees, as well as the lending of money at very moderate interest rates.

The famous Psychological Barometer, which was started in 1932, is the oldest of several excellent psychological polls which help obtain the attitudes of workers, as well as of the general public. These will prove of increasing value in the future as we adopt the "around-the-clock" personnel viewpoint. Within the factory, moreover, the "pause and praise" technique, aided by the "reversible why" and the "sandwich method" of administering reproof or correction, will do much to lessen ill will between labor and management.

When an irate employee wants to see the boss, it is also well to defer the appointment tactfully till that worker has had his

---

"Not failure but low aim is crime"   —Lowell

meal, for a full stomach lowers belligerency. Then let him get his objection off his chest. Encourage him to speak, for the act of articulating grievances helps dissipate one's anger. A skillful foreman employs the "arm in arm" strategy in such cases. Instead of meeting the employee head-on in an emotional conflict, he can say: "Why, that's too bad, Mike. Is this work too technical for you? We don't want to load you up with jobs that are over your head. So just let me know if you ever feel you can't handle your duties and I'll get you a transfer to a simpler job."

The relief of uncertainty and anxiety are two of the greatest needs among all of mankind, and especially is this true in dealing with workers, as well as military recruits. Indeed, in trying to fill its September and October draft quotas in 1950 for the Korean conflict, the Chicago draft board found that approximately 36% of those disqualified were unfit because of psychiatric disorders, with anxiety neuroses leading the list of mental disorders.

Profit Sharing And Wage Incentive Plans. When a factory worker at a lathe produces his daily output, he must always remember that he and his boss are not the only people involved as regards wages. For the lathe, plus all the other tools, and even the buildings are an essential part of that plant's productive power. Millions of widows, via their life insurance policies, and other stock holders, own the tools. They are just as much entitled to a fair wage (dividend), on their contribution to that factory output as is the actual operator of the lathe or his foreman. This broader viewpoint is much needed in American industry nowadays.

Furthermore, James F. Lincoln[24] has long advocated and put into practice a profit sharing plan in his vast company. He says it has increased production 7 times since 1933, quadrupled the wages 4 times, and tripled the dividends to the stockholders, yet prices to consumers in 1964 were still below prewar levels. The average income to employees was nearing

$7,500 per year, which was the highest in the world for that type of work. The Lincoln Electric Company had never had a strike nor lost an hour through misunderstanding. Scores of other plants have adopted the profit-sharing plan.

The tragedy about strikes is that everybody suffers. It may take 5 to 10 years for the union men to make up their losses during a 6-months to one year strike, even if they get their desired hourly increase. And during those next 5 to 10 years, a business recession may occur which will prevent them from ever breaking even. While the plants are shut down, too, the stockholders are deprived of their wages (dividends) on their investment in machines and equipment. At this late stage in our scientific age, we should apply more psychology to wage scales. If Uncle Sam could set a minimum wage scale of $1.25 per hour for all inter-state industries, he could likewise adopt a "fluid-drive" or hydromatic pay rate for coal miners vs. automobile workers, carpenters, etc.

A differential wage should thus be determined for all the major trades[17]. It could be established on the basis of the intelligence required by any given occupation, plus the minimum amount of training or apprenticeship needed, plus the hazards to life, as well as the shortness of the working season, and all other relevant factors. The differential minimum wage for all trades could then be pegged on the basis of the current commodity price index in a given city or state. Every quarter, the Department of Labor could report as to the current commodity price index and thus recommend that wages be increased or lowered proportionately. This strategy would eliminate the long periods of shut-down due to strikes, and save the housewives of those strikers the anxiety and harassment which they now undergo, for the wives suffer more than their striking mates.

The Strategy Of Building A Private Clientele.

A life insurance salesman should consider himself in the category of dentists, physicians, lawyers and other professional men, who must take the long range viewpoint regarding their personal practice. Dr. Charles Kendall, prominent Milwaukee dentist, analyzed this problem for his profession and stated that a young dentist must have treated 500 different patients in his operative chair before their repeat patronage and referral of their friends will give him an average income. To be rushed with clients, he must have had 800 different patients in his dental chair[6].

Somewhat comparable figures could be derived for other professions. After 10 years in life insurance, the average insurance salesman can count on selling about 25% of his current year's volume of business to his previous customers. But gaining those first 50 to 100 clients or customers is the toughest part of private practice. Professional men should extrovert themselves and get acquainted with the elevator men in their building, the scrub women and even the corner newsboys, for the latter occasionally are asked, "Bud, do you know a good dentist nearby?" Professional men should smile more freely and be very liberal with honest compliments. They should toot the other person's horn.

If not unduly rushed, they should let those first patients handle their technical instruments or look through their microscopes. For it is word-of-mouth talk-up which they must depend upon, since their professional ethics debar them from individually signed ads in the newspapers. But to stimulate talk-up, you must give your clients something to talk about besides your name. It inflates their ego to touch your instruments and get a peek at an x-ray or stained slide under your microscope. Show them how to make their own blood count. They'll then bring you into conversations at bridge clubs or elsewhere. A new doctor can also tap the popularity of a socially popular young woman in the town by selecting a widely known and admired girl for his receptionist or office assistant.

Since patients, clients and customers are usually recruited

from those who know the professional man and think favorably
of him, it thus behooves the young doctor or salesman or attorney to circulate socially and win many friends. If he already
has an attractive, socially minded wife, the latter may indirectly be responsible for referring many of his first clients to
him. Young professional men should invest their spare time
in constructive civic, social and religious organizations, such
as the YMCA or CYO, the Red Cross and Community Chest
Drive, as well as the church, the P-T-A, plus the Lions, Rotary, Kiwanis and other service men's luncheon clubs.

A very discouraged, though talented dentist, aged 46, recently came to my office for psychological advice. (He had
been an honor student in college but now, after 20 years in
his city of 15,000 population, he was still barely making a
living.) His net income was only $4,500. So he wondered if it
wouldn't be well for him to go to some other town and start
all over. However, I reminded him that in a strange locale
he would have all the hazards of the new dental college graduate and thus be forced to struggle for years trying to recruit
those first 500 patients.

He was a typical introvertive scientist, who spoke only when
somebody else first addressed him. He didn't smile easily, nor
did he feel happy around people, for he didn't know how to
carry on conversation. Moreover, his main hobby was raising
bees. He had a little home at the edge of town, where he kept
honey bees. Every spare minute was devoted to their care.
He was exceptionally well read on the subject.

"But bees can't talk favorably about your dental skill," I
remonstrated. "They don't attend the Ladies Aid of the local
churches in your city. They don't go to Red Cross meetings
or other civic events. So what you need right now is to develop
some extrovertive hobbies that will throw you into greater
contact with people."

Incidentally, extrovertive hobbies are the sort which young
professional men should cultivate. On the contrary, introvertive avocations like fishing, hunting, keeping bees, or puttering

around in a basement work shop, should be avoided by men who must gain those first 500 prospects or patients as soon as possible. For you simply can't expect to recruit clients unless you meet new people, or unless your present patients circulate socially and frequently talk you up among their acquaintances.

One of my medical classmates was fond of magic. He had really become an admirable amateur magician before we graduated from Northwestern Medical School. He interned with me and then headed right into New York City, to start his private practice. The large cities, however, are usually difficult spots, for too many modern doctors seem to be afflicted with what we might fittingly term "professional agoraphobia." So they cluster around the large metropolitan centers and almost starve for the first 5 to 10 years.

But this classmate of mine zoomed to the top in short order. He gained as much prestige in 5 years as most New York physicians attain in 20. And it was chiefly through his magic that he did it, for churches and men's organizations were eager to have him put on his sleight-of-hand show. Children, too, were delighted to visit his office for he would pull a rabbit out of their blouse or perform other interesting tricks. So they would talk about him among their friends until other children, as well as their parents, also consulted this young physician. His magic thus was worth thousands of dollars to him in word-of-mouth advertising. And that type of publicity is needed by those professional men who are debarred from advertising themselves in the local newspaper by paid ads. I have likewise seen priests and clergymen who attained quick popularity because of their social graces and their ability to perform even a few simple sleight-of-hand tricks for children. The latter may often contribute more to a clergyman's success than 5 years study of Greek and Hebrew or other introvertive subjects.

Many of our professional schools become so enamoured of

"Things do not happen. They are made to happen." —Gardner Cowles pure science and polysyllabic vocabulary, however, that they fail to prepare their graduates for these immediate practical demands, such as the recruiting of those first few dozen patients. Applied Psychology should be a required course for all professional students since it goes a long way to shorten this initial period when the young doctor or attorney or life insurance salesman is barely able to keep the wolf from his door. It is also vital for all Business College graduates.

Please remember, too, that the life insurance salesman has a terrific drain upon his morale, for the standard formula in his field demands 40 calls each week, 15 interviews, and ONE sale. Just think, 25 people aren't at home or will not greet him at all, and of the 15 he actually does see, 14 turn him down. He wins only once out of 15 times! Even the occupants of the cellar in big league baseball win about 1 game out of every 3. So you wives of professional men and salesmen should be "cheer leaders" instead of "wet blankets." The act of "fronting" before the public takes a great deal of energy out of a man, whether he be a doctor or a salesman.

In 1948, the median net income of dentists under 25 years of age who were in private practice, was $2,300, or approximately $50 per week. Between 25 and 29 years, their median net income had risen to $4,515, while the median for all United States dentists in private practice was $5,944 that year[16]. The median net income of the dentists in towns under 1,000 population was $4,450, while in cities of 5,000 to 10,000 size, it amounted to $5,761. It reached its maximum of $7,045 in cities of 25,000 to 50,000, but had declined in cities of 1,000,000 or above until it was $4,962. The three largest independent professions in order are law, medicine and dentistry. In 1960, the median dental income was $8,000 per year.

How Home Ownership Stabilizes Workers. Individual home ownership by workers is the antithesis of communism. The more we can thus encourage workers to purchase their own homes, the better will be our labor situation. For home owners are more stable. They lack much of the disregard for property rights which mobs and "floaters" so often demonstrate. They become a more self-respecting, law-abiding group in the community. One reason for the shifting of northern industries to the south is predicated on the greater reliability of the workers in that area. The labor market is not as "frothy" and irresponsible. Those are not the only reasons, but they are cited as among the major factors causing the modern trek southward. The Carolinas and Georgia have had a phenomenal industrial boom since the end of World War II, chiefly at the expense of New England.

It might be an excellent tactical move for modern industries to help subsidize their workers in the purchase of their own cottages. That money which corporations are now laying aside via insurance for old age pensions, might be invested in housing for their own workers, with a low interest rate for the mortgages thereon. This would keep the pension money in the same town and produce many psychological dividends, not the least of which would be the strongest type of anti-communism sentiment. Remember Jefferson's comment: "The small landowners are the most precious part of the state."

Let's Salvage The Talents In Those Past 65. Applied Psychology is a scientific name for "horse sense." It demands that we salvage the talented citizens by the millions who have remarkable skills that ought not be put into moth bags just because people happen to have celebrated their 65th birthday. If our Senators and Representatives at Washington still hold on to their offices even after the age of 80, certainly other Americans are worthy to enjoy equal respect and opportunity. A profit sharing plan in industry would thus permit each worker to turn out his own output and hence would permit older men to remain self-supporting, if they wished to continue on the job.

Others need to develop hobbies, such as more active work

"The belly will not listen to advice."   —Seneca

in the church and also in politics. It is inefficient, for example, that youth have no recreational facilities at night in many areas when the public schools, built with the people's money, have gymnasiums and swimming pools that are dark and locked up. Such youth agencies as the YMCA could expand 20-fold simply by paying a modest rent and using these public school facilities from 4 till 10 P.M., with older people as volunteer chaperones and assistants to the trained personnel of the YMCA, CYO and other youth organizations.

James F. Lincoln has ably indicted the vicious modern philosophy which intimates that "work is bad so we should escape it as much as possible." Actually, work is good insurance for long life and one of the best psychological tonics for a healthy, happy mind. It is entirely conceivable that too much idle time is now partly to blame for our zooming juvenile delinquency and the nation-wide epidemic of neuroses in the U.S.A.

If you have grandparents, therefore, don't figuratively chain them to an easy chair. Instead, tactfully encourage them in their wish to help set the table or darn your socks or raise chickens or be self-supporting. Unwittingly, however, many good-intentioned grandchildren will say:

"Now, Grandmother, you just sit still and rest, while we set the table and prepare dinner."

Is it any wonder, then, that such elderly folks soon grow dissatisfied and wish to return to their own little cottage where they are not affronted by such unintentional insults? For whenever we try to debar elderly people from a chance to work, they are likely to misconstrue our aim. They feel that we think they are beyond the age of usefulness; that we regard them as "on the shelf." And that is a most deflating thought.

With this viewpoint, you can realize why the grandchild who imposes most on the elderly grandparent, actually seems to hold her greatest interest, if not affection. On the other

"Books—lighthouses erected in the great sea of time."   —Whipple hand, the son or daughter who tries to do everything for that elderly person, unwittingly makes her feel unhappy, and hence causes her to want to move on until she finds some other relative who actually needs her services.

And don't greet your grandparents in this manner: "Hello, Grandfather. How are you feeling today?" That query immediately turns the elderly person's attention inward. So he begins to recount his aches or pains and become even more addicted to hypochondria. Instead, ask about his chickens or his garden; his workshop or even politics, and thereby extrovert his interests from his own epidermis and its contents.

According to Dr. Andrew C. Ivy, world famous modern physiologist, the duration of human life in ancient Rome averaged only 25 years. Because of modern medical discoveries and better balanced menus, we have now reached an American longevity of about 70 years. With this advancing life span, of course, we now witness many diseases that are typical of old age, such as diabetes, heart trouble and cancer. In spite of these, our average length of life is still increasing, so a new branch of medicine has developed that deals with problems of the aged. It is called geriatry (geriatrics).

Incidentally, the longevity of our domestic animals has likewise been increasing, thanks to better balanced rations plus penicillin, the sulfa drugs and other advances in medical science. Thus, the current average life span of an American dog is about 12 years whereas it was listed at 7 years in 1925. The males of sheep, cattle, hogs and poultry, however, are slaughtered for food, so their life span doesn't show much change.

Human females live longer on the average than do males, due possibly in part to the tension and keener competition of the man out in modern business and industry. For economic rivalry raises blood pressure and promotes peptic ulcers. Note the following table, adapted from Dr. Ivy[19]. It takes 100,000 girl babies, born alive, and shows their mortality rate, as well as life expectancy at different ages.

Age	Alive at start of that year	Dying that year	Future Life expectancy
0-1	100,000	3,789	67.29
6	95,203	91	64.64
11	94,824	66	59.89
16	94,443	101	55.12
21	93,848	145	50.46
26	93,059	175	45.86
31	92,116	212	41.31
36	90,958	266	36.80
41	89,475	352	32.37
46	87,460	493	28.05
51	84,617	695	23.90
56	80,601	987	19.96
61	74,894	1,399	16.28
66	66,885	1,935	12.92
71	55,893	2,610	9.94
76	41,607	3,149	7.47
81	25,757	3,034	5.53
86	12,126	2,131	4.09
91	3,890	958	3.06
96	767	248	2.35
101	85	34	1.87
106	5	2	1.53
109	1	1	1.37

"Save when you are young. The years will pass swiftly. Then when you are well on, you will find yourself well off."

—John D. Rockefeller, Jr.

(The following typical newspaper column illustrates how I attempt to increase the general public's interest in Applied Psychology.)

The Worry Clinic

George W. Crane, Ph.D., M.D.

Case W-280: Ted B., aged 32, fell in love with a girl of 24.

"But, Dr. Crane, I knew they would never be happy together," his married sister told me.

"Their home backgrounds were entirely unlike. My husband and I both realized they were simply infatuated with each other.

"But Ted is as stubborn as a mule, so I knew it would do no good to argue with him.

"Besides, it just makes a man defend his choice all the more ardently if his relatives criticize his girl friend.

"So I decided to use some of your psychological strategy. I acted as if I was in favor of the marriage and invited them to visit us for two weeks, which they did.

"THIS PLOT threw them together for breakfast, lunch and dinner. Ted enjoyed himself for the first few days.

"But his girl began to show off to disadvantage in several little ways, and Ted vaguely sensed this fact.

"He hadn't noticed it before because he had always seen her in her own setting of night clubs and dance halls.

"Now that she was in our home and thus in Ted's type of domestic atmosphere, she began to grate on his nerves.

"Ted had thought she was cute as a night club dancer. He didn't even object too much to her frequent drinking, for this seemed natural against the backdrop of a tavern.

"Besides, she now began to nag him before the first week was over, and Ted never could stand nagging.

"WELL, I ignored their restlessness and boredom. My husband and I tried to be most diplomatic. We took them to the opera and to the theater.

"But we also left them alone a great deal, too. And they both thanked us very much when Ted took her home at the end of her visit.

"Meanwhile, Ted had not received one word of criticism from us, nor had we even intimated any objection to his girl friend

"Within the next month, however, they broke their engagement. Dr. Crane, don't you think I did the right thing?"

"YES, INDEED! This tactful sister did what every such family should try when they see a son or daughter infatuated with an obviously unsuitable sweetheart.

First, don't engage in violent criticism of that prospective mate, for when his relatives attack his judgment, the young man just defends his choice that much more strongly.

But the more he recites the virtues of his girl friend, the more he will actually believe them, for a salesman thus can talk himself into believing his own sales story.

Furthermore, if everybody attacks the girl, his chivalry may cause him to go to her defense.

We parents should invite our child's sweetheart into our own home. We should be courteous and friendly.

If the stranger harmonizes, well and good. If not, our child will vaguely sense this fact.

To help objectify the rating process, send for my 100-point "Tests for Sweethearts," based on the confidential confessions of over 2,000 engaged folks.

Scrapbook these true "Case Records" taken from my professional files. Then add the various Rating Scales and bulletins. Soon you will have a practical textbook of everyday psychology.

1 BERGDAHL, HAL, *A Bonus Every Month* (Dartnell, 1966).
2 BORLAND et al., *Psych. in Dentistry* (U. S. Dept. HEW, 1964).
3 BUCKLEY, W. F. Jr., *The Committee & Its Critics* (Regnery, 1963)
4 BURGESS, T. O., "Hypnotherapy in Obstetrics" (A chapter in LeCron's *Hypno-therapy*, (Grune & Stratton, 1950).
5 CHEVIGNY & BRAVERMAN, *Adjustment of the Blind* (Yale U., 1950).
6 CRANE, G. W., "*Building a Practice*" (Cal Mag. June, 1967).
7 DIETZE, G., *In Defense of Property* (Regnery, 1963).
8 EDGERTON, A. H., "Vocational Education" *(Newsweek,* Apr. 1, 1940)
9 FLOYD & WELFORD, *Symposium on Fatigue* (London: Lewis, 1953).
10 FOSS, BRIAN, *Determinants of Infant Behavior* (Wiley, 1962).
11 GASTAUT, H., *The Epilepsies* (Thomas, 1954).
12 GORDON, E. E., "Exercise Equivalents" *(Modern Medicine,* 12/15/57).
13 GUILFORD, J. P., *Psychometric Methods* (McGraw-Hill, 1960).
14 HANNA, J. V., "The Test-Obsessed Client" *(Occupations,* 28, 1950)
15 HARBISON & MYERS, *Management in the Industrial World* (McGraw-Hill, '60)
16 HAYES, S. P., JR., "Some Psychological Problems of Economics" *(Psychol. Bull.,* July, 1950).
17 HILL, L. H., & HOOK, C. R., *Management at the Bargaining Table* (McGraw-Hill, 1945).
18 HUSBAND, R. W., *Psychology of Successful Selling* (Harper, 1953).
19 IVY, A. C., "Length of Life" *(World Book Encyclopedia,* 1948).
20 JOHNSTON, SENATOR O. D., "Establishment of Wage Scales" *(Congression-al Record,* Feb. 25, 1949, p. A1111).
21 KANT. F., *Treatment of the Alcoholic* (Thomas, 1954).
22 KELLEMS, V., *The Golden Jacka$$* (Kellems Co., Saugatuck, Conn., 1950)
23 LAWSHE, C. H., *Psychology of Industrial Relations* (McGraw-Hill, 1955).
24 LINCOLN, J. F., *A New Approach to Industrial Economics* (Lincoln Co., 1963).
25 LUNDIN, R. W., *Development and Validation of a Set of Musical Ability Tests* (Amer. Psychol. Assoc., 63, No. 10, 1949).
26 MAURER, D. W., *Narcotics & Narcotic Addiction* (Thomas, 1954).
27 McCANN, I. G., *Why the Taft-Hartley Law* (Comm. Const. Gov't, 1950).
28 NEUBERGER, MAURINE B., *Smoking Hazards* (Prentice-Hall, 1964).
29 PLANT, J. S., *The Envelope* (Commonwealth Fund, 1950).
30 REMMERS, H. H., *Opinion & Attitude Measurement* (Harper, 1954).
31 RYAN & SMITH, *Industrial Psychology* (Ronald, 1954).
32 SHEFFERMAN, N. W., *Labor's Stake in Capitalism* (Labor Rel. Assoc. 1954).
33 UHRBROCK, R. S., "Importance of Psychology" *(Indus. Med.* Feb., 1934).
34 VAN PELT, S. J., "Hypnotherapy in Medical Practice" *(Brit. J. Med. Hypno-tism,* 1, No. 1, 1949).
35 VISCARDI, H., *Give Us The Tools* (Eriksson-Taplinger, 1960).
36 WEINFELD, W., "Income of Dentists, 1929-48" *(Survey Current Bus.,* Jan., 1950).
37 WELLS, W. R., "Hypnotic Treatment of Hysteria" *(Brit. J. Med. Hypnotism,* 1, No. 1, 1949).
38 WILLIAMS, C. A., *Traffic Accidents* (Thomas, 1954).
39 WALGREEN, MYRTLE N., *Never a Dull Day* (Regnery, 1963).
40 WEEKSLER, A. N., *Incentive Management — A Case Study* (Lincoln Electric 1963).

CHAPTER XXI

PSYCHOLOGY GOES TO THE HOSPITAL

"Sickness," stated Dr. Arthur S. Flemming[12], former U. S. Secretary of Health, Education and Welfare, "now causes the loss of 500 million man days a year and a 6 billion dollar annual wage loss."

That terrific yearly tribute which we still pay to disease is doubly astonishing when we realize the tremendous forward strides that medicine has made in the last few decades. Beginning with the discovery of insulin in 1922, we have witnessed the advent of the sulfa drugs, plus the many new antibiotics like penicillin, and various vaccines such as Dr. Jonas E. Salk's polio shots.

When I was attending Northwestern University Medical School, one of the professors addressed the students with this challenging statement:

"Gentlemen, 85% of your patients will get well in spite of what you do for them!"

Obviously, this figure includes the many minor ailments that send people to physicians and for which there is as yet no sure cure, such as the common cold, influenza, stomach and intestinal upsets, etc. A few days of bedrest and such patients are usually well, thanks to the wonderful recuperative forces that God Almighty has planted in the human body.

But millions of Americans are hypochondriacs who overly magnify minor aches and pains until they are convinced that they are badly in need of instant medical attention. If they read the daily medical column in their local newspaper, and it describes the symptoms of any given ailment, they are so suggestible that they soon sprout those same symptoms and then jump to the hasty conclusion that they, too, are victims of the disease in question. See the case of Joe, on Page 619.

Many leading medical educators have admitted that at

least 50% of the patients in the average medical office are purely mental cases. This doesn't mean they are in need of psychiatric care, but that they have mistaken normal twinges of pain for more serious ailments and have then jumped to wrong conclusions.

Many worried people use surgery as an escape from unpleasant inner emotional conflicts and often insist that their doctors operate on them. Thus, James[17] reports that organic disease such as appendicitis or gall bladder trouble is regarded as socially far more acceptable than nervous problems. Jittery neurotics thus subconsciously seek "emotional surgery" as a social camouflage.

In this connection, he cites the survey by Dr. James C. Doyle of the University of California dealing with 6,248 partial or complete hysterectomies. Dr. Doyle found that 40% (2 out of 5) were unnecessary and unwarranted as per pathology reports.

And Dr. Walter Alvarez studied 385 patients who had undergone appendectomies. Yet in 225 of these 385 cases, there had been no attack of acute appendicitis or there had been a mistaken diagnosis. And Dr. Alvarez further states that only 2 of the 225 were cured of their abdominal pain by the surgical operation. Many patients thus shop around from one operating room to another, when their real trouble is psychosomatic and should be relieved by removing the basic conflict.

Fear thus tends to make one introvertive and encourages this tendency to hypochondria, whereas love is an emotion that turns one's attention outward upon the external environment and thus promotes better health. You are aware of the fact that spinsters at the age of 40 are much more likely to shop around from one physician to another, dreading cancer and other dire ailments, while happily married women, with several children to look after, can hardly be persuaded to visit a medical office even for a routine annual check-up. Marriage extroverts men and women.

Since religion likewise extroverts people, the churches thus

"Kindness has converted more sinners than zeal, eloquence or learning."
—F. W. Faber

exert a very salutary influence even as regards the health and mental hygiene of people. It is an empirical fact that if you randomly select 1,000 active church members versus 1,000 non-church attendants, in which group will you be likely to find more medical patrons? The extrovertive church members are generally the healthier!

And you can indirectly derive further supportive evidence for that fact by your own personal experience since earliest childhood. Each Sunday morning, for example, an estimated 35,000,000 or more Americans spend from one to $2\frac{1}{2}$ hours in church. Yet how many of your church colleagues have you ever witnessed suffer a heart attack in church or a stroke of apoplexy, or a perforated peptic ulcer, a ruptured appendix, etc.?

Since I am an unusually active church member and have also taught a Bible Class regularly for over 40 years, I estimate that I have associated with approximately 3,000,000 fellow church attendants in my lifetime, yet I have never seen a serious medical accident occur to any of those people in church. Oh, I have been called to attend a few who had fainted, but never a fatality!

Contrast the 35,000,000 church goers each Sabbath with any other 35,000,000 Americans for an equal time interval, whether on Sunday or any other day of the week, and you will realize from your own empirical observation that religion is a remarkable aid to better health. For the church attendants usually are more relaxed in body and mind. Thus, their blood pressure falls and their hearts beat more slowly. Their inner tensions subside so even the secretion of hydrochloric acid in their stomachs is diminished and thus their likelihood of a perforating ulcer becomes less.

Changing Attitudes Concerning Medical Practice.

Even at the time of George Washington's death, leading medical practitioners still believed the ancient Greek notion that fever is to be reduced as fast as possible. Aristotle had helped advance the idea that the brain was simply a cooling chamber for the blood, operating somewhat like the modern automobile radiator. And the heart was then deemed the center of the "soul", with the blood forming the fire of life.

From this ancient notion, we still find many relics in our modern vocabulary, for we talk about hardhearted people, as well as softhearted, tenderhearted, chickenhearted. And orators "pluck our heart strings" while clergymen "appeal to our hearts" and urge us to experience a "change of heart". That's also why Valentines are heart-shaped.

When George Washington lay dying, his doctors noted that he had a fever so they bled him several times, extracting a total of 1½ pints of his blood. They acted in line with prevailing medical opinion in that late year of 1799 A.D., yet the loss of that blood very likely killed the Father of Our Country. Nowadays, we medics would be likely to give him a blood transfusion, for when patients are in need of more rapid assimilation of oxygen, we enrichen the oxygen mixture of the inhaled air by use of oxygen tanks or oxygen tents and also give them a blood transfusion to add to the oxygen-carrying capacity of their blood.

But we have learned another important medical fact, namely, that fever is a valuable curative force. For the invading bacteria usually slow down in their rate of multiplication with each degree rise in bodily temperature, whereas the curative white blood corpuscles increase in their rate of production. As a result, fever hampers the germs and helps the body's defensive forces.

Alas, our forefathers generalized from their casual experience with illness and noticed that when the body's temperature dropped to normal after a high fever, the patient usually was on the road to recovery. So they decided to help the body by artificially reducing the temperature, as by bleeding the patient and thus removing some of the "fire". In other cases, they employed alcohol rubs and ice baths, as well as drugs like aspirin which dilate the skin capillaries and thus permit faster chilling of the blood.

Unfortunately, they failed to realize that there is a big

difference between the body's own reduction of fever via the bactericidal effect of the white blood corpuscles, versus the abnormal and often physical lowering of fever by ice packs or blood letting. Thus, many of our ancestors were probably killed, albeit unintentionally, by the false ideas inherited from Aristotle. Even today they still are evident on certain radio and TV programs where pain-killing drugs are advocated as a means of "reducing fever".

Unless the body temperature rises above 105 degrees Fahrenheit, medics usually sit tight, realizing that the elevated temperatures are working against the germs and in favor of the body's defenses. Indeed, some of our drug therapy is actually more effective under fever conditions, for increase of temperature generally speeds up chemical reactions, as you will well remember from your experiments in chemical labs. There the Bunsen burner is usually employed to add the extra heat for more efficient chemical behavior.

Now that antibiotics are so effective against venereal germs, we have less use for the fever method (hyperpyrexia) in old syphilitic infections of the central nervous system. But when we used to get a positive Wassermann reaction on spinal fluid and our drug therapy would not destroy the bacterial invasion, we would wrap a patient in hot packs and electric blankets, elevating his body temperature to 105.8 degrees, where it was kept for as many as 8 hours. And with this extra benefit of the artificial fever, our drugs would then become far more effective.

The danger of letting temperatures rise well above that 105-degree mark is the fact that nerve cells possess protein, and an irreversible gel tends to occur, like that in the white of an egg when dropped in a hot skillet. A reversible gel occurs with gelatine, which will go back to a liquid when warmed and then become solid again when chilled, etc. but not the protein in neurones. When they are "cooked" by too high a temperature, the I.Q. may be subnormal thereafter if the patient happens to survive the ordeal. But don't become unduly alarmed as long as temperatures stay under 105. Also remember that

"Preaching is personal counseling on a group scale."　　—Harry E. Fosdick children usually run higher temperatures than adults with the same type of ailments. Thus, tonsillitis in an adult may register 101 or 102 but hit 104 or higher in a child. Rectal temperatures, as usually taken in young children, also are at least one degree higher than oral temperatures so keep that fact in mind to relieve your parental apprehension, if you are worried at the bedside of an ailing youngster.

Modern medical research has also banished such old-fashioned maxims as "Feed a cold and starve a fever". Instead, we have learned that the patient's appetite is usually a pretty safe guide as to what his body needs. Certain exceptions occur, as in diabetes or gall bladder disease, but as a general rule we now let the patient determine his own menu.

We even employ soft drinks to tempt youngsters to consume more liquids, for during illness, plain water and even milk may seem rather "flat" and unappealing, whereas the "bite" produced by the carbonated beverages, plus the various colors of the soft drinks, may tempt the child to drink far more freely.

And no longer do medics show excessive concern about insomnia, for people don't die of sleeplessness. As long as they lie abed in the horizontal position, they obtain most of the benefits of sleep, even though their eyes are open. For in that recumbent posture, their vertical height is reduced from possibly 6 feet to less than one foot, and this very fact gives their heart a definite rest. The heart gains in two ways, for the blood pressure drops and the rate of the pulse may be reduced one to 3 beats per minute.

Neurotic and worried Americans still consume tremendous amounts of sleeping pills and it is estimated that the current annual bill for tranquilizers and anti-insomnia potions exceeds a quarter of a billion dollars annually. And this figure doesn't include the terrific outlay for tobacco and liquor, both of which function indirectly as tranquilizers for American neuroticism.

It is thus a common sight to witness restaurant patrons sipping strong black coffee or cola beverages, which also contain caffeine, to prod themselves into a more jittery state, while they meanwhile are sucking on a cigaret to relieve some of their unexpended inner energy. And this demand for sedative drugs is not limited to the U.S.A. for Dr. R. A. Hunter[16], of London Hospital, says the British public is likewise on a sedation "binge". .

In England, the Ministry of Health reports that almost 10% of all prescriptions now call for barbiturates. Dr. Hunter adds that sedatives have now come to be regarded as a placebo for patients who are not seriously ill. Once the patients find that the barbiturates have a soothing effect, they often demand more of them as their right under the British mental health service. If the doctor refuses to repeat their prescription, they coerce him by threatening to consult another physician. Another leading British medic, Dr. Sidney Locket, says some 7,000 cases of barbiturate poisoning are treated in British hospitals every year and suicides from barbiturates have increased sharply.

America's Greatest Epidemic Is "Hospitalitis". At the beginning of this 20th century, the vast bulk of all medical practice occurred in private homes or the offices of family doctors. Hospitals were used only for extreme cases requiring surgery or other unusual medical techniques. To use an old analogy, the hospital was then simply the "tail" on the "dog" of medical practice.

But a radical change has occurred, at least as regards the physician though the dental surgeons are still able to hold most of their patients to office care. The modern medic has found himself relegated almost to the minor position of caudal appendage on the "dog". For our latest American epidemic and the most widespread, is what may be termed "hospitalitis". Patients now want to be sent to the nearby hospital for almost every conceivable medical examination, even for such simple things as a routine medical check-up. Thus hospitals are beginning to dominate the public's thinking as regards health care.

This change has been accentuated in recent years by the remarkably comprehensive types of hospitalization insurance urged upon all families. And such insurance has been a great boon in most cases, but it acts somewhat like the proverbial two-edged sword. For it likewise has changed millions of Americans into hypochondriacs. For example, a generation ago, if a patient had a minor ache or pain, or even a fairly major disability, he waited for a few weeks for nature to effect a cure, as was generally the case.

Nowadays, however, he says, "I've been paying premiums on my hospital insurance policy, so why not go there and get some returns on that money I've spent?"

And this attitude is glutting our hospitals with neurotic folks or those who formerly would have dismissed their petty ailments and been back on their job at farm or factory with little concern for their "innards". As a result, hospital insurance companies are facing bankruptcy and are now considering the addition of a $50 or even a $100 deductible clause in such policies.

Under this new plan, the patient pays the first $50 or $100 while the insurance company then shoulders the remainder of the bill. Such a restriction has long been in effect with reference to automobile insurance and has proved effective in reducing the exaggerated claims for minor dents in fenders. Perhaps it will help generate more "horse sense" in the millions of patients who are now cluttering up hospitals unnecessarily. Actually, our present hospitals could probably handle all urgent cases that merit hospitalization, without millions of additional appropriations for bigger and better new hospital buildings, if we could thus weed out the patients who should be channeled back into private medical offices for the simple care they may require.

Dr. R. A. Hunter, quoted above, says of the British public, "Since at least 50% of patients have symptoms that originate in the mind or emotions, the number of barbiturates prescribed is enormous." A conservative estimate would probably place the same figure on American patients, so our hospitals could doubtless reduce their occupied beds by 25%, if not 50%, if Americans could be cured of the "hospitalitis" craze.

And this tendency to "institutionalize" medical practice has had other dangerous effects. For instance, it has promoted the excessive specialization of doctors with something approaching "assembly line" care for patients. In 1959, for example, the newspapers carried the account of an American girl who woke up from anesthesia to find her breast amputated, when all she had been sent to the hospital for, was a minor bit of surgery on her foot. As she lay on the cart, waiting in the corridor to be wheeled into an operating room, apparently the card on her cart had dropped to the floor and become mixed up with that of another patient.

While such errors are not common, they do tend to show the "assembly line" principle, with specialists sometimes so unfamiliar with their surgical referred cases that they can make such flagrant mistakes. A generation ago the General Practitioner or GP, as he is now called, combined a keen understanding of psychology and medicine, with a lifelong familiarity with the patient and even her family background for maybe two previous generations. The GP then combined psychiatry and medicine with surgery and obstetrics. He employed the "organismic" method instead of the "organic" and thus treated the total personality instead of the gall bladder or appendix, eye or heart.

In recent years, there has been a trend within the medical profession to go back toward the broad viewpoint of the General Practitioner, but this has been offset in a large degree by the "hospitalitis" epidemic. The latter has thus helped accentuate the ultra specialization within medicine, and as a further change, it has subconsciously educated the public toward socialization of medicine.

For when people start looking to vast buildings such as hospitals for their medical cures, or to otherwise laudable but financially dominant foundations such as the American Cancer Society, they meanwhile tend to ignore the vital contribution of the individual medical practitioner and relegate him to an ancillary function. Thus, doctors are becoming simply glorified attendants at vast healing centers called hospitals. Research laboratories are also gaining the spotlight. Bureaucracy is creeping into medicine via the salaried officials of the many fund-raising bodies in this country which are often self-perpetuating.

To be specific, though they are doing a great deal of good, we now find our calendar almost totally preempted by "Polio Week" or "Diabetes Week" or "Cancer Week," or "Multiple Sclerosis Week," etc. Each of those laudable financial drives is sponsored by a national headquarters, generally in Washington, D.C. or New York, where the funds are then doled out to medical schools or private research doctors by the salaried executive staff of the respective organizations sponsoring such drives. Newspaper editors are actually hounded by the paid publicity agents of such "drives" for free space, and medical columnists like myself are deluged with press releases in the hope we can sandwich some of their publicity into our syndicated newspaper columns.

Please do not misinterpret my remarks as being hostile to the altruistic aims of millions of people who ring doorbells to raise the money for such medical research. And the home offices of those foundations in Washington or New York likewise merit a great deal of praise. However, they are insidiously, though unwittingly, preparing the American public for socialization of medicine and dentistry by thus "conditioning" our citizenry to bow down toward the East for medical discoveries, medical information and medical research grants. Soon Uncle Sam will be expected to dictate medical policy.

And sometimes these "drives" overly dramatize a medical entity beyond its proper place in the over-all medical perspective. For example, polio is an ailment that visually lends itself to plucking the heart strings because of the pathetic tots wearing leg braces or depicted in an iron lung. Actually, even before the Salk vaccine, polio was not as serious a threat to American health as measles! So how did it suddenly usurp the limelight while measles is still relatively ignored? Partly be-

"The best exercise for strengthening the heart is reaching down and lifting people up."   —Ernest Blevins cause paralyzed President F. D. Roosevelt dramatized polio whereas measles had no such magnetic exponent.

On May 13, 1959, the American newspapers received a notice from Harshe-Rotman, Inc., prepared for The American Association of Fund Raising Counsel, Inc., marked "For Immediate Release". It listed the annual input of funds raised by 10 of the major health agencies. The total was $161,843,030. That is a great tribute to the generosity of the American public, for those 10 agencies are only a few of the groups soliciting contributions for medical education and welfare. The following table shows the number of expenditures in each area:

1. Medical Treatment . . . . 39.5 per cent
2. Community Service . . . . 20.5 per cent
3. Lay & Medical Education. . . . . 18.5 per cent
4. Research Grants . . . . 12.5 per cent
5. Fund Raising . . . . 12.5 per cent
6. Other Purposes . . . . 10.5 per cent

The above report added that the promotion of medical care and health services in the United States totals some $20.5 billion a year, which was stated as being nearly 5 per cent of our gross national product. It further noted that the current national budget for the promotion of health provides $678 million, of which 40.7 per cent, or $276 million, will come from taxes.

Incidentally, The American Association of Fund Raising Counsel, Inc. is a non-profit organization of 28 professional firms engaged in counseling, directing, and organizing fund raising activities in the United States and Canada, so you can see what a major operation such fund raising has now become. Is it any wonder that "hospitalitis" has become our Number One epidemic?

More "Horse Sense" Needed In Hospitals. Scientists in the field of medicine, dentistry, physics and chemistry are generally too introvertive. As children, they often had chemical sets in their basements and enjoyed mechanical gadgets, power tools, tinkering with motors, etc. But they seldom had much experience in such extrovertive fields as salesmanship, so they failed to acquire the art of motivating people gracefully via the proper use of words. They are also more inclined to have what is popularly termed a "one-track" mind.

After an extensive education in a professional college, they finally become so familiar with the terminology of their specialty they don't even realize they may often be talking over the heads of their patients. Because their technical jargon is A-B-C stuff to them, they can't imagine it is still X-Y-Z or "Greek" to patients, even of the college graduate variety.

Thus, they have unwittingly offended many patients and indirectly occasioned the filing of many malpractice suits, just by their ineptness in the field of human relations or Applied Psychology. This fact was aptly illustrated in Berg's[5] caustic exposé of American hospitals. He cites many examples where lack of "horse sense" or gumption made patients irate at both their phsyician as well as the hospital where they were treated.

"A hospital is not a fit place in which to be sick," Berg comments in summarizing a recent secret California survey of hospitals. He further adds, ". . . hospitals are run for the convenience of doctors and nurses—not for the benefit of the patients."

Berg's challenging essay is based on a report obtained by the California Medical Association which sought to find out why patients sue their doctors. A team of skilled psychologists, psychiatrists and sociologists was commissioned to study all factors involved in the malpractice claims. The investigators thus interviewed both the doctors as well as the patients who had been implicated in such suits. They found that many of those they questioned—both patients as well as physicians—were emotionally ill.

Psychological reactions were found to be more important factors in malpractice lawsuits than either the quality of treatment or whether the doctor made a mistake in medical judgment. One very frequently sued doctor, for example, was guilty of racial bias. Another had a persecution complex. Another had misdiagnosed a pregnancy as a tumor and had operated on the woman. Then, instead of apologizing for his mistake, he ignored his error altogether and actually sent the patient a bill for his surgery! She said she wouldn't have sued him if he hadn't sent that bill.

Others resented the fact they were not informed as to the nature of their ailment but were treated as know-nothings. Some complained about excessive hospital charges for drugs given them, while others said they were billed for medicines they never received. The investigators covered 8 hospitals, of which four were called "good" hospitals with few malpractice suits, whereas the other four were designated as "bad", since many malpractice suits resulted therefrom.

Few patients complained about hospital conditions while they were still patients therein. The investigators attributed this to the fact the sick patient felt frightened and helpless in the strange surroundings. And his individuality was further reduced by having his clothes, jewels and money removed, while his privacy was invaded by all the white-coated staff members and attendants. The patients even lost their names, so to speak, and reported that they were likely to be referred to as the "Ulcer in Room 912" or the "Gall bladder in 615".

Because the patients thus tend to be regarded as specimens instead of personalities and are abruptly ordered or directed what to do, even though they temporarily are submissive, a subconscious resentment builds up in them which later explodes in criticisms and malpractice lawsuits. A number of patients, when asked to describe what they would consider to be their "ideal" type of hospital, stressed the fact it should be "warm and friendly". Few patients ever mentioned hospital equipment or standards!

The child psychiatrists quoted in the final report also stressed the fact that a youngster has a great need for its mother and that an arbitrary separation from her may cause emotional damage that carries over into the child's adulthood. The report adds this further illuminating comment: "The sick

child at home is seen to need his mother and no one else—-
but if he comes to a hospital, his mother is said to 'upset' him
. . . and although it has been common knowledge in the community that young children are acutely unhappy in hospitals
and are often changed for the worse on a return, until recently
little attention has been given to this matter in medical and
nursing literature—and still too little in the training of doctors and nurses."

Dr. James Robertson, child psychiatrist, added, "The more
children can be kept out of hospitals or nursed at home, the
better. The next best thing is to have mother and child together in the hospital. If this can be achieved, the mental
health problem of the welfare of young children in hospitals
is virtually solved."

In the final report of the investigators for the California
Medical Association a succinct Bill of Rights for Hospital
Patients was formulated. I have digested it as follows:

(1) Let the patient save face and maintain his identity,
as well as remain as active physically as his condition permits.

(2) Permit him to stay clothed unless it is imperative that
he wear a hospital gown or be confined to bed. And even
then, it is preferable to let him wear his own pajamas or
nightgown. If he must shed his own street clothing, leave
them handy in a closet where he has access to them.

(3) Let him retain his money and personal effects so he
can buy a daily newspaper or other items which he needs
without having a hospital attendant supervise him as a
guardian over a child.

(4) Keep him informed as to his condition, even to the
extent of permitting him to help chart his own temperature,
weight, etc. unless such information is contraindicated because of his emotional or mental condition.

(5) Allow more flexibility as regards routine, such as time
for taking his meals. And don't waken a sleeping patient to
give him a sleeping pill, just because of the inexorability of
former hospital ritual!

Those 5 major items are usually within the reach of hospitals but as a physician as well as psychologist, I wish to defend some of the hospital practices being indicted. For we often have a serious shortage of nurses and many patients act like prima donnas, expecting a great deal of coddling from floor nurses. They seem to think they are the sole responsibility of that over-worked nurse, and act as if she should be their private, full-time attendant.

Many hospitals have already modified their routine so they now permit members of the patient's family to visit more freely and bring in food to the patient, if the latter is not on a fixed caloric menu or fasting for some laboratory test.

A marked change has also affected hospitals regarding the former austere white colors of the walls as well as the apparel of interns and nurses. Now many pastel shades are making hospital rooms as cozy and attractive as the home bedrooms of the patients. And the apparel of hospital staffs has been modified to permit a variety of colors for coats and nurses' uniforms.

One of the simplest remedies for the malpractice problems cited above would be a realization by introvertive doctors, lab attendants and the nurses, of the vast importance of human relations in professional practice.

"I WANT TO FEEL IMPORTANT," is thus the invisible tattoo that is indelibly branded on the chest of EVERY human being, child or adult.

Since people are not likely to sue their friends, physicians, dentists, nurses and other hospital staff members should consider themselves salesmen for the private practice of medicine in its various branches.

An axiom of applied psychology states that if you can make your companion (or patient) feel more important as a result of his contact with you, he will like you. If, however, you reduce his feeling of importance, he will dislike you and your hospital, too.

So doctors of all types should immediately learn to treat patients by the organismic method which involves recognition of their total personality, and not employ the impersonal organic method of noting only the organ that falls within the special field of the ophthalmologist or internist, genito-urinary expert et al.

Thus, a brief course in the hospitals on how to remember names and faces would not only benefit the hospital personnel by generating far more goodwill in the entire community, but would actually zoom the practice of the physicians on the staff when they get back to their own offices for afternoon consultation hours with their private patients.

The Anabolic-Catabolic Tug-of-War re Longevity.

Two hostile forces are in conflict regarding mankind's longevity. The anabolic, which is of the positive, upbuilding sort, pertains to the many helpful advances in medical research and the discoveries by our great pharmaceutical firms. They include insulin and sulfa drugs, antibiotics and vaccines, as well as pasteurized milk and pure city water, plus the recent fluoridation of water to prevent dental caries and even the addition of iodine to our table salt to check the malfunction of the thyroid gland.

Moreover, the emphasis on frequent medical check-ups has helped in the early detection of cancer so that surgery, X-ray and radium have been able to produce a cure in thousands of formerly hopeless cases. All of these anabolic contributions have added additional years of life to our middle aged. Recently Dr. Crowe[8] stressed this point in his remarkable book, saying that in the year 1850, a person who had then attained the age of 60 had a future life expectancy of 15.6 additional years. How great a life expectancy would you guess lay ahead of the 60-year-old person in the year 1965? In short, after the passage of more than a full century, how much had we added to the lifespan of our aged citizens?

Well, it may shock you to find that in 1850, the 60-year-old had a right to expect 15.6 more years, while in 1965, he still could count on only about 15.8 years. "What is wrong?" you may protest as you remember the many medical aids to old folks cited just above.

"If we have not peace within ourselves, it is vain to seek it from outside sources."
—Rochefoucauld

Alas, those anabolic forces have apparently been pretty well offset by catabolic or destructive influences. For example, automobiles now slay nearly 50,000 people every year on our highways and injure approximately 2,000,000 more. Most of those injured do not carry serious disfigurement for life, but tens of thousands are crippled to such a degree their life expectancy is actually shortened.

Meanwhile, as medical science is helping checkmate cancer, the tobacco industry seems to be zooming cancer of lungs, lips and mouth, throat and stomach. But lung cancer, as from cigarets, is not the major catabolic effect of tobacco, for its damage to heart and blood vessels is its greatest threat to longevity. For example, our Public Health Service in the 1963 World Almanac listed 269,820 deaths from all types of cancer, whereas the deaths from cardiovascular (heart and blood vessel) ailments totalled 928,670. That means heart disease kills 3½ times as many Americans as all types of cancer, combined!

Despite the fact that the vested tobacco interests try to minimize the hazards of smoking and claim that medical researchers have no specific laboratory tests to confirm their indictment of tobacco, we have the same valid statistical method that has long been relied upon to prove that women live longer in the U.S.A. than men. That same statistical method was used to vindicate the effectiveness of the Salk vaccine on polio, as well as diphtheria inoculations, smallpox vaccination, etc. Almost 2,000 American cities have fluoridated their drinking water, relying on the statistical analysis of decayed teeth among the children in the fluoridated cities versus the non-fluoridated areas. And the dental cavities are reduced approximately 65% among the children who have been reared in cities with one part of fluorine per million in their drinking water.

Many physicians and other scientists still smoke, having developed the nuisance habit in the teens when they were trying to act like supposed big shots. Then, having become addicted to this habit, they find it difficult to free themselves.

But physicians in general are so solidly against tobacco that for several years the Journal of the A.M.A. has refused to accept a single tobacco ad, feeling that it is a disgrace to medical science even to lend, by intimation, the endorsement of modern medicine to such a dangerous health menace.

The medics and other scientists who pooh-pooh the hazards of tobacco are usually afraid to face their own conscience or else are profiting from the tobacco industry, either by research grants or stock investments on which they hope to receive continued dividends.

Modern medicine considers tobacco, and especially cigarets, to be one of the primary causes of high blood pressure and coronary attacks from thickening of the blood vessel walls. Obviously, non-smokers may have high blood pressure from other toxins absorbed from infected teeth, tonsils, prostate, etc. but tobacco certainly ranks at the top as the cause of heart attacks and lung cancer.

Dr. E. Cuyler Hammond[14] of the American Cancer Society recently informed the medical section of the National Tuberculosis Association that lung cancer death rates are approximately 10 times as high among cigaret smokers as among the non-smokers. And, on the basis of verified cases of bronchogenic carcinoma, the death rate of two-pack-or-more-a-day cigaret smokers was roughly 60 times as high as the death rate of non-smokers. He adds that death rates from pulmonary tuberculosis are higher among smokers while those from pneumonia and influenza are four times as high among the cigaret users as among the non-smokers. Moreover, he reports that the death rate from heart disease is twice as high among smokers as for non-smokers.

Dr. Hammond's findings are based on three studies, one of which was conducted by two British physicians, Dr. R. Doll and Dr. A. B. Hill, while the second was by Dr. Hammond and his associate, Dr. Daniel Horn, on 187,000 American men between the ages of 50 and 60 years of age, while the third survey, by H. Dorn, was made among American veterans holding government life insurance. In each study, moreover, the subjects were traced for several years after they first answered the questionnaire on their smoking habits. Dr. Hammond also stated that cigar and pipe smokers likewise run a greater risk of lung cancer, but such death rates among them are lower than among the cigaret users.

Apart from the medical angle, smoking is an unwarranted habit from the view of practical economics. The latest figures show that the average cigaret smoker now burns up $115 per year on the ends of his cigarets. That outlay might be justified if he gained enough extra food calories or had several years added to his longevity or even was able to think more accurately for final exams. But smoking offers no calories whatever; shortens the average cigaret user's lifespan an estimated 5 to 7 years, and mildly dulls precise mental functions. It also seriously reduces visual acuity and especially depth perception so it predisposes to auto accidents.

"Dr. Crane," a worker caustically bemoaned the unfairness to his high school daughter at her graduation last June, "I can't afford to send my girl to college but those white collar guys can always send their kids to the university."

But I reminded him that he had already burned up four $500 college scholarships the past 18 years on the ends of his cigarets! For 18 years addiction to cigarets at $115 annually, amounts to $2,070. And this isn't the entire cost, for if you shorten your productive lifespan by even 5 years, with average earnings of $4,000 per year, you have also cheated your family out of an additional $20,000 income because of your cigarets. Thus, if you become a slave to cigarets in high school and use them for 50 years, you not only burn up $5,750 via the cigarets, but lose that extra $20,000 by dying prematurely, so those cigarets thus cost the smoker a total of $25,750, which means well over $500 per year, not just $115. A recent issue of *Medical Science*[20] dealing with the cost of medical care in the U.S.A. mentions that the aged person spends on the average well over 50% more for personal health services than the general population. It lists $122 a year for the aged, against $78 annually for the general population. Thus, the average cigaret smoker wastes far more money annually than average health services cost.

In order to understand the medical channels by which tobacco exerts its ill effect on the human body, we must first realize that smokers have a much higher carbon monoxide content of their blood stream. It may run as high as 10%, yet even a 3% content reduces acuteness of vision and depth perception. The smoker is thus hampered at shooting baskets on the basketball court and driving a car.

The A.M.A.'s Committee on Medical Aspects of Automobile Injuries released its report Mar. 12, 1959, warning us that "The relative oxygen deficiency from smoking 3 cigarets is equal to that of traveling at a 7,500 foot altitude . . . drivers should be advised to refrain from frequent smoking prior to and during periods of night driving or at high altitudes."

The carbon monoxide "fixes" the hemoglobin of the red blood corpuscles so that they can no longer pick up oxygen in the lungs and release it in the muscles. Those inactivated red blood cells simply clutter up the blood stream thereafter for they are inert or deadheads. Smoking thus produces a functional type of anemia which is just as harmful as if the smokers actually cut their wrists and hemorrhaged a corresponding volume of blood.

No athletic coach would normally consent to having his players donate a pint of blood prior to a gruelling game or track meet, for that reduction in oxygen-carriers would make the athletes short of wind and also inclined to fatigue more quickly. Smoking exerts a similar effect to that of actual blood hemorrhage. For the resulting shortage of available red blood corpuscles makes the heart beat faster. So smoking produces a similar extra load on the heart to that resulting from sudden hemorrhage.

For example, smoking makes the heart produce as much as 20 extra beats per minute. And this occurs for as long as 20 minutes after only one cigaret is smoked. A somewhat comparable effect is caused by cigars. In a test case of a man smoking 6 cigars per day, his heart averaged 82 beats per minute. Then he abstained from his tobacco for 6 months. During this tobacco-free period, his pulse rate averaged only 75 per minute, so his heart thus salvaged 7 extra rest periods per minute or 10,080 per day.

Dr. C. W. Leib, in commenting on this case says: "You don't have to be a physiologist to appreciate the significance of such wasted energy. Any mechanic will tell you what happens to a motor when it's overworked! There is evidence, too, that heart rate and life rate run fairly parallel—a slow heartbeat and pulse rate for a long life. Even in animals there seems to be a relationship between pulse rate and longevity—the elephant, whale and turtle (Methuselahs of the animal world)—having slow pulse rates."[19]

In addition to the ill effects of the higher carbon monoxide content of the smoker's blood stream, the vessel walls also tend to become irritated. And irritation is followed by local edema, plus scar tissue and extra thickening. You can remember what happens when you do a lot of manual work during summer vacations from college. Your hands get very red and then blister. Fluid forms and later callouses will occur.

A somewhat similar result causes the arterial walls to thicken. We designate this condition as hardening of the arteries. But with the thickening, there comes a consequent narrowing of the lumen (diameter), so the effect is much like that of changing 1-inch water pipes to $\frac{1}{2}$-inch size. Since the heart must send the same volume of blood through those smaller arteries (pipes), and in the same period of time, then the only alternative is for the heart to increase its pressure greatly. Many a man whose normal systolic blood pressure was 125 before he became a chronic smoker, later finds that his blood pressure may zoom to 175, or 200 and sometimes as high as 300. Since the heart is the motor in the entire human machine, is it any wonder that habitual smokers die on an average 5 to 7 years sooner than non-smokers?

Another reason why smoking makes a person short of wind, is the fact that the moisture layer that coats the lungs becomes thickened due to the chronic irritation from the tobacco fumes.

Since the passage of gases, such as oxygen and carbon dioxide, through a liquid becomes slower as the layer of fluid grows thicker, it is again obvious why a smoker becomes short of wind in a crisis, even if the carbon monoxide had not also inactivated a certain percentage of his red blood cells. This thicker layer of fluid bathing the irritated lungs, bronchial tubes and trachea also helps explain the excessive coughing of smokers. It also aggravates the problems of the asthmatic, too. See the accompanying illustration.

Smoker's windpipe during the day   Same when he lies down   Same when he arises

When the smoker has been standing all day, the fluid is uniformly spread over his windpipe and bronchial tubes. But when he lies down, gravity tends to peel off the fluid in drops. They swing down from the upper layer of the horizontal windpipe, resembling stalactites in a cave. The tickle effect of this shift in fluid is intensified because the cells lining the windpipe are ciliated (hairy). So the smoker experiences a severe

"I cannot consent to place in control of others one who cannot control himself."
—Robert E. Lee (Who never promoted a man who drank)

bout of coughing that continues till such shifts of fluid have become stationary once more. But next morning, when the smoker springs out of bed, he again causes a radical shift in fluids that precipitates another coughing bout.

Facts and Fallacies About Heart Attacks. In the previous section, we outlined some of the physiological and mechanical reasons why the human heart wears out prematurely. But prolonged apprehension, fears, anxiety, chronic irritability, anger and hate can likewise elevate the blood pressure and thus penalize the heart.

Love and even the mere presence of the opposite sex, will likewise zoom the pulse and blood pressure. Public speakers find that the same joke told to a one-sex audience will not evoke as much laughter as when told to a mixed audience. For the two sexes exert a reciprocal stimulating effect on one another. Thus, the resulting explosion of laughter is much greater in the mixed audience.

But lack of love exerts a somewhat negative influence on the tone of the body. Although it is not medically true to say that you die of a broken heart, severe unhappiness can hamper the heart's stamina by reducing appetite, producing insomnia, etc.

In those patients who die of cancer or pneumonia, tuberculosis or other diseases, the immediate cause of death is the heart's inability to contract and force the blood out of its muscular ventricles. To understand this, please recall the last time your automobile motor stalled or "died" on a steep hill.

What happened to your auto motor is similar to the condition in the human "motor" at death. In the case of the automobile, the power from the exploding gasoline was not adequate to move the pistons against the opposing pressure that gravity was exerting due to the steep grade.

In like manner, when your heart muscle is so weak that it cannot squeeze down on the blood within its chambers and eject that blood, it stops right in the middle of a contraction. And the reason your heart muscle grows weak is generally lack of enough oxygen or such an inadequate input of protein that the worn out muscle fibers in the heart wall could not be rebuilt. If your heart were to receive its normal input of oxygen and food, even though you were supposedly doomed by cancer or other severe ailments, the heart would generally keep on beating.

With this simple picture of what happens internally, coach yourself and your friends to develop a fighting morale. Don't surrender to the negative idea that you must die because you have cancer or TB, etc. Even if you don't relish your food, take it, like medicine, because your heart needs it. And team-up with God Almighty more fully to slow down your heart.

For example, suppose you suffer a heart attack while you are all alone in the house. (This terror lurks chronically in the subconscious of spinsters, bachelors or other middle aged folks who live by themselves). If you then fall to the floor beyond reach of the telephone, what is your proper sequence of action?

First, reassure yourself by realizing that if you are still conscious, then your attack is probably a light one, for severe attacks render you unconscious at once. This comforting thought will retard the undue rise in blood pressure which fear and panic otherwise produce and thus can save your heart the extra labor of beating against a possible 200 blood pressure instead of your normal 125 to 150.

Second, the pain which heart victims suffer is due to lack of enough oxygen to the muscle fibers in the heart wall. But you can render your own "cardiac first aid", so to speak, by indulging at once in forced deep breathing. When we medics reach you, we offer you more oxygen by bubbling it into your nostrils via a tube or by placing you in an oxygen tent at the hospital.

During the first 5 or 10 minutes you may thus tip the scales in favor of life vs. death just by your own rapid deep breathing which builds up an oxygen surplus. Many patients are so petrified with fear and severe pain under the breastbone that they hesitate to move. But your deep breathing will not hamper your heart at all and may actually save your life.

Meanwhile, stay in a recumbent position to keep your blood pressure as low as possible.

Realize, too, that many patients survive repeated heart attacks so don't grow panicky. And if you have been "playing ball" on God's team by constructive efforts in your full time job and by helping fulfill Lincoln's wish to "plant roses where thistles grew before," as in your spare time work with Boy Scouts or church activities, then just relax and talk to your Senior Partner as follows:

"Lord, I've tried to be a good Junior Partner and help make this world a better place for everybody but now I'm in a tough spot. I'll try to give my heart some quick extra oxygen by rapid deep breathing so will you please pull me through?"

Indeed, God is still the best medicine that modern physicians can ever prescribe. And if you are inclined toward insomnia, He will also give you much deeper slumber than barbiturates and all the other sedatives on earth, if you will just lift your hand above the covers, as if to place it in that of the Almighty, and then whisper this prayer:

"Lord, I'm trying to be a good member of your team but I have a heavy day tomorrow and must get up early, so I need a good night's sleep. Will you please take over the night shift for me?"

Then let your lifted hand drop back limply on the covers. It is surprising how relaxed you will become, for God never refuses to take over the night shift for anybody who is a member of his team! If you have a Doubting Thomas attitude concerning this bit of psychiatric advice, just try it sincerely tonight. It will widen your cosmic perspective and dwarf most of your supposed "mountains" of worry into the "molehill" size which they really should be.

If you will also engage in athletics in your youth, and thus build up your heart via cross-country, or the longer races, whether in track or swimming, your heart will actually enlarge. Thus, it can squirt more blood through the aortic valve per beat than does the small heart of the non-athlete. The athlete thus may have a normal pulse rate of only 66 to 68 instead of the usual 72.

"After crosses and losses men grow humbler and wiser."   —Franklin

His coronary arteries become bigger than those of the non-athlete with the smaller heart. As a result, a small floating clot (embolus) that will plug the coronary artery in the non-athlete, will flow farther along the larger coronary artery of the athlete and the farther along the branches of the coronary artery the plug occurs, the less the likelihood of death during the resulting heart attack.

A thrombosis acts much like the floating clot, except it results from the local thickening of the coronary artery wall. Ultimately, there develops a narrowing in the coronary. Like the stalactites and stalagmites in Mammoth Cave, these thick surfaces may finally touch. Such a plug is then called a coronary thrombosis. Again, you can see why the athlete with the larger coronary arteries is not as likely to suffer from a coronary thrombosis.

If your heart is hampered, you should favor it by avoiding strenuous activity. So don't try to run upstairs to bed if you suffer a heart attack. In fact, lie down right where you are or slump in the nearest easy chair. Keep the load on your heart reduced as much as possible. And to realize more vividly the indirect strain on the human "motor", please observe the relative difficulty of the various tasks shown in the accompanying chart. It is adapted from Dr. Edward E. Gordon's[13] challenging essay in *Modern Medicine*.

At the left you will find the type of task involved, while at the right is the number of calories used per minute by an average person. As you will note, many supposedly simple types of exercise are more fatiguing than hard manual labor.

Task	Calories per min.	Task	Calories per min.
Lying abed	1.0	Pushing wheelbarrow with 100-lb. load	5.0
Seated, reading	1.2	Playing golf	5.0
Fast typewriting	1.8	Walking downstairs	5.2
Playing piano	2.5	Dancing	5.5
Making pies	3.3	Sawing lumber	6.8
Walking at 2.5 m.p.h.	3.6	Pushing lawn mower	7.7
Making beds	3.9	Chopping trees	8.0
Laying bricks	4.0	Riding horse at trot	8.0
Taking shower bath	4.2	Climbing stairs with a 17-lb. satchel	9.0
Ironing	4.2	Shoveling coal	10.2
Bowling	4.4	Playing tennis	10.2
Hanging laundry on line	4.5		

Dr. Gordon warned that the energy equivalents given in that table are based on precise measurements of oxygen consumed. And he advises medics to beware of letting serious tuberculosis patients take a shower bath under the misconception that such a task is a light one. Actually, as the data show, it is more severe in energy requirements than laying bricks!

Indeed, many a wife whose burly husband minimizes her household labors should jolt him out of his complacency with these tabular data. For the wife of a bricklayer expends more energy ironing the laundry than he does laying bricks! Yet Chicago bricklayers recently established a union wage scale of about $5 per hour!

When President Eisenhower was also convalescing from his heart attack, he soon was permitted to play some golf. Yet this activity is actually more strenuous than laying bricks! Dr. Gordon suggests that a doctor would be reprimanded for letting a recent heart patient work as a bricklayer, yet may unwittingly assign him to a heavier physical recreation under the mistaken notion the latter is just "light" exercise.

In case you wonder why management and employers often drop over with heart attacks beginning at the age of 40, please recall that they carry their workaday worries over into their evening hours. For employers can't throw aside all their planning just because the quitting whistle blows! And with the many modern "feather bedding" practices by unions, is it any wonder employers develop insomnia or ulcers as they try to keep their businesses solvent against the heavy competition of rival firms? Moreover, they are also hampered by Uncle Sam's red tape regulations that even require those employers to compute and collect the income taxes of their workers, with no remuneration from Uncle Sam for thus serving as Collectors of Internal Revenue.

In May, 1959, the Chicago Journeyman Plumbers local union 130, signed an agreement for an additional 22¢ per hour pay hike that raised the hourly pay scale of journeymen plumbers from $3.73 to $3.95. But the contractors said they had finally gained a little benefit themselves because the union at last agrees to let contractors cut and thread pipe in their shops where power tools make it more efficient and thus cheaper for the ultimate home buyers.

And the new agreement now permits the "use of power tools in work other than making pipe fittings, such as making openings in walls where until now they used a hammer and chisel."

Imagine how hamstrung contractors have been because of the former inefficient policy of having to pay high wages to a man to sit and chisel by hand a hole through a basement wall, just because the union refused to permit modern power machinery to speed up the job! You college men and women must realize the dangers facing this Republic and our "free enterprise" system when employers are not free to use the business efficiency which has previously brought American industry and living standards to the forefront.

In many industries, two men are still forced on the payroll to do the work of only one, just because of "feather bedding" union practices. And such hampering of America's progress is permitted in part because politicians figure the working men have more votes than the employers. But the sheer majority of votes is no sure index of justice, as you can recall by the 100% vote in Pontius Pilate's court that sent an innocent Christ to the Cross on Calvary.

In February, 1959, a majority vote of only 80 attendants out of 322 newspaper guild members in St. Louis, closed down the great Globe Democrat for over 3 months. And the basic demand in that tragic strike was a pension plan that totalled over half a million dollars per year. Yet the 5-year guild members were already drawing approximately $9,250 per year in wages and fringe benefits for a mere 37½ hour week. Even so, they closed a patriotic newspaper by their impossible demand for extra pensions.

Richard H. Amberg,[3] the publisher and outstanding Christian leader, pointed out that the newspaper didn't even net half a million dollars per year, so the union's demand was preposterous! Besides, Social Security has now come into vogue to eliminate the need for such luxurious private pensions, since

Uncle Sam furnishes all workers a liberal pension at 65, or even earlier.

So why did that newspaper union close the Globe Democrat with such an impossible and illogical demand? Remember, too, that the average college professor in America nowadays makes barely $8,000 per year, despite 7 or more years of college training for his Ph.D. degree. And the average American dentist, lawyer and physician hardly net $9,250 yearly, which was the earnings of those newspapermen even before their glib demand for extra pension benefits.

Alas, most people are recipients of a weekly or monthly pay check. They take all of it home. So they fail to realize that a businessman or grocer or farmer or professional man cannot similarly take all of his gross income home. The general public thus has almost no conception of overhead, including wages to other employees, rent, taxes, insurance, obsolescence on equipment, etc. No, Mr. Average American still seems to have the juvenile idea that a grocer empties ALL the cash register's contents into his own pockets and takes the day's gross sales straight home to spend just as he wishes!

Sometimes, too, communistic planners spot strong, patriotic newspapers like the St. Louis Globe Democrat and plant a little coterie of their sympathizers in ringleader posts of the union. Then the latter deliberately make impossible demands in order to force the paper into bankruptcy so it will be compelled to sell to a more liberal rival newspaper. In this manner, communism can kill off powerful patriotic newspapers and thus make easier its unAmerican policy of national regimentation.

So you college men and women better open your eyes and realize the terrific strain under which management and private employers now function in America. For private industry still furnishes most of the wages to workers. Every man and woman could thus profit greatly from a year's tutelage in any leading Business College, just to gain a true perspective of this marvelous economic system that our forefathers created and tried to protect for our advantage and that of our posterity. We are rapidly verging on socialism in this country, largely because our average citizens have so little comprehension of the difference between a union man's weekly pay check vs. an employer's gross income.

For example, sometimes a $1,000,000 gross business may still not leave a $10,000 "net" for the employer, yet Mr. Average American looks only at that $1,000,000 gross and calls his boss a bloated economic royalist. On Page 686, you saw how the average American voter thus overrated industrial profits by 600%. This constantly increasing strain on management is a serious threat to America's future industrial expansion, for employers are dying early of coronary attacks or withdrawing their inventive brains from the shop and factory, to stagnate in California, Florida or some other health resort. Russia and other nations may thus overtake us just by our loss of top men in management. Suppose Henry Ford, Firestone, John D. Rockefeller and other geniuses of that sort had been driven into premature retirement! We might never have had sufficient industrial power to have weathered World War I and World War II.

Psychosomatic Medicine and Mental Illness. Psychosomatic medicine has been zooming under that new name, though it has always been a big element in all previous medical practice. And psychosomatic patients are those whose physical ailments spring from emotional or psychological cores.

For example, many patients will show almost a mania to have a physician pin a diagnosis of heart trouble on them, when their basic problem may be a family feud that makes them fear emotional rejection. A widow of an only son, on learning of his approaching marriage, may thus suffer what is purely psychological "heart ache" at the thought of losing the Number One place in her son's affections. But "heart ache" cannot win a great deal of sympathy. Nor can she talk about it publicly lest her friends label her as a selfish dog-in-the-manger.

So she may subconsciously translate "heart ache" into a

synonym called "heart pain" or "heart trouble". This new diagnosis has a much more medical flavor and acts as a convenient camouflage to hide her selfish refusal to let go of her son to the younger woman whom he plans to marry. Many a widow will thus suffer an apparent heart attack just before the wedding, and it is surprising how many marriages have been deferred because of "Mother's sudden illness".

Similarly, people who feel that they have violated one of God's divine laws, may thereafter imagine that the Almighty will strike them down suddenly. And the usual types of malady associated with God's retribution are apoplexy, heart attack, insanity and lightning. Oddly enough, these patients are not likely to fret about diabetes or typhoid or even tuberculosis.

Thus, a young wife who feels that she is at least partially responsible for the interruption of her pregnancy via a miscarriage, will often grow jittery about her sanity or her heart or sprout a phobia of lightning. Sometimes, however, she may worry at a later pregnancy lest her child be born defective. And if she never gets pregnant again, she may vow her sterility is God's way of striking back at her for her previous imagined sin.

Many a harassed wife will grow irritated at her child, especially if it is a baby girl and her husband, plus the in-laws, devote most of their attention to the new infant. That is doubly true if the wife has been a pampered only child who monopolized the attention of her own parents and preempted the spotlight in her own home after the wedding. All during her pregnancy, therefore, she still is the center of solicitude and inquiries. When her husband telephones from the office, he anxiously asks "How are you?" And that is also the query of her doting parents.

But as soon as she and her new baby girl get home from the hospital, her husband now is more likely to ask "How is the baby?" And when the delighted grandparents telephone they inquire, "How is she?" meaning the new granddaughter. So mamma may grow vaguely irritated and secretly somewhat jealous of her own child, for mamma used to be the prima donna on the family stage and now she has suddenly been demoted to a secondary role in the "chorus".

"It used to be so much more peaceful before baby came," she may thus think. "I wish it were like that again," may be the conclusion of this furtive train of thought.

Then she may consciously realize the fact she has expressed an indirect wish for the baby's death. (See the Death Wish section in the Appendix).

"Why that is terrible! I must be a monster and a heinous criminal even to think such a vague thought about my own baby," is her revulsion of feeling. "I must be abnormal as a mother."

And this self-diagnosis of "abnormal" soon may be translated into its synonym, "insane", after which she shops around among various medics, including finally a psychiatrist. She may complain of forgetfulness and wonder if her memory is being destroyed. Or she may state a number of other symptoms which she imagines are linked with the approach of insanity. Despite the reassurance from her family doctor that she is healthy and quite O.K., she refuses to accept his verdict. For she feels "I OUGHT to be punished with insanity."

When patients insist on having a certain ailment in spite of competent medical assurance to the contrary, then you can feel fairly certain that the patient is "holding out" on the doctors. She probably has some psychosomatic problem that makes her feel she OUGHT or MUST have such a malady as a divine punishment for some secret sin.

Dr. Walter C. Alvarez[2] has admirably delineated the province of psychosomatic medicine when he recently told the Vermilion County (Ill.) Medical Society, "We doctors must remember that no lab tests will show us that a woman has a broken heart because her son died in Viet Nam. Time and again, it takes only one question to uncover why a person is suffering. We need to make a more complete diagnosis."

Dr. Alvarez, who was a famous expert at the Mayo Clinic for many years, added that "Dr. Charles Mayo once told me if you can't make a diagnosis, ask the wife what's wrong with the husband."

Newsweek[6] recently reported that of the 19,000,000 Americans who consult a physician each week, 50% will not have any diagnosable ailments but will be suffering from the most puzzling problem in medicine, namely, hypochondria. "They constitute a vast class of 'medical shoppers' who receive no benefit from tons of pills, shots, operations, and examinations which they solicit from harassed doctors."

Dr. William C. Menninger adds, "Today, all diseases are psychosomatic. I wish we could use this term not as a 'specialty' but as a point of view in all medicine."

Most experts agree that hypochondriacs (Worry Warts about their health) are "conditioned" to that negative attitude by early childhood experiences, such as the real or imagined loss of a loved one or a much prized posession. Some doctors advocate letting the "hypo", as the modern hychochondriac is often labelled, go on believing in his poor health. Among the methods used in treating such cases are psychoanalysis and therapeutic interviews.

The non-directive interview is one such device widely advocated. In it, the patient talks freely without being steered by the doctor. This method is helpful but often not as efficient in economy of time as the directive interview wherein the doctor tactfully steers the conversation along lines that more quickly get at the core of the difficulty.

In lecturing to conventions of clergymen on this vast problem of pastoral counseling, I remind them that priests, rabbis and Protestant ministers MUST be available to everybody for personal interviews, because that help to distressed folks is inherent in the clerical profession. But the busy, harassed modern clergyman hasn't enough time to handle all the people who will impose upon his graciousness.

Besides, many of those patients would have their problems solved if they'd wait just another 24 hours. For example, a fearful mother with a son in Viet Nam or Germany having failed to receive her weekly letter today from the boy, may wish to barge in upon her clergyman for sympathy and consolation. But if she'd wait till tomorrow, probably the expected letter would arrive, thereby saving that busy pastor the 30-minute imposition on his time.

Other blue and depressed men or women may find that a change from rain to sunshine by tomorrow will alter their mood. Or even a good laxative can obviate the need for that time-consuming personal interview. So I have urged clergymen to let it be known publicly and from the pulpit that they are available to anybody who needs private consultation on family or personal problems, but they should then insist that the applicant follow the standard counseling pattern which the clergyman prescribes, namely:

(1) Write out your problem in advance and submit it to the clergyman so he can peruse it at his convenience.

This weeds out the majority whose problems are so trivial they will not go to the trouble of writing out their own case history. People are notoriously lazy concerning use of a pen or typewriter. As a consequence, the clergyman frees himself from unwarranted imposition on his valuable time by those people who just want to "gab" for an hour or figuratively weep on a sympathetic shoulder or have a distinguished leader of the community rub their psychological fur the right way and buoy up their ego. Moreover, the clergyman can derive the problem in 5 minutes by quickly skimming through the written case history, and thus save hours of time otherwise required for non-directive interviewing.

(2) Then the clergyman's secretary can set a convenient time for the interview in the case of the small percentage who have followed through on writing out their problem. Often not over 10% will write their cases.

In not over 15 minutes, the clergyman can thus get down to "brass tacks" and offer his recommendations. A great many patients, however, will have already made up their minds as to what they want to do. In short, they have secretly rendered their own verdict. But they wish to "pass the buck" to their clergyman or doctor so that their own conscience will not twinge them later on. For if anything goes wrong, they can then shift the blame by saying, "My pastor (or doctor) told me to do so-and-so." Experienced counselors avoid this common trap.

(3) As a follow-up from the personal interview, set the patient a definite task and give him some written prescription of a psychological nature that he is to employ before his next visit. Often the "Compliment Club" project is ideal to extrovert the shy or timid introvert, preoccupied with his own "innards", so that he will widen his perspective and thus gain new insights. If he thus will faithfully pay three sincere and premeditated compliments per day and repeat the process for 30 consecutive days without a break, meanwhile recording the reactions of those receiving such praise, he will then be entitled to a return interview.

Often, the first interview, supplemented by the extroverting effect of the "Compliment Club" or some of those other Rating Scales in the Appendix of this text, will obviate the need for a return interview. But even if he comes back, he has meanwhile been helping work his way out of his psychological dilemma. "God helps those who help themselves," runs our pioneer maxim that modern clergyman have a right to adapt to their current counseling technique.

On October 6, 1958, an epoch occurred in Indiana when the Indianapolis Care and Counselling Center was opened with a special commendation from both the White House as well as from Dr. Arthur S. Flemming, Secretary of Health, Education and Welfare. Using this memorable occasion to highlight his views on the role of counseling in the pastor's program, Bishop Oxnam said:

"I would not for a moment discount pastoral calling. I regard it as fundamental. No man can preach without knowing his people. On the other hand, it must be evident that the man who gives the time necessary to counseling is rendering a pastoral service far more significant than the formal call of a few minutes when there is little opportunity to move into the mind and heart of the person visited."[23]

Four years earlier, in 1954, came the establishment of the Institute of Religion at the Texas Medical Center in Houston. It united the facilities of Baylor University School of Medicine with the resources of the 5 Texas seminaries that cooperate in this dynamic program. Such worthy milestones in medical advancement simply emphasize the modern stress on viewing the patient as a total organism, rather than as a sum of many organs. The final cure of patients consists not alone of physical healing but also of mental, emotional and spiritual healing.

New Trends in Health Education. While I was at Goldey Beacom College to deliver the Commencement Address, its versatile president, Dr. Jay W. Miller, told me about the newest and most popular course among the coeds. It is a Medical Secretarial Course.

The coeds spend half a day at the local hospital receiving a general knowledge of medical techniques, ranging from the obstetrical ward to pathology, and also including the office administration of the hospital. Thus, the girls acquire a first hand experience with the medical terms and concepts about which they will later be writing when they accept positions as secretaries to physicians, medical clinics, hospitals, pharmaceutical offices, etc.

This practical internship, as it were, is then supplemented by rigorous training the balance of each day on such subjects as Applied Psychology, English, Public Speaking, Accounting, Stenography, etc. A number of other leading Business Schools are likewise adopting this same innovation. And the idea is expanding, for girls who plan secretarial careers in engineering are being given a similar type of internship in such professional schools.

Meanwhile, family doctors are likewise taking postgraduate courses on mental health. Typical of such splendid innovations in medical curricula is that co-sponsored by the Mental Health Association of Delaware and the state chapter of the

"The worst bankrupt in the world is the man who has lost his enthusiasm."
—H. W. Arnold

American Academy of General Practice. The physicians enroll in a series of 10 weekly 3-hour lectures on such topics as[10]:

(1) Recognition of depressions and potential suicides and their danger signals.

(2) Uses and misuses of sedatives, tranquilizers, hypnotics and anti-depressants.

(3) Emergency management of the acute psychotic.

(4) Recognition of the stage where a patient might need referral to a psychiatrist or an institution.

(5) Differential diagnosis from conditions which simulate psychiatric problems.

(6) Geriatric considerations.

(7) Alcoholism and drug addiction.

(8) Pitfalls in diagnosis and management of paranoia and the psychopath.

(9) Pediatric and adolescent psychiatric problems.

(10) Normal mental health.

The National Association for Mental Health, Inc. recently launched another splendid project called "Operation Friendship". It is a cooperative venture receiving the enthusiastic participation of 38 national organizations with close to 50,-000,000 members. And its aim is to bring 750,000 visitors—as many visitors as mental patients—to the nation's mental hospitals during Mental Health Week. The aim of this "Friendship" project is to acquaint laymen by first-hand views with the problems of the mentally ill and help remove some of the false stigma which has so long handicapped mental patients in their convalescence back to normalcy.

Leonard Engel[11] has a splendid book in this field which outlines four great advances in the care and treatment of the mentally ill. First, is the "open hospital", where bars are now being removed from the windows and the locks from the doors, thus permitting patients freedom to move from ward to ward or out upon the hospital grounds and even, in certain cases, into the community.

Second, psychiatric patients are now being accepted more widely by general hospitals instead of having the psychiatric patients sent away to a distant mental hospital. This encourages the mentally sick to seek treatment, lets him remain near his family and keeps psychiatry a part of everyday medical practice.

Third, there has come an increased emphasis on treatment instead of mere custodial care. Such treatment includes tranquilizer drugs, shock therapy, psychotherapy, occupational therapy and recreational therapy, too.

Fourth, many cities are now experimenting with "day hospitals" or "night hospitals" where the patient can go for a brief course of treatment and then return home at night. Or, if he works on a day shift, he can visit the hospital for treatment during the evening and remain there till next morning.

Since we have 750,000 mental hospital patients and more than 50% of them are victims of schizophrenia, the matter of mental health is a tremendous challenge to our medical profession in America nowadays. Each year more than 500,000 patients, many of them teen-agers, reach our mental hospitals as new patients. It is even becoming a serious tax problem for Dr. Menninger says the largest single item on the budget of the average state nowadays is the outlay of tax money for the care and treatment of mental patients.

The Menningers report that when they started their great work at Topeka, only one patient out of 8 returned home. Now they have been able to release 7 out of every 8 patients. They find that cosmetic aids to the ego of the patients work wonders. So they encourage colorful frocks and use of manicure sets, perfume and rouge. Since insanity is a flight from an apparently cold, cruel or forbidding external reality, then one of the best ways to prevent a psychosis is to extrovert a person's interests so that he likes the world and thus will not want to flee inward from contacts with it.

By the same token, love and praise, plus compliments and

affection, even from pet dogs, help elicit interest from the patients who have previously withdrawn into a psychic shell. When Marian Parker thus was studying conditions at a mental hospital in the South, she found that the patients were pathetically eager to have her little dog lick their hand and wag its tail in gratitude when they fed it scraps from the table.

"Dr. Crane," Mrs. Parker said, "even on cold wintry days, the patients would stand outdoors along the path I would take just to hear my dog bark gleefully when we approached them and they gave it some crumbs from the table. They seemed to come out of their shell more easily because of my dog than because of anything else."

It is shocking to find that the 8-year study by Columbia University on World War II conditions revealed that one of every seven men in the United States was rejected or discharged from our armed forces for mental or emotional reasons. Concentrating their analysis on 72,000 of some 2,500,000 such cases, these researches concluded that:

"The least educated, as those with only a few years of grade school, had an ineffectual rate in the Army four times greater than the high school and college man.

"In every regard, the farm population showed up more poorly than the city population — they had higher rates of rejection, higher breakdowns in the Army, and lower recovery rates after the war."[22]

Why We Need More Professional Symbiosis.   In bacteriology when we find two dissimilar organisms that live together to the mutual advantage of both, we call this symbiosis. But it is likewise good psychology for the kindred professions in the health field to demonstrate more of this same symbiosis, both for their own welfare and the greater protection of the general public.

For example, when a physician performs a routine check on the throat of a youngster, if he then observes badly decayed teeth, he should put in an immediate recommendation that the child visit a dentist. His remarks will carry additional weight, moreover, since he is not a dentist himself, for he is then credited as being a neutral bystander, so to speak, instead of a biased professional man who is tooting his own horn.

Literally millions of supposedly educated parents, including many college graduates, still mistake the 6-year molar for a deciduous (baby or "milk") tooth. Since it erupts at about the 6th year, parents often ignore decay therein, figuring it will be replaced by a second and permanent tooth later. This molar is the 6th tooth from the midline in front, above and below and on both sides, so there are four of them. As a mnemonic system in this regard, just recall the number 66 — meaning the 6th tooth erupting at the 6th year.

Dentists, too, can reciprocate medical "assists" by noting badly infected tonsils or other observable symptoms of ailments that fall within the field of the physician. Optometrists often are the first to note cataracts and thus refer thousands of such patients to ophthalmologists for surgery. Many a chiropodist likewise detects evidence of varicose veins and helpfully steers his patients to the appropriate physician. Chiropractors, too, detect many tumors, including possible cancer of the breast, so they send such patients to medics for biopsy and X-ray or other hospital treatment. The osteopathic physician, moreover, takes the same program of study as the M.D., and interns similarly so they are now practically identical fields of medicine.

And all of these professions are integrated by the pharmacist who often combines the introvertive research chemist's functions with the typical extrovertive behavior of a salesman. Pharmacy also is a good field for women, since the nation is in need of salaried pharmacists for the prescription counters. If they also have business acumen and know how to apply psychology in social relations, they may soon be managing a chain drug store or operating their own business. Pharmacists, too, are consulted for advice on medical as well as family matters, so they often are the counselors of their entire community.

Another medically trained professional man is the mortician who renders a versatile service to the community. By his cosmetic talent and plastic surgery on many victims of auto crashes, modern morticians buoy up the morale of parents and other relatives of the deceased. They deftly handle the various problems suddenly confronted by a family who are often stunned by the sudden, unexpected death of a loved one.

Many Americans unfairly malign the mortician and get the notion he, too, pockets the full $500 or more that may be spent for the casket. Actually, the average mortician handles but 36 funerals per year and the net profit BEFORE TAXES is $92 per funeral. He offers the family a valuable real estate site for 3 days and nights while the body occupies a large room at his funeral establishment. A chapel and pipe organ are often included. Meanwhile, as a college trained mortician, he spends as much time embalming the body as a surgeon devotes to removal of an inflamed appendix.

He also furnishes an ambulance and transports the body from the home or hospital to the funeral parlor; then back to a church and finally to a distant cemetery. He arranges the flowers, has the obituary printed, telephones the relatives and helps select pall bearers, a soloist and a clergyman.

The total charge for all of his versatile services is linked with the price of the beautiful half casket with its soft lining in pastel shades. Because the public recognizes that the casket doesn't cost $500 the public erroneously decides the mortician makes maybe $400 on the casket and thus may attack morticians as "economic royalists". If the overhead and many other functions of the mortician are included, it is evident that his $92 profit for 3 days of work, is not exorbitant. But most people fail to break down all the expense involved and still gripe about the high outlay for the casket. That casket is simply a symbol, so maybe it would be good psychology to itemize a few dozen of the other items covered by that casket price. Morticians render over 70 services to their patients for that casket charge yet the general public can hardly name 7.

Krieger[18] has the best book I have ever seen on psychology in professional practice. It is slanted for the mortician but applies with but slight changes to all the other related professions in

"To be trusted is a greater compliment than to be loved."   —George McDonald the health field. Therein he gives this terse advice: "Even if you have a big automobile for use in your work—*walk,* when you go to the bank or the post office. Not only will the exercise be good for you, but you will be able to say 'Good morning' or 'Hello' or pass the time of day with a lot of people. If you drive, you must watch traffic rather than your friends."

Medicine's Debt to Good Nurses. Busy doctors are so preoccupied that they often forget to smile or assume a jovial tone on the telephone, but their excellent nurses generally pour psychological oil on the troubled waters and put the patients back into a cheerful mood.

It would be wise for all professional men to hang a mirror behind the telephone so they could view that sour puss and arbitrarily force it into a smile before they speak to the stranger on the other end of the wire. Instead, many a busy medic or dentist literally "barks" at his patients and thus alienates the prospective patients who may be making their first contact with him via telephone.

In dentistry, the Dental Assistant serves as a versatile nurse and human relations expert. To show what a wide variety of duties she assumes, just analyze the data below that are taken from DENTAL SURVEY[9]. Dentists were asked to indicate the person who regularly does the following jobs in their office.

	Dentist	Assistant		Dentist	Assistant
Answer telephone	12%	48%	Prepare impression		
Make appointments	14%	51%	material	39.3%	45.5%
Collect receipts	14.5%	51%	Invest inlays and		
Bookkeeping	20.6%	39.5%	crowns	47.8%	12%
Banking	40%	31%	Pour models	44.2%	21.6%
Order supplies	35.3%	36.3%	Mount models	52.3%	6.2%
Recall appointments	11.3%	46.7%	Set up teeth	38%	1%
Sterilize instruments	12.7%	72.4%	Take radiographs	68.6%	9.7%
Seat patients	13%	68.6%	Developing		
Prepare filling			radiographs	23%	56%
material	24.3%	57.4%	Mount radiographs	26%	51.3%

Other workers, such as dental hygienists, technicians and receptionists usually accounted for the remaining percentages where the total of the dentist and his assistant did not add up to 100%, but this table shows the variety of duties within the province of the modern Dental Assistant.

Importance of Vitamin "R" in Psychosomatic Medicine.

One reason for the tremendous success of Dr. Karl Menninger has been his moral soundness, for patients "sense" whether a doctor's personal life backs up his verbal utterance.

The Menninger Brothers in the realm of mental medicine and psychiatry compare equally well with the famous Mayo Brothers. Dr. Karl Menninger is an active church member and teacher of a Bible Class. He has likewise found that Sunday School classes wield a powerful curative influence on the patients in his great sanitarium.

For Vitamin "R" is Religion. And religion stresses the extrovertive emotions of love, charity, unselfishness, and the Good Samaritan policy. When neurotic Silas Marner was wrapped up in himself and his nightly ritual of counting his gold pieces, he was doubtless a typical hypochondriac. But as soon as he lost his concern for SELF by finding little Eppie on his hearthstone, he grew mellow, kindly and neighborly, with a vital interest in his community.

Vitamin "R" is thus the greatest antidote for the rapid trend toward national neuroticism and psychotic imbalance. Barbiturates and other sedatives, tranquilizers and placebos cannot solve the snarled inner emotional life of a patient until he gets in tune with Divinity, and then starts playing on God's team. Indeed, the adjective "good" comes from the word "God". It is spelled without a capital letter and has the extra "o" added simply to avoid confusion. Thus, a "good man" is "God's man", in the literal meaning of the phrase.

Spiritual tonics are just as vital to the health of a human being as liver and iron tonics or other organic compounds. But far too many Americans either have a chronic negative‑ outlook or else are stuck on "dead center" so they fail to experience the rejuvenating effects of positive thinking, supported by its corollary, namely, positive action.

Dr. Karl Menninger has said in this regard, "Love is the

"No man is poor who has had a Godly mother."   —Abraham Lincoln greatest thing in the world . . . To give one's life away to what one knows to be of the highest worth, not only for oneself but for all mankind, is the most mature experience open to man."[21]

Lincoln aptly summarized it when he said we should try to "plant roses where thistles grew before."

Since the most convenient vehicle for harnessing our idealism is the local church, link up therewith. Recommend a similar prescription to "Worry Warts" and other fearful souls. You can soon change a 'fraidy cat into a vibrant, constructive personality by the "Weekly Check List For Active Church Members." Test yourself each Sabbath with this Rating Scale and use it on your friends. See how accurately its norms will differentiate the hypochondriac (chronic pill taker) from the healthy, happy "Spark plug" personality. (See next page).

REFERENCES

1 ALEXANDER, F. G., *The History of Psychiatry* (Harper & Row, 1966).
2 ALVAREZ, W. C., *Danville (Ill.) Commercial News* (5/6/59, p. 15).
3 AMBERG, R. H., "The 99 Days in St. Louis" (*Editor & Publisher*, 6/6/59).
4 BAILEY, H., *A Matter of Life or Death* (Putnam, 1958).
5 BERG, R. H., "A Report on Hospitals" (*Look*, 2/3/59).
6 CLARK, MARGUERITE, "Hypochondriacs at Large", (*Newsweek*, 12/8/58, p. 53).
7 CRANE, G. W., "Symbiosis in the Professions" (Cal Mag., Sept., 1, 1964).
8 CROWE, C. M., *Getting Ready for Tomorrow* (Abingdon, 1959).
9 *Dental Survey* (5/59, pp. 646-649).
10 "Operation Friendship Wins Support" (NAMH *Reporter* 3/59).
11 ENGEL, L., *New Trends in Care & Treatment of Mentally Ill* (Nat. Assoc. Mental Health, 1959).
12 FLEMMING, A. S., Address at National Health Forum (*Chicago Tribune*, 3/18/59, p. 12).
13 GORDON, E. E., "Exercise Equivalents" (*Modern Medicine*, 12/15/57).
14 HAMMOND, E. C., "Death Rate of Cigaret Users" (*Chicago Tribune*, 5/28/59).
15 HUDSON, R. L., *Sir, I Have A Problem* (Crowell, 1959).
16 HUNTER, R. A., "British Medics Hit Sedative Splurge", (*Chicago News*, 9/19/58).
17 JAMES, T. F., "Emotional Surgery", (*American Weekly*, 6/7/59).
18 KRIEGER, W. M., *Complete Funeral Management* (Prentice-Hall, 1962).
19 LEIB, C. W., "The Heart of the Matter", (*Smoke Signals*, July-Sept. 1958).
20 *Medical Science*, "Cost of Medical Care" (4/10/58, p. 438).
21 MENNINGER, K. A., In Ikeler's "Accent on Love" (*Presbyterian Life*, 6/15/59, p. 9).
22 *Miami Herald*, "1 U.S. Man in 7 Rejected", 5/3/59, p. 28-A).
23 OXNAM, G. B., Indiana Area News (*Together*, Dec., 1958, p. A-2).
24 SLOAN, R. P., *Today's Hospital* (Harper & Row, 1966).
25 ZIMMER & BIDERMAN, *Manipulation of Behavior* (Wiley, 1964).

WEEKLY CHECK LIST FOR ACTIVE CHURCH MEMBERS

- ☐ Attended a church service this week.
- ☐ Attended Sunday school this week.
- ☐ Attended Young People's Society Meeting.
- ☐ Attended midweek Prayer Meeting.
- ☐ Attended Women's Society Meeting of church.
- ☐ Attended Church Men's Meeting.
- ☐ Have contributed this week either cash, food or clothing, to my church or its allied organizations.
- ☐ Have helped this week in serving church meals, as by cooking, waiting tables, dish washing, etc.
- ☐ Am an officer of some church group.
- ☐ Am a tither (10% annual donor) to church and related altruistic projects.
- ☐ Have made a personal visit this week for the church, as on the sick or for finance campaign, etc.
- ☐ Have either telephoned (or sent "Get Well" card) to the sick, strangers or other church prospects.
- ☐ Have helped chaperone or sponsor some related church group, as Scouts, Sunday School class party, Camp Fire Girls, Young People's Society hike, picnic, etc.
- ☐ Have performed musically for church group, as by singing, playing piano or other instrument.
- ☐ Have helped usher at a church meeting.
- ☐ Have helped conduct a church meeting, as by speaking, reading Scripture lesson, etc.
- ☐ Have prayed aloud in public this week.
- ☐ Have prayed silently this week.
- ☐ Have read some in the Bible this week.
- ☐ Have said grace at the table this week, either aloud or silently.
- ☐ Have used automobile to bring other people to church meetings (not my own family).
- ☐ Have helped operate movie machine, loud speaker or other church technical equipment.
- ☐ Have invited somebody to come to church or other religious meetings this week.
- ☐ Have smiled at and greeted strangers at church.
- ☐ Have helped with church collections this week.
- ☐ Have helped with secretarial duties of church groups.
- ☐ Have helped operate Nursery for youngsters while their parents listened to sermon.
- ☐ Have paid one sincere verbal compliment this week.
- ☐ Have apologized or said "I'm sorry" to anybody this week with whom I've quarreled or whom I have wronged.
- ☐ Have helped with church mimeographed magazine, as in typing, stencil cutting, gathering news, etc.

☐ Have helped with such church chores as distributing song books, carrying or arranging chairs, sewing or cleaning, etc.
☐ Have not used tobacco this week.
☐ Have not used alcoholic beverages this week.
☐ Have not used profanity this week.
☐ Have attended a Hi-Y, Tri-Hi-Y, CYO, YMCA, or YWCA meeting this week.

On the foregoing WEEKLY CHECK LIST, you aren't expected to make a perfect score. You'd be a saint to do so. In such psychological tests we usually employ a set of "norms" against which you can then interpret your raw score.

Credit yourself with 4 points for each item on that CHECK LIST which applies to you for the week in question. A very high score two weeks ago, however, cannot carry over to help bolster this week's rating!

Then tally your total score for the week. This is your raw score. Suppose you have checked 13 items as applying to your behavior this past week. At 4 points apiece, this gives you a raw score of 52. Interpret it according to the following norms. You will find that the resulting total of 52 points puts you in the "Enthusiastic" group.

Raw Scores	Interpretation
0 to 12	Anemic Christian
16 to 24	Lukewarm Christian
28 to 36	Average Christian
40 to 52	Enthusiastic Christian
56 and Up	Real "Spark plug"

If you wish to inject some wholesome competition into your Sunday school class, divide into several teams and employ this WEEKLY CHECK LIST as the basis for computing the total team points.

Genial rivalry of this type can soon convert an anemic, sickly church into a robust, red blooded moral organization. Indeed, churches often need a "booster shot" of Vitamin "R". And just one member who attains the "Enthusiastic" or the "Spark plug" rating on the test previously mentioned, can infect an entire congregation.

So get on God's team and play valiantly. That will enable you to drain off your surplus nervous energy in constructive channels

Are You an Introvert or an Extrovert?

Place a check mark in the square at the left of the description applying to you. If you cannot decide, leave it blank and go on to the next set below.

A B

☐ Prefer books; or
  ☐ Prefer social affairs

☐ Prefer to struggle alone on a problem; or
  ☐ Prefer to ask help on a problem

☐ Slowly make friends with the opposite sex; or
  ☐ Easily make friends with the opposite sex

☐ Carefully hang up your clothes at night; or
  ☐ Throw your clothes over a chair

☐ Feel embarrassed in front of a crowd; or
  ☐ Feel at ease before a crowd

☐ Dislike sales work; or
  ☐ Like sales work

☐ Worry a great deal; or
  ☐ Seldom have a worry

☐ Are your feelings hurt easily; or
  ☐ Not easily offended by what is said about you

☐ Prefer being a bookkeeper; or
  ☐ Prefer being a sales clerk

☐ Find it difficult to start a conversation with a stranger; or
  ☐ Find it easy to start a conversation with a stranger

☐ Slowly adopt new slang; or
  ☐ Quickly adopt new slang

A B

☐ Blush easily; or
  ☐ Blush rarely

☐ Squeeze the tooth paste tube from the end; or
  ☐ Squeeze it from the middle

☐ Find yourself among the last 50 per cent who adopt the new fashions; or
  ☐ Find yourself among the first 50 per cent who adopt new fashions

☐ Easily remember all your expenses for the day or week; or
  ☐ Forget many of the expenses of the day or week

☐ Forget almost all of the funny stories you hear; or
  ☐ Remember most of the funny stories you hear

☐ Save grocers' twine; or
  ☐ Discard it

☐ Dread asking for a loan; or
  ☐ Feel little hesitation in asking for a loan

☐ Prefer to deliver a written report; or
  ☐ Prefer to deliver an oral report

☐ Find yourself a "standpatter" in religion and politics; or
  ☐ Find yourself broad-minded in religion and politics

Exhibit 60. If your check marks in the "A" columns are double the number in the "B" columns, you are an introvert. If "B" is double the "A" total, you are an extrovert. Most people fall in between with a 10-10, 11-9, 12-8, or 13-7 ratio, and are ambiverts.

Personal Rating Scale for Extroversion

EXHIBIT 61. Introverts will regularly attain scores of 1 to 9 points in this test. Ambiverts will consistently maintain averages from 10 to 20, while extroverts from week to week will be found with scores of 21 points or more. Since happiness and emotional stability correlate very highly with the multitude of bonds which tie us to our external environment, we can employ this rating scale to measure egocentric personalities. Silas Marner and Scrooge would have scored at best 5 and 7 points, respectively. Old people also tend to have fewer external ties, so their scores decline. But a person of 20 may be socially as "shut in" as his grandfather of 70.

THIS PAST WEEK I HAVE: Total Points

Taught—(2 points for each line that applies):
    Day School ....
    Sunday School ....
    A settlement group, dramatics class, etc.................

Presided at, directed, or entertained for—(3 points per line):
    A Boy Scout or Girl Scout meeting.......................
    Kiwanis, Rotary, Lions or committee meeting.............
    Church, charitable or philanthropic group...............
    Fraternity, sorority or social group, as bridge.........
    Board of directors, sales meeting, etc..................
    Professional meeting, as medical, dental, teachers......

Attended a public gathering—(2 points per line):
    Religious, charity or social service meeting............
    Business or professional meeting........................
    Athletic, theatre or social, as a dance, bridge, etc....
    Fraternal, literary, political or educational...........

Performed in public—(2 points per line that fits):
    Speech, oration, declamation, prayer....................
    Musically, as vocal or instrumental.....................
    Athletically, as dancer, gymnast, skater, ball player...
    Dramatically, as actor, magician, cartoonist, etc.......
    As a salesman, or solicitor for charity, church, etc....

Performed an unselfish deed—(2 points for each line):
    Visited sick or friendless..............................
    Sent flowers, gifts, greetings (not Christmas)..........
    Contributed to church or charitable cause...............

Paid 3 sincere compliments in one day—(1 for each day).........

Been living with my husband or wife—(2 points)................

Been parent or guardian of adult children—(2 points)..........

Been parent or guardian of minor children—(3 points for first; 1 for each other; maximum 5 points).............................

Had outside date (theatre or dinner) with friends or mate or sweetheart—(1 per date; maximum 3 points)......................

Entertained relatives or friends at home—(1 point per day with maximum score of 3 points)...............................

Been a member of a church—(1 point).........................

Been employer, supervisor or foreman—(2 points)..............

Mr. Edward Hopkins, Jr.,
The Hopkins Syndicate, Inc.,
520 North Michigan Avenue,
Chicago, Illinois.

Dear Mr. Hopkins:

Since I am looking for a position with a company which holds out a future for a person of my experience, I wish to cite the following qualifications:

1. BUSINESS EXPERIENCE
   Director, Michigan Red Cross Campaign 19___ to 19___.
   Publicity director U. S. Bureau of Health 19___ to 19___.
   Publicity director George Washington University 19___ to 19___.
   Assistant advertising manager Cramill Publishing Company 19___ to 19___.

2. EDUCATIONAL EXPERIENCE
   A.B., 1943, Northwestern University.
   Editor-in-chief of college newspaper.
   Fraternity man and member of numerous clubs.

3. PERSONAL DATA
   Age 34; unmarried; excellent health;
   Height 5' 10", weight 168;
   Carry $15,000 insurance; free of debts.

4. REFERENCES
   Judge Arnold B_____, Federal Court, Chicago, Illinois.
   Mr. Melvin V_____, President, First National Bank.
   Mr. C. E. M_____, Advertising manager, Cramill Publishing Company.

If you have a position in your organization for which the above qualifications would seem to fit me, then I should appreciate an early reply.

                              Sincerely,
VHB/T

EXHIBIT 62. This kind of letter was sent out to 120 randomly chosen presidents and high executives of large business firms in the East in mimeograph form, with their names typed in, and brought 70 replies with 19 requests for immediate interviews.

THE FORMULA FOR BEING AN INTERESTING CONVERSATIONALIST

Benjamin Franklin once said, "As we must account for every idle word, so we must for every idle silence."

Too many of us go through life relatively tongue-tied. We are guilty of keeping quiet when we should be complimenting our associates for their good deeds. We should express our appreciation while they are alive, instead of waiting till the funeral before we give them bouquets.

Conversational skill is an art, but all art has a scientific and precise foundation. I shall present three major steps in becoming an interesting conversationalist.

First, train yourself to become a social detective. Look for good things in your companions, such as artistic fingers, beautiful complexions, melodious voice, unselfishness, etc., and then pay a sincere and deserved compliment. People are starving for appreciation, but the average person doesn't pay one compliment a day to anybody, relatives, business associates, or casual acquaintances. Don't let timidity deter you. Go up to your companions and tell them you admire their new tie or frock, curly hair or attractive teeth. Like all beginning salesmen, you may feel panicky and frightened at your own boldness, especially if you've been a colorless wallflower heretofore, but go ahead, anyway. You will develop poise and assurance if you just keep forcing yourself to start conversations.

Second, learn to be skilful with what I have termed the "reversible why". When somebody asks you a question you cannot answer or don't wish to answer, tactfully reverse the question. Don't do this bluntly or it will appear like a slap in the face. Be deft. For example, if a man asks a girl, "Who do you think will win the World Series?" the girl can smile sweetly and say, "I really don't know, for they are both strong teams. If I were going to bet on one team, which would you advise?" It is apparent that a girl need know nothing at all about baseball to employ this method. Ideally, however, it is wise to have a little information on many topics in order to reverse questions more adroitly. It is a help if a person will skim the newspaper for the high spots both in local city affairs, foreign news, politics, athletics, and the financial pages. It doesn't take 15 minutes for us to get enough late information to start conversations.

Third, a skilful conversationalist is one who can get other people to talking. In fact, it is an axiom of psychology that people feel happy and inflated in their ego if we can set the conversational stage, and then give them ardent and rapt attention. We need to steer the subject of conversation so that our companion will finally take our cue and become enthusiastic about his hobby or his work, his children or his new automobile. But all of us from time to time find ourselves in a social situation where we want to keep conversation moving smoothly, but we can't think of anything to say. To meet just such a dilemma I am offering you a little mnemonic system or memory scheme by which you can always probe around till you strike the subject which will set your companion talking.

The key phrase to remember is "DEAR HOME PALS". Each letter stands for a field of conversation. By tactfully probing around from one topic to another, you can always get your companion to talk, unless he is literally a Sphinx. The key phrase is broken down into the following:

"D". This stands for "drama", including movies and the legitimate stage. You can lead into this topic by exclaiming about some recent show which you have attended. Then ask your companion for his or her favorite actor or actress. It is always better, however, to give a person a choice, in case he is tongued-tied or his mind is a blank. So ask, "Do you like Rock Hudson better than John Wayne?" Or inquire, "Which singer do you enjoy more, Elvis Presly or Pat Boone?" If your companion blushes and seems uncertain or acts as if he knows about neither, then save him embarrassment by rushing on, "Oh, I'll bet you're one of those strong, silent men that refuse to commit themselves." If your companion doesn't pick up a cue by this time on the subject of drama, then deftly move along to

"E". This stands for "entertainment". Probe this field, asking which form of recreation he would choose, "Athletics, fishing, movies, chess, or reading a book." Find out if he prefers being with people or going on a hike by himself. If she is tactful, a girl can often set her male companion talking on one of these subjects and get him to ask her for a date to go horseback riding, hiking, etc. If you get no response on this letter, proceed to

"A". It stands for "athletics" and is a further extension of "E". Here, however, focus attention upon various sports, such as baseball, football, tennis, swimming, handball, bowling, billiards and the like. Find out if your companion enjoys the game simply as a spectator or "fan", or if he or she actually plays the game. Commend the broad shoulders and height or strength of your male escort. And always keep up a friendly, bantering tone. Be delicate in your probing so that you do not embarrass your companion. If he doesn't respond to "athletic" probing, veer over to

"R". This stands for "relatives". Inquire about his or her family, or early home environment. Ask if he or she has brothers or sisters. What are they like? "Do they all have blue eyes like you?" The latter question is revealing because it shows how to keep your conversation on a personal basis. Some people converse for hours but it is coldly analytical, like a professor's lecture. Always try to break through with personal, friendly queries so that the conversation has warmth and jollity. Your bantering tone will also prevent the conversation from "going intellectual". By this time you will ordinarily have a lively discussion going on. If, however, the key word "DEAR" has not loosened the tongue of your associate, then move on to the next key word, "HOME", beginning with

"H". This letter stands for "hobbies". These may be of the present or go back to childhood and adolescence. Stamp collecting, the keeping of scrapbooks, photographs and snapshot albums, recipes, or old coins, birds' eggs or butterflies. Reading poetry or writing, painting or cartooning, cooking or tap dancing. Knitting, sewing, teaching a Sunday school class or directing the Girl or Boy Scout Troop. Tinkering with gasoline engines or building model airplanes and old sailing ships. This is a rich field which I shall only sketch here. You can go on adding additional items. If you simply cannot elicit any response on the subject of hobbies, past or present, then skilfully swing into

"O".   This stands for "occupation". Get your companion talking about her home or her children, her office job, etc. Or try to start your male companion explaining the problems he meets as a salesman or factory worker, accountant or physician. You can lead him on to talk of his ambitions and dreams of the future. Even if he has a menial job at present, he may have a high goal. If you obtain no response on this topic, move to

"M".   This represents "music". Does he prefer cowboy ballads to Hawaiian guitars, or the violin to piano? Did he ever sing in a quartette, or choir? Does she prefer a symphonic orchestra or hillbilly music? In a home situation you may thus get your companion performing at the piano before the evening is over. If your companion "muffs" these cues, then gracefully lead on to

"E".   This letter stands for "engineering" in its broad sense, covering especially modern automobiles. Find out if your companion has a car, or which type of low-priced automobile he or she considers best. Ask for advice regarding the advantages of six-cylinders vs. eight, or power brakes, air conditioning, etc. Inquire about the making of electricity, or the value of tubes in a radio, etc. A tactful girl can play "dumb" even if she knows mechanics thoroughly, and let her introvertive boy friend parade his supposedly superior knowledge. If your companion does not react to various cues in the field of automobiles and engineering, then shift to the final key word of the formula, "PALS", beginning with

"P"   This is the key letter for "politics". Older people will probably pick up this cue, especially as regards taxes. Various related topics fit into this field, such as the Supreme Court, the UMT and labor difficulties. If your companion becomes too worked up on the subject and you wish to get away from dangerous zones, make an incisive thrust with a disarming smile and get upon

"A".   This stands for "appearance", and is a lifesaver as a means of getting away from debates and logical discussion. Compliment the man's tie, as "That certainly is an attractive tie. Did you buy it or is it a gift from one of your many girl friends?" Praise a girl regarding her party dress or slender ankles, or kissable mouth, etc. You can check a heated political discussion in the very middle of a sentence by one of these complimentary verbal thrusts. And you can bring a flush of pleasure to a girl whose evening has been boresome, by such personal compliments. If you are tactful and keep up a bantering tone, you can short circuit an old fashioned 3-year courtship by such methods and get a girl to say "yes" within a few weeks or months. Furthermore, a girl can jolt a steady, phlegmatic suitor out of his complacency and pep him up by such clever verbal manipulation. Many popular men and women start out with the subject of "appearance" in their opening comments. This is a sure-fire field of conversation, regardless of whether you have traveled widely, are a college graduate or finished only the fifth grade in grammar school. If you haven't the courage at the outset to get upon personal topics, then you may want to try the intellectual approach, beginning with

"L".   This represents the field of "literature". You deftly lead the conversation into modern literature and the latest best seller. Or you ask, "Which current magazine do you like best—Reader's Digest, or Saturday Evening Post?" Remember my previous warning and don't ask, "Which magazine do you like best?" This may be vague or catch your companion wool gathering, so that he cannot respond. Always lay down a selection before your prospect, whether in the field of selling or conversation. He will be much more likely to respond, for it requires much less effort to choose than to originate ideas. If you don't like this intellectual topic and your companion cares little for magazines or books, then slip into

"S".   This stands for "sex differences". You can develop all sorts of discussions, ranging from whether or not women are as intelligent as men, or should smoke and drink whiskey, to the male opinion of red fingernails on girls, their use of slang and profanity. A man can ask his girl companion for advice about a present which he wants to buy for his sister or mother. Girls react very favorably to masculine requests for help and advice. This is one of womankind's most vulnerable spots, but most men never utilize this psychological advantage. A girl can ask a man what present she should buy for her brother, and soon have him window shopping with her down the avenue.

Many cynics will sneer at this keyed method of being an interesting conversationalist, but don't let their scoffing deter you. These same people will protest about using "canned" sales talks in selling, but most star salesmen always use "canned" talks. You cannot rely on inspiration of the moment. You must prepare in advance and rehearse and practice at every opportunity. Physicians and dentists don't rely on inspiration, either, but laboriously practice during college and interneship until they are deft. For a shorter formula, use H-E-L-P (Hobbies, Entertainment, Literature, Politics).

Sit down for half an hour and memorize the key phrase DEAR HOME PALS. You need not employ it always in that order. You can start with the letter "H" or "L" if it seems advisable, but be sure you learn the individual letters and can employ them with companions of both sexes. You will then be surprised at the ease with which you can carry on a conversation, and you will no longer be guilty of "idle silences".

A TEST FOR SWEETHEARTS (FEMALE)

This test represents the composite likes and dislikes of 1,144 unmarried men, ranging in ages from 17 to 46. They were asked privately to list the chief merits and demerits regarding their girl friends. They talked frankly. I have compressed and summarized the most frequently mentioned flaws and virtues, weighting those items which were most common or most fundamental.

In computing a girl's score, check the various items under DEMERITS which apply to her, and add the total. Each item counts as one point unless specifically weighted, as in the parentheses. Then check off the items under MERITS which apply to her. Now subtract the DEMERIT score from her MERIT score. The result is her raw score. Interpret it according to this table:

Raw Scores	Interpretation
0 — 29	Very Poor
30 — 47	Poor
48 — 69	Average
70 — 88	Superior
89 and up	Very Superior

DEMERITS

1. Wears bright red nail polish. ☐
2. Seams in her hose are often crooked. ☐
3. Is very suspicious and jealous. (5) ☐
4. Flirts with other men at parties or in restaurants, etc. (5) ☐
5. Talks too much about her other boy friends, or the shows and places to which they have taken her. ☐
6. Uses profanity. (5) ☐
7. Smokes or gambles. (5) ☐
8. Uses alcohol or dope. (10) ☐
   If ever drunk. (20) ☐
9. Tells risque or vulgar stories. (5) ☐
10. Corrects boy friend's speech or actions in public. (5) ☐
11. Apologetic regarding her parents. Seems ashamed to have boy meet them. ☐
12. Applies make-up in public. ☐
13. Permits too many sex liberties. Too easy. A "good time Gertie". (10) ☐
14. More than 15 pounds overweight. ☐
15. Comes from divorced parents. ☐
16. A wallflower. Excessively timid or shy. ☐

MERITS

1. Is fond of flowers. ☐
2. Can carry on an interesting conversation. ☐
3. Has a good sense of humor. Jolly and gay. ☐
4. Religious—has high ideals and takes an active part in church work. (10) ☐
5. A good hostess. Makes people feel welcome and comfortable. ☐
6. Wears her clothes well and dresses to fit her figure and personality. ☐
7. Praises her boy friend in public. ☐
8. Has spunk—will defend her ideals and religion. ☐
9. A good cook. Knows the culinary arts. (5) ☐
10. Writes interesting and jolly letters. Has originality and cleverness. ☐
11. Considerate of boy friend's pocketbook. ☐
12. Healthy and athletic. Likes outdoors. (5) ☐
13. Has same religion as that of her boy friend. (5) ☐
14. Loves children and a home. (10) ☐
15. Good seamstress. Can make her own clothes. ☐
16. Is dainty and feminine. Doesn't adopt mannish clothes or customs. (5) ☐

17. Speaks poor English or uses an excessive amount of slang. ☐

17. Helps boy friend with his work or lessons, and encourages him to advance. ☐

18. Catty and unsportsmanlike. Too free with gossip and unpleasant remarks about people. (5) ☐

18. Considerate and tactful with people, including boy's parents and his former friends. (5) ☐

19. Bites her finger nails. ☐

19. Interested in cultural things, as art and music, good books. ☐

20. Confides too freely in others. Tells private affairs to her girl friends. ☐

20. Honest and faithful. Is true to her steady boy friend or fiance. (10) ☐

21. Fussy about her food at a restaurant. Makes trouble for the waitress, etc. ☐

21. Adaptable. Can be serious or jolly and frivolous as time and occasion demand. ☐

22. Talks during a movie, play or concert. ☐

22. Has musical ability. Can sing or play some musical instrument. ☐

23. Has poor table manners. Gargles her soup, eats with her fingers, picks her teeth, etc. ☐

23. Always gives her escort the impression she is having a good time, so he feels well repaid for his efforts. ☐

24. Is a "peacock personality" or show-off type. Always plays to the galleries. A grandstander. ☐

24. Is usually a "cheer leader" instead of a "wet blanket" regarding her boy friend's ideas and ambitions. ☐

25. Chews gum too much, as during dancing, church, at parties, etc. ☐

25. Retains a wholesome enthusiasm for life instead of acting bored and cynical. ☐

26. Uses "Oh, yeah?" or "I'll never tell" and other stopgaps for lack of conversational ability. ☐

26. Has many friends of both sexes, and enjoys being with people. ☐

27. Has no mind of her own. A perfect slave of fashion. ☐

27. Knows how to swim, or play golf, tennis, badminton, etc. (one point for each) ☐

28. Extravagant. Cannot live within her salary, budget, or allowance. (5) ☐

28. Likes the same kind of movies, music, plays or other entertainment as her boy friend. ☐

29. Too superstitious. Believes in luck, fortune telling, etc. (5) ☐

29. Has pretty white teeth. Uses a toothbrush. ☐

30. Snobbish and affected in speech or actions. Tries to "highhat" people. (5) ☐

30. Uses mild perfume suited to her personality. Doesn't try to drown "B. O." in strong perfume. ☐

31. Makes boy friend feel she is condescending or doing him a favor by granting him a date. ☐

31. Occasionally invites him to her home or apartment for dinner. ☐

32. Has a "spoiled child" temperament or is an "only" child. (10) ☐

32. Can take shorthand or operate a typewriter by the touch system. ☐

33. Will not explain or talk things over at a quarrel. Simply pouts or sulks. (5) ☐

33. Sympathetic and tender hearted. Tries to help the unfortunate, whether a wounded bird or tenement baby. ☐

34. Has body odor, halitosis, dandruff, dirty finger nails, etc. (one point for each) ☐

34. Even tempered and has good self-control. Doesn't fly off the handle easily. (5) ☐

35. A "projector". Blames others for her own faults. Refuses to faces facts or admit her errors. (5) ☐

35. Comes from a good family, honest and industrious. Parents are gracious and friendly. ☐

36. Too serious minded and bookish. Tries to show off her superior ability, talents, or education. ☐

36. Prompt for appointments. Rarely is late. ☐

37. Flashy in her dress. Wears too much jewelry, race track plaids, red shoes, bizarre hats, backless gowns, etc. ☐

37. Laughs at her boy friend's jokes and clowning, or pays rapt attention to his speech. ☐

38. Artificial in appearance owing to mascara, bleached or dyed hair, and excessively plucked eyebrows. (5) ☐

38. Has a good figure, including shapely legs and bust, and erect carriage; not stoop shouldered. (5) ☐

39. Uses too much make-up or is careless in applying rouge or lipstick so she looks streaked. ☐

39. Will blush in an embarrassing situation, or shed tears when confronted by pathos, or unusual unhappiness. ☐

40. Too quiet and reserved. Will not let her boy friend know how she feels or what she likes. The "Sphinx" type of girl. (5) ☐

40. Comments frequently about her boy friend's masculinity and physical strength, his broad shoulders, strong muscles, etc. (5) ☐

41. The nagging or scolding type. Gets into frequent quarrels. ☐

41. Has social accomplishments, such as playing bridge, dancing, declaiming, leading group games, etc. ☐

42. Has strong prejudices regarding race, religion, politics, etc. ☐

42. Has similar home and educational background to that of her boy friend. ☐

43. Thoughtless of boy friend. Deserts him when he's at a strange party to chatter with her girl friends. ☐

43. Now belongs, or else once belonged, to YWCA, Girl Scouts, literary or other constructive school organizations. (one point for each) ☐

44. Gets her feelings hurt too easily. Thinks people are deliberately trying to affront or insult her. (5) ☐

44 Is generous and unselfish. Gives a reasonable amount of her money and time to civic, charitable and religious enterprises. (5) ☐

45. Permits herself to get into very dangerous or compromising situations, and then blames the man if she is mistreated. ☐

46. Whines instead of taking her medicine from life. Will not play fairly. Cheats at cards and otherwise. (20) ☐

47. Emotionally cold or frigid. Lacks that warm hearted, humanness and wholesome amiability. Stiff and formal. ☐

48. Keeps digging up unpleasant things from the past. ☐

49. Addicted to the "career complex" or worship of money. (5) ☐

50. Cynical. Disbelieves everybody simply because she was once deceived or mistreated. (5) ☐

45. Has a sweet and attractive voice. Not strident, harsh, or chronically faultfinding. ☐

46. Acts her age. Doesn't use baby talk and try to be "cute" or kittenish when her age or size or the situation make her appear ridiculous. ☐

47. Self-assured and poised. Gives her boy friend an occasional kiss but knows when to stop. (5) ☐

48. Always thanks her boy friend for dates and favors shown her. (10) ☐

49. Well read so she can converse on current events. ☐

50. Competent in handling children or in caring for a baby. Knows something of child welfare or child psychology. (5) ☐

A TEST FOR SWEETHEARTS (MALE)

This test represents the composite likes and dislikes of 1,187 unmarried girls and women, ranging in ages from 16 to 42. They were asked privately to list the chief merits or demerits regarding their boy friends. They talked frankly. I have compressed and summarized the most frequently mentioned flaws and virtues, weighting those items which were most common or most fundamental.

In computing a man's score, check the various items under DEMERITS which apply to him, and add the total. Each item counts as one point unless specifically weighted, as in the parentheses. Then check off the items under MERITS which apply to him. Now subtract the DEMERIT score from the MERIT score. The result is his raw score. Interpret it according to this table:

Raw Scores	Interpretation
0 — 29	Very Poor
30 — 47	Poor
48 — 69	Average
70 — 88	Superior
89 and up	Very Superior

DEMERITS	MERITS

1. Criticizes his girl friend in public. ☐
2. Tries to flirt with other girls while on a date. ☐
3. Fails to bathe or change socks often enough. ☐
4. Belches without apology, picks nose or teeth in public, etc. Ill mannered. ☐
5. Uses profanity or tells vulgar stories. ☐
6. Is very suspicious and jealous. ☐
7. Uses alcohol. (5) If ever drunk. (10) ☐
8. Tells lies — unreliable, unfaithful. ☐
9. Too possessive. Dislikes for girl to go out with anybody else, even her girl friends. ☐
10. A "mamma's boy" or an "only" child. (10) ☐
11. Stubborn—rarely admits that he is wrong. Seldom apologizes. ☐
12. Tells embarrassing things about his girl when they are out in public. ☐
13. Is guilty of halitosis, dandruff, dirty teeth, etc. (one point for each) ☑
14. Frequently borrows money from girl friend, or "sponges" on others. (5) ☐
15. Too fresh. Tries to "paw" a girl. Has "Roman" hands. ☑
16. Expects girl to be at his beck and call even if he fails to ask for a date till 7 P. M. of that night. ☑
17. Pouts or sulks if he cannot have his own way in everything. ☑
18. No time sense. Stays too late even when he knows girl must be up early to get to work. ☑
19. Uses tobacco. ☐

1. Remembers birthdays, holidays, etc. ☑
2. Frequently compliments girl friend on her looks, clothes, cooking, etc. (10) ☑
3. Polite and courteous to girl's parents and friends. ☑
4. Neat in appearance — shoes shined, hair cut, suit pressed, shaved, etc. ☐
5. Healthy and athletic—likes sports. ☑
6. Is fond of children. (5) ☑
7. Is a careful automobile driver. ☐
8. A steady worker or good student. ☑
9. Ambitious — works or studies on his own time to gain promotion. (5) ☑
10. Surprises girl occasionally with candy, flowers and other gifts. ☐
11. Attends church or encourages girl friend if she is an active member. (10) ☑
12. Has a good sense of humor, and can take a joke on himself. ☑
13. Generous with his money but not a "show off" or "splurger." ☐
14. Self-confident and positive in his personality. Assured and poised. ☑
15. Considerate and artistic in his love making. Not a glutton for kisses. ☑
16. Always knows where he is going on a date. Rarely asks, "Where'll we go tonight?" ☐
17. Uses good English with a minimum of slang. ☐
18. Writes interesting and jolly letters. Has originality and cleverness. ☑
19. Interested in cultural things as good books, music and art. ☐

20. Cynical. Believes everybody is bad until proved otherwise. ☐

20. Has high ideals and firm convictions about right and wrong. (10) ☒

21. Argues with waiters, taxi drivers, other motorists, sales clerks, etc. ☐

21. Looks directly at a person when conversing. Frank, not shifty in gaze. ☒

22. Too introvertive. Dislikes double dates, parties, dances, and such social affairs. ☐

22. Never goes home angry. Willing to talk things over fairly and concede a point if he is wrong. (5) ☑

23. Has rarely earned any money of his own. Lives on a "dole" from indulgent parents, sister, brother, etc. (5) ☐

23. Has respect and consideration for other women besides his girl friend. ☑

24. Tactless and blunt. Doesn't make friends easily. Gets on people's nerves. (5) ☐

24. Is respectful and considerate concerning his parents and sisters or brothers. (5) ☐

25. Has poor table manners. Licks his fingers, gargles his soup, eats with knife instead of fork, etc. ☐

25. A good sport. Willing to adapt himself to altered plans without getting angry, grouchy or pouting. ☐

26. Wears flashy clothes, as pink or purple shirts, loud ties, race track plaids, etc. ☐

26. Is romantic and when he kisses, bestows real movie kisses instead of timid pecks on the cheek. ☒

27. Accepts defeat too easily. Lacks persistency and spunk. (5) ☐

27. Lets girl drive his car or teaches her how, if she lacks ability. ☒

28. Indecisive. Can't make up his own mind. Vacillates. ☐

28. Sympathetic and tender hearted. May even show a tear at pathetic climax in a movie. ☒

29. Too superstitious. Believes in luck, fortune telling, etc. (5) ☐

29. Even tempered and has good self-control. Doesn't fly off the handle easily. (5) ☒

30. A chronic "projector" or buckpasser. Always blames others for his own faults and mistakes. ☐

30. Mixes well with people. Gets along well with girl's mother. Will go out into kitchen and help with dishes. (5) ☒

31. Comes from divorced parents. ☐

31. Usually good humored and jolly. ☒

32. Fails to stand when a girl leaves their table; fails to hold coat for girl or open doors for her, etc. ☐

32. Prompt for appointments, or if detained, will telephone to inform the girl. ☐

33. It's very obvious when he is bored. He doesn't try to conceal his irritation. ☒

33. Asks definitely for a date instead of leaving the girl in uncertainty, and asks far enough in advance to let her make her plans. ☐

34. Teases girl too much. ☐

34. Is a good dancer. ☒

35. Sings or whistles while dancing. ☐

35. Is courteous and manly. Well liked by men. ☒

36. An egotist. Talks about himself most of the time. ☐	36. Tells girl his secrets. Confides in her and asks for her opinion. ☑
37. Lets girl have her own way too much, till he appears spineless or sissy, and she loses respect for him. ☐	37. True to one girl if engaged or going steadily. Doesn't try to "two-time" her. (5) ☑
38. Boasts about his sex conquests or affairs with other women. (5)	38. Always speaks well of everybody. Not prejudiced or narrow minded. ☐
39. Toots horn in front of girl's home instead of coming to door. ☐	39. Comes from a good family—gracious, kindly and unprejudiced. ☐
40. Not forceful or masculine enough. Has weak handshake, nervous giggle, and excessive timidity. (5) ☐	40. Encourages a girl to maintain her ideals instead of trying to break them down. (5) ☐
41. Always trying to say things that will shock people. A grandstander, or show-off type. ☐	41. Industrious and can hold a job, so a girl feels she can lean upon him. Gives her a sense of security. (10) ☑
42. Dreams too much and flees from reality. Then tries to bolster his ego by tall tales and bragging. (10) ☐	42. An interesting entertainer. Takes girl to various places of amusement and tries to make her evening happy. ☑
43. A gambler. Thinks he can "win" success instead of "earning" it. (5) ☐	43. Is well read. Can discuss current events in addition to athletics. ☐
44. Dishonest. Cheats at cards or thinks it smart to "gyp" or short change people. (20) ☐	44. Has musical ability, as singing, playing piano, guitar, etc. ☐
45. Too serious minded, and bookish. Tries to show off his intelligence or superior education. ☑	45. Brave and strong, but gentle and courteous. ☑
46. Tries to put on airs. Is a snob. Has affected speech. ☐	46. Likes wide range of foods. Not a finicky eater. ☑
47. No business ability, and can't hold on to his money. Usually broke. (10) ☐	47. Enthusiastic and vital. Not a sluggish or anemic type. ☑
48. Too attentive and gallant to the point of effeminacy. A "yes" man. ☐	48. Gives her presents which are appropriate or useful. ☑
49. Embarrasses girl by cleaning or filing nails in public; talking with food in his mouth; spitting or dropping ashes on floor, talking loudly, etc. ☑	49. Shows some executive ability. Can make a speech or lead the singing, or get people to work for him. Inspires confidence in himself. ☑
50. Ashamed of his parents or home, and will not introduce girl to them. (5) ☐	50. Is morally and physically clean. Free from venereal disease. (10) ☑

This test is based upon the confidential reports of 1,348 men and women employees from all types of occupation. I have sorted their most frequent criticisms and compliments, and have finally compressed them into the 100 items listed below. Those items which were most frequent of occurrence or most fundamental have been "weighted" and given 5 or 10 points credit, as in the parentheses. Unless so weighted, every item counts as one point. To compute an employer's score, add the total DEMERIT items that fit him, and then subtract this figure from his MERIT total. The result is his raw score. To interpret it, consult the table of norms as follows:

Raw Scores	Interpretation
0 — 17	Very Poor
18 — 29	Poor
30 — 58	Average
59 — 77	Superior
78 and up	Very Superior

DEMERITS

1. Afflicted with halitosis—tobacco, alcohol, onion or garlic breath. ☐

2. Claims entire credit for new ideas, inventions or improvements originated by his subordinates. (5) ☐

3. A "projector" or buck-passer—always blames employees for his own errors. ☐

4. Tries to be too affectionate or use threat of discharge as a club to coerce girls in his employ. (5) ☐

5. Tries to humilate or "show up" a college employee because he is a "self-made man." Ridicules education. ☐

6. Unwilling to transfer a good worker from his department though it means a promotion for the employee. (5) ☐

7. Poor letter dictator—mumbles, enunciates poorly, speaks out of corner of mouth, turns back to his stenographer, etc. ☐

MERITS

1. Never reprimands an employee until they are alone. (5) ☐

2. Thoughtful of employee's comfort in re proper lighting, water coolers, fans, towels, illness, rest periods, etc. ☐

3. Knows his immediate employees by name and shows interest in their families, their personal advancement, etc. ☐

4. Pleasant and courteous to employees; always says "Good morning" and "Good night" and treats them as social equals. (5) ☐

5. Praises or rewards employees for new ideas or methods which they advance for improving output and efficiency. ☐

6. Intelligently criticizes employees, showing them why they made the error and how to avoid it in future. ☐

7. Will "go to bat" for his employees, defending them before his own superiors. Has backbone and is not afraid of the "big boss". ☐

8. "Chisels" salesmen and tradesmen for a personal rake-off on goods purchased for the firm. ☐

8. Is loyal to his company and honest with both his employees and the customers. (5) ☐

9. Sarcastic and bitter—browbeats or terrifies employees so they dread his approach. (5) ☐

9. Pays fair wages and adjusts them as profits rise or as employee grows more efficient. (10) ☐

10. Curses at employees re mistakes or at telephone operator re wrong number. ☐

10. Encourages employees to improve themselves, as by night school work, special reading, etc. ☐

11. Jealous of employees lest they advance faster than he did, or get promoted to an equal post. ☐

11. Knows how to do his employees' work and can show them the right way to do their tasks. Not just a theorist. ☐

12. Stirs up friction by playing one employee against another. ☐

12. Always keeps promises regarding days off and vacations, etc. ☐

13. Scolds the whole force for the error of just one employee. ☐

13. In rush periods will work shoulder to shoulder with employees to help catch up. ☐

14. Poor manager—waits till nearly quitting time; then piles on a lot of "rush" work. ☐

14. Accommodating—lets you off a little early for a date, an errand, or even a ball game. ☐

15. Miserly—gives little or nothing to charity, religious organizations, etc. ☐

15. Loyal and devoted to his wife and family, setting a good example to his employees. ☐

16. Expects employees to work overtime without pay or even a "thank you". ☐

16. Is fair about granting employees vacations with pay. ☐

17. Throws or breaks things when angry, and acts like a spoiled child. (5) ☐

17. Grants promotions or pay increases without being asked for them. (5) ☐

18. Sets bad example by gambling, drinking or telling vulgar stories before employees. (5) ☐

18. Never fires employees save as last resort, and then explains why it is necessary. (5) ☐

19. Handles too many family and personal affairs in business hours. ☐

19. Permits employees to do things in their own way as long as it is efficient. ☐

20. Intolerant. Doesn't want your honest opinion unless it agrees with his. Demands "yes-men". ☐

20. Very tactful. Phrases his orders as suggestions instead of arbitrarily barking commands. (5) ☐

21. Plays favorites or shows partiality to his relatives who are employees. ☐

21. Doesn't interrupt employee while he is busy but asks him to see him when he is through. ☐

22. Always looking for trouble—seems unhappy if he can't "bawl out" an employee. (5) ☐

22. Is a cultured man, and encourages employees to develop liking for good music, art, literature, etc. ☐

23. Too exacting, petty and "old-maidish." Lacks a sense of perspective. Over-magnifies minor errors. ☐

23. Even-tempered. Never "bawls out" an employee in anger or "hollers" at his workers. ☐

24. Rude to employees, treating them as "know-nothings" or dumbbells. ☐

24. Considerately apportions work during slack season so all can be employed. ☐

25. Yells about tardiness but fails to notice unpaid overtime that far offsets the few minutes late. ☐

25. Is willing to admit when he is wrong and always welcomes suggestions or new ideas, etc. ☐

26. Airs his domestic problems and private affairs before employees. ☐

26. Always sees that workers get their wages on time. (5) ☐

27. Promises promotions and salary increases for the future, but easily forgets his promises. (5) ☐

27. He really works hard. Doesn't put on a scowl and fuss around for the effect. ☐

28. Has a soured, dyspeptic personality and always takes a gloomy or pessimistic view of everything. ☐

28. A cheery, dynamic personality who infuses his employees with confidence and enthusiasm. ☐

29. Personally repulsive owing to "B.O.", greasy skin, dandruff, etc. ☐

29. Delegates a reasonable amount of responsibility and trusts employee's judgment. ☐

30. Delegates too much responsibility so employees miss his leadership, and training. ☐

30. Is frank and above board about checking up on employees' work. ☐

31. Constantly spying and snooping around to catch employees in error. ☐

31. Always remembers employees at Christmas with a gift or present of some sort. ☐

32. Impatient—wants everything in a hurry. Doesn't make allowances for office routine. ☐

32. Dresses well and to fit his superior position, so employees do not feel ashamed of their boss. ☐

33. Shows prejudice regarding race, color, religion, politics, etc. ☐

33. Employs the merit system for granting promotion, wage increases, etc. ☐

34. Lets his secretary try to boss the other employees and direct their work. (5) ☐

34. Always specific and thorough in his instructions, so employees are not confused. ☐

35. Practical joker—tries to make employees the butt of his jokes. ☐

35. He is considerate of new employees. Doesn't "ride" them or make their first days on the job miserable. (5) ☐

36. Unkempt re haircut, shave, shoes, fingernails, etc. ☐

36. Cooperates with efficiency experts, auditors, examiners, etc. ☐

37. Hires and fires on basis of phrenology, physiognomy, astrology, graphology and similar unscientific methods of character analysis. (10) ☐

37. Has a good sense of humor and can laugh at a joke on himself. Doesn't take himself too seriously or think business cannot go on without him. ☐

38. Coughs and sneezes in employees' faces, or "burps", picks his nose or his teeth before them. ☐

38. Frequently pays his employees sincere compliments regarding their work, their clothing or other virtues which they possess. (10) ☐

39. Discourteous and gruff to salesmen, scrubwomen, elevator boys, etc. ☐

39. Doesn't attempt to dictate or coerce his employees in their private life, political views, etc. ☐

40. Jealous of employees who dress better, drive better car, have lower golf score or better education. ☐

40. Has good taste regarding ties, socks, clothes, window drapes, pictures, etc. ☐

41. Borrows money from his employees and forgets to repay them. (5) ☐

41. Sets good example by coming to work on time and tending to business. ☐

42. A henpecked husband who takes it out on his employees and tries to be a "bearcat" boss, thus compensating for his "housecat" behavior at home. ☐

42. Doesn't reprimand his employees if they don't happen to be working when he enters the room. ☐

43. Stands and looks over the shoulder of employees while they work. ☐

43. Considerate during illness of employee or his family, holding his job for him, sending flowers or calling on him in person. ☐

44. Gets personal while dictating to stenographer; pats her knee, etc. (5) ☐

44. Encourages employees to participate in company band, athletics, dramatics, etc. ☐

45. Mutters or talks to himself when he is disturbed or excited. ☐

45. When his employees fail to understand a point, he doesn't become irritable at them but blames himself for failing to put his idea across properly. ☐

46. Jealous of employees who seem to have more "it" or sex appeal. ☐

46. Doesn't expect the impossible from his employees, nor overwork them. ☐

47. "Sissy" and vacillating. Afraid of his own superior. ☐

47. Keeps abreast of the times in regard to equipment, new methods, etc. ☐

48. Coerces employees by threat of discharging them. (5) ☐

48. Looks on his job not as that of slave driver, but as leader and teacher. ☐

49. Procrastinates about buying needed equipment, supplies, etc. ☐

49. When he pays good salaries for experts, he doesn't try to tell them how to do their work, but gives them free rein. ☐

50. Makes employees do errands for him after working hours. ☐

50. Has his employees working "with" him instead of "for" him. (5) ☐

The foregoing data represent the essence, gleaned from thousands of criticisms which I have obtained from 1,348 employees. The latter represented both sexes and almost every conceivable kind of work from that of house maid to bank cashier, farm laborer to accountant, office boy to laboratory technician, private secretary to salesman. It required six months to complete this research project.

Privately these 1,348 employees were asked to state freely the things which they liked best concerning their immediate superiors or employers, and then what they disliked most. I have sifted and sorted, weighed and evaluated their comments until I have condensed them into the 100-item rating scale described above. Those criticisms do not represent my own personal theories or opinions, but are the actual data obtained from these 1,348 men and women employees.

I commend this completed test to all those who have men and women under their direction, whether it be a housewife with only a cook, maid or gardener, or a busy executive with thousands of men under his supervision. Labor difficulties can be largely eliminated through keen psychological insight and fair play. May this test prove fruitful in promoting greater harmony between employer and employee!

A TEST FOR MOTHERS

This test is based upon the reports of 1,500 children and teenagers, ranging in age from 4 to 18, and interviewed in the absence of their parents. I have sorted their most frequent criticisms and compliments, and compressed them into the 100 items below. Those items which were most frequent of occurrence or most significant from the viewpoint of child psychology, are weighted in the parentheses. Unless so weighted, each item counts as one point. To compute your score, add the total DEMERIT items that fit you and subtract this total from the MERIT total. The result is your raw score. To interpret it, consult the table of norms as follows:

Raw Scores	Interpretation
0 — 15	Very Poor
16 — 27	Poor
28 — 59	Average
60 — 75	Superior
76 and up	Very Superior

DEMERITS

1. Uses tobacco, alcohol, dope or profanity. (5 for each) ☐
2. Plays favorites among children or stepchildren. (10) ☐
3. Doesn't let child entertain friends in the home. (5) ☐
4. Seldom kisses or tells child she loves him. (5) ☐
5. Chronically nags, scolds or "hollers" at child. ☐
6. Talks about child's faults, such as bedwetting, before outsiders. (5) ☐
7. Fails to tell foster child of his adoption till the teens. ☐
8. Doesn't belong to Parent-Teacher association or visit child's school. (5) ☐
9. Bemoans having married and prejudices child against it. (5) ☐
10. Wears dirty clothes and is rather "sloppy" in appearance. ☐
11. Lets child feel it isn't wanted or she'd rather have the opposite sex. (10) ☐
12. Babies child too much, or uses baby talk before its playmates. ☐
13. Makes little boys wear curls or sissy clothing. (5) ☐
14. Reads older children's letters. ☐
15. Objects to child's going to camp or house parties. ☐
16. Slaps or strikes child in the face. ☐
17. Chronically farms out child to maid or relatives. (5) ☐
18. Monopolizes daughter's boy friends. ☐
19. Calls child a liar or thief. (5) ☐
20. Teases child re opposite sex. ☐

MERITS

1. Sends "Only" child to nursery school. (5) ☐
2. Lets young children climb in bed with her in the morning. ☐
3. Reads or tells good stories to her children. ☐
4. Excellent cook and housekeeper. ☐
5. Always keeps her promises and tells the truth. (5) ☐
6. Permits child to stay at friend's home overnight. ☐
7. Personally tucks young children into bed at night. ☐
8. Speaks good English in the home with minimum of slang. (5) ☐
9. Teaches child to say its prayers and attend religious services. (10) ☐
10. Lets young child help her bake or makes him little pies and cakes. ☐
11. Lets child go to a movie, concert or theater up to once per week. ☐
12. Encourages child to join Scouts, glee club or school societies. ☐
13. Lets child scrape pan after cake frosting or candy has been made. ☐
14. Good natured, jolly and happy. (5) ☐
15. Lets child help select his own clothes. ☐
16. Lets child keep a pet. (5) ☐
17. Takes child on shopping trips or holiday excursions. ☐
18. Encourages child to use dictionary, encyclopedia and reference books. ☐
19. Lets child know she trusts him. (5) ☐
20. Gives child its own room. ☐

21. A chronic "No, no, don't do that," or "Run along now, I'm busy" mother. ☐

21. Teaches child to cook, sew, dance or sing. ☐

22. Prejudices child against its father or latter's relatives. (5) ☐

22. Teaches child to put its toys away after playing. ☐

23. Chronically tells about all the sacrifices she makes for child. ☐

23. Keeps plenty of peanut butter, jelly or cookies on hand. ☐

24. Objects to or scolds child re its hobbies, as stamp collecting, etc. ☐

24. Teaches child good table manners. ☐

25. Objects to advisable medical care, such as vaccination, etc. (5) ☐

25. Introduces child to guests instead of ignoring it. ☐

26. Recites child's naughtiness to the father at supper table. ☐

26. Gives child thorough and scientific sex instruction when child asks. (10) ☐

27. Develops in child fear of the dark, ghosts, lightning, etc. ☐

27. Honors child's secrets and his confidences. ☐

28. Speaks foreign language in the home, embarrassing Americanized child. ☐

28. Encourages taffy pulls, family singing and group games at home. (5) ☐

29. Encourages race, color or religious prejudice. ☐

29. Gives child an allowance or pays for work. ☐

30. Surprises child with the new baby instead of preparing him in advance. (5) ☐

30. Helps child with his school work and games. ☐

31. Dresses child beyond the average so his pals make fun of him. ☐

31. Lets young child run vacuum cleaner, wash dishes, operate phonograph. ☐

32. Sends child to bed without his meals for punishment. ☐

32. Uses the "sandwich" plan for correction—a criticism between two compliments. ☐

33. Always complaining about aches and pains—a neurotic. ☐

33. Encourages child to study hard and go on to high school or college. ☐

34. Threatens child with insanity, etc., for self-sex practices. (5) ☐

34. Encourages "amateur night" and home dramatics. ☐

35. Always butts into child's quarrels and takes its part, regardless. ☐

35. Lets child take part in family discussions and planning. ☐

36. Sends child to boarding school to avoid parental responsibilities. ☐

36. Writes regularly or sends surprise boxes to child while separated from it. ☐

37. Has child or maid say she isn't in when child knows she is. ☐

37. Encourages nature study—birds, flowers, insects or animals. ☐

38. A bridge fiend or matinee addict. ☐

38. Lets toddler talk over telephone. ☐

39. Too lax in discipline and overindulgent. (5) ☐

39. Encourages toothbrush habit and clean hands. ☐

40. Pushes child too much re reading, dancing or music for "show off" purposes. ☐	40. Cooperates with teacher and talks of school as pleasant and good fun. ☐
41. Worries over child's appetite and coaxes, threatens, or argues; thus prolonging meals. ☐	41. An "expressive" instead of "repressive" parent, urging mental exploration instead of passive obedience. (5) ☐
42. Makes child too dependent—a "mamma's boy or girl". (5) ☐	42. Lets child prepare entire meal alone or order for family at restaurant. ☐
43. Chronically scolds child about its posture. ☐	43. Dresses attractively and in good taste so child is proud of her. ☐
44. Objects to child's having dates when others his or her age do. ☐	44. Shows children she loves their father and is happy in his company. (5) ☐
45. Tries to bribe child's affection away from the father. (5) ☐	45. Gets child a manicure set and praises its nails instead of scolding re nail biting. ☐
46. Shouts "No, no, the other hand," when left-handed child fails to use right hand. ☐	46. Has a date with husband at least once a week. This enables child to feel its parents aren't old fogies. (5) ☐
47. Sleeps too long in morning or is crabby. ☐	47. Plays tennis, golf, or swims, hikes, skates, etc., with child. ☐
48. Is jealous of child and vindictive. ☐	48. Teaches good songs and poetry to child. ☐
49. Chronically whines about the child's dirty clothes and upset house. ☐	49. Lets older child help with baby, as in holding bottle, pushing cab, etc. ☐
50. Punishes school child in public or before his pals. ☐	50. Doesn't hold punishment over for father to administer at night. ☐

A TEST FOR FATHERS

This test is based upon the reports of 1,500 children and teenagers, ranging in age from 4 to 18, and interviewed in the absence of their parents. I have sorted their most frequent criticisms and compliments; compressed them into the 100 items following. Those items which were most frequent of occurrence or most significant from the viewpoint of child psychology, are weighted in the parentheses. Unless so weighted, each item counts as one point. To compute your score, add the total DEMERIT items that fit you and subtract this total from the MERIT total. The result is your raw score. To interpret it, consult the table of norms as follows:

Raw Scores	*Interpretation*
0 — 15	Very Poor
16 — 27	Poor
28 — 59	Average
60 —75	Superior
76 and up	Very Superior

DEMERITS	MERITS
1. Scolds child for things he himself does or says. ☐	1. Takes child on fishing trips or to athletic contests, as ball games. ☐
2. Punishes child for low marks in school. ☐	2. Lets young child occasionally sit in front seat of auto with him. ☐
3. Breaks his promises re circus, boat trip, etc. (5) ☐	3. Goes on walks or hikes with his children. ☐
4. Growls at mamma about expenses and how she'll send them to poor house. ☐	4. Reads comic strips to young children deleting slang and "ain'ts". ☐
5. Will not let child have a pet, as puppy, kitten, etc. (5) ☐	5. Lets young children climb in bed with him in the morning. ☐
6. Chronically answers child with, "I'm busy now; don't bother me!" ☐	6. Plays with children and teaches them athletic games. ☐
7. Jealous of child and vindictive. ☐	7. Reads or tells stories to child. ☐
8. Plays favorites among children or stepchildren. (10) ☐	8. Gives child tool box, sewing kit or educational toys. ☐
9. Insists on having newspaper first, including section with the comics. ☐	9. Takes child on educational trips, as to museum, zoo, circus or aquarium. ☐
10. Will not let child have dates though others of that age have them. (5) ☐	10. Urges religious education, Sunday school attendance, etc. (10)☐
11. Poor table manners—belches without apology, eats with knife, etc. ☐	11. Encourages child to join Scouts, 4-H club, school societies, etc. ☐
12. Inclined to be autocratic, domineering or bullheaded. ☐	12. Lets child help him wash car, rake leaves, paint garage, etc. ☐
13. Fights or quarrels with mother before the children. (5) ☐	13. Takes child on "flower", "bird" or camera hikes. ☐
14. Gives child money on the sly, or countermands mother's orders. (5) ☐	14. Lets child entertain friends in home without complaint. (5) ☐
15. Teases, humiliates or punishes child for bedwetting, nail biting. (5) ☐	15. Takes family out to dinner or to a show occasionally. ☐

16. Forces child to study for a career which the father picks out. ☐

16. Kisses child or shows he loves him; that he is wanted. (5) ☐

17. Teases child, as by threatening to give him away, desert him, sell him. ☐

17. Uses "sandwich" method of correction—a criticism between two compliments. ☐

18. Opposed to vaccination, diphtheria immunization, needed surgery, etc. (5) ☐

18. Lets child start the fire at picnics, wiener roasts, etc. ☐

19. Prejudices child against mother or her relatives. (5) ☐

19. Arranges for child to spend some time on a farm and in the city. ☐

20. Expects too much of child for its age—holds too high goals for it. ☐

20. Helps child repair broken toys or make kites, scooters, etc. ☐

21. Lets child feel it isn't wanted, or he'd rather have opposite sex. (10) ☐

21. Gives child collegiate dictionary, encyclopedia, typewriter. (3 for each) ☐

22. Gives child idea policemen are his enemies instead of friends. ☐

22. Gives child musical training, or phonograph and good records. ☐

23. Reads newspaper at table instead of talking to family. ☐

23. Does magic tricks, gymnastic stunts, etc., for children. ☐

24. Develops prejudice in his children re religion, race, color, etc. (5) ☐

24. Tells interesting stories of his own boyhood experiences. ☐

25. Ignores or is rude to child's friends or guests. ☐

25. Goes outside to admire child's cave, snowman, hut, garden, etc. ☐

26. Habitually leaves family to golf, hunt, fish, etc., on holidays, Sundays, etc. ☐

26. Always hears both sides of quarrel before deciding — fair and just. ☐

27. Forgets child's birthday. (5) ☐

27. Praises child for good deeds. (5) ☐

28. Accuses child of being sexually bad. (5) ☐

28. Writes child special letter occasionally when he is away. ☐

29. Teases child about opposite sex. ☐

29. Brings home souvenirs or "surprises" occasionally. ☐

30. Insists on pulling in the fish that child catches. ☐

30. Lets child use his typewriter or tools, etc. ☐

31. Too quick tempered and irritable—"hollers" at child too much. ☐

31. Draws pictures, cartoons, etc. for child and encourages him to do so. ☐

32. Irritable and grouchy when asked questions while listening to radio. ☐

32. Teaches adolescent children how to drive the automobile. ☐

33. Sends child to boarding school to avoid parental responsibilities. ☐

33. Helps child occasionally with the dishes or its other chores. ☐

34. Gives young children gifts of money vs. toys and then banks it. ☐

34. Gives child an allowance or pays it for work. ☐

35. Robs child's bank or reneges on his promise to pay child money. ☐

35. Takes child to visit his office or place of business. ☐

36. Strikes child in face or uses excessive corporal punishment. ☐

36. Dresses well, keeps shaved, etc., so child feels proud of his looks. ☐

37. Uses foreign language in the home, thus embarrassing Americanized child. ☐

37. Carries adequate insurance to protect home from dissolution. (5) ☐

38. Objects to child's attending camp, respectable house parties, etc. ☐

38. Shows child he loves and respects its mother. (5) ☐

39. Plays with child's toys so it can't use them, as electric train, etc. ☐

39. Teaches child first aid, how to swim, etc. ☐

40. Ridicules child for its fears, calling it "yellow", etc. ☐

40. Buys child good books, educational toys, etc. ☐

41. A poor or reckless auto driver; or prone to curse and blame other drivers. ☐

41. A steady worker, bringing check home to family regularly. (5) ☐

42. A chronic "projector", always blaming others for his own faults. ☐

42. Good natured—children look forward with pleasure to his homecoming. (5) ☐

43. Tries to bribe child's affection from mother by overindulgence, lack of discipline, etc. (5) ☐

43. Plays duet or sings with child, or urges educational games, like "Authors", charades, riddles, etc. ☐

44. Lets child know of father's unfaithfulness to wife. (5) ☐

44. Speaks good English in the home with minimum of slang. (5) ☐

45. Uses tobacco, dope, alcohol or profanity. (3 for each one.) ☐

45. Visits child's school or belongs to Parent-Teacher association. ☐

46. Gets drunk. (5) ☐

46. Lets child know he trusts it. ☐

47. Makes a public issue of child's stuttering, nervousness, etc. ☐

47. Doesn't interfere with mother's correction of children; cooperates. (5) ☐

48. Encourages child to be cynical or suspicious of women, morality, etc. (5) ☐

48. Sets an example of good sportsmanship, honesty and fair play. (5) ☐

49. Too affectionate to daughter's girl friends, kissing or "pawing" them. ☐

49. Encourages child to study hard and go on to high school or college. ☐

50. Tries to dominate child's choice of mate by threats, money, coercion, etc. ☐

50. Gives child truthful and scientific sex information when it asks. (10) ☐

Did you ever slide the tip of your tongue into a cavity of your tooth?

It probably felt very large — almost a Mammoth Cave, so to speak. But when you checked with a mirror, you may have found it very small — hardly large enough to hold the head of an ordinary pin. Do you know why you misjudged its size?

Because our valid judgments usually consist of a double-checking by vision and touch. Our eyes and fingers keep tab on each other. But the tongue is seldom checked by the eye, so it gives a distorted sense of space.

Similarly, "horse sense" results from a mutual cooperation between brain and fingers. Brilliant mental plans must be modified by the trial and error of experience in order to produce success. The best stratagems of the general must go through the test of cooties, mud and bayonet charges on the front line trenches before they become effective realities.

Horse sense, therefore, refers to that logical set of values acquired in actually meeting the practical problems of life at first hand. There is, furthermore, no better way of acquiring it than by callouses, but these should preferably be on the palms instead of on another portion of the anatomy so overworked by those who sit exclusively in swivel chairs.

"Brain trusters" and many college professors are long on theory but short on practice. Pick and shovel workers, on the contrary, are long on practice but short on theory. Neither of these extremes is desirable. A well balanced personality should have enough intelligence to evolve new ideas or theories, but also sufficient practical experience to pass judgment upon them before they lead to futile waste of billions of the hard working taxpayers' money.

Horse sense is the most valuable educational attainment you can ever obtain. And you don't have to attend college to procure it. In fact, much of our present university teaching seems actually to obscure it.

If your child doesn't have at least an average amount of horse sense by the time he graduates from high school, please don't send him on to college and make a worse theorist out of him.

The more education a pure theorist gains, the greater his potential danger to society, for his college diploma and possibly a Ph. D.

degree may fool people into entrusting him with undue responsibility or public funds.

For several years I have been trying to evolve a psychological examination which would roughly measure a person's horse sense. The following battery of tests is my best effort to date. I trust it will encourage other psychologists to further research upon this profound subject so that even better rating scales may later be evolved.

Allow yourself but ONE HOUR for this test, which covers five important fields. Like other psychological tests, this one assumes you are meeting it as an original contact, not having been "primed" on its contents. After you have scored yourself, interpret your result by the norms accompanying this test to learn if you are Superior, Average or Below Average.

Test I. RANGE OF PRACTICAL INFORMATION

This is called a TRUE-FALSE test. Some of the following statements are true. Some of them are false. If you think a statement is true, draw a circle around the "T". If you consider a statement false, then place a circle around the "F". If you cannot be sure, guess. Try every one of the statements. The two samples are already marked as they should be:

SAMPLES

ⓉF		1.	Christmas falls on the 25th of December.
T Ⓕ		2.	February has 30 days.

Ⓣ F		1.	The white of an egg is more fattening than the yolk.
T Ⓕ		2.	Yeast should be dissolved in boiling water to make dough rise.
T Ⓕ		3.	A gallon of water weighs more than a gallon of oil.
T Ⓕ		4.	A carp is a prized game fish.
T Ⓕ		5.	Your intelligence can be read from the bumps on your skull.
T Ⓕ		6.	Cream is lighter than an equal volume of skimmed milk.
T Ⓕ		7.	Rayon is made by the Japanese silk worms.
T F		8.	A bushel of Irish potatoes weighs exactly 60 pounds.
T F		9.	A bushel of sweet potatoes weighs exactly 46 pounds.
T F		10.	Glazed tiles are used for draining wet farm land.
T F		11.	An ounce of pure alcohol is more fattening than an ounce of sugar.
T F		12.	Steel will crack more easily than iron.
T F		13.	The father of a mule is a horse.
T F		14.	A woman looks thinner in white fabrics than in dark fabrics.
T F		15.	Women can float on water more easily than men.

T   F   16.   A girl usually closes her eyes when her sweetheart kisses her.
T   F   17.   Fast workers are usually more inaccurate than slow workers.
T   F   18.   Dispensing machines usually offer 12 oz. coke bottles.
T   F   19.   A quart of milk contains 32 ounces.
T   F   20.   The linotype is a farm implement.
T   F   21.   Women usually prefer a woman employer to a man employer.
T   F   22.   "Crepe de Chine" refers to a brand of wine.
T   F   23.   There are usually about 15 wieners in a pound.
T   F   24.   Cane sugar is usually higher priced than beet sugar.
T   F   25.   In silk hosiery, a 3-thread looks dressier than a 5-thread.

Test II. SOCIAL INFORMATION TEST

(Underline one of the words in large type which makes the truest sentence)

1. A "spare" is a term in FOOTBALL BASEBALL BRIDGE BOWLING
2. A "ringer" is a term in POLO HORSESHOES BILLIARDS PINOCHLE
3. A "royal flush" is a term in POKER HOCKEY BADMINTON BOXING
4. An "offside" is a term in BASEBALL FOOTBALL GOLF WRESTLING
5. A "rosin bag" is used in CROQUET TRACK BASEBALL BASKETBALL
6. A "slice" is a term in POKER GOLF CROQUET HORSESHOES
7. The "crawl" is a term in SKATING FISHING SWIMMING SAILING
8. A "spinner" is a term in BADMINTON POKER SWIMMING FISHING
9. A "half nelson" is a term in BOXING TRACK WRESTLING BILLIARDS
10. An "uppercut" is a term in AVIATION BOXING WRESTLING GOLF
11. Rossini is famous in POLITICS SCIENCE MUSIC SCULPTURE
12. Galsworthy is famous in EDUCATION LITERATURE ART RELIGION
13. Pasteur is famous in POETRY OPERA RELIGION SCIENCE
14. John W. Bricker is famous in ART SCIENCE MUSIC POLITICS
15. Burbank is famous in BUSINESS HORTICULTURE RELIGION DRAMA
16. Gutzon Borglum is famous in POETRY POLITICS OPERA SCULPTURE
17. Victor Mature is famous in LITERATURE DRAMA MEDICINE LAW
18. Mary Baker Eddy is famous in RELIGION MUSIC MEDICINE ART
19. Disraeli is famous in SCIENCE INVENTION OPERA POLITICS
20. Orville Wright is famous in LAW INVENTION POLITICS PHILOSOPHY
21. Millet is famous in ART MUSIC LITERATURE INVENTION
22. Sousa is famous in LAW SCIENCE MUSIC EDUCATION
23. Emily Post is famous in MUSIC JOURNALISM NURSING MEDICINE
24. DeWitt Wallace is famous in ENGINEERING BANKING ART PUBLISHING
25. The present Pope is called PAUL II PAUL IV PAUL VI PAUL XII

A TEST OF HORSE SENSE

Test III.   BUSINESS JUDGMENT

(Imagine yourself a publisher, selling books to the general public. Which one of each pair of book titles below, would you select for your advertising campaign in order to sell the greater number of volumes? Place a check mark before one of each pair of titles.)

1. __Battles of a Seaman
   __Privateersman

2. __None Beneath the King
   __None Beneath the King Shall Enjoy This Woman

3. __Facts to Know About Music
   __How to Improve Your Vocabulary

4. __Eating for Health (Vitamins)
   __Care of the Skin and Hair

5. __The Art of Controversy
   __How to Argue Logically

6. __Ten O'Clock
   __What Art Should Mean to You

7. __How to Write Letters
   __100 Best Books to Read

8. __The Truth About Mussolini
   __Facts About Fascism

9. __Pen, Pencil and Poison
   __The Story of a Notorious Criminal

10. __Markheim's Murder
    __Markheim

(Three answers are given to each of the following business situations. Place a check mark in front of the answer you consider best.)

11. A woman drives into a gas station in a Packard and after you have filled the tank with ethyl gasoline says, "Yesterday one of your service men checked my tires but left all the valve caps off." You should:
    __Tell her she must be mistaken.
    __Tell her she can't get away with a trick like this.
    __Offer to replace them at once.

12. A business house decides to do a great deal of direct mail advertising. It needs a machine to print its form letters. It should buy:
    __A mimeograph.
    __A linotype.
    __A comptometer.

13. A fellow worker arbitrarily orders you to perform your work in a different way than your custom. He has no authority over you. You should:
    __Tell him not to stick his nose in other people's business.
    __Tell him "O. K." but do it in your own way.
    __Follow his advice.

14. Bill Smith is an efficient worker but resents taking orders. He is likely to be a troublemaker. It would be wise to:
    __Discharge him at once.
    __Place him on probation for a month.
    __Make him a straw boss.

15. It is necessary for you to reprimand an employee under you. It would be best to:

____Criticize him before the other workers.

____Bawl him out in your private office.

____Privately sandwich your criticism between two compliments.

16. Harry Brown, aged 30, has five children. He makes $75 per week, and would like to take out some insurance. The best kind for his needs would be:

____Straight life insurance.

____A 20-year endowment.

____An educational policy.

17. A high school graduate can find no regular work. An aunt left him $1,000 in her will. He should use it to:

____Buy a used car to help him look for work.

____Take one year at a Liberal Arts College.

____Take one year at a Business College.

18. A prominent eastern psychologist has written many popular magazine articles showing the value of applying psychology in daily life. His university colleagues will most likely:

____Tender him a vote of thanks for thus elevating the prestige of applied psychology.

____Urge him to continue with his constructive popular writings.

____Criticize him behind his back.

19. Harvey is manager of a chain grocery. He dislikes formality and wants to be a friendly type of boss, so he lets his clerks call him by his first name, and furnishes them coffee and cookies each afternoon. They will likely:

____Be 100% loyal to him personally.

____Take advantage of his generosity.

____Try to imitate his unselfishness.

20. In applying for a job, it is usually better to:

____Ask for a specific type of job.

____Ask for any kind of work they will offer.

____Agree to work for nothing until you have proved your value.

21. A chronic borrower asks you to lend him $10. You know he seldom pays his debts, yet you don't wish to be rude. It is best to tell him:

____He is a deadbeat, so you wouldn't risk it.

____Tell him your wife handles the cash, so he'll have to see her.

____Lend him the $10.

22. A butler accidentally opens the bathroom door while the lady of the house is bathing. He should say:

____"Oh, excuse me, Madame. I didn't know you were in here."

____"You should have locked the door."

____"Oh, excuse me, Sir."

23. A secretary finds that her elderly employer is a little too affectionate. He pats her knee, etc., while dictating letters. She should:

___Sit across the desk from him while taking his dictation.

___Tell him she'll report the situation to his wife if he doesn't stop it.

___Slap his hand every time he tries to become too familiar.

24. Alice is secretary to a self-made man whose grammar is very poor. But he is egotistical and resents correction, yet she doesn't like to send out such letters. It would be best to:

___Tell him he should take a course in Business English.

___Say nothing, but make the corrections when she writes his letters.

___Quit her job and try to get another one somewhere else.

25. Jason Jones has owed your company a large bill, and hasn't remitted after 30 days. It would be best to:

___Threaten to take legal action if he doesn't remit by return mail.

___Offer to knock off 25% if he'll remit at once.

___Write him a courteous letter saying you'd appreciate his check so you can pass it along to the people *you* owe.

Test IV. MECHANICAL AND TECHNICAL JUDGMENT

The first two words in each line below, are related to each other in some way. You are to see what the relation is between the first two words, and then underline the word in LARGE TYPE which holds this same relationship to the third word. If you cannot be sure, guess. The samples below are already marked as they should be.

SAMPLES

(a) Arm : Hand : : Leg — NECK FOOT ELBOW HEAD

(b) Bird : Flies : : Fish—WALKS BASS SWIMS TROUT

1. Horse : Shoe : : Automobile — FENDER BUMPER TIRE HORN
2. Hammer : Nail : : Wrench — BOARD NUT SCREWDRIVER FILE
3. Glove : Hand : : Mortise — FOOT MITTEN ELBOW TENON
4. Finger : Thimble : : Bolt — NAIL RIVET SCREW NUT
5. Sow : Pig : : Goat — LAMB COLT KID CALF
6. Reel : Line : : Bobbin — NEEDLE THREAD THIMBLE BUTTON
7. Hone : Razor : : **Whetstone** — SCYTHE WAGON TRACTOR SAW

8. Plow : Farmer : : Shuttle — ENGINEER WEAVER PAINTER LAWYER
9. Screwdriver : Screw : : Brace — SAW NAIL CLEAVER BIT
10. Anvil : Blacksmith : : Chain — PHYSICIAN CHEMIST SURVEYOR TAILOR
11. Brush : Painter : : Scalpel — GROCER BARBER LAWYER DOCTOR
12. Automobile : Garage : : Oats — SILO GRANARY CELLAR WELL
13. Mutton : Sheep : : Veal — HOG LAMB DEER CALF
14. Straw : Hay : : Wheat — TIMOTHY CAULIFLOWER TEDDER RYE
15. Flax : Cotton : : Linen — MOHAIR CALICO SATIN WORSTED
16. Wool : Cotton : : Tweed — DENIM FLANNEL MOHAIR SATIN
17. Carbohydrate : Protein : : Banana — APPLE LETTUCE BUTTER HAMBURGER
18. Mason : Trowel : : Machinist — MORTAR MICROMETER HARROW MATTOCK
19. Bile : Liver : : Insulin—THYROID SPLEEN PANCREAS KIDNEY
20. Malaria : Medicine : : Arson — LAW DENTISTRY ENGINEERING MUSIC
21. Dough : Baker : : Iron — AVIATOR CHEMIST PUDDLER JUGGLER
22. Acid : Vinegar : : Alkali — TEA SOAPSUDS ASPIRIN MOLASSES
23. Wheat : Flour : : Corn — CRACKERS COOKIES HOMINY OATMEAL
24. Steam : Pressure : : Electricity — OHM VOLT ALTERNATING DIRECT
25. Horse : Percheron : : Cow — ORPINGTON MERINO PEKINESE HOLSTEIN

Test V.   TEST OF LOGICAL THINKING

On the two dash lines below write the two numbers which should come next. The samples are already marked as they should be:

S A M P L E S

5	10	15	20	25	30	35	40	45	50
3	3	4	4	5	5	6	6	7	7

9	8	7	6	5	4	3	2	___	___
4	4	6	6	8	8	10	10	___	___
9	1	7	1	5	1	3	1	___	___
1	2	4	5	7	8	10	11	___	___
2	5	8	11	14	17	20	23	___	___
1	3	9	27	81	243	729	2187	___	___
47	38	30	23	17	12	8	5	___	___
19	16	18	15	17	14	16	13	___	___
2	4	8	14	22	32	44	58	___	___
26	23	21	18	16	13	11	8	___	___

(Solve the following problems. They count as one point apiece except for the last problem, which counts 10 points if you solve it.)

11. A farmer bought some hogs for $1,800, and sold them for $2,700, making $6 on each hog. How many hogs were there?...................( )

12. A boy asked his father to buy him a Boy Scout uniform, but the father said he couldn't afford it. Yet the father spends 30 cents per day for cigarettes. How much money does the father thus burn up each year? ( )

13. A motorist is driving 60 miles an hour when he sees a child dart into the road ahead. If it requires one-half a second for him to lift his right foot from the foot throttle to the brake pedal, how far will his auto continue to travel before he starts to apply his brake?...................( )

14. A hunter pitched his tent; then walked 5 miles due south and shot a bear. He proceeded 8 miles due east and ate his lunch, but he was then no farther from his tent than when he shot the bear. What kind of bear did he shoot?...( )

15. Bill Smith wanted a new hat. But the one he liked cost $3.
"I have only this $2 bill," he told the clerk, "but you hold the hat for me and I'll be right back with the money."
Then Bill walked across the street to a pawn shop.
"Here's a good $2 bill I'll pawn for $1.50," he said.
"O. K." said the pawnbroker, taking his $2 bill, and giving him back a pawn ticket, plus the $1.50 Bill had wanted.
Next, Bill accosted a stranger on the street.
"I have a pawn ticket good for $2 which I'd be willing to sell you for only $1.50," he said, and the stranger gladly bought the $2 ticket for $1.50.
Whereupon, Bill re-entered the hat shop and made his purchase, for he now had a total of $3, having received $1.50 from the pawnbroker and $1.50 from the stranger for the pawn ticket. Who lost in this transaction? ....( )

16. Consider all the following statements, for they are relevant and essential to a correct solution of the problem:
A conductor, a brakeman and a porter are employed on a Pullman train running between New York and Chicago. Their names are Tom, Dick and Harry, but not necessarily in that order. Meanwhile, on this same train are three passengers of the same names — Tom, Dick and Harry. We shall distinguish them from the trainmen of the same names by using the prefix "Mr." in front of their names.
(a) Mr. Tom lives in New York City.
(b) The brakeman lives half-way between New York and Chicago.
(c) Mr. Harry earns exactly $4,700 per year.
(d) Dick beat the porter in a pool game.
(e) The brakeman's nearest neighbor, who is one of the three passengers mentioned above, earns exactly three times as much as the brakeman.
(f) The passenger living in Chicago has the same name as the brakeman. What is the name of the conductor?......( )

ANSWERS

TEST I	TEST II	TEST III			TEST IV
1. F	1. Bowling	1. 10,000 copies sold			1. Tire
2. F	2. Horseshoes	7,500 " "			2. Nut
3. T	3. Poker	2. 6,000 " "			3. Tenon
4. F	4. Football	34,000 " "			4. Nut
5. F	5. Baseball	3. 37,000 " "			5. Kid
6. T	6. Golf	76,000 " "			6. Thread
7. F	7. Swimming	4. 36,000 " "			7. Scythe
8. T	8. Fishing	52,000 " "			8. Weaver
9. T	9. Wrestling	5. 100 " "			9. Bit
10. F	10. Boxing	30,000 " "			10. Surveyor
11. T	11. Music	6. 2,000 " "			11. Doctor
12. F	12. Literature	9,000 " "			12. Granary
13. F	13. Science	7. 53,500 " "			13. Calf
14. F	14. Politics	32,000 " "			14. Timothy
15. T	15. Horticulture	8. 14,000 " "			15. Calico
16. T	16. Sculpture	24,000 " "			16. Denim
17. F	17. Drama	9. 5,000 " "			17. Hamburger
18. F	18. Religion	15,000 " "			18. Micrometer
19. T	19. Politics	10. 7,000 " "			19. Pancreas
20. F	20. Invention	100 " "			20. Law
21. F	21. Art	11. 3rd answer			21. Puddler
22. F	22. Music	12. 1st "			22. Soapsuds
23. F	23. Journalism	13. 2nd "			23. Hominy
24. T	24. Publishing	14. 3rd "			24. Volt
25. T	25. PAUL VI	15. 3rd "			25. Holstein
		16. 1st "			
		17. 3rd "			TEST V
		18. 3rd "	1	0	(11) 150
		19. 2nd "	12	12	
		20. 1st "	1	1	(12) $109.50
		21. 2nd "	13	14	
		22. 3rd "	26	29	(13) 44 ft.
		23. 1st "	6561	19683	
		24. 2nd "	3	2	(14) Polar
		25. 3rd "	15	12	
			74	92	(15) Stranger
			6	3	
					(16) Dick

Test	Method of Scoring	Total Possible	Your Score
I.	Rights minus wrongs	25	
II.	Number right	25	
III.	Number right	25	
IV.	Number right	25	
V.	Number right	25	
	TOTAL	125	

NORMS OF HORSE SENSE

103 — 125	Very Superior
88 — 102	Superior
59 — 87	Average
39 — 58	Poor
0 — 38	Very Poor

CAUTION! DO NOT LOOK AT THIS PAGE TILL YOU
SPEND *ONE HOUR* WORKING THE TESTS!

THE COMPLIMENT CLUB

The COMPLIMENT CLUB is a psychological society which everybody can join. In fact, you can launch it by yourself. Or you can make it a family organization.

Many people also set up a COMPLIMENT CLUB among the members of their Sunday School class or a Boy Scout Troop, or a High School Hi-Y or Tri-Hi-Y group.

Business people tell me they likewise made it an office affair for improving the friendship and happiness of all the folks employed therein.

Many churches and schools have started COMPLIMENT CLUBS for large groups, and some have even developed large luncheon or dinner groups called THE COMPLIMENT CLUB, and operated much after the fashion of the Kiwanis or Lions clubs.

The COMPLIMENT CLUB simply involves the paying of honest compliments to the people around you. You must pay one compliment per day to each of at least three different people, and keep up the process for a minimum of 30 consecutive days, to be eligible for full membership and a diploma.

And don't limit your compliments to friends or relatives. It is perfectly proper to praise casual acquaintances or even strangers. For paying compliments is simply putting the Golden Rule into effective daily action. It means you are trying to brighten the little corner of the world where you circulate socially, by taking a positive attitude.

Gossips simply take a negative outlook on life and say things about their companions which will belittle the latter or show them up as inferior, incompetent or undesirable.

POSITIVE PERSONALITIES

But COMPLIMENT CLUB members look for good things in everybody. And when they find a desirable trait or characteristic, they immediately praise the owner thereof. They are positive personalities.

It was this positive approach to social problems that Jesus demonstrated so beautifully. And it works miracles, too, as the early American Quakers so well proved.

For their friendly, positive attitude toward the American Indians resulted in permanent treaties and amicable relations. Historians tell us that the Quakers and the Indians got along very well without the firing of a single shot in combat with each other.

The world is still fraught with suspicion and political gossip whose intent is to depreciate other nations or belittle foreign people or malign and criticize.

The COMPLIMENT CLUB, if faithfully applied on an international basis, would soon show rich dividends in better world relations, plus smaller appropriations for armies and Atomic Bombs!

But let's go back to the origin of the COMPLIMENT CLUB. Among the various psychological classes which I taught at Northwestern University was one large section in Social Psychology, which met on our downtown campus in Chicago. It convened at night.

COMPLIMENT CLUB'S ORIGIN

The students in these evening courses were usually employed during the day in Chicago department stores, offices or factories. And they were generally somewhat older than the college man or woman on the daytime campus at Evanston. I should judge their average age in this Social Psychology class was about 25 years.

Following one of my lectures, a girl named Lois asked if she could have a conference with me. I agreed, so Lois followed me across the hall into my faculty office.

"Dr. Crane, this may seem like a trivial matter," Lois began, "but I am so lonely, I could almost end my life right now," and she started to cry.

"I come from a little town in Wisconsin, where I took a Civil Service examination. My marks were very high, and as there was an immediate opening in Chicago, I was sent here.

"But I don't know anybody, except a few girls at the office. At night I go to my room and write letters home. The only thing that keeps me living from day to day is the hope of receiving a letter from my friends in Wisconsin.

"Millions of people surround me in this great city, but I feel as desolate as if I were Robinson Crusoe.

"One of the chief reasons I enrolled in your course here at the Downtown

Campus, was my desire to meet some congenial people and make friends.

"But everybody in the class seems to be so poised and self-assured, while I am so shy and lonely. They don't engage me in conversation, and I am afraid to push myself forward.

"Oh, if I only were as nonchalant and sophisticated as that Miss Miller who sits across the aisle from me!"

She had ceased dabbing at her eyes with her lacy handkerchief, so I broke in at this point.

"I'm glad you mentioned the poise and self-assurance of Miss Miller," I began, "for Miss Miller came in here just two weeks ago, and began to cry, too, for she was so lonely and devoid of friends.

"Actually, she felt just the way you have described yourself. And most lonely folks are in the same boat with you. But out in public, you all put up a front, so to speak, and act indifferent or snobbish, even when your heart is almost breaking with loneliness.

"Miss Miller, oddly enough, had mentioned how aloof and distant you seemed, so she said she had been afraid to start a conversation with you.

She is from a small town in Indiana, and imagined that you were a sophisticated Chicago girl, bred and born here in this great metropolis."

"Why, I'm just the opposite, Dr. Crane!" Lois protested in disbelief. "I am anything but self-assured."

PSYCHOLOGY APPLIED

"Well, something must be done to remedy the matter," I admitted. "Psychology would be a farce if I let you students sit here in loneliness and unhappiness while we dealt with Social Psychology in theory."

"We must bring psychology down out of the clouds and put it to use. Just give me a week to think the matter over, and I'll guarantee you a solution."

Lois thanked me profusely. She felt better, of course, just to get her troubles out in the open, for sharing worries divides their weight. That is why confession of a problem is almost half the cure.

The following week when our class in Social Psychology convened, I made the following announcement:

"In order to keep this class from being a theoretical discussion of Social Psychology, I am going to assign you students various practical outside problems.

"You are to use your psychology every day either at home or at work or on the streetcars and buses. For the first

month, your written assignment will be called the COMPLIMENT CLUB.

"Every day you are to pay an honest compliment to each of three different persons. You can increase that number if you wish, but to qualify for a class grade, you must have complimented at least three people every day for 30 consecutive days.

"Keep a record of those to whom you pay your three compliments. You need not give me their names, but list them as 'Newsboy' or 'Streetcar Conductor' or 'Sales clerk'.

"And observe what they say in response to your compliment, for most people encounter praise so seldom that Emily Post hasn't even told us how to receive compliments.

"Some will blush prettily and murmur or gurgle. Others will quickly try to repay you by saying your hat or tie looks attractive, too.

"Another type of person will laugh and tell you he knows you are just looking for a quarter. So keep an accurate record of how people acknowledge your compliments.

"Then, at the end of the 30-day experiment, I want you to write a theme or paper on your experiences. Include the changes you have noted in the people around you, as well as your own altered outlook on life. This will be a month's assignment and will carry college credit."

The students laughed self-consciously, but they seemed to relish this new kind of assignment.

"Dr. Crane, are we to limit our compliments to people in our own family or our immediate associates at the office?" Miss Miller inquired.

"No," I replied, "I'd rather you distributed your compliments over a wider range of people. And include casual acquaintances or even strangers, for they will not resent a word of praise, even if they haven't been formally presented after the fashion of Emily Post."

"But I would be scared to address a stranger," Miss Miller confessed. "Besides, I might not know what to say."

"Grit your teeth and force yourself to pay the compliment," I answered. "Every beginning salesman is also frightened at ringing the doorbell. But he must compel himself to go through with his job or he will never become successful.

"You students might think over the list of prospects whom you expect to meet tomorrow. Each night sit down and plan the three people you hope to compliment the next day.

"You can even analyze them in your mind and pick out the virtue or talent on which you expect to pay them an honest compliment. Rehearse it before the mirror, if you are shy or tongue tied, so it can be uttered casually."

PRAISE YOUR ENEMY

"But suppose we meet somebody we dislike," one of the men asked. "Wouldn't it be insincere to praise our enemy?"

"That is an excellent question," I replied. "No, it is not insincerity when you compliment your enemy, for a compliment is an honest statement of praise for some objective trait or merit that deserves commendation."

"You will find that nobody is entirely devoid of merit or virtue, so try to take a detached view and analyze your companions for merits."

"But, Dr. Crane, won't people discount our compliments," Lois objected. "I'm afraid my compliments will be so apparent and obvious that people will not believe me."

"The recipient of a compliment always enjoys it," I replied, "even if he discounts it considerably. Remember, too, that it is far better to give people verbal bouquets while they are alive, for your praise may buoy up the morale of lonely souls who are almost ready to give up the struggle to do good deeds.

"You never know when your casual compliment may catch a boy or girl, or man or woman, at the critical point when he would otherwise toss in the sponge. So you will really be putting the Golden Rule into action."

Well, the experiment turned this class into a jolly, friendly crowd. Once per week I would let a few students volunteer comments on their most interesting experiences in complimenting people. At the end of the month, they wrote their reports and handed in their tally sheets.

Lois was typical of the rest in her report. She remarked that she had now lost her lonely feeling, and furthermore didn't dread meeting strangers.

SHYNESS OVERCOME

"I always was shy and tongue-tied until I began this COMPLIMENT CLUB experiment," she said. "But it taught me to forget myself in trying to ferret out good things in the people around me. I became a social detective.

"And people almost invariably smiled when I paid them a compliment. They were more friendly to me afterwards, and often went out of their way to be kinder.

"But the greatest improvement is in myself. I have found that I can be happy in any social group. No longer do I shyly wait for other folks to talk to me. I have learned to initiate the conversation.

"Other people are also shy, so somebody must start the conversation. I now look forward to meeting people so I can quickly analyze them for good points.

"Maybe they have a new hat or new frock, or beautiful teeth or a lovely complexion or artistic fingers or a melodious voice, or a deft way of handling children.

"Or possibly they are good cooks or have a beautiful home, or an artistic color scheme in their interior decorating.

"This COMPLIMENT CLUB has removed my terror and loneliness and given me new zest. It has altered my entire outlook on life."

Lois wasn't exaggerating, either. After this experiment, she would hardly get inside the classroom before she and a half dozen other students would be conversing gaily.

Before she finished the semester, she was engaged to one of the men who sat two rows behind her!

And what happened to Lois, can happen to most of us, regardless of our shyness or loneliness. For friendship is a flower.

But to obtain a lovely flower, somebody must do the initial work of planting the seed, watering and cultivating it. Neither friendships nor flowers miraculously burst into full bloom in an instant of time.

So plant your three daily compliments and you will be delightfully astonished within 30 days time, by the friendships that will flower in your social environment.

SALLY'S DILEMMA

During the depression year of 1938, when business was at a low ebb, one of my former students rushed into my office with a serious problem. Her name was Sally.

She had not been in my Social Psychology class, however, so was unacquainted with the COMPLIMENT CLUB.

"Oh, Dr. Crane, I'm in a terrible state of mind," she began, "and I don't know what to do."

"What's your trouble, Sally?" I inquired.

"It's my health and my job," she answered. "I just went through the medical clinic, and the doctors told me I'd end up in a sanitarium within three months if I didn't quit my job.

"I'm anemic and afflicted with indigestion so I get terrific pain if I eat lunch. And they say I have spastic colitis, too.

"But it is all a result of my work. I am employed by two law partners. One of them is wonderful to work for. But the younger partner is simply awful.

"He is the meanest, most irritating man I ever met. He keeps me so upset it is no wonder I am nearing a complete breakdown.

"Just to show you the type of petty tyrant that he is, Dr. Crane, let me tell you what happened yesterday. I had finished typing a long letter, single-spaced. It contained numerous legal terms.

"But in the very middle of the page, I apparently made a slight typographical error. Instead of spelling 'T-H-E' in that order, I had spelled it 'H-T-E'.

"Every good typist may make a simple mistake like that from time to time. And it can easily be erased without spoiling the entire letter.

"But this junior partner, named Sam, seems to delight in picking flaws with people. He must be a sadist at heart.

"For he gleefully ruined the entire letter by making a big question mark in blue pencil that was almost the full length of the page. Then he made blue dash lines over to the right margin and added four more question marks.

"Naturally, I had to re-type the entire letter. And this is just typical of him. Every day he is meaner than the day before. I simply hate the sight of him, Dr. Crane, and I really mean that.

"He gets me so worked up emotionally that I can't eat lunch, and if I do, I have violent cramps and indigestion. He is the reason why I am in poor health and threatened with a complete nervous breakdown."

"Then why don't you quit your job and get a position in a more congenial environment?" I asked.

"Because I'm afraid I can't," Sally replied mournfully. "Jobs are scarce. Besides, I make a better salary than most girls, and my mother is dependent on me for support, so I am afraid to quit.

"But if I stay where I am, the doctors say I'll probably have a complete breakdown, so I don't know what to do. Dr. Crane, if you were in my place, what would you do?"

FORCED COMPLIMENTS

So I told Sally I would try to use some good Applied Psychology on this young attorney.

"Actually, I think he secretly likes you," I informed her.

"Humph! He hates me as much as I detest him!" she retorted caustically. "If he liked me, why would he be so nasty about picking on me all the time? Why would he gloat every time he finds me in error?"

"Because he wants you to look up to him as a big shot," I added. "He wishes to show off his own importance. He hopes you will pay more attention to him.

"Why don't you join my COMPLIMENT CLUB and pay him at least one sincere compliment every day?"

"I—pay HIM a COMPLIMENT?" she protested incredulously. "Dr. Crane, surely you must be joking. Why, I detest the very sight of him. Besides, it would be insincere to pay a compliment to somebody you dislike."

But Sally was wrong on this point, for I explained to her that a compliment is not flattery. Instead, a compliment is a statement of praise for some actual virtue or talent that is present and deserves commendation.

Indeed, we can thus compliment our enemies in all sincerity if we but divorce ourselves from our own petty prejudices and size them up in a scientific, detached fashion until we find a good point. Nobody is so devoid of merit that he doesn't have SOME good qualities!

Besides, there is no other way to explain Christ's admonition about loving our enemies, except by this COMPLIMENT plan.

For love cannot replace hatred of an enemy on a moment's notice. Emotions don't work that rapidly. We cannot turn them on or off, as we do the faucet at the kitchen sink.

Emotions must be developed by a definite technique. And they require some time to reach their "peak" or climax.

So I urged Sally to analyze Sam for some good points and then force herself to pay him an honest compliment thereon, even if she had to grit her teeth the first few days to control her basic dislike.

"We physicians don't feel deep affection for all of our patients," I added. "In fact, sometimes we treat people that we don't like at all.

"But we can still practice scientific medicine on them.

"For example, suppose a diabetic patient came to me and was almost in a coma. Suppose, too, that I disliked that patient as much as you hate your boss. I could still take a hypodermic syringe, fill it with some insulin, and then inject this insulin under the skin, thereby protecting the life of my patient."

That hypodermic syringe is an objective tool or instrument of modern medicine. We can use it in all sincerity on people we don't like.

Compliments are likewise objective tools of psychology. We can employ them in all sincerity on people we dislike. And they will make dramatic changes.

By dint of these arguments and much coaxing, I finally persuaded Sally to try this COMPLIMENT CLUB technique on her boss.

HATE TURNS TO LOVE

The next afternoon at 10 minutes till 5, Sally called me on the telephone.

"Well, Dr. Crane, I've done it," she stated bluntly.

"You mean you paid him your first compliment?" I inquired.

"Yes," she went on. "But I had to force myself to do it over clenched teeth, and even then it took me till 4 o'clock."

"What did you say to him?" I continued.

"Oh, he had on a new suit, so I told him the cloth was very good in quality.

"Why didn't you personalize your compliment a little more by telling him how well he looked in the new suit?"

"I—should inflate his ego that much —NEVER!" she expostulated with vehemence.

"Well, keep up the good work," I admonished, "and let me know what happens."

A week later she informed me that she was able to force herself to pay him a compliment even before noon. But it still was an effort and required will power on Sally's part.

I heard nothing more from Sally for three months, when one afternoon she walked gaily into my office, looking like a million dollars.

"Oh, everything worked out as you predicted," she admitted rather sheepishly.

"After about a week of my forced compliments, Sam thawed out enough to grunt an acknowledgment.

"At the end of the second week, he even began asking my advice about which brand of stencils we should purchase or what kind of letterheads we ought to order.

"And one noon he asked me if I'd care to have a bite to eat with him. Dr. Crane, you could have knocked me over with a feather. I was so startled and shocked that I accepted before I knew what I was saying.

"Then last month, he and my other employer split up their partnership, and I stayed on with Sam."

"You stayed on with Sam?" I asked, in astonishment.

Sally's gaze had dropped to her lap, and she nodded her head affirmatively.

"Oh, well, I might as well confess it all," she said with a laugh. "Look here," and she held up her left hand.

On the ring finger was a beautiful diamond engagement ring.

"It's from Sam," she added. "We're getting married next month, too!"

If psychology can transform a neurotic girl, almost ready for a sanitarium, into a radiantly happy woman, you can readily see how effective it can be in your own home, whether in dealing with your husband or your children, your neighbors or even your in-laws.

Delinquent children could generally be salvaged if their parents and teachers would join the COMPLIMENT CLUB and pay them a little honest praise regularly.

Most divorces would never have occurred if husband and wife would give each other even ONE sincere compliment per day.

The world is starving for appreciation. It is hungry for compliments. But somebody must start the ball rolling by speaking first and saying a nice thing to his companion.

Even if you must force your compliment across clenched teeth, it will still work a miracle, for not only will your enemy begin to think you are pretty nice yourself, but, lo, you will also begin to think he is wonderful, as Sally's case proves.

"Love your enemies!" can then become a reality. You will win friends and even improve your health by the happiness that develops around you. Try the COMPLIMENT CLUB technique every day of your life. It is simply the Golden Rule in action.

A RESOLUTE WOMAN

The paying of compliments can ultimately become a habit, but at the start it requires diligence. Most people who start out paying 3 compliments per day, are likely to forget their quota within a week or two.

Not long ago the wife of a Judge in Ohio launched upon the COMPLIMENT CLUB. But one evening at the dinner table, she happened to remember that she had paid only 2 compliments that entire day.

Being a resolute woman, after the meal was over she put on her hat and coat. Then she strolled down the street looking for somebody to whom she could pay a compliment.

She finally stopped at a drug store, where she heard a sales girl deliver an excellent sales talk for a new brand of cosmetic.

Thereupon, this Judge's wife paid the girl an honest compliment on her skilful salesmanship, and went home to chalk up her third compliment for the day.

"Dr. Crane," said the Judge's wife later on, "I used to be very active in social work and church affairs, so I could have paid a dozen compliments per day, for I met so many people.

"Your COMPLIMENT CLUB has shocked me out of my complacency. It has proved that I have been gradually withdrawing from life.

"The fact that I almost ended the 17th day of your 30-day experiment with one compliment lacking, has made it imperative that I get back into action once more.

"So I have again taken a Sunday school class of young women and am beginning to invest my life in more useful pursuits than just sitting at home and growing more involuted each day."

LAURA'S TEARS

A 45-year old woman named Maude was a member of my Sunday school class. She decided to join the COMPLIMENT CLUB. But about midway of the 30-day period, she remembered that she, too, had paid only 2 compliments that day.

Maude worked in a millinery shop in Chicago. Across the room from her sat a woman named Laura, aged about 45 to 50. Maude didn't like Laura very well, for she felt that Laura was snobbish and aloof.

But Maude remembered I had said it is possible and quite proper to compliment even an enemy, if you simply search for a commendable trait which merits praise. And Laura did have beautiful hair.

"Do you know, Laura," Maude began, "I've worked in this room with you for nearly 15 years.

"And almost everytime I glance up, I see your head silhouetted against the window. I think you have the prettiest profile and hair I have ever seen on anybody."

Laura looked up, quite startled. Then she began to cry.

"What's the matter?" Maude inquired. "I didn't mean to offend you. I meant it as a real compliment."

"Yes-s-s, I know," Laura tearfully acknowledged, "But that's the first kind word anybody has said to me in all the 17 years I have worked here!"

Well, Maude soon found that Laura's apparent aloofness or snobbishness was just a pose, adopted, as many shy people do, to hide a lonely heart from the external world.

So Maude invited Laura to luncheon. Soon Laura was being included in office parties and other good times of her co-workers.

She blossomed out like a flower that for the first time obtains adequate sun-

light. For compliments are simply the Golden Rule in action. They emphasize the POSITIVE outlook that Jesus illustrated.

HEED BENJAMIN FRANKLIN

"As we must account for every idle word, so we must account for every idle silence," stated sage old Benjamin Franklin.

Most of us fail to reach the heights of social, professional or even domestic success largely because of errors of omission or "idle silences."

We fail to say the right thing at the right time. We stand relatively tongue-tied when a few tactful phrases might spell the difference between success and failure.

From our first birth cry, therefore, we become involved in a lifelong love affair but the object of whom we are so enamoured is SELF.

We are thus so blinded by our own problems and interests, our ambitions and daily tasks, that we seldom appreciate our neighbors. We fail to notice their pleasant characteristics and good deeds.

Alas, it often requires a funeral to jolt us out of our selfishness and make us realize the virtue in those with whom we have previously been long associated.

COMPLIMENTS MAKE WEDDINGS

The most powerful word in the English language is not "LOVE" but is "COMPLIMENT", for love develops from compliments and dies without them.

In order to pay an honest compliment, however, we must develop a broader perspective so that we are not dominated by our own selfish interests. We must train ourselves to become social detectives, ferreting out the good points in our associates.

Then we must teach ourselves to speak up and voice our praise while our neighbors are present and capable of being encouraged or buoyed up by our appreciation.

Criticism deflates the ego or vanity of our associates and makes them bitter. Then they draw within themselves. But praise makes people expand and feel happy.

You doubtless recall the old story from our grammar school reader about the sun and wind, who were arguing as to which could make the traveler remove his coat.

The wind blew violently, but the man simply pulled his cloak more tightly about him. Then the sun came out and soon he opened his coat, finally removing it altogether.

Compliments make people open up, much as the sun acted on the traveler, where criticisms do the opposite. These actions are not only observable in children, but almost equally well in adults.

It costs but little in energy and thought to train ourselves to become appreciative of our neighbors, our family, our employees or even the strangers, whom we meet on the street. Compliments are of the verbal and the non-verbal variety.

Non-verbal compliments consist of such behavior reactions as a smile of greeting. Did you ever witness a young couple on a date? Did you notice how continually smiling they were? Why?

Because subconsciously . they realize that a smile is a form of compliment, showing our delight in the arrival or presence of our companion. The wizened face of a chronically dyspeptic person, now popularly called a "sour puss", is anything but a compliment.

Gallantry regarding holding a woman's coat, offering a seat, giving the other motorist the right of way at a corner, gifts and other forms of consideration and thoughtfulness, belong in the category of non-verbal compliments.

How many of you male readers have demonstrated such non-verbal compliments for your wife or office assistants in the past week?

Among the verbal forms of compliment, I shall delineate FIVE BASIC LAWS which will prove invaluable when measured by the social, as well as financial, returns thereon for all who follow these rules diligently.

THE FIRST LAW

First, pay direct, personal compliments. These may be discounted somewhat because of their bluntness, but it is far better to have a compliment discounted from par to, let us say, a mere 25% of face value, than to stand tongue-tied and make no effort at all to make our companions feel happier.

Notice a woman's new frock or hat, her new slippers or purse. Compliment her on her complexion or wavy hair, her beautiful profile, or artistic fingers, her trim ankles, or dancing skill.

Commend her deftness in handling an automobile or dealing with a child: her tact in pacifying an irate client or in causing an old account to pay up in full.

Praise her healthy skin, her pretty teeth, free from cigarette stains. Her tennis skill or ability at the piano, her pies or cakes or jellies and jams. Her needlework or good housekeeping.

Obviously, when invited to a dinner party, one should always express appreciation for the meal, and commend it. But don't limit yourself to a perfunctory compliment about the food.

To gain social distinction, learn to be a bit different from the other guests. Say something appreciative about the drapes or rugs or pictures or whatnot.

Then, when all the guests have departed, and the hostess wearily drops into a chair, her roving eyes will rest upon those same drapes. Perhaps she will gloatingly call out to her husband:

"John, did you hear what Dr. Brown said about those drapes?"

Perhaps John has criticized them for one reason or another. Do you think she will forget Dr. Brown, or feel hostile toward him? Not on your life!

He buoyed up her morale by vindicating her good judgment. And Dr. Brown gained distinction among the dozen dinner guests, for all 12 may have commended the meal, but he went further, so he stands out alone.

THE SECOND LAW

Second, ask people for information or advice, for direction or an expression of opinion. A question is one of the most subtle forms of compliment and slips under the guard of even the most diligent psychologist.

The reason why a question is so valuable, is the fact that the questioner indirectly acknowledges the superiority of the questioned by coming to him for assistance.

That is one reason why mothers are so enamoured of their children, for the helplessness of the youngster is a constant compliment to the ego of the parent.

By habit we tend to reply as soon as questioned. And we delight in expressing our opinions. Just observe how freely a pedestrian will spend 15 minutes trying to give you directions when you stop in a strange city to inquire.

But when asking questions, be sure to offer your prospect a choice. An axiom of applied psychology is contained in the department store's method of laying out two or three bolts of cloth for the customer. It is far easier to select the better idea of two which are presented, than to evolve an idea.

An office girl, for example, should not ask her employer what courses she should take in night school, but should give him a choice. Inquire if a course in bookkeeping or public speaking would be more helpful to her.

Her boss can easily make a choice of two, but finds it more difficult to recall all the various courses listed in a night school curriculum.

THE THIRD LAW

Third, impute knowledge and experience, strength and maturity to your associates.

A public speaker will compliment his audience by saying, "You well remember that statement from Benjamin Franklin about complimenting, etc., etc."

Maybe the audience doesn't recall the statement, but it has been imputed with having such knowledge. It may feel much like the penniless actor who was approached by a pedestrian and asked if he could change a $20 bill. "I can't change it but thanks for the compliment," replied the actor.

People are eager to be thought intelligent and well educated. They are delighted by compliments which fall in this field, so be careful not to appear too preachy with clients, but tactfully carry them along in your sales talk or explanation so they are made to feel equally intelligent.

"You are a senior this year? Oh, your sophomore year? Well, nobody would ever know it from the looks of you." (Boy thinks, "I look grown.")

Girl 17, to boy of equal age, as she rubs his cheek, "I don't believe you shaved tonight. Aren't you ashamed!" (Does anybody really think he is?)

THE FOURTH LAW

Fourth, be sure to intimate that the other person has, or at least at one time had, phyical charm or "it".

One of the quickest ways to make a modern male strut is teasingly to allude to his "past", or to suggest that the girl will leave a string of broken hearts behind her when she finally marries.

Most men preen themselves on being called a Don Juan or Romeo, and rarely will a woman seriously resent the title of Cleopatra. On the other hand, the surest way to incur lasting enmity is to lower a person's sex vanity.

Women of sixty are almost as vulnerable to cosmetic compliments as are those of twenty. If the compliment cannot be made of them in the present, at least it can be used with reference to their youth.

"You can't fool me, Grandmother. I'll bet you were the life of the party before you married Grandfather."

"One has only to look at your wife's happy face to know what kind of a husband you are."

THE FIFTH LAW

Fifth, compliment the products or children of your associates, or their dogs and cats, goldfish or even the geranium. This is a subtle form of inflating the ego.

Alexander Pope once said that the best way to compliment a man is to comment favorably on the thing in which he aspires to be proficient, rather than the routine tasks or job in which he is obviously adept.

For example, the salesman who always hoped to be a fiction writer would probably relish compliments about some of his short stories more than praise for his sales record, though be sure to compliment him on both when deserved.

Older people are easy to compliment under this heading for they possess homes or gardens, automobiles or children.

Remember, the old adage to the effect that when you lay your hand upon a child's head, you place it on the mother's heart. Similarly, when you pay a verbal compliment to her child, you have indirectly praised the mother.

"Your children have such good manners, Mrs. Johnson. I wish mine were half as polite."

"Really, Mrs. Brown, dentistry would be a pleasure if all boys were as brave and well trained as your Richard."

CONCLUSION

Please note that I have not employed the words "flatter" or "flattery" herein. Compliments are considered honest statements of praise about virtues that really exist.

If, by training ourselves to commend our family and neighbors, we find our popularity rising and our financial success zooming, we are entitled to these desirable by-products, for the Bible states a workman is worthy of his hire, and an intelligent man or woman who knows how to obtain happiness and success, should obviously be entitled to those desirable goals if he earns them.

Resolve to give verbal bouquets while your companions are alive and can be inspired or encouraged to better things. Never permit yourself to be guilty of "idle silences".

MAKE YOUR PEN GOLDEN

A corollary experiment that ably supplements the COMPLIMENT CLUB is an ingenious idea that was developed by a great American psychologist, Dr. Karl T. Waugh.

It is called the LEAGUE OF THE GOLDEN PEN. Everybody can join. It requires that you send out a minimum of one letter each week to somebody who merits condolence or sympathy or praise.

Dr. Waugh originated this plan while teaching at Beloit College many years ago. He told his students that their written words would be golden in influence; hence, the name, LEAGUE OF THE GOLDEN PEN.

So, in addition to giving your 3 oral compliments each day to your associates, you can very profitably add this weekly letter to some deserving person. But your normal letter to your parents or family does not count. This letter must be to somebody whom you would not normally address, such as a stranger in your community.

100-point Behavior Test for Teen-agers

Your score on this test is based on your "usual" or typical behavior; not on an isolated example. Thus, a person who says "Darn it" when he strikes his thumb with a hammer, is not necessarily addicted to an excessive use of slang.

Check off all those items under the MERITS heading which apply to you. Then add the total score. Each item counts one point unless given greater value, as in the parentheses, where it might be listed at 5 points or more.

Next, tally all the items under the DEMERITS heading which apply to you. Subtract your total DEMERITS score from the MERITS total. The remainder is your raw score and can be interpreted by the following norms:

    0 - 29 . . . . . . Kindergartener, emotionally.
    30 - 46 . . . . . . Junior High, emotionally.
    47 - 68 . . . . . . Senior High, emotionally.
    69 - 94 . . . . . . College level, emotionally.
    96 & up . . . . . Mature adult, emotionally.

DEMERITS		MERITS	
1. Uses tobacco. (5)		1. Brushes teeth twice daily.	
2. Uses profanity. (3)		2. Makes own bed regularly.	
3. Crashes parties to which not invited.		3. Attends Sunday school or church regularly. (20)	
4. Untruthful - tells lies. (5)		4. Makes passing school grades.	
5. Cuts classes unnecessarily.		5. Keeps school homework up to date.	
6. "Sticky fingered" - steals. (5)		6. On the honor roll at school. (5)	

DEMERITS		MERITS	
7. Takes souvenirs from public places, as restaurant spoons, ash trays, etc.		7. Attends Young People's Meetings at church regularly. (5)	
8. Often tardy at school or at work. (3)		8. Officer of a church Youth Group. (3)	
9. Plays radio or TV loudly long after others' bed time.		9. Has belonged to Scouts, Camp Fire Girls, etc. (3)	
10. Tells vulgar stories or writes on public toilet walls. (2)		10. Represents your school, as in athletics, debating, dramatics, etc. (2 each)	
11. Careless about flushing toilets.		11. Teaches a Sunday school class. (10)	
12. Drinks alcoholic beverages. (10)		12. Plays a musical instrument.	
13. Argues over running household errands.		13. Member of a "Y" or CYO group. (5)	
14. A bed wetter.		14. Officer in the "Y", CYO, Scouts, etc. (3)	
15. Sassy or impolite.		15. Keeps own bank account.	
16. Accepts foolish dares to try to prove one's bravery.		16. Earns own money instead of being on an allowance or "dole". (5)	
17. Chronic borrower of clothes, money, etc. (3)		17. Has operated a newspaper route. (10)	
18. Talks too long on telephone.		18. Can prepare an entire meal alone. (5)	
19. Does unnecessary work on the Sabbath, as homework, etc.		19. Phones home when unavoidably late, as on a date, etc.	
20. Slams doors and makes noise after getting home late at night.		20. Not ashamed of family - brings friends home to meet parents.	
21. Social climber - puts on airs re wealth, social status, etc.		21. Replenishes gas tank after using family car on date. (3)	
22. Tosses coats on living room chairs when arriving from school or work.		22. Dresses neatly - shoes shined, seams in hose straight, etc.	

"There is a time in the affairs of men,
Which, taken at the flood, leads on to fortune;
Omitted, all the voyage of their life
Is bound in shallows and miseries." —Shakespeare

DEMERITS	MERITS
23. Fails to wash the ring of dirt from bath tub or wash basin after using them.	23. Tells parents where going on a date and approximately when to expect you home. (5)
24. Careless about personal cleanliness - "B.O.", dandruff, halitosis, etc.	24. Hangs up clothes at night instead of tossing them on chair.
25. Fails to throw soiled clothes in laundry chute or hamper.	25. Carries out garbage without excessive nagging.
26. Fails to come to meals promptly.	26. Sings in a chorus or choir.
27. A bully - picks on weaker companions or teases them excessively. (5)	27. Pays frequent compliments to family for favors and help. (5)
28. Grabs for food at table without waiting for it to be passed.	28. Asks to be excused when leaving the table early.
29. Grumpy or caustic in the morning.	29. Says grace (prayer) before meals. (5)
30. Fails to wash and clean car before using it on a date.	30. Abides by standard college curfew - not over 2 late dates per week.
31. Fails to change into old clothes when getting home from school.	31. Depends on alarm clock instead of mamma to get up in mornings. (5)
32. Shows race, religious or color prejudice. (5)	32. Says prayers at night, and not just selfish "gimme" prayers. (5)
33. Fails to clean comb after using it.	33. Maintains high moral standards. (10)
34. Indulges in excessive or promiscuous petting. (5)	34. Has stayed overnight at home of friends or relatives.
35. Indulges in illicit sexual relations. (20)	35. Can typewrite by the touch system.
36. Rude - fails to say "Thank you" or "Please", "Excuse me," etc.	36. Has lived away from home for at least a full week, as at camp, etc. (3)

DEMERITS		MERITS	
37. Fails to replace tools, books, etc. after using them. (3)		37. Plans to enter college or take special job training beyond high school.	
38. Catty, gossipy or unsportsmanlike.		38. Knows how to swim.	
39. Bets and gambles. (3)		39. Does NOT stick gum under chair, table top, or theatre seat.	
40. Reads obscene literature or carries nude pictures to show friends.		40. Generous with money but not a "show-off" or "splurger."	
41. Has temper tantrums - flies off the handle often; breaks things or tears up clothing, books, etc. (10)		41. Calls for dates long in advance instead of on the day of the dance or party. (3)	
42. Flirts with others while on a date or a "two-timer". (5)		42. Writes parents at least once per week while away from home. (5)	
43. A grandstander or boaster, who tries to show off by loud talk, reckless driving, arguing, etc. (5)		43. A careful auto driver who obeys the speed laws; doesn't race up to a stop light and then jam on brakes. (5)	
44. Speaks poor English or uses slang excessively.		44. Wipes toothpaste specks from bathroom mirror.	
45. Cheats in school work or at play. (10)		45. Confides in parents and asks their advice. (5)	
46. An egotist - talks about himself most of the time.		46. Deft conversationalist - fades out with a question so companion can re-enter dialogue easily. (5)	
47. Purposely makes embarrassing remarks. (3)		47. Helps look after younger children in the family.	
48. Gripes about the food, furniture or other home situations.		48. Has many friends among both sexes - popular and well liked.	
49. Very suspicious or jealous: spies on sweetheart. (5)		49. Smiles freely and takes the lead in being friendly.	
50. A buck-passer, blaming others for his own misfortunes. (5)		50. A "finisher" who neatly completes his tasks instead of leaving them half done. (10)	

THE PSYCHOLOGY AND MEDICINE OF THE FACE

Those of you who saw Joan Crawford's excellent acting in the movie entitled, "A Woman's Face," will recall how her scarred cheek led to an embittered personality with a cynical attitude toward all of her fellowmen. It even drove her into criminal activities.

That screen characterization was not a great exaggeration of the personality conflicts that can be traced to defects of the human face. Psychologists frequently find that people with unsightly complexions either become wallflowers, robbed of the confidence so necessary for success in life, or else they grow suspicious of the men and women around them. The latter suspicion may develop into a definite antisocial attitude as a result of which they actually try to strike back at the world in general. Many juvenile delinquents and young criminals have thus become embittered and launched into criminality, as a sadistic attempt to get revenge.

These opposing reactions of wallflowerism versus criminality, might very aptly be classified under the terms "masochism" and "sadism." The former applies to the "whipped dog" personality in which the boy or girl feels beaten, so withdraws from social contacts as much as possible and even sheds copious tears in recurrent fits of self-pity. The masochist indulges in melancholy and almost enjoys his misfortune.

The sadist, on the contrary, fights back. He may develop a cruel, vindictive mental outlook which drives him into sarcasm and higher criticism, whether of the religious or political sort. He may be a rabble rouser or anarchist. With a chronic antisocial viewpoint, he delights in throwing monkey wrenches into machinery of various types.

He may, however, attempt to compensate within constructive fields, and try to highhat his fellowmen by attaining superiority in science or invention, literature or even athletics.

As a rule, people who suffer from any stigma, whether real

or imagined, tend to lose their perspective, and therefore their sense of humor. They may become so worried about their defect that their conscious attention is chiefly focussed upon themselves and their skin, instead of upon the people around them. This narrowed perspective gives them a distorted view of life. Because they overly magnify their defect to such a serious degree, they likewise imagine the world holds that same point of view. On the contrary, the world at large, possessing a more normal outlook, seldom feels the revulsion or shows the ridicule which the victim of the defect generally imputes to those around him.

Acne Vulgaris (Pimples). One of the most common causes for the development of social inferiority complexes by young people, is the presence of a crop of pimples on the face. Sometimes these may extend to the chest, shoulders and back. Some of the pimples may have pus in the center, while others are simply red papules or hard pimples. In medical circles, this condition is termed acne vulgaris, but is popularly called acne. It seems to be associated primarily with puberty when the glandular changes are taking place in the young adult.

In order to get a better appreciation of the various functions of the skin, it is necessary to remember that it is one of the primitive tissues in embryological development. Though in the human adult its uses are chiefly to regulate the temperature and serve as medical armor against the entrance of bacteria, it can assist our health in other ways.

The skin, for example, is a basic destroyer of toxins or poisons. When other glands of the body are unable to perform their functions properly or destroy overwhelming masses of germs and toxins, as in the case of violent diseases, the epidermis comes to the rescue. You are probably familiar with the blotches on the skin during measles, or the pimples and pustules of smallpox, or the watery blisters of chickenpox and shingles, and the lumpy welts or wheals caused by allergy. We would all probably have died in childhood if the skin had not thus come to our rescue and helped destroy the massive toxic reactions of contagious diseases.

But the skin does not limit itself solely to destroying the toxins of bacteria. If normal individuals eat too much candy or chocolate, they may notice some pimples on their backs or faces. And people who are especially allergic may find that in addition to chocolate, they are also likely to show skin reactions to wheat and tomatoes, eggs and strawberries, as well as a dozen other common foods.

Mistaken Ideas About Acne. Acne must not be regarded as a contagious disease, but as an attempt of the skin to destroy bacteria and toxins of some sort which are in excess within the body. Acne is certainly not a venereal disease, though many young people imagine that it is a sign of gonorrhea or syphilis. It is not!

Gonorrhea does not produce skin pimples or pustules at all! Occasionally syphilis may produce skin eruptions something like acne, but they are not likely to appear in young people who have had no sexual relations. Besides, the syphilis pimples are not inevitably associated with blackheads (comedones). Moreover, the syphilis pimples come on suddenly as an acute disease, and are not a chronic affair lasting for months or even years.

Many young people have an inferiority complex because of their pimples, thinking that those are an indication of self sex practices such as masturbation. Masturbation, however, does not produce such skin eruptions. In fact, if it has any influence, it probably is exerted in the opposite direction.

Acne Vulgaris affects rich and poor, intelligent and stupid. It is no respecter of persons. And don't think that the "Vulgaris" part of its name, means that acne is vulgar. The root meaning of "Vulgaris" is "commonplace."

Acne is not contagious. It does not spread from one patient to another. But it does seem to be aggravated by dust and dirt, plus the heavy sweating typical of summer. Some men have suggested that it is caused by exposure to sunlight.

It would probably be more correct to say that during the sunlight months of spring and summer, we leave our shirts open at the throat and by our participation in outdoor athletic events, subject the skin to more dust.

Acne Vulgaris is medically defined as a papular eruption due to inflammation of the sebaceous glands and is almost invariably associated with "blackheads" or comedones, as physicians term them.

Blackheads, in turn, are simply plugs of sebaceous matter, capped with dust, that fill the mouths of the sebaceous follicles. The sebaceous glands produce an oily substance for softening the skin, and are a separate set of glands from those which generate sweat. They are especially abundant in the skin of the face and scalp, which is where the acne pimples are likewise most prolific. A wen is also simply a large, plugged sebaceous gland that may grow as big as an egg or even larger. You have often seen these lumps on the scalps of baldheaded old men.

The Treatment for Acne. Under this heading of treatment we shall make two classifications, called "Local" and "Systemic."

The local treatment consists primarily of keeping the skin free from oil and dust. Plugged sebaceous glands become infected with the bacteria normally on the skin and may develop pus in their centers.

To keep the skin clean, it is advisable that acne patients steam their faces every night after the manner followed by barbers in softening the beards of their customers. If possible, this process should be duplicated each morning so that the skin is cleansed twice every 24 hours.

You can employ any good soap that does not irritate your skin. Lather the face and neck thoroughly, even to the extent of using a soft brush. Then steam the face with hot towels placed on top of the lathered skin. Keep repeating this process for at least 15 minutes.

An alternative procedure consists of making a solution of borax in hot water, using two teaspoons of powdered borax to a quart of water. Use a large wash pan or bowl and make 3 or 4 quarts of the borax solution. Keep it as hot as your skin will tolerate and lean over the bowl for 15 minutes applying hot towels soaked in the borax solution.

Both the borax as well as the soap remove the grease from the skin and the necks of the sebaceous glands, as well as millions of bacteria that might get lodged in the glands.

Before going further with the local treatment, I should remind you that dandruff and oily scalps seem to complicate acne and prevent its cure, so be sure you have frequent shampoos with rich soapsuds to remove the oil and scales of dandruff.

After the face has been steamed with borax or soapsuds, examine the skin in a good light before your mirror. Notice all of the plugged glands, especially those with blackheads. Express them, not by squeezing their contents between thumb or fingers, but by use of a blackhead extractor, such as that sketched herewith.

It can be purchased at drug stores for about 25 cents. It is far more advisable to use this little metal extractor than to employ the fingers, for the latter injure the skin around the blackhead and are more likely to make it form a deep, hard pimple or lump that persists for months or years afterwards.

The blackhead extractor has two circular openings of different sizes which permit you to exert uniform pressure all around the blackhead and thus squeeze it out with a minimum of harm to surrounding tissue.

After you have cleared the skin of all visible blackheads and whiteheads, which are sebaceous plugs with the dust cleaned off, then wash the skin with very cold water or rub it with ice. The latter will help cause constriction of the skin and help close the follicles against dust.

Side View   Top View
BLACKHEAD EXTRACTOR

Since the skin of acne patients is usually quite oily, refrain as a rule from using ointments and greasy cleansing agents. Don't massage the face, either, for this may spread the bacteria on the skin and work them into the mouths of other sebaceous follicles.

There are several additional medical aids that your physician can prescribe or employ to help recalcitrant cases of acne, but the above procedures should produce remarkable improvement in your complexion, if you follow them faithfully! But "faithfully" means at least once per day, and seven days per week!

Systemic Treatment for Acne. Acne must not be regarded as a minor local condition of the face. Modern medicine realizes that the entire body is involved in all infections, so the acne patient whose case has been chronic, should make certain that his general resistance is not low because of some focus of infection elsewhere in the body which keeps feeding toxins into his blood stream.

The teeth should be X-rayed and the tonsils examined. His blood should be checked to guard against lowered resistance due to anemia. And his elimination by bowel should be regular to avoid resorption of toxins from the intestines.

He should likewise watch his diet to see if any foods seem to accentuate his acne. If he finds these, he can eat sparingly of them or avoid them altogether. Rich foods, such as candy and pastries, fats and gravies, should be avoided.

By a careful and diligent attention to the local and systemic methods of treatment, the great majority of persons suffering from acne can eliminate this trouble almost entirely.

But in addition to medical treatment, we must give the patients a broader psychological perspective and thus divert their attention from themselves. One of the best methods for so doing is to join the COMPLIMENT CLUB and pay three different people honest compliments every day for the 30-day period of this experiment in social psychology.

Other Skin or Facial Defects. Although acne is the most common cause for social inferiority complexes, a variety of other factors likewise distort personality. Some children have scars from burns. Others have obvious birthmarks on the face or neck. A certain percentage shun parties and tend to become wallflowers because their teeth are uneven or protruding, or yellow and decayed.

Some are embarrassed and thrown into an acute state of self-consciousness because of cross-eyes or large ears or a prominent nose or receding chin.

In all such cases, the first step to take is the development of a sense of humor, which is really a correlate of a broadened outlook on life. These people take themselves so seriously and feel that their life is not worth living, thus showing that they worship their own vanity to such an extreme degree they have forgotten the really important problems of life.

Religion is one of the best antidotes for all such myopic persons who can't see beyond their own little problems, for it lifts their eyes to distant realms and keeps their attention focussed on the great goals of civilization, beside which their facial problem is actually picayune.

Capitalize Your Defects as Assets. In many cases, a large nose or big ears can be capitalized on, as witness the success of Joe E. Brown, Martha Raye, Jimmy Durante and others. But you must develop a sense of humor and a wider perspective in order to treat yourself lightly or joke at your own expense, like the obese girl who laughingly says: "Well, fat people give more shade in summer and more heat in winter!"

If, however, you have cross-eyes or a bad scar or birthmark, medical science can usually remedy these conditions. The fee is generally set within the limits of your income. Tell your doctor the facts and he will be reasonable. But by reasonable, I don't mean he will charge you $25 when you have paid $295 for an electrical refrigerator or $2,500 for a new automobile. Restoration of your crooked or decayed teeth to a condition of beauty and health, or the straightening of your cross-eye will require hours of talented dentistry or surgery, so you must learn to evaluate fees in comparison with the importance to health and happiness of the respective services which you purchase.

If you don't know whom to consult, get in touch with the superintendent of any large hospital and state your case, asking him to give you the names of one or two competent doctors in your community or nearby city. Don't think, moreover, that you must go to a distant state or clinic for your operation, for you generally have just as good doctors in your own city as are in any clinic in the country.

The famous clinics usually have good men, plus a lot of advertising. Your own practitioners may be equally good, but they haven't the advertising. As a result they can do the same work more reasonably in price. It is usually silly to waste money running around the country to consult so-called "experts," when you have those experts in your own city.

Squint, also called strabismus or cross-eye, can usually be remedied in childhood by the use of properly chosen eyeglasses. But if the condition has gone unchecked till adulthood, or if the case is a difficult one to treat in that manner, don't hesitate to have an eye surgeon shorten the muscle and thus pull the eye back into line. This operation is not serious, for the work is all done outside of the eyeball itself. The patient doesn't even need a general anaesthetic, unless he is very nervous or youthful.

Straighten Cross-eyes Early. One very good reason for correcting cross-eyes early, is the fact that otherwise the patient begins to ignore the visual impressions from the cross-eye. As a result, the retina does not get properly stimulated, so ultimately that eye loses much of its sensitivity. It becomes partly blind from disuse. Don't delay in beginning some corrective measures for eye defects in your children. Here is an excellent illustration of the old adage that "a stitch in time saves nine."

You parents of babies, however, must not grow unduly alarmed if the youngster's eyes don't always toe-in uniformly. Infants do not have perfect coordination of both eyes at all times, but they will normally be all right within a few years, even without any eyeglasses or surgery, especially if their squint is only occasional.

In conclusion, may I remind you that in all cases of personality upsets traceable to facial or complexion defects, please encourage the victim to get a true perspective of life. This generally involves turning his attention from himself to the external environment. He has been making mountains out of molehills by such excessive focussing of his attention upon SELF.

Next, take advantage of the medical or dental aids which will eliminate or reduce to a minimum the actual defect itself. After surgeons and dentists have done all that modern science can perform to help you or your child, then take a philosophical attitude and turn your interest upon other people. Learn how to carry on an interesting conversation. Join the COMPLIMENT CLUB and extrovert your attention beyond your own epidermis.

Begin to worry about constructive things, such as writing a good letter of application for a job, or the formula for a good public speech. In short, teach yourself to have a sense of humor. If necessary, capitalize on your defects or large mouth or big nose, as did Joe E. Brown and Jimmy Durante. Develop a joking retort in case you are kidded about your condition.

Remember, SELF-consciousness means you are keeping SELF in the focus of your thoughts. To win friends or sweethearts, you must keep the other fellow in the spotlight of your attention!

Advertising Age, April 18, 1966

SIMMONS ADVANCE REPORT ON
AUDIENCES OF 59 MAGAZINES: 1966

	Total People 10 Years of Age and Over	Total Adults	Total Men	Total Women
American Home	10,526,000	9,249,000	2,131,000	7,118,000
American Legion.	4,568,000	3,892,000	2,644,000	1,248,000
Argosy	4,675,000	3,945,000	3,179,000	766,000
Better Homes & Gardens.	21,994,000	18,611,000	5,012,000	13,599,000
Business Management . .	960,000	893,000	713,000	180,000*
Business Week	3,851,000	3,510,000	2,742,000	768,000
Cosmopolitan	3,490,000	3,036,000	665,000	2,371,000
Cue	737,000	656,000	333,000	323,000
Dun's Review	533,000	507,000	416,000	91,000*
Esquire	5,673,000	4,956,000	3,676,000	1,280,000
Family Circle.	15,866,000	13,059,000	2,023,000	11,036,000
Field & Stream.	8,117,000	5,885,000	4,511,000	1,374,000
Forbes	1,557,000	1,406,000	1,137,000	269,000
Fortune.	1,867,000	1,737,000	1,247,000	490,000
Good Housekeeping. . . .	19,113,000	15,884,000	2,839,000	13,045,000
Harper's/Atlantic	2,451,000	2,179,000	1,045,000	1,134,000
Holiday.	4,715,000	3,945,000	1,734,000	2,211,000
Hot Rod	7,626,000	3,889,000	3,178,000	711,000
House & Garden	6,238,000	5,214,000	1,485,000	3,729,000
House Beautiful	4,924,000	4,357,000	1,067,000	3,290,000
Ingenue	2,928,000	1,275,000	144,000*	1,131,000
Ladies' Home Journal . .	17,181,000	14,508,000	2,144,000	12,364,000
Life	43,170,000	33,272,000	16,925,000	16,347,000
Look	37,308,000	29,915,000	14,989,000	14,926,000
McCall's	22,818,000	18,335,000	3,212,000	15,123,000
Mechanix Illustrated . . .	6,154,000	4,483,000	3,946,000	537,000
Modern Romances	3,181,000	2,312,000	406,000	1,906,000

(Continued on Page 846)

NOTE: In connection with these figures, an asterisk (*) indicates that the projection is relatively unstable because of small sample base.

A RATING SCALE FOR EMPLOYEES

When asked to rate an employee or write a letter of recommendation for him, we are usually inclined to deal in generalities. But a specific and detailed list of his virtues and faults would be of far greater value to his prospective employer.

The following list of MERITS and DEMERITS constitutes a specific "check list" by which we can give more clarity to vague terms like "character," "personality," "ability," "stability" and the like. It can serve as a blueprint for good workers. As such, therefore, it should be of aid not only to employees themselves, but likewise to their employers and labor union leaders, as well as trade school and vocational teachers.

In computing a worker's score, check the various items under DEMERITS which fit him, and add the total. Some items have more significance, so they are "weighted" as in the parentheses. Unless so weighted, each item counts as one point. Then check off the MERITS which fit the worker, and add the total. Finally, subtract the DEMERIT total from the MERIT total. The resulting number is his raw score. Interpret it according to the following norms.

Raw Scores		Interpretation	
0 - 12		Very Poor	
13 - 25		Poor	
26 - 43		Average	
44 - 58		Superior	
59 and up		Very Superior	
DEMERITS		MERITS	
1. Addicted to alcohol (5).		1. Owns or is buying his home (5)	
2. Frequently late to work.		2. Has clean, attractive teeth.	
3. Frequently tries to borrow money from his associates		3. Belonged to the Boy or Girl Scouts as a child.	

4. A chronic gambler (5).	4. Has a farm background.
5. A clock watcher—afraid he'll work an extra minute without being paid for it (5).	5. Admits his mistakes. Doesn't try to "bull" his way through them.
6. Careless or slipshod in his work (5).	6. Attends church regularly (5).
7. Likes to indulge in horse play or practical jokes.	7. Has cheery personality and frequent smile (5).
8. Thoughtless—spits on floor; throws paper on floor or into street, etc.	8. Voluntarily b u y s Defense Stamps and Bonds (5).
9. Chronically argues politics, religion, etc. at every opportunity.	9. Cooperates with his union leaders to avoid violating negotiated contracts.
10. Airs his marital or private affairs in public.	10. Suggests ideas for improving the efficiency or output.
11. Has "B.O.", halitosis or unkempt hair and appearance (5).	11. Carries adequate life insurance.
12. Breaks or throws things when angry, thus lacking adult emotional control (5).	12. Gives his wife the pay check or an ample allowance.
13. Frequently engages in profanity or vulgar story telling.	13. Participates in company activities, as band, athletics, dramatics, glee clubs, etc. (5).
14. Tries to "ride" new workers instead of helping them get on to the ropes (5).	14. Has a good credit rating in the community (5).
15. Lacks initiative. Requires constant supervision. Must always be told what to do (5).	15. Studies on his own time to become a better worker. Takes night school or correspondence courses (5).
16. Tries to flirt with members of the opposite sex who work with him.	16. Is a very efficient worker, being swift and accurate (10).
17. Chronic trouble maker. Likes to stir up friction (5).	17. Holds an office in some society, as his union, church, or social organization (5).
18. Forgets his tools or fails to keep them in order.	18. Is happily married (5).

19. Thinks he is a Don Juan; so keeps boasting of his flirtations and female conquests.	19. Regards the ballot as a patriotic duty; so votes at every election.
20. Curses at or argues with other auto drivers.	20. Prefers to take his recreation with his family, instead of with his own sex.
21. Is dishonest or undependable (10).	21. Makes friends readily. Well liked (5).
22. A chronic buck-passer. Always blames others for his own mistakes (5).	22. Belongs to some outside organization, as fraternal order, P-T-A, glee clubs, etc.
23. A grandstander type. Shows off by fast driving, loud talk, breaking rules, etc.	23. Is an oldest child, thus having been taught responsibility in childhood (5).
24. Chronically suspicious of people. Thinks they are all trying to gyp him.	24. Turns out his full share of acceptable work while on duty. No shirker (5).
25. Tries to take advantage of his union membership to cover up his own deficiencies as a workman (5).	25. Is resourceful. Can adjust to unexpected problems, for he thinks in terms of the "whole" instead of the "part".

DARTNELL'S LETTER COST ANALYSIS

Executive who dictates reply	$0.42
Stenographer who types letter	0.92
Fixed charges per letter	0.60
Mailing expenses per letter	0.14
Materials per letter	0.07
Non-productive labor per letter	0.20
Filing carbon copy per letter	0.09
Total cost per dictated letter	$2.44

INCORRECT FORM   CORRECT FORM

Double Negative

"I don't have *none*."..................."I don't have *any*."
"He can't hardly work."..............."He can hardly work."

Wrong Tense

"It ain't me."........................"It isn't I."
"He has went."....................."He has gone."
"He could of gone.".................."He could have gone."

Wrong Number

"He don't like it.".................."He doesn't like it."
"Everybody did their work.".........."Everybody did his work."
"Neither of us are going."............"Neither of us is going."
"None of them are working.".........."None of them is working."

Wrong Case

"It is me." ...."It is I."
"It is us.".........................."It is we."
"Him and I are going"..............."He and I are going."
"They invited she and I" ...."They invited her and me."
"It fell between you and I."..........."It fell between you and me."
"Who did they send?"..............."Whom did they send?"
"Whom did you say was going?"......"Who did you say was going?"

Wrong Degree

"Which of the two boys is strongest?".."Which of the two boys is stronger?"
"Which of the two do you like best?".."Which of the two do you like better?"

Miscellaneous

"She was dark complected."..........."She was dark complexioned."
"She liked him real well."............"She liked him very well."
"His naughtiness aggravated her."......"His naughtiness irritated her."
"He learned me to swim."............"He taught me to swim."
"It made me mad."..................."It made me angry."
"Set down and visit awhile.".........."Sit down and visit awhile."
"Leave him do it by himself.".........."Let him do it by himself."
"She is laying down for a nap.".......“She is lying down for a nap."
"She raised six children."............"She reared six children."
"That is a funny building."..........."That is an odd (unusual) building."
"I'm tired on account of I've worked
    hard." ...."I'm tired because I've worked hard."
"He said he would go, irregardless.".…"He said he would go, regardless."
"I said I'd borrow him my book."....."I said I'd lend him my book."
"Can I borrow your umbrella?"......."May I borrow your umbrella?"
"Raise up the window.".............."Raise the window."
"It was audible to the ear."..........."It was audible."
"Hurry and we'll wait on you."........"Hurry and we'll wait for you."
"I am anxious to go." ...."I am eager to go."
"Listen at the music."..............."Listen to the music."

THE DEATH WISH

In order to understand this mental phenomenon it is well to remember that basically we are animal-like and selfish. In the pig lot the sturdy pigs do not stand back, unselfishly, while the runt or weakling comes up to the feeding trough. No, they push the weaker pig away and try to monopolize the trough. If he dies, so much the better for them.

Because of our intelligence, we have evolved high ethical and moral ideals, which have been superimposed upon our primitive selfish desires. Parents, teachers, and the Christian church have tried to build up in our minds a set of habits which are unselfish. We teach generosity, magnanimity, and the Golden Rule.

But our basic or primitive animal desires come into frequent conflict with our acquired habits of generosity and altruism. To avoid this conflict we try to forget the selfish and socially taboo desires. There are two ways to keep an unpleasant thought out of mind; namely, dress it up in a disguised fashion so that we will not recognize it as the unpleasant thought, or else keep another more pleasant idea in the focus of our attention.

During our waking hours we can frequently exert enough active control over our attention so that we think about the good things and therefore disregard the unapproved ideas. But when we go to sleep, our critical control of our thinking is reduced. Basic hungers then tend to appear in our dreams.

A woman whose childhood has been made miserable by having to act as nursemaid constantly to six or eight younger brothers and sisters, may develop a secret hatred of babies. Why? Because they stood in the way of her fun and good times as a child. Later in life she may still cherish this basic dislike for babies, even after she has children of her own. During the day, she keeps such unapproved ideas out of mind. But at night she may dream of funerals involving her babies. She awakens, possibly terrified, and then consciously does penance for her subconscious wishes, by becoming overly attentive and solicitous regarding her babies. She frets and worries lest they become ill. She feels their chests at night to make sure they are breathing regularly.

Or a child who resents his father's dominance of his mother may destroy the parent during a dream. He may then wake up in terror, for his acquired habit of respect for parents is at war with his dream. He feels remorseful and may even think that he has committed an unforgivable sin.   Thereafter, he may fear to leave the house or to be away from the protection of his home, all because he dreads divine retribution.   He fears God will strike him down for his sinful dream. And all of these cases are just like the analogy of the pigs, except that our basic selfishness is in conflict with our acquired ethical codes, so we worry.   Pigs do not.

Carefully study the following actual cases and you will see how perfectly the previous psychological principles are borne out by both men as well as women.

Case B-135:   Miriam B., aged 28, is the mother of three children.   The last baby is only 15 months old and is a girl.

"I am frightened to death over my baby," Miriam said to me.   "I wake up at night and climb out of bed to feel her chest to make sure she is breathing.   Some nights I get up at least five or six times just to see that she is all right.

"About three months ago she had a bad cold and she had a convulsion while I held her in my arms.   Ever since then I have been scared to death for fear something would happen to her.

"At night I dream a lot and almost always my dreams have something to do with the baby.   Often I dream of funerals and death and coffins.   Then I wake up terrified and hop out of bed to see if the baby is still breathing.

"Dr. Crane, if this doesn't stop soon I shall be a nervous wreck.   I can hardly concentrate on my work now.   And my husband would be wild if anything happened to the baby, for he simply worships her.   What is wrong with me, anyhow?"

Diagnosis

Miriam came from a coal mining town where she was the oldest of nine children.   Naturally, she became nurse maid to all the eight who followed her.   Her girlhood freedom was ruined by such adult responsibilities.   At the age of 16 she fled to Chicago.

Here she met her husband.   They got married, but she didn't want any children, and only married with the understanding that she was to have no family.

Miriam demonstrates what is termed the "Death Wish".   She hated children because of her childhood experiences with them.   But she got children of her own.   They were attractive youngsters, of course, and being her own, she felt somewhat drawn to them, consciously.

Subconsciously, however, she was hostile to children. They cramped her style. They prevented her from enjoying life as she had wished to live it. They were fetters which bound her down to a slavery which she had early escaped when she fled her home and came to Chicago. Basically, she didn't want children, not even her own.

Such a thought would be impossible to tolerate if she were to think it consciously or express it openly. In her dreams, however, she repeatedly showed the death wish by associating corpses and coffins with her little girl.

Fear Is Penance

Her great nervousness and fear were a form of conscious penance which conscience inflicted. She would dream of the death of her little girl; then jump out of bed in terror for fear the child really was dead. She punished herself consciously by means of her fear and her many check-ups on the baby's breathing.

Moreover, the little girl had almost usurped her place in her husband's affections. The baby girl was, therefore, a rival. We have here a peculiar love triangle again, with mother pitted against daughter. It may sound radical and unbelievable to some of you readers who haven't seen great numbers of these cases, but it is no more abnormal than appendicitis or gall stones.

Case K-152: Millicent T., aged 29, is mother of a little girl.

"Please tell me what I can do to get over this terrible fear," she began in a panicky voice.

"Everything seems unreal to me, and I wonder if I am not somebody else. People look strange to me, and I keep thinking I must be losing my mind.

"I feel dazed and can't concentrate on a thing. I hardly know what I am doing all day. And when my husband comes home I just sit and cry, for no reason at all. He is very good to me, but still I cry.

"When I start to tell him all the cute things the baby does, my mind just goes blank. Oh, Dr. Crane, please tell me if I am losing my mind! I can't stand it much longer."

Origin Of The Death Wish

When Millicent had her baby girl, she often felt secretly jealous of the child. As she told me, her mind went blank whenever she tried to tell her husband about the baby's cute tricks.

Because she felt that some of her husband's love was being diverted to the baby, and because this situation was quite similar to her own childhood dilemma when a baby sister stole part of her Daddy's attention, Millicent felt a surge of irritation and anger.

Being an adult, she recoils from such unChristian ideas. She thinks she must be an inhuman monster. The next thought is, "God will surely punish me for such evil thoughts."

And the two chief forms of divine punishment which next come to mind are insanity or sudden death. Hence, she begins to assume various attitudes which she thinks the insane may adopt, because she thinks she ought to be punished.

Case L-175: Orville J., aged 17, is a high school senior.

"During the last few years I have been panicky whenever I pass a house where there are flowers and crepe outside, indicating a person has died," he began our discussion.

"I simply cannot look at a coffin. My grandfather died recently, but I couldn't force myself to enter the house, and I wouldn't attend the funeral, although my parents were shocked at my behavior.

"At night I become afraid, for I keep thinking of coffins, so that I cannot go to sleep. Often I'll waken out of my sleep, and immediately I visualize a coffin beside my bed, with the lid open and flowers piled within.

"Dr. Crane, what is wrong with me? Other people don't seem to have this fear. I've tried to reason with myself, but it doesn't do much good."

Diagnosis

People don't develop fears without a cause. Therefore, we must try to place our diagnosing finger on the specific event or fact which started Orville's dread.

A coffin itself does not produce fear or pleasure unless it is associated with the corresponding emotions. I remember reading about a star salesman in the East who sold something like 200 coffins in one summer.

He went around among the farmers and townsfolk selling them by the house-to-house method.

"Why shouldn't a coffin be an intimate, friendly part of the family?" he argued. "Why not use it for a piece of furniture, or as a cedar chest? Let your children grow up with it. Learn to look upon it as a friend, as a member of your household.

"Then, when one of the family passes on, let him be gently laid in this friendly piece of furniture. Don't import a strange box, but let him be accompanied with an intimate piece of furniture, a warm household friend, over which he has romped and played throughout the years."

The salesman's arguments were sensible. He sold over 200 coffins to be used as cedar chests until they were later needed for their original purpose.

Why do most people feel afraid of coffins and death? Because from earliest childhood they have associated tears and gloom with such subjects. And what do tears mean to a child? Why pain, of course! But pain is a synonym for punishment, so the youngster normally views with dread and shuddering such things as death, funerals and all associated objects, including the casket or coffin.

A Cause For Abnormal Fears

But most children don't lie awake at night conjuring up visions of a coffin. When we encounter a patient like Orville, we can assume that he must have some special reason for torturing himself with such frightening thoughts. Perhaps he feels he OUGHT to be alarmed at the possibility of an early demise. Modern medicine is replete with cases of hypochondriacs who shop around from one physician to another trying to get a doctor to pin a serious diagnosis upon them. Although the examiner says there is nothing organically wrong, they still maintain that this specialist must be in error, so they consult a second or a third. They actually seem to WANT something to be radically wrong, for they think they OUGHT to be punished for some real or imagined sin that they have committed but never previously confessed. Clear up their sense of guilt and they will often get well with miraculous speed.

Two common explanations underlie a case like Orville's and they are both rooted in a guilty conscience. Either Orville has felt sinful because of self-sex practices and therefore thinks God will kill him. This is the Onanism complex of Biblical report.

Or he may have cherished a deep jealousy or animosity toward his father or a brother, so that he has subconsciously wished for the death of the latter. His conscience may thus be punishing him with this abnormal fear of coffins. When I had an interview with him, he finally confessed that he had indulged in auto erotic practices occasionally. They had become more frequent just about the time of his grandfather's sudden death from apoplexy. He even wondered if God didn't strike down his grandfather as an indirect way of punishing Orville, for the lad was very fond of his grandfather. Besides, the latter had agreed to pay Orville's college expenses.

At night when Orville felt a recurring urge to indulge in self sex practices, his conscience thus conjured up this vision of the coffin. The latter was simply a psychological symbol of a deep emotional conflict that this young man was undergoing. After Orville's thinking was clarified on the matter of auto eroticism his visions of coffins promptly disappeared.

Advertising Age, April 11, 1966

TOP MAGAZINE, NETWORK TV ADVERTISERS IN 1965
Compiled by Leading National Advertisers Inc., Publishers
Information Bureau and Broadcast Advertisers Reports

COMPANY	Total Expenditure	COMPANY	Total Expenditure
1. Procter & Gamble Co.	$ 98,136,502	51. Consolidated Cigar Corp.	$ 9,054,006
2. General Motors Corp.	78,886,044	52. Nestle Co., Inc.	8,940,962
3. Bristol-Myers Co.	72,295,228	53. Standard Brands, Inc.	8,918,260
4. American Home Products Corp.	51,058,071	54. Smith, Kline & French Labs.	8,794,222
5. General Foods Corp.	48,420,663	55. Goodyear Tire & Rubber Co.	8,545,320
6. Ford Motor Co.	46,794,900	56. National Distillers & Chemical Corp.	8,415,682
7. Colgate-Palmolive Co.	44,264,864	57. Sunbeam Corp.	8,265,835
8. R. J. Reynolds Tobacco Co.	42,040,577	58. Polaroid Corp.	8,016,095
9. American Tobacco Co.	39,800,114	59. Norwich Pharmacal Co.	7,884,539
10. Chrysler Corp.	37,720,127	60. Shell Oil Co.	7,672,284
11. Lever Brothers Co.	37,487,941	61. Borden Co.	7,615,475
12. Gillette Co.	34,410,144	62. Purex Corp., Ltd.	7,584,373
13. Phillip Morris, Inc.	30,054,066	63. Columbia Broadcasting System, Inc.	7,362,263
14. Brown & Williamson Tobacco Corp.	27,278,732	64. Union Carbide Corp.	7,307,760
15. National Dairy Products Corp.	25,926,856	65. Revlon, Inc.	7,287,532
16. Liggett & Myers Tobacco Co.	23,543,963	66. Shulton, Inc.	7,125,492
17. Sterling Drug, Inc.	22,817,003	67. Chas. Pfizer & Co., Inc.	7,103,252
18. General Mills, Inc.	22,208,571	68. Firestone Tire & Rubber Co.	7,022,174
19. Kellogg Co.	22,127,399	69. Mennen Co.	7,014,979
20. American Telephone & Telegraph Co.	21,223,988	70. Volkswagenwerk, A.G.	6,944,861
21. Alberto-Culver Co.	20,668,330	71. Kimberly-Clark Corp.	6,791,183
22. Carnation Co.	18,750,405	72. U. S. Rubber Co.	6,682,097
23. General Electric Co.	18,687,619	73. Noxzema Chemical Co.	6,676,797
24. P. Lorillard Co.	18,530,553	74. Hiram Walker-Gooderham & Worts, Ltd.	6,592,951
25. Warner-Lambert Pharmaceutical Co.	17,450,386	75. Carter-Wallace, Inc.	6,467,023
26. S. C. Johnson & Son, Inc.	17,303,072	76. Scott Paper Co.	6,429,849
27. Miles Labs., Inc.	16,750,409	77. Lehn & Fink Products Corp.	6,260,792
28. Campbell Soup Co.	16,576,137	78. Aluminum Co. of America	6,259,121
29. Eastman Kodak Co.	16,483,688	79. Sears, Roebuck & Co.	6,255,493
30. J. B. Williams Co., Inc.	15,609,725	80. California Packing Corp.	6,231,364
31. Distillers Corp.-Seagrams, Ltd.	15,347,371	81. General Cigar Co., Inc.	6,194,380
32. Block Drug Co., Inc.	13,772,338	82. Philadelphia & Reading Corp.	6,177,976
33. E. I. Du Pont de Nemours & Co., Inc.	13,580,597	83. Mattel, Inc.	6,163,214
34. National Biscuit Co.	13,465,945	84. Heublein, Inc.	5,961,061
35. Coca-Cola Co.	13,397,191	85. Beecham Group, Ltd.	5,773,400
36. Armour & Co.	12,351,965	86. Falstaff Brewing Corp.	5,736,755
37. Ralston Purina Co.	12,232,023	87. Sperry Rand Corp.	5,446,745
38. Corn Products Co.	12,091,778	88. Morton International, Inc.	5,431,697
39. Quaker Oats Co.	11,676,977	89. Reynolds Metals Co.	5,400,868
40. Radio Corp. of America	11,486,780	90. General Telephone & Electronics Corp.	5,201,056
41. Johnson & Johnson	11,133,900	91. Richardson-Merrell, Inc.	5,171,481
42. Pillsbury Co.	10,923,865	92. Jos. Schlitz Brewing Co.	5,150,298
43. Stanley Warner Corp.	10,904,135	93. Monsanto Co.	5,147,370
44. Hunt Foods & Industries, Inc.	10,454,881	94. Admiral Corp.	5,120,711
45. American Cyanamid Co.	10,236,393	95. Anheuser-Busch, Inc.	5,035,535
46. Armstrong Cork Co.	9,948,981	96. Canada Dry Corp.	4,968,402
47. American Motors Corp.	9,314,628	97. Standard Oil Co. of Indiana	4,866,615
48. Westinghouse Electric Corp.	9,204,634	98. Socony Mobil Oil Co., Inc.	4,853,759
49. PepsiCo, Inc.	9,141,463	99. Olin Mathieson Chemical Corp.	4,686,895
50. Chesebrough-Ponds, Inc.	9,127,078	100. Max Factor & Co.	4,645,461
		Total	$1,561,754,714

LOGICAL PROOF OF GOD

Young people nowadays crave scientific proof and logical arguments, even in the realm of morality.

"Mother, is there really a God?" many a teen-ager will thus inquire, since it is perfectly natural for intelligent youth to question the validity of long accepted concepts.

"Certainly there is a God," the mother will probably reply.

"Yes, but how do you *know* there is?" persists the young person.

"Oh, I just know it," affirms the mother. "I feel it. Besides, it's one of those things you must take on faith."

However, modern young people don't like this type of answer, for they think that "faith" is inferior to "logic."

When they get into a high school debate, moreover, on such subjects as the existence of God, or the influence of whiskey or cigarettes, they wish for some more acceptable evidence than "faith."

For they regard the retort, "You must take it on faith", as the weak alibi of a "cornered" person who cannot muster objective facts in support of his hypothesis.

Besides, modern youth dislike the "goody goody" connotation. They are inherently interested in goodness, I feel positive, but they want terse, logical evidence to support such inner feelings.

In short, they wish to be moral but they want to be able to demolish their opposition with invincible logic which they can utter with a casual but very telling effect. And they figuratively wince when they must weakly fall back on "faith".

All of us adults have sensed this same thing, I am sure, which is one reason why we so eagerly seize upon any report from a scientist or research laboratory which helps supplement our "faith" arguments about religion. An article by Dr. Compton is thus reprinted widely, for every adult subconsciously wants logic to bolster his faith.

At a banquet meeting in the Hilton Hotel a few years ago, I happened to be seated beside a magazine editor. During our dinner conversation, the latter suddenly asked me:

"Dr. Crane, do you believe in God?"

"Certainly I do," was my immediate response. "Don't you?"

Please notice, too, my use of what I have long described as the "reversible why" technique, by which you dominate the interview through the clever device of reversing the question and thus wage an "offensive" instead of a "defensive" campaign.

Too long we moralists and educators have let advocates of immorality and atheism take pot shots at us, after which we have attempted to defend ourselves.

Isn't it high time, therefore, that we took the offense, and thereby placed our opponents on the defense, where the burden of proof is on their shoulders? I have always believed in waging a militant campaign for Christianity, by which I mean that we should attack ignorance and immorality and constantly keep them on the defensive. So I used this "reversible why" strategy and asked my companion if he didn't believe in God?

"No, I can't say that I do," he answered.

"Then how do you explain the universe?" I persisted in shooting the questions at him, instead of letting him take the initiative.

"Oh, it's just the result of a cosmic accident," he replied, with a shrug of his shoulders.

But I refused to let him stop with that apparently invincible answer.

"Brother, I'm going to give you the logical proof of God," I went on. "And we'll begin with your suggestion that an accident produced the world.

"But first of all, may I remind you that all laws, whether in the field of chemistry and physics or in ethics, are simply derived from human experience and human observation.

"What is the Law of Gravity? It is simply a generalization based on human experience that when we release a heavier-than-air object in a normal atmospheric environment, then the object will fall toward the center of the earth.

"You and I have seen that happen. So have our parents and grandparents, and at least our fellow men back since the beginning of recorded history. Thus, we simply generalize and say that since such an object will fall when we look, then it will also fall when we don't look! And that is the Law of Gravity, which is basic to our physical sciences.

"All other laws are likewise predicated on human observation. You have just said that the world was produced by accident. Have we, therefore, any evidence to suggest that accidents produce *anything* at all?

"Well, you think back and so shall I. We might also investigate the realm of printed experience of the human race for the past few thousands of years, and lo, somebody will come up with this bit of evidence. A young man named Goodyear, experimenting with latex, the sap of the rubber tree, accidentally knocks over a can of this latex with some sulphur on a hot stove lid, and presto, we have rubber. This was obviously a result of accident.

"In our Ancient History courses, too, we studied about the Bronze Age. But long before the Bronze Age there was a Copper Age. However, copper was too soft to have much utility until some of our ancestors mixed a little tin or zinc with it, after which they had bronze and brass, respectively. These are accidental products.

"Moreover, our forefathers used pig iron for many years before they refined it down to a certain carbon content, after which they found that their product had more resiliency. Instead of breaking, as the old stove lid would do when it was dropped on a concrete sidewalk, this new substance could be rolled into a saw blade and then bent into a complete circle, for this new alloy was steel.

"So it is quite evident that we have a law, predicated on human experience, that accidents *do* produce things. But what kind of things? Why, *substances* like rubber and *alloys* like bronze and brass and steel.

"But does human experience support the derivation of a law that accidents produce synchronizing systems or even a simple machine with two cog wheels, the teeth of one meshing into the grooves of the other?

"Again, let us fall back on human experience for our evidence, since that is what is used for our Law of Gravity and other scientific rules. Has anybody in the course of recorded history ever seen any cataclysm of nature, whether a volcanic eruption or tidal wave, earthquake or hurricane, produce an airplane or a vacuum sweeper or even a wheelbarrow?

"No sir, there hasn't been a single instance to show that a synchronizing system or machine has *ever* been accidently produced. On the contrary, we have thousands of examples to show that *every synchronizing system or machine has always had a creator behind it!*

"This law, based on human observation, is just as scientifically derived as the Law of Gravity! For both are simply generalizations from human experience.

"Now we are left with the last leg of our syllogism. Is the universe just a wastebasket or hodge podge of the odds and ends of creation, or is it a precisely integrated synchronizing system?

"Can we, for instance, make our calendars for next year? Certainly! We can make them for 100 years or for 1,000 years in advance and predict to a split second when there will be a full moon or when the sun will rise or set on September 23rd of the year 2061, or on any other future date.

"Elgin Watch Company gets its time from the stars. During the recent war, we taught our naval officers celestial navigation because of the precise movements of the heavenly bodies. Why, the cosmic universe operates on such an exact system that it puts to shame as a rank crudity the most delicate watch on the wrist of any woman today.

"Since, therefore, the world is a synchronizing system, and since human experience has shown that every synchronizing system has always had a creator behind it, ergo (as we say in high school geometry) there is a Creator behind this cosmic universe, whether we call him Elohim or Jahve, as did the ancient Hebrews, or the Great Spirit or Manitou, as did the American Indians, or just Lord God Almighty, as do we moderns.

"Henceforth, any would-be atheist will have to take on pure *Faith* his predication of the non-existence of God, for he cannot adduce one shred or fragment of scientific evidence to support such a bizarre hypothesis."

May I remind you parents and Sunday school teachers that this logical proof of God is invaluable insurance for your children before you send them off to college.

They not only relish this argument, but are then able in later years to confront any sadistic college instructor, though he may be fortified with his Ph.D. degree, and figuratively pin him to the wall with their verbal shafts, just as precisely as the old knife-thrower on the vaudeville circuit used to delineate his accomplice with his whirring darts.

For your teen-agers can then confound and refute any cynicism or sarcasm that a smart aleck Ph.D. may attempt in his efforts to undermine your children's firm religious anchorage.

THOUGHT FOR TODAY

"The truth shall set you free," stated Jesus, and I find that this logical proof of God sets young people free from their secret inferiority complex based on having to take the existence of God on "faith".

Faith is a very vital and valuable element in religion, but when we can fortify our children with logic and scientific arguments, they feel much more secure.

So insure their religious loyalty all throughout their college years by simply giving them this logical proof of God even before they graduate from high school.

It was a few years ago that H. L. Connelly, Instructor in Political Science at a prominent Michigan School, suggested that I construct a Rating Scale for Teachers, based primarily on the students' point of view, and stressing practical considerations rather than college degrees or the teacher's research background, as stressed in Dr. Reymert's admirable Rating Scale reproduced on page 490 herein.

Connelly had already developed a brief test of his own which he had employed with his seniors, deriving the items on his test from a previous survey of several classes. He then let the students hand in their reports unsigned, so they would have complete anonymity, which is always a good plan.

Since then, I have interviewed 600 students, distributed between grammar school, high school and the college levels. I asked them to list all the "Demerits" or faults which they had to find with their teachers. Then I reversed my query and urged them to report all the "Merits" or virtues they had found in their instructors.

The following 50-point Rating Scale represents their condensed judgments. The various items are weighted, as shown in the parentheses. In computing a teacher's score, check off the items under the DEMERIT heading which apply. Then do the same under the MERIT category. Next, subtract the DEMERIT total from the MERIT total. The result is that teacher's raw score. Interpret it according to these tentative norms:

RAW SCORES	INTERPRETATION
0 to 9	Very Poor
10 to 21	Poor
22 to 54	Average
55 to 80	Superior
81 to 159	Very Superior

DEMERITS	MERITS
1. "Bawls out" or ridicules students before the other pupils (10).	1. Makes scrapbook of everyday practical applications of his subject matter (5).

2. Poor speaker; Fails to deliver interesting lectures—dull, boring (5).	2. Attends athletic and dramatic functions of the school (3).
3. Seldom attends P-T-A meetings (3).	3. Obviously active in a local church (10).
4. Has a sex prejudice either against boys or else against girls (10).	4. Makes sincere effort to meet the parents of his students (5).
5. Injects political bias into the classroom (3).	5. Dresses neatly—clean shaven, well manicured, shoes shined, etc. (3).
6. Uses alcoholic beverages (5).	6. Very liberal with compliments (10).
7. Chronically bemoans low teachers' salaries or is critical of higher incomes of business men (3).	7. Proctors exams rigidly to avoid letting cheaters take advantage of the conscientious students (10).
8. Often digresses during class time to tell of his dates or family matters (3).	8. Develops mnemonic or memory devices to help students remember facts (5).
9. Uses tobacco (3).	9. Sincerely interested in youth, and greets students on the street (3).
10. Gambles — bets on athletic games (5).	10. Stresses fundamentals on exams (5).
11. Employs profanity or excessive slang (3).	11. Admits his own errors (5).
12. Calls class dumb when it does poorly on an exam, failing to realize that this usually means poor teaching (10).	12. Uses objective exams (true-false, "multiple choice," etc.) to lessen the personal opinion element (5).
13. Chronically wears a sourpuss or grim expression (3).	13. To avoid futile debate over true-false items, he makes them read: "The author of our textbook says..." (5).
14. Holds class overtime so students are then late to next classroom (3).	14. Teams up with other teachers so all the heavy homework of several courses will not fall on the same night (10).
15. Penalizes entire class for the violations of one or two therein (10).	15. Awards grades on the basis of the class average; not on an arbitrary standard of perfection (5).

16. Piles on heavy homework or outside reading for holidays (3).		16. Prepares practical lectures so they tie-in with current problems (10).	
17. Too easily influenced by silken calved coeds on the front rows (3).		17. Has sense of humor—not unduly upset by chewing gum or other minor infractions of rules (5).	
18. Plays favorites, as by catering to social leaders, athletic heroes, et al. (5).		18. Urges students to participate in school activities, as debate, glee club, athletics, dramatics, etc. (5).	
19. Makes dates with students in the class (3).		19. Is usually pleasant and smiling (5).	
20. Lets physical condition, as peptic ulcer or thyroidism, prevent his judicious treatment of students (5).		20. Shows class at the outset his objective plan of awarding grades so they can compute where they stand at all times (10).	
21. Doesn't cooperate with other teachers (3).		21. Urges students to think in terms of further education (5).	
22. Tells risqué or imprudent stories and jokes to students (3).		22. Uses the "Pause and Praise" method of meeting questions (5).	
23. Shows a soured, communistic or anti-American attitude (10).		23. Has a missionary fervor or salesman's zeal for his field of education (10).	
24. A poor disciplinarian—either too severe or else too lax (5).		24. Helps students overcome their personal problems or complexes (5).	
25. Carries grudges against students (10).		25. Active leader in Boy or Girl Scouting, YMCA, YWCA or CYO (10).	

(The following editorial from the Anderson, S. C., DAILY MAIL, Sept. 13, 1954, presents a challenge to church people).

THE CIO KILLS 2,700 JOBS

The death of a big industry in Yonkers, N. Y., was brought about by the CIO Textile Workers Union, judging from details now available on the closing of the Alexander Smith carpet plant employing 2,700 men and women, more than half of them with a quarter century of service.

The CIO had so many barnacles on the union contract that the company couldn't compete in a trade which for some years has been operating unprofitably.

One of the CIO shop stewards, on the day the plant closed—the CIO struck the plant June 15—told the unvarnished truth when he said "the union would rather have there be no jobs than insecure jobs. We feel it is better to take a chance on going out and finding a better job."

But employees spoke differently, those who did not have a voice, many of them with pensions ahead of them, or with 25 years of service accumulated. One woman, Ann Delahanty said she wasn't so bad off with but seven and a half years "but how about the old timers who spent their lives in the mill? I predicted this would happen when the last strike was called."

Mrs. Bridget Treiber, a carpet setter for 48½ years said "this is an awful funeral. I could have been pensioned off any time I wanted. They were wonderful people to work for. I am heartbroken. The company sent us individual contracts and it seemed very fair. But we were in such a position that we couldn't say a word to the union. Members of the union were not free to express their sentiments."

When the plant closing was announced, a union member for 25 years, on the picket line remarked, "then we don't have to picket any more," but a union boss told him "you're still on strike detail." The worker replied, "I've paid my union dues. I have the right to speak up." The union boss asked "What do you mean? If it weren't for the union where would you be?"

The reply was: "I don't care. There's just me and my wife. I'm worried about all those guys with children. But you try to speak up at union meetings and you get kicked out."

Two women on picket duty said "we just want to work. We're poor people. But we have nothing to say."

The disaster to Yonkers, N. Y., is a repetition of the CIO Textile Workers Union in numerous New England cities. The company lost more than eight and a half million dollars in three years, owed 23 million dollars and last year the Yonkers plant lost close to two million. The CIO wouldn't budge in a request to remove the many barnacles to a contract which made operations financially impossible, so a huge industry closed—to come South to the Citadel of Free Enterprise, in the Piedmont area of South Carolina to locate at a modern plant and a good community, with a good name—Liberty.

(Continuation from Page 814 of 59 Magazine Audiences)

	Total People 10 Years of Age and Over	Total Adults	Total Men	Total Women
Modern Screen	6,016,000	4,401,000	733,000	3,668,000
Motor Trend	4,671,000	3,220,000	2,996,000	224,000
Nation's Business	1,900,000	1,746,000	1,347,000	399,000
National Geographic	15,148,000	10,571,000	5,837,000	4,734,000
National Observer	2,094,000	1,745,000	968,000	777,000
Newsweek	12,876,000	10,124,000	6,454,000	3,670,000
New Yorker	3,269,000	2,907,000	1,717,000	1,190,000
Outdoor Life	7,515,000	5,315,000	4,111,000	1,204,000
Parade	27,519,000	23,063,000	10,968,000	12,095,000
Parent's Magazine	5,413,000	4,390,000	916,000	3,474,000
Photoplay	6,761,000	5,164,000	879,000	4,285,000
Playboy	10,007,000	9,000,000	7,338,000	1,662,000
Popular Mechanics	7,795,000	5,575,000	4,675,000	900,000
Popular Science	7,016,000	4,647,000	3,884,000	763,000
Presbyterian Life	1,988,000	1,723,000	581,000	1,142,000
Reader's Digest	44,576,000	37,231,000	17,554,000	19,677,000
Redbook	10,684,000	9,153,000	1,552,000	7,601,000
Saturday Evening Post	28,081,000	22,322,000	11,190,000	11,132,000
Saturday Review	1,723,000	1,506,000	832,000	674,000
Sport	5,042,000	3,314,000	2,909,000	405,000*
Sports Afield	6,197,000	4,729,000	3,960,000	769,000
Sports Illustrated	8,865,000	6,520,000	4,414,000	1,106,000
Teen	3,870,000	1,128,000	231,000*	897,000
This Week	27,327,000	23,342,000	11,047,000	12,295,000
Time	17,987,000	14,449,000	8,117,000	6,332,000
True	7,242,000	5,897,000	4,168,000	1,729,000
True Story	8,339,000	6,532,000	1,026,000	5,506,000
TV Guide	33,441,000	25,493,000	11,540,000	13,953,000
U.S. News & World Report	8,252,000	6,712,000	4,292,000	2,420,000
Wall Street Journal	2,978,000	2,840,000	2,245,000	595,000
Woman's Day	15,071,000	12,774,000	1,530,000	11,244,000

NOTE: In connection with these figures, an asterisk (*) indicates that the projection is relatively unstable because of small sample base.